Dictionary of Painting and Decorating

Relevant Griffin titles

Painting and Decorating A. E. HURST & J. H. GOODIER

Outlines of Paint Technology W. M. MORGANS

Vol. 1 Materials

Vol. 2 Finished Products

Dictionary of Painting and Decorating

Covering also allied industrial finishes

A detailed reference work for
craftsman, student and teacher

J. H. GOODIER

Justice of the Peace · Holder of the Queen's Silver Jubilee Medal · Holder of the City and Guilds Insignia Award in Technology · Fellow of the Royal Society of Arts · Fellow of the British Institute of Interior Design

CHARLES GRIFFIN & COMPANY LTD
London

CHARLES GRIFFIN & COMPANY LIMITED
16 Pembridge Road, London W11 3HL, England

First published	1961
Reprinted with supplement	1966
Second edition	1974
Reprinted	1983
Reprinted	1985
Third edition	1987

British Library Cataloguing in Publication Data

Goodier, J.H.
Dictionary of printing and decorating : covering also allied industrial finishes : a detailed reference work for craftsman, student and teacher. —— 3rd ed.
1. Decoration and ornament, Architectural —— Dictionaries
I. Title
698'.03'21 TT305

ISBN 0–85264–279–2

Typeset in Great Britain by Latimer Trend & Company Ltd, Plymouth
Printed and bound in Great Britain by Redwood Burn Ltd, Trowbridge, Wilts

Preface

Why should anyone write books about trade subjects? To me, the answer lies in the words of Francis Bacon—"I hold every man a debtor to his profession". I certainly owe a tremendous debt to my profession as a painter and decorator. It has given me a long working life packed with interest, satisfaction and enjoyment. It has enabled me to pursue this, the most diverse and fascinating of all the crafts. It has given me the means of doing a creative job with so many facets that no two days have ever been alike. It has brought me into contact with some admirable people, and some of the most perfect gentlemen imaginable. How else can I repay that debt but by providing the means of helping a new generation of painters?

My own studies were helped by books written by great technical authors of former days, especially those of the incomparable James Lawrance and that splendid character John Parry. It was natural that I should want to take up the task where they laid it down. That is what makes for continuity. In the same way, I rejoice to continue the work done by the great craft teachers I have known in the past. But my vision is of the future, not the past. One of my great personal joys is to see how many of my own students have carved out for themselves a useful and satisfying career, here in Britain and all over the world. Many of them regularly correspond with me and are firm friends. Several have achieved positions of great eminence, and that is as it should be; it would be foolish of any teacher to imagine he is on a pinnacle that nobody else can reach—every teacher worth his salt hopes that his students will go further than he himself has done. Many of my students are themselves passing on their own expertise to the rising generations, and that is how knowledge is constantly extending and expanding.

In writing this book, as with everything else I have written, I have had one clear aim from which I would not be deflected. That aim is to provide a full and comprehensive coverage of the subject and to put it into a readable and understandable form without ever sacrificing accuracy. I do not subscribe to an educational system of cutting a syllabus down to bare essentials and giving the absolute minimum of information that is just enough to enable a student to get by. I believe in raising standards, not lowering them. I am opposed to any form of technical writing that merely states the facts without giving an explanation of their underlying principles. The only form of knowledge that is of real value is the kind that is based on understanding. Of course, it is very much easier and quicker to present a subject as a series of formulae to be memorized by the student, but I discovered the fallacy of that system a very long time ago while I was still a schoolboy. I was fortunate in having many masters who loved their subjects and taught them well, but the exception was a highly qualified man whose subject was chemistry; his method was to provide in each lesson twenty chemical equations to be learned by rote without ever explaining the nature of the chemical reactions involved. I now know that he was a brilliant scientist, but he was also the worst teacher

I have ever known, who succeeded in killing any interest the students might have had in the subject. It is possible to reduce painting technology to a formula, listing various types of surface and giving a brief phrase by each to indicate the preparation, type of primer, and so on. There are two snags; one is that memory is fallible and if you get the formula wrong you can easily make a mistake that is very expensive to rectify; the other is that the formula is of no help to you when you're faced with unusual circumstances or problematical surface conditions. There is no substitute for the ability to think the matter out in a logical manner—for which a range of background knowledge is required.

I also have a profound mistrust of the slick jargon phrases that are so popular today. Jargon is lazy speech that obscures the truth. People use jargon because it enables them to sound knowledgeable without taking the trouble to make an accurate and carefully considered assessment of a situation. My desire is to see that painters and decorators are thoroughly competent in their craft and sufficiently well informed about it to command the respect of their customers and clients and the community as a whole.

We live in difficult times. In the preface to earlier editions of this book I said that painters now have less time to master the intricacies of their craft due to a drastic reduction in the period of apprenticeship and the fact that basic training is limited to the mere elements of the work. This is even more true today, and is compounded by massive unemployment which has degraded the whole concept of manual work. As painters we find ourselves in competition with people made redundant from all sorts of industries and with no training in our craft, who offer their services to the public as painters and decorators and who by the execrable quality of their work give the whole craft a bad name. Much of the output of decorative materials is deliberately aimed at the amateur market rather than the professional painter, requiring the minimum amount of skill in application but inevitably sacrificing quality. On contract work, in nearly every case the painting is regarded by the specifying authorities and the finance departments as the least important factor; the emphasis is on highly expensive eye-catching constructional devices, and the painting accounts for less than 2 percent of the contract price, consisting generally of cheap white emulsion paint on the ceiling and wall areas and a totally inadequate paint system on the woodwork and metalwork. Couple this with some ill-judged youth training schemes and you have the perfect recipe for reducing the painting craft to the level of a semi-skilled or an unskilled occupation.

As professionals we have the remedy in our own hands. It does not lie in skimping work nor in cutting costs; by those methods we shall destroy our own livelihood because our work will be no better than that of the amateur—in fact it will be worse, because the amateur can afford to spend a lot more time on the work since no labour costs are involved. The remedy lies in promoting the highest possible standards of workmanship, because then the superior quality of the professional's work is obvious for everyone to see and is clearly such that no amateur can hope to achieve. The decorating craft has a far greater variety of techniques and materials than any other craft, and that is what we should exploit. Our opportunity lies in advertising and selling our expertise and thereby making the public aware of the endless possibilities we can offer. In innumerable ways experience shows that when highly attractive things are available the public is prepared to pay a high price for them, and good quality creates its own demand.

This is not some rosy dream. We have risen above difficult times before now. Unemployment in the late 1920's and 1930's was on a disastrous scale, living conditions were poor, and salary levels and spending on luxury goods were minimal compared with today, yet there was a constant demand for high-class decorating work. The purpose of this book lies in my conviction that the success of the painting and decorating craft depends on the quality of the work it produces and the ability of its practitioners. The key to all this is knowledge—knowledge of the techniques, the materials and the new developments, based on real understanding. This book aims to supply that knowledge and understanding.

Newcastle under Lyme
May 1986

J. H. GOODIER

Acknowledgments

Writing a book is a long and lonely task, working in solitude, isolated from other people, but it is cheered and enlivened by the friendliness one encounters when one looks for advice to someone who can throw extra light on some specialist subject or new development.

I want to thank the following firms, and in particular the individual people in those firms, who have been so kind and have gone out of their way to provide information on various specialized topics.

Mr Michael J. Levete, Director of the Wallcovering Manufacturers' Association, for his lively interest.

Turner Wallcoverings (Ernest Turner (Northdown House) Ltd) and particularly Mr Michael D. Wild the Sales Director, who has given me considerable help on the subject of contract wallcoverings.

Manders Paints Ltd, and especially Mr Jim Deaville, manager of their Stoke on Trent branch, who has always been ready to discuss present trends and to give me the benefit of his long experience.

Graham and Brown Ltd, Blackburn, for the information they have supplied about various types of vinyl wallcoverings.

Century Oils Ltd, Hanley, Stoke on Trent, and especially Mr A. J. Hayman, a director of the firm, who has been extremely helpful about recent safety legislation and about skin protection.

Helen Sheane Wallcoverings Ltd, Banbury, for supplying me with many samples and descriptions of their products.

Hamilton & Co (London) Ltd, and especially Mr J. Stanbridge, Managing Director, for information about present-day brushes.

J. H. Ratcliffe & Co. (Paints) Ltd, Southport, particularly Mr J. M. Ratcliffe for information about recent legislation and present-day trends, and his great support for craft education and especially for the craft of graining.

The staff of the County Reference Library, Hanley, Stoke on Trent (under the auspices of the Staffordshire County Council) for their unfailing courtesy and helpfulness on my many visits.

And above all my wife, without whose continual help and tremendous patience I should never have been able to achieve anything.

To my very dear EDITH, with my unending gratitude

CONVERSION FACTORS

To convert	Multiply by
Inches into millimetres	25.4
Millimetres into inches	0.039
Feet into metres	0.305
Metres into feet	3.281
Yards into metres	0.914
Metres into yards	1.094
Miles into kilometres	1.609
Kilometres into miles	0.621
Square inches into square feet	0.007
Square feet into square inches	144
Square inches into square centimetres	6.452
Square centimetres into square inches	0.155
Square feet into square metres	0.093
Square metres into square feet	10.764
Square yards into square metres	0.836
Square metres into square yards	1.196
Cubic inches into cubic feet	0.0006
Cubic feet into cubic inches	1728
Cubic inches into cubic centimetres	16.387
Cubic centimetres into cubic inches	0.061
Cubic yards into cubic metres	0.765
Cubic metres into cubic yards	1.308
Cubic feet into gallons	6.235
Gallons into cubic feet	0.160
Cubic inches into gallons	0.004
Gallons into cubic inches	277
Cubic feet into litres	28.32
Litres into cubic feet	0.035
Cubic centimetres into pints	0.0018
Pints into cubic centimetres	567.936
Pints into litres	0.568
Litres into pints	1.760
Gallons into litres	4.544
Litres into gallons	0.220
Ounces into grams	28.349
Grams into ounces	0.035
Pounds into kilograms	0.454
Kilograms into pounds	2.205
Tons into kilograms	1016
Kilograms into tons	0.00098
Tons into tonnes (i.e. metric tons)	1.016
Tonnes into tons	0.984
Pounds per square inch into bars	0.069
Bars into pounds per square inch	14.504

CONVERSION TABLE

Feet and inches into metres, centimetres, millimetres, and vice versa

For centimetres move point two to right *For millimetres move point three to right*

	inches											
	0	**1**	**2**	**3**	**4**	**5**	**6**	**7**	**8**	**9**	**10**	**11**
feet	**metres**											
0	—	0.025	0.051	0.076	0.102	0.127	0.152	0.178	0.203	0.229	0.254	0.279
1	0.305	0.330	0.356	0.381	0.406	0.432	0.457	0.483	0.508	0.533	0.559	0.584
2	0.610	0.635	0.660	0.686	0.711	0.737	0.762	0.787	0.813	0.838	0.864	0.889
3	0.914	0.940	0.965	0.991	1.016	1.041	1.067	1.092	1.118	1.143	1.169	1.194
4	1.219	1.245	1.270	1.295	1.321	1.346	1.372	1.397	1.422	1.448	1.473	1.499
5	1.524	1.549	1.575	1.600	1.626	1.651	1.676	1.702	1.727	1.753	1.778	1.803
6	1.829	1.854	1.880	1.905	1.930	1.956	1.981	2.007	2.032	2.057	2.083	2.108
7	2.134	2.159	2.184	2.210	2.235	2.261	2.286	2.311	2.337	2.362	2.388	2.413
8	2.438	2.464	2.489	2.515	2.540	2.565	2.591	2.616	2.642	2.667	2.692	2.718
9	2.743	2.769	2.794	2.819	2.845	2.870	2.896	2.921	2.946	2.972	2.997	3.023
10	3.048	3.073	3.099	3.124	3.150	3.175	3.200	3.226	3.251	3.277	3.302	3.327
11	3.353	3.378	3.404	3.429	3.454	3.480	3.505	3.531	3.556	3.581	3.607	3.632
12	3.658	3.683	3.708	3.734	3.759	3.785	3.810	3.835	3.861	3.886	3.912	3.937
13	3.962	3.988	4.013	4.039	4.064	4.089	4.115	4.140	4.166	4.191	4.216	4.242
14	4.267	4.293	4.318	4.343	4.369	4.394	4.420	4.445	4.470	4.496	4.521	4.547
15	4.572	4.597	4.623	4.648	4.674	4.699	4.724	4.750	4.775	4.801	4.826	4.851
16	4.877	4.902	4.928	4.953	4.978	5.004	5.029	5.055	5.080	5.105	5.131	5.156
17	5.182	5.207	5.232	5.258	5.283	5.309	5.334	5.359	5.385	5.410	5.436	5.461
18	5.486	5.512	5.537	5.563	5.588	5.613	5.639	5.664	5.690	5.715	5.740	5.766
19	5.791	5.817	5.842	5.867	5.893	5.918	5.944	5.969	5.994	6.020	6.045	6.071
20	6.096	6.121	6.147	6.172	6.198	6.223	6.248	6.274	6.299	6.325	6.350	6.375
21	6.401	6.426	6.452	6.477	6.502	6.528	6.553	6.579	6.604	6.629	6.655	6.680
22	6.706	6.731	6.756	6.782	6.807	6.833	6.858	6.883	6.909	6.934	6.960	6.985
23	7.010	7.036	7.061	7.087	7.112	7.137	7.163	7.188	7.214	7.239	7.264	7.290
24	7.315	7.341	7.366	7.391	7.417	7.442	7.468	7.493	7.518	7.544	7.569	7.595

The letters "(NLC)" following an entry signify a material or procedure that is no longer in current use, but which may sometimes be specified to meet a particular need, e.g. in restoring an old or historic building.

Abrade A word which means to rub away or wear down by friction. Abrasion is the act of rubbing away or wearing down, and from this is derived the word "abrasive".

Abrasive In painting and decorating the term has two connotations.

(i) A material which, by a process of rubbing down or grinding down, tends to make a surface become smooth, and very often at the same time imparts some degree of "tooth" which improves the adhesion of paint to the surface. Such materials are of the utmost importance to the decorator, because it is most essential that every surface should be adequately and correctly prepared if a good finish is to be obtained.

The abrasives used by the painter include such materials as abrasive papers, emery cloth, pumice stone, pumice blocks, steel wool, etc. Some of the older traditional abrasives such as rotten stone, cuttlefish bone, etc., although obsolete in general practice, are still occasionally used for certain specific types of work.

(ii) In industrial painting the term "abrasive" is used to refer to the various types of grit or shot employed in the process of blast-cleaning, "shot" being used to describe small, rounded abrasive particles, and "grit" referring to small angular particles with a sharp cutting edge.

The types of abrasive which are used include ferrous metallic substances such as chilled iron shot or grit, and steel or malleable iron shot or grit; various non-ferrous metallic substances such as aluminium, brass or copper, and non-metallic substances such as sand (which needs to be carefully controlled because of the health hazards involved). On site work, where it is not feasible to reclaim or recycle the abrasive, cost becomes a highly significant factor, and an abrasive called "mineral slag" is often used because it is cheap enough to be regarded as expendable; mineral slag is produced in the course of refining iron or copper.

Abrasive papers These include garnet paper; glass paper and sandpaper for dry rubbing down; waterproof abrasive papers of various kinds which are generally made from silicon carbide and are used for wet rubbing down; self-lubricating papers made from silicon carbide coated with zinc stearate which, because of their convenience, are to some extent replacing waterproof papers in vehicle painting and similar work; and emery paper used for the etching of metal surfaces. In modern practice garnet as an abrasive has largely been superseded by aluminium oxide.

Abrasive papers—how they are graded Abrasive papers (with the exception of sandpaper and emery) are graded by a numerical system which indicates the fineness or coarseness of the grit. The numbers correspond with the size of mesh through which the grit particles will pass; thus, paper graded as 100 indicates that the grit will pass through a mesh with 100 holes per square inch, the system having been codified before metric measurements were adopted in this country; 400 indicates that the particles will pass through a mesh with 400 holes per square inch, and so on. Some papers are marked on the back with both the grade number *and* the grit number, which may be confusing; in this case it should be noted that the higher grit numbers indicate the coarser grits whereas the higher grade numbers indicate the finer grits. The backing paper is also graded; the finer grades of abrasive particles are bonded to a lightweight flexible paper backing, grade A, to facilitate rubbing down by hand, while the coarser grades of grit are bonded to a heavy rigid backing paper, grade D, which is suited to both hand and mechanical working.

The ordinary "wet-or-dry" abrasive papers used by the decorator are supplied in five grades ranging from 120, the coarsest, to 600, the finest. Self-lubricating abrasive papers which are widely used in vehicle re-finishing are also available in five grades, but these range from 220 to 500. For certain specialist purposes, however, there are very much finer grades of abrasive paper available. The ultimate degree of fineness at the present time is an abrasive paper of grade 1000. This is far too fine (and too expensive) for any normal decorative work, but it is used where the quality of the painted work is absolutely critical. Usually this applies to small areas of the finest pieces of ornamental work, but occasionally it is required on quite large areas. One example of this is the quality of the paintwork on the vessels designed for the highest levels of boat-racing. In order to cut down wind and water resistance to the minimum, every possible means is employed to ensure a completely smooth and nib-free surface, and to achieve this the paintwork is brought to an extraordinary degree of perfection. During the summer of 1983 the USA was so intent on trying to maintain its unbroken sequence of success in the America's Cup that the use of grade 1000 abrasive paper was regarded as part of the regular painting procedure, and great quantities of this particular grade were employed.

The coarser grades of garnet papers, for dry rubbing down, range from 40 to 100, the natural garnet being bonded to a grade D paper; the finer grades range from 130 to 240 on a grade A paper.

Glasspaper and sandpaper used for dry rubbing down are graded on a different system. They are sold in grades ranging from "0" or "00" (very fine) to "No. 3" (coarse). But there is no uniformity, and the significance of the grade numbers varies from one manufacturer to another. Some manufacturers have abandoned numbers and use initial letters instead; the grades are F (fine), M (medium), C (coarse) and S (strong) although the finest grade is sometimes termed "Flour".

An abrasive is now available for the dry rubbing down of rough painted surfaces and new timber which consists of tungsten carbide particles bonded to a thin metal sheet, and this is graded as fine, medium or coarse.

Absorbency The extent to which a surface will absorb or "suck in" a liquid. The absorbency of a surface has a great bearing on the quality of the painter's work, and the object of many of the priming coats and preparatory processes he employs is to reduce or equalize the absorbency. For example, the priming of softwoods and certain forms of plaster is directly intended to reduce their absorbency, because if undercoatings were applied to a highly absorbent surface the thinner and binding medium would be sucked into the surface, making it impossible to level the paint out quickly enough and therefore leading to "ropiness". In the same way a gloss finish applied to an absorbent surface would lose some of its binding medium and the gloss would be reduced. The absorbency of plaster surfaces is often patchy and variable and one object of applying size before papering is to help to equalize the absorbency. The painter often speaks of highly absorbent surfaces as "hot", and he experiences difficulty in applying paint coatings to them.

Abstract design Anything which is abstract is separated from any particular thing—an idea which exists only in the mind—and abstract design is the formation of pattern which relies for its effect on the interplay of masses, shapes or colours rather than on naturalistic or conventional shapes. It may, of course, be *based* on some natural object or form, but the treatment is such that the basis is often hidden in the interrelation of the shapes.

Accelerated weathering Anything which speeds up or hastens the natural process of decomposition. The paint manufacturers make great use of what are termed "accelerated weathering tests" in which paints which are under review are applied to small panels and placed in a revolving drum where they are subjected alternately to ultra-violet light rays and to soaking with a spray of cold water in constant succession. This imposes a great strain on the paint and the effect of several months' normal outdoor exposure can be reproduced in a few days. Paints do not necessarily behave under such tests exactly as they will under normal conditions, but any paint which gives a good performance under test is shown to have possibilities which are worth further consideration and experiment.

Accelerator A term sometimes used instead of the more precise term "activator" in relation to two-pack products. See *Activator*.

Accelerators in plaster The anhydrous plasters (i.e. anhydrous gypsum plaster—Class C, Keene's and Parian —Class D) have accelerators such as alum or zinc sulphate added during manufacture to speed up their setting, because they do not combine with water very quickly and there is a danger of the water used to mix with them evaporating before the setting action is complete. This leads to a fault known as "dry-out", which may have serious consequences for the decorator. The actual fault may not be observed but if water is introduced during the decoration the plaster may absorb some of it and resume the setting action which was not completed, causing the skimming coat to buckle and flake off. A form of dry-out sometimes caused by impatience on the part of the painter or his customer is dealt with under the letter "D".

Access equipment Any type of ready-made mobile equipment which can be manipulated by the operative craftsman in order to convey him/her to where the working surface is situated. The term covers all the various kinds of cradle, whether they be fixed, travelling or winch-operated, bosun's chairs and skips, and hydraulic or electrically operated platforms and towers. See *Powered access equipment*.

A

Accident An accident is an unexpected or unplanned happening which results in damage or personal injury and which may have fatal consequences.

But although *all* accidents are unexpected, most of them *could* have been foreseen and could therefore have been prevented. Accidents don't just happen without a definite reason. Accidents have a definite cause, and finding out what causes them is the first step towards preventing them.

Accidents in painting work Every human activity involves some risk, but clearly there are some occupations where very little risk is involved and others where there is a very high degree of risk. Building and civil engineering works are recognized as having a high risk factor, higher than that of most other occupations. But even within this grouping the individual trades vary considerably, and it is an unfortunate fact that the craft of painting and decorating has a very high accident rate indeed compared with that of other building crafts. The main reasons for this are as follows:

(i) The majority of painting firms are very small units serving a fairly restricted local area. There are, however, large numbers of painting firms and the total workforce is very great. It is far more difficult to supervise working conditions and enforce the observance of safety regulations when several hundred workers are operating in small groups scattered over a wide area than when a single firm employs the same number of workers on a single site.

(ii) It is regrettably common for people with no craft background at all to change from some other totally different kind of occupation and set up in business as painters and decorators. Apart from the fact that they bring the whole craft into disrepute, because they are untrained they do not recognize the risks, nor do they understand the elementary rules of craft procedure.

(iii) Most of the individual operations in painting are of very short duration. The time taken to apply a coat of paint to a wall surface is very slight compared with the time taken to erect the structure. So the painting of the structure consists of a number of individual operations each of which is performed quickly, and the painter's work is characterized by a much greater degree of mobility than that of other building trade workers. In addition, a lot of the work consists of painting small unconnected items. It follows that the amount of time required to paint the structure does not justify the cost of erecting an elaborate scaffold, and indeed it would be quite uneconomic to do so. The result is that much of the painter's work is done with impermanent forms of scaffold that can easily be moved from place to place, so that the risk of mishap is much higher than in the case of more lengthy building operations. But the fact that the risks are higher does not mean that the work is inherently more dangerous; it simply means that the risks must be recognized and proper precautions taken to avoid them.

Accident prevention Usually an accident is the last link in a chain of events, the chain consisting of a series of dangerous conditions and dangerous actions, all operating at the same time. In effect, what happens is very similar to the sequence of events which occurs when several dominoes standing on end are arranged so that when the first one is pushed over it causes each of the others to fall over in succession. The fall of the dominoes could be prevented by lifting out one of the dominoes, thus breaking the sequence. In the same way, the chain is broken by removing some of the links; in other words, by removing the dangerous conditions and cutting out the dangerous actions the sequence of events is interrupted, and the accident cannot happen. This is the basis of accident prevention.

Accident prevention is something that everyone can practise and should practise. It consists of being able to recognize when a condition is becoming dangerous and knowing when an action is unsafe, and knowing also what steps to take to remove the danger. Learning to spot these dangerous conditions and actions is not at all difficult, because accidents follow a regular pattern. The same kind of accident happens over and over again. Every day of the year on thousands of sites all over the country, the same set of dangerous conditions builds up and the same unsafe acts take place.

Accident prevention is not just the concern of the management, it is the concern of everybody engaged in any capacity in the craft, from the most junior to the most senior members of the workforce.

Acetate A compound which may be considered as derived from treating a substance with acetic acid. Those of interest to the painter are the group of slow-evaporating solvents used in the preparation of nitrocellulose lacquers and which include amyl acetate, butyl acetate, ethyl acetate, propyl acetate, etc. When paints were hand-mixed on the site, lead acetate (sugar of lead) was used as a drying agent.

Acetone A strong solvent, water-white in colour, which has several applications to the painting trade. It is an ingredient in some makes of paint remover, and is also used in the preparation of cellulose ester lacquer. The use of acetone to scrub the surface of "greasy" woods such as cedar and teak before they are painted is often recomended.

Acetylene A gas, obtained from calcium carbide and water, which burns with a very white light. It is highly flammable, and in contact with air it produces an explosive mixture. Its important to the painter is its use in various processes such as flame-cleaning and in equipment such as blowtorches. The construction, maintenance and carriage of acetylene cylinders are subject to statutory regulations; the cylinders should be stacked upright on the site.

Acetylene blowtorch A piece of burning-off equipment comprising a cylinder of compressed acetylene gas, a flexible rubber hose and a lightweight metal handpiece with burner attachment and regulator for controlling the proportions of gas and air. The flame can be adjusted from a broad fan to a narrow pencil. It was the first type of blowtorch to be fuelled with bottled gas, but in recent years has largely been superseded by butane and propane blowtorches and other types of burning-off equipment.

Achromatic Free from colour; transmitting light without decomposing it into its three primary colours. To the decorator the term might be used to apply to white and neutral greys.

Acicular A term used to denote the crystalline form of a pigment, indicating that the particles are needle-shaped, giving increased durability and tint retention to certain pigments such as zinc oxide.

Acid A substance with a sour, sharp taste and which changes the colour of litmus dye from blue to red. It is compounded of hydrogen and another element or elements. If neutralized by an alkali it forms a salt, and similarly an alkali can be neutralized by an acid. Because of their corrosive nature, acids present certain problems to the painter.

One of these is the problem of atmospheric pollution. Sulphur dioxide is generated from the combustion of all but the most refined of the fossil fuels. In industrial areas the pollution is such that a deposit of soot and grime accumulates on the surfaces the painter is required to treat. These deposits are of an acid nature, and they are activated by rainwater. The rainwater itself is polluted and mildly acid, because a small part of the emitted sulphur dioxide is dissolved in it to form sulphurous acid. Consequently the deposits bite into the paintwork and if they are not removed before repainting is begun they will attack the new paint film from beneath.

Legislation such as the Clean Air Act and the introduction of smokeless zones, together with improved methods of treating flue gases, have considerably reduced the incidence of smog in industrial conurbations, and the pall of smoke that used to envelop the manufacturing towns has greatly decreased. As a result, there is a tendency for people today to think that atmospheric pollution is no longer of much significance, and in the painting trade the importance of thorough preparation is sometimes ignored. This is, however, a mistaken view. The emission of sulphur dioxide from industrial plants is immense. It was reliably stated at a public meeting (Royal Society of Arts, September, 1983) that the industrial plants of Europe and the USSR currently emit some 60 million tonnes of sulphur dioxide into the atmosphere every year. The chief concern in this respect was the precipitation of "acid rain" causing environmental damage in areas hundreds of miles away from the sources of emission; this is a totally different problem, but it would be quite wrong to suppose that because the incidence of smog is so much reduced, the painter no longer needs to exercise care in the preparation of existing paintwork before redecorating.

The painting of industrial premises is often complicated by the presence of acids, both as regards surface preparation and the selection of a suitable paint system. Problems of preparation occur not only in chemical laboratories and chemical producing plant where such conditions can be expected, but also in such places as the factories where certain man-made fibres are produced, where the chemicals used in the manufacturing processes combine with the humidity of the air, so that what appears to be normal condensation of moisture upon a surface is actually a mildly acid solution which would be destructive to a paint film. The correct and thorough preparation of the surface is most important. The selection of a suitably resistant painting system is obviously of major importance where the painted surfaces are to be exposed to acid conditions, such as for instance in chemical plants, sewage plants, etc., where there is acid fume attack, and in situations where the surface is subjected to splashing from battery acid or other liquid acid solutions. Certain pigments are affected by acids, which again emphasizes the importance of the correct choice of paint to prevent subsequent trouble due to discolouration of the finish.

Acid, as shown under another heading, can be used in certain decorative treatments.

Acid-catalysed clear finishes A group of two-pack clear wood finishes for interior work, based upon acid-catalysed resins. They offer the advantage of excellent resistance to abrasion, and are also highly resistant to acid, alkali and detergent fumes and liquids. The proportion of the base material in relation to the activator or curing agent is critical; unless they are mixed in the correct ratio the quality of the dried film will be adversely affected. The pot-life is short, and whatever quantity is mixed must be used within the time limit specified by the manufacturer, generally within one day. When used on new woodwork, a three-coat system is usually advocated, and slight thinning of the first coat is sometimes recommended. When used on previously varnished work it is necessary to strip off all the existing finish. For spray application it may be necessary to add thinners in the proportions recommended by the manufacturer. During spray application respirators should be worn.

Acid etching A process used in a specialized branch of signwriting whereby glass is etched or partially eaten away by the action of hydrofluoric acid. Parts of the glass are protected by means of an acid resist and other parts exposed to the action of the acid, producing a contrast between the polished surface and the texture created by the etching process. Acid etching is used to produce decorative effects on windows and mirrors, and the contrast of textures is frequently enhanced by gilding and other treatments.

Acid-refined linseed oil Linseed oil which has been refined by mixing with strong sulphuric acid to char out the mucilage and other "break" materials, producing an oil of very pale colour.

Acid resist A term used in connection with acid etching, as described in a previous paragraph. The acid resist, which usually consists of Brunswick black, is the protective coating applied to those parts of the glass which are not intended to be etched.

Acid-resisting paints Coatings with greater resistance to acid than normal alkyd resin paints, and which can be used in areas and on surfaces where the acid concentration demands a higher degree of resistance. There are various materials which have this capacity, each with its own particular advantages and disadvantages; they include (a) bituminous compounds which have good resistance to inorganic acids but which tend to be brittle at low temperatures and to become thermoplastic and to soften up under hot conditions; (b) chlorinated rubber paints which have good resistance to most acids but are not resistant to acetic acid and certain organic fatty acids; (c) two-pack epoxy finishes which are resistant to most acids, even at high concentrations; (d) polyurethane finishes which in some circumstances have greater resistance than epoxides; and (e) epoxy coal-tar finishes which have a high build and give excellent results under extreme conditions of exposure, but which need the surface to be very carefully prepared. Advice should be obtained from a reputable paint manufacturer to select the most suitable form of coating for the particular conditions or situations which are to be treated.

Acoustic From a Greek word meaning "to hear", from which is derived the word "Acoustics" which means the science of sound and the phenomena associated with sound. This is of importance to the decorator because of the factors which influence the reception of sounds, especially in public halls.

Before the scientific principles of acoustics were properly understood it was a common experience to find that concert halls, theatres, lecture halls, and similar places designed for public gatherings were quite well laid out with regard to such matters as the seating, visibility, heating, lighting and so on, but were hopelessly unsuited to their main purpose because it was impossible to hear clearly the sound either of the human voice or the musical instruments. This was generally due to the hardness and smoothness of the wall and ceiling surfaces, whereby the sound waves rebounded from one area to another in such a way that the overall sound effect became blurred and distorted. Various materials have been developed with a view to overcoming this defect, but their effectiveness can be reduced or completely lost if they are coated with unsuitable decorative materials.

Acoustic materials—(1) structural These are the sound-deadening materials which have been developed to ensure that the acoustical properties of a hall are satisfactory, or to improve those properties in an existing hall where sounds are not heard clearly.

New buildings designed for public gatherings are usually rendered in one of the various kinds of acoustic plaster which are available. These plasters have a porous texture and a rough surface so that they absorb sound. What the decorator must appreciate is that any surface coating which dries to a hard impervious film will seriously detract from the effectiveness of this material. Gloss paint would be most unsuitable, and in fact it is better to avoid the use of any alkyd-based paint, as even semi-gloss or eggshell finishes will reduce the properties for which the plaster was specified. Decoration should preferably be with emulsion paint, possibly mixed a little thinner than usual, and it is highly desirable that it should be applied by spray.

Various other materials are supplied which may be incorporated in a new structure or used to line the interior surfaces of older premises in order to improve their acoustic properties. These include a range of fibre insulating boards, compressed straw slabs and strawboards, and thick insulating wallboards which are supplied with either a flat or a moulded surface (the moulded type giving some extra advantage because its irregular surface deflects the sound-waves at different angles). These, too, should be coated with emulsion paint which might with advantage be thinned a little more than usual and which should be applied by spray. It is desirable that such boardings should be primed on the backs and the edges before fixing, to reduce the risk of their buckling in the event of condensation.

Sometimes, on the grounds of economy, the walls of a public hall where the acoustics are unsatisfactory are lined with pegboard, a thin type of hardboard perforated with a large number of regularly spaced holes. This is a depressing material from the decorator's point of view, as it is difficult to mask its stark and unpleasing appearance. It should for preference be coated with emulsion paint, spray applied, and the important point to notice is that a build-up of paint in the perforations should be avoided, otherwise any advantage gained from using this paltry material will be lost. For some reason the general public seems to think that pegboard ought to be finished in gloss paint, so it is likely that both the builder and the client will exert pressure on the decorator to apply a gloss finish. This will not matter greatly, as the newly supplied raw board itself has a smooth shiny surface; it is the perforations that provide the acoustic properties, so when a gloss paint is used it is doubly important to avoid bridging the holes with paint.

Acoustic materials—(2) for the decorator In addition to the acoustic material applied or fixed by a builder there are many materials specifically designed to be applied by the decorator. These offer much greater possibilities of interesting effects. So many types and patterns are available that a choice can be made to fit in with any kind of decor or to satisfy the precise needs of the client, and the quality of finish is generally far superior to any of the materials mentioned in the section headed *Acoustic materials* (1).

The kinds of material available include mineral fibre panels which absorb nearly 70% of the sound that strikes them, hollow-backed panels stamped or moulded into geometric patterns and high-relief goods with deep indentations to break up the surface and form a striking ornamental feature. The manufacturers of the various moulded or shaped relief materials describe them as having "non-directional fissures", which indicates that the sound-waves rebound from them at random angles, thus avoiding the resonance that leads to the echoes which mar the audibility. The materials vary in size from small ceiling panels of 600mm square to large wall panels measuring 2700 × 900mm. Many of them are supplied in finished form with a wide range of attractive colourways, while the relief goods that are painted after application can be finished in any degree of sheen which suits the particular scheme; these of course have the advantage that they can be redecorated when a change of colour is desired.

A number of firms produce wall-linings, folding partitions, sound-reducing doors and sliding wall systems for use in hotels, offices, conference rooms, medical centres, etc. Some of these are of a kind which the decorator can manipulate while others are clearly intended for specialist application, and the firms that manufacture these materials usually have a contracts department which will undertake the fixing. The materials are made from a variety of substances including PVC-coated steel, solid timber, veneered panels, etc.

Acrylic paints for murals and decorative work Acrylic paints are being increasingly used by artists in preference to oil colours, the reason being that they dry so quickly that work can proceed steadily without any delay caused by waiting for sections of the paintwork to dry. They offer the same advantage to the mural painter and decorative artist. It is most useful to be able to complete a fairly small area so that the overall effect can be judged and any adjustments of colour or technique be made before starting the main body of the work. It is also very handy to be able to complete sections of the work piece by piece instead of having to work over a relatively large area because of the slow drying of the paint, because it cuts down considerably on the quantity of scaffold required. An extremely wide range of colours is available and all the colours can of course be freely intermixed. A further advantage is that there is no risk of any of the colours fading. Many decorators maintain that the colours are brighter and cleaner than many of the tube oil colours they were accustomed to. The latest move in the art world is to use acrylic colours as an alternative to the normal pigments when painting in water colour. The advantage here is not the speed of drying (water colour itself is very rapid), it is the possibility of laying washes on top of each other without the risk of disturbing the previously applied colour. Interior decorators are finding acrylic paints useful for the production of perspective sketches and working drawings and for the sort of quick colour sketches that convey the idea of the intended scheme to a client.

Acrylic resin emulsion and priming paints Because it is possible to vary the formulation of acrylic resins to provide widely differing degrees of flexibility, and because they can be combined with other polymers so as to exploit the advantages of both, these resins are extensively used in many differing brands of emulsion paint. Since every brand has its own particular formulation, it is impossible to be specific about the properties of an acrylic emulsion beyond saying that it can be expected to provide an economical non-toxic finish which will give good results on most types of surface.

What is of special interest is the use of acrylic resins as the basis of wood primers. It is their flexibility and powers of adhesion that make them suitable for this purpose, but these factors alone would not have justified developing a material so totally different from the existing range of primers. There are, however, sound practical considerations which sway the issue.

On any construction site there is usually a considerable amount of debris in the form of dust and wood shavings, the wind is continually swirling through the doorways and window openings, and workers in several different trades operating in a fairly small area are constantly on the move. Under these conditions, any newly applied paint is subjected to an endless deluge of dirt and grit, and it is practically impossible to produce a decent standard of work. The advantages of using a paint which is touch-dry within minutes are obvious. The disadvantages are equally clear; a very quick-drying paint cannot be expected to penetrate the surface to the same extent as the traditional primers, nor can it provide as good a foundation on which to build a first-class painted finish of the quality we should like; while for exterior work a tough, elastic medium is needed to withstand the weather conditions of the British Isles. The fact remains that on new constructional work there are serious problems and difficulties, and the painter has to decide what is the best solution possible in the circumstances of the particular job in hand. It was for this reason that acrylic resin primers were introduced. At first there was a lot of prejudice against them and this was increased as a result of the wildly exaggerated claims made for the new products, but there was sufficient in their favour for the manufacturers to think it reasonable to improve and develop them. So at the present time there is a good range of quick-drying water-thinned acrylic resin primer-undercoatings available, all having the properties of high opacity, good adhesion and flexibility.

These paints may be applied by brush, roller or spray. If they are to be sprayed in poorly ventilated areas, respirators should be worn. When being used for priming they should preferably be applied by brush. The limitations on their use are as follows:

(a) They are not suitable for exterior work.

(b) Even when used on interior woodwork, any metal fittings or nail-heads need to be touched in with metal primer and allowed to dry before the acrylic primer is applied.

(c) They should not be used as primers on metallic surfaces, asbestos-cement, brickwork, plasterwork, nor on rough surfaces of any kind.

(d) On highly resinous timber an aluminium primer is more suitable than acrylic.

(e) No matter how carefully they are laid off it is not possible to eliminate the brushmarks, and these detract from the appearance of the finished paintwork.

Acrylic resins These are a group of co-polymers made from a variety of acrylic ester monomers. According to the nature of their formulation they vary considerably in their properties of elasticity, ranging from flexible to extremely hard. Their main use originally was in plastics such as perspex. After this they came into use in the leather and textile industries, but for a long time now they have been widely used, either on their own or in combination with other polymers, as the film-formers in many kinds of emulsion paint. As such they are notable for their rapid drying, adhesion, flexibility, durability, and freedom from yellowing. They have also become popular in recent years as the media for artists' colours, their quick-drying properties being a great asset compared with the very slow drying of the traditional artists' colours in oil.

Actinic light The actinic or ultraviolet rays, those components of the sun's light which exert a very destructive effect upon the organic binder of a paint, leading to breakdown of the paint film. To some extent they are filtered by the smoke pall which blankets industrial areas, so that their influence is more pronounced in coastal districts.

Certain pigments, notably red oxide of iron, have the property of absorbing ultraviolet radiations and this protects the binder from their harmful effects; for this reason red oxide is sometimes incorporated into finishing paints.

Activator A substance which, when added to some mixture or material, sets in motion a chemical or physical process which could not hitherto have taken place. In painting and decorating the term is used specifically in reference to certain products such as epoxy and polyurethane paints, etc., which are supplied as two-pack materials and which cannot develop their distinctive properties until the two packs are mixed together, i.e. until the activator is added. The film-forming material is called the "base". When the base and the activator are mixed together a chemical process of polymerization known as "curing" or "cold curing" begins. The pot life of the mixture is very short, generally between 8 and 12 hours, so it is important not to mix more than is required for one day's working. It is also most important that the base and activator should be mixed in exactly the right proportions. Because of the acid nature of the activator in some products, the manufacturers recommend that the mixing should be done in a non-metallic container.

Adam style The Adam style of decoration is the brilliantly inventive interpretation of Roman antiquities, especially those of Pompeii, Herculaneum and Spalato, developed in the latter part of the 18th century by the Adam brothers, of whom the second eldest, Robert Adam, was the acknowledged leader. It is seen in its perfection in the interiors of Kedleston Hall in Derbyshire (1764) and Kenwood House, Hampstead (1767–8). Among the characteristic features of the style are the delicate lines and mouldings of the ornamental plasterwork of the ceilings, cornices and walls, the use of inlaid marble and scagliola, and the interlacing trails of stucco branches and foliage, enhanced by the masterly use of coloured paintwork (especially the distinctive secondary colours such as pink, pea green, light blue, lavender and rose, picked out with gold leaf). One of Robert Adam's greatest talents lay in his genius for the interior planning of rooms, and he loved to incorporate the work of the gifted artists and craftsmen of the time. He employed many well-known painters such as Angelica Kauffmann, Antonio Zucchi, Francesco Zuccarelli, Biago Rebecca and Giovanni Battista Cipriani to paint decorative scenes in the ceiling and wall panels, and the stuccoist Joseph Rose and the sculptor Joseph Wilton also worked for him. Adam, like Christopher Wren, had the capacity for collaborating on the friendliest terms with his craftsmen; he respected their abilities and was happy to give them a free rein to develop their ideas, and the mutual trust that existed between them meant that they produced their finest workmanship. At this period, decoration reached great heights. Many people would maintain that Christopher Wren in the 17th century and Robert Adam in the 18th century were the most accomplished and inventive designers that Britain has ever known; men of supreme genius, both of them. Every aspiring decorator should make a point of studying the work of the Adam brothers.

Additive colour mixtures These relate to the effect of mixing the primary colours of light. When two light primaries are mixed, a secondary colour is produced (red plus green producing yellow, red plus blue producing purple, green plus blue producing blue-green). The light secondaries are of higher luminosity than the primaries that produce them, due to the additive effect of mixing coloured light. When a light primary is mixed with its contrasting secondary, white light is produced because all three primaries are now mixed.

It is important not to confuse the primary colours of light with the primary *pigment* colours; in this case the effect of mixing the colours is totally different, the secondary pigment colours being darker than the primaries which produce them.

Adhesion This, to a painter, means the extent to which a material will stick or adhere to a given surface. It is a matter of great concern to the painter, since many failures of decoration such as the blistering of paintwork, flaking of emulsion paint, and the springing and peeling of wallpaper are failures of adhesion that might well have been foreseen and prevented.

The adhesion of paint is the result of molecular attraction between the paint medium and the surface to which it is applied. It is therefore most important that the surface should be clean and perfectly dry at the time of painting. Any dirt or moisture that is present forms a barrier between the two and interferes with the adhesion. The adhesion of the paint is improved if the surface is roughened or is of a porous nature. When liquid paint is applied to blast-cleaned steelwork it penetrates the profiles in the surface, and when the paint dries it is anchored into these profiles; as a consequence it adheres more tightly than it would do to a smooth steel surface. Similarly a paint applied to an absorbent plaster surface penetrates the pores, and when it dries is securely locked in them, whereas a paint applied to the smooth glass-like surface of Keene's cement receives no such help. Occasionally another factor is involved, when some constituent in a liquid coating produces a chemical attack on the surface to which it is applied, such as when an etch primer is applied to steelwork. This may be summed up by saying that good adhesion requires a clean dry surface, free from grease or loose powdery matter, and that roughening the surface provides an additional mechanical bond.

Adjustable base plate A base plate, for use with tubular scaffolding, which incorporates a screw jack which enables it to be adjusted to suit varying levels.

Adulterant Something which is added to a substance or a mixture in order to cheapen it or degrade it.

Sometimes the term is used incorrectly to imply that anything added to an existing substance is an adulterant, and this can result in a perfectly legitimate operation being classed as wrong and harmful. The judicious thinning of paint, for example, is generally acceptable and at times is in fact really necessary to avoid the paint being applied too thickly and to assist the paint to penetrate. Occasionally an officious engineer controlling a painting contract or an obstinate site foreman on constructional work will refuse to allow any thinning of paint on the ground that such thinning constitutes adulteration; this can lead to a painter attempting to use a priming paint in far too round a condition, when a glance at the manufacturer's instructions would reveal that the addition of a reasonable proportion of thinners is actually recommended. This in itself is serious enough, but it becomes an intolerable imposition when the work is then condemned on the ground that the paintwork is ropey.

Advancing colours Colours generally on the yellow to red range, which when used on a particular surface tend to make that surface appear more prominent so that it "advances" or asserts itself.

Advice note A printed form which a merchant sends to a customer to indicate that the goods listed thereon have actually been despatched and warning the customer to expect them. In the case of small items sent by post, the advice note is sometimes enclosed in the package. When the customer is a painting contractor it often happens that goods ordered from a merchant are delivered direct to the site where they are to be used, rather than to the contractor's premises; in this case, the merchant's driver who delivers the goods brings an advice note in duplicate with a carbon slip between the two parts. The foreman on the site signs the note and retains the top part while the driver takes the second copy back to the merchant's office as proof of having delivered the goods. When this is done, it is most important that the foreman or whoever has signed for the goods should keep the advice note carefully and hand it as soon as possible to his/her employer. The employer files all the advice notes and in due course uses them to check the accuracy of the invoice or the bill for the goods received from that merchant. Should one or more of the advice notes be lost, the employer is unaware of what has actually been delivered to the site, and may dispute the invoice, which could lead to relations between the merchant and the contractor becoming strained.

Aerosol spraying A method of spray application for the refinishing of small articles and for touch-up work on motor vehicles, intended chiefly for the amateur and house operator. The aerosol pack, which is supplied complete and ready for use, contains a mixture of fluid paint and a liquid propellent gas, the free space above the fluid being saturated with the vapour of the gas which is sufficient to eject a stream of fluid from the spray aperture when the valve is released. The liquid gas acts as a thinner to the paint and vaporizes rapidly when it emerges into the atmosphere, thereby atomizing the paint.

Spraying with an aerosol pack must be carried out intermittently to allow some of the gas inside the container to vaporize and fill the space vacated by the paint; continuous spraying results in momentary loss of pressure. If the pack is held too close to the work, runs and sags will form in the paint film and the film will be unduly wet, since the gas will not have had time to vaporize completely before reaching the surface. The pack must be shaken well before use to disperse any pigment which has settled in storage; pigment settling is more likely to occur than in a conventional paint container because of the low viscosity of the paint/gas mixture. Care should be taken to ensure that the empty containers are not thrown away in any place where they are liable to become overheated or they may explode.

Aerosol packs are expensive, but against this must be set the fact that they can be used without any expenditure on spray plant, and also the fact that there will be no time to be spent on cleaning out containers and equipment after use.

After-image The phenomenon which is experienced when a person concentrates his gaze for a length of time upon one figure or object and then transfers his gaze to a blank surface; for a little while afterwards the shape of the figure or object appears to be still present before his eyes, though in a completely different colour. Gradually, of course, the after-image fades away. Usually the colour of the after-image is complementary to the colour of the original object. Thus, a person staring at a blue-green shape for any length of time tends to see the same shape in red when he transfers his attention elsewhere, especially if the surface to which he transfers his gaze is achromatic, i.e., white or neutral grey. The appearance of the after-image is due to the fact that part of the eye's mechanism, the receptors which respond to certain colours in light, become fatigued under the influence of continual stimulation; when the gaze is transferred elsewhere they tend to rest for a time while the receptors which respond to the complementary colours come into play.

After-tack A term used to describe a condition of a film which dries normally up to a point but which permanently retains a slight degree of tack. It is a defect associated with long-oil compositions, especially those in which a soft drying oil predominates; the painter may encounter the condition if a long-oil outdoor quality varnish has been used for indoor work. With present-day materials the condition is unlikely to occur, but it is sometimes found when work is taking place on old property decorated several years previously.

Agate burnisher An agate is a precious stone. An agate burnisher is a tool used by the decorator for burnishing gold leaf in the process of water gilding, rubbing the gold gently to bring it to a brilliant polish as lustrous as solid gold.

The tool has an overall length of 200mm. 185mm of that is the slender wooden handle, which the decorator grips between the thumb and fingers. Securely attached to the end of the handle is a piece of agate 25mm long, but curved round like the tail of a letter J. See *Water gilding*.

Ageing The term is sometimes loosely used by the painter to mean the natural process whereby an exposed film grows older and undergoes the gradual changes associated with growing older; the term is actually one used by the paint manufacturer to mean the storage of a material (e.g., a varnish) in order to mature it and allow it to stabilize itself before it is offered to a customer. This term has very little application to present-day practice.

Agitator Used in two connections.

(a) In one sense it is applied to a mechanical device for the rapid shaking of tins of paint, whereby paint kept in stock can be periodically shaken up to prevent the contents from settling.

(b) The term is also applied to a device fitted to the pressure tank of spray painting plant whereby the material is kept constantly stirred while in use. On some plant the agitator may be operated by hand when required; on other types of equipment the agitator is mechanically driven.

Air brush A very small spray gun, not much larger than a fountain pen, designed for use as an artist's tool. Its application to the decorating trade is mainly in the preparation of perspective drawings.

Air cable The air cable in electrostatic spray equipment, which connects air and high voltage from the power supply to the spray gun and provides a ground connection from the gun handle to the power supply. It consists of a high-voltage cable within the air hose, and a braided copper wire woven into the air hose.

Air cap The front part of the type of spray gun used in air-propelled (conventional) spraying. The air cap directs the air into the paint stream to "atomize" it—that is, to split it up into fine particles—and to form it into a suitable spray pattern. The usual type of air cap has three holes, but multiple jet caps can be used when spraying highly viscous materials.

Air compressor A piece of equipment which takes in air, compresses it to a given maximum pressure, and then delivers it as and where required. The sort of air compressor of most interest to the painter is probably the type used in spray painting by the air-propelled (conventional) method, although the industrial painter is also concerned with blast-cleaning plant and various kinds of tools for mechanical cleaning.

Air drying The drying of a paint due to exposure to the air at a normal temperature, as opposed to forced drying and stoving.

Air flotation Sometimes called "dry levigation". A term used to describe a method of preparing certain pigments; it consists briefly of feeding dry ground pigment into a current of air in order to separate the finer particles from the coarse.

Air hose Any flexible tubing that conveys air from one point to another as part of an industrial process. In paint spraying by the air-propelled (conventional) method, the air hose is the tubing which conveys the air from the compressor to the pressure tank and to the spray gun, or (when the paint is being fed to the gun from the feed cup) direct from the plant to the gun. To avoid confusion, the air hose is coloured red or orange whereas the hose which conveys the paint is coloured black.

Air leakage In air-propelled (conventional) paint spraying, this denotes air leaking from the front of the gun before the trigger is pulled, a fault which is caused by defective assembly of the gun, broken or worn gun parts, or the presence of dirt on the valve or seating of the gun.

Airless spraying A paint-spraying system using modern and highly sophisticated equipment but which consists basically of subjecting the fluid paint to an extremely high pressure and then forcing it through a tiny aperture in the gun, so that the release of the paint causes it to explode into a cloud of very fine particles. It has many attractive features which have made it an important factor in present-day painting practice and in a comparatively short space of time have led to its widespread adoption both in decorative and industrial work.

Airless spraying is radically different from the previous methods of spraying which depended on feeding paint into a flowing stream of compressed air, and it therefore has several advantages. These include the following:

(1) Speed of application. This is far higher than that of any other method of application, and consequently there is a considerable saving in labour costs.

(2) Cleanliness and absence of spray-fog. The atomized paint as it emerges from the spray cap in a cloud of minute particles is slowed down by the resistance of the air as it travels towards the surface which is being painted; it settles down gently on the surface. There is no moving airstream to make the paint hit the surface and then bounce off again as with other spraying systems. Thus, instead of the premises becoming charged with spray-mist which settles on furniture and fittings quite a considerable distance away from the scene of the operation and which penetrates behind and between the dust sheets and sometimes causes damage to items that were supposedly being protected, the whole operation is very much cleaner.

(3) Penetration of angles and corners. Because of the absence of a moving airstream, there is no build-up of compressed air in the corners and angles creating a cushion which repels the paint; on the contrary, the paint settles evenly on all the surfaces, and gives a level coating of uniform thickness.

(4) The production of an even coating. The application of the paint can be controlled so closely that a very high-quality finish can be obtained. The paint film is so level and uniform that one coat applied by airless spray is often equivalent to two coats applied by brush or roller.

(5) Precision work in situations where the quality of finish is critical. Where complete accuracy and the utmost degree of efficiency is required, the fact that the output of the paint is precisely controlled by the tip orifice size and angle means that it is possible for the wet and dry paint films to be monitored to comply with the most exacting specification.

(6) Suitability for the application of almost any type of coating. The airless spray system can be used to apply almost any type of paint, however heavy or viscous. The possibilities extend to the spraying of bitumens, mastics, masonry paint, etc., and in fact there are several materials which are too heavy or viscous to allow of brush or roller application but which are quite capable of being applied by airless spray.

Airless spraying units of various capacities are available; they range from the small types suitable for domestic work to the very big plant with outlets for several guns operating simultaneously and suitable for large-scale work such as bridges, dock installations, warehouses, storage tanks, etc.

Air pressure In spray painting by the air-propelled (conventional) method, the term relates to the pressure, measured in lb/in^2 (British) or kg/cm^2 (metric) or bars (SI)*, of the air delivered by the spray plant. In general, the higher the pressure the more finely the paint will be atomized. In the air-volume method of spraying comparatively low pressures are employed, dependent on the size and speed of the fan which blows the current of air along. In a high-pressure unit the air is compressed to a higher pressure and pumped into a cylinder from which it is drawn as required, and regulators are fitted so that the pressure actually fed to the gun may be considerably lower. If a pressure tank or a regulator-type paint cup is being employed, further regulators are included in the system, so that one pressure is used to force the paint along the hose and a different pressure is used to atomize the paint. The pressure on the paint is not very high unless a heavy-bodied material like spray plastic is being used, but needs to be stepped up if the work is at some height above the plant; the pressure on the air line varies according to the viscosity of the material, the length of the hose in use and the effect desired.

The industrial painter's interest in air-pressure also extends to blast-cleaning processes, and to the driving power of mechanical cleaning equipment.

Air-propelled spraying Any form of paint spraying where the equipment is such that the paint is conveyed by a forced stream of air from the spray gun nozzle towards the surface which is to be painted. The term covers the old-fashioned air-volume system of spraying and also the system in which compressed air plant is used. Originally *all* spray painting depended on the paint being conveyed in this way, and to differentiate between the air-volume

* 1 bar = 10^5 N/m^2 = 10^5 pascals = 1·02 kg/cm^2 = 14½ lb/in^2

and the compressed air methods, the compressed air method was called "high-pressure" spraying. Unfortunately, later developments have made these terms misleading and meaningless. The invention of airless spraying introduced a totally different method of propelling the paint from the gun to the paintable surface. In airless spraying, it is the paint which is pressurized, but the pressures involved are extremely high, so that the term "high-pressure spraying" as related to the compressed air system may well lead to confusion.

It is a pity that nobody at the time was sufficiently alert and forward-looking to anticipate the difficulties that would arise. As it was, the manufacturers of spray equipment began to call the new system "airless spraying" and at the same time they began to call the existing methods "conventional spraying". But the word "conventional" means "following the generally accepted practice". This was reasonable enough when airless spraying was a new thing and a novelty, but we are now in the situation where it is the airless spraying that is normal and commonplace, and the older methods such as the air-volume system that are practically obsolete. Today it is the airless spraying which is the conventional method, but the painting and decorating trade has got itself saddled with a completely misleading way of describing spray systems.

Once a wrong term is adopted it is very difficult to change it. As decorators, we already have too many terms that were introduced in this thoughtless manner and which give a mistaken impression—the term "emulsion paint", for example, which was introduced to differentiate between a new product and the old-fashioned water paint; but an emulsion paint is not strictly speaking an emulsion in the true sense of the word. Further back still, when synthetic resins were first introduced as binders when most paints were based upon a drying oil medium, it quickly became the habit to call the new materials "synthetic paints", but happily this grossly misleading term is now dying out. It would be a good thing if general agreement could be reached and the misleading use of the term "conventional spraying" be banned forthwith.

The term "air-propelled spraying" is not greatly used at present but is far more sensible than "conventional spraying".

Air regulator A pressure-reducing valve which allows an operative to reduce the air pressure delivered by a compressor to a level which suits the particular type of paint in use.

Air storage tank or air receiver The cylinder in which compressed air is stored. When maximum pressure is reached in this tank, the motor driving the compressor cuts out and runs idle. As air is drawn off from the tank, when a certain level is reached the motor cuts in again. The purpose of the tank is to provide a steady supply of air whenever required, with the utmost economy in the running of the plant.

Air transformer A device incorporated in spray plant of the air-propelled (conventional) type in order to condense air, oil and moisture, to strain the air, to indicate the pressure, and to provide an outlet for the guns and air tools.

Air valve A valve in the body of an air-propelled spray gun, which is opened and closed by the action of the trigger, thereby controlling the supply of air.

Air volume system A type of spray-painting equipment, now practically obsolete, which does not require the use of a compressor. It is operated by a pump or blower which propels a stream of air along the air line at a moderate pressure and flows continuously through the gun; when the trigger is pressed, paint is released into the stream of air and is split up and directed towards the wall surface. Because the pressure is so low, the paint is not so finely split up as in the sort of plant operated from a compressor, but on the other hand there is considerably less rebound and spray-fog. It is quiet and simple in operation, and is useful for decorative work, but it no longer has any place or significance in general paint-spraying practice.

Aisle A word which literally means "a wing", but which is generally applied to an open space or passageway which divides up—and gives access to—blocks of pews or seats as found in a church, a theatre, or some other kind of building used for public assemblies.

Alabaster A very pure form of the rock gypsum, sparkling white and translucent. When calcined it is reduced to a powder which has the same chemical composition as Plaster of Paris but without the impurities which give plaster its pinkish colour. Alabaster is used as the basis for certain good-quality powdered filler compositions, and has given its name to various proprietary fillers such as Alabastine, etc.

Alcohol The name given to a large and important group of solvents; the most important from a practical viewpoint is ethyl alcohol, so much so that when the word "alcohol" is used without being qualified it is generally assumed that it refers to this.

Alcove A deep recess in a room (and often containing a seat), or a recess in a wall.

Alga (singular), Algae (plural) Algae are plants which have no flowers and no true roots, although some forms of algae (seaweeds, for example) do have a part which enables them to hold on to a rock surface. They contain chlorophyll, a substance by means of which plants make sugar from carbon dioxide and water.

When algae are present on old exterior wall surfaces they must be removed by scraping and brushing before redecoration takes place. Residual growth should be killed by washing the affected area with a solution of domestic bleach in water. The solution should be applied liberally during a spell of dry weather and should be left for 48 hours, at the end of which time the surface should be washed and scrubbed with clean water to remove the dead growth and any bleach remaining in the surface.

Alkali (a) A compound of hydrogen and oxygen with sodium, potassium, calcium or other bodies, which is soluble in water and which produces caustic and corrosive solutions capable of neutralizing acids and changing the colour of vegetable substances.

(b) A knowledge of the action of alkalis is of the utmost importance to the painter for the following reasons:

(i) Many of the vegetable oils used in paints are badly affected by contact with alkaline materials; they react with the alkali to form a soap, and the effect seen by the painter is that the dry paint film softens up, becoming sticky, soft and soapy.

(ii) Several of the materials used in building (for example, lime plaster, Portland cement, asbestos-cement sheeting, etc.) are of an alkaline nature, so that when painting such surfaces the risk of alkaline attack on the paint must be considered and countered.

(iii) The paint may be attacked on the face by contact with an alkaline solution, a danger often met with in the painting of factories, workshops, and other industrial premises. Faulty procedure in washing down a paint film with mildly alkaline materials can also lead to the film being attacked.

(iv) Certain of the pigments used in paint are subject to alkaline attack.

Alkalinity Many building materials, such as brickwork, cement rendering, concrete, and lime plasters are highly alkaline, and gypsum plasters which in themselves are inert can become alkaline if lime is added to them. Alkalis present in the backing materials may also be brought to the surface in solution as the structure is drying out.

When an oil-based paint is applied over an alkaline surface which still contains moisture, the oil is liable to saponify. This is a form of chemical attack which causes the paint film to soften and become sticky; in acute cases the film may liquefy and develop runs or tears of an oily soapy nature, because in effect the oil has been converted into a soap and has thus become water-soluble. In addition, the alkalinity of the surface may result in certain pigments becoming bleached or discoloured.

Alkaline surfaces when thoroughly dry are not harmful to oil-based paints, but although they may be dry at the time that they are painted there is always the risk of moisture being introduced by means of water penetrating an outside wall or from leaking roofs, burst pipes or a faulty damp-proof course. It is therefore always desirable to prime such surfaces with an alkali-resisting primer.

Emulsion paints are not affected in this way because they do not contain oil, but in the presence of moisture the alkaline content of the surface may discolour the paint film or otherwise affect it.

Alkalinity, testing for A surface may be tested for alkalinity by moistening a very small area with distilled water and then pressing a piece of pink litmus paper into contact with it. Should the surface be alkaline the litmus will immediately turn blue.

Alkali-resisting paints These are finishing materials intended to withstand the attack of chemical concentrations and dust in the atmosphere, caustic soda spray, etc., in other words, alkaline attack on the outer face of the paint film. There are various materials available which are resistant to alkaline attack, including certain synthetic resin paints, chlorinated rubber paints, and bituminous paints; the actual choice for any particular area would be dictated by local conditions and requirements.

Alkali-resisting primer A primer intended to prevent damage to the paint film from alkaline materials present in the actual surface which is to be painted, i.e. attack on the paint film from below. (In a previous paragraph lime plaster, concrete, asbestos-cement, etc., were instanced as such materials.) The primer may be based on tung oil reinforced with coumarone resins, tung oil being more resistant to alkaline attack than linseed oil, but today primers are more likely to be based upon heat-treated oils, various synthetic media, or chlorinated and de-polymerized rubber. Some of these primers produce a fairly impervious film; for this reason it is desirable that the surface should be dry before they are applied, since no paint film can be expected to resist the pressure of a build-up of water trying to escape from the surface.

Alkyd resins The largest group of resins used in the paint industry at the present time, and they form the basis of both air-drying paints and stoving finishes. They are made by reacting a polyhydric acid such as glycerol or penta-erythritol with a polybasic acid such as phthalic anhydride and fatty acids of linseed oil or other oils. In air-drying paints, acids from drying or semi-drying oils such as linseed, tung, tall oil and soya are used. In stoving finishes acids from coconut and castor oils, which produce non-drying alkyds, are used. Unlike the familiar hard solid resins, alkyd resins take the form of thick syrups which are supplied to the paint manufacturer as solutions in solvent. The long-oil alkyds which are used as the medium for brush-applied gloss, semi-gloss and flat paints are thinned with white spirit. Short-oil alkyds which are used in spray-applied quick-drying paints or stoving finishes are thinned with xylol.

The features which render alkyd resins so useful and important in all classes of painting and decorating and in marine work are their durability, weather resistance, paleness of colour, colour retention, and flexibility. Although they have good properties of flow and are fairly easily applied by brush, they tend to set up quite quickly in warm weather which reduces their wet-edge time, so that speedy application and good brushing technique are called for when painting large areas.

Finishes based on alkyd resins are sensitive to moisture during the drying period and, to a lesser extent, when dry. If the dried film remains in contact with water for long periods it is liable to swell and blister. For this reason alkyds are not suitable in situations where the surfaces are to be immersed in water for long periods.

Alligatoring A clumsy term to denote the extensive cracking of paint in which the surface resembles alligator hide.

Alloy A mixture of metals. Alloys are of interest to the painter and decorator in two connections: (a) the metallic paints produced by mixing aluminium and bronze powders or, in the case of gold bronze paints, by mixing copper, zinc and aluminium, and (b) the various substitutes for gold leaf, such as Dutch metal, which is an alloy of copper and zinc. These substitutes are generally thicker and more brittle than real gold leaf, and they tend to tarnish if not protected with lacquer.

Alphabet (a) A series of symbols by which the form of a spoken language can be set down by one person and interpreted, or read, by another. In the case of a picture alphabet, each symbol represents an object, but what we use in our Western civilization is a "phonetic" alphabet, in which each symbol represents a sound. It will be seen that a phonetic alphabet such as ours, with only 26 symbols, is far less cumbersome and is easier to learn and read than a picture alphabet composed of several thousand characters. When we consider what a vast influence the written and printed word exerts upon the spread of every kind of knowledge and learning, it does not seem an exaggeration to describe the invention of a system of writing as probably the most important and far-reaching invention of all time.

(b) The term "alphabet" is often used to refer to a particular style in which the shapes of the letters of the alphabet are painted or depicted; for example, we speak of a "Roman" alphabet, meaning that the characters are slender and elegant with strokes of varying thickness, and of a "block" alphabet, in which characters are in a bolder and heavier style. Examples of various styles are described under the appropriate headings.

The painter when called upon to reproduce the letters of the alphabet in the medium of paint should be concerned to make them convey their meaning as readily as possible, in as pleasing a form as possible; this involves a careful study of the various kinds of alphabets, the ability to select those best suited to the work in hand and harmonizing best with the surroundings, and a sound knowledge of colour and design.

Alum A double sulphide of aluminium and potassium.

It used to be the common practice for the painter to add a lump of alum to a mixing of non-washable distemper to make it less soluble in water and to ease the labour of applying the distemper to a "hot" surface. This practice is now obsolete.

It was also the custom among some paperhangers to add a small quantity of alum to the paste that they were using, and to the glue-size. This was never a practice to be encouraged, as the alum tended to affect the colours in the wallpaper, and with present-day materials it is totally unnecessary and quite harmful. In spite of this, there are still some paperhangers who have heard of these old techniques and believe there is some virtue in using them. It needs to be clearly understood that materials such as alum should never be introduced into modern kinds of fixatives and pre-treatments.

Alumina The oxide of aluminium, forming the basis of alum and a constituent of all clays. It is a soft fluffy white powder which becomes transparent when mixed with oil. It is sometimes used as a suspending agent with heavy pigments to prevent them from settling.

Aluminium A white ductile metal. Combined as silicate it is very abundant; as a metal it is extracted principally from the ore bauxite, but also to some extent from nepheline, felspar, corundum and leucite.

Aluminium is widely used in constructional work in the form of sheetings, lightweight structural members, extruded sections and castings. In recent years it has been very widely adopted in the manufacture of window frames and is being increasingly used on domestic properties. Aluminium is also used as a sprayed metal coating for steel, especially in severely corrosive conditions. In all these circumstances it is very often required that a protective or decorative coating should be applied to the metal, and this matter is dealt with in the next few pages under the headings listed as *Aluminium units*.

Aluminium in various forms also has several applications to the craft of painting and decorating, and these are discussed under the next series of headings.

Aluminium foil A material frequently used in the thermal insulation of buildings because it combines the properties of high reflectivity of radiant heat and low emissivity of transmitted heat with lightness of weight and resistance to fire, and is also vermin proof. It may be obtained both as plain and corrugated sheets and is often supplied in rolls of 533mm width. Although it does not normally come into his province, the decorator is sometimes called upon to apply the foil. When this is the case, it should be remembered that aluminium is affected by contact with alkalis, wet brickwork, plaster, cement, etc., and should there be any doubt as to the conditions to which the foil is to be exposed it should, before application, be coated with a special thin transparent lacquer which protects it without seriously reducing its reflective properties. The fixative may be a bitumen compound or a synthetic rubber adhesive which is produced for the purpose. The insulating value of the foil is increased by using two layers with an air gap between, but this involves a method of fixing which is outside the decorator's normal practice. There is a form of aluminium foil for use on damp surfaces, designed for application by the decorator; it consists of sheets 3m long by 762mm wide, which are coated on the back with a particular form of synthetic rubber adhesive; the sheets are applied direct to the surface with a hot domestic iron.

Aluminium leaf A thin foil of the metal, used for decorative purposes, is sold in books in similar form to gold leaf. Each book contains 25 leaves, the size of the leaf varying from 82mm to 152mm square. It is much thicker than gold leaf and is therefore less delicate to handle. The fixative used is Japan gold size.

Aluminium paint—non-leafing There are certain finishes in which the leafing characteristics are not required, and if the particles are non-leafing they remain in the body of the paint film as it sets instead of rising to the surface; the result is that the flakes, being set at random, catch the light at varying angles, producing a satin or silky effect.

Aluminium paints These are made from aluminium paste or powder mixed with a suitable medium, and fall into three main categories:

(i) Decorator's finishing quality.
(ii) Decorator's priming paints.
(iii) Industrial or pyroxylin type.

The most widely used medium for (i) and (ii) is varnish, which can be made from a variety of resins including phenolin, paracoumarone and alkyd resins, ester gums, resins made from crepe rubber, chlorinated rubber, etc. Cellulose and synthetic gums can be combined to form binders for the pyroxylin type.

Aluminium paints—properties of Apart from the characteristic "leafing" referred to elsewhere the features of aluminium paint may be classed as follows:

(a) *Mechanical strength.* The aluminium flakes within the dried film act as a reinforcing pigment, strengthening the film.

(b) *Opacity.* Being actual metal particles, the flakes are themselves opaque, and as the paint film is composed of numerous overlapping flakes it will generally hide the underlying surface perfectly in one coat.

A further point that follows on the fact of the flakes being opaque is that they do not transmit light or other forms of radiant energy (including the damaging ultra-violet rays of the sun) so that the flakes in the upper layers of a paint film tend to protect the underlying layers of medium.

(c) *Moisture resistance.* The individual aluminium flakes, although very thin, do not permit the passage of liquids nor even of gases; in a paint film composed of such flakes moisture can only penetrate by the devious means of finding a path across and around the edge of each flake it encounters. Since the length and width of a flake are generally several hundred times its thickness it follows that such penetration is slow and difficult, giving the film great resistance to water.

(d) *"Sealing" properties.* The thin foil of metal which results from the overlapping of the flakes when set in a suitable medium is of value in sealing materials which have a tendency to "bleed". Aluminium powder added to shellac knotting will check the penetration of creosote, bitumen, bleeding reds, soot, etc., and when very resinous timber is to be treated aluminium paint is often found to have enough mechanical strength to hold back the resin where a normal wood primer would soon be blistered and lifted off the surface.

(e) *Reflectivity.* This is almost as great as that of the metal itself, which reflects up to 75% of the radiant energy which strikes it. This is an important factor in lowering temperatures inside various kinds of structure—for example, the painting of storage tanks with aluminium to prevent losses by evaporation.

(f) *Emissivity.* Very low, since emissivity is the opposite of reflectivity; the radiation of heat from hot sources can be reduced by painting them with aluminium. This factor is made use of when it is required to conserve heat, but is often overlooked when radiators are being painted; coating radiators with aluminium paint for decorative purposes seriously reduces their efficiency.

(g) *Spreading capacity and ease of application.* Very good, the average being usually in the order of 18 to 22 square metres per litre.

Aluminium paste The finest aluminium powders are usually mixed with sufficient liquid to form a paste, since in this form they are easier to handle and use, and quicker to mix.

Aluminium powder There are two main classes of aluminium powder; flake and granulated. The length and breadth of a flake particle are much greater than its thickness (often several hundred times greater), whereas the length, breadth and thickness of a granulated particle are all roughly the same; it follows that flake particles are essentially flat whereas granulated particles are spherical or ovoid.

Granulated powder is produced by "atomization"; the aluminium is melted and blown into a stream of cold air which breaks it up into minute solid particles. Flake powders for use in paint are made by feeding granulated powder into a ball mill with a suitable lubricant; here the particles are flattened into flakes. (Flake powder can be produced by a stamping process, but this is only used in the chemical and explosives industries.) The type of powder and its method of manufacture have a great bearing on its use, e.g., it is essential that the flakes of the powders used in primers should have "leafing" properties, whereas non-leafing flakes of various grades are needed to produce satin finishes, polychromatic paints, and hammered, crackle or wrinkle finishes.

Aluminium powders are often polished during manufacture to give extra brilliance.

Aluminium powders—"leafing" properties The minute metal flakes of the powders used in most aluminium paints are polished and coated during manufacture so that the surface is not readily "wetted" by normal paint media. This produces a high degree of interfacial tension between the flakes and the liquid medium, with the result that the flakes, although heavier than the liquid, tend to float to the surface and arrange themselves parallel with the surface, overlapping each other. This phenomenon, which resembles the way in which fallen leaves overlap one another in flat layers on the ground, is known as "leafing". The paint film therefore consists of innumerable layers of overlapping metal flakes with layers of medium between them. The extent of the leafing has a great bearing both on the appearance and the characteristic properties of the film.

Aluminium primer A very useful wood primer, composed of flake aluminium powder (the leafing form, that is) and a varnish medium. It is especially valuable for the priming of timbers with a highly resinous content, such as Columbian pine, pitch pine, etc. In such timbers the resin tends to exude freely, not only from the knots but also from the whole surface area of the wood; this prevents the paint from adhering and results in the formation of great numbers of blisters. The aluminium primer clings to the surface because of the strongly adhesive nature of the medium, and the leafing effect of the aluminium forms a metallic barrier powerful enough to hold back the resin.

Another purpose for which aluminium primer is exceedingly useful is in the priming of plywoods faced with Columbian pine and similar woods. A feature of these plywoods is that large areas of soft absorbent whitewood alternate with bands of dark brown and highly resinous hardwood. Ordinary wood primers are unsatisfactory for such surfaces; should the primer be oily enough to satisfy the whitewood it will not obliterate the darker bands and may fail to dry on them, but if it is adapted to dry on the hardwood bands it will fail to penetrate the softer areas. Aluminium primer creates what is virtually a continuous layer of thin metallic flakes over the whole surface, and this levels up the porosity.

On new construction work and when property alterations are in progress, aluminium primer is of great value for "back-priming" the timber, i.e. the priming of those parts of the window and door frames which are in contact with wet brickwork, because the impervious nature of the primer prevents the penetration of water.

Aluminium primer is also useful in situations where woodwork that is to be painted has previously been creosoted or painted with bituminous compounds. In such cases the tarry content of the previous finish tends to bleed through the new paint coating, but the leafing properties of the aluminium primer act as a sealer to prevent this from happening. It is important, however, that the creosote or bitumen should be old and weathered, otherwise the painting of the surface could not be guaranteed to be a success, due to the tendency of any kind of hard paint-coating to crack when applied over a soft elastic ground.

It is necessary to recognize the limitations of the primer as well as the advantages. Aluminium primer is definitely not suitable for use on unseasoned timber. The application of an impervious coating would prevent the evaporation of the moisture, and would imprison water inside the wood. This would generally lead to the paint flaking off, but in some circumstances there could be more serious results in that wood rot and similar undesirable conditions might develop.

It should also be noted that difficulty sometimes arises when aluminium primer is used because the subsequent coats of paint may not adhere very well to the primed surface.

Aluminium products—safety in use It is a feature of all aluminium paints that there is a tendency for pressure to build up inside the paint container. For this reason, great care should be taken when the lid is being removed. Because of their flammable nature, aluminium paints should be stored in areas remote from heat or sources of ignition. Apart from these factors, and provided there is a reasonable degree of ventilation, there is no need for any particular precautions to be observed when using these paints for normal painting and decorating work.

In the case of industrial painting the position is less straightforward. The work may involve areas of very high temperature such as steam radiators and pipes, furnace installations, metal smoke-stacks, boilers, etc., and very often there are added complications because of severely corrosive and destructive conditions, while sometimes the work is in confined spaces with rigorously restricted ventilation. Particular hazards may exist as a result of welding or burning through dried paint-films producing a variety of toxic gases and the possible presence of aluminium ions.

It is not feasible within the space of this paragraph to deal individually with all the hundreds of possibilities that might arise. Where any doubt or difficulty exists, the correct information should be obtained by consulting a recognized authority, which in most cases would be the area office of the Health and Safety Executive. Where the work is situated in a confined space, the operatives should wear the type of breathing apparatus which is supplied with fresh air from an outside source; the ordinary respirator is not adequate for the purpose and would indeed be dangerous. PVC gloves or gauntlets should be worn to protect the skin from splashes. Eye protection should conform to BS 2092 and *The Protection of Eyes Regulations, 1974.* Calculating the quantity of air required to dilute the solvent vapours to a safe level is extremely complicated; Her Majesty's Stationery Office supplies a guidance pamphlet, EH 15, which was prepared by the Health and Safety Executive, and a similar pamphlet EH 9 concerning *The Spraying of Flammable Liquids* should also be consulted.

Aluminium sealer A type of styptic sealer consisting of a manilla gum base pigmented with aluminium powder, which is produced by some manufacturers for application over bituminous surfaces, dry creosoted surfaces, bleeding colours, gold bronze paints, nicotine stains, and similar surfaces which are liable to stain or discolour newly applied coatings.

Aluminium stearate A complex salt of aluminium and stearic acid, incorporated in several preparations used by the painter. It is chiefly used as a flatting agent, but is also used as an anti-settling agent to keep pigments in suspension, as a water repellent for use on porous structural surfaces, and as an ingredient in transparent glazes for use in broken colour work.

Aluminium units—the painting of The metal aluminium has a great affinity for grease, and absorbs a fair amount of grease during the process of rolling or fabrication. Before it is painted, a thorough degreasing is essential, and it is also necessary to etch the surface of sheets and extrusions to provide a "key" for the paint. This is very often done during the production process, but if it has not been done then site treatment is needed.

Degreasing is best done with one of the proprietary materials sold for the purpose, although for small areas white spirit may be used and is equally effective. To provide a key, a good-quality etching primer should be used, although here again it is quite acceptable to use a fine abrasive paper and white spirit or fine steel wool and white spirit where only small areas are involved. The use of alkaline detergents must be avoided because the metal is dissolved by contact with caustic solutions. After degreasing and etching, a zinc chromate primer is applied. Aluminium castings do not need pretreatment, beyond ensuring that they are clean and dry, and they are also primed with zinc chromate.

In the case of aluminium units which require repainting, any defective paint should be removed, care taken to see that the surface is clean and dry, and then a coat of zinc chromate should be applied. If the existing paintwork is in poor condition, and especially if it is flaking extensively due to inadequate pretreatment before it was originally painted, the whole of the paint should be stripped with a spirit paint remover and a thorough degreasing and pretreatment programme carried out as for new metal.

Aluminium is frequently used in industrial painting as a sprayed metal coating for the protection of steelwork, especially where severe corrosive conditions exist. The value of the sprayed metal coating is enhanced by the subsequent application of a normal paint system, and if the paint coating is regularly renewed the protection it gives is practically permanent. When the sprayed metal coating on the steel is to be protected in this way, an etching primer should be applied within 48 hours, otherwise corrosive products may develop which impair the adhesion of the paint.

Sometimes aluminium units are anodized by one of the various patented electrolytic processes to produce a thin surface coating of aluminium oxide, but although this coating is highly protective (except in severe corrosive conditions) it is customary to reinforce it with paint or lacquer coatings. See *Anodizing* below.

Aluminium—used for scaffolding Aluminium alloys are used in the production of scaffold tubes, prefabricated scaffold units, and ladders. Tubular scaffold and prefabricated units of this type are not as strong as their steel counterparts but they are very much lighter in weight, and this is a great advantage in everyday use for the painter and decorator, and of vital importance in the scaffolding of lofty structures and areas where access is difficult. Aluminium scaffolding is also preferable to steel units on buildings of historic importance, because there is no risk of its causing rust stains on the fabric of the building. On the other hand, in situations where the scaffold is in contact with new cement or concrete or where the work involves the use of chemical detergents, steel scaffolding is preferable since aluminium alloy is softened by alkaline action. See *Tubular scaffold.*

Ladders made of aluminium alloy have certain advantages over wooden ladders because they are lighter in weight and are not subject to rot or decay. They do tend to slip more easily than wooden ladders on hard smooth floor surfaces, but this can be counteracted by the use of non-slip feet. Like the aluminium alloy scaffolding discussed in the last paragraph, they may be damaged by alkaline action. The greatest drawback to their use is that they are good conductors of electricity, which is a source of danger in situations where they may come into contact with exposed electrical installations. See *Ladders.*

Amber A yellow translucent fossil resin, found chiefly on the southern shores of the Baltic, and the hardest resin known.

Amber varnish A very pale varnish. The name refers to the colour and quality of the varnish and not to the type of resin used in its manufacture; amber would be too expensive to be used for this purpose.

Ambient A word that means "surrounding". For example, one can speak of "the ambient air", meaning "the air which is on all sides" or "the surrounding air".

American cloth A glazed cotton fabric of the oilcloth type, which at one time was frequently used as a wallhanging in kitchens and similar rooms where a strong, waterproof, hygienic surface was required. (**NLC**)

American turps A volatile solvent distilled from the oleo-resin which is obtained from certain species of pine and fir trees. It has many qualities which make it practically the ideal paint solvent, but it is no longer in such general use due to its cost. It used to be commonly held that American turps was of higher quality than that produced elsewhere, but this opinion was largely due to prejudice and seems to have no valid basis in fact.

Amino resin A synthetic resin of the thermosetting type produced by reacting urea, melamine, and similar compounds with formaldehyde. It is cured by stoving, and is blended with alkyd or epoxy resins to make paints used in the motor industry.

Ammonia A colourless gas with a pungent smell and strong alkaline reaction. At one time it was the practice to add a little liquid ammonia to water for the purpose of washing down and preparing old paintwork, in preference to sugar soap; it was milder in action but less positive in removing grease.

Ammonia is also used as a chemical stain for wood, as in the process of fuming oak.

Amorphous pigments Pigments whose particles are of shapeless structure and lack definite form, as opposed to crystalline pigments.

Ampere The unit for measuring the rate of flow of an electric current; the current that one volt can send through one ohm.

Amplitude A term used in connection with the indentations which roughen the surface of blast-cleaned steelwork. The amplitude is the vertical distance between the deepest parts of the troughs or hollows and the highest points of the peaks.

Amyl acetate A substance with a fruity smell, used for dissolving nitrocellulose.

Anaglypta An embossed paper made from good-quality rags, produced in both high and low relief designs to give the appearance of modelled plaster, plastic paint and other effects. The high relief is supplied in hollow-backed panels, the low relief in rolls of normal length and width. Normally it is coated after hanging with emulsion paint or flat oil paint, but it can also be obtained in ready decorated form. It has largely been supplanted by more modern types of relief materials.

Analogous colours Colours which lie close to one another on the colour circle.

Anatase One of the crystalline forms of titanium dioxide.

Anchor pattern A term sometimes used to describe the roughening of a surface—especially a metallic surface such as steelwork—by the process of blast-cleaning, thereby improving considerably the adhesion of the subsequent paint film. The term "profile" is another name for anchor pattern.

The effect of the blasting operation is to roughen the surface into a series of tiny indentations, which enables the paint to cling to the surface by anchoring itself into the hollows; hence the name "anchor pattern". The nature of the pattern or profile depends largely on the type of abrasive used. The small round particles known as "shot" produce a rounded anchor pattern or profile, while the small angular particles known as "grit" produce an angular pattern or profile.

Angle iron An L-shaped iron beam, or an L-shaped iron member to strengthen a corner. The term is generally used to refer to a standard iron or rolled steel section in structural work.

Angle roller A paperhanger's roller, usually 25mm in width, the drum of which is supported on one side only to enable it to be used close in to an angle.

Anhydrite Sulphate of lime, an anhydrous form of gypsum; that is to say, a form of gypsum with no water in its composition and which occurs naturally as a mineral.

Anhydrite plaster A plaster made by grinding the natural mineral anhydrite and adding an accelerator. It behaves like the moderately burnt anhydrous plasters when setting and gives an extremely hard but fairly porous finish.

Anhydrous gypsum plaster A group of plasters and cements made by heating the rock gypsum to a temperature of 400° Celsius* in order to drive off the whole of the water of crystallization. When water is added by the plasterer it combines with them to replace the water of crystallization which was expelled. The group includes the plasters known by the trade names of Sirapite, Glastone, Statite, Victorite and Xelite; it also includes Keene's or Parian cement and those varieties of Keene's sold under the proprietary names of Astoplax, Pixie Keene's and Superite; and in addition it includes anhydrite which, as mentioned in a previous paragraph, is not made from gypsum but from a naturally occurring mineral form of anhydrous calcium sulphate.

In BS 1191:1972, which is the basis of the present-day terminology about plasters, anhydrous gypsum plasters are classified as belonging to Group C, while Keene's is classified as Group D.

None of these materials combines readily with water, and an accelerator is added during manufacture; otherwise they would take too long to set and harden. The various types of plaster in the group differ from one another in detail, but it may be said, as a general characteristic of the group, that their set is slow and continuous; this is an important point for the decorator, because should they for any reason dry before they are completely hydrated (i.e., before the water of crystallization has been completely replaced) defects such as "dry-out" and "delayed expansion" may occur. Another consequence of their slow setting which is of importance to the decorator is that the plasterer, having plenty of time to trowel them, often brings them to a smooth glassy finish which presents very little "key" to paint coatings or emulsion paint.

The anhydrous gypsum plasters, when used as they are sold, rarely have any chemical action on paint, but, if they are gauged with even a small

---

*The word "Centigrade", for the unit of temperature, has been changed to "Celsius" to avoid confusion with Continental practice. The units remain the same, as does the abbreviation, °C.

quantity of lime, caustic alkali is formed which will give rise to saponification. They should be tested for alkalinity before painting.

Annexe An addition to a building structure.

Annual rings The concentric light and dark rings of wood fibre added each year to a growing tree, which are disclosed when the tree is sawn through. The annual rings determine the grain markings in wood, as imitated or represented by the grainer.

Anode The positive plate in electrolysis.

Anodizing The covering of an aluminium surface with a layer of aluminium oxide by the process of electrolysis. The layer protects the metal, and can be dyed in various colours.

Anti-bacteria paints Paints to which poisonous metallic salts (e.g. salts of sodium, mercury, zinc or magnesium) have been added to check the growth of bacteria and fungus. See also *Fungicidal paints*.

Anti-climb paints Paints which instead of drying after application remain wet and slippery. They have been developed for the specific purpose of combating crime and vandalism and are used in such situations as the painting of downspouts (to deter cat-burglars) and the painting of marker buoys and posts to prevent removal and theft. Their properties are due to the use of a medium based upon non-oxidizing castor oil. They are applied in heavy coatings, by brush, and have a very low spreading capacity.

Anti-condensation paints Materials made to minimize the condensation of moisture on cold surfaces such as metal or plaster. Several proprietary brands are on the market, consisting of an absorbent material suspended in a suitable emulsion; these are applied in a thick coating of about 4.5 to 5.5 square metres/litre, and are often stippled as a finish. To increase the thickness two coats are often preferable to one. Applied in this way their effectiveness is due to three factors: the provision of a thick buffer layer which insulates the surface; the absorption of some of the moisture; and the fact that air tends to stagnate in the pockets or cavities formed by the stippling, providing further insulation. Another form of anti-condensation paint, which however is purely functional and does not present so pleasing an appearance, is formed by painting the surface with a strongly adhesive material on to which, when it has become tacky, granulated cork is blown.

Anti-fouling paints Materials devised to minimize the loss of speed caused by the accumulation of barnacles etc., on the hulls of ships. They consist of highly poisonous substances such as copper salts or arsenic, bound in a very tenacious non-drying medium. Their effectiveness is due to the salts leaching out into the water to poison any marine growth. There are three types in general use: (a) a dark red/brown paint supplied in ready mixed form which is more expensive than normal industrial paints, (b) a bright metallic copper material which is more expensive than (a) and in which the bronze powder is mixed in the medium immediately before use, and (c) a white paint which is twice as expensive as (a) and which is supplied in ready-mixed form. All these materials can be applied by brush, roller or spray. Care is needed in their use because of their toxic properties.

Anti-graffiti paints Paints produced and used in the hope of saving newly decorated premises from being defiled with ugly and obscene markings. Several brands are available, but they all fall into one of two categories: (i) Textured systems, consisting of paints with a hard aggregate in their composition, upon which it is difficult to write with ballpoint or felt-tipped pens, crayons or lipstick, but which unfortunately give no protection against aerosol sprays; and (ii) Smooth systems, which present a smooth hard surface which is resistant to staining and from which graffiti can be cleaned off; some of these are pigmented, others intended for hardwoods or masonry are clear and free from pigment.

Anti-skinning agent A material added to a paint in order to prevent or delay the process of oxidation or polymerization whereby an insoluble skin forms on the surface of the paint in the container.

Antimony Antimony white, an oxide of antimony, is produced by roasting the black mineral called stibnite (sulphide of antimony) in the presence of air, the fumes being condensed to form an amorphous white pigment. It is fine textured and very opaque, has a tendency to discolour in the presence of sulphur, and has a retarding effect on the drying of linseed oil but is improved by combination with zinc oxide. When combined in this way, it is used to reduce the chalking of titanium oxide; it is also considered to offer good protection against sea air.

Antimony orange and antimony vermilion are sulphides of antimony, rather unstable as pigments and nowadays rarely used in paint.

Antiseptic washes Chemical solutions, of which several proprietary makes are on the market, used to eradicate mould growth, etc. from a surface prior to decoration.

Antwerp blue Used principally as an artists' colour. It consists chemically of zinc ferrocyanide; its properties are very similar to those of Prussian blue, but it is a lot paler in colour and is a more greenish blue. (**NLC**)

Applied decoration A term which covers all forms of surface decoration, from simple stencils and lining to hand-painted ornament and mural painting.

Appliqué motifs Strictly speaking, this means any ornamental work cut out of one material and applied to the surface of another. In painting and decorating this gives an opportunity for an enterprising and skilful craftsman to show his/her ingenuity by using a wide variety of materials to create some distinctive feature to enhance what would otherwise be just an ordinary scheme. The possibilities are very wide, and include such things as monograms, heraldic devices, roundels, floral emblems, etc., which can be cut from metal, wood, cork, felt, polystyrene, card, paper, metallized plastic, wire and metallic thread, etc. In the ordinary course of domestic decoration it can apply to paperhanging treatments whereby such things as perforated corner pieces, nursery and bathroom cut-outs, high-relief motifs and metallized plastic devices are superimposed on to the finished papering, their placing being at the discretion of the decorator.

Apprentice Strictly speaking, a young person bound by indentures to serve an employer for a recognized term of years in order to learn a craft.

Apprenticeship The system whereby an employer and a young person enter into a legally binding agreement, the employer undertaking to provide regular employment and to train the young person in every branch of the craft as far as lies in his power, the young person undertaking to serve the employer faithfully and to strive diligently to learn the craft as thoroughly as possible.

The system originated in this country in the 13th century; prior to this the knowledge and practice of the craft was passed from father to son. At that time the craftsman was a person of substance and occupied a position of respect in the community. There is documentary evidence that craftsmen were generally freemen and were often freeholders of considerable properties. Throughout the Middle Ages the master craftsmen in each of the building trades were responsible for the organization of that trade's activities on every building project. It was in the 17th century that the idea was mooted that one individual should plan the whole operation of a building project, but it was well on into the 18th century before it gained any degree of acceptance. Even so, it was only the tremendous wave of building activity in the 19th century that depressed the crafts into a subservient capacity, with the overall planning of all aspects of the work coming under the control of one person, usually an architect, and this was a situation that occurred by chance since the profession of architecture was developing on haphazard lines—the Institute of British Architects was not founded until 1834 and had only 82 members in 1835; it did not receive royal status until 1866.

Although craftsmen were no longer in a position to exercise their own originality and creative expertise, their work being mainly planned and directed by a person with no first-hand craft experience, the desire to uphold the high standards of craftsmanship was still the uppermost consideration. The essential factor in this was the well-defined system of apprenticeship. Various bodies were set up to supplement the on-site training of apprentices; in our own craft, evening classes were established to give apprentices an insight into the skills of lettering, gilding, graining, decorative painting, etc., which in many cases were outside their normal everyday range of working experience, and eventually a National Joint Education Committee was set up which organized an examination system to encourage students to progress towards a wider range of craft knowledge. But it was recognized that the finest training any young entrant to the trade could receive was that of working under the constant daily tuition of experienced craftsmen, well versed and thoroughly competent in the practice of the craft. Naturally the standard of tuition varied greatly; it does not follow that because a person is a sound craftsman, he/she is capable of imparting that knowledge to others.

The fact remains that an employer with a keen sense of responsibility plus the kindly guidance of older employees with long years of working experience can implant a knowledge of craft practice in a young person in a way that cannot be surpassed.

Up to the outbreak of World War II the traditional craft procedures had undergone remarkably little change, with the result that when the war ended there seemed no obvious reason why the recognized system of apprenticeship should be disturbed. Since then, the craft of painting and decorating has changed dramatically. Modern methods of manufacture have revolutionized trade practice, notably in the fact that surface coatings are no longer prepared on the site with traditional ingredients but are now invariably supplied in ready-made form and consist of vastly superior products developed by scientific research. There has been a tremendous extension in further education, with day classes available to supplement the site training of apprentices by offering them knowledge of modern materials and the chance to practise modern techniques which may be beyond the range of their everyday work experience. Unfortunately as economic conditions have deteriorated, the expansion of further education has been curtailed, and by a paradox many apprentices today are deprived of the opportunity of engaging in further education to the extent that they need or desire.

There are other factors at work. Modern marketing methods put the emphasis on stocking and selling only those mass-produced lines that can be sold in bulk, and the materials needed for specialist decorative lines are no longer available. This is exacerbated by the preference of many manufacturers for catering for the amateur home decorator rather than for the needs of the small professional decorator. The training of decorators has passed into the departments of construction where it is regarded as being of minor importance, since painting work averages at only 2% of the cost of new construction work; what is overlooked is that the vast majority of painting operations are concerned with the upkeep of existing buildings and involve a much wider range of skills and materials never used in new building where totally different criteria apply. The changing economic and social climate has brought the organization of craft education under the control of people and bodies with no first-hand experience of the traditional training in craft skills.

Many of the present-day schemes of training aim primarily at increasing the productivity of the students; to this end they are concerned with providing the bare minimum of basic skills that will enable the student to take his/her place on the production line rather than equipping the students with a proper understanding of the craft. The period of apprenticeship has been reduced to a point where it no longer has any real meaning. Of course, there is no particular virtue in requiring that an apprenticeship should last for seven years, five years or any other period of years unless it is realized that the apprenticeship has a definite purpose to fulfil and is not just a means of obtaining relatively cheap labour. The really important thing to recognize is that in a very short training period the young entrant can only be brought into contact with a very small proportion of the many operations that a craftsman needs to be familiar with, and certainly does not have the time to reach a reasonable level of proficiency.

Nobody could predict the course that craft training will take in the future. Clearly it will change considerably. It needs to be recognized that painting and decorating by its nature is still largely a hand craft, a manual skill, relying on a fine combination of knowledge and manual dexterity, and that nobody has yet evolved a better way of teaching those skills than by placing the young trainee under the personal care and tuition of an older and experienced craftsman.

Arabesque Surface decoration of a rhythmic linear character composed of scroll work and foliage.

Architectural drawing Precise and accurate drawing of rooms, the exteriors of buildings, or architectural features, usually relying for its effect upon good line work and neat draughtsmanship.

Architrave The moulded frame around doors or windows.

Archrome range A range of colours specially recommended for use in schools, and introduced by what was then called the Ministry of Education in its Bulletin No. 9, *Colour in Schools* published in 1953. The range was incorporated in the BS 2660 range of colours, but BS 2660 was withdrawn in 1973. In spite of this, the term is still often seen in technical literature. See also *Paint Colours for Building Purposes*, below.

Argent The heraldic term for silver, which is very often depicted in heraldic painting by white.

Armenian bole A red earth powder dusted on to the thin tissue pages which separate the leaves of gold in a book of gold leaf; its purpose is to prevent the gold from sticking to the tissue.

Aromosol The trade name for a solvent used for chlorinated rubber paints, similar to the coal-tar naphtha formerly used for this purpose but with a much more pleasant odour.

Arris A sharp external edge formed when two faces of a structural member meet; the external angle on wood, stone, plaster, or steelwork. Paint tends to recede from a sharp angle, leaving a thinner coating on the arris which thereby becomes a weakness in the film.

Arsenic yellow A pigment derived from the mineral orpiment, used in tempera paintings in the ancient world; also known as king's yellow. (**NLC**)

Arylamide yellows A group of organic yellow pigments with the properties of bright colour, fastness to light, soft texture and good tinting strength. Because of their relatively low cost and non-toxic nature they are used in place of the lead chromes, but they have the disadvantage of low opacity.

Asbestine An extender with a fibrous texture, used to control the rate of settlement of the denser pigments and to prevent them from forming a compact mass in the paint container.

Asbestos A fibrous crystalline material, a form of the mineral hornblende, which possesses the property of resisting fire very strongly and is often woven into fireproof fabrics.

Asbestos cement Asbestos, when mixed into a slurry with cement is pressed into sheets of various sizes or moulded into the form of spoutings, etc., which when dry compose prefabricated units used in the building trade. They are easy to assemble and have a high resistance to fire. The factor of greatest importance to the painter is their alkaline nature, since cement forms 85 percent of their content, but their alkalinity decreases as the material becomes weathered.

In recent years there has been a great deal of adverse publicity about the health hazards associated with the use of asbestos products, and the link between them and cancer is well known. As a result the sale and use of these materials has declined dramatically. This will mean that the number of buildings in which asbestos cement products are used will become progressively fewer. Meanwhile there are of course many buildings in existence where the painter is still required to treat asbestos-cement surfaces. Apart from the technical factors concerned in painting the material, it is important to realize the health hazards concerned, and to comply with the provisions of the Asbestos Regulations when handling or working with materials containing asbestos. The Asbestos Research Council issues information about the general safety precautions that are needed and about the wearing of protective clothing.

The painter should also remember that in addition to the health hazards, asbestos-cement sheeting is extremely brittle, that it fractures very readily, and that it shatters without giving any warning. Under no circumstances is it safe to walk or put one's weight directly upon it. The common practice of walking along the line of sheeting bolts where there is a double thickness of sheeting gives no protection at all. It is never safe.

Asbestos wood This material is supplied in sheets and is used in the making of fire-resisting walls and ceilings. Its composition is 50% asbestos and 50% cement by weight. It is less brittle than asbestos cement sheeting, and is more adaptable in the sense that asbestos cement units are used as fabricated whereas asbestos wood sheets can be sawn to shape with a handsaw, can have circular holes cut in with a padsaw, and can be nailed or screwed into position. To the construction team concerned with the fixing, it clearly presents a significant health hazard.

Asbestos wood is much more absorbent than asbestos cement, and before painting, it requires coating with a proprietary brand of primer.

Ash (1) A hardwood which is not used greatly in building but because of its resilience is widely used in coachwork. In colour and grain markings it is very similar to light oak, and in fact the two are very often confused. Its colour is a little lighter than oak, and the heartwood markings are more smoothly rounded, but it requires a practised eye to distinguish between the two.

Ash (2) See *Fly ash.*

Ashlar A term in masonry to denote squared hewn stone laid in regular courses with fine joints.

Ashlar effects The imitation of ashlar in decorative materials; for example, with stone paints or plastic paint, the ashlar joints being scored out with a small screwdriver or shaped piece of wood while the paint is wet, or by setting out the joints with narrow masking tape before applying the paint and removing these before it is set. The effect can be enhanced by emphasizing the joints with white or any colour desired.

Asphaltum Mineral pitch, a dark brown or black form of bitumen, the purest varieties being used in the manufacture of black Japan, and various grades and qualities being used in the production of bituminous paints.

Assertive colours See *Advancing colours.*

Atomized paint Atomization is the basic principle upon which spray-painting depends. It is the term used to describe the action which takes place when a stream of liquid is subjected to a force which breaks it up into very fine particles. In the case of spraying, paint is fed into a spray gun, and the gun is designed to provide the means both of atomizing the paint and conveying the resultant particles towards the surface which is to be painted. When the particles reach the surface they merge together again to form a coherent film.

In air-propelled spraying, atomization is produced by feeding a controlled trickle of paint into a forced airstream, with a vacuum area breaking up the liquid flow. In airless spraying, atomization is produced by releasing the paint which is being held under great pressure, and changing its directional flow at the point of release, which causes it to spread over a larger surface area than the surface tension can maintain, thereby breaking it up. In electrostatic spraying, atomization is produced by using centrifugal force to stretch the paint over a wider area than its surface tension can maintain, causing it to break up.

Atrium A forecourt or open court in front of the entrance to a building.

Automatic spraying A system of spraying used in industrial coating when a large number of identical or similarly shaped objects is to be painted and where high-speed production is required. The spray guns are mounted either on a fixed bar or on a movable carriage, and are controlled mechanically, a device being fitted which prevents them from spraying unless some object is within range. The carriage and mountings can be adjusted to cope with changes of contour such as are found, for instance, on a car body. The object to be treated can be made to rotate while being sprayed so that the whole area is painted.

The principle of automatic spraying has been extended by the introduction of robots, which are far more sensitive and adaptable and which are already widely used in the car industry, especially in West Germany. A new generation of "intelligent robots" is now being developed which will have far-reaching effects on assembly line work. The new robots are equipped with sight and a delicate sense of touch, and are capable of performing a wide range of operations which could previously only have been done by human beings. It is probable that in the next few years they will have taken over many of the operations at present carried out by human labour.

Axonometric projection A projection is a method of linking together the plan and elevations of a room, building or other object, so as to present a three-dimensional picture. An axonometric projection is produced by drawing the plan to scale (and, in the case of a room, all the furniture, etc., is also drawn in on the plan). The plan is set at an angle, usually 30, 45 or 60 degrees, from the horizontal. Vertical lines are drawn from each corner (and through the corner of each object in the case of a room) to the same scale as the plan. The drawing of rooms is stressed because the principal value of this projection to a decorator is to show the interior of rooms. It gives a good idea of the solid shape of the room and its contents, and also, because the plan is indicated and everything on the plan and elevation is to the same scale, it can be referred to as an accurate working drawing.

Azure The heraldic term for blue.

B

Back priming This refers to coating up, for protective purposes, those parts of a structure and those materials which will be out of sight when the building is completed. Door frames and window frames, for instance, should be primed before fixing, because their back edges, when fixed in position, are in direct contact with the brickwork and therefore liable to absorb a great deal of water from this source; the water thus absorbed might very well seek to escape through the outer face of the woodwork after the painting has been completed, leading to blistering and peeling of the paintwork. An aluminium primer, being almost completely impervious to moisture, is eminently suitable for the back priming of such frames, and two coats are to be recommended in preference to one.

The term back priming also refers to the very sound practice of painting the backs of such materials as asbestos sheeting before they are fixed; the alkaline content of such materials (which may be dormant when the paint is first applied) can be reactivated by the re-introduction of moisture at a later date, and back priming with, say, bituminous paint is a wise safeguard to prevent this occurring.

Back putty Otherwise known as bedding putty; the putty which is run into a window frame and into which the pane of glass is bedded.

Background stencil Otherwise known as a negative stencil, one in which the background is cut out and the design itself forms the ties. Background stencilling is very important to the decorator; for such things as the running bands which are often applied around large halls, churches, etc., a negative pattern is more satisfying than a positive pattern, in which the design is cut out, largely because it avoids the spotty effect which a positive pattern produces when repeated several times.

Backing up A term used in glass gilding. It is impossible to apply loose leaf gold exactly to the size and shape of the lettering or ornament that is required; it is laid in such a way as to extend beyond the bounds of the shape that is actually required and then, when it is dry, the shape is painted on to the gold with backing-up paint applied with a writing pencil. When the backing up is dry the surplus gold is removed. Paint for backing up may be made by mixing black Japan and red lead, or one of the proprietary materials sold by the gold beating firms may be used.

The term is also sometimes applied to a coat of paint given to the whole of a glass window after it has been lettered; the object of this coat is to make the lettering more prominent and the window opaque.

Bactericidal paint A paint which contains additives which prevent the growth of bacteria on its dried film.

Badger hair A very soft hair, derived, as the name implies, from the badger. The peculiar feature of badger hair is that it tapers both at the root and the tip and is broadest in the centre; for this reason, when a group of hairs is bunched together and secured at the roots it forms a compact and sturdy mass for most of its length, but the tips are more widely separated. This principle is followed in the making of softening brushes for graining, which are very soft and light at the tips.

Badger softener A brush with a filling of badger hair and having a long slender handle; it is used for softening the markings in water colour graining, but is too delicate to be used for oil colour.

Ball mill A revolving drum, containing steel balls or pebbles of varying sizes, which is used in the preparation of pigments and paints. As the drum rotates, the continual tumbling action of the balls subjects the pigment to extremely fine and uniform grinding and blends it very thoroughly with the medium.

Ballotini Very small transparent glass spheres which, when backed by a suitable paint, reflect back any light which is directed at them. They are either incorporated in or superimposed upon paint films or plastic coatings to give them increased visibility. One example of their use is on signs illuminated by car headlights, another being their use in road-marking paints.

Balsam Oleo-resinous matter obtained from coniferous trees, consisting of resin, essential oils and other compounds. See *Oleo-resin.*

Baluster A column or pillar supporting a handrail or coping; a series of these forms a balustrade.

Bandstand A colloquial term for a splithead. See *Splitheads.*

Barge board A broad board extending along the edge of a gable to cover the ends of the rafters.

Barrelling A method of paint application used in industrial finishing; it is otherwise known as tumbling (q.v.).

Barrier coat A coating intended to prevent a new paint system from being affected by some harmful substance in the surface to which it is applied. Examples of barrier coats would be an alkali resisting primer preventing new cement from saponifying the paint applied to it and stop-tar knotting preventing creosote from bleeding through a new film.

Barrier cream A smooth paste applied to the skin to form a protection against toxic or irritant materials. There is a wide variety of these creams, affording protection against many types of chemical; they are used in several industrial processes in factories, the operatives spreading the creams on their hands before commencing work. They could, with advantage, be used more freely in the painting trade for the less pleasant operations (such as those involving the use of caustic materials) where rubber gloves would be a hindrance but some form of protection is desirable. For further details see *Skin protection.*

Barytes A crystalline substance, its chemical composition being a normal sulphate of barium, which occurs naturally in the form of a mineral called heavy spar. It is used as an extender in the manufacture of paint. It has no value as a pigment, being practically transparent in paint media, but is opaque in water and is used by commercial artists and decorative designers under the name of "Process White".

Base The term which refers to the constituent in a two-pack coating (consisting of the film-forming material plus the pigment) to which the activator is added.

Base plate A square flat metal plate with 150mm sides (22,500mm^2 area) used in tubular scaffolding to distribute the load from a standard or raker; it has a central shank over which the tube fits loosely. There are two small holes in the plate through which spikes can be driven to secure the fitting to a sole plate.

Bastard flat A painters' term for a semi-flat paint as opposed to a completely matt finish.

Batch number The number printed on every roll of wallpaper to indicate the batch in which it was manufactured. Before commencing work in a room the paperhanger must check that the batch numbers on all the rolls of paper are the same, as there may be slight differences of colour and shade between one batch and another and these would be very obvious when the paper was hung on a wall and had dried.

Bath enamels Enamels designed for brush application and used in the renovation of the old-fashioned type of bath; they are hard-drying enamels with high waterproofing qualities and resistant to alkaline attack to enable them to withstand the action of hot soapy water for a reasonable length of time. They are supplied in small tins containing just sufficient for the painting of one bath. Before any paint is applied it is essential that the bath should be very carefully and thoroughly cleaned to remove all traces of soap, scum, etc. All traces of rust must also be removed, and the bared metal should be coated with zinc chromate primer. The bath is then painted with thin undercoatings which must be allowed to dry hard between coats; when the grounding is sufficiently solid the enamel is applied, and this must be allowed to harden completely before the bath is put back into use. It is very important that no moisture be allowed to enter the bath at any stage after the initial cleaning; the usual custom is to suspend a small empty jar beneath each of the taps to catch any drips.

At one time the use of bath enamel was an everyday routine, but the material is no longer used to any great extent.

Batter A term applied to a wall with an inclined face.

B

Bays Compartments into which the roof of a building is divided; the spaces between columns; projecting windows.

Bead A small cylindrical moulding, frequently carved with an ornament resembling a string of beads.

Beading A length of bead moulding.

Bed A painters' term for a flat recessed surface, such as the bed of a ceiling as distinct from the cornice or frieze.

Bedding putty The putty into which a pane of glass is bedded; see *Back putty*.

Beer Stale beer was commonly used by the old-time grainer as a binder for water graining colour. Today when there is a revival of graining techniques for decorative purposes, people are referring to the old recipes in the manuals and textbooks of former days, so a note about the use of beer is timely. The beer needs to be diluted; if used in too strong a form it will produce a crop of small blisters. As a general rule, the proportion should be in the order of one part of beer to two parts of water. There is no point in letting the stuff go stale; there is no magic virtue in stale beer as such. The old ragged-trousered grainers were operating in times of great hardship and deprivation, and rather than spend good money they would go to a public house and get the dregs and the tray drippings free of charge, these being sufficient for what they needed.

Beeswax A material secreted by bees in the construction of the honeycomb; for commercial purposes it is obtained by extracting and melting down the combs. It is usually deep yellow in colour but may be refined to make a bleached wax or "white wax". At one time it was an ingredient in a number of painters' materials but is now principally used in wax polishes and stains.

Belt sander A sanding machine with a continuous belt of abrasive paper driven round a series of rollers. It has a straight-line action and can be used when long runs of new woodwork need to be sanded before priming, and it can be adapted for sanding floors.

Bench An essential item of workshop equipment. For the greatest convenience in colour mixing and matching, it should be placed beside a North light window; it should for preference be zinc covered to facilitate cleaning.

Benzene One of a number of volatile solvents obtained from coal tar.

Benzidine A yellow pigment with greater staining strength than arylamide yellow but with only moderate fastness to light.

Benzol A material similar to benzene but not so pure. It is occasionally used in small quantities to increase the solvent power of turpentine substitutes and as a solvent for oil-soluble dyes in wood stains because of its high penetrative power.

Berries' graining tools These are tools which produce a strikingly good representation of oak grain by cutting or incising the grain markings into the painted ground; after the markings have been cut, the ground is coated with graining colour which is allowed to set and is then gently wiped over with a soft cloth to give subtle variations of colour. The tools are in sets. Each individual tool consists of a series of circular steel cutters with irregularly spaced notches cut into them, the cutters being mounted on a spindle which is firmly set on to a strong handle; the tools vary in width from very narrow to broad. These tools were immensely popular in the 1930's but have not been made for many years. They were very expensive and very much cherished by their owners. They were so strongly made that many sets are still in existence, in good condition. The present vogue for graining is resulting in some of these fine tools being brought into use again, and there are decorators who are rediscovering the art of producing these faithful imitations of wood grain.

Bill of Quantities This is a contract document relating to a projected building scheme. It is drawn up by a quantity surveyor. There are preliminary pages which deal with important financial matters concerning the contract as a whole, after which the bill sets out fully and accurately every single item which will form part of the entire finished structure. The pages are divided into columns in which the dimensions of every item and the number of such items are entered. The bill of quantities is generally a thick and bulky document, and very often runs to hundreds of pages. A copy of the bill is sent to a selected number of contractors, and it is upon the contents of the bill that they base their estimate of the cost.

Many building firms are self-sufficient in that they employ members of every trade or craft engaged in the operations. Such firms usually employ their own quantity surveyors to process the bills of quantities that they receive, entering their estimated prices for every item in the work, and submitting them to the people responsible for placing the contracts. But there are other building firms who only employ members of the constructional trades such as bricklaying, carpentry and joinery, etc., and who arrange for the works of the other trades such as painting and decorating to be carried out by sub-contractors. When this is the case, the building firm is known as the main contractor. When the main contractor receives a copy of a bill of quantities he retains the sections relating to constructional work but makes photocopies of those sections relating to the other trades; usually the main contractor will approach a small number of sub-contracting firms in each of the other trades. In this way there might be four or five painting and decorating firms who each receive a copy of the painting section of the bill, and who each submit an estimate of the cost to the main contractor. The main contractor selects one of these, thus appointing one painting firm as sub-contractor. The main contractor collates all the estimates for all the sub-contracted work, adds them to its own estimate for the constructional work, and sends off the completed bill of quantities to the company or body which is having the premises built. At a stated time and place all the completed bills are opened and inspected, and one of them is selected as the successful firm to be entrusted with the contract for the building.

Bill of Quantities, purpose of There are four main reasons why the Bill of Quantities contract is such an important feature of present-day organization in the construction industry. They are as follows:

(i) To ensure that all contractors seeking to gain a contract are basing their prices on exactly the same information.
(ii) To provide a basis for variations which may occur during the progress of the contract.
(iii) To provide an itemized list of the components required, thus enabling the contractor to order the necessary materials and to assess his labour requirements.
(iv) To provide the contractor with the basis for "cost planning" and "cost analysis".

Binder A word sometimes used to describe a paint medium, an adhesive material which binds together the particles of pigment in any kind of paint, holding them in suspension while the paint is wet and then drying to form a skin which keeps the particles together and binds them firmly to the surface.

Binding down The application of a viscous binding material over a loosely-bound, chalky or powdery film in order to form a stable surface for the reception of a new film. The term has two connotations.

(i) In general trade practice "binding down" usually refers to the preliminary treatment in situations such as (a) where an existing coating of cement paint has become powdery on a cement-rendered wall (indoors or outdoors) or on a pebbledashed exterior wall, and where a good-quality masonry paint or emulsion paint is to be applied; (b) where there is loose powdery limewash on either an outdoor or indoor wall and especially where some superior painted or emulsion painted finish is required; (c) where an existing coat of water-thinned material such as emulsion paint on interior walls is to have a heavy relief or heavily embossed wallpaper hung upon it, even if the painted surface appears to be in good condition; (d) where an existing coating of water-thinned material has become powdery, either on interior or exterior surfaces, before any kind of paint coating is applied; (e) where a surface is coated with a loose powdery distemper coating—but this is rare nowadays.

In some of these instances, it would be wise to wash the surfaces as thoroughly as possible before any other treatment is used, but it is recognized that washing alone would not be wholly successful in forming a stable base for the new coating. The material used for binding down such surfaces generally takes the form of a penetrative primer of a highly viscous nature, consisting either of a varnish medium (when it is known as a stabilizing fluid) or an oily composition, or in some cases with a proprietary brand of sealer recommended by the manufacturer for some specific problem area.

(ii) The term "binding down" is also used in connection with the process of graining in water-colour medium. The graining colour is loosely bound, either with a weak solution of beer (as described in a previous paragraph) or with some similar composition (such as vinegar and water, skimmed milk and water, etc.). The pigment when dry is bound together sufficiently for it to remain in place and resist mild rubbing, but is not bound firmly enough for more graining colour to be applied and for further operations to take place without "rubbing up" with consequent blurring or loss of the grain markings already applied. To fix the graining colour before the next stage is begun, it is bound down with a mixture of varnish and turps in equal parts, which, when applied quickly, binds it securely to the surface and makes it proof against further disturbance.

Birch A fairly hard tough timber, pinkish-brown in colour, which stains and varnishes well. Birchwood can be imitated by the grainer by a process similar to that used in reproducing the more familiar mahogany. The ground is yellowish white, and the graining colour is made from raw sienna, burnt sienna and raw umber, overgrained with blue-black or ivory black.

Birdcage scaffold An interior scaffold used in the decoration of churches, public halls and similar structures with large unbroken ceiling areas; in such situations it provides the only practicable method for the painter to keep the edges alive. It consists of a framework based upon rows of standards which are spaced at approximately equal distances apart both lengthways and breadthways; ledgers are spaced at vertical intervals of about 2 metres, and the top ledgers support a close-boarded working platform at approximately 2 metres below the ceiling. Narrow working platforms can be supported on the intermediate ledgers around the perimeter of the hall, providing the means of painting the walls from the same scaffold.

Bird's eye maple A light-coloured wood with considerable possibilities for the decorator. Its characteristic features are a softly mottled background, small clusters of "bird's eyes" (i.e., small horseshoe-shaped markings of darker colour), and curly irregular grain markings of soft colouring. It can be imitated in oil colour, but grainers generally prefer to work with water colour on a white or cream ground colour; the mottling can be imitated with a washleather or mottler, the bird's eyes inserted with a small brush called a "dotter", shaped for the purpose, and the curly markings run in with Conté crayon. Because the two later stages do not disturb the mottling, binding down between coats is unnecessary and a satisfactory imitation of this wood can therefore be achieved quite economically.

Bismarck brown A spirit-soluble dye used sometimes as the colouring agent in a spirit stain.

Bittiness A defect in painting whereby bits of grit, fluff and other foreign bodies contained in the paint mar the appearance of the finished film. Although there are times when it occurs in spite of the utmost care, in the majority of cases it is caused by carelessness. Bittiness can often be traced to the use of dirty brushes; to brushes which, through careless storage, have become caked with hard paint in the stocks and which have then been "cleaned" with a scraper or wire brush; to dirt and grit being picked up during painting; to failure to remove grit from the surface after rubbing down; to the use of dirty pieces of wood for stirring paint; to the inclusion of broken skins in the paint during stirring; to the failure to strain paint on which skin has formed; to the use of badly cleansed spray equipment; and so on. Occasionally the paint in an unopened tin may become bitty during long storage, but in this case careful straining will remove the trouble.

Bitumen A non-crystalline, semi-solid or viscous substance, intensely dark in colour, consisting of a mixture of complex hydrocarbons derived from petroleum deposits. There are many varieties of bitumen, known somewhat loosely by the names "asphalt", "asphaltum" and "pitch". In general, the terms "asphalt" and "asphaltum" refer to the natural bitumen associated with mineral matter, while the term "pitch" is applied to artificial bitumen obtained by the distillation and refining of crude petroleum.

Natural rock asphalt is found in many parts of the world, most of the present-day supply coming from localized regions of Switzerland, France and Sicily. Lake asphalt also occurs in several parts of the world such as Bermuda, Cuba, Texas and Venezuela, but easily the main source is Lake Trinidad in the British West Indies. This lake has been in production for more than four hundred years and the supply seems to be practically inexhaustible; vast quantities of bitumen are produced and are exported throughout the world. Paints made from bitumen have properties which are of great importance in the protective coating of steel and other surfaces.

Another source of supply comes from natural seepages of bitumen through veins in the earth, occurring in many parts of the Middle East from Egypt to Pakistan; it was from these deposits that the ancient civilizations obtained their supplies of bitumen for bonding their brickwork, lining their drains and baths, and making their floor coverings.

Pitch is the residue obtained from the distillation of tars which may be derived from coal or petroleum; it is the solid matter left when all the lighter oils have been extracted. Certain grades of pitch are highly compatible with epoxy and polyurethane resins, and as such they are of great importance in the production of high-build coatings for use in industrial painting.

Bitumen-impregnated board A type of building board used to support slates and tiles, and as such is very rarely painted. If, however, painting is required, the board should first be coated with aluminium sealer to prevent the bitumen from bleeding.

Bituminous paints These range in quality from the highest grade black Japans to the cheaper black varnishes, Brunswick blacks and tar blacks. Black Japan, a non-bleeding material, is dealt with in a later and separate paragraph.

The term "bituminous paint", as used in the trade generally, usually implies a material widely used in industrial painting for the protection of steelwork and for anti-corrosive purposes. It is made from pitch, asphaltum or coumarone resin in combination with heat-treated oils and suitable solvents. The distinctive properties of bituminous paints include their great tenacity, their very high degree of resistance to water penetration, their high measure of resistance to acid or alkali attack, their great flexibility, and their durability. After application they tend to remain soft and plastic, and it is for this reason that many authorities claim that they are eminently suitable for the finishing of iron and steel since they can readily adjust to the expansion and contraction of the metal caused by changes in temperature. The available range of colours is very limited, being restricted mainly to black, dull reds, browns, sombre greens and aluminium, although other colours can be obtained on request. To some extent these coatings are disintegrated by light, but this defect can be overcome by adding aluminium powder to the bitumen. It is most important to notice that conventional paint coatings should not be applied on top of existing bituminous coatings, because the bitumen will without doubt bleed through into the applied coating. For the same reason, when the time comes to renew the coating a further application of bituminous paint should be used, otherwise bleeding will occur. It is also important that bituminous paints should not be applied on top of ordinary paint coatings, as the thinners used in the bituminous product—often solvent naphtha—may well dissolve the previous paint film. In the case of bituminous paint applied over a red lead primer, sufficient time—three or four weeks—must elapse for the primer to become thoroughly hard before the next coat is put on.

Bituminous paints are in considerable use for the painting of bridges, cranes, steel and chemical works installations, dock installations, gas-holders and gasworks, sewage plant, colliery head gear, etc. Their use is not confined to the treatment of iron and steel surfaces; they are also used on a variety of surfaces where protection is of greater importance than a decorative finish.

As mentioned in the previous entry, there are some grades of pitch which blend very successfully with epoxy and polyurethane resins, and these are being extensively used at the present time in the formulation of high-build coatings for situations where extremely harsh conditions are encountered. Particular interest attaches to the epoxy-pitch compounds which are being used to produce high-build coatings for the protection of steelwork, especially when it is submerged in salt water. These coatings have been of tremendous importance in the initial treatment and the subsequent maintenance of the North Sea oil rigs, where any paint system is exposed to conditions of the utmost severity. It should be noted, however, that these products behave in exactly the same way as other bituminous paints in that they bleed into any conventional coatings that may be superimposed upon them.

At one time there was a lot of interest in a range of bitumen emulsion paints for the exterior treatment of cement stucco, concrete renderings, etc. These were prepared from bituminous materials emulsified with an agent such as soap so that they could be thinned with water, and pigmented with lime-resisting pigments and dyes. However, since they were subject to the inherent drawbacks of all bituminous materials in that they were only available in a very limited colour range and had a marked tendency to bleed into subsequent coatings, they are no longer a significant factor in present-day production.

Bituminous paints for special purposes The firms which specialize in the production of bituminous paints supply a range of special materials for use where normal conditions do not apply. One example is a tasteless, odourless, non-contaminating bitumen solution of great anti-corrosive power, supplied in the form of an enamel, for the internal treatment of water pipes, tanks, reservoirs, pressure filters, brewery vats and food containers. This product is marketed in two forms; in one it can be applied by brush or spray, in the other it is applied hot by a process carried out by specialist operatives employed by the manufacturers of the product. Another example is heat-resisting bituminous paint supplied for the painting of smokestacks, boiler fronts, ducts and pipe systems, which will withstand heat up to a temperature of 260°C (500°F). As indicated in an earlier entry, certain "super-service" bitumen paints are also available for use in extreme corrosive conditions.

Black and gold marble Also known as "Porter". A marble which was very popular at one time for the decoration of string-courses, chimney pieces, etc. It is worked from a black ground with a palette of raw and burnt sienna, black and white. The characteristic feature of the marble is that the veins follow a chain-like formation, which can be imitated by using a writing pencil with a rolling, dragging motion.

Black ash A strongly alkaline material sometimes used as a constituent of caustic paint remover.

Black Japan A bituminous black made from the finest grade of asphaltum cooked with oil and blended with a good copal varnish, thinned with turpentine. The best black Japans were made for high-grade coachwork; they dried slowly to a thoroughly hard but elastic film and were non-bleeding; they could be varnished without any greenish discolouration occurring. Such materials are now only made for a highly specialized market.

Black Japan is heat-resisting and can be used as a stoving enamel; even when not made for stoving it withstands heat well enough to be used, if so desired, as a radiator paint. It has other applications; it can, for instance, be mixed with turpentine or white spirit to produce a rich walnut floor stain.

Black varnish This is a very cheap bituminous black made by neutralizing tar and thinning it down with naphtha or similar solvent. Such things as rainwater spouting, when made from iron or asbestos-cement, were often dipped in black varnish before leaving the works, which led to a great deal of trouble from bleeding when ordinary paint was later applied. (**NLC**)

Blackboard paint A slightly thixotropic paint containing a high proportion of slate powder, which dries to a matt finish to produce a non-slip surface well suited for the reception of chalk. When the paint is properly compounded, it is possible for the chalk to be removed easily without polishing the surface. Although known as blackboard paint, it is available in various colours as well as black, and in fact a dull green is often used because it has been proved to be less tiring to the pupils' eyes.

Blanc fixe An artificially produced form of barytes; chemically it is the same as barytes but differs in its physical structure, which is amorphous instead of crystalline. It is produced by precipitating solutions of barium salts by means of sulphuric acid, and is bulkier, finer in texture and more opaque than the natural pigment. Like barytes, it is practically transparent in paint media. In water, however, it has good opacity, and it is used by decorative designers under the name of "Process White".

Blast cleaning A method of cleaning and preparing steelwork which is of considerable importance in industrial painting. The term covers the range of operations known variously by such names as abrasive blasting, abrasive cleaning, grit-blasting, shot-blasting, etc. The process consists of directing various kinds of abrasive particles towards the steel at a very high velocity by means of compressed air or centrifugal force. It produces a clean and slightly roughened surface which provides good adhesion to the paint film. It is extensively used on site work, and where the conditions are suitable it is a most effective way of removing mill scale, rust and corrosion products from steel. The efficiency of the operation depends on the rate of working and on the nature and coarseness of the abrasive.

Blast cleaning is generally done on the site by an open blasting process, the abrasive particles being loaded into a hopper, from which they are passed into a pressurized pot and thence through a metering device into a stream of compressed air or to the centrifugal ejector, to be directed to the work surface. On erected steelwork the open blasting process might well constitute a safety hazard to other operatives on the site, and might also give rise to very high operating costs due to the wastage rate of the abrasive; these difficulties are overcome by the use of the type of blasting equipment which includes a vacuum device to reclaim the abrasive after impact and then to clean and recirculate it. It is important to remember that steelwork cleaned by either of these processes must be primed immediately, otherwise the whole value of the treatment will be lost.

The main purpose of blast cleaning lies in the treatment of steelwork, but the process can also be used for the cleaning of stonework, concrete, metal alloys, etc., and is occasionally employed for decorative purposes by blasting motifs and patterns into the face of brickwork, concrete, stonework, etc.

Bleaching Not to be confused with fading. The whitening of a substance due to exposure to light or to chemical agent. Certain colours are bleached by chemical action: Prussian blue, and any mixture of colours containing Prussian blue, are bleached by alkaline attack; ultramarine is bleached by exposure to acid fumes, etc.

Bleaching of wood Lightening the colour of wood when stains caused by exposure to the weather need to be removed or when variations in the natural colouring of the wood have to be corrected. The old-time painter used to be adept at these operations, and very often had his own treasured recipes which he regarded as top secret. Bleaching was often done with an oxalic acid solution (100 grams of oxalic acid crystals to one litre of water) used hot, applied by brush or with a cloth, allowed to stand for half an hour and then rinsed off. Other recipes were based on hydrogen peroxide, sodium perborate, or sodium bisulphite. It is fashionable among present-day householders to strip down the woodwork in old property and restore it to its natural colour, and to renovate old furniture by bleaching it by the authentic old processes. There are in fact a number of proprietary wood bleaches on sale which are far more effective, more certain and more consistent than home-mixed solutions.

Bleeder type gun A spray gun designed for use with low-pressure (air-volume) spraying equipment in which a current of air is flowing all the while the plant is in operation. The gun is so called because it allows the air to "bleed" or flow through constantly; pressure on the trigger releases paint into the airstream, whereas in the non-bleeder type of gun air does not flow until the trigger is operated.

Bleeding The action of any material in penetrating and discolouring coatings applied on top of it. There are many substances which will bleed and stain new coatings in this way. Red pigments used to be notorious in this respect and, although with modern materials the danger is not nearly as common, certain red lakes and dyestuffs still give trouble, particularly when the old paint containing them has been rubbed down and the new coatings applied before the abraded surface has had time to harden off again. Water-soluble dyes in some types of wallpaper can give rise to trouble, and when such paper is being stripped off, care is needed to prevent the dye soaking into the plaster or penetrating the surrounding woodwork.

Bituminous products can cause a great deal of trouble; if oil paint is applied over them it rapidly develops brown stains and its drying is impeded. Anything derived from tar can be expected to bleed; old tar and creosote coatings on exterior work may become weathered to the point where oil paint can be applied without damage, but there is no means of knowing or guaranteeing when the safe point has been reached.

Other materials which will bleed through new coatings are the resinous content of knots, certain kinds of timber heavily impregnated with resin which exudes freely from all over the surface, soot penetrating through cracks in the vicinity of chimney breasts, nicotine deposits on the ceilings of public halls and hotel rooms, and copying ink pencil markings. Vandyke brown when ground in oil also shows a tendency to bleed.

The main difficulty with bleeding is that it is usually impossible to remove the offending coating completely, and the only remedy is to apply a buffer coat between the old and new systems. But while such materials as shellac, stop-tar knotting, etc., will often seal the bleeding material quite effectively, they will, if applied over elastic films such as bitumen paint, very soon develop cracks.

Blender A short square-ended brush, generally made of sable or ox hair, for blending light and dark colours in shaded effects in signwriting.

Blending The operation of producing a gradation of colour from light to dark or from one colour to another. Blending on small scale work can be achieved with a spray, and decorative spraying consists largely of using masks and templates to produce an alternation between hard distinct outlines and soft edges where the spray colour blends into the ground. But on large scale working, when it is required to blend colour either in water paint, oil paint or glaze, the best method is to apply the colours by brush, make the preliminary blending with the brush and complete the blending with hair stipplers.

Blistering A defect in painting in which the paint film rises away from the surface in bubbles due to lack of adhesion. Among the factors which give rise to blistering are the following:

(a) Moisture contained within the surface such as when new plasterwork, etc., is painted before it has had time to dry out, when unseasoned wood is painted, or when timber has been fixed in a new building with inadequate priming or without back priming so that moisture is absorbed into the timber from the brickwork.

(b) Moisture introduced into a surface, such as when a surface is painted during wet or foggy weather, or when work which has been washed down is painted before it has had time to dry.

(c) Water introduced into the paint, by means of paint brushes which have been stored in water overnight and put into use before all the water has been removed from them.

(d) Resin exuding from knots.

(e) Resinous matter becoming gaseous when heated, such as when timber with a very high resin content is painted and, under the influence of sunlight, develops numerous small blisters which are found to contain no moisture when opened.

(f) The use of soft oily undercoats and old fatty colour.

(g) Surfaces which offer little adhesion to paint being painted without the correct pre-treatment, as in the case of galvanized iron and other zinc coated surfaces.

It has been noticed that dark colours are more prone to blistering than light ones because they absorb more heat.

Blockboard A type of composite board built up with whitewood strips sandwiched between two layers of hard plywood; it is used in the making of doors, partitions, signboards, etc.

Blooming A milky white cloudiness which sometimes occurs on, or in, work finished in gloss materials; varnish, enamel and hard gloss paints are all liable to be affected.

The term "blooming" covers two distinct types of defects. One, called "crater blooming", takes the form of small pits and depressions in the dried gloss film which cause the light which falls on the surface to be scattered instead of being reflected evenly, giving a hazy appearance. The other type, called "crystalline blooming", is much more common; this consists of a crystalline layer—generally of ammonium sulphate crystals—on the surface of the gloss film. Crystalline bloom can often be removed from the surface by rubbing, but when a surface is pitted by crater bloom its lustre cannot as a rule be restored without recourse to felting down and refinishing.

Considerable research has gone into the subject of blooming, and the exact causes have not yet been fully established. It seems likely that crater blooming is caused by condensation of moisture or dew deposition on the surface before the gloss film is completely dry. Crystalline blooming is known to originate from the presence of sulphur dioxide and ammonia in the atmosphere, but the bloom only occurs when certain atmospheric conditions prevail, and it seems that the conditions leading to condensation of moisture are a factor in this type of bloom also.

The gloss film is most susceptible to these various influences during its drying period, when it is tacky but not fully set. To some extent the formation of bloom can be avoided if attention is paid to this fact. In spite of the wide range of quick-drying paints now available, and in spite of the fact that such quick-drying paints are generally used for exterior work, it is still good sound trade practice to refrain from applying gloss finishes out of doors late in the day, when a rapid drop in temperature would cause sudden chilling of the partially dried film. In this connection it should be remembered that a rapid fall of temperature can occur just as easily in the summer as in the winter months, and the temptation to proceed with glossing late in the afternoon should be resisted. Of course, no attempt should be made to apply gloss materials during foggy or misty periods.

On indoor work, gloss finishes should not be exposed to draughts or chills during the drying period. Blooming often occurs near to open gas jets; adequate ventilation is needed to prevent this, but direct draughts should be avoided.

When blooming has occurred it is sometimes possible to restore the lustre. Mild cases may respond to sponging down with lukewarm water and a brisk rubbing over with a wash-leather. More obstinate cases may yield to treatment by polishing with a mixture of linseed oil and vinegar. If these methods fail the only remedy is to felt down the work and refinish it with gloss under good dry conditions.

Blowing A defect in plastered surfaces caused by the use of imperfectly slaked lime. It takes the form of small craters formed by the blowing of flakes of plaster due to the expansion which takes place when the particles of unslaked lime gradually combine with water after the main body of the plaster has set and hardened. Quite often the defect does not become apparent until the surface has been decorated, and the blowing may continue for a number of years. It is beyond the control of the decorator. The treatment is to cut out the craters and fill them with Keene's or a lime-free filler; if the trouble is too widespread for this, it may be necessary to line the surface.

Blowlamp A portable appliance which directs heat upon a given spot and is used to soften up old paintwork in the process known as "burning off". Some types are designed for use with petrol, others with paraffin or methylated spirit. Blowlamps have largely been superseded with blowtorches of various kinds.

Blowlamp pricker A small tool for clearing the nipple of a blowlamp when it becomes clogged with carbon.

Blown oils Drying oils, such as linseed oil, castor oil, etc., which have been thickened by a process whereby a rapid stream of air is passed through heated oil without the addition of driers.

Blown vinyl The name given to a wallpaper of a three-dimensional type in which one or more parts of the design are printed on to the base with PVC foamable pastes, the other parts being printed with compact plastisols. The three-dimensional effect is produced by passing the material through a foaming oven at a temperature of between 180°C and 210°C (356°F and 410°F).

This is a high-quality product made in a wide range of attractive patterns, and it possesses many distinctive features. One outstanding feature is its resilience to crushing. If subjected to undue pressure through being impacted, through being kept tightly rolled for a long time, or by reason of a heavy weight being laid upon it, the emboss may be badly marked or flattened, but the apparent damage is only temporary and the material reverts to its original contours without leaving any visible defect. It also resists other forms of damage, being highly flexible and tear-resistant. It has good heat-insulating and sound-insulating properties, and has a high degree of flame resistance. It does, however, discolour in an atmosphere polluted by tobacco smoke.

The blown vinyls produced in this country are excellent materials. Regrettably a number of very inferior imitations are now on sale in the shops catering for the amateur market, many of them imported from Spain. They bear no comparison with the British products, but by reason of their poor quality they could bring the whole range into disrepute.

Blowtorch An appliance used to soften up old paintwork in the process of "burning off", which has largely superseded the blowlamp for this purpose. As a general rule blowtorches are operated on LPG fuel, i.e. liquefied petroleum gas (butane or propane), and they have many advantages compared with blowlamps; for instance, they light instantly and can be used at full power immediately whereas blowlamps need filling at regular intervals and need to warm up before their full power is developed; there is no loss of pressure whilst work is in progress, adjustment of the flame is more precise, there is no residue left on the surface to affect the adhesion of the paint film and the flame is hotter than a blowlamp flame which makes for quicker working. Some blowtorches are fully portable, others are fed from a large fuel container by means of a flexible hose, and for some purposes the type of blowtorch operated from a disposable cartridge is highly convenient.

Blueing The addition of a trace of blue to certain white pigments or paints in order to neutralize their yellowish cast and make them appear to be whiter. At one time this was a procedure familiar to every decorator, but of course it is now part of the manufacturing process. Virtually the only time it is ever seen done on the site is when lime blue is added to limewash to improve its whiteness.

Blue wool scale A means of assessing the lightfastness of a pigment. The pigment is dispersed in a paint medium, which is applied to a strip of metal or card. When it is dry the strip or card is exposed to ultra-violet light in a fugitometer, together with a monitoring sample painted on a separate strip to provide a basis for comparison. Full details are to be found in BS 1006.

Blushing A milky white filming (the equivalent of "blooming" in varnish and enamel) which spoils the appearance of nitrocellulose lacquers, spirit varnishes and French polish, and is caused when these materials are applied in cold or humid weather. Moisture deposited on the surface reduces the solubility of the resins or the cellulose so that some are precipitated out of the solution; the defect is generally confined to lacquers, etc., which dry solely by the evaporation of the solvents.

Boat varnish A varnish with outstanding properties of water resistance, being made with tung oil and 100% phenolformaldehyde resin; it is also highly resistant to attack by alkali. It is very similar to spar varnish; both these materials derive their name from the fact that originally they were used on ship spars.

Body A term which is used freely and rather loosely, so as very often to lead to confusion.

(a) In one sense it is taken to mean the consistency or viscosity of a material, not as measured exactly against some standard, but judged according to the ease with which the material can be spread, the way in which it pours, or the "feel" of the material as it is being stirred. This is perhaps the most usual implication, hence the terms "full-bodied" and "heavy-bodied" as applied to various varnishes and paints.

(b) The term is sometimes used to describe the covering power or hiding power of a paint, although in this connection the word "opacity" would be a better term to use, being less ambiguous.

(c) The term can also be taken to mean the "build" or thickness of a dried paint film.

Body colour (a) As applied to oil paint the term refers to a pigment of great opacity or obliterating power.

(b) When applied to artists' materials the term is used to denote an opaque poster colour, as opposed to ordinary water colour which relies for its effect upon its transparency.

Bodying An increase in the apparent viscosity of a paint, resin or lacquer which may be introduced deliberately during manufacture, or may occur unintentionally while the material is in storage.

Bodying-up A term used in French polishing to describe the building-up of a thickness of shellac before the final spiriting off. Bodying-up is carried out with a "rubber", a pad of cotton wool wrapped in linen.

Boiled linseed oil Linseed oil which has been heated to a fairly high temperature for a number of hours, and to which a small proportion of driers has been added so as to increase its property of absorbing oxygen. Boiled oil has a higher viscosity than raw oil, is more resistant to moisture, is darker in colour and tends to darken further on exposure to sunlight, and dries more rapidly. (**NLC**)

Bonderising A chemical treatment whereby small steel units used in building are rendered rust-inhibitive and suitable for the reception of paint.

Bone black A black pigment produced by burning bones and other animal refuse in closed retorts; a good-quality bone black is also known as drop black. It is of good black colour and produces a bluish grey when mixed with white. (**NLC**)

Bosun's chair A simple type of seat suspended by means of pulley blocks and operated by one man who is able to lower himself as required. It is used in the painting of small items in elevated positions where access from ladders is not possible and where the expense of erecting a scaffold or suspending a two-man operated cradle is not justified, such as, for example, isolated rainwater pipes or narrow metal strappings on lofty buildings; there are also some types of work where apart from any question of expense or convenience the chair provides the only reasonable form of access, which is often the case in the painting of either the inside or outside of metal smoke-stacks. Flagpoles are another item sometimes painted from the bosun's chair.

Brace A tube inserted diagonally in a scaffold to give stability and to prevent the tendency for the framework to fold up.

Bracket Something which projects to support a weight, as for example the member supporting the cornice of a building, or a light construction supporting a shelf, etc.

Break Vegetable oils are said to break if, when they are heated, a mucilage-like material separates; such a material once separated usually remains insoluble and cannot be re-dissolved with the oil. The term "break" is also applied to the actual mucilage or insoluble matter itself.

Breaking in Generally used in connection with brushes. The process of making a new brush assume a certain shaping or certain characteristics, as when a new paint brush is used in such a way that a compact chisel edge is formed.

Breathing apparatus See *Respiratory protective equipment.*

Brèche violet A very decorative type of marble quarried in the Carrara Mountains; although the quarries are exhausted and the marble no longer produced, examples are often to be seen in public buildings and its colour and pattern make an appeal to decorators. Its basic colour is generally a clean creamy white clouded with delicate tones of blue-grey and it is broken into irregular angular shapes by a system of veining, the main veins being of blue-violet and the secondary veins being in a great variety of colours.

Bridging A term used when a continuous film of paint is not in complete contact with the surface to which it is applied; it generally implies too thick a coating put on without sufficient attention to preparation or application. Common examples of bridging are (a) when paint is applied over unfilled cracks or small holes in plaster or woodwork in such a way as to conceal the gaps, and (b) when thick paint is applied over riveted or bolted portions of steelwork without being forced into the corners around the boltheads or rivets, so that the coating appears complete but is not actually in contact with the steel at these points. Bridging causes a weakness in the paint film which soon leads to the lifting and cracking of the dried film.

Bridle A horizontal scaffold tube secured between two putlogs to give support to intermediate transoms across window openings.

Bridling The process of binding a new paint brush with string in order to shorten the effective length of the bristles. Bridling is essential before a round brush of the old-fashioned type—sash tool, seconds tool or pound brush—is put into use, but such brushes have been superseded by the flat paint brush with a metal ferrule, which cannot be properly bridled. A great advantage of the old-fashioned brush is that the bridling can be released a few turns at a time as the bristle wears down so that, when it is once broken in it retains its most efficient length for quite a long time and outlasts the flat brush by a wide margin. (**NLC**)

Bring forward (a) A term used in the repainting and redecoration of old work when it is felt that certain local areas need an extra coat of paint to make them conform with the rest of the work before undercoating is commenced. For instance, some areas may be noticeably more absorbent than the main body of the work, various parts may have needed stripping and in some places new pieces of timber, etc., may have been inserted. When such areas are picked out and separately painted in order to bring them into line with the rest they are said to have been brought forward.

(b) In some districts the term is used more loosely to mean the general painting of any particular area. For example, in decorating the interior of a house it may be decided to bring one particular room a stage nearer to completion, in which case the painting of that room is referred to as "bringing the room forward"; again, it may be decided to concentrate on completing all the ceilings throughout the house before proceeding further with other parts of the work, in which case the ceilings are said to have been brought forward.

Bristle A term which is used exclusively for the hairs of the hog, pig or boar, hairs which are of the utmost importance in the making of paint brushes. The hairs are those obtained from the neck, shoulders and back of the animal. Bristle possesses certain unique features which make it an outstandingly suitable filling for most types of paint brush. These features are: (a) its resilience. (b) The fact that the filament tapers from root to tip, the root being the stiffest portion. (c) The surface is serrated or barbed with the serrations pointing towards the tip; it is the barbed surface which has an affinity for paint and holds the paint, for bristle is not absorbent. (d) The tip is split, forming what is called the "flag" and, as the bristle wears down, the flag is constantly renewed. (e) The hair is curved.

All these features combine to give a brush filling which is tough and springy and capable of standing up to hard wear, yet which has a fine soft tip enabling paint to be laid off without brush marks; the barbed surface holds the paint but the taper of the hair and the direction of the barbs force the paint to flow outwards toward the tip rather than inwards towards the handle, thereby assisting even distribution of the paint on the surface. The curve of the bristle is used by the brush manufacturers to produce a brush of good shape with a narrow chisel edge.

"Pure bristle" and "All bristle" are terms protected by law, guaranteeing that the brushes so marked contain 100 percent hog bristles with no adulteration.

British Standards Institution A non-profit-making body set up in 1901 and incorporated by Royal Charter in 1929. It is an organization which plays a vital role in British industry by defining acceptable standards in manufactured goods and working methods, standards which are of benefit both to the manufacturers of goods and to the consumers. Its findings are continually under review in order that they shall keep abreast of progress. It is generally recognized that any article or product that conforms to the appropriate British Standard is the best of its kind that is obtainable.

Among the many thousands of documents which the Institution has published there are several which are of interest and concern to the decorator, including a number relating to paints, colour, scaffold materials, etc., together with a most comprehensive *Code of Practice for the Painting of Buildings*, BS 6150: 1982.

British Standard sections Rolled steel structural sections which conform to the dimensions recognized by the British Engineering Standards Committee and, as such, a matter of great importance to the estimator in industrial painting.

Broken colour A term describing any multi-coloured effect in which the patches of various colours are irregular in size, shape and distribution because their production is to some extent accidental. Such effects can be produced in a variety of ways, including the following:

(a) Blending of various wet opaque colours on a previously prepared ground colour.

(b) Use of transparent glazes, suitably tinted and applied over a solid ground colour and subsequently stippled with the hair stippler.

(c) Partial lifting of wet colour or wet glaze (in order to expose the ground colour in irregular patches) by means of manipulation with absorbent rags, wash-leathers, pieces of crumpled paper, steel combs, rubber stipplers of various patterns, sponges, etc.

(d) Distribution of spots of colour by means of sponge stippling, etc.

Broken white White paint—or other decorative material—which has been modified so as to avoid the somewhat harsh effect produced when a large area is treated in pure white and yet which is not tinted sufficiently to produce any definite colour. Generally (although not always) the pure white is broken by the addition of a very small quantity of a yellow pigment when broken white is required.

Bronze powders Metallic powders made from alloys of copper and zinc or aluminium. Ready mixed bronze paints become dull and leaden when stored for any length of time; to achieve a good lustre it is better to mix the bronze powder with a suitable medium immediately before use. For display work, exhibition work and other types of work where durability is not an important consideration, bronze powders are available ready mixed in quick-drying media in aerosol packs.

Bronzing A term with two connotations.

(a) The application of imitation gold or other metals either in powder form or in leaves.

(b) The characteristic metallic lustre displayed by certain highly coloured pigments, such as Prussian blue, when used in full strength.

Bronzing lacquers Transparent lacquers intended for application to bright metals in order to preserve their lustre amd enrich their colour.

Bronzing medium or liquid A medium specially formulated for use with aluminium or bronze powders.

Brunswick black A bituminous black, which dries very quickly by the simple evaporation of the solvent, presenting a glossy brittle finish with a fairly high degree of heat resistance.

Brunswick blue A reduced quality of Prussian blue.

Brunswick green Brunswick blue combined with a pale chrome yellow.

Brush The traditional tool used for the spreading and distribution of paint and consisting of either animal hair, vegetable fibre or synthetic filament secured to a suitable handle.

Brush cleaner and renovator A fluid which is used to clean paint brushes and rollers after use; most decorative paints respond to it, as do many of the paints developed for industrial purposes, but it is not effective with cellulose paints. Some types of brush cleaner will also remove emulsion paint. The method is to work the brush or roller into the liquid and then rinse out under a cold water tap, after which it is allowed to dry. When paint brushes have been neglected and paint has hardened in them, the technique is to allow the brush to soak in the fluid until the paint has softened and then to clean off any remaining paint with a wire brush before rinsing in water. Brush-cleaning fluids are also effective in removing tar, grease, oil stains and substances such as chewing gum from surfaces.

Brush filler A filling composition, used for producing a smooth level surface by filling up small indentations, thinned down to such a consistency that it can be applied with the brush.

Brush graining The simplest form of wood effect obtained by drawing a clean duster brush or drag through newly applied graining colour.

Brush keeper A metal container, fitted with a hinged lid, in which paint brushes may be suspended in a suitable liquid while not in use; when the lid is closed dust is prevented from entering and the evaporation of the liquid is checked. As a general rule, far too little attention is paid to the care and maintenance of brushes, and brush keepers are not used as freely as they should be.

Brush marks Ridges left in a paint film by the brush.

Brush marks in enamel When this defect is seen it may be due to a fault in the enamel, which ought to flow out and eliminate all brush marks, but it is usually due to faulty application of the undercoat. Brush marks in the matt finish of an undercoat are not very noticeable, but become extremely prominent when a gloss coating is applied.

Brush-out cards Also called "Hiding-power charts". They are cards printed with alternate black and white stripes or with a black-and-white chequered pattern like a chessboard. When a sample of paint is applied on such a card in a normal coating it is possible to assess the degree of obliteration or hiding power of the paint. The cards are mainly used to compare the hiding power of one sample of paint as against another.

Bubbling A defect caused by bubbles of air or bubbles of solvent vapour appearing in a paint film.

Buffer coat Any coating which serves to insulate one material from another. For example, if an oil scumble or a coat of clear varnish is to be applied over a metallic paint, a buffer coat consisting of a thin coating of clear lacquer is necessary between the two. In most metallic paints the metal floats to the surface of the medium, and unless a buffer coat is used the metal particles may "work up" in the scumble or varnish; moreover, the oil in the scumble or varnish would have an oxidizing effect upon the bronze. The buffer coat provides the insulation which prevents this. Other examples of buffer coats are the coatings used to prevent creosote or red dyes from bleeding into new paintwork, to prevent a paint coating used on a cloth fabric from coming into contact with the cloth fibres and making them brittle, etc.

Buffing The polishing of a finishing material, usually a nitrocellulose finish, with abrasives and polishes.

Buffing compounds Materials for the buffing or polishing of a finishing coating, available in bar, paste or spray composition form. They are composed of various abrasives of very fine grit size, typical abrasives being powdered pumice, tripoli, rouge, lime, magnesium oxide, silica, silicon carbide and emery.

Build The thickness of a dry paint or varnish film.

Paints which are specially formulated to give an abnormally thick dried film are sometimes known as "high build paints". Certain pigments are notable for producing an unusually thick coating, e.g., micaceous iron oxide provides a coating equivalent in thickness to two coats of conventional paint (a fact which makes it valuable in the preparation of undercoatings for use on iron or steelwork).

Building boards Also known as wallboards. There are many types of building boards used for lining walls and ceilings; they are made from such varied materials as gypsum, straw, sawdust, wood pulp, etc., with various kinds of face finish, and are available in many sizes and thicknesses. Details are given under the appropriate headings.

Building Regulations The regulations which lay down the standards governing the general stability of a structure, and such matters as the fire resistance and resistance to flame-spread of materials used in the building (which includes paints, wallhangings and other decorative materials), the thermal insulation, the drainage, etc. They should not be confused with the

Construction Regulations which are totally different and relate to the safety, health and welfare of operatives. The Building Regulations are the requirements laid down by law in the United Kingdom with separate by-laws in London. This legislation is contained in England and Wales in The Building Regulations 1976 (As Amended), in Scotland in The Building Standards (Scotland) Regulations 1971–80, in Northern Ireland in The Building Regulations (Northern Ireland 1977) (As Amended), and in Greater London in the London Building Acts 1930/1978 and Construction Bylaws.

Burlap A coarse kind of canvas occasionally used as a wallhanging and sometimes subsequently painted. It can be supplied on a stout paper backing or in the unprepared and unbacked form. When backed it is trimmed with a knife and straightedge and is pasted and hung like wallpaper; when unbacked it is hung dry, the wall being pasted, and the pieces are allowed to overlap, a good joint being obtained by cutting through the overlap with a sharp knife.

Burning off The softening of a paint film by the application of heat, and its removal by scrapers or shavehooks.

Burnisher See *Agate burnisher*.

Burnishing Polishing or improving the lustre of a material by means of friction. In the painting trade the term is generally used in connection with the polishing of gold leaf. Gold leaf which has been applied with a mordant of either Japan gold size or old oil gold size is burnished with a wad of cotton wool to give it as lustrous a finish as possible. Gold leaf used for glass gilding with a mordant of isinglass is burnished when dry with a small pad of warmed cotton wool before it is backed up with paint. Water giding is burnished with an agate burnisher.

Burnish size A composition of parchment size or gelatine size, pipeclay and blacklead, used in water gilding to produce a very brilliant lustre. See *Water gilding*.

Burnt sienna An orange-red pigment obtained by the calcination of raw sienna (an earth colour found in Sicily and Italy). See also *Raw sienna*.

Burnt umber A rich reddish-brown pigment obtained by the calcination of raw umber. See also *Raw umber*.

Burr walnut The burrs in walnut generally occur in a fairly old tree. Often they are caused by a growth which the tree puts out to surround an insect which is boring into it and causing irritation; sometimes they are the result of the trunk being bruised, or of a side shoot which has been struck off causing local damage to the trunk. The wood displaying these markings is found in the lower part of the trunk and is generally cut as a veneer. The graining of burr walnut is worked on a deep warm cream ground; water colour graining is employed, the palette consisting of Vandyke brown, burnt sienna and black.

Butane A flammable gas derived from petroleum; it provides one of the fuels that can be used to operate a blowtorch. See *LPG containers*.

Butt joints A term used in paperhanging to indicate that the paper is hung with the edges lying side by side and not overlapping at all.

Butting tube A very short piece of tube used in tubular scaffolding to make it possible for a diagonal brace to be fastened to a standard with right-angled couplers instead of with swivel couplers, thus giving extra strength.

C

Cadmium A bluish-white metal resembling tin, and from which various pigments are derived, all of them being produced by precipitation from cadmium sulphate solution. They are bright in colour with a high degree of lightfastness, but their main feature is their outstanding property of resistance to heat. It is this which makes them so important as an ingredient of heat-resisting paints, in spite of their relatively high cost.

Cadmium red This is a compound of cadmium, sulphur and selenium; a brilliant red pigment, very opaque and with good staining power, stable, fast to light, unaffected by exposure to sulphur fumes, and with considerable resistance to heat. Used as an artists' colour and also in the making of vitreous enamels. Reduced qualities, lower in cost than the pure pigment, are used as a replacement for vermilion.

Cadmium yellow A sulphide of the metal cadmium; a fine permanent pigment ranging from pale yellow to orange, more expensive than lead chrome but not affected by exposure to sulphur fumes as the lead chromes are, and used as an artists' colour and for high-class decorative work.

Cadmopone yellow or cadmium lithopone A durable pale yellow lower in cost than pure cadmium yellow; by modifications in the manufacture a range of colours extending from yellow to deep crimson can be produced. Unlike the chromes, cadmium lithopone is heat-resisting, but if mixed with lead or copper pigments will cause discolouration.

Caking The settling of the pigment particles of a paint into a hard mass which cannot readily be redispersed by stirring.

Calcination The process of burning or roasting a substance with great heat in order to produce certain chemical changes. It is used in the production of several pigments, in reducing limestone to lime, etc.

Calcium A chemical element; the basis of lime; a component of many chemical compounds. Hence:

Calcium carbonate A substance of great importance to the decorator since it provides a common material used in painting and also a surface on which decoration is applied. Calcium carbonate is derived from natural chalk or limestone and is the substance commonly known as whiting. Lime plaster, used as a skimming coat, is made by adding water to quicklime which in turn is obtained by calcining chalk or limestone, and when the skimming sets and hardens, it does so by a process of carbonation, whereby it reverts to the form of calcium carbonate.

Calcium hydroxide Calcium hydroxide or slaked lime is formed by adding water to calcium oxide.

Calcium oxide Calcium oxide or quicklime is obtained by burning chalk or limestone.

Calcium plumbate A metal primer in which the main pigment constituent is calcium plumbate prepared in a polymerized oil vehicle or in a medium based on phenolic resin and tung oil, producing a paint film with considerable weather resistance. Its properties make it a very useful primer for galvanized iron, zinc sheeting, iron and steel. Its particular value for galvanized iron and zinc sheeting lies in the fact that it is the most convenient material for priming these metals on site work, since it can be used successfully direct upon the metal without the need for any prior etching or phosphating and without waiting for the surface to become weathered. On steelwork its protective and rust-inhibitive properties are due to both cathodic and anodic action, and it has far less tendency to blister than a red lead primer; it possesses good covering capacity and opacity, and its pale buff colour is more easily obscured by the subsequent paint coatings than is the strong colour of red lead.

Calcium sulphate The basis of a number of the plasters used in building, including the types referred to as plaster of Paris, retarded hemihydrate plasters, anhydrous gypsum plasters, Keene's and Parian cements and anhydrite. Such plasters are derived from the rock gypsum except in the case of anhydrite, which is obtained from naturally occurring anhydrite (or calcium sulphate with no water in its chemical composition).

Calor gas A trade name for butane (and propane). See *LPG containers.*

Camel hair Animal hair used as a filling in certain types of brushes, but not, as its name would imply, obtained from the camel. It is actually *squirrel hair*, obtained from the tail of this animal, and its misleading name is said to be a corruption of "Keml's Hair" from the name of a Dutch artist who introduced it. It is very soft and when it is moistened has no springiness, so that for ordinary paint brushes, water colour brushes, or writers it is of no value at all; for glass work, however, its lack of spring may be an advantage and some signwriters prefer a camel hair pencil for this work because of the way it clings to the glass. For the same reason it is used for the mops and size brushes used in glass gilding, when its soft floppiness enables the isinglass to be flooded on to the glass very freely just where it is required. The softness of the hair also makes it ideal for the dabbers which are used to press gold leaf into moulded and carved work.

Canada balsam Resinous matter, exuding from conifers, which solidifies when exposed to the air but which remains plastic and is used as a plasticiser in certain spirit varnishes. Fairly pure and transparent. (**NLC**)

Candlenut oil Similar in properties to tung oil: obtained from the fruit of the tree *Aleurites triloba* found in Fiji.

Cannoning A process in brush manufacture whereby the brush is given a bevel so that it is shaped ready for immediate use without having to be broken in.

Cantilever scaffold Also called a jib scaffold or trussed scaffold. A scaffold formed with tubes cantilevered out of a window or other opening so as not to obstruct the pavement on a busy throughfare.

Canvas A coarse unbleached cloth made of hemp or flax, used in a variety of ways; for example (a) as a wallhanging, which is often subsequently painted, (b) stretched over a wooden frame, as a surface upon which easel pictures are painted, and (c) stretched over a light framing to form screens, light roofing for caravans, etc.

When canvas is to be painted it should first be given a coat of hot weak size in order to insulate the fabric from the paint; this is because the vegetable oils used in paint have a hardening effect upon the fibres and make them become brittle and easily torn. Strong coats of size should be avoided; the object is to impregnate the fabric, not to stop the suction.

Capacitance meter A type of instrument designed to measure the moisture content of a surface, and consisting of two flat electrodes which are pressed against the wall surface to produce a reading on a scale. It is not very reliable as it only measures the moisture at the face and gives no indication of the condition below; the accuracy of the reading is also influenced by the presence of soluble salts.

Capillarity The force of attraction between dissimilar substances. The phenomenon is seen when a fine tube is placed vertically in a liquid, the surface of the liquid inside the tube assuming a different level from the liquid outside the tube; if the liquid is water, it will be found that the level of the water inside the tube is higher than the level outside. The condition only occurs if the diameter of the tube is small, and the smaller the diameter the higher the water will rise; hence tubes which exhibit this property are called capillary or "hair-like" tubes. The condition also occurs between two flat plates of glass or similar material which are vertical and parallel. All substances with pores of sufficient size are capable of sucking up water by virtue of capillarity; hence the importance of the subject to the painter.

Capital The crowning feature of a column or pilaster.

Carbazole violet A violet pigment with very high staining strength and with excellent properties of lightfastness whether used in the pure state or reduced with white to form a tint.

Carbolic acid Otherwise phenol. Of considerable importance to the painting trade because, when treated with aqueous solutions of formaldehyde, it forms the basis of certain synthetic resins from which paints and varnishes with good resistance to alkaline and corrosive conditions and to the effects of industrial atmospheres and sea air are obtained.

Carbon black or gas black A pigment composed of practically pure carbon in an extremely fine state of division, produced by burning petroleum gases or oils in a limited supply of air so that the combustion is incomplete. It is an intense black of good staining strength (but giving a brownish-grey when reduced with white); it is light in weight and has a high degree of oil absorption. It is non-greasy, works well with water and fairly well with oil.

Carbonation The process by which a substance combines with carbon or carbon compounds to become a carbonate. As mentioned in a previous paragraph, lime plasters undergo a process of carbonation; the drying and hardening of such plasters consists of the evaporation of their water content and a slower and more gradual process of absorbing carbon dioxide from the atmosphere. This is of importance to the painter because if such plasters are painted too soon and are sealed with an impervious layer of oil paint they will be prevented from hardening properly and will always remain weak.

Cardiglio marble A highly decorative type of marble, quarried in Sicily; a grey variety of the better known cipollino, with markings similar to the strong veins and bands of the latter but in grey instead of green.

Carlite plaster A lightweight plaster based on retarded hemihydrate gypsum plaster with the addition of a lightweight aggregate consisting of perlite or vermiculite or both. A small amount of free lime is present, so it is slightly alkaline; it is more porous than other gypsum plasters and therefore holds more water initially and takes longer to dry out. If it is not plastered evenly it creates difficulties for the painter because the patchy surface together with the slow rate of drying out leads to emulsion paint coatings being unequally absorbed; there is a further complication in that additional coats of emulsion, instead of levelling the surface, tend to pile up and produce sheary patches.

Carmine A brilliant deep fiery scarlet pigment prepared from cochineal; it works well in oil or water, and is used as an artists' colour and as a glaze colour, but fades badly.

Cartoon A word that is frequently misunderstood and misused; it is a full-size working drawing, generally on strong detail paper. On important mural work the design is fully worked out on the cartoon and then transferred to the wall. Very often cartoons are brought to a high degree of finish; the most famous cartoons in art history are probably the Raphael cartoons in the Victoria and Albert Museum, which are of great interest and importance to mural painters and interior designers.

Cartouche An ornamental scroll, usually providing space for a lettered inscription.

Cartridge paper A stout rough-surfaced paper, originally used for cartridge making and now used for drawing, stencil cutting, etc. It is available in numerous weights and grades.

Casein The albuminoid or protein in milk, extracted by treating skimmed milk with hydrochloric acid. It used to be of great importance as a binding agent for washable distempers, which are now obsolete. (**NLC**)

Casement window A window casement which is hinged vertically to the frame, opening inward or outward.

Casing wheel A circular cutter, mounted on a wooden handle, used in paperhanging. Its purpose is to cut and fit the paper rapidly and cleanly around architraves, door casings, etc., instead of the more laborious process of finishing with the scissors. See also *Corner knife*.

Cast iron Iron which has been shaped by being poured into a mould; it is brittle and is therefore easily broken. It has a spongy texture to which paint adheres very well provided the iron is dry when painted.

Castor oil Derived from the castor plant which grows wild in nearly all tropical and sub-tropical countries, and which is cultivated chiefly in India, Brazil and East Africa. The oil remains liquid at low temperatures, it does not thin rapidly with a rise in temperature and it is notable for its high viscosity. Untreated castor oil is a non-drying oil and is used as a plasticizer; when polymerized and dehydrated it develops good drying properties; dehydrated castor oil has properties intermediate between linseed and tung oil. It produces a paint film which is flexible and durable, and when blended with synthetic resins gives good resistance to moisture and to chemical conditions.

Castor wheels Wheels which enable a mobile tower to be formed from a tubular steel frame or a wooden scaffolding frame. Castor wheels can be fixed or swivelled, plain or fitted with tyres, and can incorporate a locking device.

Catalyst A substance which, without undergoing a change itself, assists in producing a chemical change in other bodies or substances. The term is often seen in technical literature and is of importance to the painter. Many of the modern two-pack materials (such as the epoxy resin paints and the clear wood lacquers familiar to the decorator) rely for their setting and for the development of their distinctive features upon the addition of a catalyst immediately before the material is required for use; and such an additive is usually known to the decorator by the term "activator".

Catalyst spraying The process of spraying simultaneously a protective coating and a catalyst additive, where the two materials cannot be premixed because of incompatibility or where the materials have insufficient pot life to permit of application by conventional spraying equipment. A twin-headed spray gun is used so that the two materials are mixed in the spray pattern after they have left the gun and before they reach the surface. The gun has its head fitted with a standard atomizing and fluid nozzle but has another nozzle at the side of the head which feeds a controlled amount of catalyst into the atomized paint when the trigger is depressed. Two pressure feed tanks are used, one for the basic material and the other for the catalyst. The pressures are regulated separately, and because the proportion of catalyst to material is critical the catalyst tank has two regulators to compensate for any fluctuation in the main air line pressure. In addition there is a flow meter in the catalyst line so that once the correct rate of flow has been established it can be verified visually when required.

Cathode Electrically, the negative pole of current. In the process of electrolysis, the cathode is a negative electrical plate, negative ions flowing away from the cathode through the liquid. In an X-ray tube, electrons pass out from the cathode through the gas (or vacuum) towards the anode or positive plate. This has some bearing on the behaviour of certain paint coatings and other protective films.

Cathodic protection A means of protecting a ferrous metal (e.g. steel) against corrosion, by passing a small electrical current between the metal surface and the surrounding moisture. In the world of industrial painting, such protection is provided by hot metal spraying and by zinc-rich primers, the primers being those with which the painter is more familiar. These primers consist of a high concentration of metallic zinc-powder (between 90% and 95% of the dry film by weight) in a non-saponifiable medium such as chlorinated rubber or epoxy resin. Under damp conditions an electrolytic cell is formed with the zinc as the anode and the ferrous metal as the cathode, and it is the zinc which is attacked rather than the ferrous metal. It is for this reason that zinc-rich paint is known as a sacrificial film—it is sacrificed in order to preserve the other metal. This action is linked with another of the properties of zinc-rich paint, namely that it forms a film which is two or even three times as thick as a normal paint film, and it dries very quickly. Even if the film is scratched or scored so as to expose bare metal, the cathodic protection is strong enough to prevent the bared metal from corroding for quite a considerable time, long enough for the damaged film to be repaired.

It should be noted that there are certain difficulties relating to the use of zinc-rich paints which mean that careful thought is needed before deciding whether or not to use them in any particular situation; these reservations are dealt with more fully in the section headed *Zinc-rich paints*.

Caulking gun A mechanical device for sealing joints by injecting them with compounds such as mastic, etc.

Caustic When used as an adjective the word means "burning", "hot", or "corrosive".

Caustic paint removers Strong caustic solutions, thickened to a paste by the addition of whiting, flour or starch to make them hold to a surface and to prevent them from splashing; they soften old paint films by saponifying them. They are rather crude materials and there are several drawbacks to their use.

(a) If used on porous surfaces, such as wood or plaster, the solution is absorbed into the surface and it is very difficult to remove it completely; any that remains is liable to discolour or saponify the new paint coating.

(b) A thorough wash down is necessary to try to remove all traces of the alkaline material and sometimes a wash with weak acid (such as vinegar) is used to try to neutralize the alkali; but this is very haphazard as there is no means of control or of knowing when the point of neutralization is reached.

(c) The plentiful use of water for washing down raises the grain of wood, so that extra time has to be spent in rubbing down and filling.

(d) These paint removers have a harmful effect upon the skin and are destructive to clothing and to bristle brushes.

(e) They have a solvent effect upon aluminium and zinc.

Caustic pickle A time-saving system whereby a large cask containing a caustic soda solution is kept in the paint shop. Dirty paint cans returned from site work are immersed in the cask so that the alkaline solution will soften the paint and make them clean; in this way the time that would otherwise be wasted in burning them out is saved. (Aluminium and zinc should not be placed in pickle because these metals are softened by alkali.)

Cedar A type of wood which sometimes presents difficulties to the painter; it has an oily nature which affects the drying and adhesion of paint. Generally the trouble can be overcome by scrubbing the wood with pure turps and a stiff brush to remove the oily residue; sometimes a wash with acetone is recommended. Following this treatment an aluminium primer should be used.

Ceilings, decoration of Unless some special reason presents itself, it is correct when painting or papering ceilings to begin at the window and work away from it.

Cellulose The principal carbohydrate constituent of many woody plants and vegetable fibres.

Cellulose coatings—paints and lacquers These are based on chemically treated cellulose compounds with suitable solvents to keep them in solution, plasticizers to give flexibility, resins to give gloss and adhesion, and suitable pigments to provide colour. They are widely used in the motor car industry and in industrial finishing; their application to house painting and decorating is more limited.

The fundamental difference between cellulose materials and oil paint films is that cellulose paints dry entirely by the evaporation of the volatile solvent. They are more suitable to application with the spray than the brush (a) because their rate of drying is so rapid, and (b) because the dried film remains soluble in the cellulose solvents so that each coat softens the previous ones; this can be an advantage because each succeeding coat is welded into the previous ones, resulting in a completely homogeneous film. Special qualities are formulated for brush application, but their use on large surfaces is still limited. The speed of drying is an advantage owing to the saving of time which is effected, several coats being applied with only a short interval between. But, of course, the fact that spray application is generally necessary means that considerable masking up is required, so some of the time advantage is lost.

Cellulose paints produce hard films resistant to abrasion and general wear and tear, but although this hardness is often an advantage it can lead to cracking and flaking if the materials are used on softwoods or surfaces subject to much expansion and contraction. They have the advantage of being unaffected by alkalis and are immune to fungoid and mould growths.

Cellulose pastes A number of cellulose-based adhesives for use in paperhanging are available. They have the advantage that even if not used for some time after mixing they do not deterioriate or putrefy. They are clear and colourless and it is claimed that they will not stain the most delicate paper even if the face of the paper is smeared, but this claim, although correct up to a point, should be treated with reserve.

In the case of a traditional type of wallpaper printed with water-thinned colour, any paste which encroaches on the face will loosen the colour, and when the papering brush is passed over the surface it will dislodge some colour and leave an unsightly smear. In the case of vinyls, any paste left on the surface may remain undetected for a time but will soon reveal itself as a shiny smear which eventually deepens in colour and becomes very noticeable. It is just as important for the paperhanger to be skilful and scrupulously clean when using cellulose paste as when working with any other kind of fixative.

When a cellulose paste is being used, it is desirable to use the same product, suitably thinned, for sizing the surface prior to papering.

Cement A term used to describe various adhesive substances which are applied as a paste and which harden to a stone-like consistency. To the painter and decorator these are the commonest applications of the term:

(i) Portland cement. Calcinated lime and clay used as an external rendering to buildings in the form of cement stucco and also used in the floating coats for Keene's cement and other gypsum plasters, as well as being the essential ingredient in concrete, asbestos-cement sheeting, etc. It is made by burning limestone and clay together at a high temperature until a clinkered mass is formed, which is then ground to a powder; when water is added to the powder it replaces the water driven off in the burning and combines chemically with it to set into a hard mass. It is highly alkaline and is very destructive to oil paint; very often it remains very strongly alkaline for a considerable time.

(ii) Gypsum cement. A name often used to describe anhydrous gypsum plasters.

(iii) High alumina cements, often known as ciment fondu, and made by burning limestone and bauxite, the cooled mass being ground to a fine powder. They are very dark in colour and harden rapidly. Though not nearly so alkaline as Portland cement, it is wise to test them for alkalinity before painting. Their moisture content, however, is as great as that of Portland cement, and if not given adequate time to dry out the pressure of moisture may be sufficient to force off an impervious coating. Before painting, they should be brushed down with a stiff fibre brush to remove any loose particles of efflorescence.

(iv) Hydraulic cements, or Roman cement, made by burning a naturally occurring cement rock and reducing it to a powder. They vary in colour from yellow to reddish brown. The exterior rendering of stucco fronts during the 19th century was of this type and some natural cements are still marketed under the name of "Roman" cement or "Natural Portland" cement. They should be tested for alkalinity before painting.

(v) Fixative cements of various kinds, such as, for example, those used for fixing lead foil, etc.

(vi) The cements used for securing the bristles into the binding of a brush, for which purpose vulcanized rubber or synthetic resins are generally used nowadays.

Cement paint A material composed basically of Portland cement with the addition of extenders, waterproofers and accelerating agents. It provides a reasonably cheap treatment for such surfaces as concrete, cement rendering, stucco, etc. because it is similar in composition to these materials and is therefore not adversely affected by them. It can be used where the presence of steam or continuously moist conditions would preclude the use of other types of coating. It is intended for brush application, but is not an easy material to apply; on absorbent surfaces it is necessary to control the porosity by wetting the wall before applying the cement paint. When used on textured surfaces like roughcast or pebbledash, the first coat can be reduced by the addition of sand, thus lowering the cost and at the same time actually improving the performance of the paint by reducing the roughness of the texture, and making it easier to apply the second coat.

On exterior work, cement paint chalks very freely if exposed to severe conditions of exposure, and its rough surface tends to harbour algae and lichen. It is not suitable for use on gypsum plaster, and should not be used on top of existing coatings of paint, emulsion paint or limewash. But the main difficulty with cement paint is not so much what happens at the time of application, but what will happen when the time comes to re-decorate. Because it is such a loose and powdery material it gives a most unstable base for any other kind of paint, which severely limits its use.

Unfortunately this can lead the decorator into a lot of trouble. Customers sometimes assume that because the paint is composed of cement it must be as strong as a solid slab of cement, and the decorator is blamed when faults develop; others are attracted by its cheapness, and specify a first coating of cement paint followed by a second coat of a high-class material, and again the decorator is blamed when the coating breaks down. Nor can the average customer understand why it should be necessary to remove all the cement paint coating before attempting to re-decorate, and this leads to the situation when the painter's price is considered unduly high; if the painter sticks to his guns he doesn't get the job, or if against his better judgment he fails to prepare the surface properly he is faced with the expense of putting the faulty work right.

Centrifuging An industrial finishing process somewhat similar to barrelling or tumbling, except that the items to be painted are placed in a cylindrical basket and rotated at very high speed; at a certain point in the process a drain cock is opened and surplus paint allowed to run out. It is essentially a one-coat process.

Centring of wallpaper This becomes necessary when a paper with a large prominent pattern is being hung; it means plotting beforehand where the various lengths of paper will lie so that the pattern appears nicely balanced in relation to the shape of the room. For example, in hanging a ceiling paper with big pattern, the exact centre of a pattern—or the edge of a pattern—is made to coincide with the centre of the ceiling, so that the number of repeats on either side of the centre is exactly balanced. Another example concerns the hanging of wallpaper; on a prominent feature of the room, such as the chimney breast, the paper is centred so that the repeats are balanced symmetrically. Again, when walls are panelled with a stiling border the pattern will be centred in each panel. A variation may occur when the mantelpiece is not placed centrally on the chimney breast; the paperhanger here must use his judgment and may decide that the mantel is a more important feature than the chimney breast itself and centre the pattern on the mantelpiece.

Ceresine wax Used as a substitute for beeswax; a petroleum product obtained from Galician "earth wax", harder than paraffin wax and dazzling white in colour.

Cessing An alternative form of the term "cissing". For full details see *Cissing*.

Chalk Soft white limestone, carbonate of lime. A composition made from this is used in marking and setting out signs and decorative work. Coloured chalk is available as well as white chalk, but for setting out on paintwork the use of coloured chalk should be avoided wherever possible, as it contains dyestuffs which stain the paint and leave permanent marks upon it.

Chalk board paint See *Blackboard paint*.

Chalk line or snap line A length of thin string or twine which when rubbed with a block of chalk provides the means of setting out a straight line.

Chalking The process whereby the surface of a paint film breaks down and becomes loose and powdery, due to the disintegration of the binding medium. Generally it is caused by the action of the weather; paint rarely chalks on interior work.

Chalking, unless it occurs prematurely, is not necessarily a drawback, firstly, because the paint retains some measure of its protective power and, secondly, because a chalking surface is easily prepared for repainting by means of a good rubbing down. But the early development of chalking is a serious fault due either to the quality of the paint, the use of an unsuitable paint or inadequate preparation.

Chamfer The bevel which is formed by cutting off an arris diagonally, or by paring the arris. A hollow chamfer or concave chamfer, formed with the gouge, is a groove instead of a flat bevel. The word is derived from French roots which mean literally a "break-corner".

Charcoal Wood which has been partially burnt. Sticks of willow charcoal, supplied by artists' colourmen, are excellent for the preparation of cartoons and the marking out of mural or decorative work on light-coloured grounds.

Charring The charring which occurs when woodwork is carelessly burnt off destroys the resinous nature of the wood and makes it greasy, so that the adhesion of the new paint film is affected.

Check roller A tool used in graining, to suggest the dark-coloured pores in oak. It consists of a number of serrated metal discs mounted on a wooden handle. One type of check roller is sold with a clip-on attachment of a mottler, which moistens the discs as they rotate. End finishers are a small type of check roller which permit the top and bottom angles of a panel to be completed without leaving a gap.

Checking A form of cracking in which very fine cracks which do not penetrate the top coat of paint are distributed over the surface like a fine pattern.

Cheesy A paint or varnish film is said to be cheesy when, although dry, it is rather soft.

Chemical changes A chemical change is said to occur when a chemical combination takes place and the properties of the product or products are different from those of the constituents, or when a chemical action is accompanied by a change in the properties of the combining substances (the formation of new substances being due to the regrouping of atoms to form different molecular groups), and when the change is *permanent* in the sense that it is impossible to reverse the change by mechanical means. An example of a chemical change relevant to painting and decorating is the change which takes place when a vegetable drying oil, such as linseed oil, is exposed to the air, absorbing and combining with oxygen from the atmosphere in order to change from a liquid to a dry, tough, leathery substance called linoxyn.

Chemical reaction The chemical action of one substance upon another.

Chemical symbols These are used as a convenient form of shorthand when describing chemical reactions, etc., and an understanding of their use is essential if the full benefit is to be derived from technical literature. The principle involved is that each element is given a distinctive letter of the alphabet, or a recognized combination of letters, e.g., O for oxygen, C for carbon, H for hydrogen, Pb for lead, and so on. As a simple illustration of their use, we might instance the symbol for water, H_2O, representing two atoms of hydrogen and one atom of oxygen combined to form a molecule of water.

Chemically resistant paints Paints formulated for use in situations where contact with chemicals (e.g. acids, alkalis, alcohols, mineral oils etc.) is to be expected.

Chilling Subjecting a material to the effects of a low temperature. Some materials are very susceptible to chilling during storage; for example, varnish which has been exposed to severe cold will be found to contain innumerable small lumps of hard coagulated matter and will not be fit for use, and emulsion paint if not protected from frost will break down and become unusable.

Chilling can also have an adverse effect on materials after application. Gloss finishes are very sensitive to temperature changes during their drying period, and if they become chilled at a certain stage they are very liable to bloom (see *Blooming*). Certain bituminous emulsions are liable to break down when exposed to severe frost, causing free water to be released, and for this reason it is safer when using these materials on steelwork to apply them over a protective primer rather than direct to the metal.

China clay A fine white amorphous powder formed as a result of the decomposition of granite, and found extensively in many parts of the world, including Devon and Cornwall in the UK. It is used to some extent as an extender in paints because of its low specific gravity, which helps to prevent heavy pigments from settling, but if used in excess it gives the paint a "soapy" working quality and weakens the dried film. It is also used as a flatting agent in flat oil paints and undercoats, as a base for the preparation of lake pigments, and in the production of ultramarine blue.

China wood oil A binding medium obtained from the seed pods of the Aleurites or tung tree. It is pale amber in colour, dull in appearance, and has an unpleasant taste and smell. It has a high specific gravity and a very high refractive index. The heat-treated oil has great resistance to water and is very resistant to alkaline attack. It is used in conjunction with both natural and synthetic resins in a wide variety of paints and finishes, and is an important ingredient in many alkali-resisting primers, marine paints and boat varnishes.

Chinese blue A refined form of Prussian blue with good colour and a fine bronze lustre.

Chinese insect white The deposit of an insect, a parasite on Asiatic trees. Used in the East like a beeswax, and sometimes exported from there. (**NLC**)

Chinese lacquer Obtained from the sap of a tree which is native to China; it is in the form of a thick, milky emulsion. When purified, this is applied thinly to a surface and hardens to a tough dark film which is very durable and takes a good polish. The famous Chinese lacquer ware relies for its effect on the application of numerous thin coats of this material. (**NLC**)

Chinese red Also known as American vermilion, chrome red, Derby red and Persian red; it is a chromate of lead. (**NLC**)

Chinese white The name under which zinc oxide was first introduced. Chinese white is now the recognized term for zinc oxide used in water as an artists' colour.

Chipping A term with two meanings:

(i) A fault which takes the form of a dried paint film flaking off to expose the previous coatings, generally as the result of accidental damage or severe wear and tear. For instance, chipping is likely to occur on skirting boards, the bottom rails of doors or on stair treads and risers as a result of these surfaces being kicked, particularly after redecoration has taken place without the old paint coatings having been stripped. The possibility of chipping taking place is increased if at the time of redecoration the old paintwork is not thoroughly prepared to give "key" to the new paint coating. Where a drastic change of colour is intended from a light-coloured finish to a dark one, or vice versa, it is safer to strip those parts of the work which are liable to be knocked or chipped; otherwise, the chipping which is almost bound to occur will be most unsightly. Floor finishes are very liable to chipping because of the constant pounding they receive from the passage of feet; paints and varnishes intended for application to cement or concrete floors or to lino should be sufficiently tough to withstand the abrasion, and the cement must be bone dry before painting. Stained floors need thorough preparation before fresh coatings are applied and the use of cheap brittle stains should be avoided because of the danger of chipping.

(ii) Chipping, to the industrial painter, means the removal of paint, rust or mill scale from steel or ironwork by means of striking the surface rapidly and repeatedly with chipping hammers or pneumatic tools. Chipping followed by wire brushing is easily the most widely used method of cleaning steelwork for painting; it is tedious work and rarely effects a complete and efficient removal of the scale, but very often it is the only practical method that can be employed on an existing structure.

Chipping hammer or scaling hammer A hammer sold for the purpose of scaling steelwork by hand, consisting of a boat-shaped or wedge-shaped head with a sharp nose, set on a wooden handle.

Chlorinated rubber Chlorinated rubber paints are of considerable importance in present-day practice, and are of great value as protective films on surfaces exposed to severe chemical and corrosive conditions, or where heavy condensation is present. They are made by treating natural rubber with chlorine, under heat and pressure; the resin which is thus obtained is brittle and lacks adhesion, but the addition of a plasticizer produces a tough adherent film with remarkable resistance to moisture and chemicals.

These paints, when properly applied to correctly prepared surfaces, will tolerate immersion in sea water and fresh water, dilute acids and alkalis, and lubricating oil, but are not suitable for surfaces in contact with drinking water. They resist splashing with alcohols and concentrated acids and alkalis. They can also be used in situations where atmospheric pollution would retard the drying of conventional paints, or cause such paints to become discoloured.

Chlorinated rubber paints have a very wide range of uses. The types of premises on or in which they are typically used include dye and bleach works, factories devoted to chemical manufacture and mineral water manufacture, breweries, fertilizer works, farms and dairies, bottling and bottle-washing establishments, ships' hulls, concrete swimming pools, gasworks, laboratories and research establishments, including those where nuclear materials are involved.

A full range of paints is available, in the form of primers, undercoatings and finishes, and they may be applied by brush, spray and airless spray. They can be used over existing paint coatings, provided these are hard and in good condition, but the old paint film should be tested first and if there is any indication that it will soften or lift it must be stripped off.

Certain precautions are required when using chlorinated rubber paints. There should be good ventilation, and it is advisable to wear eye protection and gloves or gauntlets. In confined spaces, breathing apparatus with a fresh air supply should be worn. The material is flammable and should therefore be stored away from heat.

Chroma The Greek word for colour. In American publications on colour theory the term "chroma" is used to denote the purity of a colour, that is its strength, intensity or saturation. In the Munsell system the chroma of any colour is specified by a number placed under the value number of the colour.

Chromated red oxide A primer suitable for both aluminium and steel, consisting of a mixture of zinc chromate and red oxide in an appropriate medium. Provided it contains a substantial proportion of chromate it possesses good corrosion-inhibiting properties.

Chromated red oxide primer A good corrosion-inhibiting primer for iron, steel and aluminium, quick drying and non-toxic, composed of zinc chromate and red oxide.

Chromatic scale The whole range of colour generally arranged in a series of graduated wedges in a colour circle, passing from yellow through green, blue, violet, purple, red and orange and back to yellow.

Chromating The treatment of light alloys with chemical solutions containing chromic acid and/or chromates in a suitable acid medium in order to give increased protection against corrosion and to provide a good base for subsequent paint treatment.

Chrome greens Known also as Brunswick Greens; they are made by combining Prussian blue with pale yellow chrome and precipitating them together. According to the proportion of blue to yellow, their colour varies from pale yellow-green to deep blue-green. They are toxic and are badly affected by alkalis, so they are unsuitable in situations exposed to alkaline conditions. They are opaque and they possess good staining power, but the wet paint film tends to deepen in colour before it is dry; this is caused by the Prussian blue rising to the surface and is known as "flooding"; sometimes the surface dries with a mottled appearance, due to the same reason, and this is termed "floating" or "flotation". Their use in paints has declined considerably because of this defect and also because of their toxicity, and they have been largely replaced by a non-toxic mixture of phthalocyanine blue and organic yellow.

Chrome red See *Chinese red.*

Chromes The chromates of lead, zinc, barium and strontium are generally classed under this head.

Chromium oxide A very opaque green pigment with a rather yellowish or sage-green cast; it consists of anhydrous chromium oxide. It is extremely durable, is quite fast to light, withstands acid and alkaline attack, is unaffected by sulphur and resists heat; it is reasonably low in cost. Originally introduced as a colour for the pottery industry, it is now used as a pigment in paints (especially for those intended to be exposed to adverse conditions) and as a colouring agent in rubber, concrete, roofing tiles and plastics.

Church oak varnish This has always been a recognized trade term for the best quality of indoor varnish. It denotes a short-oil varnish, generally made from Congo or Kauri gums, which gives a hard film that does not soften when warmed and may therefore be used on seats, pews, etc. It is rarely used now, having been superseded by more modern types of clear wood finish. (**NLC**)

Ciment fondu High alumina cement made by burning a mixture of limestone and bauxite, cooling it rapidly and grinding it to a fine powder. For further details see *Cement*.

Cinnabar Natural vermilion, consisting of mercuric sulphide; a pigment used from ancient times. (**NLC**)

Cipollino A highly decorative marble with a whitish ground traversed by veins or bands of green.

Cissing This is a term applied when a coat of paint, varnish or water colour refuses to form a continuous film, recedes from the surface, collects in beads and leaves the surface partially exposed. It occurs very often in graining when water colour is applied over an oily ground; it can also occur when a second coat of varnish is applied over a varnished surface which has not been flatted down, when varnishing is delayed so long that the undercoats have become unduly hard, and when paint or varnish is applied over greasy surfaces (such as surfaces which have been wax polished, or old painted surfaces, which have not been thoroughly washed down). In all these cases cissing can be prevented by "cissing down", or by rubbing the surface down with fine waterproof sandpaper.

A delayed form of cissing can also occur in varnished work some time after application and may be caused by mixing different kinds of varnish together, by applying the varnish too vigorously or by using a brush which has not been properly worked into the varnish and which still contains turps. When delayed cissing occurs the varnish must be removed with turps and the surface allowed to dry before rubbing down and revarnishing.

Cissing down This is the process employed when it is known that cissing is likely to occur, such as for example in graining when water colour is to be applied over an oily ground. The surface is rubbed over with a damp sponge lightly powdered with fine whiting or fuller's earth used very sparingly.

Cladding A thin facing of some material used externally as a non-load-bearing covering to the structure of a building. The name derives from the old English version of "clothing". Originally it was applied to thin slabs of stone or to brickwork covering the structure in order either to improve the appearance of the building or to improve its resistance to the weather. In present-day building it is applied to a wide variety of materials including cement, concrete, weatherboarding, ceramic wall tiles, heavy-duty laminates, mirror glass, etc.

Claircolle or clearcole At one time this was a common material, part of everyday working life; it has no place at all in present-day practice. It consisted of diluted glue size to which a small quantity of whiting had been added. It was used on ceilings and walls to reduce the porosity before a coating of soft distemper was applied. Sometimes a little alum was included in the mix to make the distemper work more easily on a "hot" surface; the alum hardened the glue size and made it less soluble, but this made the subsequent removal of the distemper more difficult when the time for redecoration arrived.

Soft distemper is a thing of the past, and so is claircolle. The reason for including the term is that it still occasionally crops up in painting specifications. It would appear that some of the people who draw up specifications still refer to old-fashioned painting manuals for their information, and imagine that this is the correct form of preparation to be used before water-thinned materials are applied. Under no circumstances should claircolle, or indeed glue size in any form, be used when emulsion paints and other present-day finishes are to be applied. If it appears in a painting specification the decorator should point out that its use would be disastrous; if the specifying authority insists on its use the decorator should disclaim in writing all responsibility for the failure and breakdown of the finish. (**NLC**)

Clapboard A thin narrow board, usually of cleft oak, but nowadays often made from sawn deal, used for covering the exterior of timber-framed buildings. The term is still used in America but is no longer as common as it was in the U.K.; the term more generally used now is "weatherboarding".

Classification, packaging and labelling of dangerous substances A great deal of attention has been given to this subject in recent years. In 1978 a Statutory Instrument entitled "The Packaging and Labelling of Dangerous Substances Regulations" was passed. In September 1984, however, these regulations together with all the previous existing legislation were revoked and replaced by a new Statutory Instrument with wide-ranging terms of reference, bringing the law in Great Britain into conformity with a series of EEC Directives. This new Instrument is SI No. 1244, entitled "The Classification, Packaging and Labelling of Dangerous Substances Regulations 1984". There was a short interim period during which goods marketed under the previous legislation were regarded as complying with the law, but all the old regulations were superseded and the new Regulations became fully operative on 1st January 1986.

Certain parts of the Regulations are of considerable importance to the painter and decorator, especially those dealing with the classification and identification of dangerous substances and the fact that warning notices and pictorial symbols must be displayed on products which until recently had been supplied in plain containers. These matters are dealt with in Regulations 5, 7 and 8. The main features of Regulation 5 can be summarized as follows:

(i) A product classified as EXPLOSIVE is defined in Schedule 1 as a substance which may explode under the effect of flame, or is more sensitive to shocks or friction than dinitrobenzene. The symbol indicating an explosive substance is an exploding bomb, depicted in black upon an orange background.

(ii) A product classified as OXIDIZING is defined as a substance which gives rise to highly exothermic reaction when in contact with other substances, particularly flammable substances. The symbol indicating an oxidizing substance is a flame surmounting a circular ring in outline, depicted in black on an orange background.

(iii) A product classified as EXTREMELY FLAMMABLE is defined as a liquid having a flash-point of less than 0°C and a boiling-point of less than or equal to 35°C. The symbol for such a product is a flame depicted in black on an orange ground.

(iv) Several types of product are classified as HIGHLY FLAMMABLE; they are defined as a substance which

(a) may become hot and finally catch fire in contact with air at ambient temperature without any application of energy;

(b) is a solid and may readily catch fire after brief contact with a source of ignition and which continues to burn or to be consumed after removal of the source of ignition;

(c) is gaseous and flammable in air at normal pressure;

(d) when in contact with water or damp air evolves highly flammable gases in dangerous quantities, or

(e) is a liquid having a flash-point below 21°C.

For all these the symbol is exactly the same as the symbol for "extremely flammable" materials, namely a flame depicted in black upon an orange ground.

(v) A product classified as FLAMMABLE is defined as a substance which is a liquid having a flash-point equal to or greater than 21°C and less than or equal to 55°C (except a liquid which when tested at 55°C in the manner described in Schedule 2 of the "Highly Flammable Liquid and Liquefied Petroleum Gases Regulations 1972 (a)" does not support ignition). No symbol is required, but the word "Flammable" should appear on the risk phrases on the label.

(vi) A product classified as VERY TOXIC is defined as a substance which, if inhaled or ingested or penetrates the skin may involve extremely serious, acute or chronic health risks or death. The symbol is a black skull and crossbones upon an orange ground.

(vii) A product is classified as TOXIC if when inhaled, ingested or penetrates the skin, it may involve serious, acute or chronic health risks or death. The symbol is exactly the same as for the "Very Toxic" classification.

(viii) A product is classified as HARMFUL if when it is inhaled, ingested or penetrates the skin, it may involve limited health risks. The symbol for such a product is a black St Andrew's Cross on an orange background.

(ix) A product classified as CORROSIVE is defined as a substance which may on contact with living tissues destroy them. The symbol shows test tubes from which drops are being poured, showing the damaging effect of a corrosive substance, the symbol being in black on an orange background.

(x) A product classified as an IRRITANT is defined as a non-corrosive substance which through immediate, prolonged or repeated contact with the skin or mucous membrane may cause inflammation. The symbol is a black St Andrew's Cross on an orange background.

There are special classification provisions for new substances within the meaning of the Notification of New Substances Regulations 1982 (SI No. 1496) which include solvents, paints, varnishes, coatings, adhesives, jointing compounds, putties, undercoats, paint-strippers, degreasing agents, artists' colours, release agents, preservatives and primers. There is also specific mention in the Regulations of paints and varnishes containing more than 0.5 percent lead, cyanoacrylate adhesives, preparations containing isocyanates, and certain preparations intended for spraying.

Coupled with the above, there are other sections of the Regulations which concern the painter. Regulation 8, based on Schedule 6, gives particulars of the manner in which products are to be labelled. The principal features of the supply label are (i) the designation of the substance, which generally means the chemical name, (ii) the classification (e.g. "Harmful", "Corrosive", "Toxic", etc.), and the corresponding hazard symbol, (iii) the appropriate "risk phrases" (e.g. "may cause fire", etc.), (iv) the "safety phrases" (e.g. "keep container dry", etc.), and (v) the name and address of the manufacturer, importer, wholesaler or other supplier.

Another section which is of interest, although it does not have a direct bearing on the painter's work, is Regulation 7 which relates to the packaging of the product and states that (a) the receptacle containing the substance, and any associated packing, must be designed, constructed, maintained and closed so as to prevent the escape of any of the contents when subjected to the stresses and strains of normal handling, and that a suitable safety device such as a pressure release valve may be fitted; (b) the receptacle and any associated packings must be made of materials not liable to be adversely affected by the substance; and (c) when the receptacle is fitted with a replaceable closure, this must be designed so that the receptacle can be repeatedly reclosed without the contents escaping.

Of course there are other sections, including some of the major parts of the Regulations, that have little relevance to painting and decorating, although clearly they are of prime importance to other branches of industry. A very considerable part of the Regulations is devoted to the safety hazards of transporting dangerous substances by road haulage, both as regards the packaging of the materials in drums, bottles, carboys, boxes and crates, and the risks to the health or safety of any person during the course of their conveyance. Regulation 6 deals with these matters in great detail. Regulation 9 is devoted to the matter of labelling for conveyance by road; the Regulation is derived from Schedule 2 and defines the designation and identification numbers of substances under such headings as Flammable Gas, Flammable Liquid, Flammable Solid, Spontaneously Combustible, Dangerous when Wet; Toxic, etc. The appropriate hazard warning symbols are supplied and illustrated. These are of no relevance to the painter and decorator, although they would obviously impinge on the work of the vehicle painter and signwriter, who should refer to the Statutory Instrument itself (available for inspection in the reference library section of the main public library in any large town) for full information about the nature of the symbols and the required colour systems.

Further developments

Another step has been taken in connection with the packaging of dangerous substances, bringing certain substances under the scope of BS 6652: 1985 (b). This is the British Standard which relates to packaging designed to be resistant to opening by children; it was introduced as a safety measure to protect young children from the risk of inadvertently swallowing harmful medicinal and pharmaceutical products. Since September 1985 it has been compulsory for such tablets, medicines, etc., to be supplied in child-resistant packaging. The intention is that from 1st December 1987 various products, including some which are applicable to painting processes, must be supplied in child-resistant packaging.

There is a Schedule of products covered by this extension of the law comprising

(a) all substances defined in the Classification, Packaging and Labelling of Dangerous Regulations as "very toxic", "toxic" or "corrosive";

(b) turpentine, and any solvent used as a substitute for turpentine.

(c) white spirit;

(d) products containing, in concentrations of 25 percent or more by weight, methylene chloride, toluene or xylene;

(e) products containing methanol in concentrations of 4 percent or more by weight.

The Regulations prohibit the supply of products listed in the Schedule where the products are contained in packaging, and are supplied in a quantity of 2 litres or less, unless the packaging satisfies the requirements of BS 6652 or where, in the case of products imported from the EEC, the packaging has been approved as resistant to opening by children by a competent body in an EEC Member State, or is at least as resistant to opening by children as the packaging approved by the British Standards Institution.

The prohibition does *not* apply to

(i) products listed in the Schedule which are solids, gells, or liquids of a viscosity specified in the Regulations;

(ii) products contained in aerosol cans or in spray containers, or in containers which can only be opened by the use of a tool;

(iii) toluene below a certain concentration contained in small volumes of liquid which is not any product listed in the Schedule; and (iv) most important from the viewpoint of the painter and decorator, the prohibition does *not* apply to products supplied exclusively for business or professional purposes.

See also *Skin protection.*

Clean colour A term used very vaguely by painters and decorators and even by the writers of textbooks; at various times it is used to imply light colours of high light-reflective value as opposed to dark sombre colours, strong primary colours as opposed to secondary or tertiary colours, and so on. A term of more definite meaning is "cleaner colour".

Cleaner colour Used to express a comparison between two samples of colour, in which there is an apparent difference due to the presence of less black in one than the other.

Cleanliness The most important factor in painting and decorating, and a vital factor in such operations as glass gilding, paperhanging, etc.

Clear finishes A rather loose general term covering varnishes of all types, clear lacquers (one-pack and two-pack), timber dressings, varnish stains, varnish medium, glaze, etc.

Clouding A defect which is sometimes apparent in varnished work due to the use of poor quality varnish or to a measure of blooming after application.

Coal tar Materials from which various substances such as benzene and naphthalene are distilled from which are derived a number of dye-stuffs used in the paint industry.

Coal-tar paints Phenolic resin-based paints of this kind are highly resistant to dilute acids and alkalis and also possess outstanding water resistance. Various combinations of coal-tar pitch and epoxy resins (some of them two-pack materials) are produced for situations demanding resistance to heat as well as to water and chemical attack, and such paints are eminently suitable for lock gates and chemical plant where exposure to water is severe. In recent years they have been used with great success in painting the structural work on the North Sea oil rigs, which present the most rigorous conditions of exposure imaginable. Normally before these paints are used the surface needs to be blast-cleaned.

Coat The term given to a film of paint, water paint, varnish or other similar liquid decorative material, applied to a surface in one single application. A paint system consists of a number of coats, separately applied, with a reasonable interval between each to allow for drying. The painter often adds to the term in order to describe the type of coat more fully, e.g., full coat, mist coat, sharp coat, etc.

Cobwebbing The production of fine filaments instead of the usual atomized particles when certain materials are sprayed. Normally it is regarded as a fault which can be overcome by the use of suitable solvents and by adjustment of the spray equipment, but it is sometimes used deliberately to provide a protective covering for certain articles during storage. The process is used for the protection of aeroplane engines, for example; the article is encased in a cocoon of cobwebbed lacquers prepared specially for the purpose, the cocoon then being sprayed with a complete film of lacquer.

Codes of practice A code of practice is a document drawn up by a recognized authoritative body which defines fully and comprehensively, without any ambiguity, the correct forms of procedure governing any particular set of operations.

In the strict sense of the word, a code is a systematic collection of statutes and laws, assembled in such a way as to avoid any inconsistency or overlap. Every reputable organization in today's complex society is governed by such codes, and for the protection of society it is desirable that any type of work which is carried out should conform to recognized standards.

There are codes of practice governing the organization and activities of the construction industry as a whole, and codes of practice relating to the activities of each individual craft—such as, for instance, those controlling the day to day organization of the employers' federations.

The British Standards Institution has, over many years, performed a valuable public service in assessing and defining the most satisfactory methods of work procedure in many branches of industry, and these include several documents relating to painting and decorating. The most recent of its publications to be of importance to the decorating craft generally was produced in 1982. It is BS 6150: 1982, entitled "Code of Practice for the Painting of Buildings". It replaces the former code published in 1952 and revised in 1966 and takes into account the enormous changes in techniques and materials that have taken place in recent years. These codes, together with the codes of practice relating to the Health and Safety at Work Act, should be known and understood by everybody engaged in the craft.

Cohesion The forces which bind together the particles of paint or varnish into a coherent film as opposed to *adhesion*, the forces which bind the film to the surface to which it is applied.

Cold checking A process used in industrial finishing to produce hair cracks in a lacquer coating by subjecting the coating to defined cycles of alternating hot and cold temperatures.

Cold cracking The defect of cracking or checking in a gloss paint film caused by a sudden drop in temperature.

Cold cure materials These are two-pack materials such as epoxies and polyurethanes in which the two packs or components are mixed before use; a chemical reaction takes place in the applied film so that it "cures" (i.e. it becomes solid) and will no longer dissolve in the original thinners.

Cold galvanizing A term sometimes used to describe the application of zinc-rich primer.

Colloid A gluey substance of a non-crystalline semi-solid nature, the particles of which form a permanent suspension in some medium, e.g., starch, flour paste, etc. China clay, used as a flatting agent in undercoatings, etc., can be prepared artificially in the form of a colloid.

Colophony Also known as rosin. The residue which remains when turpentine has been distilled from the oleo-resin exudation of pine trees. It is a brittle and highly acid resin with low melting point.

Colour (i) The sensation produced by waves of decomposed light upon the optic nerve. White light, or sunlight, is composed of innumerable different wavelengths or colours of light; when a beam of white light passes through a prism, or a beam of sunlight passes through raindrops, it is decomposed or split up into its constituent parts producing the familiar colour spectrum.
(ii) That property of bodies by which rays of light are decomposed so as to produce certain effects upon the eye. When light falls upon a body it may be reflected or absorbed or transmitted; in practice it never occurs that only one

of these actions takes place at once, and the colour which the body appears to be depends upon the particular absorption properties it possesses. Thus the colour of a piece of stained glass will depend upon which rays are absorbed and which transmitted, and the colour of an opaque body upon which rays are absorbed and which reflected. In general, the light that is absorbed by a substance is complementary to the light that is reflected or transmitted by it.
(iii) Any one of the hues into which light can be decomposed, or a tint or a shade, so that, for example, we term one hue red, another blue, and so on, and refer to a tint of red as pink, or a shade of orange as brown, etc.
(iv) That which is used for colouring or altering the apparent colour of a body. A pigment, for example, produces a certain sensation of colour because of the particular rays which it absorbs and the rays which it reflects. That pigment can be applied in the form of a film over an object of a different colour; for example, if a film of paint pigmented with green is applied to a length of white wood, we speak of "painting the wood green" or "applying a coat of green".
(v) The term is also used very loosely in the trade to refer to any coat of paint after the primer as a "coat of colour".

Colour circle Colours arranged in a graduated scale, useful in the planning of colour schemes and an invaluable help to those who are trying to develop colour sense.

Colour coding The painting of objects to a recognized colour scheme so that their contents or functions may be identified at a glance. Colour coding is widely used in industrial painting both for reasons of safety and for the convenience of maintenance staffs. Moving parts of machinery and danger areas are picked out to give them prominence, and service pipes and conduit systems are coded so that throughout a factory one colour will denote a pipe carrying hydraulic oils, another for diesel oils, others for steam, acids and alkalis, and so on. Water pipes are coded in twelve different ways to indicate the various types such as drinking water, untreated sea or river water, boiler feed supplies, etc.

Until recently many firms had their own identification codes, but obviously in the interests of safety it is most desirable that there should be a universally recognized system. An EEC directive required that from January 1981 onwards all safety signs and symbols should conform to a uniform system, and legislation to this effect was introduced in all places governed by the Health and Safety at Work Act.

The British Standards Institution has produced detailed information covering various aspects of colour coding, notably BS 1710: 1975, "Identification of Pipelines". In this there are basic identification colours indicating the essential nature of the contents, with optional coding colours indicating the precise nature of the contents. Until recently, safety signs were covered by BS 5499: 1978 and BS 5378: 1976. It should be noted that from January 1986 it became compulsory for all safety signs to comply with BS 5378.

Colour combing The production of patterns by means of lifting wet colour to expose a differently coloured ground. It is done with either steel, rubber or celluloid combs, and it may be carried out in scumble, glaze, flat oil paint, coloured plastic paint or metallic paint.

Colour theories The subject of colour is complicated by several factors, such as the fact that a person's reaction to colour stimuli is a highly individual matter, the loose manner in which colour terms are applied, the great number of imprecise terms which exist and the difficulty of relating experiment with coloured light to the effects obtained with coloured pigments. Since it is obvious that any faculty of the human mind can only reach its fullest development by undergoing some discipline and training, various attempts have been made to establish a set of principles by which the subject of colour can be approached logically and its use regulated by system as opposed to more fortuitous methods.

The basis of these systems is that the colour of a surface has three attributes, namely, hue, tone and saturation, and upon these attributes, considered in conjunction with each other, depends the position of that colour within an orderly arrangement of all possible colours. Various authorities differ in the details of their approach; in the Ostwald system the chromatic scale is divided into eight basic hues, the Munsell system rests upon ten basic hues, while other systems are based upon twelve, fourteen and so on.

Colour wash A term applied to the treatment of broad areas with inexpensive water-thinned materials for the sake of economy. At one time it was generally understood to mean the use of soft distempers on interior walls and various kinds of "washable" distempers for exterior use, but these have been superseded by the almost universal use of emulsion paints. The term colour wash, however, is still sometimes used to refer to a coating of limewash, tinted with dry colours, on exterior walls.

Columbian pine Also known as Oregon pine or Douglas fir, a softwood frequently employed in building work, and one which often gives rise to trouble in painting. It is extremely resinous and the resin exudes not only from the knots but over the whole surface, causing extensive lifting and blistering of the paint system. A further complication is that the wood presents a surface of uneven absorption, especially when used as plywood, part of the grain being hard and impervious while the other parts are very porous. A priming paint which is intended to penetrate cannot gain a hold on the hard parts, and in any case the resinous nature of the wood has the effect of retarding the drying of the primer. The most suitable primer for Columbian pine is aluminium, which has sufficient mechanical strength to seal the resin and which has good adhesion as well as presenting a film of even porosity for the subsequent coats of paint.

Combination lacquers Nitro-cellulose lacquers into which a proportion of melamine or other polymerizable resin is incorporated. The effect is that for a short space of time after application the surface may be pulled over in the same way as a normal nitro-cellulose lacquer but that it soon becomes resistant to pullover solvents and forms a non-reversible film.

Combing Lifting wet colour with rubber or steel combs to expose the ground, as explained in "Colour Combing". Combing is also used in the process of graining and provides a simple method of portraying coarse grain, especially of woods such as oak and pitchpine. A considerable degree of realism can be achieved by following the use of a broad toothed rubber comb (or broad steel comb wrapped in rag) with slanting strokes of a fine comb.

Combs The combs used in the process just described take many forms. Steel combs may be bought in sets ranging from wide to narrow and from broad teeth to fine teeth. Rubber combs of various patterns are also available. Many craftsmen, however, prefer to make their own rubber combs in order to get greater variation of pattern than is possible with the machine-made article. Celluloid combs for use with tinted glazes in colour combing are easily made to suit the requirements of the particular job in hand.

Compatibility The state of being compatible, whereby two separate things are able to exist together and agree with one another. Paint materials are said to be compatible if they can be mixed together without causing gelling, coagulation or other undesirable results, and paint films or coatings which can be safely applied on top of an existing film or coating without causing any damage and without leading to defects such as cracking, etc., are also said to be compatible.

Complementary colours A pair of contrasting colours. The word "complement" can be defined as "that which completes". In dealing with paint mixtures, complementary colours are so called because each completes the other by reflecting those components of white light which the other absorbs.

Compressed straw boarding A type of building board, usually supplied with a facing of paper ready for immediate painting.

Compressor A device which draws in air and compresses it to a pressure at which it will drive various tools and pieces of equipment. So that the operation of these tools may be properly regulated, a compressor is designed to provide a continuous supply of compressed air at a predetermined maximum pressure and minimum volume in cubic metres per minute. For workshop use, the most efficient and economical type of compressor is a stationary one with a large air receiver for ample air storage, but for normal painting and decorating work the portable type mounted on a handled and wheeled chassis is essential. The plant may be driven by electricity, petrol engine or diesel engine.

Compressors—source of supply Compressors can be powered by electricity, diesel engine or petrol engine. Electrically driven compressors are relatively cheap to buy, are very convenient to operate, provided there is electric power of the correct voltage and phase on the site, run very quietly, and do not produce any noxious fumes. Petrol-driven compressors can be used on any site regardless of whether electric power is available or not, but they are noisy and produce poisonous exhaust fumes; for these reasons and because of the fire risk their use may not be allowed in public buildings. Diesel-driven compressors are the most powerful of the three and can produce the whole range of pressures sufficient for any type of pneumatic appliance; they are also the most expensive.

Concentrated size Glue size in powdered or granulated form. Because of its convenience and the fact that it is readily prepared for use it is much more popular than cake glue or jelly size. It should be protected from deterioration by storing in a dry place at an even temperature. It is important that concentrated size should be bought from a reputable manufacturer as this type of size lends itself to the inclusion of impurities which might retard the setting and lower the adhesive qualities of the material. It should be noticed that the size should be prepared with hot, but not boiling, water; if the size is made too hot it will not gell properly when cool.

Concrete A material widely used in modern building construction. Basically it consists of a mixture of cement, a fine aggregate in the form of sand, and a coarse aggregate of crushed stone or gravel; the sand fills the voids between the particles of coarse aggregate, and the cement fills the voids between the particles of sand, so that a compact mass is formed. When water is added to the mix a chemical reaction takes place which causes the whole mass to set hard. The required shape of the concrete is formed by erecting a shuttering of timber or metal; the wet concrete is poured in, and when it is set the shuttering is removed. Alternatively the concrete can be precast and delivered to the site in the form of solid slabs or blocks.

There are various ways in which the basic material can be adjusted to increase its tensile strength, its water-repellent qualities, and its speed of hardening. Reinforced concrete has steel rods or mesh embedded in the mix; in prestressed concrete the steel is stretched before the concrete is poured in, and the tension is released after the concrete has set. Several techniques are used to produce lightweight concrete in its various forms. These matters are of great interest in terms of structural methods but they are not of direct interest to the decorator.

On the site the painter and decorator is called upon to treat concrete both as a load-bearing structural material and as non-load-bearing slabs or blocks used in framed structures and in partition walls. Building costs are frequently reduced by leaving the bare concrete exposed, even on internal walls.

The painting of dry concrete does not present any great difficulty, but if the structure is wet there can be serious problems because of the highly alkaline nature of the material, and efflorescence can also be a serious difficulty because of the presence of salts and organic matter. On new property the concrete should be left undecorated for as long as possible to enable it to dry out, especially if an impervious paint system is to be used. Even mature surfaces may be wet as a result of leaking rainwater gutters or structural defects. If early decoration is required, a good quality of emulsion paint is often the best choice of material. Where there is staining because of leaks or building defects marring an external wall, a good quality masonry paint would be preferable. If an oil-based paint system is to be used, an alkali-resisting primer must be applied first, even if the concrete surface is dry at the time of application; there is always the risk of moisture being introduced at a later stage because of some building defect and this would re-activate the alkaline content.

There may be difficulty because of the presence of mould-release oil (the oil which is used to help in separating the shuttering and moulds from the concrete after erection). In this case a cleaning agent should be used to remove the oil. This is particularly necessary on internal wall surfaces where wallpaper is to be hung.

Lightweight aggregate concrete takes longer to dry than high-density concrete, and is more porous.

Concrete floors are very often painted, not only to improve their appearance but also to prevent the surface from "dusting up". Special floor paints are available for this purpose, and such paints are usually applied by roller.

Condensation A matter of considerable importance to the decorator. The principles involved are as follows:

All air contains water in the form of vapour; this moisture is always present and is diffused throughout the atmosphere, but there is a limit to the amount of water that any given quantity of air can contain. If the temperature of the air remains unchanged its water content can be increased until the limit is reached; at this point the air is said to have reached *saturation point*, and if any more water is introduced it will no longer be held in the air but will condense. If the amount of water in the air remains unchanged but the temperature of the air is lowered, a temperature is reached at which the air becomes saturated; this temperature is termed the *dew point*, and any further cooling of the air beyond this results in condensation. As a general rule, the higher the temperature of the air the greater its capacity for holding water, and the lower the air temperature the less its capacity.

Condensation of moisture on the structural surfaces of a building occurs when the temperature of the surfaces falls below the dew point of the air which is in contact with them. This may be brought about by a surface being cold—plaster and steelwork, for instance, are good conductors of heat, and by drawing heat away from the air they tend to present a cold surface—or by abnormally high humidity, such as in kitchens, canteens, washhouses, etc., or in textile factories where humidifiers are installed to keep the air moist. Whether the condensation shows as water on the surface depends on the nature of the surface. On a non-absorbent surface the moisture will appear as droplets but on a more absorbent surface it will still form but will be absorbed. This is an important point to remember; in a room such as a kitchen or bathroom, where the atmosphere becomes steamy at intervals, a surface coating such as soft distemper or water paint may not show condensation as much as gloss paint, but such a coating will tend to disintegrate very quickly due to the repeated soakings it receives.

The problem of condensation of moisture inside buildings can only be cured by providing adequate thermal insulation and by improving the ventilation. Surface treatments applied by the decorator can only have a limited value, and depend for their efficiency upon the extent of the condensation and whether it is intermittent or constant.

This problem of condensation also arises in connection with the blooming of gloss finishes and the deposition of moisture upon surfaces—especially metal surfaces—if too long an interval elapses between cleaning and priming, and in recent years there has been a considerable increase in the staining of walls and ceilings due to the condensation of moisture in domestic chimneys.

Condensation is a factor to be considered in spray painting, too, since the sudden expansion of the air leaving the gun nozzle causes a drop in temperature which may lead to moisture deposits.

Conductivity meter An instrument designed to measure the moisture content of plaster, concrete, etc., consisting of probes connected to an electrical device that measures the conductivity of the material. Several types are available; some give a reading on a graduated scale, others indicate the conductivity by means of coloured lights and/or a colour scale ranging from green (safe to paint), through yellow, to red (unsafe to paint). They are not always reliable because the presence of soluble salts in the material increases the conductivity and gives a distorted reading, and also because at a certain stage in the drying of the material the atmospheric conditions may either increase or decrease the rate of evaporation in a way that produces a false reading.

Conductivity tester A battery-operated device designed to measure the electrical conductivity of a paint that is being used in electrostatic painting, and to assist in controlling and adjusting the conductivity. It consists of a probe and cable assembly connected to a meter with a graduated scale. The probe is inserted in the paint container, the reading taken, and the required adjustments made by altering the proportion of polar solvent, i.e. electrically conductive solvent, in the paint.

Condy's fluid A solution of sodium permanganate used by French polishers as a chemical stain for wood.

Consistency The degree of density, firmness or solidity of any thick liquid. The consistency of paint is understood to mean its condition when mixed for application; too thick or "round" a consistency will be difficult to spread with the brush and will produce ropiness, while if the consistency is too thin the binder will be so attenuated as to lose some of its cohesive power, the opacity will suffer and the paint will tend to run. For spraying, the consistency of paint is very often slightly thinner than brushing consistency. The degree of consistency is generally determined by practical application but can be measured more accurately by means of the Plastometer or the Consistometer.

"Consistency" is also applied to the other fluids and semi-fluids used by the painter, such as fillers, paste, etc. A considerable part of the skill of the paperhanger is the ability to judge the correct consistency of paste for any given sample of paper.

Construction regulations Regulations introduced under the provisions of the Factories Act of 1961 to provide a complete code of safety, health and welfare for the building and civil engineering industries; they supersede the 1948 Regulations which only dealt with building operations and which specifically excluded works of engineering construction. They lay down detailed and explicit requirements covering, amongst other things, the provision, maintenance, and examination of scaffolds, the use of lifting appliances, chains, ropes, lifting gear and hoists, the dangers inherent in excavation and demolition work, the use of vehicles, the provision of first-aid equipment and shelters, the protection against dust, fumes and poisonous compounds. Together with the Compressed Air Regulations and the Diving Operations Regulations of 1960 they form a code embracing every aspect of the industry. The measurements in the Regulations were amended under the terms of the Construction (Metrication) Regulations which came into force on 9th November 1984.

Construction regulations—statutory instruments The word "statutory" indicates that observance of the regulations is imposed by statute; in other words it is the law of the land. This means that the requirements of these regulations are enforceable by law. There are six sets of regulations which together comprise a comprehensive code applying uniform requirements for safety, health and welfare to all types of construction work; the titles and numbers of the statutory instruments which relate to these are as follows:

(1) The Construction (General Provisions) Regulations 1961 (S.I. 1961 No. 1580).
(2) The Construction (Lifting Operations) Regulations 1961 (S.I. 1961 No. 1581).
(3) The Construction (Working Places) Regulations 1966 (S.I. 1966 No. 94).
(4) The Construction (Health and Welfare) Regulations 1966 (S.I. 1966 No. 95).
(5) The Work in Compressed Air Special Regulations 1960 (S.I. 1960 No. 1307).
(6) The Diving Operations Special Regulations 1960 (S.I. 1960 No. 688).

The ones that are of particular relevance to painting and decorating are numbers 3 and 4, those dealing with working places and health and welfare.

To these six sets of Regulations a new Statutory Instrument has now been added, namely S.I. 1984, No. 1593. Its title is The Construction (Metrication) Regulations 1984. It takes the form of a series of tables and schedules by which metric measurements are substituted for all the Imperial measurements which appear in the previous six sets of Regulations. This came into force on 9th November 1984.

Contact adhesives Adhesives intended for the fixing of rigid materials such as plastic sheetings, etc., which set immediately when the sheets coated with them are placed in the selected position.

Contract An agreement or compact, an undertaking to do certain work or supply certain articles for a specified payment, which the law recognizes as binding. Although a contract need not necessarily be set down in writing, in actual fact most business contracts *are* recorded as a written agreement to prevent any misunderstanding.

In construction work (which includes painting and decorating) there are two main forms of contract; they are the fixed-price contract in which the contract price is fixed in advance subject to certain adjustments on an agreed basis, and the cost-reimbursement contract in which the price of the work is determined by the actual cost incurred by the contractor plus an agreed sum to cover overheads and profits. Within these two types there are various specific kinds of contract which are dealt with in this book under their respective headings.

Contract wallcoverings Wallcoverings specifically designed for large-scale work, especially in public buildings where they will be exposed to very much harsher conditions of usage than the materials used in domestic decoration, and where they will be subjected to rigorous cleaning methods.

The traditional response to the demand for a hard-wearing form of decoration in public buildings was to aim primarily for a material that would resist knocks and abrasion, its appearance being of only secondary consideration. This generally took the form of a gloss paint finish or a spray-applied multi-fleck paint, with coarse hessian subsequently coated with paint as an alternative. In recent years, however, the public has become much more discriminating. The big hotel chains catering for the tourist industry have realized that an important factor in attracting custom is the provision of an atmosphere of luxury and comfort. Commercial undertakings, banks, etc. see it as a mistake to entertain their clients in dingy surroundings. Business houses feel that their directors and managerial staff deserve well-appointed board rooms and offices befitting their position, and from this point it is only a short step to recognizing that the shabby appearance of the general run of office suites is bound to have a depressing effect on those who work in them and that pleasant surroundings make for greater efficiency.

This change of attitude towards the decoration of public buildings has become a considerable factor in the provision of suitable wallcoverings, and a number of firms now specialize in producing and marketing these materials, coupled with an advisory service to assist in the selection and supply of the products. A very large range of wallcoverings is available, including both natural and man-made textiles, wood products, natural and simulated leather, vinyl hangings, glass fibre, metallic finishes, etc. Many of them are specially produced to provide acoustic and thermal insulation, and in all cases great emphasis is placed on providing an attractive appearance. The most important factor, however, is that because they are specifically designed for use in public buildings they must conform to the various statutes which control fire precautions and the spread of flame, etc. in public places, both as regards the wallcoverings themselves and also the adhesives used in their application.

Information bulletins which give details about new contract wallcovering developments, together with technical data on suitability for particular wall surfaces and about adhesives and application methods, are published regularly by Ernest Turner (Northdown House) Ltd, one of the best-known firms operating in this field.

Contractile Tending to contract, having the power of shortening, shrinking or drawing together. Certain painting and decorating materials are contractile, glue size and paste being examples. There is an obvious danger in allowing size or paste to dry on a painted surface as the strong shrinkage might lead to deep cracking of the paintwork. There is a danger, too, in the practice of adding size to plaster stopping in order to retard the set; the size may cause such strong contraction that the stopping is loosened and drops out.

Contraction The act of shrinking, shortening, drawing together.

Contractor A person who undertakes a contract, or an employer of labour who contracts to perform work for an agreed sum of money.

Contrast ratio A method of measuring the opacity of a pigment after it has been made up into a paint. The paint is applied to a colourless sheet at a known film thickness, and the reflectance measured when the dry film is placed on white and on black substrates; this indicates the amount of light passing through the film and being absorbed by the black substrate. The contrast ratio or opacity is the reflectance over black expressed as a percentage of the reflectance over white.

Contrasting colours Colours which lie opposite or nearly opposite one another on the colour circle. When placed side by side they intensify one another.

Control of Lead at Work Regulations See *Lead Paint—Statutory Regulations.*

Controlled cracking The defect of cracking in paintwork may be caused, among other things, by applying a hard brittle coating over the top of a soft, elastic coat; this principle is put to practical use in order to obtain a wrinkled or "crackle" effect in the industrial finishing of small objects such as typewriters, etc. Of course, the process is carefully regulated, as opposed to the accidental effect from which it is evolved, and is usually carried out with stoving paints.

Convection The transfer of heat through a gas or a liquid by means of movement of the heated particles; e.g., in a convection stoving oven the air surrounding the object which is to be stoved is heated, being circulated from the source of heat to the object and returned for reheating.

Conventional A very misleading term which is frequently used but which ought to be avoided.

The word "conventional" can properly be defined as meaning "following the accepted pattern or the normal usage". What tends to happen in painting and decorating when some new material or technique is introduced is that the existing products are immediately referred to as the "conventional" products. For a while this doesn't matter because everybody knows that the term is used for purposes of comparison. Difficulties begin to arise when the more recent product gains wider acceptance. And if in the course of time the newer product becomes a commonplace and the older one becomes outdated, we find ourselves in the ludicrous position of speaking about an obsolete material or process as the conventional one whereas it is now the more recent product which is conventional.

This may not seem to matter, but in fact it causes a lot of confusion. For example, when airless spray plant first appeared on the market very few people took it seriously; they spoke about airless spraying as if it were something quite unimportant which would have little or no impact on the trade, and talked about the existing methods as "conventional spraying" to imply that these were the only methods that really mattered. Airless spraying is now very important indeed, and is a subject of major concern in the application of many products both in industrial and decorative painting. The fact that we still speak of the older methods as "conventional" has led many craftsman painters to believe that the word "conventional" means something that needs air pressure to apply it. But now another factor is appearing. New forms of paint coatings, primers, etc., are being developed and already the paint manufacturers are beginning to refer to the existing materials as "conventional paints" to distinguish them from the new products. Unless this is checked it will lead to a lot of misunderstanding among craftsmen. The word "conventional" has now been completely distorted to the point of becoming meaningless. It would be far better if we adopted the habit of describing our materials and processes by their proper names. This is the only way by which people can have a real understanding of the materials and techniques of their craft.

Conversion factors and table See pages x and xi.

Convertible coatings These are paint coatings which dry or cure by means of a chemical reaction taking place in the film. When the coating is applied to a surface the thinner evaporates, and then the binder which remains in the coating undergoes a chemical reaction and becomes solid. The solid film is therefore a different chemical substance from the original oil or resin, and does not dissolve in the original thinner.

This term and its opposite term "non-reversible coating" are not very easy to understand, and lead to a lot of confusion. Briefly then, the distinctive feature of convertible coatings is that they can be re-coated without softening up.

Copal A generic name embracing a number of resins, both fossil and recent, which are found in many tropical and subtropical regions of the world and are commonly named after the country of their origin. These resins, which are usually hard and somewhat brittle, formed the basis of most oil varnishes until the introduction of synthetic resins.

Co-polymer See *Polymerization.*

Copper A reddish-coloured, malleable, ductile metal.

Copper sulphate Solutions of copper sulphate were widely used by the old-time painter in a number of ways—as a wash to discourage mould-growths, as a means of etching the surface of galvanized iron sheeting, etc. Their value was problematical, and there are now materials which do all these things far better. They have no place in modern practice. (**NLC**)

Copper, the painting of Copper and copper-based alloys such as brass and bronze are sometimes painted so that they will match their surroundings;

there is little need to paint them for protective purposes unless they are exposed to some specific form of chemical attack. Painting them with traditional materials is unsatisfactory as there is a chemical reaction between the metal and the oil medium which retards the drying of the paint (although synthetic resins are not affected); furthermore, acid drying oils and varnish media sometimes dissolve traces of the metal and produce a green stain, and may also impair the adhesion of the paint.

The metal surface may be degreased and etched simultaneously by roughening it with emery cloth or abrasive paper, used wet or moistened with white spirit; it should not be abraded dry. Moistening with white spirit prevents the dispersal of metallic dust, which has a tendency to produce green or grey spots on any painted surface on which it settles. Aluminium pigmented primers and etch-primers are both satisfactory; some authorities recommend zinc chromate or calcium plumbate primer; in all these cases a normal decorative gloss paint can be used as a finish. On indoor work it is possible to paint directly on the metal with an alkyd gloss paint, followed by a second coat if obliteration has not been complete. Special lacquers are available which preserve the original colour of the metal and prevent both discolouration and the formation of a patina.

Copper, toxic properties of Various compounds of copper are used to repel the attack of insects and fungi. Copper rosinate, made by heating rosin with copper acetate and combining it with linseed oil, forms a durable varnish which is used in a poisonous paint for the protection of timber; copper naphthenate and similar solutions are used as a protection against woodworm, furniture beetle, etc., and there are various proprietary solutions made for the same purpose which are based on copper.

Corbel A block of stone, often carved or moulded, projecting from a wall and supporting the beams of a roof or other feature.

Cork The outer layer of the bark of a type of oak tree, *Quercus suba*, widely cultivated in Spain, Portugal and France. Because of its thermal insulation properties it is used to reduce the incidence of condensation on wall and ceiling surfaces (see *Anti-condensation paint*). Thinly-cut sheets of cork are also used to produce decorative wallhangings, much favoured by interior decorators because of their attractive appearance; unfortunately they have the disadvantage of bleaching in a patchy way when exposed to light and air, so that they assume a dingy and unpleasant colour.

Cork paint See *Anti-condensation paint*.

Corner knife A broad sharp-ended knife mounted on a light wooden handle and used in a similar manner to a casing wheel for the rapid trimming of surplus wallpaper from around skirtings and architraves. See *Casing wheel*.

Cornice Strictly speaking a cornice is a moulded horizontal projection crowning a wall, pillar, entablature, or other part of a building, but most people think of a cornice in terms of the interior rooms of a building in the form of a plastered moulding separating the wall from the ceiling.

In the 16th and 17th centuries such cornices were very richly ornamented with modelled and moulded work on which the plasterer lavished considerable skill and ingenuity, and these were enhanced when the decorator picked them out in attractive colouring. In Victorian buildings the plastered cornices were a notable feature, although the ornament was somewhat mechanical and repetitive and was often rather heavy-handed. With the present-day interest in Victorian properties many householders delight in restoring the ornamental features of the rooms, and the decorator is often called upon to enrich the cornices by picking them out in gold and colour.

In the 20th century, cornices became much plainer, until they generally took the form of a simple coving which the plasterer produced by means of a metal template mounted in a wooden frame and handpiece. Eventually it became the fashion to dispense with the cornice altogether, partly because of a swing in fashion away from ornamental work, but chiefly for the sake of economy—especially in the days of austerity following the 1939–45 war years.

At the present time there is a distinct reaction against the rather stark appearance of rooms totally devoid of ornament, and it is evident that many householders wish to have a cornice in the main rooms of a house, to relieve the monotony. To cater for this demand, various lightweight relief goods moulded into the shape of a cornice are available in long sections, to be fixed in position by the decorator in rooms where the walls and ceiling meet at right angles. They are usually made of polystyrene, but some are made of a material similar to Anaglypta.

Corrosion The wasting away of a metal due to the chemical attack which it undergoes when exposed to the action of oxygen, water, acid or salts. Most of the metals used industrially do corrode but the effect upon non-ferrous metals is extremely slow compared with the rapid deterioration of iron and steel. When iron and steel corrode, rust, which is hydrated ferric oxide, is formed; this is very often due to an electrochemical action (galvanic action), which can only occur when moisture is present. Efforts to check the corrosion of structural steel are directed towards coating the steel while it is clean and dry with a suitable primer of rust-inhibitive qualities and building up a paint film, which will resist the ingress of moisture. These conditions, however, are not easy to achieve. Rust itself contains moisture and active rusting ingredients; its moisture content makes its complete removal from a surface very difficult, but if it is not completely removed further rusting proceeds to take place under the new paint film. As rust occupies a greater volume than its parent metal it swells when forming and eventually pushes the paint film off, leaving the metal open to the weather and allowing further corrosion to proceed very rapidly.

Neither dry air nor pure water will in themselves corrode unprotected iron, but moist air readily induces corrosion; this is particularly the case when the atmosphere is smoke-polluted because of the acid nature of the dust and soot deposits and the acid content of the rainwater. Dilute salt solutions such as sea water are also highly corrosive. Alkalis tend to suppress rusting.

Corundum abrasives Abrasive papers made by coating the paper with a natural mineral called corundum, the crystals of aluminium oxide. Corundum is extremely hard, second only to the diamond in hardness.

Cost and fixed fee contract A form of cost-reimbursement contract, in which a fixed lump sum based on an estimate of the cost is agreed between the contractor and the architect, engineer, or appointed agent of the customer. The contractor receives this sum, whatever the ultimate cost of the work, subject to any agreed variations. This form of contract is rarely used in decorating but is sometimes used in industrial painting.

Costing The system of calculating the exact cost of producing an article or a process in any type of industrial work, in order to ascertain the profit gained or the loss sustained by the employer of labour.

Cost plus percentage contract Generally known as the "Cost-plus contract". It is a form of cost-reimbursement contract where the contractor and the customer agree beforehand on a percentage figure to cover overhead expenses and profits; at the completion of the work the contractor is paid a sum equivalent to the wages he has paid out and the materials he has bought plus the agreed percentage. It is used in emergency situations where work must proceed immediately, because it is the quickest way of arriving at an agreement and avoids any delay in commencing operations.

Cost-reimbursement contract A general term covering various types of contract. The essential feature is that the price to be paid for the work may be left open at the time that the contract is entered into, to be determined on completion on the basis of the actual costs incurred by the contractor (for payment of wages, purchase of materials, etc.) plus an agreed amount to cover overheads and profits.

Coumarone–indene resins Resins derived from coal-tar distillates by direct polymerization under the influence of a suitable catalyst. They are soluble in drying oils and provide varnish media of low acid value. They are usually blended with tung oil, and such varnishes are alkali-resisting and do not react with metals. They are used in metallic bronze paints and alkali-resisting paints.

Coupler A term used in connection with tubular scaffolding; it is a fitting used to grip the external surface of two tubes in order to hold them together.

Courlene ropes Polythene ropes, resistant to acid and alkali. See *Synthetic ropes.*

Covering power A very loose term, the use of which is best avoided. It is sometimes used to refer to the spreading capacity of paint and at other times to mean the hiding or obliterating power.

Cracking A defect occurring in paintwork, usually due to the application of a hard-drying coating over a softer and more elastic film, so that the top coating is unable to keep pace with the expansion and contraction of the undercoat. This may be because of using undercoats in too round a condition, or through not allowing the undercoats sufficient drying time. Another cause of cracking in paintwork, frequently seen in domestic decoration, is that glue-size or paste or other wallpaper adhesives have encroached on to the painted surface and instead of being immediately removed have been allowed to dry. In industrial work a common cause of cracking is the use of shellac solutions such as knotting, etc., to seal bituminous paints, or using hard-drying gloss paints over bituminous materials which are much more elastic. Sometimes cracking occurs simply because of the ageing and embrittlement of the whole paint film.

There are various degrees of cracking, varying from the fine cracks mentioned under the headings of "crazing" and "checking", to deep cracks which penetrate the entire film. Slight surface cracking may sometimes be treated by sandpapering the surface, applying filler if necessary, and then re-coating, but it must be recognized that this is always a risky procedure and is not to be recommended; besides being time-consuming it cannot be guaranteed to be effective. In severe cases of cracking there is no remedy except to strip off the entire film.

Crackle finishes Paints employed in the industrial finishing of small objects such as typewriters, radio components, etc., and which simulate such defects as cracking and turn them to decorative use. See *Controlled cracking*.

Cradle A type of suspended scaffold for exterior use, in which a cradle or boat composed of wood, metal or polyester fibre is occupied by two men who have the ability to raise or lower it as required. In many cases it is the easiest, cheapest and most practicable form of scaffold for painting and decorating and maintenance work. It is especially useful over a busy thoroughfare because it does not cause any obstruction on the ground, and on a building rising above a river bed or some other feature which would preclude the use of a scaffold rising from the ground, or on very lofty buildings which would not be accessible from the ground.

Hand-operated cradles are suspended by a system of ropes passing over pulley blocks; the men occupying the cradle raise or lower themselves as required and then tie off the ropes to hold the cradle in the desired position. They fall into three main types. A fixed cradle is suspended from outriggers and is capable of upwards and downwards movement only. A travelling cradle consists of a track suspended from outriggers, with the cradle itself suspended from jockeys which are able to run laterally along the track; this type of cradle provides movement upwards and downwards and also sideways in either direction. A third type of cradle is suspended from a mobile tower; the cradle itself is fixed and only capable of upwards and downwards movement but the tower supporting the cradle can be moved sideways.

Cradles may also be operated mechanically. In many cases nowadays, especially for very lofty buildings, a winch is mounted on the cradle decking and suspension is by wire ropes; upwards and downwards movement is controlled by the winch. There is also an electrically operated type of cradle designed to be incorporated into modern buildings in the construction stage or added to existing buildings for maintenance purposes, which runs along the roof track and is placed out of sight on the roof when not in use.

Crawling A very pronounced form of cissing, which is sometimes due to faulty materials or to working on an extremely greasy or oily surface. See *Cissing*.

Crayons Often used in the production of figure markings in graining (and sometimes in marbling). Conté crayons are suitable for oil-colour work; for water-colour work, crayon pencils in a wide variety of colours may be bought, although some grainers prefer to make their own from a mixture of pipe clay, dry pigment, gum and glycerine. Crayon should always be tested before use to ascertain how it will behave when varnished; some varieties may be found to "work up" in the varnish, while very waxy crayons will give rise to cissing.

Crazing A form of cracking in which the surface is covered with fine cracks which give the appearance of a small pattern; the term is understood to mean cracks that are deeper and broader than those indicated by the term "checking".

Creeping Another term for *crawling*, q.v.

Creosote An oily liquid with a penetrating smell and strongly antiseptic properties, obtained by the distillation of wood-tar or coal-tar, and ranging from light brown to a tarry black in colour. It is used as a preservative for timber when for any reason ordinary paint treatment would not be suitable, especially when the timber is to be in contact with the ground (on garden fencing and posts, for example) and where protection from fungoid growths, mites and woodboring insects is desired. It is also used in the treatment of such things as telegraph posts, etc., but in such cases as this it is forced into the wood under pressure. Certain proprietary brands are marketed which are available in other colours than brown and which, when dry, may be varnished. Normally, creosote cannot be painted or varnished unless sealed with a stop-tar knotting; otherwise, it would bleed through.

Cresylic acid A coal-tar derivative used for outdoor fencing and for the forced impregnation of timber which is to be in contact with the ground.

Crevice brush A brush mounted on an angled handle 400mm long, used for applying paint in narrow spaces, deep crevices and other areas which would be inaccessible with a normal paint brush. Various patterns are available ranging from 15mm to 30mm in width and a thickness of from 12mm to 20mm, with the length-out of the bristles ranging from 50mm to 60mm.

Crinkling A fault in paintwork which takes the form of a puckering or gathering of the surface, and very often due to too thick an application of the paint or to applying paint over a greasy surface. Also termed "wrinkling".

Cripples A colloquial term for ladder brackets; by means of their use a scaffold can be erected with stave ladders and planks. They are of sturdy construction; the arms are adjustable to the angle of the ladder and are secured when adjusted by means of a chained pin. The method of fixing is to hook them over the rungs of the ladders; the safest type are those which hook over two rungs as opposed to those which rely on one rung only.

Crocodiling An extreme form of cracking whereby the surface is so badly affected as to resemble crocodile hide.

Cross lining The hanging of a lining paper as a foundation for a good quality wall or ceiling paper, the lining paper being run at right angles to the direction taken by the finishing paper.

Crossing The means whereby paint applied with a brush is distributed evenly over the surface. The paint is brushed on and then the brush is taken across the work at right angles to the direction of the previous stroke. Each time the work is crossed the pressure on the brush is decreased, in order to eliminate brush marks.

Crow's footing A defect in a paint or varnish film whereby small wrinkles, similar in appearance to a crow's foot, appear; it is often caused by the formation of a surface skin.

Crutch The name given to a roll of paper used by a paperhanger, when working on a ceiling, to support the folded portion of the length he is actually hanging.

Crystal paper varnish A very pale varnish made for the purpose of providing an impervious gloss finish to the old-fashioned "sanitary" wallpapers which were printed in oil colours. Now completely obsolete. (**NLC**)

Crystalline deposits Deposits which appear on the surface of plaster, brick, cement, stonework, etc., and which are due to the presence of soluble salts.

Most building materials contain small quantities of such salts; when the materials are drying out the salts are brought to the surface and are left there in the form of a white crystalline growth as the moisture evaporates. On a surface decorated with emulsion paint the salts may percolate through the coating and be deposited on the face, where they will do little damage apart from presenting an unsightly appearance. If, however, the salts are deposited beneath a paint or emulsion paint film the coating may be disrupted and flaking or peeling will take place.

When such deposits appear they should be brushed off and the surface kept under observation until no further growth occurs, before any impervious paint coating is applied. Washing off deposits is inadvisable as the water is liable to dissolve further salts and bring them to the surface. Sealing the surface with an impervious coating will aggravate the trouble. See *Efflorescence*.

Curing The process by which a convertible type of vehicle or medium undergoes a chemical reaction whereby it becomes solid when applied to a surface. Curing takes place in a normal decorative paint by absorption of oxygen from the air, and in the stoving materials used in industrial finishing by the application of heat, but the term is now being more generally used to describe the chemical reaction whereby two-pack materials such as epoxies and polyurethanes develop their distinctive properties. In this case the two packs or components are mixed before use and the chemical reaction takes place in the film. Full curing may not occur until some time after the coating is dry.

Curing agent Another term for the activator in a two-pack material, the catalyst which is added by the decorator immediately before the material is required for use and which sets in motion the chemical reaction whereby the material cures. See *Activator*.

Curtain coating A method of paint application used in industrial finishing; it is somewhat similar to flow coating, the items to be treated passing on a conveyor beneath a curtain of falling paint. It produces an even coating of accurately controlled film thickness. It is simple, there is no wastage and the production rate is rapid.

Curtain wall In mediaeval building, a wall connecting two towers or strong points; in a modern framed building, a thin wall between, and often in front of, the main structural members of steel or of reinforced concrete, and bearing no load.

Curtaining Sagging; the occurrence of curtains in paint, enamel or varnish films.

Curtains A defect which occurs in paint coatings, particularly gloss paints and varnishes, when applied to a vertical surface. It is due to uneven application. It takes the form of a downward movement of the paint film between the time of its application and its setting which results in the formation of a thick line of paint like a slung curtain. Also known as "sags".

Cushioned vinyl Another term sometimes used for blown vinyl.

Cutting down A term applied to the rubbing down of a painted surface with abrasives, and generally taken to imply the grinding down of a glossy surface.

Cutting in Finishing off a section of paintwork in a neat line. Hence, "cutting in windows"—finishing the paintwork in a neat edge where it meets the glass of a window pane; "cutting in to a colour"—where a sharp line of demarcation is formed in parti-coloured work; "cutting in skirtings"—where the paintwork is performed neatly without encroaching on the flooring. Hence also the term "a clean cut" applied to neatly finished paintwork.

Cutting tool A brush used for the cutting in of windows, etc. It was the traditional term for the round brush approximating in size to the modern 25mm paint brush; the term is still sometimes used to refer to the modern 25mm equivalent. Also known as a "sash tool".

Cuttlefish bone Used as an abrasive for cutting down paintwork, especially the cutting down of gloss paints in between coats. The hard outer shell needs to be removed, to avoid scratching the surface. Cuttlefish bone is used with water and is very clean in use; it grinds well and does not become clogged. It is very rarely used today, and then only when a really first-class finish is being produced by traditional methods. It is never used in ordinary trade practice. (**NLC**)

Cyclized rubber Also known as "isomerized rubber". It is made by heating rubber with phenol and a catalyst, which causes a change in the structure of the rubber and gives a product which is soluble in white spirit. When used alone as a binder, cyclized rubber requires a plasticizer, but it is compatible with a number of alkyds and is often mixed with them to improve their chemical resistance.

D

Dabber A very soft camel-hair brush, used in the process of gilding for pressing loose-leaf gold leaf into mouldings and quirks.

Dado When the walls of a room are divided horizontally into separate sections, the lower part of the wall is described as the dado, as distinct from the upper portion which is called the filling. Usually the dado is capped with a moulding, known as the dado rail or chair rail. The top of the dado is between 600mm and 900mm from the ground. Generally the dado is decorated in a darker colour than the wall filling, and it is often finished with some form of surface coating or wallhanging with greater resistance to knocks and abrasion.

Dado rail The moulding which separates the dado from the wall filling. Also called the "chair rail".

Damar or dammar A soft resin found in Malaya and Thailand, which was used in the manufacture of crystal paper varnish and map varnish. (**NLC**)

Damask effects Damask is a rich silk fabric or linen fabric with raised figures woven in the pattern. There are various ways of producing an attractive representation of damask in painted decoration at an economical cost. One of the simplest and most effective is to finish the wall surface in gloss paint and then superimpose a pattern by means of stencilling or silk-screening, using a flat paint of the same colour as the gloss paint or a colour very similar to it.

Damp Dampness, whether due to humid weather conditions or present in the structure of a building, is always a source of trouble. If paint is applied while rain is falling moisture will be trapped beneath the paint film leading to blistering and flaking. Fog and mist cause considerable surface deposits of moisture which may penetrate to such an extent that even if the surface is dried off before paint is applied there is sufficient moisture present to impair the adhesion. Moisture condensing on a partly dried paint or varnish film may cause loss of gloss or blooming and during damp weather conditions the drying rate of most paint is retarded, particularly the drying of water thinned coatings such as emulsion paints.

The presence of moisture in the wall and ceiling surfaces of a building may be due to a number of factors; the chief causes of damp in building may be summarized as follows:

(a) *Damp in new building materials*. There is a considerable amount of free moisture in the brickwork, mortar, plaster, etc., of a new building which takes a long time to dry out; evidence of damp during the first year or two may be due to this rather than to any structural faults that can be rectified.

(b) *Penetration from outside*. This may be due to defective slates or tiles, damaged lead flashing or broken guttering or downspouting, or the brick-work or stonework may have become porous, absorbing the rain instead of repelling it, or in the older type of house there may be no cavity wall so that once penetration occurs there may be no barrier to the ingress of moisture, or the pointing of the building may be faulty, or in a building faced with cement rendering fine cracks may have developed in the rendering, or water may have lodged on a flat roof or parapet or may be entering because of faulty window-sill construction or through the jointing of prefabricated panels.

(c) *Rising damp*. This may be caused by a faulty or fractured damp course, or in the older type of house the absence of any damp course at all, and sometimes by the fact that soil has been allowed to encroach on the outside wall above the damp course level; moisture is drawn from the ground by capillary action and rises to a considerable height.

(d) *Condensation*. The tendency for water to condense when warm moisture-laden air strikes a cold plaster surface is increased if the ventilation is inadequate.

(e) *Condensation in domestic chimneys*. A fault which is becoming increasingly troublesome with the extended use of small domestic boilers.

(f) *Deliquescent salts*. Some of the building materials used in the construction of the house may contain mineral salts, etc., which have a special affinity for water and which remain permanently moist.

The essential thing in the treatment of damp surfaces is to find out the cause of the damp and, if possible, to remove the cause, and allow ample time for the surface to dry out before decorating. In most cases the removal of the cause of damp will be outside the province of the decorator and will definitely be a job for the builder. It must be emphasized that any surface coating applied by the decorator can only be a temporary palliative and not a substitute for curing the trouble.

While it is possible in some cases (e.g. in the case of faulty pointing or a leaking roof) to effect a complete cure, there are other cases where such a cure is impossible or impracticable. There are various measures that can be adopted to hold back the moisture, such as the fixing of lead foil, the hanging of pitch paper, etc., but except in mild cases these measures will only give a temporary relief.

In the case of rising damp, it will be found that the damp will climb beyond the level of any damp-proofing that is applied. Various proprietary damp-proofing solutions are made; it will generally be found that directions are given indicating the conditions under which these materials will be effective. Provided they are used on the type of work for which they are appropriate they fulfil the claims made by their manufacturers. But damp-proofing solutions should not be used indiscriminately; in the case of damp caused by condensation of moisture on a wall surface, for example, if the fault is wrongly diagnosed as being due to penetration of moisture and a damp-proofing solution is applied to the inner face of the wall, the effect will be to increase the amount of condensation (due to making the surface more impervious) and the trouble will be aggravated.

Damp-resisting paints Usually composed of a vehicle formed by dissolving paraffin wax, rosin, bitumen and gutta-percha in varying proportions in mineral solvents, with tung oil added.

Dangerous substances Many of the materials used in painting and decorating present health and safety hazards unless suitable precautions are taken.

The link between the use of asbestos compounds and the incidence of cancer is recognized and most workers are aware of it, but on site-work operative painters often seem to ignore the risks involved in the preparation and painting of asbestos lagging on pipe systems. Asbestos-cement sheeting presents physical hazards due to its brittle nature; it is often used for roofing, especially on factory buildings, and serious accidents involving operatives falling through shattered roof lights are very common. Cellulose products present both fire and explosion hazards. Hydrofluoric acid, whether used for glass embossing and etching or more commonly as a constituent of stone-cleaning fluids, is a highly dangerous substance, especially as its effects are not immediately noticeable. The solvents used in certain paints, stains and stripping compounds produce vapours which in high concentrations can cause unpleasant symptoms such as headache, dizziness and nausea, and may in some cases become dangerous if inhaled for any length of time; in normal working conditions there is no serious risk, but when the work is taking place in confined spaces it is important that there should be enough ventilation to disperse the vapours, or else a suitable form of respirator should be used.

Some protective coatings used in modern industrial painting present particular hazards. Nuclear power reactors are treated during construction with a special rust-proofing compound, because once the installation is put into use it is no longer possible to reach these parts. The treatment consists of blast-cleaning the metal followed by the application of a rust-inhibitive compound suspended in a volatile liquid such as carbon tetrachloride. Carbon tetrachloride and other solutions in the group known as chlorinated hydrocarbons possess highly toxic and anaesthetic properties. Accidents have occurred when men working in confined spaces have discarded the breathing apparatus supplied to them and have been exposed to the vapour. Carbon tetrachloride and other chlorinated hydrocarbons are sometimes used in the manufacture of water-miscible cleaning agents and paint removers. They produce highly toxic vapours which are heavier than air; ventilation at floor level is needed to clear them. There is an added danger in that the vapour produces phosgene if it comes into contact with a naked flame; it is extremely dangerous to use these materials near to an open fire or to smoke whilst using them.

Epoxy-based resin coatings, used for such purposes as the interior surfaces of rail and road tankers and the tanks of ships, consist of partially polymerized resins to which a curing agent is added just before use, producing toxic vapours of a highly flammable nature. In the spraying of certain polyurethane coatings, free isocyanates of a very toxic nature are produced.

These matters are mentioned under the appropriate subject headings, and detailed information is provided under the headings of (a) Lead Paint, Statutory Regulations, (b) Protection of Eyes Regulations, (c) Protective Clothing, (d) Respiratory Protective Equipment, and (e) Skin Protection.

Darkening of paints Often due to a chemical reaction affecting certain pigments, as, for example, when white lead paints, lead chromes or chrome greens are exposed to a sulphurous atmosphere, when black lead sulphide is formed. A similar reaction takes place when lead pigments are mixed with sulphide pigments such as vermilion and ultramarine. Some pigments darken when heated, and care is needed in selecting paints for hot surfaces.

Data The information relating to some project. To the decorator the term generally means the preliminary information to be obtained before commencing operations, such as the height, accessibility, customer's requirements, etc.

Daven process A method of imitating oak grain by means of notched cutting wheels, similar to that described under *Berries' graining tools*.

Daybook A large ledger kept in a decorator's workshop, in which all materials and items of equipment sent out to the various job-sites are recorded and against which all items returned to the shop are checked off. It is most important to keep such records, and the use of a daybook is reasonable for a decorator just starting up in business, but it is a cumbersome procedure. It is better, when once a business is well established, to use a good filing system with properly designed job-cards printed according to the requirements and methods of the particular firm.

Daywork Work valued on the actual cost of labour and materials with an agreed percentage added to cover overheads and profit. On daywork jobs it is customary for the operatives' timesheets to be made out in duplicate, one copy being retained by the customer and the other by the contractor.

Decorative canvas Closely woven jute canvas, attractively coloured and mounted on a waterproof backing; it is extremely durable and is a material of distinctive appearance with many applications in modern schemes, especially where a background is required for pictures, displays, etc. It is usually 0·9 metre wide and is ready trimmed. The walls should be cross-lined with a tinted lining paper; the adhesive may be of a stiff flour paste but a proprietary adhesive of the type recommended by the manufacturer (usually the PVA type) is preferable; the adhesive is spread on the lined wall and the dry canvas pressed on to it. Alternate lengths should be reversed and the edges butted; any attempt to stretch the material to force the edges together will result in shrinkage and open joints. Application is by felt-covered roller; over-rolling must be avoided, otherwise moisture from the paste will penetrate and stain the fabric. The canvas can also be obtained on a paper backing in rolls of the same dimensions as wallpaper; here the normal procedure for paperhanging is followed, using the adhesive recommended by the manufacturer.

Deemed-to-be-included items This term is used in connection with a bill-of-quantities contract, and signifies those items which are so commonplace and so much an essential part of the job that they don't need to be specifically mentioned. For instance, the contractor's price includes the materials to be bought, but there is no mention in the contract of storing the materials safely until such time as they are to be used; similarly the contractor's price includes applying the materials but there is no mention in the contract of using a duster brush to dust down the surfaces before paint is applied—it is understood that this will be done as an integral part of the job.

Defect A fault or blemish which spoils the appearance of any piece of work.

Degradation Derived from the word "degrade", in the sense that to degrade means to reduce or wear away. The term "degradation" is being increasingly used in trade literature and handouts to mean the deterioration of a surface coating or the wearing away of a surface that is to be painted—for example, the degradation by micro-organisms is said to be a reason for the deterioration of a wooden surface to which paint is to be applied.

"Degradation" is also used as an art term, as for example in mural painting when certain objects are partly obscured or are painted less sharply in order to convey the effect of distance.

Degreasing A term generally taken to mean the degreasing of metals, i.e. the removal of grease from the metals before painting. Obviously the presence of grease would adversely affect the adhesion of the paint film and would also affect the drying and the protective properties of the paint film. The methods of degreasing may be summarized as (a) wiping over with solvent, (b) emulsion cleaning, (c) the use of trichlorethylene, and (d) alkali degreasing. Of these (c) and (d) are not applicable to the treatment of large areas and are not therefore of major interest to painters; in any case alkalis have a softening effect upon aluminium so their use for this purpose is precluded. Emulsion cleaning is used in the preparation of machinery before painting in industrial work; rinsing with water is necessary afterwards, followed by a thorough drying. Very often on site-work the only feasible method is that of washing or wiping over with white spirit or other suitable solvent; the cleaning swabs should be changed at very frequent intervals, and care is needed to see that the grease is actually removed and not just spread around over the surface. Certain proprietary degreasing agents are available, and these should be used strictly in accordance with the manufacturer's instructions.

Dehydrated castor oil Untreated castor oil is non-drying, but when processed by chemical or heat treatment it becomes a useful drying oil with properties intermediate between tung and linseed oil. When combined with phenol–formaldehyde resins it produces a flexible film with good properties of water and chemical resistance.

Delayed expansion A term referring to a defect in plaster. It takes the form of a buckling or blistering of the plaster; in mild cases it consists of a slight rippling of the face but in severe cases there is a wholesale rotting and lifting of the skim coat. It is due to plaster which is suffering from the effect of "dryout" becoming wet again, and because the wetting is frequently caused by the application of decorative material the subject is an important one for the painter and decorator.

Dry-out occurs in anhydrous gypsum plasters when they do not remain wet long enough for the setting, that is their chemical hydration, to be completed. This may be caused by rapid evaporation of moisture due to a spell of hot weather, or by the absorption of moisture from the skim coat into the backing, the backing being unduly porous; sometimes, too, it is caused by lighting fires or circulating heat in order to speed up the rate of drying. The plaster becomes friable and powdery and lacks strength and hardness, but the fault may easily go unnoticed until the decoration is applied. When, however, water-thinned materials such as emulsion paint are used the water which is introduced into the surface is absorbed by the plaster and the setting action which was interrupted may be resumed, causing the buckling of the surface, which is known as delayed expansion. It is important that the decorator should be aware of these facts because it sometimes happens that he is unjustly blamed for the defect when it occurs.

Deliquescent salts Literally, this means salts which liquefy and which melt away gradually by absorbing moisture from the atmosphere. Many building materials—mortar, bricks, plaster, etc.—contain small quantities of soluble salt, but some materials, such as sea-sand, contain quite considerable quantities. When we speak of the presence of deliquescent salts in a building we are generally referring to cases where materials unduly rich in such salts have been used; the salts, being hygroscopic, attract moisture from the atmosphere and the tendency is for the affected areas either to appear permanently damp or, in certain cases, to become damp during spells of humid weather.

Denatured alcohol Methylated spirit; alcohol adulterated for industrial use with some noxious substances to render it unfit for drinking.

Dental plaster An unmodified hemi-hydrate gypsum plaster similar to plaster of Paris except that it is much more finely ground and is generally made from a pure sample of gypsum (alabaster) to produce a good pure white colour. While, as its name implies, it is prepared primarily for use in dental surgery, it has an application to painting and decorating; for those who prefer a home-made plastic paint to a ready made bought mixture, dental plaster is a useful ingredient mixed in equal proportions by weight with oil-bound water paint, and for this purpose plaster of Paris would be too coarse.

Dermatitis An inflammation of the skin which, though it cannot be classed as a serious disease, is very unpleasant and can only be cured by a long course of treatment. It can be caused, among other things, by the careless use of solvents; and almost any solvent used in such a way as to remove the natural oils from the skin may produce it. Some people are more susceptible to the action of solvents than others, but the risk of contracting the complaint should be recognized. The practice of washing the hands with white spirit to remove paint splashes, common among some operatives, should be strongly discouraged, and when any process involving scrubbing down with solvent is required it is a wise precaution to use a barrier cream before starting work.

Descaling The removal of rust and mill scale from iron and steelwork preparatory to painting it; complete removal is essential before any permanent paint film is applied.

When steel comes off the rolling mills it is covered with a layer of iron oxides known as mill scale, generally adhering tightly but in some places fairly loosely; if the layer were continuous and intact it would provide a good basis for paint but as in practice the scale is broken in places the metal is exposed and corrosion spreads rapidly, the whole of the scale eventually becoming loose. Very often it is specified that steelwork should be left to weather, unpainted, for a period of six months to allow the scale to loosen and to facilitate the process of descaling.

The principal methods of descaling are:

(a) Chipping and wirebrushing. By far the most usual method, but not an efficient one. Wirebrushing is a tedious task and rust is very difficult to dislodge; the complete removal of rust and scale by this means is a practical impossibility.

(b) Mechanical chipping and brushing, by means of pneumatic hammers and rotary wire brushes. Again, not completely effective; the pneumatic tools tend to cause pitting of the surface of the metal and the rotary wire brushes tend to burnish the rust instead of removing it.

(c) Flame cleaning—rapid heating with an intensely hot oxy-acetylene flame which dehydrates the rust and dislodges the scale by means of differential expansion. Very efficient, but unfortunately very expensive.

(d) Blast cleaning. Very effective, leaving a clean and slightly roughened surface which offers good adhesion to paint. Regarded mainly as a factory process, but extensively used on site-work where conditions are suitable. On erected steelwork, especially occupied sites where production work has to be maintained, there is a problem because of danger to other operatives on the site, unless the plant incorporates a vacuum attachment to withdraw the loosened scale and reclaim the abrasive, increasing the already high cost. (e) Acid etching, and (f) Passivation, are in general unsuitable for the treatment of erected steelwork.

Descaling pistol A pneumatically driven piece of equipment suitable for cleaning small areas of steelwork. It consists of a group of hardened steel needles, propelled and retracted from an open valve by a spring-loaded piston; the needles adjust to the contours and uneven surfaces of the steel. The action is trigger-controlled and a continuous flow of air blows away the loosened rust. This equipment is of some interest to painters and decorators for occasional use on small-scale work, but the process is so slow that on work of greater size it is not economically viable. On the heavy work extending over the huge areas undertaken by industrial painting contractors it would never be considered.

Detail paper A thin semi-transparent paper generally used by designers and interior decorators for detail drawings, and as a substitute for tracing paper.

Detergent A substance used for cleaning; used in painting work for loosening or rubbing away dirt and grease so that it is carried away with the water.

Determination This term is used with reference to contracts in the construction industry to mean the act of bringing a contract to an end. For instance, under the R.I.B.A. Standard Form of Contract, an architect or the customer for whom the work is being carried out can determine the contract if the contractor has failed to observe certain well-defined rules, or has engaged in corrupt practices. In the event of the contractor becoming insolvent (bankrupt) the appointment of a receiver gives grounds for the automatic determination of the contract. Similarly, a contractor can give notice of determination if, for example, certificates of payment are not honoured when due, or if the customer interferes with or obstructs the issue of a certificate.

Dextrin A strong adhesive derived from starch, prepared by heating the dry material to a temperature of 200°–250°C (392°–482°F), or by moistening flour with a mixture of dilute nitric and hydrochloric acids and heating it to 125°C (257°F). It varies in colour from nearly white (pure dextrin is quite white) to a dark brownish yellow and is soluble in water. It is used by the decorator when panelling with realwoods and relief materials, for fixing mouldings, strappings and similar members. In the past it was sometimes added to ordinary paste to improve its adhesiveness when fixing heavy materials. It has now been largely superseded by the modern range of adhesives.

Diagonal A line extending from one angle of a quadrilateral or multilateral figure to a non-adjacent angle, or from one edge of a solid to a non-adjacent edge.

Diaphragm pump A type of pump used to pressurize the paint in an airless spraying unit. It is driven by electric motor, but can be adapted to be driven by a petrol engine or sometimes by a diesel engine. The diaphragm pump has numerous advantages compared with pneumatic or hydraulic piston pumps, e.g. it needs less power to drive it, it takes up less space, and is easier to move and transport, and easier to clean and maintain because it has fewer moving parts. It may not, however, provide sufficient pressure for high-viscosity paints.

Dibutyl phthalate A plasticizer or softener which can be added to a cellulose compound to make it more flexible.

Diluent Strictly speaking, something used to dilute a substance making it thinner and more liquid and increasing the proportion of fluid.

The term is used rather loosely by writers on painting and decorating and may be considered in three different ways.

(a) When the term is used to describe a liquid which dilutes another fluid. For instance, in the production of cellulose lacquers, diluents are used to dilute the solvents, being cheaper than the solvents and therefore of importance in lowering the price of the product; as an example, ethyl acetate, a solvent (a liquid capable of dissolving nitro-cellulose) can be diluted with benzole (a liquid incapable of dissolving nitro-cellulose but which when added to the solvent does not cause the precipitation of the nitro-cellulose).

(b) When the term is used as a synonym for an "extender". Some text books describe as "diluents" or "diluent whites" those white pigments such as barytes, blanc fixe, terra alba, etc., which have little opacity in oil and which are incorporated into paints, among other reasons, in order to cheapen the material.

(c) When the term is used as a synonym for "solvent" or "thinner". The word "diluent" is sometimes used rather loosely to mean white spirit in the case of oil paint or water in the case of emulsion paint; and some writers use all three terms, diluent, solvent and thinner at random without drawing any distinction between them. It is better to avoid using the term so loosely; the word diluent sounds pretentious compared with the much more expressive terms thinner and solvent, and its use contributes nothing whatever to the cause of clarity of expression.

Dimension paper An item of stationery used by quantity surveyors and by other people concerned with "taking off" dimensions in order to prepare a bill of quantities. It consists of A4 paper divided down the middle by a vertical line. Each half is divided into three narrow columns and one wide column, and on these, every item in the structure is recorded. The first column shows the multiplying figure where there is more then one identical item, the second column indicates whether the measure is linear, square or cubic, the third column is where the length, area or volume is recorded. The wide column is where the description of the item is written; the first few words in this column indicate the precise nature of the work. Recognized abbreviations are used to reduce the length of the description—for example, k, p & s for knot, prime and stop.

On large-scale work most of the information is now recorded by computer.

Dip tank The tank in which dipping is carried out, which naturally varies in size according to the object to be treated. Several factors are involved in the design of the dip tank; it must present as small a surface area as possible in order to cut down the evaporation of the paint solvents, and a means must be provided to circulate the paint continually in order to prevent settlement at the bottom of the tank. The evenness of the paint finish depends on the rate of withdrawal of the painted object from the tank, and this rate is carefully governed, the object being withdrawn by mechanical means. Generally there is a conveyor system included in the installation so that the dipping of numerous objects may take place in smooth rotation.

Dipentene A solvent used in the paint industry, obtained by a process of distillation. It is an excellent solvent for several synthetic resins, and is also used to increase the solvent power of white spirit. It possesses anti-skinning properties, and because of its low rate of evaporation is used to extend the wet-edge time of decorative finishes and undercoats.

Dipper A small pot or tin used whenever it is desired to hold small quantities of paint, medium, gold size or thinner for a variety of uses. Dippers may be bought which have a clip attachment enabling them to be clipped to a palette board; these are very useful in mural work for holding the thinners, and in graining or marbling work for holding medium or thinners as required. The dipper is an essential tool in signwriting; it allows a full dip of paint or gold size to be taken and the signwriting brush thus charged to be drawn across the edge of the dipper to remove surplus paint and bring the writer to a good shape. The practice of dispensing with the dipper and using a palette board instead is to be deplored, as it leads to the inefficient use of the writer.

Dipping A method of paint application, used in mass production work, which consists of immersing the objects that are to be coated in a tank of paint and allowing them to drain during and after their removal. A wide variety of articles, ranging from motor-car bodies to quite small objects, is treated by this technique. The advantages offered by the process compared with spray application are (a) its speed, (b) low labour costs, (c) low paint losses, most of the surplus paint draining back into the tank, and (d) the fact that surfaces such as the interior of pipes and tubes which could not be reached by spray or brush are coated successfully by this method. Against these advantages are to be set the high initial cost of the dipping installation and the difficulty of coating objects of irregular or complicated shape.

Dipping lacquers, dipping paints, etc. Paints formulated especially for dip application. The viscosity of the paint is of vital importance; it must be exactly suited to the rate of withdrawal of the object, and once fixed must not be allowed to vary. It is necessary, too, that the paint should be able to withstand the constant circulation and exposure to air.

Direct labour Productive labour as distinct from administration and supervision. The term is also widely used when a corporation or local authority employs its own workforce for constructional works—including painting and decorating—instead of allocating the work to specialist contractors.

Dirt retention The extent to which dust and dirt become embedded in a dried paint film thereby masking its true colour and spoiling its appearance; it is very closely related to the hardness of the film.

Disc sander See *Rotary disc sander*.

Discolouration Some slight change of colour may be expected when any paint or water-thinned coating is drying; as a general rule, flat paints and undercoats tend to dry lighter, while enamels and gloss paints tend to darken on drying. It may also be expected that some slight darkening of colour will occur gradually over the passage of time, due to the vehicle darkening, etc. Anything more rapid and drastic in the way of a colour change, sufficient to constitute a fault, may be caused in a variety of ways. For instance, there is the discolouration or whitening of a paint due to bleaching, the discolouration which occurs when some substance penetrates the paint from beneath, or the darkening which occurs when certain pigments are exposed to sulphurous atmospheres, which are dealt with under the headings of *Bleaching, Bleeding* and *Darkening* respectively. Discolouration may also take the form of fading, which certain colours undergo when exposed to strong light, or "floating", whereby certain pigments separate and rise to the top of the material while it is still wet. Another cause of discolouration is the action of free alkali which may attack the medium of a paint to cause a change of colour without affecting the pigments, or which may attack certain pigments irrespective of the medium.

Discord Discord, when the term is applied to colour, is produced when the correct tonal order of colours is reversed. In the natural order of colour there is an orderly progression from yellow, the lightest, to violet, the darkest colour, all intermediate colours between these extremes becoming progressively darker in tone. If the natural order is reversed so that, for example, a pale purple is placed against a strong orange, the sensation of discord is produced.

Dispersing agent In the formulation of a paint the dispersion of the pigment in the medium is bound up also with the "wetting" of the pigment. A simple mixture of pigment and medium would not produce a satisfactory paint, as the pigment particles would tend to fall through the medium and settle in a hard mass at the bottom of the container. In order that the particles may remain in a state of dispersion they must also be "wetted" by the medium. In cases where the pigment or medium is not likely to produce good wetting, dispersing agents consisting of aluminium soaps such as stearate and oleate, sulphonated oils or modified rubber are added to prevent hard settlement from taking place.

Dispersion The state of being dispersed, i.e., diffused or scattered. To the decorator the term refers to the dispersion of a pigment in a medium or vehicle; in other words, the distribution of the particles of pigment throughout the liquid constituent of a paint.

In modern paint manufacture various kinds of mills are used to disperse the pigment in the medium—e.g. ball mills, sand mills, single-roll finishing mills—according to the type of paint which is being prepared. High-speed dispersers are used where a high degree of dispersion is not needed or where the pigments are readily wetted, as in emulsion paints and certain kinds of primer.

Disposable face masks Paper face masks intended primarily for the use of doctors and nurses, but which are very useful to painters and decorators during short spells of spray painting and in situations where otherwise the unhygienic practice of sharing a respirator by several persons would need to be resorted to.

Disposable products Items or pieces of equipment designed to be discarded after use. They are cheap enough for this to be a real economy. In most cases the labour cost involved in cleaning out a more permanent product after use is very much higher than the price of the disposable article.

Disposable strainers See *Strainer*.

Distemper Strictly speaking the term distemper means a composition of common whiting bound with either glue size or casein. The size-bound type is known as "soft distemper" because the dried coating remains soluble in water and is easily removed by washing. The casein-bound variety is known as "washable distemper" because it has some limited resistance to moisture which allows it to be sponged down. Casein, a product of skimmed milk, is insoluble in water but soluble in alkalis, so the distemper includes a proportion of borax and lime. When water is added the casein is dissolved by the alkaline action of the lime, but when the water has evaporated from the applied film the action of the lime ceases and the casein gradually reverts to its hard insoluble form.

Distempers used to be of immense importance to the painter and decorator, being the principal material for the decoration of ceilings and also being used to a great extent for the treatment of walls. They were superseded by oil-bound water paints which in time were themselves superseded by emulsion paints. Distempers are now completely obsolete in normal trade practice in this country. Washable distempers, however, are still used in some parts of Europe and are also sold in the USA under the name of calcimine.

Both soft and washable distempers are used to a certain extent in theatrical work for scene painting, their complete absence of sheen and their excellent light-reflectance being ideal in conjunction with the brilliant lighting used for stage productions. When used for the coating of canvas back-drops, which need to be rolled up, the distemper is generally plasticized with glycerine (or sometimes treacle) to prevent it flaking off.

The term "vinyl distemper" is sometimes used to describe the cheaper grades of emulsion paint which are only suitable for indoor work. (**NLC**)

Distemper brush The brush used for the application of water-thinned paints, especially emulsion paints, to the broad areas of a structure such as the walls and ceilings. The nature of these paints is such that a very different brushing technique is needed for their application from that required for an oil paint. In general, it may be said that they are best applied liberally with good firm strokes, and the size and shape of distemper brushes is governed by what has been proved by long years of experience to lend itself most successfully to this technique. Broadly speaking, although there are many different sizes and types according to local usage, the dictates of price, etc., the essential features of any distemper brush are the length of its hair filling, its width, and its weight. Flat distemper brushes, known in some areas as kalsomines, kalsoes or whiteners, vary in width from 150 to 200mm, the weight of their filling ranges from about 170 to 227 grams, and the length of hair visible above the ferrule varies from about 110 to 150mm. The brush with the conventional shape of handle and copper ferrule is sometimes known as the Yorkshire pattern. In some regions a brush known as the Lancashire pattern was preferred; this type of brush had a triangular stock and a leather binding, but it is rarely seen today. Two-knot distemper brushes consist of two knots of bristles, bound with copper wire or copper strip, attached to a common handle; the weight of their filling is in the order of 283 grams. Two-knot distemper brushes were always more popular in the South of England than the North, but their use in general painting and decorating work has declined considerably. They are still used, however, for such purposes as scenic painting.

Bristle is to be preferred to any other material at present available as a filling for a good distemper brush, but the supply of bristle, especially in lengths exceeding 100mm, is steadily decreasing. It follows that a good-quality distemper brush is bound to be an expensive item, and it is a pity to see brushes being spoiled by mishandling and by careless cleaning, etc. Today the filling of many of the distemper brushes on sale consists of mixtures of fibre, hair and bristle, or bristle, hair and man-made filament, and a good proportion consist entirely of synthetic filament.

Distillation The process of heating a solid or a liquid in a vessel so constructed that the vapours thrown off from the heated substance may be collected and condensed. The product of this process is termed a distillate. A number of paint materials are obtained in this way, turpentine being distilled from the semi-liquid resinous exudations of the pine tree, white spirit being a petroleum distillate, naphtha and benzole being coal tar distillates, and so on.

Distressed painting A term sometimes used to describe a broken colour effect in which a glaze applied over a light-coloured ground is treated with a brush-graining technique. The effect is also known by the name of "dragging".

The ground is generally white, although it may be lightly tinted if so wished; it is desirable that the ground should dry with an eggshell sheen. The glaze can consist of a proprietary glaze medium, its setting time adjusted as required by the addition of raw linseed oil or white spirit; alternatively, a home-made glaze medium can be used consisting of one part of linseed oil, or two parts of white spirit and a small quantity of liquid driers. The important thing is that the glaze should remain fluid long enough to be dragged successfully but should set up without any tendency for the drag marks to flow out. The glaze is tinted with appropriate stainers of semi-transparent type.

The broken colour effect is obtained by drawing a clean duster brush, paperhanging brush or distemper brush through the glaze. The essential feature of the process is that all these brush marks should be in a vertical direction.

Most people would regard distressed painting as a totally obsolete technique, but it is astonishing how often, in the author's experience, inquiries are received from decorators who are required to use the process in the course of renovating or restoring period houses; also how often inquiries come from architects who are anxious to specify the technique for restoration work and need information about it.

Dope A type of lacquer used for the tautening and protection of stretched linen fabric, and for the waterproofing of canvas. The term originated in the early days of aeroplane manufacture when fabric was extensively used for the wings, etc.

Dormer window A window projecting vertically from a sloping roof; usually the window of a sleeping apartment, hence the name.

Dotter A brush used in graining for obtaining the "bird's eyes", the small horseshoe shaped dots, in the imitation of maple. The tool is generally a homemade one; an old water-colour sable, the centre of which has been scorched out with a red hot knitting needle, serves the purpose admirably.

Double gilding A term used in glass gilding. When gold leaf is applied to glass, no matter how carefully the work has been done it will, when dry, reveal a number of blemishes such as open joints, pin-holing of the leaf and so on. It is customary on commercial work to lay in small pieces of gold over the blemishes, an operation known as "faulting", but in good quality work the whole of the gold surface is gilded a second time. The process is referred to as double gilding.

Double-insulated tools Appliances which give protection to the operative because there is no electrical connection between the body of the tool and the motor; if the electrical part of the tool develops a fault there is no possibility of the operative receiving an electric shock. A two-cored flex is used for double-insulated tools; no earth wire is needed.

Double priming As the name implies, this means applying two coats of primer to a surface instead of the customary one coat, and then following it up with the normal system of undercoats and finishing coat. This method is used principally in the treatment of steelwork, for which purpose it offers many advantages. The reason lies in the fact that it is quite impossible to produce with one coat of primer a continuous paint film of regular thickness and which is free from pinholes, and the pinholes are the points at which corrosion begins. A second coat of primer ensures that the surface is completely covered with all pinholes eliminated. It is more logical, and far more likely to increase the effective life of the whole paint film, to apply an extra coat of primer rather than an extra undercoat or an extra finishing coat. It is also much more economical. At some future period a new coat of finishing paint can readily be applied to the existing coating to keep the whole film in good condition, which is much easier and far less expensive than having to carry out a complete repainting programme with all that this entails in the way of cleaning, preparation, undercoating and finishing. The double priming system is being specified with increasing frequency as more people realize its great advantages.

Douglas fir A softwood frequently used in joinery work. See *Columbian pine*.

Downhaul That part of the suspension rope by which the up and down movement of a cradle or chair is controlled.

Dr. Angus Smith's process A method of treating ferrous metal articles in order to prevent corrosion. It consists of heating the articles at a temperature of 149°C (300°F) as soon as they are cast, and then immersing them in a prepared solution of coal tar which is then brought to the boil and allowed to continue boiling until all the ammoniacal liquor, water and lighter oils are expelled. The articles remain in the solution for some time and are then removed and allowed to drain.

Dr. Angus Smith's solution A term which is sometimes used loosely and incorrectly in the trade to refer to any black bituminous composition applied by brush.

Drag (a) A small wire-drawn brush with a handle shaped for easy gripping with the fingers, resembling in appearance a paperhanging brush in miniature; it is used for the purpose of brush graining, as a brush to pull through the wet stain.

(b) The pull on the bristles which is experienced when paint is applied by brush.

Dragging See *Distressed painting*.

Dragon's blood The resinous product of an Asiatic tree, used as a spirit stain and yielding a deep red colour. (**NLC**)

Drawing A most useful accomplishment for any decorator to possess. Very often it is impossible to convey to a client in words what the effect of a projected piece of decorative work will be, whereas to present it visually in the form of a drawing or sketch overcomes the difficulty immediately. The interior decorator needs to take the matter a stage further and deal with it in a professional manner, which means submitting ideas in a competent and attractive way in the form of colour sketches, vignettes and perspective drawings. On a decorative project, working drawings are required so that the operatives know how to set out the scheme and prepare it properly. On big-scale painting projects, drawings are necessary for the organization and control of the work. On bill-of-quantities contracts drawings are often needed to locate specific areas referred to in the schedule. Drawings are required in the planning of sign work. An estimator often needs to do quick sketches to identify specific details of the structure. There are innumerable ways in which drawings are an integral part of the decorator's work.

Yet most operative painters firmly believe that they are unable to draw, as if the ability to draw was some kind of rare inborn talent. In fact, of course, practically anyone can learn to draw quite competently. Drawing simply consists of moving a pen or pencil across a piece of paper in a predetermined direction, and can be mastered by anyone who approaches the matter with confidence. Anybody who is able to write has already mastered a skill which is for more difficult than drawing, since writing consists of drawing certain symbols but with the added complication that they must be drawn accurately enough for other people to recognize them instantly.

Drier, electric The use of an electric hair drier can save a lot of time in glass gilding, particularly in wintry conditions. As each stage of the gilding is completed it can be dried off rapidly and the next stage carried out, so that the work can be set out, gilded, faulted and backed up all in one operation where without the aid of a drier three separate visits probably on three separate days might be needed to reach the same stage.

Driers Materials added in small quantities to drying oils, or to paints based upon drying oils, in order to increase the absorption of oxygen by the oil and thereby accelerate the speed of drying. They consist of compounds of certain metals, mainly lead, cobalt and manganese, combined with organic acids to render them soluble in paint media. They have no place in present-day painting practice, except when traditional materials and methods are being used in processes such as graining, distressed painting, etc., when a small proportion of liquid oil driers may be required.

Dripless paints A term sometimes used for thixotropic paints, q.v.

Drop black A good-quality bone black, produced by calcinating animal bones in closed retorts. The name refers to a former method of manufacture when the pigment was squeezed through perforated plates, forming drops. Drop black is a good intense black colour; it is generally ground in turpentine and used as a spirit colour, because if mixed with oil it retards the drying of the oil. It is seldom used in modern painting practice, but is still sometimes employed when coach painting is being carried out by the traditional methods.

Drop pattern A term used to describe a wallpaper in which the full pattern extends across two widths of the paper. This means that the matching points on each side of the paper are at different levels, the repeat on one side coming between two repeats on the other side.

When cutting up a drop pattern paper into lengths it is generally advisable to work from two rolls at a time, cutting alternate lengths from each. By this means a great deal of waste is avoided. A drop pattern paper is sometimes described as an "offset match".

Dry colours Pigments which have been ground, dried and prepared in powdered condition for use as stainers for water-thinned paints. Pigments which are unaffected by alkali are used for this purpose. They should be soaked thoroughly in water and mixed to a smooth paste before they are added to the coating which is to be stained. If they were added in their dry state it would be found impossible to mix them in completely and streakiness would be the result. They are very seldom used today in painting and decorating, but are sometimes used in scenic painting, limewashing, etc. (**NLC**)

Dry-out A fault which occurs in anhydrous gypsum plasters, due to the fact that they do not combine very readily with water. If they do not remain wet long enough to absorb all the moisture they need in order to achieve complete hydration, the plaster does not attain its full hardness and strength and in severe cases it assumes a powdery friable condition. Dry-out may be caused in various ways, such as by the too rapid evaporation of the water in hot weather, the absorption of water from the skimming coat into a backing which is too porous, or by the use of artificial heat to speed up the drying of the plaster. The subject is an important one for the decorator. See *Delayed expansion.*

Dry-peelable papers Wallpapers which are very easily stripped when the time arrives for the room to be redecorated; the top surface peels away, leaving the paper backing intact.

Dry rot Decay in timber, especially in softwoods, caused by the fungus *Merulius lacrymans*, which feeds on the timber and reduces it to a dry brittle mass. Once established, the fungus has the power to create the ideal conditions to promote its own growth. It does this by throwing out conducting strands called *hyphae* which derive from chemical action on the timber; the hyphae release an acid which combines with the moisture to produce an environment in which the fungus can flourish. The hyphae can quickly penetrate through brickwork, masonry and concrete, and can travel considerable distances to reach and infect new areas of woodwork.

It is desirable that the decorator should be able to recognize dry rot, so that if its presence is detected on a site the customer can be informed and suitable measures put in hand. The treatment and elimination of dry rot is essentially a matter for a specialist firm experienced in this type of work.

Dry-strippable papers Wallpapers which are very easily stripped without any wetting or soaking. An edge is lifted and the paper is then pulled away completely, leaving the wall surface bare.

Drying The change which takes place whereby a film of paint ceases to be a liquid and becomes solid.

There are three main ways in which paints dry: (i) by evaporation of the solvent, (ii) by oxidation of their oil content, and (iii) by a change in the structure of the medium which occurs irrespective of the oxygen supply.

In some cases a paint dries almost entirely by one or other of these actions. Cellulose, for instance, dries entirely by the evaporation of the volatile solvent, and two-pack (cold cure) materials such as epoxies and polyurethanes dry by the chemical reaction which takes place in the film when the two components are mixed together. In some cases, however, the drying occurs by a combination of two or more of these causes; the traditional oil paints, for example, dry partly by the evaporation of the solvent, partly by the oxidation of the oil, and ultimately by polymerization of the oil.

Paints which dry by exposure to the air at normal temperatures are said to be "air drying"; materials which need the application of heat either in convection ovens or by infra-red plant in order to develop hardness and protective powers are called "thermosetting paints" or "stoving paints". When the drying of paints is accelerated by applying a moderate degree of heat, 65°C (150°F) or less it is called "forced drying".

Drying oils Oils which are secreted in the seed pods of plants and in the liver and other organs of animals, which when spread out in a thin film and exposed to the air have the property of combining with the oxygen in the air to undergo a chemical change, changing from a liquid to a solid state. Such oils are the basis of oil paints and varnishes. Well-known examples of drying oils are linseed oil and tung oil; other examples are perilla, walnut, poppyseed, etc.

Drying time The length of time which elapses between the application of a coat of paint and the point at which it achieves a certain degree of hardness. There are certain recognized terms which indicate the degree of hardness achieved by a paint film; for instance, it is said to be "surface dry" when a surface skin has formed which is dry although the paint underneath is still soft and tacky, "dust dry" means that dust will no longer embed itself in the paint, but can be removed, "hard dry" means that it is dry enough for a further coat of paint to be applied, "touch dry" means that the paint will bear gentle pressure from the fingers, and "tack free" means that it is no longer tacky even under pressure. The drying time of a paint is affected by numerous factors such as the temperature of the air, the presence or otherwise of light, and so on.

Ducat gold An alloy of copper and aluminium, used in imitation of gold leaf. It is supplied in books, the leaves varying in size between 82 and 120mm square. It is liable to tarnish unless protected with lacquer.

Ductile A term used to describe a material which can be pressed or pulled into shape whilst cold. Copper is one example of a ductile metal, hard steel an example of a metal which is not ductile. Sometimes the term "ductile" is used rather loosely to mean the opposite of "brittle".

Duplex papers Good quality embossed wallpapers, which are reinforced with an additional backing paper, the two layers being pressed together while wet. The backing paper takes a lot of the strain when the paper is pasted, with the result that there is less tendency for the embossing to be stretched and levelled out during hanging.

Durability The length of time that a paint, paint system or decorative material will last before it needs to be renewed; in the case of protective materials, the length of time that they continue to be effective.

The factors affecting the durability of a paint system are:

(a) That the correct types of paint are used; that there should be an adequate build for the purpose, and that the paints should be properly compounded and of good quality materials.

(b) That the paint should be applied with a high measure of skill.

(c) That the surface should be adequately prepared to remove any deposits in the way of soot, dirt, rust, etc., that would be harmful, to remove surface imperfections, and to insulate the paint system from any chemical activity of the surface.

(d) That the paint should be applied only under suitable weather conditions and not during periods of fog, rain, mist, etc. Factors outside the control of the painter or manufacturer are the conditions of exposure, the presence of polluted atmosphere, the extent to which actinic rays can penetrate to the paint, the presence or otherwise of local chemical concentrations that might affect the film, etc.

Duster A term with two entirely different meanings.

(1) The "Duster brush" or "Jamb duster". A brush, some 100mm wide, 25mm thick and with bristles some 85mm long out of the ferrule, which is an essential part of the painter's equipment. It should be carried at all times. It is used to remove dry loose grit or dirt from a surface before paint is applied, and it should be the instinctive act of every painter to pass the duster over any surface he is painting. Far too often the duster brush is a neglected tool; it will not do its work properly if it is clogged up with dirt and dried paint. It should be washed regularly and kept in good condition.

The duster brush is frequently used as a drag for brush graining.

(2) The "Air duster". A small compact tool for use when compressed air is available. It can be used to blow grit and dust from a surface before painting—a great advantage when places inaccessible to a duster brush are to

be sprayed. The tool has several other applications to industry, such as in garage work, etc.

Dutch enamel An enamel prepared from linseed stand oil. Stand oil, which is very pale and slow drying, is obtained by heating a fine quality oil for a long period (without the addition of driers) until it has thickened or polymerized, and the production of viscous oils by this method without any appreciable oxidation taking place originated in Holland. Enamels prepared from stand oil may contain a proportion of resin to harden them, but this is unnecessary in the case of white enamel, in which the pigment which is used, zinc oxide, has a hardening effect upon the oil. Only a small proportion of pigment is added, rarely more than 600 grams of pigment to one litre of oil; otherwise the gloss and the flow will be impaired, and for this reason Dutch enamels possess little opacity. It is therefore essential that the surfaces on which they are used should be well prepared and free from blemishes and that the undercoating should be perfectly solid. These enamels are not very easy to apply, and are rather slow drying, but they offer many advantages in compensation—they dry with a beautiful brilliant lustre, they have exceptionally good flow which results in a smooth surface free from brush marks, and they produce a very tough, durable and elastic film.

Dutch enamel is not used in present-day practice except in those rare cases where the highest class of finish is required regardless of expense. (**NLC**)

Dutch pink A yellow pigment; it is obtained from quercitron, the bark of a tree found in North and Central America. The extract from this bark is precipitated with alum on to a base of alumina or Paris white. (**NLC**)

Dutch process Otherwise known as the "stack process", for a very long time the principal method by which white lead was prepared. (**NLC**)

Dye A coloured substance in the form of a liquid or a soluble solid, which is capable of imparting its colour to any porous material, such as wood or fabric, which is immersed in the solution.

E

Ear plugs Protective equipment to be worn when the working conditions are such that the operatives are exposed for long periods to noise, e.g. in close proximity to heavy plant and machinery in a factory area or when using a compressor. It is now recognized that such exposure can lead to progressive and permanant deafness. The old-fashioned solid rubber ear plugs have been superseded by much better fitting and more comfortable ear protectors, supplied by the manufacturers of safety equipment.

Earth colours The name given to those pigments which are mined or derived from the earth, as opposed to chemically manufactured pigments. They are prepared by grinding and levigation, and are very stable and permanent. They include ochre, sienna, umber, red oxide, malachite, etc., and the range of colours obtained naturally is increased by calcining some of these materials to obtain a deeper, warmer hue, e.g., burnt sienna, a reddish brown obtained by calcining raw sienna, burnt umber from raw umber, etc.

East India gum A gum resin similar to fossilized damar, used in flat lacquers. (**NLC**)

Eaves The projecting edge at the bottom of a roof, beyond the face of the wall.

Ecru A name given to a creamy-yellow colour. The term is derived from a French word which refers to the colour of unbleached cloth of any kind, cotton, linen, silk or wool.

Efflorescence A term which means, literally, "bursting out into flowers" and which is used to refer to a white crystalline deposit which forms on the surface of plaster, brick, cement, etc., giving the appearance of a white growth. It is due to the presence of soluble salts in the various building materials; the salts, dissolved in free moisture, are brought to the surface and are left behind when the water evaporates.

The salts may be wiped off or brushed off quite readily, but often continue to develop for quite a long time. If the surface has been decorated, the deposit may form on the surface of the paint film, in which case it can be brushed off without causing much damage, but generally the paint film is pushed off and broken and will flake and peel.

The treatment for efflorescence is to brush off the deposit, wipe the surface with a damp sponge, and keep the surface under observation for a few days. Should no further crystallization occur it may be assumed that it is safe to decorate. It should be noted that the crystals should be brushed off dry; if they are washed off more water is introduced into the surface and the formation of crystals will be renewed and increased. Should it be insisted that some form of decoration should be applied in spite of the risk of efflorescence, the decoration should take the form of water-thinned paint such as emulsion paint. On no account should an impervious paint film be applied.

Egg glair A material used in the process of gilding to prevent gold leaf from sticking to varnished or enamelled work other than where required. However hard drying the varnish or enamel may be, it retains for a surprisingly long time enough tack to allow gold leaf to adhere to it; if lettering or ornamental work is applied directly on such a finish, the edges of the gilding will be blurred and marred by the gold which adheres around them.

Egg glair is prepared by blowing a new-laid egg to separate the white from the yolk, the white of the egg being added to half a litre of lukewarm water which is then shaken up well to produce a froth. The glair is applied all over the surface that is to be gilded and is allowed to dry; it may be applied with a clean sponge which is quite adequate for normal large-scale sign work, but on small-scale decorative work some authorities prefer that it should be applied with a flat camel hair size brush. It is important that the glair should be applied all over the surface and not just where the gilding is to be done; otherwise, a slight difference in lustre may be detected on the parts treated with glair.

The lettering or ornament is set out in the usual way and run in with gold size which, when it has reached the right degree of tack, is gilded with transfer gold. The solvent in the gold size destroys the egg glair with which it comes in contact. When gilding is completed the egg glair is washed off with lukewarm water and a sponge, taking with it the gold which has infringed beyond the edges of the gold size. Egg glair must not be allowed to remain on the surface longer than is necessary for the gilding to be completed, because if it is left too long cracking of the paint film may take place.

Eggshell finish A rather vague term for a finish which is not completely flat or matt, but which presents instead a slight sheen or lustre, similar to the sheen on an eggshell. The precise degree of sheen which is implied by this description is difficult to determine, as the term is applied by various authorities to finishes which range from almost matt to semi-gloss; the British Standards Institution suggests in one of its publications that two degrees of eggshell finish are recognized, "eggshall flat" having slightly more lustre than a flat finish, and "eggshall gloss" having more lustre than eggshell flat but less lustre than semi-gloss.

Eggshell finishes This term is generally understood to mean a group of finishing paints, intended for interior use, based upon highly bodied alkyd resins or upon a mixture of these and other resins, including the thixotropic types. The nature of the pigment and the proportion of pigment to resin are of vital importance, since they have a significant bearing upon the gloss, flow and levelling properties of the finish. Care is needed in the application of eggshell finishes, as over-brushing and poor brushing technique results in the defect known as sheariness. Similarly, failure to keep the edges alive results in the defect of flashing. Sheariness may also occur if the undercoating has not been adequate to satisfy the porosity of the surface.

Eggshell varnish An interior quality varnish which dries to an eggshell sheen. It may take the form of a gloss varnish which has been thinned and modified by the addition of paraffin wax, or it may be made from saponified beeswax, but modern eggshell varnishes are usually made with an alkyd resin medium incorporating a special matting agent.

Eggshell varnishes are intended for decorative effect and do not offer a great measure of protection. To obtain the best results, a coat of full-gloss varnish should be applied to the surface and allowed to dry, and the eggshell varnish applied on the following day while the gloss finish still possesses a certain degree of tack. Unlike gloss varnish which should be disturbed as little as possible, eggshell varnish should be vigorously shaken up before application and in cold weather the varnish bottle should be allowed to stand for a while in warm water before any varnish is poured out. Eggshell varnish needs to be applied quickly and confidently, each section of the work being cut in cleanly, and once applied it must not be brushed again or disturbed while setting; otherwise, "flashing" will result.

Egyptian blue This was the first pigment ever to have been prepared by artificial means, and was for many centuries the most important blue pigment in use. It is a crystalline silicate of copper, a fine rich blue that is eminently suited to fresco work, and a small amount is still manufactured. (**NLC**)

Elasticity The degree of flexibility possessed by a paint or varnish film. It is a factor of considerable importance in a varnish or gloss paint, which depends on its elasticity for its ability to conform without cracking to the expansion and contraction of the surface to which it is applied. The degree of elasticity is also an important feature of undercoats, since the application of a hard-drying coating over a softer and more elastic undercoat will cause the defect known as cracking.

Electrical equipment—safety precautions Electricity is an unseen hazard. Any electrical gear is a potential source of danger. Electric shock is a major hazard which strikes without giving any warning. The effects of electric shock are directly related to the amount of current passing through the body in a given time. At low levels, these effects may not in themselves be serious, although they may cause an involuntary reaction whereby a person makes a sudden jump and is thrown off balance; if the person is working on a scaffold he or she may fall and sustain serious injuries. At higher levels, the effects take the form of muscular tension so that the person is unable to release whatever equipment he or she is grasping, and this in turn causes fibrillation of the heart which is almost invariably fatal. The danger of electric shock is increased by the presence of moisture. The passage of electrical current through the body can also cause severe burns.

The safe use of electrical tools depends upon being aware of the risks and taking precautions to avoid them.

The amount of current passing through the body is determined by the voltage; reduced voltage lessens the severity of electric shock. Wherever possible compressors, hand tools, spray equipment and other electrical gear should be operated from a reduced voltage supply of 110 volts through a transformer centre tapped to earth and thereby having a maximum differential of 55 volts. It is always worth while to incorporate in the electrical system a residual current contact-breaker, which detects even the most meagre flow of electricity to earth—through the human body for example—and instantaneously cuts off the current. (Where double-insulated equipment is in use, if the electrical part of the tool develops a fault the outer casing protects the user from shock.)

Before using any equipment, it is essential to operate a regular safety routine. Check that the correct type of plug is fitted, and don't try to force a plug into a socket not designed for it, otherwise the earth pin may enter a live contact tube. Don't try to make do without a plug by the dangerous practice of inserting the cable wires into the socket and holding them in place with matchsticks. Don't use broken plugs. Don't use lamp-holder adaptors for equipment that needs to be earthed. Check that the fuses are of the correct rating. Check that the equipment itself is in sound condition. Check that the cables and leads are in good condition; beware of frayed leads, broken insulation and bared wires.

When using equipment, assume that all cables, plugs, etc., are live; don't make any adjustments without making sure that the current is cut off. When removing a plug from its socket, grasp the plug itself firmly—don't attempt to remove it by pulling at the leads, and above all don't snatch at the leads. Don't attempt to make any adjustment to the equipment without first disconnecting the plug. See that trailing cables can't be caught up or damaged in the scaffolding; see that they will not be trapped in the fittings or window openings; don't allow the cable to lie in pools of water.

On domestic work look out for bared wires and rotting insulation in lighting flex, etc., especially when washing paintwork or stripping wallpaper. When stripping wallpaper take special care when working around the light switches; avoid jabbing with the stripping knife in such a way that the knife goes behind the protective cover—accidents have occurred through a stripping knife shorting across the wires inside the switch.

On factory work avoid contact with live conductor wires on crane tracks, etc., and prevent metal ladders from touching bare conductor wires (remembering that wooden ladders may also be a risk because of the wire reinforcement running along the stiles); take care that ladders, poles, etc., do not come into contact with overhead cables because of the possibility of a high voltage charge jumping a wide gap.

When an accident has occurred and someone has sustained an electric shock, the action to be taken will depend on whether it is domestic current or high-power current that is involved. In the case of domestic current, switch off the current immediately and do not touch the victim before doing so. If the current cannot be disconnected, avoid touching the victim and try to remove him or her by means of a dry non-conducting material such as a wooden pole, chair leg, etc. If nothing else is available, pull the victim clear by using a thick dry material such as a rug or blanket. In the case of a high-power current do not attempt to approach the victim; stay at least 18 metres away until it has been confirmed by a competent authority that the power has been cut off. When the victim has been moved clear, apply artificial respiration until medical help arrives.

Electrolytic white lead There are various methods of producing white lead by electrolysis, and the pigment which is obtained, similar in chemical composition to stack or chamber process white lead, is generally of very good colour and texture with a high degree of oil absorption. It is also sold as "flake white" as an artists' colour. (**NLC**)

Electro-painting A system introduced in the USA in 1976 for the priming of car bodies, trucks, etc. and now widely used not only in the car industry but also for domestic appliances and architectural products such as metal window frames, etc. It is a development of the electrophoretic coating process; in the cathodic electrocoat system a single primer coat provides considerable resistance to corrosion, and it is of particular interest in view of the trend towards zinc-coated steel because it gives increased resistance to saponification.

Electrophoresis A process in which two electrodes are immersed in a solution of colloidal particles dispersed in a conducting fluid; when an electrical potential is applied to the electrodes the particles migrate and under certain conditions adhere to the electrode to which they are attracted. The process has been widely used since the early 1970's as a means of applying protective and decorative coatings in the car industry and in many aspects of industrial finishing.

Electrostatic de-tearing The principle described in the next paragraph on electrostatic spraying is employed to prevent the formation of the tears and fat edges which frequently mar the finish of articles painted by the dipping process. The dipped article, after a short period of draining, is passed over a grid, and both the grid and the article are electrically charged but with charges of opposite sign. The tears and thick edges are removed by the attraction of the grid.

Electrostatic spray A method of paint application which depends on the principle that, when bodies are electrically charged, those of similar charge repel each other while those of opposite charge are attracted. An electric field of very high voltage is set up through which the paint is sprayed, the atomized particles of paint becoming charged by the absorption of electrons from the ionized air; the article to be painted is earthed, so as to attract the particles of paint. By this means, the paint not only reaches the side of the article which faces the spray but also passes round to the far side of the article; this is termed the "wrap-round effect".

Elevation A side or end view of the vertical surfaces of an object, wall or building, which may be sketched in perspective or may be drawn to scale without reference to perspective.

Ellipse A regular oval.

Elm A wood used in furniture making, panelling and artistic joinery, and one which therefore lends itself to reproduction in painted treatments. The grain markings are conspicuous; according to whether the wood is cut longitudinally or obliquely they take the form of zig-zag lines or a distinctive feathery formation known among woodworkers as "partridge breast".

Emblems One of the most interesting branches of the decorator's craft is that which concerns the use of emblems and symbols as motifs for decoration, and the selection of such symbols as are appropriate for any particular building. In earlier days, when a large proportion of the population was illiterate, the visual arts of painting, sculpture, etc., were also required to serve as a medium of instruction, and the various figures could often be identified by symbols which they bore. The signs displayed by shops and business premises were also pictorial in character, bearing symbols to represent the trade in which the owners were engaged.

Not only has this symbolism persisted to the present day, but its use is still extending, as may be seen by the trade marks which modern business firms employ as distinguishing marks for their goods. The decorator who is alive to the possibilities of this traditional branch of the craft is never at a loss for suitable and appropriate motifs as a basis for design. Church decoration teems with symbolism, such as the dice, nails and thorns which are the emblems of the Passion, the keys of St Peter, the eagle of St John, the winged bull of St Luke (who is also the patron saint of painters), and so on. Emblems suitable for other types of public buildings include the scales of justice, the torch of learning, the serpent and rod representing medicine, the crown, orb and sceptre of royalty, etc.

Embossed wallpaper A paper which has been passed through rollers which mould it so that either the pattern is raised in relief or a raised background texture is produced. When these papers are being hung, care must be taken that they are not oversoaked during the pasting and that they are not subjected to undue brushing or stretching during application; otherwise, the embossing may be stretched and levelled out. See also *Duplex papers*.

Embossing of glass The process of etching glass with hydrofluoric acid so as to produce a pattern or piece of lettering raised in relief. The glass must be perfectly clean, and the parts which are not to be etched are protected with acid-resist. The glass is then set perfectly level upon a bed of sawdust on a workbench—it must be laid horizontally; the process cannot be carried out on vertical or sloping surfaces—and a wall of cobblers' wax built around it. Dilute acid is poured in and allowed to remain until the required depth of etching has been obtained, when it is poured off and the glass thoroughly cleaned. See also *Acid etching*.

Emerald green A pigment compounded from the arsenite and acetate of copper. Its brilliant blue-green colour is a useful addition to the decorator's range, but it has many drawbacks, being coarse in texture, liable to settle and, like all the copper pigments, easily discoloured. Its chief drawback, however, is its highly poisonous nature. It is rarely used nowadays for decorative work, but is included in anti-fouling paints for the hulls of ships and is also prepared as an insecticide known as Paris green.

Emulsifying agent A material added to substances which are not normally miscible in water in order to form a stable emulsion, such as the soap or glue used to emulsify an oil to form the medium of an oil-bound water paint. See *Emulsion*.

Emulsion An emulsion is a substance consisting of two liquids which normally would not mix together, but in which one of the liquids is dispersed in the other so that they *will* mix and will *remain* mixed and will not separate. A common example of an emulsion is milk, which is composed of water and cream-fat.

Emulsions of oil and water were at one time of very great importance in painting and decorating, being the basis of oil-bound water paints. Such paints are no longer used in ordinary trade practice, but the principles underlying their manufacture are still of interest, as a grasp of them will enable the decorator to understand certain terms used in technical literature. These paints consisted of a vegetable drying oil and water. Oil and water are not normally "miscible", which means that if they are shaken together the oil will break up into small particles or droplets, but when the shaking stops the liquids separate again and the oil particles flow together; the oil, being lighter in weight than water, will then float on top of the water. To overcome this, an "emulsifying agent" such as soap or glue was dissolved in the water; this was then mixed with the oil and the mixture was vigorously agitated for a long time. The agitation caused the oil to break up into tiny droplets, and these became coated with a film of the soap or glue, so that when the shaking ceased the particles of oil could no longer "coalesce"—meaning that they could no longer flow together. The oil thus remained in a state of "permanent suspension" in the water. Since it was a relatively small proportion of oil that was dispersed in the water, the oil was described as being the "disperse phase" and the water as the "continuous phase". But certain of these paints were formulated for exterior use, and in these the oil content was considerably greater than the water content; in this case it was the water that was dispersed in the oil, so the water was the "disperse phase" and the oil was the "continuous phase".

Emulsion paints These are water-thinned paints with so many useful properties that they have completely superseded the distempers and oil-bound water paints formerly used by decorators, and are now a major factor both in paint manufacture and in painting and decorating work. To be precise, they are not really emulsions, although they have always been known by this name ever since their introduction. As explained in the previous entry, an emulsion consists of two liquids which are not normally miscible, one liquid being dispersed in the other to enable them to be mixed. An emulsion paint, however, consists of particles of resin dispersed in water, and the resin is closer to being a solid than a liquid. When the emulsion paint is applied to a surface, the water evaporates and the resin particles flow together or coalesce; this is a non-reversible process, producing a washable film.

The most important synthetic polymers used in emulsion paint are polyvinyl acetate (PVA), co-polymers of vinyl acetate with other monomers, and polyacrylic esters. The preparation of the polymer emulsion is carried out in two stages; first, an emulsion is made of the liquid monomer (e.g. vinyl acetate) in water with an emulsifying agent, and this is then polymerized by heating in the presence of a catalyst, to give a colloidal dispersion of the resin particles.

The emulsion paint is made by dispersing rutile titanium oxide or suitable coloured pigments in water together with various additives such as wetting agents, thickeners, preservatives, etc. This dispersion of pigments is then added to the polymer emulsion and the two are thoroughly mixed.

PVA gives a hard brittle film, and needs the addition of a plasticizer to make the film flexible. Gradually, however, the film loses the plasticizer and becomes brittle again as it ages. But if vinyl acetate is co-polymerized with a second monomer such as ethyl acrylate or ethylene, a co-polymer resin can be produced with any degree of flexibility that is required according to which second monomer is used and in what proportions, and no additional plasticizer is needed. Most PVA emulsion paints today are produced by this method and they have considerably greater adhesion and durability than the earlier types.

Acrylic emulsions contain co-polymers of various acrylic esters. By selecting appropriate monomers it is possible to produce co-polymers of any desired degree of flexibility. The manufacture of the polymer emulsion and of the emulsion paint are carried out by processes similar to those used for the vinyl types, but there are significant differences between the respective products. Acrylic emulsion paints have greater powers of adhesion and durability and can be more flexible. They are less popular than vinyl emulsions for interior decoration, probably because of their characteristic odour, but their flexibility and adhesion make them highly suitable for use as wood primers; they also adhere well to some plastics. On alkaline and absorbent surfaces they tend to give better results than vinyl emulsions.

Several different grades of emulsion paint are available to suit particular locations or conditions of exposure. Some are so formulated as to be equally suitable both for interior and exterior work, and to be capable of withstanding vigorous washing and scrubbing; others whilst only suitable for indoor work can still be subjected to fairly robust cleaning, whilst others again will only tolerate occasional light washing. There are differences, too, in the level of condensed moisture that can be tolerated and in the degree of chemical resistance that they offer. The cheaper grades are sometimes known as vinyl distempers or vinyl water paints and these are only suitable for interior work and can take only very occasional light cleaning. Another point of difference concerns the lustre of the finish. Emulsion paints are supplied in various types ranging from a completely flat finish, through varying degrees of matt, silk and eggshell, to a finish with a considerable amount of sheen. The most recent development has been the production of emulsion paint in "solid" form. It is a thixotropic material with a consistency resembling that of an unmelted cube jelly. It is supplied in a plastic paint-tray pack. The paint liquefies as soon as the roller is applied to it, and it spreads easily whilst retaining its drip-free properties. It is useful in situations where there is difficulty in protecting the interior fittings of the premises.

Emulsion paints are very versatile and can be applied by brush, roller or spray with equal success. The containers in which they are supplied must be protected from frost, and the paint should not be applied at temperatures lower than 4°C. They have a relatively short shelf life and should not therefore be kept too long in storage. Since they dry very rapidly and become hard and insoluble, it is important that any splashes should be removed promptly with water. It is also necessary that they should not be allowed to harden in the tools or equipment used for their application; brushes and rollers should be rinsed immediately after use with clean water, followed by thorough washing with soap and water. Prompt and rapid cleaning of spray plant is essential, and on no account should emulsion paint be allowed to harden in the guns, hoses, etc.

The attractive properties of emulsion paints which have made them such an important part of present-day practice can be summarized as follows:

(a) Rapid drying and hardening, which means that further coats can be applied without much delay—a useful point when premises have to be brought back into use in as short a time as possible.

(b) Ease of application, which makes for reduced labour costs.

(c) The absence of unpleasant or lingering odours during application—an important feature in the decoration of restaurants, hospitals, etc.

(d) Resistance to alkaline action, which makes them suitable for use on new plaster, cement rendering, concrete, etc.

(e) Ability to reduce to a very marked extent the porosity of highly absorbent surfaces such as various types of building boards, etc., thereby reducing the number of coatings required to complete the finish on such surfaces.

(f) Ability to withstand washing and scrubbing within a reasonable time of application (except in the case of vinyl distempers, etc.)

Emulsion paints possess other qualities which are often quoted in their favour, but these need to be accepted critically and with some reservations:

(g) Tolerance of damp. The structure of the dried film permits the passage of water vapour (a property more marked in the matt and eggshell finishes than in the types with a higher degree of sheen). For this reason they are of value in the decoration of new property, but it should be emphasized that the risk of breakdown is always greater on a damp surface than on one which is reasonably dry, and it is not wise to make too great a demand on the material.

(h) Resistance to mould-growth. Emulsion paints contain nothing to provide the nourishment needed for mould spores to develop, but on the other hand they are not fungicidal and will not destroy any fungoid growths already present—in fact, the presence of moisture will encourage the growths.

(i) Resistance to bleeding. Many type of emulsion paint can be used successfully over coatings of bitumen, creosote, etc., and no bleeding takes place—but they do *not* seal the surface. If oil paint is subsequently applied, the solvents penetrate the emulsion and the film will almost certainly be discoloured by bleeding.

(j) Opacity. Although emulsion paints normally have good obliterating properties, some of the strong colours in the BS 4800 range are recognized as having only low opacity, and the manufacturers' instructions regarding the number of coats and suitable undercoats must be observed.

There are some purposes for which emulsion paints are *not* suitable:

(i) They should never be applied to bare metal, as the free acids which they contain will attack non-ferrous metals, and in the case of ferrous metals their water content will promote rusting.

(ii) They have no power to bind down loose or powdery material. If applied upon such material they will inevitably flake off.

(iii) Although they are tolerant of moisture they are susceptible to damage when exposed to severe conditions of humidity or condensation.

(iv) They do not penetrate the surface to which they are applied to any marked degree. For this reason, emulsion paints do not have powers of adhesion comparable with those of oil paint, although as already stated they do have the power of sealing the absorbency of a porous surface. Their comparative lack of adhesion can lead to serious difficulties. Decorators should be very cautious if they are required to hang heavy wallcoverings—such as, for example, a thick embossed wallpaper, a relief material such as Anaglypta or Supaglypta, or a contract textile wallcovering—upon a wall surface which is already finished in emulsion paint. Very often in such cases the wallcovering loosens and becomes completely detached from the wall; although it has adhered perfectly well to the underlying emulsion paint, it is the emulsion paint itself which has parted company with the wall plaster.

(v) They should not be used on heated surfaces, and this includes radiators.

Enamel Originally meaning a vitreous compound with which articles of metal or porcelain are coated by fusion, the term is used in several connections to refer to a hard, smooth, glossy coating.

The word is now used rather loosely in the painting and decorating trade. Until recently its meaning was more precise; it was applied specifically to a material made with a limited quantity of finely ground pigment in a medium of linseed stand oil with or without the addition of resins; such materials, which possess little opacity and are rather slow drying, produce a very durable film of considerable smoothness and lustre and are described under the heading of *Dutch enamels*. A distinction was drawn between these enamels and the materials with greater powers of obliteration made with a higher proportion of pigment in a varnish medium, which were known by such names as "hard gloss paints", etc.

In today's world of synthetic resins and highly opaque pigments there has ceased to be any clear-cut distinction between the materials variously termed enamel, enamel paint, hard gloss paint, full gloss paint, gloss enamel, etc., and the term "enamel" is generally taken to imply a superior quality of full gloss finishing paint.

Various materials are used for specific purposes (e.g. see *Bath enamel*) and in the field of industrial finishes there are numerous thermosetting enamels.

Encaustic painting An ancient method of painting, practised by the Greeks and Romans, whereby melted beeswax was applied, the colours being blended with heated spatulae. (**NLC**)

End finisher A small type of check roller used in graining, which allows the top and bottom angles of panel work to be completed without leaving a gap.

End grain The pattern seen when a piece of wood has been cut across the grain. The end grain of wood is considerably more absorbent than any face which runs parallel with the direction in which the fibres run. This is because the cells which conduct moisture up the trunk from the roots have been cut across, leaving their open ends exposed in the form of pipe-like ducts; these ducts act as capillary tubes, through which liquids will rise. It is essential when painting timber that end grain should be properly primed to check this absorption; otherwise, moisture will enter and will be conveyed into the very heart of the wood no matter how well the rest has been painted. Because of its great absorbency, end grain should, wherever possible, be primed twice.

Epon The name under which epoxy resins are marketed in the USA.

Epoxy esters These are made by reacting an epoxy resin with the fatty acids from oils, from drying oils to produce air-drying finishes, and from non-drying oils to produce stoving finishes. The air-drying types are similar in many respects to alkyd resins but have greater adhesion and resistance to chemicals. Although they are not as highly resistant as the two-pack epoxy systems they are useful under conditions of mild chemical attack, e.g. industrial atmospheres. They are used as binders in gloss finishes, undercoats, and primers for metals.

Epoxy floor paint A one-pack epoxy resin paint with good properties of adhesion which is an excellent finish for various types of flooring such as wood, concrete and steel. Under all normal conditions it presents a durable coating which is not affected by ordinary maintenance cleaning with soap and detergents. There are, however, certain situations for which it is not suitable. It will not withstand conditions of frequent or prolonged wetting, it is not recommended for areas that are subjected to the spillage of solvents, dairy products, etc., and it is not suitable for floors upon which rubber-tyred vehicles are parked or stacked for long periods because it tends to be softened by the anti-oxidants in rubber.

Epoxy paint A rather loose term which includes any paint, whether one-pack or two-pack, in which the medium is based upon epoxy resin.

Epoxy pitch compounds Also known as coal-tar epoxy coatings, etc. These are materials with outstanding properties of water resistance as well as a high degree of resistance to chemical attack. Two-pack materials of this kind have made a significant contribution to present-day industrial demands; they have been used with great success in the most severe conditions of exposure, such as in the protection of structural steelwork subjected to continual immersion in salt water in dock and harbour installations, and in the particularly harsh conditions associated with the steelwork of oil-rigs in the North Sea and elsewhere. It should be noted that the effectiveness of these coatings depends on a meticulous pretreatment programme of blast-cleaning. See also *Coal-tar paints*.

Epoxy resins These are polymers made by reacting together epichlorhydrin and diphenylol propane, both of which are by-products of petroleum refining. The reaction can be controlled to give a range of products varying from hard resins to syrupy liquids. The features which they offer include a very high resistance to alkalis, extreme hardness combined with great flexibility and toughness, excellent adhesion, and resistance to abrasion. They are rarely used on their own but are combined with other resins or resin-forming materials to produce both stoving finishes with considerable chemical resistance and high-grade air-drying finishes. When combined with suitable amines as "curing" or polymerizing agents a surface coating is produced which, either at normal air-drying temperatures or at the slightly higher temperatures obtained by forced drying, has the durability and chemical resistance of a stoved finish—a factor of great importance when the object to be painted is sensitive to heat or is too large to be treated in a stoving oven.

Epoxyester paint A single pack material designed to resist mild chemical attack. It is resistant to water, acids, oils and to many solvents, but is usually adversely affected by alkalis.

Erosion The wearing away of the top surface of a paint film, by means of chalking, etc.

Establishment charges A term meaning the same as "overhead expenses"—a highly significant item in estimating for painters' work. They are the costs that are bound to be incurred in operating a business, but which are not directly chargeable to any particular job or contract. They are the essential items of expenditure which continue irrespective of whether the firm is busy or is undergoing a slack period. They include the salaries of the supervisory staff and the office staff, the upkeep of the firm's premises including the rent, rates, lighting, heating, and cleaning of the office, workshop and stores, the cost and maintenance of the firm's cars, vans and other vehicles together with the requisite road tax, etc., and the drivers' wages, the cost of plant and equipment, the cost or hire of office equipment, telephone charges, printing, stationery, insurances, advertising, etc.

The usual procedure is for a firm of contractors to assess its establishment costs over a given period of time, generally twelve months, and to compute them as a percentage in relation to its turnover for the same period. This percentage is then added to the estimated labour cost of any piece of work for which it is tendering, so that the establishment charges are included pro rata, whereas the cost of materials and the desired profit margin are variable figures.

Ester copals Soft copals of high acid value, such as Congo copals, esterified in the same way as the rosin described in the next paragraph. (**NLC**)

Ester gums Glyceride esters of naturally occurring acid resins; generally the term is understood to refer to rosin esters. They are of very low acid value, and because they do not "feed" with basic pigments they are used in the preparation of mixing varnishes and enamel media; they are also used in nitro-cellulose lacquers. (**NLC**)

Ester interchange A chemical reaction which occurs when two or more resins are heated together under suitable conditions; a factor of great importance in the varnish industry, as it produces films with better performance than the natural resins. Other examples relating to the paint industry are (a) when linseed and tung oils are heated together, a range of new glycerides is produced; (b) when polyamide resin is introduced into an alkyd resin cook, an ester and amine interchange takes place whereby a thixotropic alkyd paint is produced.

Esters Compounds formed by replacing the hydrogen of an acid by a hydrocarbon radical of the ethyl type. Examples relevant to the painting trade include a number of materials used industrially as solvents, such as ethyl, propyl, glycol, amyl and butyl acetates (the latter two being the chief solvents used in the manufacture of nitro-cellulose lacquers), ethyl carbonate, ethyl, amyl and butyl formates and lactates, etc.

Estimate A contractor's statement of the sum for which he will undertake a specified piece of work, based essentially on his knowledge of the length of time required to perform the various operations of the trade and his judgment of the area covered by a given quantity of material. When the labour cost has been arrived at, the cost of the materials is also worked out, and the establishment charges and the profit margin are added to provide the complete estimated price of the work.

Etch primer Also known as "wash primer", and sometimes referred to as "pretreatment primer".

Etch primer is available either as a one-pack or a two-pack material, and it is used chiefly as a pretreatment for non-ferrous metals, to improve the adhesion of the paint system. It can also be used to give immediate protection to steelwork which has been blast-cleaned, but in this case it needs to be followed up promptly with a coating of a recognized metal primer as the etch primer alone would not provide long-term protection.

Etch primers consist of vinyl resin reduced with solvents to a thin "wash" consistency, lightly pigmented with zinc chromate or other similar rust-inhibitor, and with an acid additive such as phosphoric acid. The two-pack type is usually more effective, but it is less resistant to water than the one-pack type.

When etch primers are used on new non-ferrous metals it is essential that the metal should first be thoroughly cleaned and degreased.

Etching This term means literally "eating away", being derived from a Dutch word meaning "to eat". In art circles an etching is a picture produced by printing on paper from a copper plate into which lines have been etched or eaten away by an acid, but to the painter and decorator the word has two quite different connotations. One of these is a process used in signwriting whereby the surface of a sheet of glass is etched or slightly eaten away by means of hydrofluoric acid—see *Acid etching*. The other applies to industrial painting, and describes the action of blast-cleaning whereby the surface of structural steelwork is etched by the impact of the stream of abrasive particles; the effect is to "eat away" or roughen the steel surface into a series of minute indentations resembling a series of peaks with tiny troughs or valleys between them. The etching process is of great importance because it enables the paint to cling to the surface by anchoring itself in the hollows—hence the term "anchor effect". The etching of the metal thus improves the adhesion of the paint.

Ethyl acetate A solvent—one of the group known as "esters"—with a strong smell of fruit, used in cellulose lacquers and in two-component systems.

Evaporation The transformation of a liquid into a vapour; the process of driving off moisture by heating or drying.

Examination A means of assessing the capabilities and knowledge of a student. Various institutions hold recognized examinations for this purpose and provide documentary proof of the candidates' attainments. Those of greatest concern to the painter and decorator are the City and Guilds of London Institute (the largest examining body in the world) and the British Institute of Interior Design.

Expanded metal Metal which has been cut and then pulled out to make the cuts into diamond-shaped holes.

Expanded polystyrene or foamed polystyrene A material prepared in such a form that it can be applied by the decorator to improve the thermal insulation of structural surfaces and thus help to eliminate condensation and minimize the occurrence of pattern staining. It is extremely light in weight and is available in various forms and several thicknesses to suit varying purposes. The usual forms in which it is supplied are as follows:

(a) In sheet form, in various thicknesses, for application to plastered walls and ceiling surfaces, after which the surface can be hung with wallpaper or decorated with water paint or emulsion paint; it should be noted that oil paint is not a suitable material to be applied directly to foamed polystyrene because of the damaging effect of the solvent upon the plastic.

(b) As a moulded coving, which enables the decorator to add a cornice to a room at the junction of the wall and ceiling surfaces; such coving may be finished with a coating of water paint or emulsion paint.

(c) As acoustic tiles of various dimensions and thicknesses, which present a pleasing appearance even when no further decorative coating is applied.

(d) As acoustic tiles in ready decorated form with a simple geometric pattern applied in colour to the surface.

All these materials are very easy to handle and can readily be affixed with the special adhesive supplied by the manufacturers. In some cases it is necessary to seal the plastered surface with a coat of alkali-resisting primer before fixing the polystyrene.

The surface of the foamed polystyrene is easily dented and damaged; when wallpaper has been superimposed, and re-decoration is necessary, no attempt should be made to use a knife for stripping the old paper; the paper should be well soaked with water until it is loose enough to be pulled away by hand.

While the main purpose of the material is to reduce condensation, it also provides a good measure of sound insulation, and also by retaining the heat in the room helps to cut down on fuel costs. Expanded polystyrene is available in large slabs of considerable thickness, some of them patterned with a cross cut design for ornamental effect, as well as in the forms stated above. The fixing of such slabs, however, is usually carried out by constructional staffs rather than by the decorator.

It should be noted that it is inadvisable to apply expanded polystyrene to wall or ceiling surfaces in a kitchen because of the flammable nature of the product. There is a tendency for it to soften and liquefy, and if the drips fall on or near to an exposed gas jet or electrical ring, or indeed on any very hot surface, they blaze up very rapidly and present a serious fire hazard.

Expansion An increase in volume due to an increase of temperature or moisture content, e.g. the expansion of metal when heated, the swelling of timber when it absorbs moisture, etc.

Exposure rack A frame upon which painted panels are exposed for durability tests. The panels are generally arranged at an angle of 45° and facing due south so that the full severity of the weather and the action of sunlight is encountered.

Exposure tests Tests carried out by paint manufacturers in order to determine the durability of paint products under various conditions of exposure. Panels painted with the material under test are mounted on exposure racks in various parts of the country, generally in chemically polluted atmospheres, coastal districts and other places where the conditions destructive to paint are severe, and an overall assessment of the material is arrived at by keeping the several panels under observation. Similar exposure stations are set up abroad by manufacturers engaged in overseas markets.

Extended elevation The elevations of the several wall surfaces of a room arranged so as to read as a long continuous strip; this device is useful in preparing working drawings for decoration.

Extenders Materials which have little or no opacity when mixed with varnish or oil, and which are incorporated into paints for a variety of technical reasons, such as to prevent the settling of heavy pigments, to harden the film, to increase the body, to arrest the flow, and in some cases to cheapen the material. Among the principal extenders used are barytes, blanc fixe, China clay, asbestine and silica.

Extending scaffold boards Scaffold boards which can be adjusted in length.

Extension ladder A ladder consisting of two or more sections, each of the standing ladder type, made so that the height can be adjusted by telescoping the sections. Each section can be used separately if desired. The two main types are (a) the hook-and-clip catch type, which is ropeless, and (b) the rope-operated, safety catch type, which is operated by means of pulleys. Type (b) is heavier and stronger, and should be used where a considerable height is required. Extension ladders consisting of two sections are used for heights of up to 15 metres, and of three sections for heights of up to 22 metres.

Extension spray head A device used in industrial finishing to enable the interior of small-necked vessels, tubes, pipes, etc., to be sprayed. The head can be arranged to give a disc spray, cone spray or fan spray as required.

Extra-over items A term used in the preparation of bills of quantities for contract work to describe certain processes which involve additional cost over and above ordinary working practice; such as, for example, providing an extra degree of finish to the paintwork on an area of wall surface by stippling it.

Eye protection Eye protective equipment should always be used by the painter when carrying out operations such as chipping, scraping, scurfing or wire-brushing which might cause damage to the eyes through the entry of solid particles, or through impact, or when using caustic materials with the possibility of splashing. Various kinds of equipment are available including goggles, face masks, spectacles and visors. For details of the legislation controlling eye protection, see *Protection of Eyes Regulations*. For information about suitable equipment see *Goggles*, etc.

F

Fabric wallhangings There are very many fabrics used today as wallhangings, the number having increased enormously in recent years. They include: (a) Highly expensive fabrics of the utmost luxury, such as silk, tapestry and velvet. (b) Coarser materials such as canvas, glass fibre, hessian, jute, linen and wool, and various synthetic materials such as polypropylene, acrylic dralon, etc. Some of these are high-class decorative fabrics in their own right; there are, for instance, many attractive canvas hangings with subtle colouring, available either with a backing ranging from paper to a thick polyurethane foam, or simply as unbacked materials. Others of a much coarser type are intended to be painted after hanging. A fine muslin cloth known as scrim cloth is supplied to be hung on surfaces such as tongued-and-grooved woodwork as a basis for the subsequent hanging of wallpaper (see *Scrim*). (c) An extremely wide range of decorative hangings consisting of various combinations of fabrics such as cotton, jute, linen, polyester, silk, viscose and wool, attached to a suitable backing material. Among these it would be logical to include grasscloth which is usually classed as a wallpaper but which consists of long strands of convolvulus stems bound with metallic thread and attached to a rice-paper backing. (d) Specialized fabric hangings produced for specific purposes, such as some glass-fibre hangings which have been developed solely for their fire-proofing properties.

Façade The face or elevation of a building.

Face screen A piece of equipment having a protective screen which extends over the eyes and covers part or all of the face.

Fad A pad used in the application of French polish.

Fadding The application of polish by means of a fad.

Fading The loss of colouring matter in a painted surface, which may be due to ageing, weathering or exposure to sunlight. Colours which fade under the action of sunlight are known as "fugitive" colours; the lakes are notorious in this respect. Certain colours which are tolerably fast to light when used at full strength will fade badly when reduced to a tint with white. Fugitive colours tend to fade more in flat finishes than when protected by a gloss medium. Sometimes a paint which is chalking gives the appearance of fading but the colour may be restored by the application of a coat of varnish.

Fall The suspension rope passing through the pulley blocks in a suspended chair or cradle.

False body A condition whereby a paint appears to be full-bodied but undergoes a sharp drop in viscosity when agitated or brushed out, resuming its original condition when the agitation stops. It may be produced by the addition of such materials as aluminium stearate, bentonite, etc., and is a feature of materials such as transparent glaze medium. False body should not be confused with thixotropy, although it appears to be a similar condition. When thixotropic materials are subjected to the shearing action of a brush there is a lapse of time before the original viscosity is resumed, during which the brush marks flow out; in the case of false body the original viscosity of the materials is resumed immediately the shearing action ceases, and the brush marks do not flow out.

Fanlight A glazed oblong or semi-circular window over a door; so called because in the late eighteenth century, when they became a popular feature in English architecture, such windows had glazing bars radiating from the centre like a fan.

Fantail overgrainer A long-handled brush the bristles of which are splayed out into the shape of an open fan, used in graining.

Fast to light A term meaning that the paint or pigment so described will not fade on exposure to light.

Fastening The binding down of loose particles of pigment, etc. For example, the water-colour pigments used in graining are loosely bound by the addition of stale beer, vinegar or fuller's earth, but will not withstand any vigorous rubbing; before any further working in the form of overgraining, etc., can take pace, they must be bound down with a coat of varnish and turps in equal quantities, applied with speed. This process is described as "fastening" the graining colour.

Fat edges A fault in application whereby a thick ridge of paint occurs on a corner or arris; it can be avoided by laying off at the corners with an almost dry brush. The fault may also occur on an article coated by dipping, due to the paint accumulating at the edges when draining.

Fattening A thickening up of fluid paint which sometimes occurs in the interval between its being mixed and being put into use. Probably the term conveys very little to those who are only accustomed to using ready-mixed paints, but those who remember when most paints were mixed on the job will recall it as a very expressive phrase, suggesting very forcefully the fatty feel of the paint under the brush when for some reason it was kept too long before use.

Fatty acids The acid components obtained by the hydrolysis of fats, used in the preparation of various resins, etc.

Faulting A term used in glass gilding. When the gold leaf has been laid in, a number of blemishes reveal themselves as the mordant dries; some of the joints will be open, in some places the leaf will be seen to be pinholed and here and there cracks will have opened. Before the leaf can be fixed with the backing-up paint it is always necessary to inspect the work and touch in the blemishes, where they occur, with further pieces of gold leaf. This operation is known as "faulting".

Feather The characteristic figuring found in mahogany (and certain other woods) when the timber is cut from the topmost part of the tree trunk through the actual base of the main branch.

Feather, the use of A long wing-feather from a fairly large bird such as a swan or goose is frequently used by grainers to put in the more open grain markings of woods such as walnut, etc.; when used with a dragging motion through wet stain it produces effects which cannot be obtained by any other type of tool or appliance.

Feathered edge The irregular joint invisible beneath the completed decoration obtained by the process described in *Feathering*.

Feathering A method of producing joints in lining paper, etc., in such a way as to avoid showing a distinct edge or ridge. When the paper is applied to the surface the last few inches are folded back at right angles to the surface; when the paste has dried out the projecting fold of paper is firmly seized and torn off, leaving a joint which is imperceptible beneath the completed decoration. The method is also of value when it is desired to cover only a small portion of a surface with lining paper, such as when covering a stain or making a neat and tight finish after making good the defective plaster on an external angle.

Feeding A defect caused by mixing together materials which are incompatible with one another, whereby a paint thickens up to an unusable consistency. A feature of the fault is that although the paint has become very thick it loses its opacity, and that any attempt to thin the paint down with solvents tends to make it become still thicker.

Felt blocks Thick pads of hard felt sold by decorators' merchants for use as rubbing blocks. When a surface is being sandpapered down, the common practice of holding the sandpaper across the flat of the hand is very inefficient; pressure is only applied by the finger-tips, with the result that the abrasive action is unevenly distributed; and it is practically impossible to rub into the corners of panels. If the sandpaper is wrapped around a rubbing block, the abrasive face outwards, the task of rubbing down is made easier and an even pressure is exerted over the whole working surface of the sandpaper; it is possible to sandpaper the corners of panels just as effectively as the centres and the whole work is performed better and more quickly.

Felt-covered roller A broad roller, the drum of which is encased in a long cylinder of thick felt or in several short cylinders placed end to end, which is sometimes used by the paperhanger as an alternative to the papering brush in the hanging of delicate papers such as flocks, satins, etc., which are easily scratched or damaged by normal handling, and which is also used for pressing down certain materials such as vinyl wallpapers, Realwood, leathercloths, etc., to expel air bubbles.

Felting down The process of rubbing down a recently painted surface with powdered pumice and a piece of thick felt, with water as a lubricant; generally it is done with the intention of rubbing down a gloss varnish or enamel coating to a matt surface prior to the application of a second coat of gloss. It has been superseded in present-day practice because many modern paints such as alkyd resin paints do not need to be flatted down before a second coat of gloss is applied. When flatting down is still required it has largely given place to the use of waterproof sandpaper which is considered to be cleaner in use, there being less likelihood of traces of grit remaining on the surface to mar the next application of gloss paint. Nevertheless it is doubtful whether rubbing down with waterproof sandpaper flats the surface as effectively as felting down with pumice and, provided the surface is properly washed off and is rubbed over with a tack rag before being revarnished, there is no reason why any grit should remain to cause trouble.

Ferric, ferrous Words which are derived from the Latin *ferrum* meaning "iron". Both words are used to define substances consisting of or containing iron; hence "ferrous metals", etc.

Fibre A slender filament of which the tissues of plants and animals are composed; the substances composed of vegetable or animal tissue which form the raw materials of textile manufacture.

Fibre boards Materials made from pulped wood fibre or other vegetable fibre, used to form a rigid lining construction for walls and ceilings, and which provide thermal and sound insulation to the structures in which they are employed. They range from thick loosely compacted boards of the type used for acoustic purposes to hardboards closely compacted under high pressure.

Fibre brushes Brushes in which the filling consists of vegetable fibre derived from the Mexican agave plant. This fibre possesses none of the spring or elasticity of bristle, but because it is not affected by alkalis it is very suitable for a cheap form of brush which can be used for the application of limewash, cement paints, etc., and for washing down with alkaline materials, all purposes which are extremely harmful to bristle brushes.

Vegetable fibre is also used as an adulterant, being mixed with bristle to produce cheaper brushes than those made entirely of bristle. Mixture brushes do not, however, work so easily as those composed of 100% bristle, nor do they produce so good a finish; this is because the fibre does not taper as bristle does and therefore does not help the paint to flow to the tip, nor does it possess the flag which is so characteristic of bristle and which contributes so much to the laying-off of the paintwork. Brushes containing a high proportion of fibre tend to become matted in use and are noticeably lacking in spring.

Fibre hardboards See *Hardboards*.

Fibre insulating boards Building boards made from wood or other vegetable fibres, fairly lightly compressed to produce a rough and highly absorbent surface upon which it is difficult to achieve a good standard of painted finish. They are often supplied in flame-retardant grades; these sometimes contain chemicals which react with water-thinned paints to cause efflorescence on the surface, but this may be overcome by applying an alkali-resisting primer.

Fibreglass Fibreglass, bonded with polyester, epikote or polyurethane resin, is used in the manufacture of wall sheetings and mouldings and for motor bodies, ships' hulls, etc., and the painting of these products may present difficulties. Their surface is generally very smooth, and is often contaminated with a mineral oil or some other form of greasy mould-release agent, the presence of which seriously affects the adhesion of the paint. In such cases the grease must be removed by a very thorough scrubbing with white spirit. The primer itself needs to be extremely tenacious, and the paint manufacturers supply a primer specially formulated for the purpose, with the appropriate type of thinner for either brush or spray application.

Cradles for scaffolding purposes are sometimes made from moulded fibreglass; there is no need for them to be painted for protective purposes, but if it is desired for them to be finished in the distinctive colours or with the symbols or logos of the contractors who own them they will need to be prepared in exactly the same way.

Another use for fibreglass is in the production of fabric or textured wallhangings, sometimes in a highly decorative form, sometimes for fire-proofing purposes, and sometimes as a fabric to be painted after hanging.

Fibrous plaster High relief decorative plaster work which is used to form cornices, mouldings, wall panels, decorative swags, ceiling centrepieces etc., and which is cast by the plasterer from reverse moulds on the bench and then fixed in position on the site. Although it appears to be solid it is really a thin layer of plaster strengthened with scrim and wooden laths; the plaster used is generally of the hemihydrate type, such as plaster of Paris, retarded by the addition of glue size. Because of the porous nature of the plaster and the thinness of the shell, fibrous plaster units are often considerably more absorbent than the surrounding areas of ceiling or wall plaster against which they are set; they should therefore be given a coat of sealer or an extra coat of primer, otherwise when painted they may dry to a different colour from the adjacent plaster due to the variation of porosity. Difficulty sometimes arises from the fact that the moulds used in preparing fibrous plaster are coated with oil to facilitate the removal of the cast; this may retard the drying of the paint.

Filler (a) A composition used to fill surface indentations, fine cracks, etc., in order to produce a perfectly smooth and level surface prior to painting. There are many excellent proprietary brands of filler available which have superseded the older hand-mixed materials. Information about how to choose the most suitable type of filler for any particular purpose together with the method of using it is given under the following headings: *Japan filler*, *Oil-based paste filler*, *Plaster/cellulose filler*, *Plaster-based filler*, *Polyurethane foam filler*, *Spatchel filler*, *Vinyl-based filler* and *Vinyl grain filler*.

The term "filler" is often used loosely and incorrectly nowadays to include materials used for the stopping of large holes and cracks.

(b) The term filler is also used as an alternative name for "extender", a mineral pigment having no opacity in oil (see *Extender*). The term is sometimes loosely and wrongly used in this connection to refer not only to the extender but to the pigmentary content of a paint in general.

Fillet A small flat band between mouldings separating them from each other; also, the top member of a cornice.

Filleter A very long-haired signwriting pencil with a squared end, used for running in bands and fillets with colour.

Filling (a) The process of achieving a perfectly smooth level surface, prior to painting, by the use of filler.

(b) When a wall surface is broken up by various mouldings and members, the term "filling" is applied to the main portion of the wall between picture rail and dado rail.

(c) In speaking of brushes, the filling is the bristle, animal hair, fibre or synthetic filament which forms the brush head.

Filling knife A broad knife used for the application of filler when filling and levelling a surface prior to painting. The knife should be reasonably stiff but flexible at the tip. It is essential that the edge should be perfectly true and free from any twists, kinks or other defects, otherwise each stroke of the knife will produce a ridge in the filler, which will defeat the purpose of the operation; it is therefore desirable that the filling knife should be kept solely for that purpose and not used for stripping wallpaper, burning off, etc., and that the edge of the knife should be protected, when not in use, in a sheath of stout paper or leather.

Film thickness The degree of protection afforded by a film of paint depends to a great extent upon its being of adequate thickness, because there is a direct relationship between the thickness of the film and the duration of the protection. This is especially so in the protective painting of structural steelwork, and very often the specification for such work states clearly and precisely the film thickness of the system to be applied.

The film thickness can be expressed either in Imperial or metric units. The Imperial unit is a thousandth of an inch (0·001 in.) which is called either a "thou" or a "mil"; it is better to avoid using the term "mil" as this might be wrongly interpreted as referring to a millimetre. The metric unit is a thousandth of a millimetre, and is called a "micron".

The thickness of a single coat of paint applied by hand may vary between as little as 0·70 thou and as much as 2 thou, depending on the type of paint, the conditions of application, and the quality of the operative's brushing technique. The thickness of a four-coat paint system on new work may therefore be as low as a mere 3 thou, a very slender film on which to rely for the protection of wood or metal, while on the other hand the unskilful piling on of inordinately thick coatings may cause serious paint defects to develop. It should be said, however, that in the hands of a competent craftsman the average thickness of a single coat is usually about 1 thou (25 microns). It is generally acknowledged that a paint system intended for the protection of exterior woodwork and metalwork should present a film thickness of between 4 thou and 5 thou (100–125 microns) as a minimum. When the conditions of exposure are unusually severe, or when long-term protection is required (especially in the case of steelwork) a much thicker paint system in the order of 10 thou or 250 microns, or even more, may be specified. Such a thickness would obviously not be possible with normal paints unless several coats were applied. To meet these exacting demands various heavy-duty materials are available which can be applied at 4 thou (100 microns) or upwards per coat.

When a definite film thickness is specified it generally relates to the dried film. Because most paint films decrease in thickness as they dry, due to the evaporation of the solvents, it is necessary to apply the paint in coats of even greater thickness. The paint manufacturers supply the information which the painter needs concerning the application procedure, and the wet film thickness needs to be regularly monitored during application as the work proceeds. This is done by means of a comb-type gauge. The outer teeth of the gauge rest on the substrate; the inner teeth, which are calibrated in both Imperial and metric units, are situated at varying levels, and the thickness of the film is indicated by the position of the tooth which just touches the surface of the paint. Since, however, the specification is directed to the thickness of the dry film, the finished surface is tested with an instrument which is gently held in contact with the dry film. The instrument used for structural steel is a magnetic gauge which incorporates a sensing contact, and the reading on the scale indicates the film thickness. The instrument used on non-magnetic surfaces has a probe which is first placed on a clean unpainted section of the surface, and the scale set to a zero reading; it is then placed on the painted surface and the new reading indicates the film thickness. The instrument needs resetting for each type of surface it is used upon.

Fineness of grind An important quality in any pigment, the durability, spreading power and hiding power of a paint depending to a great extent upon the fineness of the particles.

Fingering A term used when a new paint brush, instead of maintaining a good shape and clean chisel edge, splays out into a bad shape. A brush tends to finger through being wrongly used, as for example by being used edgeways, or through not being properly treated during the breaking-in period.

Finial A scaffold fitting designed to hold a horizontal tube directly above the vertical tubes to form a guard rail or barrier. Two types are available, a fixed type to make a right-angled joint and a swivel type for a joint at an angle other than a right angle.

Finish (a) The final coat in a paint system; the coat which is intended to provide the required colour, texture and degree of gloss, and which offers resistance to the corrosive effects of the atmosphere, the destructive effect of sunlight and to the peculiar conditions met with in special circumstances such as in bakeries, breweries, chemical works, etc. The extent to which the finish fulfils these requirements depends upon the previous coatings being suitable, adequate and properly applied.

(b) The term is also used in a general sense to indicate the appearance of the finished work, e.g., "flat finish", "gloss finish", "textured finish", "crackle finish", etc., and in a still more general sense "good finish", "poor finish", etc.; it can also be used loosely to describe the type of finishing material, e.g., "textured finish", "bitumen finish", etc.

Fire point The temperature at which a substance will ignite and continue to burn when brought into contact with a small flame.

Fire-retarding paints Paints applied for fire protection purposes to combustible materials such as timber, fibre board, and the flammable lining and partitioning sheetings used in construction work. No paint will render a flammable substance fireproof, but fire-retarding paints can make such a material less readily ignitable, can delay and minimize the spread of flame across the surface, and may prevent the material from continuing to burn after the source of heat has been removed; in these ways the seat of the outbreak is localized and the occupants of the building given time to escape. This is of major importance in the decoration of hotels, boarding establishments and passenger vessels, where there are large numbers of rooms occupied on a temporary and usually very short basis by separate families, the rooms being connected by long corridors that create strong air currents which increase the rapidity of flame spread. The fire risk in such areas is clearly much higher than normal, and an already dangerous situation is aggravated by the fact that when a fire breaks out the corridors quickly become congested with crowds of panic-stricken people.

Fire-retarding paints fall into two main categories:

(i) Flame-retardant paints formulated to prevent the rapid spread of flame across a surface. One example which is extensively used contains antimony oxide dispersed in a medium containing chlorinated compounds which under the influence of heat combine to form antimony chloride, a flame-retardant gas, which smothers the flame. Another type is based upon zinc borate which melts when it becomes hot and forms a blanket of buffer material.

(ii) Intumescent paints which contain chemicals such as ammonium sulphate, the particular feature of which is that when heated it swells up and chars, forming a layer of cellular non-flammable foam of low heat-conductivity, which cuts off the supply of oxygen to the surface.

First coat The first coating applied in any painting system; it may be the primer coat or a sealer or binder coat.

Fish oils Oils derived from fish or fish organs; very often they possess a disagreeable odour and are liable to yellowing upon exposure; their weathering properties are poor. In the USA the term is generally used to refer to menhadin oil, which is combined with perilla and tung oils to produce finishes which will withstand fairly high temperatures. (**NLC**)

Fitch A word derived from a Dutch word meaning polecat, and originally applied to a brush made from the fur of a polecat; nowadays the term is used to refer to a brush, generally composed of hog hair, set in a metal ferrule and attached to a long slender wooden handle. Fitches are made in various graded sizes, and are supplied in three types—flat fitches which are squared at the end, round fitches which have a cylindrical section and taper slightly at the tip, and the filbert type, which have a tip shaped like a finger end. They are most useful brushes with a variety of applications; they are essential for all classes of decorative work, mural work and so on, and are widely used in sign work, etc. They are also a useful adjunct to the tool kit of the ordinary painter and decorator as there are many occasions when small touches of colour can be applied more easily with a fitch than with any other tool.

Fixative A liquid which is applied over charcoal, crayon, chalk or black lead pencil drawings in order to prevent them from becoming blurred; it is usually applied by means of a diffuser, two hinged tubes of metal, one of which is dipped in a bottle of fixative and the other placed in the mouth of the operative, the act of blowing upon the latter tube producing a fine spray, or by means of a small hand-operated atomizer like a scent spray.

The term is also used rather loosely sometimes to refer to pastes and other adhesives employed in the hanging of wallpapers and wallcoverings generally.

Fixed cradle A cradle which can be operated upwards and downwards but not in a sideways direction.

Flag A characteristic feature of bristle—hog hair—whereby the tips of the hair split into two or three separate strands. This has a great bearing on the quality of brushwork produced with a bristle brush; not only is the bristle strong and resilient enough to enable oil paints to be applied firmly and vigorously, but it also possesses a softness at the tip, due to the flag, which allows the paint to be laid off lightly and the brush marks eliminated. As bristle is worn down the tip continues to split, so that the flag is continually being renewed; for this reason a bristle brush maintains its characteristic properties throughout the time it is in use.

The word "flag" is also used in some parts of the country as the name by which a radiator brush is known.

Flaking A defect primarily due to poor adhesion, whereby the paint film lifts from the underlying surface and breaks away in the form of brittle flakes. The conditions which give rise to flaking may develop in a number of ways. Moisture is often the cause of the trouble; it may be present in the surface before it is painted or may find an entry into the surface after painting, through open joints or building defects, and may be drawn out by the action of heat or sunlight, causing the paint film to lift, or a film of moisture may be present upon the surface while painting is in progress, due to condensation or because the surface is exposed to rain, frost or fog, thus preventing the adhesion of the paint.

Flaking may also occur due to the surface being in a loose or powdery condition when painted; for example, the paint may have been applied over rust, or upon old paintwork that was chalking badly and not properly prepared, or upon weak and crumbling plaster.

Sometimes flaking may be due to the nature of the surface, such as when paint fails to adhere to the highly polished surface of a dense plaster such as Keene's cement, or to the greasy surface of certain non-ferrous metals. If dirt and grease are not removed from an old painted surface before re-painting is commenced, flaking may result, and if decoration is begun before efflorescence has ceased to form on a surface, the paint film may be fractured and flaked by the eruption of the salts. Flaking will also occur if either emulsion paint or oil paint is applied over a coating of glue size.

Flamboyant finish A type of industrial finish very popular for the treatment of such items as cycle frames, etc. The article to be painted is given one or two coats of metallic paint, usually aluminium; it is then lightly sprayed with a semi-transparent coat of very pure bright colour and finished with a coat of clear lacquer. It is generally carried out with stoving paints.

Flame cleaning A very effective method of cleaning and preparing structural steelwork for painting, consisting of applying an intensely hot flame to the surface. Until recently, oxy-acetylene equipment was used, the oxygen and acetylene being in separate cylinders and fed through individual hoses to the torch; in present-day practice a liquefied petroleum gas such as propane, contained in a special mixer, provides the fuel. The effectiveness of flame cleaning is due to several factors, which may be summarized as follows:

(a) It loosens rust and scale by means of differential expansion, that is to say the scale is heated more rapidly than the parent metal to which it is attached and therefore expands more quickly, thus being caused to flake off.

(b) The rust is dehydrated by the process; all the contained moisture, which causes rust to cling so tenaciously to the parent metal and which, if the rust were not completely removed, would cause further rusting to develop beneath the new paint film, is rapidly driven off by the intense dry heat of the flame and the rust converted to a dry powder which is easily removed by wire-brushing.

(c) Convection currents and heat radiation from the treated surface prevent impurities suspended in the atmosphere from settling before the steel is painted.

(d) The metal is still in a warm expanded condition when the paint is applied, so that as it cools the paint tends to be drawn into the irregularities of the surface, promoting good adhesion.

(e) Under certain circumstances work can be carried out during damp weather conditions which would bring other forms of preparation to a standstill.

An essential part of the treatment is that the priming paint must be applied while the steel is still hot; unless this is done the whole advantage of the process is lost. While flame cleaning is considerably more satisfactory than manual or mechanical scaling and wire-brushing, it is also unfortunately far more expensive.

Flame spread The speed with which a flame spreads over a surface when tested in the manner prescribed in BS 476.

Flammable Capable of being ignited, or kindled, or set on fire—that is the definition of the word "flammable", and also of the word "inflammable". These words have the same meaning. Until fairly recently the word "inflammable" was the one normally used in everyday speech, but for reasons of precision the term "flammable" has gained a greater measure of acceptance and is now generally used, especially in technical literature. In either case, the term is of importance to the painter.

There is no paint which will render a flammable material completely fireproof, but there are a number of coatings which can make a material less easily ignitable and can delay or minimize the spread of flame. See *Fire-retarding paints*.

The term also has a bearing upon the use, storage and transport of paint solvents. A liquid is termed "flammable" when the flashpoint, i.e. the temperature at which the liquid begins to give off a vapour which will ignite upon exposure to flame, is below 65·6°C (150°F); and under the provisions of the Highly Flammable Liquids and Liquefied Gases Regulations which came into force in June 1973, a liquid is classed as "highly flammable" if its flashpoint is 32°C (89·6°F) or less.

Flash A glossy streak in a flat or eggshell finish.

Flash dry A term used in industrial finishing. To flash dry a coating is to allow most of the volatile solvents to evaporate from a sprayed coating before re-spraying or stoving.

Flashing A defect which occurs in flat and eggshell finishes, taking the form of glossy streaks or patches which mar the appearance of the work. It is generally due to faulty application of the material, such as when a matt finish has been applied without due regard to keeping the edges alive so that wet paint is brushed into material which has partially set, or when an attempt is made to touch up slight misses in material which is setting. Flashing often occurs at the intersection of stiles and rails in woodwork which is being finished in flat varnish or flat enamel, due to careless brushwork at the joints.

The tendency of flat paints to flash is increased if the grounding is unduly absorbent or of uneven porosity, factors which cause the finish to set too quickly making it difficult to keep the edges alive. Flashing may also be caused by the addition of unsuitable thinners in the finishing material.

Flashpoint The temperature at which the material gives off a vapour which will ignite on exposure to a flame.

When the flashpoint of a substance is known the extent of its flammability may be assessed; for instance, a liquid is stated to be flammable if its flashpoint is below 65·6°C (150°F), and if its flashpoint comes within the range of normal summer atmospheric temperature it is stated to be "highly flammable" and it becomes subject to certain transport regulations. Under the terms of the Highly Flammable Liquids and Liquefied Gases Regulations, which came into force in June 1973, a liquid is classed as "highly flammable" if its flashpoint is 32°C (89·6°F) or less.

Flat (otherwise matt) Possessing no gloss, sheen or lustre.

Flat brush Colloquial term for a distemper brush.

Flat enamel A finishing material intended for use where a finish free from gloss is required on surfaces subjected to constant handling, where a flat oil paint would rapidly become finger marked. It possesses similar properties of flow to a gloss enamel, for which reason it dries with a smooth satin-like surface, but it is made with an excess of volatile thinners and is not so full-bodied as a gloss enamel, working more easily under the brush. It is applied in a full flowing coat and care must be taken to avoid flashing. Whereas most flat finishes are applied over a semi-gloss ground, the grounding for flat enamel should be a flat or eggshell undercoat.

Flat enamel is rarely seen in everyday painting practice but may still be called for in restoration work on period buildings, and in very high-class decoration.

Flat oil paint A finishing paint for indoor use, which has a high pigment-to-binder ratio so that the film dries with little or no gloss. In everyday practice it has been completely superseded by the present-day range of matt and eggshell finishes. (**NLC**)

Flat varnish A varnish made to dry to a matt surface by the inclusion of waxes, metallic stearates, etc., with volatile solvents added to reduce the viscosity imparted by these materials. It is generally thinner than gloss varnish and brushes more easily. It should be applied quickly and fairly liberally; care is needed to avoid flashing and each section of the work should be cut in cleanly so that no part receives a double application. Flat varnish has little protective power and is chiefly used for interior work. Its durability is increased and a more uniform result obtained if it is applied over a coating of full gloss varnish, preferably while the gloss varnish retains a little tack. Some brands of flat varnish need to be warmed immediately prior to application; the manufacturers' instructions on this point should be noted.

Many manufacturers now produce varnishes with a satin or a matt finish for interior work which are based upon polyurethane resins. They are generally thixotropic, but need to be thoroughly stirred before use.

Flatting (a) A flat finish for walls and ceilings, made from paste white lead mixed to a very thin consistency with turpentine without the addition of any oil. It is a thing of the distant past, never used at all today. It is included here because students sometimes see it referred to in some of the older textbooks, and are curious to know what it means.

(b) The term flatting is also sometimes used rather loosely to mean the flat undercoating used as a grounding for a gloss paint. (**NLC**)

Flatting down Rubbing down a painted or varnished surface with fine abrasives to produce a smooth surface free from gloss. See also *Cutting down*.

Flatting varnish An undercoating varnish used when a two-coat varnish system is being employed. It is a short oil varnish containing a high proportion of hard resin, and is designed to produce a hard, quick-drying film which can be flatted down with powdered pumice or waterproof sandpaper within a few hours of application without risk of scratching or "sweating up". Rarely used in present-day practice.

Flavanthrone yellow A chemically prepared yellow pigment with very good staining strength and a high degree of fastness to light.

Flexwood A type of wallhanging consisting of selected wood veneers mounted on a backing of thin flexible card, and which is stained and varnished to the required colour after hanging.

Flint A hard crystalline mineral, consisting of almost pure silica, used in the manufacture of certain grades of dry sandpaper and waterproof abrasive paper of the type employed by painters and decorators.

Floating A defect in painting, in the form of a discolouration which occurs during the drying of the film. It is caused by the pigments separating and rising to the surface while the paint is wet. The defect is most common in greens, blues, and brown shades, and is accentuated if the paint is overthinned. If the paint has not been applied evenly the discolouration appears in patches. In some brands of emulsion paint the predominantly blue colours are particularly prone to floating. In extreme cases the defect is known by the term "flooding".

Flocculence A term used to describe the puffy or woolly texture which a paint sometimes develops due to faulty mixing.

Flock Fibrous material, either cut to length or ground to a powder. Natural flocks may consist of animal hair, asbestos, bristle, cotton, mica, silk, vegetable fibre or wool; manufactured flock may consist of cellophane, nylon, rayon or spun glass.

Flock finishes Finishes obtained by spraying finely shredded rayon or similar textile fibres on to an adhesive ground to produce the effect of baize or suede. These materials are chiefly used in industrial finishing on small articles such as the insides of spectacle cases, the lining of cutlery drawers and instrument cases, the undersides of table lamps, etc., although they have occasionally been applied to the treatment of wall surfaces.

Flock gun A special type of spray gun and container designed for the application of textile fibres used in producing flock finishes. The gun can also be used for such purposes as applying French chalk to rubber goods, granulated cork in anti-condensation treatments, etc. It is used solely for dry materials.

Flock papers High-class wallpapers with a pattern of raised pile, produced by printing the pattern in an adhesive medium or coloured mordant, on to which, when it is tacky, finely shredded wool, rayon or nylon fibres are blown. The effect is that of damask, velvet or tapestry hangings. Flock papers were first introduced towards the end of the 16th century and have remained very popular ever since. Some are still made by hand, but most are now produced by machinery and are therefore within the price range of a much wider public than ever before. These papers need careful treatment in hanging to avoid damaging the pile; the surface to which they are applied must always be cross-lined.

Flogger A brush used in graining for the purpose of imitating the pores of certain hardwoods. It has a broad thin handle into which is set a row of long bristles so as to form a thin lightweight brush about 125 mm long and some 75 to 100 mm wide. Freshly applied oil stain or water stain is stippled by striking it with the flat side of the flogger in a series of sharp strokes, working from the base upwards.

Flooding An extreme form of floating, in which the pigment particles rise to the surface of a film of paint in such a way that the colour of the dried film, although uniform over the entire surface, differs considerably from the colour when first applied.

Floor paint Highly pigmented paint in a hard varnish medium, resistant to chipping. Most modern floor paints are based on epoxy resins and are supplied either as one-pack or two-pack materials. For situations where safety is a highly important factor, floor paints are now available which are suitable for harsh conditions of outdoor exposure and which contain anti-slip ingredients; they are used for the decks of ocean-going vessels and for the gantries and walkways of industrial premises.

Floor stain A variety of materials can be used for the treatment of floorboards, etc., including oil stains, water stains, spirit stains, chemical compositions such as solutions of potassium permanganate, and so on. The essential thing is that they should be able to penetrate the surface of the wood; otherwise, they will soon be worn away in places by the constant passage of feet. Glue size, which is sometimes used as a preparatory coat before staining, should not be employed under floor stain as it prevents penetration and is also liable to be softened by buckets and other wet household implements placed on the floor. Proprietary brands of spirit stain are often used much too thickly, presenting an unpleasant, treacly appearance and being liable to chipping. Varnish stains consisting of a mixture of varnish and oil stain generally present a muddy appearance; better results are obtained by applying the stain and varnish as separate coatings.

Floor varnish A hard, quick-drying varnish, in which resistance to abrasion is of more importance than clear colour.

Flotation Another term for *floating*. Also used in the sense of *air flotation* to mean a process in the preparation of certain pigments whereby the dry pigment particles are conveyed by an air stream into a device which separates them into grades ranging from coarse to fine, due to the heavier particles settling first.

Flour paste A fixative used in the hanging of wallpaper. Flour consists of gluten and starch. The paste is made by mixing pure wheaten flour with a little cold water, beating it to a smooth creamy batter and then scalding it by pouring boiling water on to it very quickly, stirring vigorously all the time. By this means the flour is cooked, the molecules being partially broken down by fermentation or heat. Flour paste can be prepared as a powder which keeps indefinitely by mixing flour and water to form a dough which is fermented at about 43°C (110°F) and then cooked, dried and pulverized.

At one time flour paste was the only fixative used in paperhanging, but it has now been superseded by the wide range of modern adhesives. It would, of course, be totally unsuitable for many of the present-day wallhangings, especially the vinyls.

Flow The extent to which a material can flow out after application to produce a smooth surface free from brush marks.

Flow coating A method of paint application in which paint from a tank with a circulating system is poured or hosed on to the object to be painted, the excess paint being allowed to drain off. It is used for objects of an awkward shape that makes them unsuitable for dipping.

Fluid A substance composed of particles that move freely in relation to one another, hence "fluidity", the ability to flow freely.

Fluid hose The tubing which, in spray equipment, conveys paint to the gun. In air-propelled systems the fluid hose is usually coloured black to distinguish it from the air-hose which is red. In airless spraying the hose is designed to resist the very high fluid pressure; the centre core is of smooth nylon or Teflon reinforced with a nylon and wire braid, into which a spiral static wire is wound to prevent sparking at the gun; the hose is covered with a vinyl sheath for protection.

Fluid needle That part of an air-propelled spray gun which stops and starts the flow of paint.

Fluid needle adjustment The adjustment controlling the movement of the needle of a spray gun, and hence the amount of paint which can pass.

Fluid regulator A device incorporated into circulating paint feed systems, a regulator being provided at each fluid outlet in order to maintain constant and correct fluid pressure at each spray gun.

Fluid strainer A device fitted either to the fluid inlet of a spray gun or to the fluid outlet of a pressure tank in order to strain the finishing material before it enters the fluid passages.

Fluid tip That part of an air-propelled spray gun which meters and directs the fluid into the air-streams. Fluid tips are available in a number of nozzle sizes to permit materials of different types and varying viscosities each to be sprayed satisfactorily, taking into account the type of paint feed (e.g. suction feed or pressure feed).

Fluid valve A valve incorporated in a spraying system in order to turn the supply of fluid on or off.

Fluorescent pigments Coarse crystalline materials, usually the sulphides of calcium, barium and strontium, which have the property of glowing in the dark after they have been activated by exposure to light. The length of time that the glowing remains visible varies considerably and depends to a great extent upon the medium in which the pigment is dispersed.

Flush doors Solid or semi-solid doors, or framed doors faced with hardboard or plywood. The face of the doors presents a level surface on one plane with no projections (unlike panelled doors which are divided into panels, mouldings, stiles and rails at varying levels).

—

Flushing (a) The application of paint to the inside of a hollow article by means of pouring it in or pumping it through, the excess being allowed to drain off.

(b) A term used in paint manufacture to refer to a process whereby an aqueous pigment paste is treated in such a way that the water is replaced by oil.

Fluttering spray A defect in spraying, the paint leaving the gun in a jerky fashion. In air-propelled systems it is caused by air leaking into the fluid line, which may be due to a variety of reasons.

Fly ash Fly ash, or pulverized fuel ash, is the residue left by the combustion of the pulverized coal that is used as the fuel in power stations, etc. The fine ash is collected for use as the lightweight aggregate in certain types of concrete and is sometimes incorporated as a constituent of lightweight screeds and building blocks; it is also used as an artificial form of pozzolana.

The composition and properties of fly ash vary considerably according both to the type of fuel from which it is derived and the type of plant in which the fuel was burnt; it sometimes contains a high proportion of unburnt fuel. In general it can be stated, however, that any concrete or building blocks containing fly ash are usually highly alkaline, even more so than Portland cement, and will rapidly attack and destroy any oil paint that is applied to their surface.

Pozzolana is a natural volcanic ash found near Rome, the peculiar properties of which largely accounted for the excellence of ancient Roman mortar and concrete. The term is used in modern concrete technology to denote a material either natural or artificial which is added to concrete to retard its hardening and to increase its resistance to chemical attack.

Foam filler An aerosol-packed foam which expands to some three times its original volume as it sets, and which because of its expansion can be used to fill irregularities in a surface or for filling holes around pipes and conduits. It will adhere to such surfaces as concrete, glass fibre, plaster, stone and wood and to most plastics. It can be cut or sawn when dry, it can be plastered over, and can be coated with paint or emulsion paint.

Foamed vinyl wallpapers These come in many forms, including (a) textured, highly foamed products such as imitation plaster, etc.; these consist of a backing of duplex paper, PVC-coated pre-printed vinyl, or a textile laminate, in each case with a white overprint; (b) imitations of ceramic tiles, fabrics and yarn laminates, and (c) wallpapers with small relief patterns.

Foam-in-place spraying The application of a polyurethane material directly to the structure of a building to form a continuous coating of rigid foamed texture for thermal insulating and sound deadening purposes. The equipment consists of a twin-headed spray gun, two pressure feed tanks of 25 or 50 litre capacity with stainless steel fluid passages and fittings to resist corrosion, an air transformer and an air compressor. The polyurethane material and the appropriate catalyst are fed to the gun in the required proportions, the fluids blending as they emerge from the gun. See *Catalyst spraying*.

Following the trowel A technique sometimes employed on anhydrous gypsum plasters in order to improve the adhesion of paint. Considerable trouble is experienced in the decoration of plasters in this group, particularly Keene's and Parian; because of their slow rate of setting they are frequently trowelled by the plasterer to a smooth glass-like surface to which paint does not readily adhere, and this fact, coupled with the presence of moisture in the plaster, often leads to the failure of the decoration through flaking and peeling.

Following the trowel consists of applying a sharp coat of paint to the newly plastered surface as soon as it is firm enough to bear the weight of the brush. The setting of a gypsum plaster is due to the plaster and water combining chemically by a process of crystallization, and at a certain stage in this process a slight suction is exerted; the object is to apply the sharp coat early enough for it to be drawn into the surface as a result of this action. Ideally it should be applied within two or three hours of the plastering being completed and if through any circumstances a much longer time has elapsed the idea of following the trowel should be abandoned.

Traditionally the sharp coat is made of white lead with just enough oil, gold size or varnish to bind it, well thinned down with white spirit, but in today's circumstances it is preferable to use a leadless paint very well thinned down; no oil should be added to the paint, otherwise the hydration of the plaster may be prevented. After the paint has been applied the plaster must be given sufficient time to dry out completely before any normal painting is begun, and on no account must it be imagined that following the trowel offers a means of carrying out the decoration any earlier. When the surface is ready for further painting it should be sandpapered down lightly to remove any loose material or any efflorescence which has formed.

It is important that the technique of following the trowel should be used only on plasters which are acid (e.g., Keene's, Parian, anhydrite, etc.) to which no lime has been added. Used on an alkaline surface it may result in the formation of a powdery layer of plaster, not properly hydrated, which is not strong enough to support paint. There is also a danger of alkaline attack. To decide whether the technique may safely be used a scraping of the plaster should be mixed with a suitable chemical indicator and the resultant colour noted. While the process of following the trowel is usually adopted to promote adhesion, it may also, by delaying the setting of the plaster, prevent the defect of "dry-out", which is caused by the too-rapid loss of moisture in the initial drying stages. Such undue loss is most likely to occur in warm dry weather and it is at such a time, therefore, that the technique is most valuable.

Opinions differ as to whether following the trowel is an effective measure or not. When it fails in its object, however, it is frequently found that faulty methods have been employed, either by making the paint too thick or too oily, by applying it too long after completion of plastering, or by following it up too quickly with the subsequent decoration. It should be noted that following the trowel is a suitable technique when the finished decoration is to be in oil paint but is not suitable when silicate paints are to be used.

Foot filter A wire-gauze plate fitted to the inlet of the pump in airless spray equipment.

Footner process A method of cleaning scale from steelwork and providing a good surface for painting by means of phosphate pickling.

Foots A term used to denote the sediment of mucilage which collects at the bottom of the tank when a drying oil such as linseed oil is being refined. Until the foots have settled the oil is cloudy and dull. (**NLC**)

Forced drying Speeding up the drying of a material by the application of a moderate degree of heat.

Ford cup A form of viscometer, used to determine the viscosity of paints, enamels, varnishes, etc., which is calibrated to conform to the cups used in the laboratories of the Ford Motor Company. It is a cup with an accurately machined orifice; the cup is filled with the material under test and a stop-watch is used to record the time from the moment when it is allowed to flow to the point at which the stream of liquid breaks into droplets.

Formaldehyde A colourless gas which, dissolved in water, becomes a substance known as formalin. This can be combined with phenol and urea to make certain plastics, e.g. Bakelite. When a modified form of phenol is combined with formalin a resin can be produced which has excellent qualities of resistance to alkalis and to the corrosive effects of industrial and coastal atmospheres, and is of value in paint manufacture.

Fossil gum Natural resin, used in the manufacture of the traditional type of varnish, which is found buried in the ground, having been secreted in trees which lived so long ago as to have now become extinct.

Foxy Hot unpleasant colour; so called from the colour of the fur of the red fox.

Free match Also called "random match". The term is used to denote plain wallpapers, woodchips, etc., or papers with a random pattern, none of which need matching.

French chalk A hydrated silicate of magnesium sometimes incorporated in paint to help to keep the pigments in suspension. French chalk is also used occasionally in signwriting; it is dusted over the gilder's cushion at intervals in order to prevent the surface from becoming greasy and causing the gold leaf to stick, and it is sometimes applied to a signboard by means of a pounce so as to provide a guide when the signwriter is using untinted gold size and to prevent the gold from adhering beyond the edge of the letter.

French ochre A good quality opaque ochre of bright yellow colour and good staining strength.

French polish A spirit varnish composed of shellac dissolved in methylated spirits, with other spirit-soluble gums sometimes added.

French polishing The production of a rich high-gloss finish by means of the application of several thin coatings of French polish, a "rubber", consisting of a pad of cotton wool wrapped in two layers of calico, being used to apply the material. In the final states the shine is due to friction rather than to the quantity of polish applied.

French polishing mop A round dome-shaped brush, composed of squirrel hair, used in "bodying-up" French polish, i.e., in applying the preliminary coating.

Fresco A painting carried out with lime-proof pigments mixed with limewater, the colour being applied directly on to a freshly laid surface of lime plaster. The surface sets and hardens by a process of carbonation, a hard layer of insoluble calcium carbonate being formed which binds the colours firmly together in a durable film. The technique of fresco painting presents many difficulties, due to the limited number of colours that can be used, the fact that the colours lighten very considerably as they dry, and the necessity for applying only as much of the ground as can be painted in one day, since anything in excess of this films over and gives a patchy appearance to the work; nevertheless some of the greatest achievements in the history of art have been carried out in this medium. Fresco painting is permanent in a dry climate, but is not suitable for work in damp industrial regions, as the film, although insoluble in water, is readily attacked by weak acids.

The term is often wrongly used to describe any form of mural painting indiscriminately.

Fresco-type wallhangings Modern hand-produced wallhangings made by coating the backing and then rapidly blending random shapes and colours into it while it is still fresh, thus obtaining luminous effects reminiscent of fresco painting.

Fresh-air breathing apparatus The type of respirator which receives a supply of clean air from an outside source, so that the wearer is independent of the air in the immediate vicinity of the working area; this is very important to the painter when using materials which give off toxic vapours. See *Respirator* and *Respiratory protective equipment*.

Fret pattern Sometimes called a "key-pattern"; an ornament consisting of straight lines intersecting at right angles. The term is derived from an early French word, *frette*, meaning a grating.

Frieze In classic architecture, the middle division of the entablature. In ordinary domestic architecture, the horizontal band beneath the cornice and above the picture rail.

Frogs A colloquial term referring to skins and other foreign bodies in paint which needs straining.

Frosting A defect taking the form of fine wrinkling on the surface of a drying film of paint, giving it a frosted appearance. It is generally due to a fault in the preparation of the medium of the paint.

Frothing Frothing occurs when certain materials are shaken or agitated and is very often a sign that the material has been handled too roughly. A creamy froth appears on varnish, for instance, if the material is poured out of the bottle carelessly, or if the bottle is shaken up, or when a brush is worked into the varnish and scraped out on the edge of the paint can. In all these cases the froth, once formed, takes a very long time to clear, and is detrimental to the quality of the finished work. The froth consists of minute air bubbles, and when a coating of the varnish is applied the air bubbles burst as the material is drying, causing pinholing of the dried film and the defect known as "delayed cissing"; the film thus presents a roughened surface instead of a smooth gloss finish, and allows moisture to penetrate instead of offering a resistant coating.

Fugitive colours Colours which fade when exposed to light. The lake pigments are notorious in this respect. Some colours which are reasonably fast to light when used at full strength develop fugitive tendencies when reduced with white. Fugitive colours fade much more quickly when used in flat paints than when incorporated into gloss paints or protected by a varnish coating.

Fugitometer A device comprising a humidifier and an arc light which approximates to daylight, and in which the combined effects of moisture and light reproduce to some extent the conditions of weathering. Samples of paint applied to small panels are inserted in the instrument, part of each panel being covered with a mask to exclude the light. After a period of exposure a comparison of the two portions of a panel reveals the amount of fading which has taken place, providing a test by which samples of paint can be compared with one another.

Full coat A single coating of paint, enamel or varnish applied as thickly as is possible without detriment to the quality of the work and the satisfactory performance of the material, as opposed to a "bare coat" or a "starved coat", in which the material has been applied too thinly.

Full colour Rich pure colour, as opposed to tints and greyed hues.

Full gloss A term used about enamels, varnishes and paints meaning that they possess a high-gloss finish when dry, as opposed to semi-gloss, eggshell or matt finishes.

Fuller's earth A kind of clay or marl of highly absorbent properties, composed chemically of hydrous silicate of alumina, so called because it is used in the "fulling" (i.e. the cleaning and felting) of cloth. It is sometimes used in graining as a binder for water stains. It is also useful in preventing the cissing which may occur if a paint or stain is applied to a greasy surface; the surface is wiped over with a damp wash-leather sprinkled with fuller's earth, and then allowed to dry.

Fully trimmed material Any kind of wallhanging which is supplied in a form ready for immediate use, without any selvedge that would need to be trimmed off. Generally such materials are individually packed in a protective wrapper to protect the edges from damage during transit. Nearly all wallpapers today are in fully trimmed form. So too are a high proportion of textile hangings, but some fabrics such as hessian and canvas may in certain cases be better trimmed after hanging, by cutting through the overlapping edges.

Fume pigments Pigments with extremely fine texture, such as zinc oxide, antimony white, carbon black, etc., which are produced by the process of sublimation. In this process the raw material from which the pigment is produced is volatilized by roasting it in the presence of air, forming dense fumes; the fumes are drawn into chambers where they condense and settle in the form of a light powder.

Fumed oak Oak which has been stained by exposure to the fumes of ammonia, a process which leads to considerable darkening of the figuring.

Fungicidal paints Surface coatings containing substances (which in some cases may be poisonous) which make them resistant to the formation of fungoid and mould growths. If such coatings are to be used in kitchens, breweries, bakeries or other premises where foodstuffs are prepared and handled, the advice of the paint manufacturers should be obtained to avoid risk of contamination of the food.

Fungicidal wash A solution of fungicide which is used to prepare surfaces affected by mould or fungoid growth before paint or any other form of decorative material is applied.

Fungicides Substances which destroy fungi. They are used in several forms in the painting trade, as antiseptic washes for the cleansing of surfaces which have become infected with mould growths, as penetrative solutions and stains for the treatment of timber and other building materials, which are to be exposed to conditions giving rise to fungoid growths, and as ingredients in fungicidal paints.

Fungoid growths The term fungus covers a wide variety of plant forms which includes moulds and mildew as well as growths such as toadstools, etc. All fungi are alike in that they are destitute of chlorophyll and so are unable to synthesize food from simple substances; instead, they obtain nourishment from various organic substances. While some of them are parasites, attacking living organisms, the ones which concern the painter are saprophytes, which attack dead organisms and break down the organic compounds which are present into simple forms in order to feed upon them. They thrive upon such materials as glue size, paste based upon flour, and the oil content of paint, etc., and their growth is encouraged by the presence of warmth and humidity. Emulsion paints contain nothing that encourages mould growth, but they are not fungicidal and will not destroy any fungoid growths already present. These growths are a frequent source of trouble in premises such as bakeries, breweries, dairies, etc., and in conservatories.

Fungus spores can be carried considerable distances by the wind and can infect plaster and timber which has hitherto been perfectly free from such growth. The spores can lie dormant for a very long time, ready to germinate should the conditions favourable to their development occur for even a short period.

The presence of fungoid growths is denoted by the appearance of spots or patches of varying colours such as black, green or fluffy white; pink and purple patches are also common, especially in greenhouses. The treatment consists of stripping all infected paper or paint (the paper, etc., being burnt to prevent the spreading of the spores), finding out the cause of any damp and taking steps to cure it, and sterilizing the infected surfaces and surrounding areas with a suitable antiseptic wash, used in accordance with the makers' instructions. Where conditions especially favourable to fungoid growths exist, as in breweries, etc., paints containing fungicidal agents may be used, precautions being taken to avoid contamination of foodstuffs with poisonous substances.

A lot of the trouble caused by fungoid growths on ordinary domestic work is due to very obvious mistakes, such as applying wallpaper over newly plastered or damp surfaces. It should be noted, too, that the same reasons which give rise to fungoid growths in decorative materials can give trouble to the painter in other ways; brushes made from animal hair or vegetable fibre, if put away damp, are very liable to be attacked by mildew.

Funnel A useful piece of equipment where petrol-driven plant is in operation, to enable the fuel tank to be filled without spillage. Similarly, on those occasions when the old-fashioned blowlamp is in use, a small funnel should be employed when filling the lamp.

Furs The furs used in heraldry are depicted by conventional patterns, and the most common are ermine and vair. Ermine is shown as a white ground with black spots which represent the animal tails. In the early heraldic records the tails are drawn with more realism than is shown in the conventional form which is usually favoured today. There are certain variants of ermine; *ermines* has a black ground with white spots, *erminois* has a gold ground with black spots, and *pean* has a black ground with gold spots.

Vair is a pattern representing the stitching together of squirrel furs, as used in cloak linings. In the earliest records vair is depicted as a series of straight horizontal lines alternating with horizontal wavy lines, but later became conventionalized into a geometric pattern of bell-like shapes of blue and white in alternate spaces. There is a variant called counter-vair. Vair is always blue and white, but the same pattern is frequently found in other colours when it is termed "vairy" of the colours concerned. Another fur, potent, originally derived from vair, is depicted as a pattern of crutch-shaped skins in blue and white, potent being an old English word for a crutch or walking staff. There is a variant known as counter-potent.

G

Gable The triangular portion of a piece of wall between the enclosing lines of a sloping roof.

Gaboon A hardwood very similar to mahogany, showing the same fine grooving as mahogany, but generally lighter in colour. Used extensively in making plywood and often encountered by the painter.

Galvanized iron, galvanized steel Iron or steel sheeting which is protected from corrosion by means of the application of a layer of zinc, the low cost and easy application of which compares favourably with other forms of metallic coating. The zinc is deposited either by electro-plating or by a process of hot dipping in which the sheets are prepared by pickling and washing before being immersed in molten zinc, known commercially as "spelter".

The painting of new galvanized iron or steel may present difficulties. These arise partly as a result of the smooth greasy surface which offers very little key to a paint film, and partly from the fact that the zinc coating has an embrittling effect upon the medium of any paint applied upon it. For these reasons there is a strong tendency for the paint film to peel and flake off in very small fragments soon after application. Sometimes, with this in mind, the sheeting is pre-treated at the works by degreasing followed by a phosphate or chromate treatment. If it has not been so pre-treated, the sheeting may be left exposed to the weather for several months, when it will eventually acquire a good key for paint. But it is not easy to determine how long the weathering process will take before this occurs; it may be only a few months or it may be well over a year. Weathering is not necessary, however, if the correct priming procedures are followed.

Galvanized iron and steel, painting of (a) New sheeting pre-treated at the works or weathered by exposure

Any rust should be removed by wire-brushing, taking care not to damage the zinc coating. The surface should then be primed either with calcium plumbate or with a metal primer such as zinc chromate or zinc dust/zinc oxide primer.

(b) New sheeting which has not been either pre-treated or weathered

After the rust, if any, has been removed, the surface may be primed with calcium plumbate primer, but if a lead paint cannot be used the surface should be given a coat of etch primer followed by a metal primer (zinc chromate, zinc dust/zinc oxide, etc.).

(c) Old sheeting, previously painted

Any paint which is beginning to flake or which is showing signs of poor adhesion should be removed; if the flaking is extensive the whole surface must be stripped. Should there be any rusting this too must be removed. The bared metal should then be primed as indicated in the previous paragraphs.

In each case, after the initial preparation and priming, a normal undercoating and finishing programme is followed.

Garnet A vitreous mineral used as the grit in making waterproof sandpaper of the yellow type employed by painters and decorators.

Gas black A black pigment of the carbon black type, produced by the incomplete combustion of natural gases. It is an intense black colour with good staining properties; when reduced with white it yields a brownish grey colour.

Gas cylinder See *LPG containers.*

Gas torch An imprecise term for a blowtorch. See *Blowtorch.*

Gauged lime plaster Lime plaster to which a small quantity of plaster of Paris has been added to accelerate the set and to prevent shrinkage cracking.

Gauntlets Strong abrasion-proof gloves, long enough to cover the wrists and to come well up the forearms, used in a variety of heavy operations such as blast-cleaning, etc.

Gel A semi-solid colloidal solution; hence "to gell"—to assume a semi-solid condition.

Gelatine A transparent substance which forms a strong jelly in water, obtained from connective animal tissues, such as skin, tendons, bones and horns. In its dry state it is horny and flexible.

Gelatine capsules Hollow cylindrical capsules of dry gelatine which are often used instead of isinglass to make the mordant for glass gilding. For this purpose one capsule is dissolved in half a litre (500 ml) of hot, almost boiling, water. The advantage of using such capsules is that the gilder is not likely to be tempted to make the mordant too strong, as so often happens when he is using shredded isinglass, the hollow capsule giving a deceptive appearance of size.

Gelation Becoming semi-solid.

Gelling As *Gelation.*

Gesso A composition of whiting and glue used for the execution of relief work on woodwork or plaster. Although it can be modelled with the fingers or with a modelling tool, and may also be carved when dry, essentially it is a brush-applied material, and finished gesso work should possess the free fluid sweeps and the smooth textureless appearance of brushwork. A gesso composition of plaster of Paris and glue or size is also used at times to produce a smooth grounding on woodwork prior to the application of paint.

G

Ghosting A colloquial term sometimes used to denote pattern staining, whereby dust and dirt accumulate on the plastered surface of a ceiling in such a way as to show the arrangement of the joists and lathing underlying the plaster. It is due to the difference in thermal conductivity between the plaster and the wood or metal of which the joists are composed, dirt being deposited on those areas which offer the readiest passage for the transmission of heat. See *Pattern staining* for a fuller description.

Gilder's compo A composition used to form relief ornament of the type favoured in the Victorian period for the enrichment of picture frames, etc. It is made up from glue, rosin and linseed oil, stiffened with sifted whiting to a dough-like consistency, and is pressed into wooden or plaster moulds from which it takes a sharp impression. While still in the mould the back of the material is cut to a level surface ready for attachment to the surface which is to be decorated.

Gilder's cushion A pad from which the gilder works when applying loose leaf gold. It consists of a flat wooden board padded with felt and covered with a tightly stretched skin of chamois leather. One end of the pad is fitted with a stout parchment screen to shield the leaves of gold from draughts; when not in use the screen is folded down to lie flat upon the pad. A few leaves of gold are emptied from the book into a corner of the draught screen, and one leaf at a time is withdrawn and placed on the centre of the cushion as required. The underside of the wooden board is fitted with two soft leather straps, one of which is a thumb strap by which the gilder holds the cushion and the other serves to hold the gilder's knife. The chamois leather face of the cushion must be kept free from grease, otherwise the gold leaf will stick to it and tear instead of lifting cleanly; this is achieved by lightly dusting it occasionally with French chalk.

Gilder's knife A long thin knife used in the process of gilding with loose leaf gold; its purpose is to cut the separate leaves of gold into strips of whatever width is required. A leaf of gold is brought to the centre of the cushion and the knife drawn backwards and forwards across it to cut it. The blade is not sharpened; if it were sharp it would cut the chamois leather cushion, and in any case a sharp edge is not needed for such a malleable metal as gold. The knife is balanced so that when it is laid on a flat surface the blade is lifted clear and is not in contact with the surface. It is essential, if the knife is to cut the gold cleanly and not tear it, that the blade should be quite clean and free from grease; it should be dusted at intervals with French chalk and should on no account be handled or fingered. A gilder's knife is usually about 250 mm in overall length, the blade being about 150 mm long.

Gilder's mop A round bushy squirrel hair brush used to press gold leaf into place in the recesses and hollow contours of carved work and enrichments.

Gilder's tip This is another item of equipment, along with the cushion and knife, used in loose leaf gilding. It is a small brush composed of a single line of badger hairs fastened in a cardboard handle consisting of two thin sheets of card glued together, and it is used to pick up the gold leaf from the cushion and transfer it to the surface which is being gilded. In order to do this the badger hair must be slightly greasy, a condition which is achieved by the gilder drawing the tip across his cheek or across his hair.

Gilder's wheel A device used for applying lines in gold leaf or for gilding single members of beads and mouldings. It consists of two wheels mounted on a handle, one wheel holding a roll of ribbon gold and the other wheel a padded one which presses the gold into contact with the mordant. Generally, the lining is carried out directly upon a varnished surface when the varnish has achieved a degree of tack suitable for gilding.

Gilder's wheels do not often appear in present-day catalogues of decorators' materials. There are, of course, many old-established sign firms and coach-painting firms who still possess them, and they have always been part of the standard equipment of public transport departments, being widely used in the ornamentation of coaches and buses. The ribbon gold which is used in them is only made to order nowadays.

Gilding The application of gold leaf to any surface by means of an adhesive or "mordant".

Gill Sans A name given to a sans serif alphabet designed by Eric Gill. In sans serif letters the short cross-line, which terminates the unconnected strokes in Roman lettering, is dispensed with. In designing this style Eric Gill was probably influenced by the letters produced by Edward Johnston for the London Underground in 1918, both these designers being concerned to raise the standard of lettering above the level which had become common in the 19th century. Gill Sans letters are of more uniform width than the modern German sans serif versions; the only points come at the feet of the V and W, and the M is square with the middle strokes descending half-way. See also *Univers*.

Gin wheel A single pulley wheel with a rope passed over it, used for hoisting materials and equipment.

Girder A large heavy beam capable of carrying both concentrated and uniformly distributed loads.

Glair See *Egg glair*.

Glass, painting of When paint is applied to glass, either in the form of painted letters or an all-over coating to obscure the glass, the results are often disappointing and the film begins to peel after a short time. This is due to (a) the smoothness of the glass and the fact that it provides no "key" for paint, (b) the fact that glass is prone to condensation which affects the adhesion of the paint and (c) the fact that glass is a good conductor of heat and the paint is therefore subjected to frequent and rapid changes of temperature affecting its adhesion.

The success of the operation is more likely to be assured if certain points are observed. These are as follows: (a) The glass must be scrupulously clean before paint is applied; in particular it must be free from all trace of grease. A thin coating of whiting helps to clean the glass and to reveal any greasy areas. (b) Thick coatings of paint must be avoided, as thick coats are more liable to peel; thin coats are more successful. For lettering work, some firms produce tubes of extra-opaque colour specially for glass writing. (c) The medium of the paint must be of an adhesive and tenacious nature; alkyd resin gloss paints are very useful in this respect and under present-day conditions are generally the most suitable materials to use.

It should be noted that the colour of the glass itself, usually a greenish hue, modifies the appearance of any paint which is applied. A little crimson lake added to the paint helps to correct the colour. A small sample of the paint should be applied and the colour examined (and modified if necessary) before the whole of the work is laid in.

Glass embossing The treatment of glass so that lettering or ornament is etched or otherwise hollowed deeply into the surface; when viewed from the other side this gives the pattern the appearance of being raised or embossed. Glass embossing may be carried out by the process described under the heading *Acid etching* or by sandblasting.

Glass fibre See *Fibreglass*.

Glass fibre, painting of Glass fibre is used, among other things, for the construction of vehicle bodies. The moulds in which the components are manufactured are lined with a wax or water-soluble material called a "parting agent" or "release agent" which facilitates the extraction of the completed mouldings. Unless this agent is completely removed it will affect the drying and hardening of the paint system and may lead to flaking. As a general rule, more filling is required on a glass fibre surface than on a metal surface.

Glass fibre wallcoverings These were originally introduced to provide an alternative to fabrics such as hessian and jute, especially where the intention was to use the fabric as the base for paint coatings, and they are now established as being superior in many respects. Probably their greatest advantage lies in their fire-resisting properties, which meet the accepted requirements of the building and fire regulations not only in this country but throughout Europe. This is of great importance in the decoration of public buildings, hospitals, hotels, etc. Other advantages are their ease of application and their stability in that they do not stretch or shrink as a result of variations in temperature and humidity. They also provide an economic way of reinforcing cracked and weakened wall areas. The most usual method of painting them is by emulsion paint applied by roller. In recent years the scope of glass fibre wallcoverings has been extended to compete with the more expensive and luxurious hangings. There is now a range of very attractive and highly decorative wallhangings in tune with modern demands in colour and design, and glass fibre is also included in the formulation of laminates, ceiling tiles and acoustic panels.

Glass gilding The application of gold leaf to glass. The work is carried out in reverse so that the gilding is viewed through the glass. Loose leaf gold is employed for the purpose, the tools being the cushion, knife, tip, and a camel hair size brush; the mordant is isinglass or gelatine dissolved and cooked in hot water. The essence of the work is scrupulous cleanliness.

Glass reinforced polyester or glass reinforced plastic Commonly known by the initials GRP. A material extensively used in the construction industry, especially in the house-building sector. It is widely used for the reproduction of period details, such as the porticos, columns, pilasters and door surrounds incorporated into mock-Georgian style modern houses, also for bow-window and dormer-window units, moulded garage doors, claddings, etc. It is supplied in a white finish and also in a variety of colours, and is not intended to be painted. No maintenance other than cleaning is required for several years. When, however, the conditions of outdoor exposure lead to its becoming shabby in appearance, or when the owner of the property desires a change of colour, painting does become necessary, and the wrong type of preparation and paint system may lead to unsightly paint defects such as peeling and flaking due to lack of adhesion.

When GRP products require painting they should be carefully prepared by scrubbing them thoroughly with a warm detergent solution, using a stiff bristle brush or a nylon pad, and whilst still wet they should be rubbed down with fine waterproof abrasive paper. Wire wool should not be used as this can cause rust stains to develop. Alkyd resin paints adhere well to GRP; chlorinated rubber paints and good-quality emulsion paints and masonry paints are also suitable.

Glasspaper An abrasive for dry rubbing down, consisting of fused alumina bonded by means of hide glue or resin to stout cartridge paper.

Glastone plaster The brand name of a proprietary brand of anhydrous gypsum plaster.

Glaze A transparent or semi-transparent coating which is used to modify or enrich a previously applied colour. There are several ways in which glazes are employed in decorative work. One of the simplest is to relieve the plainness of broad wall surfaces finished in solid colour by applying a coat of delicately tinted glaze all over the surface and stippling it evenly with a hair stippler; the effect of this is to give a richness and depth which cannot be achieved with opaque colour alone. Glaze can also be used in the production of broken colour effects, by means of rag-rolling, combing, rubber stippling, etc.; it can be used to accentuate the highlights on relief work, the carving or modelling being coated with tinted glaze, stippled and then wiped over with a soft rag; further examples include the glazing of plastic paint followed by wiping to expose the highlights, and the use of glaze in blended effects. The term "glaze" also refers to some of the thin coatings used in graining, such as the wash of Vandyke brown which is applied over figured oak graining and which is manipulated to produce lights and shadows, the thin washes of colour employed in obtaining mottled effects, flogging, and so on.

As a general rule, it may be said that too wide a difference should not exist between the glaze colour and the ground colour in any type of glazed work; otherwise, the work will appear crude and coarse.

Glaze coat Any transparent or semi-transparent coating used to modify an existing colour without obscuring it.

The term is also sometimes used as meaning any transparent finishing coat, such as varnish, etc.

Glaze medium A transparent material which may be tinted with oil stainers in order to produce glazed and broken colour effects. There are two types of glaze medium, both of which are based on light amorphous pigments such as china clay, aluminium stearate, etc., which have little or no opacity in oil. One type known as the fixed glaze type is formulated so as not to flow out after application; this type is used for effects such as rag-rolling and colour combing, where it is necessary that the crispness of the markings should be retained. Although the material appears very thick it brushes out with astonishing ease; it possesses "false body" in that it decreases its viscosity when agitated but reverts to its former viscosity directly the shearing action ceases. The other type, known as the flowing or merging type, is prepared with a medium which flows out readily after application; this type is used for the blending and shading of colours. Glaze medium of the fixed glaze type is sometimes added to graining colour to prevent the markings from flowing out.

Gloss The brightness or lustre of a painted surface; the extent to which it will reflect light, ranging from flat (absence of gloss), through the stages of eggshell sheen and semi-gloss, to the degree of smoothness and brilliance which is described as full gloss.

Gloss level The extent to which a painted surface reflects light in a manner resembling a mirror. The three main levels correspond roughly with what are described as full gloss, eggshell, and flat or matt.

Gloss meter A piece of apparatus for determining the degree of gloss of a painted surface. In general, the glossier a paint the more light it will reflect. The gloss meter works on the principle of directing a beam of light on to a painted panel and allowing the reflected beam to excite a galvanometer. The more light is reflected the higher will be the galvanometer reading. The reading is usually expressed as a percentage of the gloss that would be obtained with a glass panel painted at the back.

Gloss paint A rather vague term which covers any kind of paint which dries with a fairly high level of gloss.

Glossing up The appearance of glossy patches on a flat or matt paint finish due to the surface being handled or subjected to polishing.

Glue An adhesive substance made by boiling animal hides, hooves or bones. It consists of gelatine and chondrin, a substance derived from cartilage and which is similar to gelatine except that it does not form as firm a jelly; the adhesive properties of the glue depend on the proportion of chondrin which it contains. Glue made from skins is superior to that obtained from bones. The best quality of cake glue is called Scotch glue.

Glue size A weak form of glue, available to the decorator as cake glue, jelly size, or "concentrated size". Concentrated size, which is glue in granulated or powdered form, is by far the most popular because it is easily prepared for use, stores well, and dissolves quickly. Two kinds are produced, one to be mixed with cold water, the other with hot water. The hot water type is preferable as it gives a greater measure of penetration. It should be mixed with water that is hot but not boiling, because if mixed with boiling water it will not gel properly when cool. All the glue size sold today includes a fungicidal agent to prevent the development of mould growth. There is no advantage in buying the cheaper grades; a poor-quality size contains impurities which affect the setting and adhesive properties of the glue.

The main purpose of glue size is as a preparation for paperhanging. It helps to equalize the porosity of the surface to which it is applied, and it gives a degree of "slip" to the paper without which it would be difficult or indeed impossible for the paperhanger to slide it into the correct position. A common mistake is that of making the size too strong. Its purpose is not to *stop* the suction completely but to level it up between one area and another. Too strong a coat may lead to the paper remaining wet for an undue length of time which causes excessive shrinkage, and this in turn causes springing of the joints when the paper is drying.

Glue size is sometimes used as a thin coating to act as a buffer coat. Open-textured wallboards, fabrics, lining papers, and other fibrous materials need a buffer coat before a paint coating is applied to them, as the medium in paint has an embrittling effect on the fibres, but it is essential that the glue size should be extremely thin, preferably applied hot, and that it should penetrate the fibres without forming a continuous film on the surface. In present-day practice, however, the customary thing when wallboards and lining papers are to be painted is to use a thinned coating of emulsion paint as the buffer. Glue size is still often used, however, on canvas and similar fabrics.

Glue size has an important role in decorative work when it is properly used, but it can do a lot of damage when wrongly used. It is not suitable as a preparatory coating before paint is applied, except on fibrous materials as already discussed, and it should never be used before emulsion paint is applied. When used before paperhanging, any splashes of size which fall on the painted woodwork must be wiped off while still wet; if they dry upon the surface they cause the paint film to lift away from the wood in a most dramatic manner, this being due to the strongly contractile nature of the glue.

Glycerine or glycerol A colourless sweet liquid which is a compound of alcohol. It is contained as an ester in all vegetable oils and is released when a vegetable oil is saponified or decomposed by alkaline action. It has many applications in paint manufacture, such as, for example, when glycerine and phthalic anhydride are reacted together in the production of an alkyd resin or when glycerine and rosin are fused to produce ester gums.

Glycerine is a hygroscopic material and when it is mixed with water it resists the tendency of water to evaporate. This fact is used in various ways; glycerine is added to artists' water colours as a plasticizer, and it is also used by the scene painter to plasticize the colours used on canvas backcloths and by the decorator wishing to retard the setting of plastic paint in order to carry out modelling.

Glyptal resins Alkyd resins; "Glyptal" is the trade name applied to alkyd resins produced by the American company which was the first to develop them.

Goggles Eye-protective equipment designed to enclose the eyes; they are usually held in position with a headband of good-quality durable material at least 9·5 mm wide. The two main types of goggles are (a) the box type, which has a one-piece lens giving protection to both eyes, and (b) the cup type which has two individual eyepieces, adjustably connected across the nose. In both cases precautions must be taken to prevent misting, which would impair the user's vision; either the goggles are constructed to provide ventilation, such ventilation being designed to prevent the entry of any particles or strong radiation to the inside, or else the goggles are totally enclosed, and double-glazed or specially coated filters are used to reduce the misting.

Various types of goggles are available, each suited to particular purposes. BS 2092: 1967 identifies the following recognized types: (a) General purpose eye-protectors, in which the lens or lenses have been tested to reach an approved level of robustness; (b) Impact eye-protectors designed to withstand an approved impact test; (c) Molten metal eye-protectors which give protection against flying molten metal and hot solids; (d) Gas-tight goggles, giving protection against gases, fumes, dust and splashes of liquid entering into the space or spaces in front of the eyes and enclosed by the goggles; and (e) Chemical goggles providing protection against dust and splashes of liquid.

Gold bronze A light-coloured bronze powder made from a copper alloy, mainly used for decorative purposes on interior work. It can be obtained with the powder mixed in medium ready for use, or with the powder and medium separate to be mixed immediately before it is required, or if desired can be applied in powder form over a ground of tacky gold size. It tends to tarnish unless protected by lacquer.

Gold leaf Metallic gold beaten out into the form of a very thin leaf or sheet. It is supplied in books in which the individual leaves of gold are separated by thin leaves of tissue paper dusted with Armenian bole to prevent the gold sticking to it. Each book contains 25 leaves of gold, each leaf measuring 82·5 mm square. It is sold either as loose leaf gold or transfer gold. Loose leaf gold, as its name implies, consists just of the thin squares of leaf unattached to anything else; in this form, which is intended for tip and cushion work, the leaf is very fragile. Transfer gold is more robust and easy to handle, each leaf of gold being attached to a thin sheet of waxed tissue paper large enough to leave a margin all round it, and is intended for outdoor sign work and any other type of gilding in which the draughts or the nature of the work preclude the use of loose leaf gold. Transfer gold is also available in the form of rolls of various widths known as ribbon gold, for use with the gilder's wheel.

Gold leaf is available in various shades ranging from pale to deep, and in various thicknesses, extra thick leaf being used when the work is to be exposed to very severe conditions or is in some inaccessible place that cannot often be reached. English gold leaf, of twenty-three or twenty-four carat, is reckoned to be the best quality, being more dependable and consistent than foreign leaf. Gold leaf can be readily distinguished from cheap substitutes by holding it up against a strong light when it appears green, whereas alloys and Dutch metals appear reddish or blue-black according to their composition.

Gold size An adhesive material used as a mordant for gold leaf, the leaf being applied when the gold size has attained the requisite degree of tack.

Gold size is available in two forms; there is "oil gold size", which is a slow-drying composition prepared from a linseed stand oil or a naturally thickened linseed oil tinted with yellow ochre and thinned to workable consistency with boiled linseed oil or varnish, and there is *Japan gold size*, sometimes termed "writers' gold size", which is a quick drying short-oil varnish.

Oil gold size (sometimes called "Old oil gold size") is used for very high-class interior decorative work, for the gilding of large wooden or metal letters and carved woodwork, and on broad areas of wall surface which are to be gilded in solid gold. The work must be painted so that its absorption is completely satisfied and so that it presents a hard, smooth semi-gloss ground for the gilding. The gold size, which has a tendency to form sags, curtains and thick edges, must be brushed out evenly, and steps must be taken to prevent dust from settling on the surface. Twenty-four to thirty hours must elapse before it is tacky enough to gild, and it may retain its tack for several days. It is not suitable for use with alloys and metals other than gold as these react with the oil and become discoloured.

Japan gold size is used for lettering, lining and ornamental work on which a sharply defined outline is required, and for any gilding work which is to be carried out *in situ* in a position where exposure to dust or weather conditions would affect the gold size before the gold was applied. The proportions of oil and driers can be adjusted so that it dries at varying speeds, and writers' gold size is sold at such rates as 1-hour, 4-hour, or 20-hour size. Generally speaking, the longer the gold size takes to tack up the brighter and more lustrous the gold will appear; the drying speed is selected according to the circumstances ruling on the particular job in hand. For outdoor signwork in inclement weather a quick-drying size presents obvious advantages. The drying speed suggested on the label is only intended as a rough guide and the actual length of time required before the material tacks will fluctuate according to weather conditions; for instance, a 1-hour gold size may take considerably longer to tack up in dull humid weather but may take much less than an hour to harden if exposed to a burst of hot sunshine. For this reason it is necessary to test the hardness of the gold size at frequent intervals, laying the gold whenever the right degree of tack has been reached before proceeding to run in any more gold size. The material is ready for gilding when the back of the forefinger can be lightly laid upon it without leaving any mark. On lettering work a small quantity of tube lemon chrome is added to the gold size so that it can be seen more clearly; too much stainer should not be added or the drying will be retarded. If it is found necessary to thin Japan gold size pure turps should be used, as the material reacts unfavourably with white spirit.

Gothic lettering Otherwise known as "Old English"; a style of lettering sometimes used by signwriters which is derived from medieval manuscript lettering.

Gouache Opaque colour which is ground in water and thickened with gum and honey. It is sold as a tube colour, very often labelled as "Designers' Gouache" (the tubes are much larger than those in which water colours are marketed) and it is available in a very wide range of colours. Gouache is extensively used by interior decorators and designers in the preparation of colour sketches, drawings and colour schemes to provide their clients with an indication of the finished appearance of their proposed schemes of decoration.

The word is sometimes used to include other types of water-thinned opaque paints such as poster paints.

Gradation of colour or graduated colour Colour which passes very gradually from one shade or tone to another. Sometimes the walls of a room are graduated so that the colour gradually becomes deeper on the lower parts of the walls. Sometimes a frieze can be graduated so that the lower part tones with the colour of the wall-filling and becomes progressively lighter as it goes upwards to the ceiling. Graduated colour in small areas is very successfully carried out with spray equipment, but on a large scale as on wall surfaces it is much more easily controlled if done by brushwork and finished off with a hair stippler.

Graining A reproduction of the decorative qualities of natural wood grain, achieved by manipulating semi-transparent glazes over a painted ground of solid colour. For details of specific woods see under the appropriate headings.

Graining colour The term used by the painter to mean a thin stain, scumble or semi-transparent glaze which is brushed on to a grounding of solid colour and which is dragged, combed or otherwise manipulated to produce brush graining or figure graining.

Graining combs Steel combs with teeth of varying widths, and pieces of rubber, cork or linoleum with the edges serrated to form openings of various widths, which are used to reproduce the plainer kinds of wood markings and which are used in combination with various other effects in figure graining.

Graining horn A short piece of celluloid or perspex over which a piece of folded rag is doubled and which is used by the grainer to "wipe out" or lift wet graining colour in order to reproduce grain markings. It is a less painful and more hygienic substitute for the old-time grainer's method of using his own thumb nail, allowed to grow unnaturally long for the purpose.

Graining paper A material used as a means of imitating wood grain. It consists of absorbent paper embossed with the features of a particular type of wood grain. The surface to be grained is painted in a suitable ground colour and allowed to dry; it is then laid in with scumble and while the scumble is wet the paper is pressed into contact with it, the absorbency of the paper removing some of the stain.

Graining, the survival of Graining has been practised ever since people first used painted decoration. Egyptian painters were imitating wood-grain effects in paint as long ago as 2500 BC, and in this country numerous examples of graining have been found in the course of excavating Roman villas dating from the second century AD. Many people today dismiss graining as a thing of the past, a dead technique in terms of modern decoration. The strange thing is that in spite of being in continuous use for thousands of years it obstinately refuses to die. The question is, can it survive into the 21st century?

For any craft process to survive, four things are essential. First, there must be a demand for it; second, there must be people capable of doing it; third, it must be available at an economic cost; and fourth, the materials to produce it must still exist. It is pertinent to consider graining from these four viewpoints.

(1) Demand. In every age across thousands of years the demand has existed. In every age there have been wealthy people who liked the appearance of graining so much that they were prepared to pay for it. It is also true that in every age there have been other people who have disliked it intensely. There is plenty of evidence that opinions were sharply divided on the subject in the Middle Ages. In Victorian Britain there was an enormous demand for graining that led to a colossal output of the work, yet there was also a great deal of opposition from people who objected to it on aesthetic grounds and roundly denounced it as a sham. In our own lifetime we have seen periods when it was automatically assumed that whatever form of decoration was used for the walls, the woodwork in any room would be grained, and at other times public taste swung in the opposite direction and most customers were demanding an enamelled finish in white or some very delicate colour, but always there were some people violently opposed to the popular trend of the day. There is no reason to suppose that the pattern of human behaviour will alter. Everything indicates that there will continue to be fluctuations in taste and fashion and that periodically there will be renewed interest in graining with a consequent upsurge in demand.

(2) Craftworkers capable of graining. This again is a constant factor, based on human nature. There have always been some people who have become fascinated by the subtle patterns of the markings, colourings, and light and shade effects which occur when a piece of wood is planed to expose the grain, and who have been impelled to spend time studying these effects in various kinds of wood and seeking to discover how to reproduce them in paint. They become totally absorbed, and working out the techniques to master the complexities develops into an obsession, the main thing in their life, and leads them into an amazing degree of artistry. This happens irrespective of whether or not there is any apparent call for the work. Actually there generally *is* an outlet for their ability, because there are always householders who have similar feelings about the beauties of wood grain and are only too glad to find someone who can reproduce them in a decorative scheme.

But when the pendulum of fashion swings strongly in the direction of graining, the demand is considerably increased and the supply of highly sensitive and competent craftsmen is not adequate to satisfy the demand. At this point two things are likely to happen. The first is that some unscrupulous tradesmen with no previous experience of the work and with little or no artistic sense suddenly realize that there is money to be made in graining. Rather than miss the opportunity they immediately add graining to the list of activities they offer, without regard for quality and with no concern for the public image of the decorator. The second is that many well-meaning decorators also see the market that exists and being anxious to please their customers are prepared to try their hand at graining. They are quite content to achieve a rudimentary imitation of wood; in fact, not having devoted much time to studying the subject in depth they don't realize how pitifully weak their work is. Inevitably, it is only a matter of time before the quantity of shoddy work so far exceeds the good that the general public becomes disgusted, and the whole concept of graining is discredited. For a while graining is under a cloud, till memories fade and the cycle is repeated. The point to realize is that first-class grainers have always been scarce, and most so-called graining is wretched stuff unworthy of the name.

(3) Cost. The argument invariably advanced about this is that the old-time grainers were able to produce excellent work simply because their wages were so low; they could spend time putting on innumerable glaze coats to heighten and enhance the work, but at today's prices this would be impossible. This is a completely mistaken view. Grainers' wages in Victorian days were very low—but so were the wages of every other worker. The cost of good-quality work today in relation to the price of other commodities is no greater than it was 50 or 100 years ago. People who want the highest-quality work are prepared to pay for it.

(4) Availability of materials. If graining fails to survive this will be the main cause—and the same thing goes for other decorative processes as well. Until recently, any good firm of decorators' merchants carried a stock of the tools and materials needed by specialist branches of the trade, small as the sales would be; this was part of the service offered to the trade. Today the merchants' stock list is controlled by accountants rather than by people with the interests of the trade at heart. Accountants are only interested in stocking the most profitable lines, in the quantities required by big contractors or by the huge do-it-yourself market, so that there is a rapid turnover of goods. The grainer who needs a new fantail overgrainer or a fresh supply of Vandyke brown can no longer slip into the nearest decorators' supplier's shop to obtain them. Many of the little-used items are no longer obtainable at all. Herein lies the biggest enemy of the traditional crafts.

At present there are still a few firms catering for minority interests and from whose catalogues the tools and other requisites can be selected. A notable feature is their concern for the well-being of the painter's craft. J.H. Ratcliffe & Co. of Southport are well known for the scumbles they produce, for example; what is not so generally known is the interest they take in the training of decorating students. And good-quality graining is still sometimes specified by architects for big-scale hotel work, etc., and in high-class domestic work it is still required. But future trends in the manufacturing industries are unpredictable.

Granite A hard igneous rock used in building. It occurs in various shades of pinky-red, blue-grey and green-grey; some varieties have a coarse mottled appearance, others present a mass of fine spots.

Granite chippings Sometimes used to produce a texture treatment known as "paint harling" for the exterior protection of steel cladding.

Graniting The imitation of granite in paint. The work is grounded out in red or grey and when this is dry the surface is sponge stippled with black, blue-grey, red and white, the darkest colours being applied first. For the fine spotted varieties brush spattering is used instead of sponge stippling.

Granulated cork A material used in anti-condensation treatments. Its effectiveness is due to the fact that cork is a poor conductor of heat, so that a thick layer of cork forms a buffer coat which insulates the surface. See *Anti-condensation paints.*

Granulated size Concentrated size.

Graphite A black pigment consisting of carbon in crystalline form. Natural deposits of graphite, which is also known as "plumbago" or "blacklead", are found in various parts of the world and a very pure quality is produced artificially by calcining anthracite coal or coke residue in electric furnaces. In appearance, graphite is dark grey with a metallic lustre rather than black. The particles of which it is composed take the form of very thin hexagonal flakes, similar to the flakes of metallic bronze powder, and because of this it possesses great opacity and resistance to moisture penetration. Its outstanding property, however, is its tremendous covering power, one litre covering as much as 40 square metres; it brushes out to such a thin film that it has little value when used alone but it can be incorporated with other pigments to make them work freely.

Grasscloth A type of wallhanging consisting of the long trailing stems of plants, which after being dried and dyed are woven with metallic thread, and mounted on a paper backing. See *Japanese grasscloths.*

Gravity bucket A type of paint container which is hoisted by block and tackle and from which paint is fed downwards through a fluid hose to a spray gun below. (**NLC**)

Gravity feed cup A small paint container which is attached directly to the top or side of a spraygun (air-propelled), so that when the gun trigger is pulled a stream of paint is fed by the force of gravity into the air stream. There is an orifice in the lid of the cup by which air enters to replace the paint as it is used.

Gravity feed type gun A spray gun which can be fed from a gravity feed cup. The air cap for such a gun should be of the suction feed type. Gravity feed guns with $\frac{1}{2}$ litre (500 ml) capacity cups are very useful for decorative spraying; they would, of course, be impracticable for any large-scale work because of the low pressure employed, the fact that they would need frequent re-charging with paint and the fact that they could not be tilted to any great extent because of stopping up the air hole in the cup lid. A range of smaller type guns is available for a variety of purposes, being employed in many industrial finishing processes and as touch-up guns; very small gravity feed guns of the pencil type are made as artists' air brushes.

Gravity straining The normal system of straining paint by pouring it into a truncated cone of light metal into which a circular piece of gauze mesh is fitted, and allowing the paint to be drawn through the gauze by the force of gravity.

Green One of the three primary colours of light, and one of the three secondary colours of pigment mixture, obtained by blending blue and yellow.

Many of the green paints used today are produced from a pigment made by mixing phthalocyanine blue and arylamide yellow. Other green pigments include chrome greens and Brunswick greens (made by blending chrome yellows with Prussian blue), chromium compounds such as chromium oxide and Guignet's green, cobalt green, and copper compounds such as emerald green. Terre verte (green earth) is now only used as an artist's colour.

Green earth (terre verte) A natural earth pigment found in many parts of the world, especially in the Verona district of Italy. The colour is chiefly due to the presence of silicate of iron. It is a rather dull colour, variable in strength and tone like most of the earth colours, and possesses little opacity. The better qualities are supplied as artists' tube colours. (**NLC**)

Grinding The use of mills and runners of various types to reduce pigments to a state of uniform fineness.

Grinning A term used when a coat of paint fails to obscure the surface to which it is applied; the ground which shows through is said to be "grinning through". This may be due to the paint having been applied unevenly or too thinly, or it may be because too great a difference of tone exists between the grounding and the newly applied coating. Old painted lettering or heavily coloured ornamental painting will often grin through a new paint system unless proper steps are first taken to reduce the difference of tone. For example, in the case of a white-painted signboard with black lettering, which is to be repainted with a white or other light-coloured finish, a first coating of deep cream colour followed by a coating of white will give better coverage than two coats of white.

Grit A term used in connection with blast-cleaning to define the nature of the abrasive particles; it refers to small angular particles of either ferrous or non-ferrous metals, the particles having a sharp cutting edge.

Grit blasting Strictly speaking, the use of grit such as silica sand, etc., propelled by compressed air, for the cleaning of stonework or brickwork and for the removal of rust and scale from steelwork. The term is often used very loosely, however, to include any kind of blast-cleaning operation. In order to avoid confusion, it is better to be quite specific; the type of operations carried out by the painter should be known by the proper term of "blast-cleaning".

Ground A rather loose term used in a great number of ways to describe a surface to which paint is to be applied; for instance, to denote the condition of the surface (e.g., "The application of a hard brittle film over a soft *ground* will cause cracking", "The *ground* for gilding should be hard and non-absorbent"), to denote a colour which is to be completely covered (e.g., "A delicate raw sienna glaze on an ivory *ground*", "The room was *grounded* out in white"), to indicate the background or prevailing colour upon which a design is to be painted (e.g., "A sprig pattern in gold on a crimson *ground*"), to suggest the texture of a surface (e.g., "Painting with a dry-brush technique on a stippled *ground*"), and so on.

Ground brush Another name for the old-fashioned round-shaped "pound brush" which is now no longer used. (**NLC**)

Ground coat An opaque coat of paint over which it is intended to apply a further coating or treatment, e.g. the opaque coating used as the base for a glaze or scumble coat in broken colour effects.

Ground colour The general background colour upon which a design is painted or stencilled or a piece of lettering executed. The term is also sometimes used very loosely to mean the first coat of paint in any paint system.

Grounding A term used in many districts to mean specifically the solid colour which is the base upon which graining colour is applied and which shows through the graining colour as the lightest part of the wood which is being imitated; for instance, "medium oak grounding" to denote a buff colour suitable as the base for medium oak graining, "mahogany grounding", and so on.

Grounds Wallpapers to which a coat of background colour has been applied and allowed to dry before the pattern is printed upon it, as opposed to those on which the pattern has been printed directly upon the uncoated paper.

Grout A thin cement in fluid form or a two-pack epoxy product used for running into the narrow joints between ceramic wall tiles, or a thin liquid mortar used for filling the vertical joints in masonry.

Grouting The act or process of filling in or finishing with grout. Various kinds of grouting tools are available which help in the production of a neat finish.

GRP The term generally used to refer to glass reinforced polyester or glass reinforced plastic, q.v.

Guard-rail A protective rail placed around the working platform of a scaffold in order, together with the toe boards, to prevent the fall of persons, materials or tools from the platform. Under the terms of the Construction Regulations it is required that guard-rails shall be provided on every working platform (with certain exemptions which are listed) from which a person might fall a distance exceeding two metres. The height of the rail is to be between 910 mm and 1·15 m (3 ft and 3 ft 9 in.) and the distance between the guard-rail and the toe boards shall not exceed 765 mm (30 in.). These measurements were amended under the terms of the Construction (Metrication) Regulations which came into force on 9th November 1984.

Guide coat A very thin coating of spirit colour which is applied to a surface which has been filled and levelled, in order to indicate whether the filling has been completely and thoroughly carried out or whether there are still some indentations which require further filling. The guide coat is generally composed of turps tinted with Prussian blue or drop black; it is brushed on to the surface and allowed to dry, and the surface is then carefully rubbed down with fine sandpaper stretched over a rubbing block. The thin colour is removed from the flat surface but is not dislodged from any cavities which remain, and by this means the position of such cavities is revealed.

Obviously the use of guide coats is not part of the pattern of everyday working practice, but they *are* used not only on high-class decorating work but also on certain classes of industrial painting, e.g. in electricity power stations, in the painting of generating plant, etc., where a very high degree of finish is necessary.

Guignet's green (also called Viridian) A fine brilliant green with an almost metallic lustre, which is fast to light, stable and inert, and unaffected by sulphur or alkalis. It consists of a hydrated oxide of chromium. It is very expensive and is now chiefly used in the production of artists' tube colours.

Gules The heraldic tincture red.

Gum A viscid substance exuded from certain trees in the same way as resin, but differing from resin in that it is soluble in water but insoluble in organic solvents. In the paint industry, however, the term is used in a wide and general sense to include both resins and gums. (**NLC**)

Gum arabic A product of acacia used in the preparation of artists' water colours.

Gum thus A material which exudes naturally from American pine trees, and is essentially the same material as the oleo-resin from which turpentine and rosin are distilled. (**NLC**)

Gumwood A wood which is native to the Southern parts of the USA. The grain resembles the figure of rosewood, and is sometimes imitated by grainers. It can be grained in either water or oil media, working with raw umber and drop black on a ground colour composed of white lead, raw umber and raw sienna.

Gun filter Also called a "cartridge filter". A small cylinder of wire gauze fitted in the handle of an airless spray gun, or fitted on the hose close to the gun.

Gypsum A soft pinky-white rock consisting of hydrous calcium sulphate.

Gypsum cements A term sometimes used to mean anhydrous plasters.

Gypsum plasterboard A building board that consists of a core of set and hardened gypsum plaster, enclosed between two firmly attached sheets of strong stout paper. Various types are manufactured, including those which are termed gypsum baseboards and gypsum lathboards, both of which are designed to receive a skimming coat of plaster after fixing. Today, however, plasterboards are increasingly being used to provide a dry-lining system for interior walls. Boards for this purpose are manufactured with a tapered edge, and after fixing, the joints are filled and taped so that an overall smooth seamless wall surface is produced.

Special water-repellent plasterboards are obtainable, and there are also insulating plasterboards which are faced on one or on both sides with a thin veneer of aluminium foil. The type of plasterboard of most interest to the painter has a facing of stout paper which is suitable for immediate decoration with either oil paint, emulsion paint or wallpaper applied directly to the surface with no preparation required. When it is intended to hang wallpaper, however, it is only a matter of common sense to look to the future. It is always advisable to coat the face of the plasterboard first with an oil-based priming paint, as this makes it very much easier to strip off the wallpaper when the time comes for redecoration. The paint coating prevents water from soaking into the board, which might well cause the surface to buckle, and it also means that the water stays on the surface and soaks the wallpaper instead of being absorbed by the board, so that there is less risk of the scrapers digging into the board and damaging the surface.

Gypsum plasters Plasters used in building, which are derived from natural gypsum. They are produced by calcining the crushed rock in order to drive off the water of crystallization. When the gypsum is roasted at a moderate temperature, approximately 170°C, three-quarters of the contained water is driven off, the product being known as hemihydrate plaster. Heating the gypsum to a temperature of 400°C drives off the entire water content, and anhydrous plaster is produced.

The British Standards Institution distinguishes four classes of plaster according to their relative porosity and hardness. Class A has the highest level of porosity and the lowest level of hardness; the porosity decreases and the hardness increases from Class A to Class D.

Neat hemihydrate plaster, commonly known as plaster of Paris, sets very quickly and is used as a material for stopping holes and cracks; it is listed as Class A in the British Standard classification of plaster. It sets too quickly for use on large areas, and therefore needs to have a retarding agent added during manufacture; it is then known as a "retarded hemihydrate plaster" which is often described as a "hardwall" plaster; this is listed as Class B. Anhydrous plasters can be modified in various ways during manufacture, the products being classified either as "anhydrous gypsum plasters" which are Class C, or as Keene's or Parian cement, Class D.

The characteristic of all gypsum plasters is that they set by a process of crystallization whereby the water added to them by the plasterer combines chemically with them to replace the water of crystallization driven off during their manufacture. They expand slightly as they set and are chemically neutral. For further details of the various types see under the appropriate headings, e.g. *Anhydrous gypsum plaster*, etc.

Hair cracking When the term is used to refer to the degree of cracking of a paint, it implies the presence of fine cracks occurring irregularly and at random, and not deep enough to penetrate the top coat.

Hair cracks Very fine cracks occurring at random in a surface which is to be painted, particularly in plaster work and cement rendering. Lime plasters especially, unless gauged with plaster of Paris, are liable to shrink when drying and to develop a mass of fine hair cracks; these are not particularly noticeable until paint is applied, but then they become very conspicuous due to the absorption of the medium into the cracks. There are filling materials suitable for filling hair cracks, but when the surface is extensively affected it is difficult to fill all the cracks satisfactorily, and it is often more economical to size and line the surface with lining paper.

Hair stippler A type of brush with several applications to painting and decorating. It consists of a flat rectangular base plate into which several rows of wire drawn bristles are set, the rows being so close together that the bristles present a flat level face of the same area as the base. The base is in two parts consisting of a flat rectangle of wood to which a thin plate of either aluminium or ebonite is attached in order to keep the wood dry and prevent it from warping. Various sizes are available but the most usual sizes are those with a base plate measuring 175 mm by 125 mm or 150 mm by 100 mm. Each stippler is provided with two interchangeable handles, secured to the base with a thumb screw; one of these is a long handle projecting well beyond the base, and the other is a bridge or arch handle.

The purposes of the hair stippler are as follows:

(a) To level out the newly applied coat of paint and to eliminate the brush marks from it.

(b) To blend colours together in order to obtain a gentle gradation where a blending of colour from light to dark is required.

(c) To level out an area of tinted glaze before any broken colour effects such as rag-rolling or rubber stippling are commenced.

The method of use is that when an area of suitable dimensions has been laid in with paint or glaze, the surface of the wet material is patted or struck several times with the face of the stippler, the brush being used with short sharp clean strokes, each stroke largely overlapping the previous one. It is essential that the stippler be used systematically with a series of strokes travelling in a straight line across the painted surface, followed by another series travelling in a straight line below it and slightly overlapping the previous series, and so on; if it is used in a haphazard fashion with a series of circular movements there is a strong tendency for some small areas to be missed, and these show up very prominently in the finished work. A hair stippler is generally used with flat or semi-flat materials or glaze; it would, of course, be quite unsuitable for use with a gloss paint as it would disturb the even flow of the material and produce minute pits and hollows that would detract from the gloss.

The method of cleaning a stippler after use is not always clearly understood; the correct method is as follows: (a) A piece of lining paper or newspaper is laid down flat and a few drops of the appropriate solvent poured upon it. The stippler is gently tapped on the solvent so as to loosen the paint in the tips of the brush. (b) Once the cleaning operation has begun the stippler must on no account be turned face upwards, otherwise softened paint may flow down into the base of the brush from whence it will be difficult to dislodge it and where it will tend to set hard and stiffen the bristles; moreover, when washing commences, if water flows down into the base plate it may cause the base to warp and buckle. (c) The stippler is then washed with warm water and soap; the tips of the bristles only are dipped in the water, the stippler is kept face downwards, and the soap worked into the brush with the fingers until the paint is loosened. The washing continues until the soapsuds produced are clean and frothy, indicating that all oily material has been removed. Hot water should not be used, as it has a harmful effect on the bristles. Under no circumstances should the stippler be completely immersed in water so as to wet the base plate. (d) The tips of the bristles are rinsed in clean water to remove all the soap. (e) The stippler is well shaken to remove as much moisture as possible and is then hung up to dry with the bristles pointing face downwards. No attempt should be made to dry the stippler by artificial heat as this will lead to the base plate becoming warped.

Hammer finishes Industrial finishes, used on a variety of products ranging from office equipment to toilet articles, which give the appearance of hammered metal but with the irregularities of the surface not as pronounced. They offer the same advantages as wrinkle finishes without the drawbacks, such as the tendency to harbour dirt. They are usually produced by stoving processes owing to the difficulty of obtaining a hard film with an air drying paint.

Handboard A stout piece of wood, usually about 300 mm square, on which the painter mixes small quantities of plaster of Paris when making good the cracks and holes in plasterwork. The handle consists of a sturdy piece of dowelling fastened centrally on the back at right angles to the board.

Hanging edge The hanging edge of the door is the edge which is hinged.

Hard dry A term which is used rather loosely to denote the degree of hardness attained by a film of paint. It can mean that the film is hard enough to be rubbed down and for a further coat of paint to be applied by brushing. In the case of a finishing coat it implies that the film is hard enough to be handled without damage.

Hard gloss paint A term which has been outdated by present-day technology. It referred to full gloss finishing paints made of pigments ground in an oil-varnish medium, and it was used to differentiate between such paints and the old-style Dutch enamels in which the medium was linseed stand oil. (**NLC**)

Hard hat Slang term for a safety helmet.

Hard stopping A material used for stopping holes and deep cracks in timber and for repairing angles and mouldings in joinery work. It can be made by mixing stiff paste white lead with whiting and gold size, but this is rarely done today; there are some excellent proprietary brands of ready-mixed hard stopping available which work very smoothly and dry extremely hard. There are also two-pack stoppers available which are based on polyester, and these are suitable for stopping both woodwork and metalwork. On good-quality work a hard stopping, which dries hard throughout its mass, is always preferable to ordinary putty which hardens slowly and tends in time to shrink and crumble.

It used to be the practice to add red lead powder to mixtures of white lead and gold size, or to add red lead powder to ordinary linseed oil putty to stiffen it, and a hard stopper for ironwork was sometimes made with red lead powder and gold size or boiled linseed oil, but these materials contravene the Control of Lead at Work Regulations.

Hard water Water containing salts of magnesium and calcium, as from a chalky soil. Its characteristic is that soap will not easily form a lather in it.

Hardboard A type of building board available in the form of large sheets and extensively used as a lining for walls and ceilings and for such purposes as the erection of exhibition stands, shop fitting, the facing of signboards and the flushing of doors. It is composed of wood pulp, wood fibre or other vegetable fibre together with suitable fillers and bonding agents, and is densely compacted under high pressure to present a smooth hard polished surface. Some types of hardboard possess very little porosity while others in spite of their polished appearance are extremely porous; some types contain oil in their composition and require a special primer and filling treatment if they are to be brought to a good-quality gloss finish. Because of the varying composition and texture of different brands it is advisable to consult the manufacturers' instructions about the painting of any particular type. Hardboards are hygroscopic and it is therefore advisable that the back and edges should be painted before fixing in order to prevent the penetration of moisture.

In spite of their polished appearance, it is not necessary to rub hardboards down to provide a key before they are painted. If for any reason it is decided that they *should* be rubbed down, care is needed to avoid scratching or scoring the surface, as the scratches may absorb an undue quantity of paint and may therefore swell up to produce unsightly ridges in the finished work.

Hardness The extent to which a paint film can resist the impact of a hard object without denting and the extent to which it will stand handling without sustaining damage. Various tests such as the scratch test, the mechanical thumb and the hardness rocker are used by manufacturers in order to assess with accuracy the hardness of a paint film after a certain length of time.

Hardwall plasters Gypsum plasters of the retarded hemihydrate type are commonly known as hardwall platers, but the term is not precise and is sometimes applied also to certain plasters of the anhydrous group.

Hardwoods All timbers obtained from broad-leaved trees are called hardwoods and nearly all the coniferous trees are classed as softwoods, but certain broad-leaved trees such as the horse chestnut, the willow, the poplar, etc., are actually quite soft. Generally speaking, softwoods are timbers of fairly rapid growth, while hardwoods grow more slowly and consequently have a finer, closer grain. Sometimes, when hardwoods such as mahogany and oak are to be painted, difficulty is experienced due to the closeness of the grain resisting the penetration of the primer, which results in poor adhesion. For this reason the usual practice is to thin the primer with additional white spirit, in the proportions recommended by the manufacturer, to help it to penetrate.

Harmony A scheme or colour combination which presents a pleasing appearance because it is composed of colours which lie close to one another on the colour circle and are used in their proper tonal order.

Hawk The name given over a wide part of the country to the handboard used in making-good defective plaster. See also *Handboard*.

Haziness A term sometimes used for blooming.

Health and Safety at Work, etc., Act 1974 The legislation which came into force on 1st April 1975 to secure the health, safety and welfare of everybody in Great Britain engaged in any form of work, and to protect all members of the general public against risks to their health and safety which might be caused by the activities of persons engaged in work.

When legislation covering working conditions was first introduced in Britain in 1802 it was concerned solely with the welfare of apprentices in the textile industries, and its development from that date onward has been a very gradual and piecemeal process. Building operations did not appear in statutory legislation until 1895 and even then it was limited to the mere requirement that any accident occurring during the construction or repair of a building exceeding 30 feet in height should be notified to the authorities. One by one, regulations were passed governing certain aspects of specific trades and occupations, such as the use of woodworking machinery, etc., one example relating to painting and decorating being the Lead Paint (Protection against Poisoning) Act of 1926. The Factories Acts themselves were continually amended and widened in their scope; for instance, the 1948 Act empowered the Minister of Labour and National Service to introduce special regulations for safety and health, which led to the introduction of the Building (Safety, Health and Welfare) Regulations, and these in turn were extended in the 1961 Act to form the Construction Regulations which covered not only building but also works of engineering construction (i.e. civil engineering) which had hitherto been excluded.

The Health and Safety at Work Act of 1974 marked an entirely new concept in safety legislation, because it governs the activities of every company, every firm and every individual person employed in any kind of work whatsoever. Its powers are very far-reaching. In addition to providing for the safety and welfare of workers and of third parties affected by the operations of any workpeople, it controls the possession and use of dangerous substances, it prevents the emission of harmful and offensive materials into the atmosphere, it lays a duty upon the designers, manufacturers and importers of any articles and substances used in working processes to ensure the complete safety of such equipment and substances, it provides for the maintenance of an employment advisory service, and it clearly defines the law relating to building regulations. To implement the Act, two bodies were established, namely the Health and Safety Commission and the Health and Safety Executive.

The significant feature of the Act is that it involves everyone; it affects all employers and employees at every level. Directors and managers of firms are held personally responsible if a breach of the Act occurs as a result of their neglect or their consent, and similarly any employee who fails to observe the regulations is also personally liable and open to prosecution. This is not always fully understood. Some operatives are still under the impression that when statutory regulations are broken the responsibility lies with the employer alone, but this is not the case, and the penalties are heavy.

Under the terms of the Act every employer is required to formulate a written policy code, detailing the activities and operations of the firm as they affect both the firm's employees and the general public, and every employee must be in possession of a copy of the document and be fully aware of its contents.

Heartwood The older, inner part of a tree trunk, impregnated with colouring matter, oil, tannin, resin and mineral by-products. Heartwood markings are the grain markings seen when the log is sawn along its length from bark to bark. In graining, the heartwood is mainly employed in situations where it would be used by the woodworker, such as the rail of doors, etc.

Heat-resisting paints To some extent the term is self-explanatory, as it obviously implies paint which will withstand the effects of heat, but the actual choice of a heat-resisting paint for any particular purpose will depend upon the conditions which prevail and the temperature range likely to be encountered. The temperatures reached in radiators and pipes fed by normal hot water heating systems are not as a rule sufficiently high to cause serious difficulty, provided the finish is elastic enough to cope with the expansion and contraction of the metal and that soft undercoats are avoided. The temperatures reached in steam radiators and pipes are much higher and are more likely to present difficulty, and the painting of industrial premises includes the treatment of such items as metal smoke stacks, flues, exhausts, boilers, furnace installations and coke ovens which may reach an extremely high temperature, often in combination with other highly corrosive and destructive conditions.

Domestic hot-water radiators usually operate at temperatures below 82°C (180°F) which is within the range of heat tolerance of ordinary decorative paint products. The radiators should for preference be primed with a chromate metal primer, after which a normal undercoating and alkyd gloss finish is perfectly adequate and presents no problems.

Heat-resisting paints can be classed under three headings as follows:

(i) Paints withstanding temperatures of up to 93°C (200°F)

After priming with a chromate metal primer, a normal alkyd resin finish is satisfactory, but ordinary undercoating paints should not be used; it is better to use the gloss paint for undercoating as well as for finishing. Some colours will actually withstand temperatures of up to 120°C (250°F) but this cannot be guaranteed, and in any case there is likely to be some loss of gloss and discolouration as the temperature approaches 93°C when white or light-coloured paints are used.

(ii) Paints withstanding temperatures of between 93°C (200°F) and 260°C (500°F)

Within this range, in ordinary circumstances the usual practice today is to use aluminium paint applied directly to the bare metal (the metal having first been thoroughly cleaned of course). There may, however, be some difficulties. The results may be satisfactory if the temperature remains constant, but less so if the temperature is subject to variations; furthermore the resistance of the paint is impaired by long exposure to a high temperature, and the finish may fail if the heat is withdrawn and moisture condenses on the surface. It should also be noted that when metallic paints are used on pipes and radiators they reduce the emissivity to a considerable extent; in the case of steam pipes carrying live steam to various parts of a factory this can be an advantage by cutting down heat losses, but in the case of hot-water systems for heating domestic and public buildings it can lead to a marked reduction in the efficiency of the radiators and heating pipes. When unusual conditions prevail, alternative paint treatments are available. These include (a) Acrylic-resin based paints which in certain colourings may withstand temperatures of up to 150°C (300°F) for fairly long periods without deterioration, even in the presence of severe conditions such as on smoke stacks exposed to acid fumes. (b) Heat-resisting bituminous enamels in black, aluminium and certain colours, which withstand temperatures of up to 260°C (500°F) and are used for boilers, smoke stacks, and for asbestos cement flue-pipes subjected to rapid attack by acid condensates. (c) Cyclized rubber paints which, suitably pigmented, will withstand temperatures of 200°C (400°F), although yellowing occurs after 120°C (250°F) has been reached. Other possible alternatives are graphite in sodium silicate paint, up to 150°C (300°F) and red iron oxide/zinc chromate paint, up to 260°C (500°F).

(iii) Paints withstanding temperatures above 260°C (500°F) and up to 540°C (1000°F)

Within this range there are heat-resisting paints based upon inorganic media such as silicone resins or butyl titanate resins pigmented with earth colours, aluminium powder, etc. The resins decompose when heated and leave a firmly adherent film of inert residues of silica or titanium oxide. These paints have great resistance to heat but a less certain resistance to weather; they may withstand up to 315°C (600°F) on exterior surfaces such as chimney stacks, and up to 540°C (1000°F) on interior surfaces. Their resistance to atmospheric corrosion is increased if they are pigmented with zinc instead of aluminium, but this reduces their heat resistance from 540°C to 400°C (1000°F to 750°F). It is essential, if they are to be efficient, that the metal to which they are applied should be perfectly clean, and they need to be brought to a temperature of 260°C (500°F) very shortly after application in order to cure them. They withstand a constant temperature better than a fluctuating one, and it is found that when they have been exposed to heat for any length of time they are liable to break down rapidly should the heat be withdrawn due to a temporary closing down of the plant.

Heavy bodied A term applied to a material of thick consistency or to a very viscous material, generally one that leaves a thick coating when dry. Sometimes the term is used in a misleading and incorrect sense to refer to a material of high opacity.

Heavy spar The mineral found extensively in many parts of the world from which barytes (barium sulphate) is obtained. See *Barytes*.

Helmet See *Safety helmet*.

Hemihydrate plasters Plaster derived from the rock gypsum, and obtained by crushing the rock and heating it at a temperature of 170°C (338°F), a process which drives off three-quarters of the water of crystallization. The plaster thus formed is commonly known as plaster of Paris. When mixed with water it sets or hydrates very quickly, the water combining chemically with it to replace the crystalline water driven off during manufacture so that the plaster reverts to its original composition. Plaster of Paris sets so quickly that its use is limited mostly to the pointing of holes and cracks, but if a retarding agent is incorporated during manufacture a form of plaster suitable for skimming large surfaces and yet capable of setting very rapidly is produced; this is known as retarded hemihydrate plaster, often called "hardwall' plaster. Plaster of Paris is classified in BS 1191 as belonging to Class A; retarded hemihydrate plaster belongs to Class B.

In common with all gypsum plasters, hemihydrate plasters expand slightly when setting and are chemically inert. Theoretically they contain nothing which would set up an unfavourable reaction with any oil paint which is applied upon them, but it must be remembered that they may be contaminated by alkaline materials brought forward from the backing, and that sand and lime may have been added to them by the plasterer; they should therefore be tested for alkalinity before any paint is applied.

Heraldry The science connected with the correct use of armorial bearings; hence, *heraldic charges*, the conventionalized symbols used in heraldry; *heraldic colours*, the colours used in heraldry, known by their Norman-French names, viz., azure (blue), gules (red), purpure (purple), sable (black), vert (green); *heraldic painting*, that part of the decorator's work concerned with the representation of heraldic devices; and so on.

Hessian A strong coarse cloth made from hemp or jute. For a long time it was used chiefly by the decorator for its strength, both as a highly durable textile wallcovering in situations where the finished appearance of the hanging was only a minor factor, and also as the foundation for a painted finish where the wall surfaces needed strengthening before any treatment was applied. Eventually, however, it was introduced as a decorative hanging, the coarseness of the weave being turned to advantage by mounting the fabric on a stout paper backing so that the colour of the paper brought the weave and texture into prominence. Hessian is now produced as a luxury product in very attractive forms, its decorative qualities combined with its durability making it a useful material for public work—hotels, offices, galleries, etc.—as well as for domestic work.

Hiding power The opacity of a material, its ability to obliterate the surface to which it is applied.

High alumina cement Also known as *Ciment fondu*, q.v.

Hog hair Animal hair, generally obtained from the neck, shoulders and back of the wild boar, used in brush manufacture. Because of certain outstanding features, such as its taper, curve, serrated surface and flagged end, it is a particularly useful filling for paint brushes. See also *Bristle*.

Holding primer A primer formulated to provide a temporary protective coating to steelwork which has been blast-cleaned, especially in situations where the metal is exposed to severe atmospheric or chemical attack and where special heavy-duty coatings are to be applied. It is most important, if the blast-cleaning is to be effective, that the steel should be given a quick-drying protective coating as soon as possible.

There is often considerable delay between the time that the metal is blast-cleaned and the completion of the painting system, and the newly cleaned steel is very liable to rusting if exposed to a damp atmosphere. The holding primer gives the required protection and is designed to dry and harden quickly, so that the metal is shielded from damage during handling and transport and during the course of erection. It must be recognized, however, that the holding primer is only a temporary measure and is in no way to be regarded as a replacement or alternative to the normal priming paint. It is essential that as soon as practicable a suitable inhibitive primer should be applied.

Holidays A colloquial term for misses or areas left uncoated with paint due to carelessness on the part of the operative.

Surprisingly, the word "holiday" is now officially recognized as an accurate term in modern technical literature. In a British Standard issued in 1985 (BS 3900: Part F 11: 1985) gaps in a paint coating are described as "accidental holidays" and gaps deliberately introduced in a coating on a test-piece are described as "artificial holidays".

Horse hair Animal hair obtained from the manes or tails of horses and used in brush manufacture. It is inferior to bristle in every way, possessing neither the stiff root end, the fine taper, the flagged tip, the resistance to water nor the resilience and springiness of hog hair. It is used as an adulterant or substitute, being mixed with other hair, such as bristle, in order to produce a cheaper brush, but brushes containing more than a small proportion of horse hair are too soft and floppy to be of much use.

Hose Flexible tubing through which gases or liquids can be conveyed to a given point, for example, the fluid hose and the air-hose in spray equipment, the hose feeding a flammable gas to a blowtorch, etc. In some cases it is desirable that hose should be colour coded to prevent confusion; very often in spray equipment the fluid hose is brown or black and the air-hose red, and when oxyacetylene equipment is being used for flame cleaning, etc., red hose is used for acetylene and black hose for the oxygen.

Hose swivel end A device fitted to the fluid hose in airless spraying equipment, to provide freedom of movement to the gun which would otherwise be restricted by the stiff and rigid nature of the hose. The swivel end is fitted between the end of the hose and the gun. The inclusion of a swivel end is essential in situations where the spraying involves scaffold work or where limitations of space mean that extra mobility is needed to manoeuvre the gun.

Hot spraying A spray painting process in which paint or lacquer is heated just before application in order to reduce its viscosity, so that in effect heat is used instead of the addition of volatile solvents in order to bring the paint to spraying consistency.

Several advantages over normal cold spraying methods are claimed for the process. Heated paint has improved flow characteristics, giving a smoother finish, and is independent of fluctuation in atmospheric conditions since the temperature and the viscosity of the material are controlled. The solvent loss from the material is much greater—up to 80 percent in hot spraying compared with some 20 percent in cold spraying—so that the applied paint film has a very high solid content and therefore gives greater build, with consequent saving of costs if required. In addition, the applied film regains its viscosity so rapidly as to reduce the tendency for sags and runs to form, there is less tendency for orange peeling to occur since there is less solvent to be expelled from the film, and the coverage of surface imperfections is improved since the lower solvent content means that there is less shrinkage in the film.

There are also certain distinct economies to be considered, especially when an air-propelled spraying system is in use; there is obviously a saving on the amount of thinners used, but in addition there is a significant saving of paint, since heated paint requires less air for its atomization and consequently there is a marked reduction of overspray and spray rebound.

Several types of hot spray equipment are available, including portable hot airless-spray units, which combine the advantages of normal airless spraying with the reduction of viscosity obtained by the hot-spray process. This is a factor of great importance in industrial painting as it enables heavy material of very high viscosity to be sprayed in even the coldest weather conditions.

Hot surfaces To the painter the term "hot" is applied to any surface which is unusually absorbent or porous.

Hot wire spraying A term sometimes applied to metal spraying, a process in which steelwork is sprayed with a molten metal, such as zinc or aluminium, in order to receive protection from corrosion. The metal to be sprayed is drawn into the form of wire which is fed into a specially designed pistol operated by gas and oxygen. While zinc and aluminium are the two metals most usually sprayed there are several other metals, such as tin, copper, brass, cadmium, etc., which may be used for certain specific purposes, and in fact any metal which can be drawn into wire and melted by oxy-gas equipment can be sprayed.

In the treatment of structural steel the process is mainly used for spraying the steel before erection, but it can also be used for steelwork *in situ* and in fact several important contracts have been carried out by this method.

Although hot wire spraying is a specialized trade and is not carried out by painters and decorators, it is still a matter of interest and concern to them, as the durability of the coating is enhanced if it is painted immediately after application and repainted at regular intervals. The sprayed deposit has a matt surface ideally suited to the reception of paint. See *Metal spraying*.

Hot-air paint stripping A method of removing dry paint films by directing a stream of hot air upon them to soften them. It has many advantages over the traditional methods of stripping; unlike burning-off with blowtorches or blowlamps, there is no naked flame involved and consequently fire hazards are eliminated, a very important factor in high-risk areas; and it is quicker and much cleaner than the use of chemical paint removers.

The process was originally developed in Holland, and the equipment consists of a blower which feeds a current of air along a flexible hose and into a heater gun containing an electrical element, so that the temperature of the air is raised immediately before it is directed on to the painted surface. A control on the handle enables the temperature to be adjusted to any level between 20° and 600°C. It is of very sturdy construction, suitable for the rough usage associated with site conditions over prolonged periods, and it normally operates on a 220–240 voltage, but a 110-volt model is also available. Since it was introduced, various other models have appeared on the market, some of which are less robust and resemble an electric hair-dryer in appearance and weight; some operate at a higher temperature, up to 800°C in certain cases.

One feature of the process is that the paint film tends to lift away in clean dry strips, instead of clinging to the wooden surface in a melted and sticky form as with normal burning-off methods; for this reason the stripping operation is much cleaner, there is less risk of the surface being damaged by the scrapers, and the possibility of scorch marks on the wood is almost entirely eliminated. These advantages help to offset the fact that the process is slower than normal burning-off.

Properly handled, the hot-air stripper can be used on window frames with less risk of cracking the glass than with the blowtorch. On delicate work and for the restoration of historic buildings the hot-air stripper is especially useful. Restoration work is simplified because small areas of paintwork can be removed selectively without damage to the surrounding paintwork.

Hue Another name for colour, e.g. red, orange, yellow, green, blue, etc.

Hungarian ash A beautiful silky wood, a little deeper and richer than common ash, with a fine curly grain and strong highlights and shades. It is grained in raw umber and raw sienna on a ground of pale cream.

Hungry The painter speaks of a hungry surface when he means that the absorption of the surface has not been completely satisfied by the previous coats of paint so that it appears patchy and uneven.

Hydrate A term used in two different senses. Used as a noun, a "hydrate" is a compound of water with another compound or element. Used as a verb, "to hydrate" is to combine a substance with water. Hence, "hydration" means the adding of water to a substance.

Hydrated ferric oxide The chemical name for rust, the product of the corrosion of iron and steel.

Hydrated lime Lime which has been slaked (i.e. combined chemically with water) and then dried and ground to a powder.

Hydraulic A word which relates to water in movement, e.g. "hydraulic cement", "hydraulic platform", etc. See below.

Hydraulic cement A cement which will set and harden under water (not by air).

Hydraulic piston pump A type of pump used to pressurize the paint in airless spraying. It can be driven by electric motor or, less frequently, by petrol engine. The piston action differs from that of a diaphragm pump in that it puts oil under pressure instead of using compressed air, is self-contained, only needs to be plugged into the power socket, and is very silent in operation and therefore highly suitable for use in hospitals, schools and public buildings.

Hydraulic plasters These are a type of lime plaster rarely used as interior finishing plasters but sometimes used as exterior plasters or stucco. They may be strongly alkaline in content, and can be very destructive to paint.

Hydraulic platform A form of hydraulically operated access equipment, consisting of a working platform on the end of a crane-like boom, the boom being mounted on a vehicle turntable which can be swung around into any desired position. It is used for the painting of overhead work in busy streets, tall masts, awkwardly situated gable walls, the underside of bridges, and many other locations where painting work is essential and yet is of such short duration that the erection of a normal scaffold would be hopelessly uneconomic.

Hydro-additive paints Primers, undercoatings and finishes which have been developed for application to surfaces on which moisture is present. The principle involved is that if certain organic materials are added to paint the surface tension of the wet paint film is reduced; when this occurs the paint is able to displace the water present on the surface to which it is applied and is able to spread over the surface in its stead. The organic material used for the purpose is stearine amine, derived from stearic acid. It should be noted that these paints are only effective in the case of surface moisture; they cannot function and are not intended to function on wood or any other material which is saturated with water, and the effect of applying them to such a material is exactly what would occur with a conventional paint system, namely that there would be no possibility of adhesion and the paint film would be forced off by the pressure of the contained moisture.

Hydrofluoric acid The type of acid used for glass embossing and glass etching, and also a constituent of certain proprietary brands of stone-cleaning fluid. Because of its solvent action upon glass it needs to be stored in gutta-percha or lead containers.

Hydrofluoric acid is a highly dangerous substance, especially as the hazards connected with its use are not immediately apparent. It can cause skin burns to occur without giving any preliminary warning pain to the user; it can also penetrate unbroken skin and can cause serious bone damage unless prompt remedial action is taken. When used indoors for etching purposes, the room must be well ventilated; when used for any purpose, either indoors or outdoors, suitable protective clothing (e.g. rubber gloves, eye protection, etc.) should be worn. Any accidental splash of acid upon the skin must be immediately treated by copiously swabbing with clean water, and skilled medical attention must be obtained as soon as possible.

Hydrometer An instrument for measuring the density or specific gravity of a liquid.

Hygrometer An instrument for measuring the humidity of air. It is sometimes used to assess the moisture content of a wall in order to determine whether or not the surface can safely be painted. To do this, a sealed and insulated box is mounted on the wall with a hygrometer fastened to the box face standing opposite the wall; several hours must elapse before the reading is taken, to allow the humidity of the airspace to reach equilibrium.

Hygroscopic A word used to describe a substance which takes up water very readily; for instance, common salt is noticeably hygroscopic, and quicklime from which builder's lime is produced is extremely hygroscopic; hence "hygroscopicity"—see below.

Hygroscopicity The property of taking up moisture from, and giving out moisture to, the atmosphere. The term has a bearing upon various aspects of a painter's work, such as, for example, when deliquescent salts are present in a building and, being hygroscopic, cause the surface to appear permanently damp or to become damp during spells of humid weather.

Hypalon paint A chemically resistant paint similar to neoprene paint (q.v.) except that it is available in a wider range of colours.

I

Identification colours Colours used to denote the function of the object painted with them—e.g., the colours used to call attention to a hazard, such as a dangerous piece of mechanism—or to identify the purpose or the contents of conduits, cables or pipes in a building. See also *Colour coding*.

Ilmenite A lustrous black substance, a titaniferous iron ore, which is the principal source of titanium oxide.

Ilmenite black A black pigment derived from the mineral ilmenite and used in the preparation of fillers and undercoatings for the painting of machinery, motor cars, etc. It is also sometimes added to other paints to improve their resistance to heat.

Imitation glass embossing A method of obtaining a matt finish in glass gilding in order to imitate the appearance of gold upon glass that has been etched. It is produced by pencilling in with clear varnish those parts of the lettering or ornament which are to appear dull, and allowing the varnish to dry before proceeding to apply the gold leaf.

Imitation leather The appearance of tooled leather can be imitated in a paint treatment by the use of plastic paint, which is manipulated in various ways to produce the desired pattern and emboss and is then grounded out with bronze paint. A scumble of umber glaze is then applied and the surface wiped with a soft cloth to expose the metallic paint on the raised portions of the work.

Imitation leather wallpapers Embossed papers coated with metallic paints and scumbles to suggest antique leather hangings, and ranging in quality from cheap leatherettes to high class hand-scumbled productions. Now superseded by the modern range of vinyl wallcoverings.

Imitation stone paints Paints intended to present the texture and appearance of stone. They consist of an aggregate of granulated stone or silica sand held in suspension in an oil varnish medium or a latex emulsion, and are applied in thick coatings; any attempt to thin them down leads to a patchy and uneven finish. Their spreading capacity is low, and when a second coat is applied it becomes still lower because its application is hampered by the texture produced by the first coat. The realistic appearance of the coating is enhanced if the paint is scored, while it is drying, with a blunt steel tool such as a screwdriver to represent the joints in stonework.

Impact resistance The extent to which a paint film can withstand a sudden blow.

Impasto In mural painting and decorative work, the technique of applying paint very thickly.

Impenetrable varnish A term sometimes given to sealers such as stop-tar knotting, etc., which are used to prevent such materials as bitumen, tar, creosote and certain colours from bleeding through and spoiling a newly applied paint film.

Impervious Impenetrable; not allowing passage or entrance; for instance, when we speak of a film of paint as being impervious to moisture we mean that it will not allow moisture to pass through.

Impregnating varnishes Varnishes used in some industrial processes, and designed to penetrate the material to which they are applied; for example, electrical insulation varnishes designed to impregnate the cotton fabric covering of coil or armature windings.

Impregnation The saturation of a substance or a surface with some other material; for example, we speak of a surface which is heavily charged with machine oil or grease, thereby presenting difficulties in painting, as being *impregnated* with oil. Sometimes building materials such as timber, etc., are impregnated with fluids for preservative or fire-resisting purposes, the fluid being forced in under pressure in order to penetrate deeply.

Imprisoned moisture Free moisture which is trapped beneath the surface of such a material as wood or plaster by an impervious film of paint and which can only escape by forcing the film away from the surface.

Incompatibility Materials which are unable to subsist together are said to be incompatible. There are many instances of paint materials failing to blend together satisfactorily, due to the incompatibility of certain types of media or solvents; for this reason, it is generally unwise to mix together different brands of paint, lacquer or emulsion paint.

Indene resins Synthetic resins similar to coumarone resins.

Independent scaffold A scaffold used chiefly for painting and decorating and general repair work on existing buildings (although also used for masons' work on premises in course of erection) which does not depend upon the building for support. An independent scaffold used by painters generally consists of two rows of standards or a series of prefabricated frames with the inner row placed as close to the building as possible allowing for projections such as cornices, etc.; the standards or frames are connected longitudinally with ledgers upon which transoms are coupled to support the working platform. Although no load is carried by the building, it is essential that the scaffold should be adequately tied in to the building throughout its length.

Indian ink A waterproof ink consisting of a dispersion of carbon black in water with an organic binder, and used by decorators in the preparation of working drawings and perspective drawings for decorative schemes.

Indian red A deep red oxide pigment tending towards purple-brown, which is prepared by the calcination of crystalline ferrous sulphate. It possesses good staining power, spreading power and opacity, is permanent and will mix with all other pigments without either affecting them or being affected by them.

Indian yellow Otherwise called puree. A pigment prepared from animal sources and now no longer made. (**NLC**)

Indigo A fine rich blue pigment of subdued tone, formerly obtained from vegetable sources but now produced artificially; used in decorative work, mural painting, etc.

Induction heating An industrial finishing technique. A method of raising the temperature of a painted object in order to speed up the drying time of the paint on the same principles as those employed in stoving processes. The painted article is placed within a series of copper coils, and an electric current passed through the coils produces a magnetic field which induces a secondary current in the article itself, causing it to heat up very rapidly.

Industrial finishing Generally taken to mean the painting of machine-made articles under controlled conditions at a factory, as opposed to the painting of structures and buildings carried out on the site. It includes many techniques which could not be applied to the painting of structures.

Industrial painting The painting of industrial premises, once regarded by the painter and decorator as being largely unskilled work but now recognized as a highly organized business covering a vast range of interesting and important operations.

Industrial paints Usually understood to mean paints formulated for factory use on machine-made products, as opposed to decorators' paints intended for use on the site.

Industrial spirit Similar to methylated spirit; like methylated spirit, it is denatured to prevent its being used for drinking, but not to such an extent as to interfere with its technical properties; it is available only for manufacturing purposes.

Inert Lacking the power of reacting chemically with other substances; for example, "an inert pigment", a pigment which can be mixed with other pigments or paint materials without affecting them or being affected by them; "an inert plaster", a plaster which does not exert any chemical action upon the superimposed paint; and so on.

Inflammable A word with exactly the same meaning as "flammable", to indicate something which can be ignited or set on fire. Nowadays the word "flammable" is preferred, and "inflammable" is not often used in technical literature. See *Flammable*.

Infra-red stoving A technique used in industrial finishing, whereby heat is transferred to a painted article by radiation from a hot surface in order to accelerate the drying. The term indicates the location of this type of radiation in the complete electromagnetic spectrum, just below visible red, the wavelength of infra-red rays being beyond that of the visible spectrum.

Ingrain papers Wallpapers, commonly known as "wood-chips", the characteristic of which is their "oatmeal" or "woolly" texture. They consist of stout substantial pulp papers into which wood chips and fibres of various kinds have been introduced during manufacture in order to provide the texture. Colour is sometimes added during manufacture, or the paper may be coated with emulsion paint, etc., after hanging.

Inhibit To "inhibit" means to hinder some process, to delay it, or to restrain some action from taking place; from this, the words "inhibitive" and "inhibitor" are derived.

Inhibitive pigments Pigments which, when used in direct contact with iron or steel, inhibit or retard corrosion. Included among such pigments are zinc chromate, zinc dust, red lead, white lead, lead chromate, basic lead sulphates, etc.

Inhibitors Materials added in small quantities to compounds of various kinds in order to arrest or delay the onset of a chemical reaction. Examples relating to the painting trade include anti-oxidants incorporated into paints to prevent them from skinning in the containers, and arsenic or antimony compounds used as restrainers in acid pickling solutions to prevent the metal from being unduly attacked.

Inlay A decoration formed by inserting different materials into a groundwork and leaving the surface level. For example, in cabinet making the term is properly applied to the process of scooping shallow holes in the surface of solid wood and filling them with contrasting materials, but it is also used to refer to veneered work where the thin veneer is laid in separate pieces, a decorative pattern being produced by arranging the pieces so that the grain markings are in varying directions, or by using pieces of assorted colourings. In painters' work inlaid effects are produced in various ways. For instance, a technique very similar to that of the cabinet maker's can be used when woodgrain wallpapers are hung with bands of contrasting colour or grain pattern inserted. On the other hand, the representation of inlaid effects in graining involves a very different technique whereby all the work of one particular colour or direction is grained, fixed with varnish, and allowed to dry before the next stage is proceeded with, each colour being treated separately.

Inorganic A term often seen in the technical literature relating to paints and decorative products. It refers to substances and compounds that are of mineral origin, as opposed to those arising from natural living growth. Inorganic chemistry is the study of all the elements and compounds other than carbon, as opposed to organic chemistry which is the study of carbon compounds.

Inorganic zinc silicate A two-pack coating in which a zinc pigment, e.g. zinc dust, reacts with an inorganic silicate solution. It can be used as a primer upon which other paint coatings are applied, or it can be applied in several coats as a self-finish. It is particularly valuable for use in wet situations such as bridges, marine structures, and immersed pipes. A very high standard of surface preparation is required if satisfactory results are to be achieved.

In-registered duplex papers Duplex wallpapers in which the embossing is in register with (i.e. coincides with) the printed pattern.

Insecticidal paint A paint containing an additive which forms a bloom on the surface and which destroys any insect that alights upon it, but which is harmless to children, domestic pets, and livestock. The additive does not affect the performance of the paint, which can be washed repeatedly without reducing the efficiency of the insecticidal substance.

Insecticide A preparation for killing insects. Insecticides are sometimes incorporated into paints so that the dried film will be lethal to house flies, bluebottles, cockroaches and other insect pests; these coatings are useful not only in domestic properties but also in restaurants, hospitals, farm buildings, etc., where the frequent use of an insecticide spray in the atmosphere is either objectionable or inconvenient. Some of these paints are formulated to remain active for a long time by means of the insecticide content being gradually discharged at a controlled rate to form a crystalline bloom on the surface of the coating. There are also preservative fluids available for the treatment of structural timbers and for other constructions which for various reasons cannot be maintained by regular painting, and these give protection against the attacks of wood-boring insects, exterminating pests such as the furniture beetle and the deathwatch beetle by destroying the eggs, larvae and beetles, and preventing re-infestation by making the wood unpalatable to larvae.

Insert container A device used in air-propelled spray painting equipment consisting of a thin light metal vessel which is placed inside a pressure feed tank; the paint is placed in the insert container instead of being poured directly into the tank. The use of these containers presents many advantages; it makes the cleaning out of the tank a much simpler and quicker operation, makes the process of changing from one colour to another very much easier, and allows batches of paint to be prepared and strained in advance so that no time is wasted when the tank becomes empty and requires replenishing.

Insignia Award in Technology The Insignia Award in Technology is the premier Award of the City and Guilds of London Institute, and is a supreme and unequalled hallmark of distinction. It was established in 1952 and was immediately recognized as an exciting new concept in educational achievement.

The immediate post-war years saw the beginning of a huge and rapid expansion in higher education. Not only were existing institutions enlarged but many new ones were founded; these included various new universities and several colleges of advanced technology which later became polytechnics; student numbers increased enormously, and the training for many occupations and professions which had hitherto been to a great extent work-centred now became totally college-based. A natural consequence of this expansion was that a much wider range of courses was offered, and there was considerable extension in the provision of courses concerned with business studies, management and administration. It was desirable that the training of supervisory staff should be properly organized to increase and develop production in the quickly-changing conditions of world industry, but there was one inherent drawback. It is axiomatic that in any form of industry where production depends on the deployment of human skills and techniques the people most likely to be successful at management level are those who themselves possess a sound and thorough background of practical training. Of course, practical experience alone is not sufficient; effective management demands many other skills and attributes, and it is probably true that not enough attention was paid to the development of managerial skills in the past. But exercises in simulated work-situations are no substitute for real practical knowledge and training, and college-based courses run the risk of being theoretical and unreal, especially if they are run by people with no first-hand managerial experience in industry.

The City and Guilds of London Institute has always been the pre-eminent body in advancing technical and scientific education, and the Institute at this stage had the happy inspiration of devising a scheme which would give due recognition to people whose original training, although thorough, lay largely in non-academic areas, but whose subsequent work record and studies combined with outstanding personal qualities had marked them out as being suited for positions of the highest responsibility. The relevance and importance of the Award become increasingly apparent as time goes by, as a means of identifying those who are capable of making a real and positive contribution to industrial progress and efficiency in today's highly competitive social and economic world. It is impossible to compare it with the qualifications conferred by professional bodies since its emphasis lies upon individual competence and the successful application of knowledge to the needs of industry.

Candidates for the Award have to show that they have achieved the highest level of technical excellence and that they have proven ability to initiate technical advances in their own particular sphere of work. These advances, moreover, must be linked with practical applications to industrial efficiency, in areas such as design, safety, cost-effectiveness, etc. In addition to technical excellence, evaluation for the Award takes into consideration the candidate's education, training, background, and personal characteristics, attitudes and interests; it looks at the nature and level of the posts held by the candidate and expects to see in them the evidence of continual progress and increasing responsibility; it assesses the candidate's ability to accept responsibility and to exercise leadership, and is looking for personal characteristics of the highest order; it requires in the candidate the capacity to discuss technical problems in the chosen field of technology in such a way as to arrive at their solution.

There are three steps leading to the Award: (i) registration, (ii) the submission of a thesis or a report on a project in which the candidate has been personally implicated, and (iii) a searching interview. The whole process of testing and assessment at every stage is extremely rigorous and the failure rate is very high. If the standards were not maintained at the very highest level, the status and value of the Award would be rendered worthless. There are no age limits for entry; it is recognized that candidates below the age of 25 will probably not have had sufficiently wide experience to be able to undertake the work, but each application is judged on its own merits and candidates below 25 years of age are not debarred from entering.

Successful candidates are presented with a Warrant which specifies the subject area in which the Award has been gained. By order of the Privy Council, holders of the Award are entitled to use the designatory letters C.G.I.A. after their name.

Information about the Award and the regulations concerning application can be obtained by writing to The Secretary (Senior Awards), City and Guilds of London Institute, 76 Portland Place, London, W1N 4AA. The Institute has provided the Award as a means whereby people with suitable aptitudes and qualities, who have the ambition and determination to succeed, can have their ability recognized and be given the opportunity of progressing to the highest positions in industry, whatever their original background may have been. Readers who want to make their mark in the world are strongly advised to consider the advantages of working for the Award. There is nothing to lose and a very great deal to gain by asking for further details.

Insoluble The word "insoluble" means "incapable of being dissolved"; hence the word "insolubility" used in relation to a material which cannot be dissolved. An interesting example in the painting trade is provided by the material known as shellac, which is derived from the secretion of insects. Shellac is soluble in methylated spirit, but is insoluble in turpentine, petroleum spirit or oil. When a quantity of shellac is dissolved in methylated spirit it forms the material known as "knotting". Knotting is applied as a thin coating over the knots in timber prior to painting, and the methylated spirit very quickly evaporates when thus exposed to the air. The hardened shellac now acts as an insoluble sealer coat over the knots, and this prevents the natural solvents in the resinous knots from bleeding into the paint film and causing it to soften.

Insulating board Also known as "softboard". A fibre building board of cellular composition with good thermal insulation and sound-absorption properties. It is made from a fibrous pulp similar to that used in the manufacture of hardboard, but instead of being compressed into thin sheets it is only lightly squeezed between rollers prior to being dried off in a drying tunnel. It is supplied either in large sheets or in the form of tiles in thicknesses ranging between 12 mm and 25 mm. Wallboard, which is similar in composition but is not so thick, is supplied in large sheets, and there are also acoustic boards in the form of small panels made with insulating board which sometimes has other materials added and is sometimes perforated to increase its sound absorption.

Insulating boards are sometimes supplied in ready-decorated form, either with a factory-applied coating or with a laminate facing; sometimes, however, they need decorating after fixing, and because of their extremely porous nature it is difficult to achieve a good standard of finish. Because of the spongy open texture of the board a thin sealer coat is needed as a primer. When the finish is to be emulsion paint, a thinned coating of emulsion makes a satisfactory primer; in the case of a painted finish a suitable primer/sealer should be used, but sometimes for the sake of economy a coat of thin emulsion paint is used to prime the surface. Whenever emulsion paint is used it is important that any nail-heads should be touched in with zinc chromate to prevent rusting.

Insulating varnish A type of varnish used in electrical work for the treatment of coils to prevent the entry of water, which would break down the insulation.

Insurance A means of securing, by the periodical payment of a premium, that compensation will be received for any loss, damage or injury which may be sustained. Compulsory forms of insurance are an integral feature of industrial life; e.g., an employer is legally required to provide insurance to compensate any employees who meet with a mishap, and to undertake third party insurance for the protection of members of the general public who may be injured as a result of the firm's activities; in addition to which an employer will insure the firm's premises, plant, equipment, etc., against theft, fire and damage. Both employers and employees are compelled to pay their contributions under the National Health Insurance scheme; any person whether an employer or employee who is the owner of a mechanically propelled vehicle is required to provide third party insurance for the compensation of any member of the general public involved in an incident which causes loss, mishap or injury, etc.

Intensity The purity of a colour, sometimes called the "saturation" or, in American terminology, the "chroma". The spectrum colours are the most intense; the intensity of a pigmentary colour is reduced or weakened if it is mixed with white, black, grey or another colour.

Interim payments Part payment while work is in progress. In the case of a bill of quantities contract, interim payments may be made at certain stages to pay an agreed percentage (usually 80 to 90 percent) of the work already completed; the extent of the work qualifying for the payment is determined by the quantity surveyor.

Interior decorator—interior designer Broadly speaking, these terms have the same meaning and both refer to a person capable of planning and implementing a complete decorative scheme in its broadest terms—complete, that is, in the sense of including all the design elements required in the premises, not only the colour scheme and the choice of paints and wallcoverings but also the provision of such items as partitioning, screening and suspended ceilings, the furniture, the carpets and other floor coverings, the soft furnishings such as curtains, drapes, cushions, etc., the lighting and its accessories, together with the additional ornamentation that completes the scheme such as the china, glass and silverware, the floral decoration and such features as aquaria, etc., and the provision of paintings, prints, graphics of various kinds, sculptures and other forms of artwork.

Within this broad range it is clear that many, if not all, practitioners choose to specialize in certain specific aspects of the work. Two categories immediately suggest themselves. There are some people, for instance, who operate a consultancy service and who practise solely as designers, whilst others offer a package service and will undertake actual labour on the site in addition to preparing the scheme. Within both these categories there are some people whose chief interest lies in the designing of hotels, restaurants and other licensed premises, others with a particular feeling for shopfitting or for the planning of offices and business premises, others who concentrate on domestic work, and so on. There are also those who specialize in period decoration and who, because of their scholarly knowledge of the historic styles of architecture and ornament, can faithfully reproduce the distinctive features of any particular era; and there are those who prefer to be in the forefront of fashion and whose taste is for innovative styles and techniques. Some practitioners like to specialize in the use of one particular medium and the techiques pertaining to it—for example, some may establish a reputation because of their facility with stained glass, with modelled work and moulded concrete or fibreglass, with inlaid and marquetry work, or any one of a host of other techniques.

For a long time the people who engaged in these activities were known as interior decorators, but many of them felt that the term was not sufficiently precise—and indeed there were those whose normal work was purely and simply that of the painter and decorator but who described themselves as interior decorators because it implied a certain superiority, appealing to snobbish instincts. Today those who undertake this highly skilled work prefer to describe themselves as interior designers, a term which clearly indicates the design elements and gives some suggestion of the factors involved. It is of course true that the work of the interior designer demands a long period of training covering a wide range of subjects, and calls for a high degree of professionalism in those who practise it. Nevertheless it should not be forgotten that the profession has its roots in painting and decorating. The interior designers' professional association is the British Institute of Interior Design. The Institute was incorporated in 1899 to take over and develop the work of an Institute which had been established in 1894 by a group of leading decorators and craftsmen of that period. The Institute has always relied very heavily on its painter and decorator members for its inspiration, its driving force and its financial support.

Interlacing A form of surface decoration in which a number of strands or ribands are interwoven to produce a symmetrical design, as in Celtic art.

Intermixing The act of mixing together, intermingling. In the painting trade, the term usually refers to the mixing together of two or more ready-mixed materials, such as when the colour of a paint is modified by adding a quantity of another colour. It is not a good idea, however, to intermix different brands of paint, as the media may react together unfavourably; even with paints of the same brand, unless it is particularly stated by the manufacturer that intermixing is permissible, such intermixing may lead to defects such as gelling, fading, etc., due to the incompatibility of the ingredients.

Internal mix gun A type of spray gun which mixes air and paint within the air cap and is used with small air compressors delivering a restricted volume of air at a comparatively low pressure. The gun is suitable for spraying such materials as multicolour paint; it is not suitable for paints containing abrasive particles nor for very quick drying materials.

Intumescent paints Fire-retarding paints of a type that contain certain chemicals which swell and char when heated, forming a layer of cellular non-flammable material which cuts off the supply of oxygen to the surface. See also *Fire-retarding paints*.

Invisible moisture Moisture which is always present and is diffused throughout the atmosphere. The amount of invisible moisture in the air is constantly varying, depending upon the temperature; when the air according to its temperature contains as much vapour as it can hold in invisible state it is said to be saturated, any further addition of vapour becoming visible as cloud, fog, mist, etc., or any drop of temperature causing the vapour to be condensed. See *Condensation*.

Iridescent finishes Industrial finishes which give the appearance of *shot silk*, the hues changing with variations in the contours of the painted surface and with variations in the direction of viewing. They are produced with dyestuffs giving a semi-transparent film, in conjunction with non-leafing varieties of aluminium paste or powder.

Iron A malleable tenacious metal, with the chemical symbol of Fe, used extensively in every walk of life. Its relevance to the painter takes two main forms. (i) Iron and steel (which is iron combined with carbon in various proportions) when used for structural purposes present considerable problems to the painter and the paint manufacturer due to the rapidity with which they corrode. (ii) A number of painters' pigments are derived from iron oxides; for example, red oxide, siennas, ochre, etc.

Isinglass A very pure form of gelatine prepared from the swimming bladders of certain kinds of fish, chiefly the sturgeon (from which Russian isinglass is produced) and the cod and the hake (from which North American isinglass is derived). When cooked in boiling water it forms an extremely strong jelly. It is used as a mordant in glass gilding in the proportions of a small pinch of isinglass to half a litre of boiling water. The mordant needs to be strained before use; otherwise, it may cause a cloudy film to occur between the gold and the glass.

Isocyanate A substance derived from the salts of cyanic acid which is present in certain kinds of polyurethane paint and which can produce a toxic vapour if the coatings are applied by spray. This health hazard is obviously much greater in vehicle painting and the furniture finishing trades, where spray application is the norm, than in painting and decorating work where brush application is the general rule. When, however, it is intended to spray such materials it is not sufficient for the operative to wear a respirator; the essential thing to prevent the operative from inhaling the substance is that the respirator must be of the type with a separate air supply.

Isomerized rubber See *Cyclized rubber.*

Isometric projection A method of projecting the plan and elevations of a room, building or other object in order to present a three-dimensional picture for use as a working drawing. The lines of the plan are drawn at an angle of 30° from the horizontal, vertical lines are projected on the same scale as the plan, and the whole of the work can be carried out with a 60° set square and a T square.

Italian walnut A variety of walnut, the characteristic features of which are its curly formation, close and well-defined mottle and broad bands of contrasting tone. It is usually grained in Vandyke brown and black on a ground of warm buff.

Italic alphabet A lower case alphabet of sloping characters, derived from a cursive style developed in Italy in the 16th century. It is a beautiful alphabet which is ideally suited to the technique of the writing pencil, and is particularly useful for anything in the nature of lengthy inscriptions, being a compressed style which occupies a comparatively small space.

Ivory The hard white substance of which the tusks of an elephant are composed. The term "Ivory white" is often used to describe a colour, and in this sense it suggests a delicate colour similar to the appearance of piano keys, deeper of tone than "off-white" and cooler than "cream", although the term is very vague. "Old ivory" is a much warmer colour, approximating to the deeper colour of antique ivory carvings.

Ivory black A fine artists' colour produced by calcining ivory chippings in airtight retorts. Although some is still prepared in this manner the term is now generally used to refer to the highest quality of bone black.

J

Jamb The side post of a doorway, window, etc.

Jamb duster A brush used for dusting preparatory to painting. See *Duster*.

Japan A glossy black enamel based on asphaltum and drying oils. See *Black Japan*.

Japan black The same as "Black Japan".

Japan drier A liquid drying agent, otherwise known as "terebine", q.v. (**NLC**)

Japan filler A composition which is used to fill shallow indentations and to produce a smooth level surface prior to painting. It consists either of materials such as slate powder, pumice powder or silica, ground in Japan gold size, or of paste white lead, whiting and Japan gold size. When hard it is rubbed down wet with pumice or waterproof sandpaper. The painting of machinery often involves the use of filler to level out the roughness of the castings, and Japan filler is very useful in this respect because it withstands vibration without loosening or crumbling.

Japan gold size Sometimes called "writers' gold size". A mordant or adhesive for gold leaf, consisting of a short oil varnish containing a high proportion of driers. It is used for the gilding of lettering, lining and ornamental work in which sharpness and clarity of outline are desirable features, and for any gilding which is to be done in situations where there is a possibility of dust or weather conditions affecting the work before the gold is applied. It can be obtained in various drying speeds, such as 1-hour size, 4-hour size, etc., the variation in drying time being achieved by adjusting the proportions of oil and driers; as a general rule, the longer the drying rate the more lustrous the gilding appears. Japan gold size is also used as a binder for spirit colours, as a drier in paint, as an ingredient in fillers and stopping compositions and as a sealer coat for various purposes. See *Gold size*.

Japan wax An ingredient of oriental lacquer, derived from the berries of the sumac trees of Japan and China. (**NLC**)

Japanese grasscloths and silk cloths Luxurious wallhangings which have been developed from traditional materials used in Japan for many centuries for the decoration of shrines and palaces. The weaving of these materials was originally a peasant craft. Grasscloth is made from the inner core of the slender stems of wild honeysuckle, which was split and knotted by hand and mounted on a backing of rice paper. Modern production methods are now used; the colouring is carefully supervised and a much more robust backing paper is employed. But there is still room for considerable individuality, and there are many different ways of treating the material by interlocking the fibres with cotton or metallic strips or by cutting the grasscloth into squares or diamonds to achieve parquet or basket weave effects, and the individual nature of the product is one of the distinctive features which appeals to the public.

The wall surfaces are cross lined before the finishing material is applied. Trimming is carried out with a very sharp knife and straightedge, about 16 mm being taken from each edge. The material is cut very carefully to length before pasting. Any part that needs cutting after pasting requires careful handling, because unless the scissors are very sharp they are likely to produce a ragged untidy edge. After pasting the material is allowed to become supple before hanging, but oversoaking must at all costs be avoided. A felt-covered roller is used to press the material into contact with the wall, care being taken not to stretch it. No attempt can be made, of course, to match up the weave along the joints; the individual appearance of the lengths is part of the effect which is sought after and prized. Naturally, the appearance is improved if the lengths are centred on each wall. Sometimes the joints are covered with beading. Both grasscloths and silk cloths are supplied in rolls 2·44 metres long by 0·9 metres wide.

Japanners' gold size A synonym for Japan gold size.

Japanning The application of a stoving black Japan finish.

Jarrah An Australian hardwood widely used in building and furniture making. It is so close-grained that normal wood primers will not penetrate; it should be primed with a thin aluminium primer or synthetic primer.

Jaspé papers Wallpapers with a soft irregular pattern giving the appearance of the surface having been combed or brushed.

Jaune brilliant An artists' colour prepared from cadmium, vermilion and white lead. (**NLC**)

Jelly size One of the forms in which glue size was supplied to the decorator, but which is now rarely seen. It has the drawback of being bulky, but some decorators preferred it because it was easy to judge the amount of water needed to thin it. The stiffness of the jelly gives an indication of its strength. A good quality of jelly size needs very little added water, just enough to prevent burning when the size is heated. A great disadvantage of jelly size is its tendency to putrefy in warm weather. (**NLC**)

Jib door A door which is flush with a wall and which is painted or papered in the same manner as the wall so as to make it inconspicuous or indistinguishable from its surroundings.

Jib scaffold Alternative term for cantilever scaffold.

Joint The place at which two things are joined together, e.g., the joints of wallpaper.

Joint pin An internal connection used in scaffolding for joining two metal tubes together, end to end; it is fitted with a screw by which it can be expanded to grip the inside of the tubes firmly.

Joint roller A roller used to press down the edges of wallpaper in order to make the joints less conspicuous.

Jute The fibre from the inner bark of certain types of plant from which a coarse fabric is derived, available in various colourings or in a natural finish, which is sometimes used as a wallhanging. Prepared and backed jute fabric is hung in the same way as a wallpaper, being applied with a strong paste on a cross-lined surface; unprepared jute is usually hung dry, the adhesive being applied to the wall surface and the fabric rolled on. It is an extremely hard-wearing material which withstands brushing and scrubbing. When jute fabric is to be painted after hanging, some method is needed to insulate the fibres from the oil medium of the paint, because of the hardening effect of drying oils upon the fibre, and the customary procedure was to coat the hung fabric with hot weak size; today, jute fabrics are supplied ready for immediate painting without any such preparation.

But jute is no longer regarded merely as a cheap means of producing a hard-wearing hanging in situations where appearance is only a secondary consideration. Highly attractive jute wallhangings are now produced which are suitable for modern decorative scheming. In addition, there is a wide range of textile wallcoverings in which jute is combined with other fibres such as silk, wool, cotton and linen or with man-made fibres such as polyester. These have the advantage of being dust-resistant, and they can if necessary be lightly sponged and cleaned. In the case of woven materials, the paste is applied to the wall surface; in the case of warp-laid vertical yarn types, the paste is applied to the back of the hanging.

There is, however, one drawback about some of these textile hangings. Jute has rather poor qualities in respect of lightfastness, and textile wallcoverings in which jute is a component part may show a tendency to fade quite quickly. This in itself might not be too noticeable, but where there are wall areas masked off by pictures or pieces of furniture, the change of colour will become very obvious.

K

Kalsomine or kalso A name used in some parts of the country to indicate a flat whitewash brush.

Kaolin China clay; a porcelain clay derived principally from the decomposition of feldspar, and used in the paint industry as a base for lake pigments and in the preparation of ultramarine blue, and also as an extender and as a flatting agent.

Kauri gum A fossil resin, obtained from New Zealand, which is used in the manufacture of varnish, being easy to run and combining well with oil. There is also a recent resin called bush kauri. (**NLC**)

Keene's cement An anhydrous gypsum plaster of the hard-burnt type—composed, that is to say, of calcium sulphate to which an accelerator has been added. It is used where a hard, compact smooth plaster surface is required; sometimes when a softer grade of plaster has been used for the main body of the work Keene's cement is used to form external angles, mouldings and arrises. It is very often trowelled to a hard glass-like surface which offers poor reception for paint, and may be subject to the defect known as *dry-out*. Unless lime has been added by the plasterer Keene's cement exerts no harmful chemical effect upon paint. See also the notes under the headings *Anhydrous gypsum plasters* and *Dry-out*, and for a possible treatment to improve paint adhesion see *Following the trowel*. Keene's is also sold under various proprietary names such as Astroplax, Pixie Keene's and Superite.

Because of its hardness and its low level of porosity Keene's cement is distinguished on the BSI scale as a Class D gypsum plaster.

Kerosene The correct word for what is usually described as paraffin.

Keruing A hardwood sometimes used as an external cladding in modern construction. Its use presents certain problems to the decorator. A clear wood finish is often specified for its treatment, but in fact keruing gives off a resinous exudation which prevents varnish from adhering to it satisfactorily. Madison sealers provide a very much better finish for this and for similar woods. Decorators need to be aware of this difficulty, and for their own protection they should bring it to the attention of the specifying authority if they find themselves required to use a treatment which can only lead to failure; they should disclaim responsibility in writing, otherwise they could be held liable.

Key A surface is said to present a "key" for paint when it exhibits a slight degree of roughness which helps the paint to adhere. A perfectly smooth surface does not provide any key; for example, paint does not readily grip the close-trowelled surface of Keene's cement or the hard smooth surface of a film of shellac knotting. The failure of paint to adhere to a smooth hard surface is the reason for rubbing down a varnished or enamelled surface with pumice or waterproof sandpaper before applying fresh coatings of paint, and there are many instances of treatments such as etching or grit-blasting metal surfaces to make them provide a key for paint.

Knife filler A filling composition mixed to the consistency of a stiff paste so that it can be applied with a broad filling knife.

Knife filling The application of knife filler in order to fill surface indentations; the filler is drawn across the surface with a broad knife with a flexible blade and a perfectly level edge. It is an operation which calls for considerable skill and patience.

Knives Essential items of a painter's equipment, comprising a broad knife for general purposes such as stripping wallpaper, a broad knife with a perfectly true edge for filling, a chisel knife for working in narrow spaces, a putty knife for the application of stopping and a palette knife for mixing small quantities of colour and for colour matching. Other knives used in specialized departments of the trade include stencil knives, gilders' knives, etc.

Knocking up A term used to denote the mixing up of paint; probably dating back to the time when paint mixing was an arduous process involving the beating up of stiff paste pigments.

Knots Hard cross-grained disfigurements in timber which are formed where the parent stem puts out the shoots which develop into branches. Since the resin ducts run parallel with the growth, the resin which is in the knots flows to the surface of the planed timber. If the exposed surface of the knots is not sealed before paint is applied the resin, being the same substance from which turpentine is obtained, bleeds into the paint film to cause staining and in severe cases exudes in the form of sticky unsightly tears. The most effective treatment in the case of large knots is to cut them right out and plug the holes with sound wood. Where this is impracticable an alternative method is to cut the knot back below the surface and fill the cavity with a filler which when hard is sandpapered down to the level of the surrounding wood. The normal method employed where the knots are small and not too troublesome is to seal them with shellac knotting, although very occasionally metal foil is used as the sealer.

Knotting A solution of shellac in methylated spirit which is used to prevent resin from exuding from the knots in woodwork and softening and affecting the paint film. The knotting should be applied sparingly and allowed to extend well beyond the edge of the knots, being feathered off so as not to leave a prominent ridge. It is better to apply two thin coats rather than one thick one, as there is a tendency for the spirit evaporating from a thick film of knotting to develop pinholes through which the resin can pass, and in any case it is difficult to avoid the formation of a ridge.

Cheap grades of knotting should never be used as they are frequently adulterated with colophony (rosin), a material which is readily soluble in paint oils and thinners, and they are therefore incapable of holding back the resinous matter from the knots.

Knotting should be kept in airtight containers to prevent the thickening and darkening which takes place on exposure to air.

A variety of knotting known as stop-tar knotting, consisting of shellac and methylated spirit with the addition of a plasticizer, is used to prevent materials such as creosote from bleeding into paint.

Knotting bottle A metal container with a glass lining, with a wide neck in which a close-fitting stopper is inserted. The stopper is pierced so as to grip the handle of a small soft-haired brush, the brush and stopper being firmly joined together to form a complete unit; thus, when the stopper is replaced in the neck of the bottle the brush is suspended in the knotting.

It is most desirable that knotting should be used from a properly made container of this kind; the common practice of using discarded varnish tins and other makeshift receptacles is very unsatisfactory. Even the heaviest tin plating used for protecting the iron of cans is disintegrated in the presence of knotting, and if there are any imperfections in the lining the corrosion which takes place is very rapid indeed. This causes the knotting to become contaminated with soluble iron salts, and also sets up an electrolytic action which affects the resin by producing acidic substances. It used to be the practice for knotting to be supplied by the manufacturers in large earthenware jars: nowadays it is often sold in metal cans but the metal has been specially protected with a lining of mineral wax. It is not generally realized that when the knotting is transferred to smaller containers for use on the site its properties are often adversely affected.

Kotina The brand name of a type of foamed polystyrene used in sheets on ceilings and walls to prevent condensation, and also supplied in the form of acoustic tiles.

L

Labelling paint tins See *Classification, Packaging and Labelling of Dangerous Substances* and *Skin protection*

Lac A resinous substance secreted by an insect and from which such materials as shellac are derived. It is collected from the twigs and branches upon which the insects have swarmed.

Lacquer In present-day practice this term is used to define a coating which dries solely by the evaporation of the solvent. Chlorinated rubber coatings, which have considerable resistance to acids, alkalis, etc., and to immersion in sea-water, are examples of lacquers used in industrial painting; metallic lacquers made by pigmenting clear lacquers with "bronze" powders and other metal powders are examples relating to painting and decorating. Perhaps the most familiar types of lacquer are the nitrocellulose coatings used in the car industry, the furniture industry and many areas of industrial finishing. Other kinds of lacquer used in industrial finishing include varnishes made by dissolving various gums (chiefly shellac) in suitable volatile solvents, and the cellulose lacquers used for wood polishing and for minimizing the tarnishing of polished metal.

Lacquer, the origins of In its original sense the term "lacquer" refers to the material used in oriental lacquer work. This is a thick emulsion derived from the sap of a type of tree native to China, and is purified to produce a natural varnish which requires darkness and a cool damp atmosphere to make it dry. The varnish is applied in thin coatings which dry to a tough, dark durable film which takes a fine polish. The art of lacquer ware was first introduced in China but was perfected in Japan, and consists of the skilful application of as many as thirty or even forty thin coats of the varnish. Burmese lacquer and Indian lacquer are somewhat similar materials obtained from vegetation native to those countries. (**NLC**)

Ladder A portable device consisting of two long upright members connected by rungs or steps by which a person may climb to points which cannot be reached from the ground. Ladders may be classified under two main headings: single-section ladders, constructed as a single unit, and extension ladders consisting of two or more sections which can be telescoped so as to adjust the height. Single-section ladders may be of the pole ladder type or the standing ladder type. A pole ladder, otherwise known as a builders' ladder, has semicircular stiles made by sawing a straight pole down the centre, and is used for general building work and wherever a robust ladder or a ladder of considerable length is required. A standing ladder has rectangular stiles and is used where lightness is required. Standing ladders are obtainable in lengths of up to 8 metres, and pole ladders in lengths of up to 20 metres or even more on occasion. Extension ladders may be of the hook-and-clip catch type or of the rope-operated safety catch type. Rope-operated ladders are heavier and stronger and are to be preferred when considerable lengths are required.

Wooden ladders are made with softwood stiles and hardwood rungs; metal reinforcements are provided under the rungs and long ladders have a metal reinforcement sunk in the stiles. There are also metal ladders made from aluminium alloy, which offer the advantages of lightness, strength and freedom from deterioration and decay but which are a hazard when used in the vicinity of exposed electrical equipment.

Ladder—a painting defect Sometimes the word "ladder" is used to describe a fault in painting. The fault is due to a failure to lay off properly, and consists of a narrow strip of painted work, missed in the final laying off, in which brush marks at right angles to the direction of the laying off are exposed.

Ladder bracket A wrought iron bracket which rests upon the rungs of a ladder and supports one end of a scaffold plank; by the use of two of these brackets a light temporary scaffold can be erected between two ladders.

Several types of bracket are available; the safest type is that which has two sets of hooks so that the weight is not resting upon one ladder rung only. It is desirable that the hooks should be adjustable to fit ladders of varying rung spacings. The arm which supports the plank is hinged so that when in position it lies horizontally whatever the inclination of the ladder, and it is useful if there is sufficient latitude in the adjustment to allow the bracket to be fixed either in front of the ladder or behind it, whichever is more convenient. The pin securing the arm should be fastened with a short chain so that it cannot be detached or lost.

Ladder brackets are particularly useful for operations such as signwriting, where the work is of such short duration that it does not justify the erection of a more elaborate scaffold. They are especially valuable for operations on wall panels or gable ends where the height of the plank needs to be altered frequently as the work proceeds.

Ladder brackets are sometimes known by the term "cripples".

Ladder stay A device which hooks on to the top rungs of a ladder so that the end of the ladder is held at a distance of about 300 mm away from the vertical surface instead of resting directly upon it.

Lake colours Pigments prepared by precipitating soluble organic dyes on to a mineral base such as alumina, Paris white, China clay, etc. and fixing them chemically to form an insoluble compound. Some authorities say that the term is derived from the word "lac"; others maintain that it comes from the word "lacca", which was used by medieval dyers for the coloured scum which formed in the dye vats. Originally a large number of brilliant pigments were prepared in this way from natural mineral or vegetable dyestuffs; most of these are now obsolete but pigments prepared from cochineal, logwood, madder and indigo are still used to a limited extent. Many of the natural lakes suffered from the disadvantage of fading badly when exposed to sunlight and were very liable to bleed.

Most of the lake colours now used are made from the products of coal-tar distillation. A wide range of colours is available, the variations in colour being due chiefly to slight modifications in the arrangement of the constituent atoms of carbon, hydrogen, nitrogen and oxygen. The chemistry of these materials is very complex. (**NLC**)

Lambswool Lambswool is used as one of the covering fabrics for paint rollers. It is softer than a pile fabric, and is generally considered more suitable than the latter for the application of gloss and semi-gloss paints by roller. Comparative tests seem to indicate that the consumption of paint and the labour costs are both lower with lambswool rollers than with rollers covered in pile fabrics.

Lamina A thin plate, layer, coat, flake or stratum; from this is derived the verb "to laminate" which means to beat, press or roll a material into thin plates, or to cut or split a substance into thin layers or sheets.

Laminar pigments Pigments consisting of particles which take the form of thin flat flakes. When bound in a suitable medium, and applied as a paint film, the flakes tend to lie parallel with the surface on which the paint is being spread, and in doing so they overlap, thus making the film resistant to moisture penetration. Aluminium and micaceous iron oxide are typical examples of laminar pigments. See also *Leafing*.

Laminated lead A form of lead sheeting sometimes used in the treatment of damp surfaces.

Laminates A term used to define a range of sheetings which are of great importance to interior designers and decorators. They are widely used as wallcoverings, claddings, shelvings, working surfaces, and the facings of kitchen furniture, furniture for offices, laboratories, etc.

Decorative laminates were first developed in the late 1920's to provide hard-wearing materials for the cladding of table tops and similar surfaces. They were generally dark in colour. One of the earliest was the material with the familiar brand-name of Formica. As they gained acceptance, wood-grain effects were introduced consisting of resin-impregnated papers tightly pressed to a stainless steel caul plate, the colour and the pattern being printed on the paper, and these were followed by fabric-type designs and linen prints and by sheetings in which real wood veneer was used in place of the printed paper layer.

For a long time laminates were never even considered as decorative possibilities; they were regarded solely as substitutes for better materials in situations where a hard-wearing, scratch-resistant surface was required that would withstand heat, sunlight and chemicals. Gradually, however, their image has changed, and since the 1970's there has been a totally different attitude towards them. Today an extremely wide range of laminates is available, and they are established as important high-class decorative materials in their own right. They are produced in many different colourways (one manufacturer advertising a range of nearly sixty colours) and in a variety of metal sheetings with a polished, brushed or embossed finish; there are finely-woven linens and hessians, woodgrains, marbles, leathers, corks, and woven canes, available in gloss, satin, matt and embossed finishes. Many kinds of material are used to form the core, including asbestos-cement sheets, blockboard, chipboard, foam, plasterboards, plywoods and veneered boards as well as the usual metallic plate.

One big advance is that as well as being supplied in flat sheets, laminates can now be "post-formed" or curved, which gives an immense range of possibilities. Another growing aspect of laminates is in the production of specially designed devices created for the individual customer, ranging from a firm's logo or trademark to big decorative maps and full-scale murals. Continuous laminates can now be made which enable long walls and friezes to be decorated with pictorial designs. Probably the best known of these is the curved wall decoration at Charing Cross on the Northern Line platforms of London Underground, where David Gentleman's humorous and robust drawings depicting the history of the area have become familiar to millions of travellers since 1979. This particular scheme is quite outstanding in one respect; part of every decorator's skill consists of the ability to cope with considerable variations of size and scale, but there can be very few people indeed who could emulate David Gentleman in being equally at ease whether designing postage stamps or executing a mural that covers the entire wall surface of a tube station.

The performance levels of decorative laminates in respect of resistance to impact, scratching, smouldering cigarettes, staining, etc., are defined in BS 3794: 1982. This British Standard does not include a fire-resistance test, but certain manufacturers have introduced their own flame-retardant grades.

Lamp black A black pigment consisting essentially of free carbon, produced by the incomplete combustion of waste coal-tar products. It is not so intense a black as carbon black, but makes a fine bluish grey when reduced with white. (**NLC**)

Lancashire pattern distemper brush (**NLC**) See *Distemper brush.*

Lancaster cloth A washable coated cotton fabric of the oilcloth type which was once highly popular as a wallhanging in situations where a hard-wearing waterproof finish was required. It has now been superseded by modern materials. (**NLC**)

Lanolin Cholesterin-fatty matter which is extracted from sheep's wool. Lanolin is a constituent of certain proprietary compounds used as temporary protective coatings for steelwork, such coatings being employed when for some reason it is necessary for a time-lag to occur between the cleaning and de-scaling of the steel and the application of the paint coatings.

Lap The word is used by the decorator both as a verb and as a noun. Used as a verb, "to lap" means either to apply a coat of paint in such a way that it partially overlaps the edge of a section previously painted so that there is a double thickness of paint along the edge, or to apply wallpaper, metal foil, canvas or any other form of wallhanging in such a way that the edge overlaps the previously hung piece. Used as a noun, the word "lap" applies to the double thickness of material, whether it be paint, wallpaper, foil or anything else, which exists along the joint when the edge has been allowed to overlap.

Lapis lazuli A semi-precious stone consisting of a rich blue silicate of alumina, lime and soda, from which ultramarine blue was formerly prepared. (**NLC**)

Lapped joint A term employed when wallpaper, metal foil, or some form of fabric is hung in such a way that the edges overlap, as opposed to a butt edge, where the edges meet without overlapping.

Latex The milk-like juice of the rubber tree, often used instead of the cured crude rubber for such purposes as the preparation of adhesives, etc. Artificial latex, which is a water dispersion of reclaimed rubber, resembles latex but is softer and tackier, and is often used in the manufacture of adhesives; it is produced by swelling and dissolving the rubber in an organic solvent, treating it with an organic acid or ammonia and then emulsifying it.

Latex adhesives are recommended by the manufacturers for the hanging of various types of coated fabrics. Certain fabrics such as decorative canvas and hessian are sometimes supplied on a latex backing.

Laying gold A term used to indicate the process of applying gold leaf to a surface. When transfer leaf is being used, the process consists of holding between the thumb and forefinger of one hand the waxed tissue to which the leaf is attached, placing it so that the gold is brought into contact with the gold size which has been allowed to assume the correct degree of tack, and then rubbing the back of the tissue with the ball of the thumb of the other hand, rubbing to and fro with short firm strokes of about an inch in each direction till the leaf has completely parted from the tissue and is firmly adhering to the gold size with no pinholes to mar the surface. The laying of loose leaf gold involves the use of a gilder's cushion in the corner of which several leaves are placed; the process consists of taking each leaf in turn with the knife, spreading it flat on the surface of the cushion, cutting it approximately to size, lifting each piece with the gilder's tip and bringing it into contact with the mordant.

Laying in A term which is generally understood to mean painting or otherwise covering a surface as a preparation for some further treatment. For instance, we speak of a surface being laid in with gold size preparatory to gilding, of a wall being laid in with glaze medium which is subsequently manipulated to produce a broken colour treatment, of a surface being laid in with plastic paint prior to texturing, etc.

Laying off Part of the technique of applying paint by brush; it is the action of finishing off an area of paintwork with very light strokes of the brush in order to eliminate brush marks. The technique used by the competent painter is as follows:

(i) Several brushfuls of paint are applied with firm vigorous strokes.

(ii) When a suitable area has thus been laid in, the work is "crossed" without recharging the brush, using a somewhat lighter touch, in order to distribute the paint evenly.

(iii) With still lighter strokes the brush is taken across the area with diagonal strokes.

(iv) Finally the work is "laid off" using only the tips of the brush and working rapidly with the lightest possible touch.

The general rule when woodwork is being painted is that the work is laid off in the direction of the grain; walls are laid off vertically, and ceilings are laid off with strokes running parallel to the main window. Emulsion paints call for a different technique and are usually laid off with long semicircular strokes.

Leaching To "leach" is to make a liquid percolate through a substance in order to dissolve and remove some soluble matter that happens to be there. The term is frequently used in painting and decorating to describe operations aimed at getting rid of some offensive material; for example, we speak of leaching out deliquescent salts from plaster by washing with copious quantities of water, leaching out stains from a surface by swabbing liberally with solvents, and so on.

Lead A soft heavy blue-grey metal, with the chemical symbol Pb, obtained chiefly from the mineral galena. It is the basis of many paint materials, including the following:

White lead, a basic carbonate of lead.
Red lead, an oxide of lead.
Orange lead, similar in composition to red lead.
Sublimed blue lead, a pigment consisting of basic sulphate of lead.
Lead acetate, otherwise known as "sugar of lead"; a white crystalline salt formed by the reaction of lead oxide and acetic acid, and used as a drier in paint.
Lead borate, a white crystalline compound, also used as a paint drier.
Lead chromate, the basis of a group of pigments.
Litharge, lead monoxide used as a drier.
Calcium plumbate, a pigment made by heating calcium hydroxide (slaked lime) and litharge to a high temperature; it is used as a metal primer.

The use of lead paints has declined greatly, severe restrictions having been imposed because of their toxic nature.

The metal lead is used in various ways in the construction of a building, although here again it has been superseded to a great extent by other materials. Lead does not normally require protection by painting, and in fact it has a greasy nature and tends to reject paint, causing the paint to flake and peel. Very often, however, it is necessary to paint lead pipes, etc., so that they conform to the general colour scheme. Sometimes, too, lead and lead alloys are used for coating steel by hot-dipping and metal-spray processes, and as such coatings are often too thin to give permanent protection to the steel it may be necessary to reinforce them with a paint system. New lead surfaces should be abraded, with water or white spirit as the lubricant, or treated with phosphating solutions or phosphoric acid. Etch primers are satisfactory, and so too are the ordinary metal primers such as zinc chromate or calcium plumbate, but a primer containing a graphite pigment should not be used because if the coating were to be ruptured the graphite would make contact with the steel and would tend to cause corrosion.

"Lead and you" The title of a leaflet which, under the provisions of the Approved Code of Practice for the Control of Lead at Work Regulations, is to be given to every employee at the time when he or she first takes up employment with a painting and decorating firm.

Lead chromes A group of pigments based on chromate of lead, ranging in colour from very pale primrose yellow, through lemon, gold and orange to red, and known by various names such as lemon chrome, primrose chrome, chrome yellow, orange chrome, chrome red, Derby red, Chinese red, etc. Lead chromes possess the properties of brilliant strong colour, good opacity, considerable staining strength and moderate price, and they have useful rust-inhibitive qualities. They are fairly permanent though apt to fade in strong sunlight. When used in conjunction with Prussian blue and Monastral blue they produce a wide variety of green shades. Lead chromes become discoloured if exposed to atmospheres containing hydrogen sulphide or if mixed with sulphide pigments such as ultramarine or vermilion. They are also sensitive to alkalis.

The use of lead chrome has declined in recent years because of the general agreement to restrict the use of toxic pigments.

Lead colour The painter's term for a grey-coloured paint, generally in reference to a grey undercoat.

Lead foil Thin sheet lead which is available in various forms and has some limited applications to painting and decorating.

Lead foil sheets were at one time commonly used for the treatment of damp surfaces on interior walls and for sealing various kinds of stains. The sheets were attached to the wall with a fixative of either red lead or paste white lead mixed with gold size. This is very rarely seen today, but there is also a paperbacked lead foil for damp areas and this is attached with a latex adhesive.

Lead foil is also used as a masking material in certain kinds of glass sign work and in glass embossing. When employed in the production of painted glass signs the foil is attached to the glass with weak gelatine size and firmly pressed down. The design is traced in reverse on the back of the foil, which is then cut with a sharp knife, the letter shapes being lifted out. The exposed glass is painted, two coats usually being required to obtain a solid job, after which the remainder of the foil is removed leaving the letters clear and sharp. When lead foil is used for glass embossing, the whole of the glass is coated with Brunswick black and allowed to dry; the surface is then laid in with beeswax and the foil pressed firmly into contact with it. The design is traced on the foil in reverse, the foil is cut and the parts to be embossed are removed. The exposed portions are gently cleaned off with white spirit to remove the beeswax and Brunswick black, a wall of tallow is built up round the edge of the glass and acid is poured in and allowed to etch the exposed parts of the glass.

Lead free A self-explanatory term defining a paint or other substance with virtually no lead content. See also *Low solubility inorganic lead compounds.*

Lead paint This is defined in the Control of Lead at Work Regulations, 1980, as being any paint, paste or other material used in painting which yields to dilute hydrochloric acid more than 5 percent of its dry weight of a soluble lead compound calculated as lead monoxide when determined by the prescribed test. See also *Low solubility inorganic lead compounds.*

Lead Paint (Protection against Poisoning) Act, 1926 An Act of Parliament passed in December 1926 which came into force on 1st January 1927, to give improved provision for the protection of persons employed in the painting of buildings against the dangers of lead poisoning. It is noteworthy as being the first piece of legislation ever made specifically for members of the painting and decorating trade. It was revoked in its entirety when the Control of Lead at Work Regulations came into force on 18th August 1981.

Lead paint regulations Regulations governing the use of lead paints, made under the terms of the Lead Paint (Protection against Poisoning) Act of 1926. As such they were familiar to all but the most recent entrants into the painting and decorating craft as the statutory authority which bound both employers and employees for more than fifty-four years. They were completely revoked by the Control of Lead at Work Regulations, 1980.

Lead paint—statutory regulations

(1) THE CONTROL OF LEAD AT WORK REGULATIONS, 1980 (STATUTORY INSTRUMENT 1248) These Regulations were made on 18th August 1980, laid before Parliament on 1st September 1980, and came into operation on 18th August 1981; they have supplanted the previous Acts and Regulations of 1926 and 1927. Unlike the previous legislation which was concerned solely and specifically with painting and decorating, they cover a much wider field, being designed to control all the activities in which lead is used. Painting and decorating in fact occupies a relatively minor role, since many of the industrial operations involving the use of lead present a much greater health hazard both to the workpeople and to the general pubic who are influenced by these operations.

After the preamble, the main body of the document consists of what is termed "The Arrangement of Regulations", under which there are twenty headings. Some of these have no relevance to painting and decorating, others are only marginally relevant. The ones which may affect decorators to a greater or lesser degree are as follows:

Regulation 3, "Duty of an employer to persons who are not his employees", this duty being defined as broadly the same as the employer's duty to his employees as far as is reasonably practicable.
Regulation 4, "Assessment of work which exposes people to lead", which is concerned with the nature and degree of exposure to lead.

Regulation 5, "Information, instruction and training".
Regulation 6, "Control measures", which requires such measures for materials, plant and processes as will adequately control the exposure of employees.
Regulation 7, "Respiratory protection equipment", such equipment to be provided for employees liable to be exposed to airborne lead.
Regulation 8, "Protective clothing", stating clearly that protective clothing shall be worn by employees whilst working, but also stating that it shall not be worn whilst the employee is not engaged in work.
Regulation 9, "Washing and changing facilities".
Regulation 10, "Eating, drinking and smoking", ensuring that employees shall not eat, drink or smoke in any place liable to be contaminated with lead.
Regulation 11, "Cleaning", which relates to the cleanliness of work places, premises, respiratory equipment and protective clothing.
Regulation 12, "Duty to avoid the spread of contamination by lead".
Regulation 15, "Air monitoring", which requires the provision of adequate monitoring procedures to measure the concentrations of lead in the air to which employees are exposed, unless the extent of the exposure is not significant.
Regulation 16, "Medical surveillance and biological tests", whereby an employee shall be under such surveillance under certain conditions:

(i) (a) if the exposure is significant, and (b) if an appointed doctor certifies that the employee shall be under such surveillance.

(ii) Every employee exposed to lead at work should when required present him/herself for a medical examination, such an examination to take place during working hours.

Regulation 17, "Records", requiring an employer to keep adequate records of assessments, air monitoring, medical tests, etc.

(2) APPROVED CODE OF PRACTICE FOR THE CONTROL OF LEAD AT WORK REGULATIONS This is the Code of Practice which supports the Control of Lead at Work Regulations. It was drawn up under the auspices of the Health and Safety Commission's Advisory Committee on Toxic Substances, and approved by the Health and Safety Commission. It conveys a duty on any employer who uses lead or products containing lead to assess the level of exposure; it requires the employer to inform and protect his employees and any other persons who may be exposed to significant levels of lead as a result of his activities; it expands and clarifies the Regulations.

The sections of chief concern to the painter and decorator are as follows:

Section 3 reiterates Regulation 3 relating to the duty of an employer to persons at work who are not his employees.
Section 4 expands and explains very fully the provisions of Regulation 4 relating to the assessment of work which exposes persons to lead. A complete guide is given to the types of work where there is likely to be a significant level of exposure, and these include:

(a) The abrasion of lead, giving rise to lead dust in the air, e.g. dry discing, grinding and cutting by power tools (factors which may arise in the course of industrial painting operations).

(b) The spraying of lead paints and lead compounds other than those paints conforming to BS 4310: 1968 and low solubility lead compounds. This section also indicates the types of lead work where there is NOT likely to be any significant exposure to lead; these include

(i) Painting with low solubility paints.

(ii) Work with materials containing less than 1 per cent total lead.

(iii) *Brush painting with lead paint* This is clearly the paragraph of major interest to painters and decorators. The paragraph is bound up with a section relating to "work with lead in emulsion or paste form where the moisture content is such that lead dust and fumes will not be given off, and is maintained as such throughout the duration of the work".

This provision, however, does not absolve the employer from the obligation to assess the level of exposure, inform the workforce of the results of the assessment together with instructions about the precautions to be taken, and supply and maintain the required washing facilities.

Section 5 expands the regulations on information, instruction and training, and contains the provision that every employee when first taken into employment shall be given a copy of the leaflet "Lead and You".

Section 6 aims to control the measures by which lead can be ingested into the system or can be absorbed through the skin. To this end it stipulates that, wherever practicable, lead-free materials or low solubility lead compounds should be substituted for those with a higher concentration of lead.

This section also lays down an absolute requirement that wet methods must be used for rubbing down or scraping lead-painted surfaces.

Section 7 states that where an employee is exposed to airborne lead, suitable respiratory protective equipment must be provided and worn, and this of course applies when paints containing lead are to be applied by spray.

Section 8 expands the Regulation about protective clothing, but it indicates that for painting and decorating operations, outer protective clothing (e.g. a boiler suit or overalls) is adequate.

Section 9 about washing and changing facilities stipulates that the term "washing facilities" includes the provision of soap, nailbrushes, hot and cold water, and individual towels.

Section 10 about eating, drinking and smoking, makes the point that the term "eating" includes the chewing of gum.

The Code of Practice contains several references to "low solubility lead compounds" and provides a definition of this term. A definition of the term, together with details of the method of testing a material to ascertain its lead content, is given later in this book under the heading of *Low solubility inorganic lead compounds*.

(3) PREVIOUS LEGISLATION, NOW REVOKED When the Control of Lead at Work Regulations came into force in 1981, several of the previous measures relating to the use of lead were revoked in order to prevent ambiguity.

From the early part of the 20th century, many parliamentary orders and regulations had been made controlling the use of lead in various branches of industry, but because the new regulations were intended to cover every field of activity where lead is used, it was felt necessary for the whole situation to be tidied up, to remove any possibility of misunderstanding. But, of course, many of the trade textbooks and manuals still in use contain references to the older legislation, and since expensive books when once bought are not lightly discarded, this will remain the case for many years to come. It is therefore highly important to know which of the previous measures have been superseded.

As noted in section (1) of this entry, the whole of the Lead Paint Regulations of 1927 were revoked, and so were certain sections of the provisions of the Factories Act of 1961.

In addition to these, the following measures related to various aspects of paint and painting operations were revoked:

(a) The Regulations of 21st January 1907, in respect of the manufacture of paints and colours.

(b) The Order dated 8th November 1921, defining the expression "lead compound".

(c) The Vehicle Painting Regulations, 1926.

(d) The Rule dated 24th December 1926, for ascertaining whether or not a paint is a "lead paint".

(e) The Order made on 14th November 1927, relating to the employment of young persons in the painting trade and of women and young persons in work of decorative design.

(f) The Lead Paint (Prescribed Leaflet) Order of 1964.

Lead poisoning An occupational disease to which those employed in making or using certain lead products are liable; at one time it was a common complaint among painters but in recent years its incidence has decreased to insignificant proportions. Lead poisoning is caused by continual absorption of lead into the system over a long period, due chiefly to inhalation of lead dust or spray or to transference of lead from the hands to the mouth, although some authorities state that lead can also be absorbed through the skin. The symptoms are weakness, constipation and severe abdominal pains (painters' colic) followed by sickness and palpitation. In its more advanced stages it leads to anaemia and loss of weight; in chronic cases it may cause palsy or paralysis. One of the features of lead poisoning is the gradual weakening of the muscles which leads to the condition known among painters as "drop-wrist".

Lead restricted A term used to describe a paint which contains less than 5 percent of soluble lead, such a paint being often spoken of as "lead free within the meaning of the Act".

Lead soaps Organic compounds which are formed by the interaction of lead pigments and driers with the fatty acids of the drying oils used in paint. When viewed through a microscope the lead soap is seen to radiate outwards from the particles of pigment in a fibre-like manner; in a heavily pigmented paint the particles are so close together that the fibres intertwine, an action which reinforces the film and imparts great toughness and elasticity. The formation of lead soaps is one of the specially desirable features of a lead paint, producing a waterproof film which expands and contracts in conformity with the surface to which it is applied giving a tough, durable, protective coating.

Lead stopping A material for stopping up holes and cracks in timber, etc., to which extra properties of hardness are imparted by the addition of a lead compound. For good-quality work a hard-drying lead stopper is far more satisfactory than ordinary putty, which always takes a long time to harden and is very liable to shrinkage and crumbling.

Lead stopping can be made by mixing stiff white-lead paste with whiting and gold size, but there are excellent proprietary stoppers available in ready-mixed form. It used to be common practice to make an extra-hard stopping by adding red lead powder to a mixture of white lead and gold size or to a straightforward linseed oil putty, and a stopping for ironwork was made with red lead powder and gold size, but for all practical purposes such materials have now been abandoned because of their toxic nature.

Leaded zinc A pigment, used more freely in the USA than in this country, which consists of a variety of zinc oxide containing a certain amount of basic lead sulphate, the proportion of lead varying from 5 to 45 percent. It possesses good weathering properties and it has greater opacity than zinc oxide, although its colour is not so good.

Leadiness The defect which occurs when a paint pigmented with aluminium powder loses its initial lustre and develops the dull appearance of weathered lead sheeting.

Leadless paints The term implies that such paints are completely free from lead content, but in fact it is generally interpreted as referring to paints which conform to BS 4310: 1968, "Permissible Limits of Lead in Low-lead Paints".

Leafing A term used to describe the behaviour of certain pigments with a flaky or laminated structure when mixed in a suitable vehicle and applied as a paint film. Aluminium powder and graphite are outstanding examples of materials possessing this property. The minute flakes of which they are composed, although heavier than the vehicle, have a tendency to float to the surface and arrange themselves parallel to the surface, overlapping each other and forming continuous layers several flakes in depth with a thin film of vehicle between each layer. This phenomenon resembles the way in which leaves falling from a tree in the autumn overlap one another on the ground, and it is this resemblance which gives rise to the term.

The leafing properties of aluminium, graphite, etc., have an important bearing upon the characteristics of the paint film of which they are a part. The individual flakes, although very thin, offer a barrier to the passage of moisture, which can only penetrate the film by means of finding a path across and around the edge of each flake and, since the surface area of the flakes is very great compared with their thickness, it follows that the film has very considerable resistance to moisture penetration. Another feature of such a film is its opacity, and this in turn may serve to improve the durability of the paint since the overlapping flakes in the upper layers of the film tend to protect the underlying layers of medium. In the case of aluminium paints, the overlapping layers form a continuous film, which is an effective sealer to prevent the penetration of bitumen, creosote, soot, bleeding reds, etc., and which is also a useful sealer-primer for timbers with a high resinous content such as Columbian pine, etc.

Leather The skins or hides of animals cured by the chemical action of tannin.

Leathercloth A term used to describe a wide range of coated fabrics which are embossed and coloured to present the texture and appearance of various kinds of leather. They are available in differing weights and qualities which make them suitable for a number of purposes such as upholstery, car trimmings, coverings for tables and shelves, and wallhangings, the latter being of course of most interest to the decorator.

Modern leathercloths usually consist of PVC-coated fabrics (polyvinyl chloride) which have the advantage of being fire-resistant. They are widely used in interior decoration, not only for their attractive appearance but also because they are tough, durable, hygienic and resistant to most household chemicals. As well as being used in domestic work they are eminently suitable for the treatment of public buildings such as restaurants, hotels, hospitals, schools and offices, and they are also used in the finishing of aircraft and caravan interiors.

Leathercloths can be hung with various proprietary adhesives, according to the manufacturers' recommendations, or with ordinary wallpaper pastes; if a paste is used, it is essential that it should contain a fungicide.

Leatherette A type of embossed wallpaper which is coloured, lacquered, metalled and bronzed in various ways to represent antique Spanish and Venetian tooled leather hangings, but the term is generally used to refer to the cheaper kinds of imitation leather paper. When such papers are hung, it is important to avoid oversoaking with paste, otherwise they stretch and the relief is to a great extent lost; there is also a tendency for the metal or bronze finish to blacken, especially if the paste used to hang them was not fresh and had become sour. Leatherettes of this kind, however, have largely given place to more modern vinyl papers.

Ledger A term used in scaffolding, particularly in tubular metal constructions. The ledgers are the main horizontal members which tie the scaffold longitudinally and support the transoms and putlogs. It is very important for the stability of the scaffold that the ledgers should be checked in course of erection to see that they are perfectly horizontal, and they should be coupled to the standards with load-bearing couplers.

Lemon chrome A pale yellow pigment belonging to the lead chrome group. See *Lead chrome.*

Lemon yellow A very pale yellow pigment made by precipitating barium chloride with sodium bichromate. It has an advantage over lead chrome in that it is not discoloured in the presence of sulphuretted hydrogen, but has the drawbacks of being available only as a very pale tint and being less opaque than lead chromates, and it is used principally as an artist's colour. (**NLC**)

Lesura The brand name for a very unusual seamless textile wallcovering with a padded backing, which is applied horizontally over a whole wall area in one single piece so that there are no joints whatsoever. It is a very luxurious material, beautiful in appearance and warm and soft to the touch, with a wide choice of fabric-facings including velvet, linen, and many woven textiles both natural and man-made, and is available in more than a hundred colourings. Yet although it has such a rich effect and is obviously an expensive product, it is highly economical both in preparation and application costs because there is no need to strip off the previous decoration, and it can be applied on rough unplastered wall surfaces.

The material is supplied in a width of 2.60 m, and because it is hung horizontally the 2.60 metres represents the height. The method of application is to apply a neoprene glue adhesive in a band 50 mm wide all round the perimeter of a wall; the roll of material is unwound from one end of the wall and pushed into contact with the adhesive as it unrolls. Superfluous material along the skirting board and around door and window openings is trimmed off when the adhesive is dry.

Levelling A term sometimes used to mean obtaining a smooth level surface by the use of fillers.

Levelling-off coat A fluid applied by spray over a final coating of nitrocellulose lacquer in order to soften it and allow the irregularities to smooth themselves out.

Levigation A process used in the preparation of certain pigments such as earth colours, red oxides and mineral whites. Wet levigation has been practised from the earliest times; the plant consists of a mixing tank, below which is a further series of tanks, each tank being of greater size and capacity than the previous one and each placed at a lower elevation than the previous one. The lump ore or crude pigment is agitated with running water in the mixing tank, and the water carrying the pigment particles in suspension overflows into the lower tanks. As each tank is reached the rate of flow is reduced due to the increased capacity, and in each case the heaviest and coarsest particles settle at the bottom. When the final tank is reached the particles that remain are those of the finest and smallest size. By this means the pigment is automatically separated into grades. The particles are allowed to settle, the water drained off, and the pigment removed from the tanks, dried and ground in a suitable medium. Dry levigation is a process by which dry ground pigment is passed into an air stream and through a device which grades the particles; this process is also known as "air flotation".

Lichens Small grey, yellow or blue-green plants which consist of an alga and a fungus growing together in union, and which are found growing flat on the surface of building stonework and masonry in rural districts. The painter is sometimes called upon to remove the growth in the course of decorating country properties; an effective solution for the purpose can be made up with 125 grams of zinc silicofluoride or magnesium silicofluoride mixed into 5 litres of water, but there are also proprietary solutions available in ready-mixed form.

Life The length of time that a paint or other decorative material continues to serve its purpose completely and adequately. Not to be confused with terms such as "pot life" and "shelf life", which refer to the length of time that a material will remain in usable conditions before application.

Lifting A term used to describe the softening and wrinkling up of a dry film of paint or varnish which sometimes occurs when a further coat is applied over it. This is particularly likely to occur when materials which need a very powerful solvent to bring them to a workable condition are being used, or when materials containing a solvent which is incompatible with the previous coating are being applied: for example, when a material such as a chlorinated rubber paint is used over an unsuitable primer, when cellulose is applied over soft oil paint or when certain finishing materials are used over unsuitable undercoats. Lifting can also occur, of course, if a coat of paint is applied before the previous coat has been allowed enough time to dry and harden properly.

Lightfastness The extent to which a paint, pigment or dyestuff will retain its colour when exposed to light. Inorganic pigments which are compounds of metals have a high degree of lightfastness, but there is considerable variation between differing types of organic pigments. Some retain their colour both in their pure form and when reduced with white, but others which are satisfactory in the pure form fade very quickly when reduced with white. Lightfastness is assessed by what is termed the Blue Wool Scale, and is measured by dispersing the pigment in a paint medium and applying the dispersion to a metal strip or card; when dry, the strip is exposed to ultraviolet light in a fugitometer, alongside a standard strip for comparison purposes. Details of the test are given in BS 1006: 1978.

Lightweight staging A form of strongly constructed staging which is 460 mm wide (the width of two planks) and is available in lengths of from 3 to 7 metres. It is designed so that the amount of sag or deflection when it is fully loaded is negligible, although it is only supported at each end. For this reason it is invaluable for roof work in factories, when it can be used to span the trusses without any further support and provide a broad rigid runway without causing any obstruction to the floor below. Used as a trestle scaffold, it reduces the number of trestles necessary. It is only half the weight of the equivalent quantity of scaffold boarding.

Lily bristle The highest quality of natural white bristle, usually understood to refer to Siberian white bristle, which is now unfortunately no longer obtainable. (**NLC**)

Lime Calcium oxide occurring abundantly in nature, chiefly in combination with carbon dioxide as calcium carbonate in chalk, limestone etc. Its importance as a building material has lasted from ancient times to the present day, and it is widely used in mortars and cements, internal plastering and external renderings. It is produced by heating limestone or chalk to a high temperature in a kiln to drive off the carbonic acid gas, the residue being known as quicklime. The addition of water causes this material to slake with the production of much heat. Hydrated lime, which is made by grinding quicklime, slaking it under controlled conditions with water, and sifting it to a fine powder, is easier to handle and is more reliable.

From the decorator's point of view, the interest of lime as a building material is largely bound up with its capacity for destroying oil paint. Pure lime itself is not particularly harmful, but it becomes very destructive when contaminated with even small quantities of soluble alkalis, such as soda or potash.

Lime blue Originally this was a term applied to a copper blue, but now it is used to describe a very cheap form of ultramarine blue made by grinding the lowest-grade pigment with terra alba or by striking a synthetic dye on a white base. Lime blue is a weak stainer that is not affected by alkali. At one time it was widely used for tinting distempers, but its use is now confined to correcting the colour of limewash to make it appear whiter. It is generally supplied as a powder which needs to be soaked in water before it is added to the limewash.

Lime green A limeproof pigment formerly used for tinting distemper.

Lime plaster (a) Non-hydraulic. This is a type of plaster used as a skimming coat for interior walls and ceilings, and is usually applied over a rough lime/sand backing. It is rarely used in modern new construction work because of certain disadvantages (its slow hardening, its mechanically weak surface when new, and its tendency to shrink; see below). It is, however, still used on restoration work.
(b) Hydraulic. This is not often used as a finishing plaster for interior work, but is used sometimes for exterior plastering and for stucco work.

Lime plaster is produced by slaking quicklime by means of adding water to it, the milk of lime which is obtained being sieved and allowed to mature for a fortnight, when it fattens up into what is known as lime putty; or it can be made from a hydrated lime which is soaked to lime putty by mixing with water and then allowed to stand for a time. The process by which lime plaster dries and hardens is a dual one, combining both evaporation and carbonation. While the water is evaporating, the plaster is gradually absorbing carbon dioxide from the atmosphere to form a firm compact layer of calcium carbonate, similar in composition to the limestone or chalk from which the lime was originally derived, the depth of the layer depending on the extent to which the carbon dioxide can penetrate.

The factors involved in the successful decoration of lime plaster are as follows:

(i) The plaster must be allowed to dry out completely before the surface is sealed with an impervious layer of paint; otherwise, the paint film will be forced off in the form of blistering and flaking. The length of time that this will take depends to a great extent upon the type of construction, i.e. whether the plaster is applied to plasterboards, wooden or expanded metal lathing, old porous brickwork or new brickwork containing a large quantity of water; much will depend, too, upon whether or not the drying conditions are favourable.

(ii) The plaster must be allowed adequate time to carbonate before it is sealed; otherwise it will be prevented from ever attaining its proper hardness and strength, and a permanently weak skin will be the result. Carbonation is a very slow process which cannot be hastened.

(iii) For practical purposes all lime plaster should be regarded as chemically active, because even if the lime putty itself is relatively harmless it becomes strongly alkaline if contaminated by sodium and potassium salts brought forward from the backing; the effect of alkaline attack upon an oil paint is to saponify the oil, causing the film to become soft and sticky and causing oily runs to develop. For these reasons the decoration of lime plaster should be delayed until the surface is reasonably dry, preferably for at least a year. On non-hydraulic lime plaster, used internally, it is advisable to use a good-quality emulsion paint for the initial decoration, as this has a certain amount of tolerance of damp. When an oil paint is applied, a priming system consisting of two coats of alkali-resisting primer is generally advisable. Wallpaper should not be hung until the surface is thoroughly dry, and then the preparation consists of sandpapering down to remove mortar splashes and nibs, and applying a coat of alkali-resisting primer. On external hydraulic plasters limewash may be used, but for a better finish a good-quality masonry paint applied according to the manufacturer's instructions is preferable.

Other characteristics of lime plaster which affect the painter are as follows:

(i) The plaster, if not properly gauged and worked, tends to shrink when drying and develops a mass of fine hair-cracks, called "surface crazing".

(ii) If the lime has not been properly slaked the plaster is liable to the defect of "popping" and "blowing" due to the presence of pockets of unslaked lime which, when attacked by moisture, slake after the surface has set and erupt to cause pits and craters.

(iii) Lime plaster finishes usually possess a fairly high degree of suction.

(iv) Lime plaster rarely develops efflorescence, and gives less trouble in this respect than any other type of plaster.

Lime putty Slaked lime which has been allowed to mature, as described under the previous heading.

Lime-resisting pigments Colours which are not affected by the presence of active alkali; they include yellow ochre, the brown earth pigments, black, chromium oxide (green), cobalt blue and ultramarine blue, and red oxides of iron. (**NLC**)

Lime water A bucket of water into which a small pat of lime putty has been mixed is sometimes used in the washing down, rubbing down and preparation of old paintwork, particularly in kitchens and similar places where there are deposits of grease. Some people object to this on the grounds that any residue of lime left on the surface may have an adverse effect upon the new paint, but provided the lime water is not allowed to dry on the surface and is thoroughly rinsed off with clean water after use, there is no reason why it should raise any difficulty. Lime water used in this way has a less positive action upon grease than sugar soap but is milder in it action upon the paint.

Limed oak Oak which has been pickled by the application of a coating of lime, which is subsequently brushed off the surface but allowed to remain in the grain. The surface is usually left unpolished.

At one time, limed oak furniture was tremendously popular with householders, and the decorator was often required to match the woodwork of a room to the furniture. This is now uncommon, but even today a customer will occasionally ask for a scheme to be carried out in limed oak, and there are various methods which can be used. When the woodwork consists of real oak, whether in the form of solid wood or of a thin veneer used as panelling, a suitable treatment is to stain the wood to the required depth of colour and then apply a sealer coat of eggshell varnish. A stiff white paste is then prepared with a proprietary brand of plaster-based filler or vinyl-based filler, mixed to a consistency which will allow it to cling in the grain, and this is either brushed or knifed across the surface in such a way as to fill the pores, the surplus material being removed from the face with a soft cloth or a squeegee. Softwood doors and architraves can be matched by painting them with a suitable ground colour, incising the grain pattern by a "needle oak" process with the requisite cutting tools, staining to the required colour, applying a sealer, and then filling the grain as already described. Alternatively a straightforward graining technique can be used on a smooth painted ground with a graining colour composed of glaze medium tinted with eggshell white, combing and cross-combing the glaze with a fine-toothed steel comb supplemented where necessary by light figure-graining.

Limer A large fibre brush used for limewashing. It may have either a flat or a round head, and is designed to be fitted to a long handle, for use on factory work and industrial painting.

Limewash An inexpensive form of treatment for brickwork, plaster, stonework and similar surfaces, both interior and exterior, which has been used for thousands of years in many parts of the world and which is still employed in this country on farm buildings and domestic properties, especially in rural districts. It needs to be recoated at fairly frequent intervals, but its renewal is easy and cheap, and it very often presents quite a pleasing appearance. It also has the advantage of preventing the accumulation of lichen and mould growths and discouraging the presence of insects and vermin. For these reasons it has enjoyed widespread use in the treatment of factories and industrial premises for a very long time.

In its simplest form limewash consists of newly slaked lime mixed with water. When freshly mixed it is thin and semi-transparent, but it becomes opaque when dry. Lime blue is generally added to correct its slightly dingy colour and give a clean white, but it can also be tinted with a variety of limeproof dry pigments. There are, however, a huge number of recipes in which binders and waterproofing agents are added to improve the properties of limewash. In rural districts it is common practice to add organic matter of various kinds, and there are several recipes calling for the use of such materials as casein, linseed oil, starch, etc. Probably the most satisfactory mixtures are those based on lime and tallow, applied cool; upon lime, glue and salt, applied hot; and upon lime and Portland cement mixed to a thick slurry.

Lincrusta A low-relief composition made with oxidized linseed oil with suitable filling agents added. The most familiar form of Lincrusta is that of wood effects and imitations, which are supplied in plain buff or putty colour to be stained and varnished after hanging, or in ready decorated form. There are also patterns available in ready decorated form giving the appearance of glazed tiles, and it has also been produced in the form of ornamental patterns, leathers and plastic textures.

Lincrusta is one of the great success stories in the history of decorative materials. The process was invented by Frederick Walton in 1877, and in fact the material was always known by the name "Lincrusta-Walton" until the 1950's. Walton had been associated for many years with the celebrated Staines linoleum, and it was his innovative mind that led him to apply the floor-covering material in a totally different way to the development of a wallcovering. It was so popular that several imitations appeared on the market, but Walton introduced so many new ideas that it was always ahead of its rivals, and it has remained the premier product in its class for well over a 100 years. Although it now has to compete with a vast number of new decorative products, there is still a healthy demand for it at the time of this book's revision in 1986.

Linear measure Also sometimes called "running measure". Measurement in one dimension only, e.g. measuring the length of a line. In estimating for painting work, while most of the measurements are of areas, certain items are too narrow to be reckoned in this way and are therefore measured in linear form. Examples from various types of work are as follows: in exterior domestic painting, the guttering and downspouts; in the interior decoration of schools, hospitals, etc., painted lines run with a lining fitch or lining tool; in high-class decoration, the gilding of narrow beadings and mouldings. On a big exterior contract where many windows are identical in size, the estimator measures the total length of the glazing bars in one window, carefully reckons how long it will take to cut them in, and then multiplies by the number of windows.

Linenfold Panelling carved in low relief with a stylized representation of folded linen, developed by woodcarvers in the 16th century. Certain modern decorative materials such as Lincrusta are sometimes supplied in a form which reproduces the effect of linenfold panelling.

Liner A long-haired brush, which may be sword-shaped or may terminate in a chisel edge and which is usually set in a quill, used in the production of fine lines in paint. Liners are commonly used in coachpainting but are not often used by painters and decorators.

Lining (a) The application of paint in the form of a narrow line of regular width. In painting and decorating this generally refers to running a line by means of lining fitch and straightedge for such purposes as separating a dado from a wall filling or for lining out panels on walls or ceilings, although for picking out the mouldings on doors or around signboards it is customary to use a sable writer. In commercial painting various methods of lining are employed, including the use of sword liners and lining pencils, transfers, masking tape or mechanical lining tools.

(b) The hanging of a backing paper in order to provide a good foundation of even porosity for the reception of good quality wallpapers or relief goods, to provide a better surface for the reception of wallpaper on badly cracked or uneven walls and ceilings, or to provide a surface of regular absorbency for the reception of paint or distemper.

Lining fitch A brush used in conjunction with a straightedge in the production of narrow lines in paint, the method of lining most commonly used by the painter and decorator. It is made of hog hair and is set in a tin ferrule mounted on a long thin wooden handle which is tapered down to a narrow end. The working edge of the brush is slanted, and the ferrule is slanted in a parallel direction.

Lining fitches are available in various sizes, the smallest being capable of producing a line 1.5 mm wide. They are also sold with varying lengths of bristle. In general, it may be said that the shorter the bristle, the easier it is for the beginner to achieve a reasonably straight line, but that the man who accustoms himself to working with a short brush will never gain real proficiency and speed; fitches with longer bristle carry more paint and require recharging less frequently. A bad practice adopted by some painters is to cut down the bristle very short to that it cannot splay outwards at all, making it easier to use the fitch but also making the work tediously slow. The correct method of using the fitch is to hold it very lightly so that no weight rests on the bristles and therefore there is no tendency for them to splay outwards; the fitch, charged with colour, is then drawn rapidly along the whole length of the straightedge; with practice this produces the cleanest quickest lining.

Lining paper Plain paper applied for the purposes mentioned in paragraph (b) under the heading *Lining*. It is available in varying weights and qualities. White lining paper of a pulp type is used prior to the hanging of ordinary wallpapers, stouter brown lining papers are used for the reception of heavy relief materials and for rough walls, and there are linings faced with linen, calico or muslin for use on badly cracked surfaces or for jointed boardings. A brown lining paper coated on one side with tar, known as pitch paper, is sometimes used as a treatment for damp surfaces. Coloured linings are still available but are not widely used today.

Any piece of paperhanging work is improved by the use of lining paper, which provides the ideal surface for its reception, but in some cases lining is absolutely essential; lining paper should always be hung prior to the hanging of relief materials, delicate or expensive papers, and papers with a lustrous finish that reflects the light and therefore shows up the imperfections in the surface, and when wallpaper is to be hung on previously painted surfaces or upon surfaces treated with damp-proofing solutions or lead foil.

Lining pencil Sometimes known as a "rigger". A type of signwriting brush with extremely long hair set in a quill, and used chiefly by coach-painters for the rapid production of fine lines in paint. The best variety is made from sable. The operative holds the brush by the quill, charges it with colour, and applies it to the work by means of a deft flick of the wrist.

Lining tool or lining wheel A device used originally for the production of narrow painted lines in industrial finishing such as, for example, the lining of bicycle frames, metal furniture, etc., but now being widely used in painting and decorating and available from any good decorators' merchant. It consists of a paint container and a system of wheels or wipers which transfer the paint to the work surface. Generally the wheels may be changed to provide lines of varying widths. Usually a guiding device is incorporated to ensure the production of an accurate straight line.

The same principle is applied on a much larger scale in road lining machines, with which white or coloured lines can be painted on roads by unskilled labour.

Linoleates Drying agents produced by fusing linseed oil and metallic oxides.

Linoxyn The tough leathery substance of which a dried film of linseed oil is composed. When a film of liquid linseed oil is exposed to the air it undergoes a chemical change, absorbing oxygen and becoming the solid substance known as linoxyn; this action is commonly described as drying.

Linseed oil A vegetable drying oil obtained by crushing the seed pods of the flax plant. Until recently it was the principal oil used in the binding of paint and the manufacture of varnish, and although this is no longer the case it is still a material of importance in the paint industry. It was always considered that oil derived from the Baltic provinces of Russia was superior to any other, having a higher iodine value and therefore greater drying properties; this source of supply no longer contributes to the world market, and the chief producing countries are now Argentina, the USA, Canada and India.

Raw or crude linseed oil as expressed from the pods needs refining in order to rid it of mucilage before it is fit for use as a paint medium, and what is usually called "raw linseed oil" is actually a refined oil. In this form its colour is pale yellow which becomes paler with age and exposure to light. It works very easily under the brush and mixes readily with other paint materials. When exposed to the air in a thin film it absorbs oxygen and "dries" in three or four days, the drying being chiefly due to the process of oxidation. Since this is too slow for practical purposes the rate of drying is accelerated by the addition of drying agents. Linseed oil, like most vegetable oils, is a compound of glycerine and certain fatty acids; a small quantity of the fatty acid exists in a free state, and the degree of acidity is expressed as the "acid value" of the oil. When exposed to the action of alkalis, linseed oil is readily decomposed, free glycerine being produced, and the film becomes sticky and soapy; this phenomenon is known as "saponification".

Raw linseed oil can be modified in various ways. Its property of absorbing oxygen can be increased by heating it for several hours at a high temperature in contact with the air and with the addition of a small quantity of driers; in this form it is known as "boiled linseed oil" and is darker in colour, more viscous, quicker drying and more resistant to moisture than is raw oil. The action of heat alone produces polymerization, the oil increasing in viscosity as the heating continues. Stand oil is a thickened oil produced by heating a high-quality refined oil for a considerable period without the addition of driers, and is a pale slow-drying material with a high degree of flow. Blown oil is produced by blowing air through a heated oil, which causes it to thicken rapidly and become much darker in colour.

Lintel The horizontal beam or stone over a door or window.

Liquefied petroleum gas A fuel derived from petroleum, which is used to operate various kinds of equipment such as blowtorches, etc., and certain types of industrial burners; it is also used for some kinds of domestic equipment in situations where piped gas is not available. See *LPG containers or cylinders*.

Liquid Matter which is in a fluid state but which is relatively incompressible.

Liquid driers Driers such as terebine or liquid oil driers used for accelerating the oxidation of an oil medium. Their interest to the painter today is limited to carrying out such operations as graining, and to those rare occasions where traditional hand-mixed materials are specified for restoration work.

Liquid oil driers Liquid driers made by dissolving linoleates with turpentine and reducing them with linseed oil or wood oil. (**NLC**)

Litharge A monoxide of lead used as a drier for paint. (**NLC**)

Lithopone A white pigment produced by the precipitation of zinc sulphide and barium sulphate, yielding a very pure white with a high degree of opacity. At one time it was of great importance in the production of flat oil paints and oil-bound water paints. It has now been superseded by titanium oxide. A very small proportion of lithopone is contained in some emulsion paints, but it has ceased to be of any importance in the paint industry. (**NLC**)

Litmus A vegetable dye which is sensitive to acid and alkali, becoming red in the presence of an acid and blue in contact with an alkali. The dye is obtained from lichen and the chief source of supply is Holland.

Litmus paper A type of unsized paper stained with litmus; books of litmus paper containing a number of small leaves can be obtained very cheaply from a chemist, and provide a useful and convenient method of determining the alkalinity or otherwise of a surface which is to be painted.

Live edges A term used to denote the fact that the edges of a previously applied area of paintwork are sufficiently fluid to allow newly applied paint to blend into them without showing any lap. It is important when large areas are being painted that the edges should be kept "alive" so that no joints or laps are apparent in the work.

Livering A defect in paint whereby the paint thickens partially or completely into a jelly-like condition resembling raw liver, and becomes unusable. It is caused by a chemical reaction within the paint itself, or by the addition of an unsuitable thinner or some other incompatible ingredient to the paint; it may also occur through the continued oxidation or polymerization of the paint medium in the container during storage.

Lock rail A term used to define one of the horizontal members of a door construction, namely the member upon which the lock or handle is mounted.

Logo This word came into use in recent years as a colloquial term for a "logotype", which is a printing term meaning a word or group of letters cast in one piece. In a short space of time the meaning has altered again by common usage. The term is now generally used to refer to a non-heraldic device or symbol chosen as the distinguishing mark of some organization such as a commercial company, a local authority or a college, and used as such in advertisements and on notepaper. The decorator is often called upon to depict a customer's logo on signboards and motor vehicles, or as part of a decorative scheme in shops and offices.

Logwood The wood of the Campeachy tree grown in Central and South America and the West Indies, which is used as a dyestuff. It owes its name to the fact that it is imported in logs. The wood is hard and yellow, but turns red on exposure to air. The dye is a colourless crystalline substance extracted from the heartwood but when combined with oxygen it becomes red, and with suitable mordants it produces a range of dark red, blue, and dense black colourings. Logwood is the only natural mordant dye which is still used commercially, and is the basis of various wood stains.

Lombardic A type of alphabet characterized by bulging shapes, derived from a style employed in medieval manuscript writing.

Long oil (i) A term applied to a varnish or varnish medium indicating that it is composed of a high proportion of oil and a low proportion of resin. A long oil varnish is defined by the British Standards Institution as being an oleo-resinous varnish, other than an alkyd, comprising not less than $2\frac{1}{2}$ parts of oil to 1 part of resin by weight. Such varnishes are durable, elastic, and capable of withstanding considerable changes of temperature, and as such they are suitable for exterior work. They are generally slower-drying and less lustrous than varnishes with a higher resin content. Long oil alkyds are alkyd resins in which the amount of oil included as a modifying agent exceeds 60 percent.

(ii) The term is now also used to denote a paint in which the proportion of drying oil in the medium or binder is 70 percent or more.

Loose leaf gold Gold beaten into very thin leaves measuring 82.5 mm square and supplied in books containing 25 leaves each. The individual leaves are kept separate from one another by being interspersed with thin sheets of tissue paper which are dusted with Armenian bole to prevent them from sticking to the gold; the gold itself, as its name implies, is loose, that is to say it is not fastened down in any way to any substance which would make it easier to handle, as opposed to transfer gold in which the gold leaf is attached to a waxed tissue. Loose leaf gold is used by the decorator for such purposes as glass gilding, the gilding of carved or modelled work, and the gilding of large wooden or metal letters of the type which can be taken down and treated in the workshop instead of being gilded *in situ*. Gold in this form is very delicate and susceptible to the slightest draught or current of air; it is generally applied by means of the tip and cushion. It produces a much more brilliant lustre than transfer gold.

Low solubility inorganic lead compounds In the Control of Lead at Work Regulations and the Approved Code of Practice, a low solubility lead compound is defined as being one which does not yield to dilute hydrochloric acid more than 5 percent of its dry weight of a soluble lead compound calculated as lead monoxide when determined by the test described below.

If the lead compound is dispersed in a liquid (for example, a paint) then the soluble matter is to be separated out by a suitable method (e.g. by centrifuging) before applying the test, and the results reported as a percentage of lead in solid material.

TEST. The test to ascertain this percentage is as follows: A weighed quantity of the material in the form in which it is used or processed (see above), which has been dried at 100°C and thoroughly mixed, is to be shaken continuously for one hour at 23°C (73°F) (plus or minus 2°C (3.5°F)) with 1000 times its weight of 0.07N hydrochloric acid. The solution is allowed to stand for one hour, and then filtered, before being analysed by suitable techniques.

LPG blowtorches An abbreviation for "Liquefied petroleum gas blowtorches". See *LPG containers.*

LPG containers or cylinders Steel cylinders containing a hydrocarbon such as butane, propane, etc., in compressed and therefore liquefied form; when released from compression the substance vaporizes to produce a flammable gas. The cylinders are supplied for domestic use in situations where no piped gas is available, and they also have many industrial uses with various applications to the construction industry. They are used for a number of purposes in industrial painting, but to the painter and decorator they are probably most familiar as providing the fuel supply for blowtorches for burning off old paintwork. For practical reasons the domestic type of container, which supplies sufficient fuel for about thirty hours of continuous burning, is often used.

LPG cylinders are usually hired on a rental basis, empty containers being returned to the supplier for replenishment in exchange for refilled cylinders as needed. It is desirable that only sufficient cylinders for immediate requirements should be kept on a site. If for any reason it is necessary to maintain a stock of cylinders either on a site or in a workshop, certain safety precautions are essential. A definite area should be reserved for the storage of the cylinders, and every cylinder must be returned to this area at the end of each day's work; the local fire brigade headquarters should be notified that LPG containers are being stored on the premises, and the brigade should be informed of the exact location of the storage area. Strict observance of these rules is necessary because in the event of an outbreak of fire the explosive nature of the cylinders presents a serious hazard; firemen unaware of the presence of such containers face the added danger of explosion.

Lumigraphic The trade name used for fluorescent pigments.

Luminous paint Paint which is activated by daylight and continues to glow in the dark. It consists of a crystalline fluorescent pigment bound by a synthetic resin medium. One type, in which the pigment is either zinc sulphide, cadmium sulphide, or a combination of the two, produces a glow which is fairly bright at first but which soon declines; another type, based upon cadmium fluoride, strontium sulphide or a combination of the two, gives a glow which is not so bright in the initial stages but which persists for a longer time. A pronounced reaction takes place if luminous paint is brought into contact with lead, and it is therefore important not to apply luminous paint directly upon a surface or an old paint film containing lead. Special undercoats based on titanium are supplied.

Luminous paints may be applied by brush, roller or spray. They may be used for sign work, but their value in this respect is limited by their poor flowing properties and the coarse nature of the pigment particles.

There is another type of luminous paint which is radioactive and which is used for picking out the figures or markings on watches, compasses, etc., but this is a specialist application with no bearing upon the painter and decorator's work.

Luminous pigments There are two types of luminous pigment, which differ in the way they react to illumination.

In the type known as "fluorescent pigments" the luminosity exists only as long as the paint is exposed to the exciting radiation and disappears on its removal. These pigments are activated by daylight, and they are used in high-visibility paints. One type which is widely used contains a fluorescent dye dissolved in a hard resin which is then powdered and used as a pigment. The paints produced are translucent, and are therefore applied over a matt ground coat. The performance of the paint can be improved by the application of a protective lacquer, but its exterior durability is limited to a period of between twelve and eighteen months.

The type known as "phosphorescent pigments" consists of specially prepared sulphides of certain metals, and paints which contain these pigments retain an "afterglow" when the exciting radiation is removed. The colour which is emitted depends on the nature of the metal sulphide used in their manufacture, and its duration is very limited. Paints made with these pigments contain a very low proportion of binder, and consequently they have only a limited durability.

Lump sum contract The simplest form of fixed-price contract, and the one most frequently used in painting and decorating transactions. The quoted price is a lump sum or overall figure for the complete job; the sum is determined by the contractor, with nothing in the agreement to indicate how the price was estimated.

The great majority of painting and decorating operations are not concerned with new construction but with the redecoration of existing premises. Because the work is of an individual nature, dictated by the personal taste and whims of the customer, and because the areas involved are usually very small, it would be quite impracticable to attempt to draw up anything resembling a bill of quantities. The usual method is for the price to be based on a specification in which is listed the extent of the work, the type of preparation required for the various surfaces, the type and brand of the primers, undercoats and finishing materials, the number of coatings and the type of wallcoverings, etc. Sometimes the specification is compiled by the customer or by an agent acting on the customer's behalf; at other times the contractor draws up the specification after visiting and inspecting the premises and discussing the various options with the customer. It is very desirable that the specification should be prepared carefully so that nothing of any consequence is overlooked. A purely verbal agreement without anything being clearly defined is far too vague and can easily lead to a dispute and conflict of opinions when the work is completed. When the customer intends to approach a number of contractors in order to obtain several competitive prices, it is important that the specification should be sufficiently detailed for all the competitors to be tendering on exactly the same basis. But given a properly drawn up and detailed specification, the lump sum contract is a perfectly adequate and satisfactory method of transacting business, and it is certainly the one best suited to the particular nature of painting and decorating work. Indeed, this type of contract is used for work of quite a considerable scale such as hotel work and the decoration of churches, hospitals, offices and general painting, and in industrial painting operations it is customary for huge contracts to be allocated in this way.

Lustre Brightness, gloss or sheen. The term is often used to describe the quality of gloss and the extent to which light is reflected by a varnish, enamel or gloss paint finish.

Lustre finish A term used for a nitro-cellulose lacquer tinted with spirit soluble dye to give a sparkling effect when used on a bright metal.

Lymnato A type of decorative effect obtained by manipulating a spray gun in such a way as to produce a continuous irregularly shaped line of paint in a colour contrasting with the ground; a low air pressure is used so that the paint, instead of being atomized, emerges from the gun in a thin continuous stream.

M

Machine print Wallpaper produced by mechanical methods, as opposed to hand-printed wallpaper.

Obviously the vast majority of the wallpapers produced and sold now are processed entirely by machinery; hand-printed papers form only a very small part of the production, and their use is restricted to those situations where either a highly individual colour scheme is required or where an unusual size of pattern repeat or a personal choice of motif is called for. Until fairly recently the term "machine print" indicated a paper on which the pattern is printed from cylindrical rollers, the paper being fed into the machine as a continuous roll and passing over a revolving drum to which the printing rollers are attached, the drum and rollers revolving in unison, a separate roller being used for each colour in the pattern. Today the methods of producing and printing wallpaper are so many and varied that the meaning has become blurred; in fact the term is not very often used now, and when it *is* used it refers in general terms to all mechanically produced papers.

Machinery paints Paints formulated by the manufacturer to provide quick-drying, hard protective coatings for machinery, plant and equipment, capable of withstanding the harmful action of various substances used in industrial processes, such as mineral oil (lubricating oil), cutting oil, battery acid, fresh and salt water, etc., and to resist abrasion.

Madder A shrubby climbing plant, *Rubia tinctorum*, from the root of which a red dyestuff is obtained; the dye itself is also known by the name madder, although another name for it is alizarin.

Madison sealers (Madison formula) Madison sealers are penetrating compositions used on exterior timber as an alternative to clear varnish, lacquer or clear wood finishes. Their name is derived from the fact that they are based on the "Madison formula" which originated in the USA. They consist of a mixture of boiled linseed oil, waxes, fungicidal agents and white spirit, together with a small quantity of semi-transparent pigment to give a resemblance to the colour of natural woods.

Madison sealers are produced by all the main paint manufacturers under a variety of trade names. They provide a pleasing eggshell gloss finish which, unlike most transparent finishes, prevents the timber from developing a whitish or greyish discolouration due to the bleaching of the natural wood; they also prevent the timber from darkening due to the accumulation of mould growths. They are easy to apply and are relatively cheap, with the result that the material and labour costs are low. On planed weatherboarding a single application of the sealer is usually sufficient, although sometimes a second coating is desirable. Under normal conditions of exposure the coating lasts for about three years, at the end of which time a further single application of the Madison sealer is all that is needed, because there is no surface film in which faults such as cracking and flaking have developed; they allow the surface of the timber to "breathe".

They are especially useful on woods such as Western red cedar which contain an oil which interferes with the drying of varnish, and on hardwoods such as keruing which give off a resinous exudation which prevents the varnish from adhering properly.

Madison sealers are applied by brush, and after two hours any surplus material is wiped off with a cloth. The cloths so used should be burned immediately afterwards, as otherwise they present a fire hazard. Opened tins of the sealer should be kept out of reach of children and household pets, because of the toxic nature of the fungicide.

Magenta A brilliant crimson colour, named after the Italian city where a battle was fought in 1849 at which the French and Sardinians defeated the Austrians.

Magnesium A silvery white metal which itself is comparatively weak but which can be mixed with aluminium, zinc and manganese to produce magnesium alloys of considerable strength. These alloys are largely employed in the manufacture of aircraft parts. Most of the magnesium alloys are rapidly corroded by salt, especially when in sheet form. The treatment for them consists of a degreasing and cleaning process followed by a pre-treatment aimed at producing a surface layer rich in chromates which will give a high resistance to corrosion and provide a good base for paint. The priming paint is based upon zinc chromate or a mixture of pigments with zinc chromate predominating. Subsequent coatings, which because of the highly corrodible nature of the material need to be developed to a good film thickness, vary according to the purpose for which the metal article is to be used, but paints containing lead are quite unsuitable for the purpose.

Mahlstick Sometimes called "maulstick". A wooden rod with a round pad at the end, used by signwriters and decorative artists as a rest upon which the hand holding the brush or writer is steadied. The most convenient pattern is tapered and is divided up into two or three separate sections, each section being fitted with brass jointing-pieces. The pad at the end should be covered with a piece of clean chamois leather so as to prevent damage to the painted surface of the signboard.

The position of the mahlstick should be varied according to the stroke which is being executed. Generally speaking, the mahlstick should be at right angles to the direction of the stroke. A great many people adopt a rigid attitude and never shift the position of the mahlstick, thereby robbing themselves of most of the value of the tool. It sometimes happens that due to a misunderstanding of the purpose of the implement students develop the habit of using the mahlstick solely as a sort of straightedge along which the writing pencil is drawn to form straight lines; this practice should be firmly discouraged since it prevents the student from attaining a proper brush technique.

Mahogany A light hardwood; one of the best known and most widely used of the hardwoods. The original Spanish mahogany which in the 18th century became so popular for the production of furniture was introduced into

Britain in the first place as a ballast cargo from Cuba and Central America; it is now rare, its place having been taken by another species from Central America and by African mahogany from Nigeria and Ghana. Spanish mahogany is very close grained with a fine silky texture and is often beautifully figured particularly where forking of the stem occurs to produce the "crotch". Central American and African mahoganies are lighter in colour and coarser in texture. A number of other tropical woods which bear some resemblance to it in colour, grain and texture are sometimes described as mahogany but strictly speaking only woods of the true mahogany or Meliaceae family are entitled to the name.

Mahogany is important to the painter and decorator in two connections. In the first place the wood is widely used for constructional purposes, advantages in its favour being the fact that it shrinks very little when drying and also the fact that when dry it is very durable and largely free from twisting and warping; it is employed in the construction of doors and panelling, in high class joinery work of all kinds and in the production of veneers. A normal wood primer of the traditional type is suitable for mahogany, but some difficulty may be experienced due to the closeness of the grain resisting penetration by the paint; adhesion is improved if the primer is thinned with up to 10 percent of white spirit.

In the second place the popularity of mahogany in the making of furniture means that it is a wood that the decorator is often called upon to imitate by graining. It can be reproduced in either oil or water medium, but it is generally agreed that the effect of its characteristic silky appearance is achieved more faithfully in water medium. A common fault in mahogany graining is the use of a rather unsuitable pink ground, upon which the necessary richness of colour can only be obtained by means of a too-warmly coloured reddish glaze; far better results are achieved if the warmth is introduced into the ground colour and the glaze colour is kept on the cool side. A suitable ground can be made up with Venetian red, burnt sienna and ochre, or Venetian red and orange chrome, and the glaze may consist of Vandyke brown, Vandyke brown and mahogany lake, or mahogany lake and blue-black. There are innumerable methods of producing the figure; it is usual to build it up in stages, using the flogger to produce the pore marks, a feather, a sponge or a mottler, coupled with overgrainers, to produce the main figure, and a mottler to produce the final faint mottling, all the work being softened with the badger.

Mahogany feather The highly decorative figuring which occurs at the forking of the trunk.

Maize A type of corn which besides being used as food has important secondary products such as starch. It formed the basis of dextrin which was widely used as a fixative for hanging heavy relief goods, but which has now been superseded by modern adhesives. (**NLC**)

Making good Cutting out and repairing defective plaster or Portland cement work to present a sound surface prior to decoration; the term is often included in painting specifications, and implies that any loose or crumbly material should be removed and any holes or cracks raked out, and the cavities then patched in with sound material.

Makore Sometimes called "cherry mahogany". A Nigerian reddish-brown hardwood used for superior joinery, veneers, etc.

Malachite A green mineral, consisting of basic carbonate of copper which occurs in many parts of the world, particularly in the Urals, in Germany, France, England, the Belgian Congo, Rhodesia and Australia.

Malachite green A green pigment, used as an artists' colour, prepared by grinding and levigation of the mineral malachite.

Maleic anhydride Used in the production of certain types of alkyd resins to give very pale varnishes of good durability, the maleic anhydride taking the place of phthalic anhydride as the acid component.

Manganese A diatomic metallic element which in various compounds has several uses in the paint industry. Manganese salts are the basis of certain drying agents, and manganese is also present in various pigments such as sienna, umber, manganese brown and manganese black.

Manhelp A handle, the length of which is adjustable, which may be attached to various types of brushes in order to reach places that would otherwise be difficult or inaccessible.

Manila (a) A type of hemp used in making rope; hence "manila rope" which formerly was used in rigging cradles and other forms of scaffolding, but which has been superseded by various kinds of synthetic ropes produced from man-made fibres.

(b) A natural resin found in the Philippine Islands; the fossil resin is fairly hard, but the recent resin is soft and is used in spirit varnishes, being soluble in alcohol.

Mantling Decorative scrollwork or drapery in heraldic painting, derived from the silken mantle worn by medieval warriors to prevent the heat of the sun from striking directly upon their armour. The mantling is usually depicted in the principal colours of the charge but there are certain exceptions, e.g., the Sovereign's mantling, which is gold lined with ermine.

Maple A tree of the same family as the sycamore, the wood of which is used as a decorative veneer and is also employed in furniture making and to some extent for flooring and stair treads. Maple wood is very light and clean in colour and is characterized by a beautiful silky silvery mottle, but when exposed to air and light it darkens to an unattractive yellow colour. The grain markings are indistinct; sometimes the outer parts of the wood are dotted with "birds' eyes" where tiny branches have sprung.

The graining of maple is usually carried out in water medium on a ground of white or ivory, a very thin glaze of raw umber and raw sienna being used. After the glaze has been mottled and softened with the badger, grain markings may be inserted with a crayon. "Birds' eyes" are put in with burnt sienna by means of a maple dotter; they can also be put in with the finger-tips or with a piece of rough cork, but these devices produce an unnatural effect.

Maple dotter A simple tool with which the small horseshoe shaped "birds' eyes" can be inserted in maple graining. A useful dotter can be made by singeing the centre out of a water colour brush with a red hot needle; dotters can also be cut from pieces of rubber, chamois leather, felt, etc.

Maquette A small three-dimensional model. Interior designers very often use maquettes of rooms, including furniture, etc., either instead of perspective drawings or in addition to drawings in order to give their clients a clear indication of the probable appearance of a completed scheme.

Mar resistance The ability of a film of paint, varnish or lacquer to undergo the conditions for which it was designed without showing signs of damage—for instance, the ability of a bar counter finish to withstand the contact with alcoholic liquids, or the ability of a furniture lacquer to resist damage by normal wear and tear.

Marble Strictly speaking, a metamorphized and recrystallized limestone or dolomite capable of taking a high polish. In the building trade, however, the term is used freely to describe any crystallized calcium carbonate rock which displays a pleasing pattern and colour when cut and polished.

Marbling A surface treatment by which the texture, pattern and broken colour effect of polished marble are imitated in paint. The work is prepared and grounded out in a suitable colour, and the marbling is generally executed with opaque oil colour, blended and softened as required, although glazes are sometimes used to give added depth and the appearance of translucency, and crayons are sometimes used for the veining.

Marine paints, marine varnishes, etc. Materials formulated especially for the protection and enrichment of ships, especially ocean-going vessels, and to some extent for application to harbour installations in seaports. The conditions of exposure which such materials are expected to withstand are very severe and it is seldom possible to ensure that the materials will be applied under suitable circumstances; it is rarely possible, for instance, for a ship to be in dry dock long enough for a treatment comprising complete rust removal followed by the application of a thorough anti-corrosive system to take place, nor can it always be arranged for the repainting of the superstructure to be preceded by adequate preparation.

The various parts of a ship each present their own particular problems demanding a paint system specially designed to meet their needs. The whole of the steel structure is subjected to the severe corrosive effects of exposure to salt water, sea air and strong sunlight, the topside also being attacked by continual wetting and drying and those parts which are at waterline level being liable to physical damage due to the impact of tugs and lighters. The paint for the funnels may have to withstand high temperatures. The underwater painted surfaces must not only resist corrosion but also combat the accumulation of marine growth and barnacles. A further factor influencing the manufacture of marine paints is that they need to be elastic enough to withstand considerable climate changes ranging from arctic to tropical conditions within a few days.

The term "marine paints" also covers the compositions used for painting the holds, cargo tanks, etc.

Marking The term used in industrial finishing for the application of trade marks and coding devices or the application of the scale markings on instruments, etc.

Maroon A rich brownish-crimson red colour. There are various chemically prepared pigments producing maroon, those in the azo class tending to fade when reduced with white, but Perylene maroon has a high tinting strength and is fast to light.

Marouflage The method of affixing a painted canvas picture to a wall surface by cementing it with white lead and gold size or oil.

Marquetry Inlaid work. The term is usually applied to inlaying with fine woods, ivory or metals, but the painter and decorator can use the technique of marquetry to produce patterns and decorative motifs with low-relief materials such as Lincrusta, or with thin wood veneers.

Mask (a) Some object such as, for example, a sheet of paper or a piece of sheet metal, which is placed on a surface to prevent paint from encroaching on to it when an adjacent surface is being painted. The term is generally used in connection with spray painting rather than with other forms of paint application; for instance, the technique used for decorative spraying is similar to that used for edge stencilling, but the paper used to define the pattern in decorative spraying is referred to as a mask, whereas in the case of edge stencilling it would normally be termed a stencil plate.

(b) Term commonly used to mean a respirator.

Masking paste A paste which is used to mask off certain areas of a surface before paint is sprayed and which, after the paint has dried, is sponged away. Various proprietary emulsion types of paste are available. It is essential that they should be thoroughly cleaned off the surface as soon as is reasonably possible, otherwise there is a strong possibility that they will cause the ground coating to crack.

Masking tape A material sold in rolls of varying widths for the purpose of masking out prior to spray painting. Gummed paper and cellotape are sometimes used for the purpose but these tend to disturb the ground coat and pluck it off when they are being peeled away. Proprietary masking materials consisting of pressure-sensitive adhesive paper or linen tapes are safer, although more expensive. These are flexible and can be made to conform to the contours of almost any desired shape.

Masonite The brand name of a hardboard with a smooth polished surface, used for lining walls and ceilings.

Masonry paint Coatings intended for application to external surfaces, masonry and renderings. These now represent a considerable proportion of the paint industry's output. Every firm of paint manufacturers now offers its own particular line, and some manufacturers produce a whole range of lines.

The properties and qualities of any particular kind depend partly on the liquid media and partly on the solid matter suspended in the medium. The liquid medium may be a drying oil or a synthetic resin or a combination of the two, similar to the medium of an oil paint, or it may be a synthetic resin of the kind used in water-thinned emulsion paints. The solid particles may consist of a variety of substances, including (a) sand or granulated stone, both of which impart cohesion to the paint, (b) fine aggregates of very hard materials such as granite which produce a coating of great durability, (c) combinations of mica and such materials as sand, mineral quartz, granite, etc., in each of which the mica is intended to give improved properties of adhesion, and (d) nylon fibre which being smoother than stone particles is claimed to produce a paint which is easier to apply and which remains clean longer than other materials because there are no rough particles to trap the dirt. The actual formula of each brand is a careful selection made by the manufacturer to produce a paint with distinctive features. The choice of brand depends to a great extent on the nature of the surface to be painted and on the conditions of exposure on the particular site. It is clear, for example, that in some situations the toughness and durability of the first-named type of medium would be a distinct advantage, whereas on surfaces which are highly alkaline or which still retain some moisture the water-thinned type would be the better choice. For some brands it is claimed that a gradual and controlled erosion of the components takes place so that the surface remains constantly clean in appearance.

Some products are advertised as possessing a very high measure of durability, figures of fifteen years and upwards being quoted. Obviously the claims would not be made if they were untrue, but the inference to be drawn from them may be misleading. For instance, a very expensive product might be chosen on the grounds that over its extended life-period its average cost per year would be less than that of a cheaper material which needed renewing much earlier; if, however, the woodwork of the structure needed repainting after five or six years, it is unlikely that the customer would sacrifice the appearance of the premises by not renewing the masonry paint on the rendering, and the cost advantage of the long-life product would be lost.

The appearance of external rendering is often marred by a mass of fine cracks. Most masonry paints are thick enough in their composition to fill the cracks adequately, but for situations where the cracking is very severe some extra treatment may be necessary. Certain manufacturers produce a sealer composition for the purpose, to be used in conjunction with a thin membrane of glass fibre, forced in while the sealer is wet, with a further sealer coat applied when this has dried.

There are some firms specializing in the production of masonry paints who, instead of supplying their products to the decorator or to the general public, market them as a full application service through approved distributors. The materials are based on polyester-resin, with filling agents such as glass fibre, perlite, mica, zinc oxide, titanium and fungicidal matter, and their composition is such that they cannot be applied by normal painting methods.

Application is by high-powered spray, carried out by operators trained in this particular process. The coating is a very thick single-coat film with a heavily textured finish and is extremely tough, tenacious and elastic.

Mastic A jointing or sealing compound which is plastic when applied and which should retain the property of yielding and movement throughout its life. Mastic generally consists of bitumen, tar, resin, rubber or oil with the addition of some inert fibrous or powdered filler. If the joint is to remain waterproof the mastic should be of a form which will adhere firmly to the sides of the joint.

Mastic cement A sealing compound made from litharge and boiled oil which sets harder than most other types of mastic.

Mastic varnish A spirit varnish made from a natural resin called gum mastic, which is used for varnishing oil paintings; because it possesses the property of becoming brittle when ageing it can when old be removed by friction, without damaging the picture, which can then be revarnished.

Matchboarding Tongued and grooved boards with beaded edges to conceal any shrinkage that may occur.

Matching Making two things correspond—for example, matching one colour to another, or matching a wallpaper so that the pattern on one piece is accurately joined at all points to the pattern of the piece previously hung.

Matt Flat, substantially free from gloss or sheen.

Matt finish A finish which presents neither gloss nor sheen.

Matt gold A term usually used in connection with glass gilding, where certain areas of gold may be made to present a matt effect which contrasts with other highly burnished areas. Such an effect is seen when the gold leaf is applied to an area of glass which has been etched or sandblasted, and the effect can be simulated on a piece of plain glass by coating in the area which is to appear matt with clear varnish and allowing it to dry before the gilding is commenced.

Matt size A composition of parchment size or gelatine size with pipeclay and Armenian bole, used in the process of water gilding. See *Water gilding*.

Matting agent A material used to decrease the gloss of a paint film; it may be a material which is soluble in a medium or it may take the form of a solid extender such as magnesium carbonate, asbestine or colloidal china clay.

Maturing The process whereby varnishes are clarified and improved by storage. The process applies to varnishes made from natural resin, but not to the modern varnishes made with synthetic resins.

Maulstick See *Mahlstick*.

Maximum amplitude This refers to the vertical distance between the hollows and the peaks in steelwork that has been prepared by blast-cleaning. Where metallic abrasives have been used, a maximum amplitude of 0.10 mm is considered acceptable for painting, and when non-metallic abrasives have been used 0.18 mm is regarded as acceptable.

Measuring Ascertaining the length and breadth of a given area of work, or the length of a linear feature, by the use of a measuring tape or folding rule, so as to calculate its exact dimensions. This information is coupled with the decorator's knowledge and experience of how many square metres can be treated per hour and what allowance is needed for cutting in a linear feature, in order to arrive at a precise estimate of how long it will take to perform the work. The same information, coupled with a knowledge of the spreading capacity of various types of coating, will also determine the quantity of material required.

Careful measurement is always desirable, as it eliminates the element of guesswork from estimating prices. It is not always applied to small-scale domestic work; many experienced decorators are so accustomed to this particular type of work that they can give a fairly close assessment of how long the operations will take by merely making a visual inspection of the premises, but guesswork is always a risky process. There are times, however, when even the most experienced tradesman needs to measure the work accurately. It must be recognized that the bigger the extent of the work, the more important correct measuring becomes; the same rule applies when the work is of an unfamiliar nature. On large-scale industrial painting work, accurate measuring is absolutely vital. A contract which may take several months to complete, or where the paintable areas involve hundreds of thousands of square metres, or where as on a bridge structure there are huge supporting piers and a complex web of angled steelwork, needs to be very precisely estimated, otherwise it may lead to financial disaster. Another example of where absolute accuracy is essential is work consisting of several identical units; for instance, the decoration of rooms in the nurses' living quarters in a large hospital or the students' quarters at a university college may very easily involve scores or even hundreds of small rooms each with the same dimensions. The temptation is to measure one room in the cursory way that small rooms in domestic properties are often estimated. It must be remembered that an error of a few square metres is a relatively minor matter where one small room is being decorated and the cost will not be crippling, but on repetition work the error is multiplied many times and perhaps by many hundreds, and it now becomes a big enough error to bring financial ruin to a contractor. Few people engaged in domestic painting are aware that on large industrial painting contracts the estimator measures and records every single item however small it may be.

The subject of measuring and estimating is dealt with in considerable detail in Chapter 37 of *Painting and Decorating* by Hurst and Goodier, published by Charles Griffin & Co. Ltd.

Mechanical advantage See *Pulley systems*.

Mechanical cleaning The preparation of surfaces by mechanical means, as opposed to manual methods, prior to painting. In the field of industrial painting this includes the use of pneumatic hammers and chisels, rotary wire brushes, flame cleaning, blast-cleaning and certain other blasting processes. The methods employed in coachpainting and industrial finishing include grinding, sanding, steam cleaning, buffing, rumbling, etc.

Mechanical graining A method by which an imitation of wood grain effect can be produced without the services of a skilled grainer. The commonest method is probably the use of graining paper. See *Graining paper*.

Media The plural of *medium*.

Medium The medium, or vehicle, is the liquid component of a paint, in which the pigment is dispersed or suspended and which enables it to be spread upon a surface. Once the paint is applied to a surface the medium acts as a binder to hold the pigment particles together in a cohesive film and to make the film adhere to the surface. These two factors militate against one another so that if the cohesive properties of the medium are too great the adhesion of the film is weakened. The functions of a medium are thus interdependent, and can be defined as (i) to support the pigment particles during storage without undue settling taking place, (ii) to provide fluidity whereby the paint can be readily applied, (iii) to dry as a film which effectively binds the pigment particles, and (iv) to provide good adhesion to the substrate. The nature of the medium also affects the degree of gloss or sheen possessed by the film and the extent to which it will be resistant to water penetration.

The earliest media were the animal fats, egg yolk, glue or milk used in tempera painting and the slaked lime used in fresco painting. Oil paints have been in use for at least a thousand years, during most of which time the medium was a vegetable drying oil. The binding agent in distempers for centuries was glue size; in the second quarter of the 20th century distemper was replaced by oil-bound water paint in which the medium was an emulsified drying oil. Today there is a wide range of media many of which can only be blended under controlled factory conditions. It is in the development of the media that the most striking advances in paint technology have been made.

Modern paint media can be divided into two categories, namely the "convertible" and the "non-convertible" types. When a paint containing the convertible type is applied to a surface the thinner evaporates and the medium then undergoes a chemical change and becomes solid; the medium cannot be dissolved again in the original thinner. Paints with media of the non-convertible type dry simply by the evaporation of the thinner; no chemical reaction takes place, and the medium remains soluble in the thinner in which it was originally dissolved. Among the convertible media there are air-drying media such as vegetable drying oils, oil varnishes, alkyd-resins, epoxy esters and urethane oils, and there are two-pack or chemical cure media such as the epoxies and polyurethanes; there are also stoving media which are of more interest in industrial finishing. The non-convertible types of media include chlorinated rubber, cellulose nitrate, shellac, bitumen, and the vinyls and the acrylics used in water-thinned paints such as emulsions.

Medium pressed boards Building boards which are thinner and denser than fibre boards, presenting a smooth compact surface which is only moderately porous and on which a good standard of painted finish is readily achieved. They are sold under many different brand names; one of the best-known is Beaverboard.

Megilp A substance which is added to graining colour to prevent it from flowing together and to help it to retain its sharpness of definition after it has been combed or figured. Old-time grainers used to pride themselves on their own private recipes, but grainers today generally use transparent glaze media or scumble glazes. Megilp should always be used in moderation; an excessive quantity thickens the graining colour and produces an unpleasant relief effect which detracts from the smoothness of the finish and gives a patchy appearance when varnished.

Melamine resins Etherified condensation products of melamine with formaldehyde. Alkylated melamine finishes are characterized by good adhesion and a high degree of impact, heat and chemical resistance; they are used in the finishing of motor cars and kitchen and office equipment. Acid catalysed melamine resin finishes are used as air-drying and force-dried finishes for metal and wood.

Menhaden oil An oil sometimes used in paint manufacture, derived from a fish of the shad family, common on the Atlantic coast of North America. (**NLC**)

Mercury Sometimes known as quicksilver. A very heavy metal which at ordinary temperatures takes the form of a bright silvery liquid. Various materials used in painting processes are derived from it. Water-soluble salts such as mercuric chloride are strongly poisonous and are incorporated into fungicidal paints, wood preservatives of various kinds, and marine paints for discouraging the growth of barnacles, etc., on ships' hulls. Mercuric sulphide is sublimed to produce the fine red pigment known as vermilion. It should be noted that although the salts of mercury are virulent poisons, vermilion, being insoluble, is free from toxic properties.

Metal A material belonging to a class of elementary substances which usually present in varying degrees certain characteristic properties such as high electrical and thermal conductivity, great opacity, high reflectivity of light, malleability and ductility.

Metal leaf In addition to the more familiar gold leaf, several other metals are available in leaf form; they include aluminium, copper, platinum, silver, tin, Abyssinian gold (an alloy of copper and tin), ducat gold (an alloy of copper and aluminium), and Dutch metal (an alloy of copper and zinc). Most of these are thicker than gold leaf and can be handled and cut to shape with scissors. They all tarnish fairly quickly and therefore need to be protected with a coating of lacquer. Silver leaf is thinner, but is rarely used for decorative work because it tarnishes so very rapidly—so quickly, in fact, that the leaves tarnish at the edges while the leaf is still in the book. Platinum is very expensive and is not often used.

Metal spraying A process whereby molten metal is sprayed to form a protective coating for iron and steelwork. A specially designed type of spray gun is used and the metal is fed in in the form of thin wire (or sometimes in powdered form), melted in an oxy-acetylene or oxy-hydrogen flame and blown out in finely divided form by an air blast. Modern equipment is very mobile and the hand plant is very light in weight, so that it can easily be used on site work. Any type of metal that can be drawn into wire and melted in an oxy-gas blowpipe can be sprayed, and a wide range of metals including aluminium, brass, bronze, cadmium, copper, cupro-nickel, lead, molybdenum and tin is used for various purposes; aluminium, cadmium and zinc appear to offer the greatest protection for iron and steelwork. Sprayed coatings of zinc, like all other deposits of zinc, are highly protective to iron and steelwork because of the nature of zinc in relation to iron in the electrochemical series. Zinc protects iron and steel by a sacrificial action; in other words, zinc is normally the anode in any electrolytic cell and it therefore dissolves away preferentially to the iron. When conditions are favourable the corrosion product of zinc is insoluble and this gives added protection. It should be noted that the surface of the iron or steel must be absolutely clean; this is essential, and blast-cleaning is usually employed to achieve a suitably clean surface.

Metal spraying is a specialized industry, and the process is carried out by firms devoted to this particular branch of industry. The interest of the process to the painter lies not in the application of the molten metal but in the painting systems which follow it. Metal spraying, which has been used on some contracts of immense scale for the protection of structural steelwork in exposed conditions, always produces a matt surface which is porous and presents a key which is ideally suited for the reception of paint. Apart from the very considerable degree of protection afforded by the metal spraying itself, the addition of a single coat of paint applied in the usual manner increases the effective life of the coating for a number of years. If the surface is washed down and the coating of paint renewed at regular intervals the total cost of the anti-corrosive treatment assessed over the whole of its life is very much lower than that of normal steelwork protective treatments. The coating may consist of a chlorinated rubber paint or a paint containing a co-polymer of vinyl chloride and vinyl acetate; lead-based paints and the cheaper varieties of bituminous paint are unsuitable. But a single coating would only be feasible in cases where the steelwork was within easy reach; obviously there are many situations where it would be uneconomic in view of the cost of hiring access equipment or erecting scaffolding, and in such cases a more durable paint system is called for. Where this is so, it is recommended that an etching primer be applied within 48 hours of the metal spraying; should there have been any delay whereby corrosive products have developed, these should be scrubbed off with clean water before etch primer is used. The etch primer is followed by a normal metal primer and a suitable undercoating and finishing coat.

Metallic car finishes Finishing paints which incorporate flake aluminium to provide a sparkling effect. They contain less coloured pigment than normal paints and in fact without the addition of the aluminium they would lack opacity. Light rays penetrate the surface of the paint film and are reflected at different angles by the minute metallic particles, which means that the contours of the vehicle produce apparent differences of colour from one surface to another.

Metallic finishes for car bodies were used on a small scale in this country in the early 1930s but soon became very unpopular because of the difficulty of matching the existing finish when repairs were necessary, and for a very long time they were hardly used at all. In the 1960s they became extremely popular in the USA, and as a result they were re-introduced in Britain, but once again they failed to make any appreciable impact, largely because of the difficulty of matching any repairs. In recent years, however, due to the influence of the American market they have become very widely used in this country. In the USA they account for a substantial proportion (well over 60 percent) of the current production in car finishes, and this trend is being increasingly reflected in the British and Continental markets.

The increasing popularity of these finishes has brought problems to vehicle painters called upon to finish and re-spray repair work. These problems are accentuated by the fact that many people are unaware of the factors involved in achieving a satisfactory colour match. Since the layering of the aluminium flakes affects the appearance of the paint film, it follows that the apparent colour of the finish can be altered by varying the spraying technique. Briefly the most important factors are the viscosity of the paint and the air pressure on the spray. The wetter the paint whilst spraying, the more the flakes will tend to sink in and settle, whereas when the material is sprayed dry the flakes are trapped in the surface of the film. Matching an existing sample of metallic colour thus resolves itself into the following considerations: (a) Viscosity of the paint; the higher the viscosity, the deeper the colour; therefore to lighten the colour, add more thinners. The use of a fast thinner will lighten the colour still further; a slow thinner blended with a retarder deepens the colour. (b) Air pressure; the lower the air pressure, the deeper the apparent colour; therefore to lighten the colour, increase the pressure. (c) Gun adjustments; spreader control—a narrow fan pattern gives a deeper colour, a wider fan pattern a lighter colour; position of gun—the gun held close to the surface gives a deeper colour, further away gives a lighter colour. The colour matching must be carried out in strong daylight, and adjusting the variable factors should produce a satisfactory match without the addition of pigment tinters. Tinting with additional pigments, if necessary at all, should be kept to where chemical attack is heavy. See *lead paint* (for regulations, etc.)

Metallic lead primer A primer for iron and steel, consisting of fine particles of metallic lead in a suitable medium. Under certain conditions it may be preferred to traditional metal primers if there is likely to be a long delay between priming and painting. It is especially valuable in situations where chemical attack is heavy. See *Lead paint* (for regulations, etc.)

Metallic paints Materials made by mixing aluminium powder or bronze powder with a quick-drying varnish medium of low acid value. Aluminium powders of the leafing variety have a wide application both in priming paints for wood and in finishing paints for locations where a high degree of reflectivity of light is required; non-leafing powders are used in certain satin or silk-effect finishes. Bronze powders, made from alloys of copper and zinc or aluminium, vary in colour from pale lemon gold to deep copper bronze. The powder and medium may be supplied either mixed ready for use or separately to be mixed by the decorator immediately prior to application; ready-mixed metallic paints tend to lose their lustre when stored for long periods.

Metallic paints, being heat resisting, are often used for heating-pipes and radiators, although it is not generally appreciated that they reduce the radiation of heat to quite a marked extent. They are liable to discolouration if exposed to acid, alkali or sulphurous fumes. They are sometimes glazed to produce decorative effects and sometimes varnished for protection; before glaze or varnish is applied they should receive a buffer coat of thin shellac lacquer to insulate them from the oxidizing effects of the oil in the superimposed material.

Metallized panels Panels made of a plastic material, which has been embossed and finished with a metallic coating to simulate the appearance of hammered copper, brass, pewter, etc.; some of the panels are heavily embossed to form replicas of historic repoussé metalwork patterns such as the spirals and bosses, enriched with coloured enamels.

Metameric A word used in technical literature to describe certain paint constituents; it means that they have the same composition and molecular form but different chemical properties. The word is also used to describe colours that seem alike but have different spectrophotometric curves, with the result that they look alike under some conditions but look different from one another if the lighting conditions are changed. Metamerism in this sense usually occurs when two colours of similar appearance have different formulations.

Methyl chloride One of a group of chlorinated solvents used in the formulation of paint removers. These solvents are more volatile than ordinary paint solvents, and the vapours they produce are potentially dangerous to persons either using them or in the vicinity of their use. The dangers arise from two sources: (a) the vapours can have powerful anaesthetizing effects when inhaled, and (b) if they come in contact with a naked flame or with a red hot surface they decompose to form toxic substances. It is important when paint removers containing these solvents are in use that there should be adequate ventilation and that a strict no-smoking rule should be enforced.

Methyl ethyl ketone Methyl ethyl ketone (which paint chemists often refer to as MEK) and methyl isobutyl ketone (MIBK) are very strong solvents for a number of the resins used in paint manufacture.

Methyl isobutyl ketone See above.

Methylated spirit Alcohol prepared for industrial use. In the painting trade it is used as a solvent for shellac in knotting, and it is of course an essential constituent in spirit varnishes and French polish, although these are no longer of any real significance. Mineralized methylated spirit consists of a mixture of nine volumes of "plain" spirit with one volume of wood naphtha or wood spirit, with the addition of a small quantity of mineral naphtha to make the liquid unpalatable. Colouring-matter in the form of methyl violet is also added. When added to water a white opalescence is produced. Industrial methylated spirit, widely used as a solvent, consists of 95 percent ethyl alcohol and 5 percent crude naphtha, without the addition of any mineral naphtha or colouring-matter. No opalescence is produced when it is mixed with water. Considerable restrictions are imposed upon its sale and supply.

Mica The name given to a group of silicates which are distinguished by their perfect basal cleavage, which causes them to split readily into thin flakes, and their vitreous pearly lustre. Mica is used in paint manufacture to impart "tooth" and to increase the bulk of the product. The shape of the particles produces a leafing effect similar to that of aluminium powder or graphite, which helps to keep the paint in suspension and gives improved resistance to moisture penetration. Mica is also used in the manufacture of wallpaper.

Mica papers Wallpapers or ceiling papers in which the ground or pattern is printed with mica, giving a silvery satin sheen. They are no longer used to any great extent. If a coating of water-thinned paint is applied over a mica paper there is a tendency for the mica to bleed through.

Micaceous iron oxide A pigment which is of very great importance in the painting and protection of steel structures, especially those exposed to industrial and marine atmospheres. It is a practically pure iron oxide obtained from haematite or iron ore. It does not in fact contain mica; the name derives from the fact that the pigment particles are in the form of minute flat plates which glisten in a way that is similar to mica.

Micaceous iron oxide has several outstanding features. One of these is the leafing action of the particles, which overlap like fish scales to produce a paint film with remarkable resistance to the penetration of water (although it is not very suitable for situations where it would be continually immersed in water). Another feature is that the pigment is chemically inert.

Micaceous iron oxide paints These are based on micaceous iron oxide pigment in a linseed oil/phenolic resin medium. Their particular value is due to the very great thickness of the coatings, one coat being the equivalent in thickness of two coats of a conventional type of paint, and this is a most important factor in the painting of steel where the "build" or film thickness has a direct bearing on the durability of the paint system. Another very important factor is that they give additional protection to the angles and sharp edges of the metal, because unlike other paints they do not recede or withdraw from the edges whilst drying to leave a thinner coating here than on the flat metal surfaces. It is also useful that these paints can be stored for long periods without any problems arising, because the pigment does not settle to any marked extent.

The natural colour of the pigment is a greyish or greenish black, which means that micaceous iron oxide paints are only offered in a restricted colour range. This, however, is not a serious drawback. The paints are very often used as undercoatings, and can be finished with a top coating of any desired colour. But they can also be used as finishing coats in their own right, and on exposure to air they develop an attractive metallic sparkle which tends to increase as the weathering process continues. They can be applied by brush, roller or spray, and their spreading rate is in the order of 7 to 9 square metres per litre.

Micronizer A type of paint mill used to reduce mineral pigment particles to the size required by the paint manufacturer. The particular feature of the micronizer is that it contains no moving parts, the size reduction being obtained by attrition between the particles, brought about by compressed air or high-pressure steam in a circular chamber, the fine pigment being removed by a process of air flotation.

Microporous A term in wide use today, especially in connection with exterior wood-protective treatments of various kinds. The microporosity of a film relates to its permeability, in other words to its ability to allow moisture vapour to pass through it. The object of microporous coatings for exterior timber is to control and regulate the moisture content of the timber.

The critical level of moisture content in timber is generally considered to be around 20 percent, above which the wood is liable to rot and decay. When timber is newly felled its moisture content often accounts for 50 percent of its total weight (100 percent of its oven-dry weight) and before it can be used for constructional purposes this must be reduced to an acceptable level, which is done by the process of seasoning. Wood which is seasoned naturally in the open air has a moisture content of about 15 percent of its oven-dry weight, and this level when once achieved tends to remain fairly constant. But natural seasoning is a very lengthy process during which a lot of capital would be tied up and a considerable area of ground would be occupied for non-productive purposes. For sheer economic reasons it would be impossible to restrict the use of wood in industry to naturally-seasoned timber, and therefore virtually all the timber employed is kiln-dried. The snag is that kiln-drying reduces the moisture content to about 10 percent, but this does not remain a constant figure and the moisture content is continually fluctuating, sometimes quite considerably.

Obviously wood needs to be protected. It is easy to see that exposure to the elements brings some periods of wet weather when the timber would absorb considerable quantities of moisture, causing it to swell, alternating with other periods when it would dry out rapidly and be liable to a substantial amount of shrinkage. The application of surface coatings provides a protective barrier, and the main purpose of external painting of property is and always has been to furnish a suitable barrier, but all paint coatings of every kind are permeable to some extent, and the passage of moisture vapour through the film means that some fluctuation in moisture content takes place. It follows that unless the surface coating has been properly formulated for the purpose, applied with reasonable skill and maintained in good condition, there will in any year's exposure to the elements be the possibility that in prolonged periods of wet weather the moisture content of the timber will rise well beyond the critical level of 20 percent, and other periods when moisture is lost quite rapidly. Microporous coatings are formulated with the idea of regulating the passage of moisture and maintaining the moisture level of the wood well below that figure. Many types of microporous coatings are on sale, some being water-based and others solvent-based, some being opaque and coloured and others semi-transparent, some being intended for smoothly finished surfaces and others for rough-sawn timber such as fences and sheds. Details of individual types should be obtained from the manufacturers.

Microwave meter A highly sophisticated instrument for measuring the moisture content of a plastered or rendered wall. A beam of high-frequency radio waves is directed at the wall and passes through to a receiver on the other side; the reading indicates the extent to which the intensity has been reduced by the presence of moisture. The result is sometimes ambiguous, because the reading is for the entire thickness of the wall, and in addition the reading is modified by the presence of soluble salts.

Midsheen Another term which is now being used for what is usually called eggshell, as in eggshell finish.

Mildew A white fluffy form of mould which, like all fungoid growths, thrives under damp and humid conditions and is liable to infect and feed upon the organic matter contained in some kinds of paint, pastes and wallpapers, etc. New paint brushes exposed to damp conditions during storage are particularly prone to develop mildew growths. The term is also used in a general way to describe the rotting of paper, cloth and fabrics by fungi or moulds. See also *Mould growths*.

Milkiness A term used to describe a defect whereby a film of lacquer or varnish which should be transparent presents a whitish translucent appearance. Its most general application is to a fault similar to blooming in cellulose or spirit finishes, caused by working under damp conditions.

Mill scale A thin skin or layer of iron oxides which covers the surface of hot-rolled steel when it leaves the rolling mills, produced by the rapid oxidation of the white-hot metal in contact with the air. Mill scale is also present on the surface of new wrought iron. When first formed it adheres tightly to the parent metal but in course of time it generally becomes loose and flaky and provides an unstable basis for a paint system.

Mill scale usually has a laminated structure, and examination under a microscope reveals the fact that it consists of three separate layers each composed of a different iron oxide, with ferrous oxide (FeO) in contact with the steel, magnetite (Fe_3O_4) above this, and ferric oxide (Fe_2O_3) on the outside face.

The thickness, composition and structure of the mill scale vary considerably according to the nature of the steel to which it is attached, the conditions under which steel was rolled and the thickness of the finished steel section. These differences have a pronounced effect upon the way in which the mill scale behaves when the steel is exposed to weathering, and this in turn has a great bearing upon the pre-painting treatment. If it were possible to apply a white lead/linseed oil priming paint to the steel while it was still hot on leaving the rolling mill, a coating would be formed which would provide good protective qualities for as long as the scale remained intact. Such a course is rarely possible, however, because of the way in which it would slow up steel production at the mill. Furthermore, the process of cutting the steel to the required lengths and drilling it for fixing, together with the scoring to which it is subjected while being handled by cranes in transit, all lead to the film of scale being disrupted. Where the scale is broken, the presence of moisture causes a galvanic action to be set up between it and the exposed steel, and corrosion spreads rapidly, loosening the scale and, of course, lifting the paint film.

The manner in which mill scale is loosened by exposure to air and moisture suggests a method by which it can be removed prior to painting, and it is a common practice for engineers to specify that structural steel shall be left unpainted and allowed to weather for a period of some six months prior to scraping, wire brushing and painting. There are several drawbacks to this course, however. As already indicated, the rate of loosening varies considerably according to such factors as the type of steel, the thickness of the sections, etc.; it also happens that those parts of the structure which are sheltered in any way weather much more slowly than those exposed to the full severity of the atmospheric attack, and the extent to which the atmosphere is polluted also has a bearing on the rate of weathering; for these reasons, the weathering of the structure does not proceed at a uniform rate, and in practice it is found that while in some areas the mill scale may have loosened satisfactorily, in other parts it will still be clinging tightly to the surface, and in other parts again it may have disintegrated completely and considerable rusting may have developed, leading to an appreciable loss of metal.

It is now generally recognized that the only sound basis for a painting system for structural steelwork is to carry out complete removal of the mill scale before painting. The method most widely used is chipping and wire brushing, by hand, which in some circumstances may be the only practicable method on erected steelwork, but which for various reasons rarely results in complete descaling, and leaves a partially descaled surface which is a bad foundation for paint. Better results are obtained with pneumatic chisels and hammers and rotary wire brushes, but the use of these tools may result in the steel being pitted, and rust may be burnished over instead of being removed. A very effective method of removal, although an expensive one, is that provided by flame cleaning, which loosens the scale by means of differential expansion and which also dehydrates any rust which is present. Blast-cleaning also results in the complete removal of scale and leaves a surface which is more receptive to paint than is bare metal.

Modifications of the blast-cleaning process which can be used on erected steel include wet sand-blasting and the type of blast-cleaning equipment which incorporates the use of a vacuum attachment to reclaim the shot. The efficiency of any kind of grit-blasting is reduced if the steel has been allowed to rust before it is treated.

Complete descaling before erection can be carried out by pickling, a process whereby the steel sections are immersed in an acid bath of suitable concentration; the layer of ferrous oxide which is closest to the steel is dissolved and the remainder of the scale flakes off. Inhibitors are added to the acid to prevent undue attack upon the steel itself.

Milori blue Highest quality Prussian blue.

Mineral Any inorganic substance with a definite chemical composition, found in the ground.

Mineral green Malachite.

Mineral orange Another name for red lead.

Mineral white Also called terra alba; sulphate of lime derived from gypsum.

Mineral whites A term used in paint manufacture to indicate those substances which are used as extenders to increase the bulk and give *tooth* to paint, including barytes, barium carbonate, strontium white, Paris white, mineral white, satin white, magnesite, alumina, China clay, asbestine, mica, silica and slate powder.

Miscibility The ability of two or more substances to mix and form a single homogeneous phase.

Misses Areas which have been left uncoated with paint, generally through carelessness.

Mist (or spray fog) The haze which results from finely divided particles of paint (atomized paint) rebounding from a surface which is being sprayed or being projected into the air beyond the edge of a surface through overspray. A high-pressure spraying system produces more mist than an air-volume system (although the mist so produced tends to settle in the form of a fine dust whereas the less finely atomized paint particles produced by the air-volume system are larger and wetter and are more difficult to remove). The reduction of spray mist is one of the great advantages offered by the airless spraying and hot spray processes.

While a certain amount of spray mist is inseparable from the use of high-pressure spraying equipment, the quantity of mist commonly seen when spray painting is in progress is usually quite excessive and is due in a great measure to incorrectly regulated pressures.

Mist coat A term used in spraying to denote a very lightly applied coating. The actual nature of a mist coat is subject to considerable variation. When spraying vertical surfaces it is often an advantage, both with cellulose and synthetic resin paints, to apply a mist coat to help the main coating to hold up, and the technique is to apply the paint over an area of convenient size with rapid strokes of the gun so as to form a thin coating (which need not necessarily be a continuous film) and then immediately follow up with a full coat applied at normal spraying speed. When a cellulose surface which is in good condition is being resprayed a mist coat is very often used to help to create a firm bond between the old film and the new coating, and in this case the mist coat is made up with some three parts of thinners to one part of paint. For touch up and minor repair work on cellulose finishes a mist coat consisting of thinners alone is very often sprayed over the finished repair to help it to blend into the background.

Mixing varnish A type of varnish of low acid value, which can be added to metallic pigments without any risk of "feeding". (**NLC**)

Mix-in-the-shop colours A layman's term for the colour-mixing systems offered by paint manufacturers to provide a considerably wider range of colours than is available in the standard colour ranges. The principal systems are Berger Colorizer, Carsons Colours, Crown Colour Cue, Dulux Matchmaker and Sanderson Spectrum. These systems are generally operated through the decorators' merchants and the retail shops, where a mixing machine is installed and where there is a set of coded instructions relating to all the colours on the appropriate colour charts. To obtain a quantity of any given colour that is required, the specified proportion of one or more pigments or stainers is added to the stock base colour.

Mobile towers Towers constructed from tubular scaffolding or prefabricated frames and mounted on castor wheels. They are most useful in painting and decorating, especially for ceiling work; they enable a large ceiling area to be painted from a small working platform using only a small quantity of scaffold, and they occupy very little space where other types of scaffold would obstruct the whole floor area. Unfortunately, accidents involving the use of mobile towers are very common, most of them due to the tower tilting or overturning. The essential safety precautions include the following:

On exterior work the height must not exceed three times the shorter of the two base dimensions, and on interior work the height must not exceed three and a half times the shorter of the two base dimensions; a tower should never be moved while people are on the platform; a tower should only be moved by pressure applied to the base and men on the platform should never try to move the tower themselves by pulling on roof trusses, etc.; castor wheels should be firmly attached to the tubes so as not to drop out while the tower is being moved; and the castor wheels must be locked before work commences to prevent the tower from being accidentally moved.

Mock up A term frequently used by architects and interior designers to mean a scale model prepared in full colour to show in three dimensions what the effect of a proposed scheme of decoration or similar project will be.

Model A representation or pattern in miniature, in three dimensions, of something to be produced on a larger scale.

Modelling (a) Fashioning, shaping or moulding a pliable material in order to produce relief, as, for example, when plastic paint is worked with modelling tools in order to produce a relief motif.

(b) Form seen within a contour; representation by use of light and shade, as distinguished from drawing in outline.

Moiré Wallpaper with a watered silk effect produced by means of a delicate emboss.

Moisture content The moisture content of a material such as wood, plaster, etc., on which decorative coatings or hangings are to be applied is of the utmost importance to the decorator. The application of an impervious layer of paint on to plaster or timber in which moisture is present is practically certain to lead to problems of adhesion such as blistering, flaking, etc., and even water-thinned paints such as emulsion paint, which do possess some tolerance of moisture, cannot be guaranteed to give satisfactory results on a surface which is anything more than mildly damp. Wallcoverings applied to surfaces with any significant level of moisture content may be discoloured, can very well be loosened, and may develop stains and mould growths.

Moisture content—the measuring of Several instruments of various kinds are available to measure the moisture content of wood or plaster and to give some indication of whether or not it is safe to proceed with a painting programme.

The conductivity meter acts on the same principle as an avometer by measuring the electrical resistance between two probes inserted into the surface, and it indicates the moisture content either by a numbered reading on a calibrated scale or by a colour scale ranging from red to green; the result may sometimes by misleading because at a certain stage of the drying-out process the rate of evaporation is affected by other factors controlled by the humidity of the atmosphere.

The capacitance meter consists of two flat electrodes pressed against the plaster or timber surface and gives a reading on a graduated scale, but this instrument only measures the moisture at surface level and gives no information about the condition below the surface.

The hygrometer measures the humidity of the atmosphere, but can be adapted to showing the moisture content of a wall surface by mounting a sealed and insulated box on the wall with a hygrometer fastened to the box opposite the wall; considerable time is needed for equilibrium to be reached before an accurate reading is available.

The microwave meter operates by means of high-frequency radio waves, but this method is not very often suitable for site conditions.

Probably measurement by weight is the most effective method of assessing the moisture content of a wall surface; the wall is drilled to yield samples of the wall filling and these are weighed, dried in an oven and then reweighed to ascertain the weight loss. It is possible to determine the moisture content at varying depths. This is not a method that can be used for quick site testing, but is useful where a precise assessment is required.

Moisture repellents Colourless fluids formulated for the purpose of making porous and absorbent wall areas more resistant to rain penetration. See *Water-repellent fluids* and also paragraph 3 of *Silicone resins*.

Monastral blue The proprietary name for phthalocyanide pigment with several distinctive features. Monastral blue is completely insoluble in oils and organic solvents. It is a very powerful stainer having double the strength of Prussian blue, it is immune to acid or alkaline attack, it is resistant to heat up to a temperature of some 200°C (400°F), and can therefore be used in heat-resisting paints and stoving finishes, and since it does not react with oil media it does not feed or liver. It is an intense blue colour and is fast to light in the stronger shades although liable to fade if reduced to a very pale tint.

Monastral green A pigment dye with similar characteristics to Monastral blue.

Monochrome Of one colour only; hence "Monochromatic painting"—painting in tints and shades of one colour only. The form and contours of a three-dimensional object can be represented in monochrome by carefully placing the tints and shades to indicate which parts of the object are exposed to the light and which are in shadow.

Monomer The word is derived from *mono* meaning "one" and *mer* meaning "part" or "unit". A monomer is a unit part, a simple chemical compound, whose molecules can be made in polymers ("many parts")—that is, long chains of molecules joined together, as in plastics. The term is much used in paint technology in connection with emulsion paints; for instance, vinyl acetate is a liquid monomer which is polymerized by heating (in the presence of a catalyst) to produce polyvinyl acetate.

Montan wax A hard wax-like material obtained from lignite or peat, sometimes described as bitumen wax.

Mop A soft camel-hair brush used in the gilding of carved, moulded or modelled work for the purpose of pressing the gold leaf into the quirks and crevices.

Mordant A term derived from the French *mordre* meaning to bite; hence a mordant is a substance capable of biting or gripping some other material. It has two connotations in the painting trade.

(a) A chemical solution used to etch the surface of galvanized iron or other zinc-coated surfaces or any other non-ferrous metal in order to provide a *key* to improve the adhesion of the paint.

(b) An adhesive substance used to attach gold leaf to a surface—for example Japan gold size, or old-oil gold size or, in the case of glass gilding, isinglass or gelatine.

Mosaic A pattern or pictorial composition produced by setting small pieces of differently coloured glass, marble or stone into a bedding of cement, and owing its effectiveness very largely to the play of light reflected from the various facets. Mosaic was used in ancient Egypt, Assyria and Greece, but was not fully exploited until the Romans made it a distinctive feature of early Christian art; when the Roman empire was eclipsed the use of mosaic was brought to a tremendous peak of achievement in the Byzantine buildings of Asia Minor and the Middle East.

In present-day interior decoration the art of mosaic has been revived and is being used in light-hearted schemes of great elegance in shops, hotels and restaurants. Resins are used as the matrix instead of cement, and there is a firm centred on Bristol which specializes in using glass and translucent marble set in tinted resins and lit from the rear so as to emphasize certain parts of the design. The mosaics are set in panels of a size convenient for easy handling, and they are produced in the studio/workshop and then transported to the site for fixing. The price is said to be about a third of what a mosaic produced by traditional methods would cost.

Mosses These are a very primitive form of plant life, with stems and leaves but no roots; the stems form into root-like structures known as rhyzoids. They are often seen in roofs and walls in rural areas, and are sometimes encouraged by householders, especially when repairs have been carried out and the new work presents a raw appearance. They are not usually destructive, but they can weaken materials like asbestos-cement and will eat into limestone; they also can cause blockages in drainpipes. The painter working on exterior properties in country districts is sometimes required to remove the growths. The method is to use one of the proprietary toxic washes, and the action is hastened if the surface is wire-brushed and the toxic wash scrubbed in well with a stiff brush. Sometimes a second application of wash is necessary.

Mother of pearl The iridescent pearly substance which forms the internal layer of many kinds of sea shells. At one time it was widely used in glass sign work, providing a pleasing contrast when placed alongside gold leaf, and supplies can still be obtained from decorators' merchants for this purpose.

Motif The dominant feature or device in a decorative composition.

Mottler A type of brush used in graining for the purpose of mottling; various sizes are obtainable. The filling usually consists of hog hair, although other types of hair are sometimes used. The handle is thin and rectangular in shape and is made of tin plate packed with either wood or a compressed fibre composition.

Mottling (a) A term used in graining to describe the representation of the highlights and shades which are a characteristic feature of natural wood. Mottling is generally carried out in water medium as a glaze which is superimposed on figure graining, but it may on occasions be executed in an oil stain.

(b) A defect in a sprayed film which appears in the form of a uniform series of imperfections of roughly circular shape.

Mould growths Mould is the general non-scientific name for a wide variety of fungi, all of which flourish where moist conditions are accompanied by warmth, and the growth is encouraged by the absence of light. Once mould growths occur they are extremely difficult to get rid of. The disfigurement appears as large spots or patches which vary in colour according to the species of fungus which is present. Mildew which is white and fluffy, black mould which has an unpleasant smell, and green mould are all very common in any kind of property, and additionally pink and violet coloured fungi are often seen in greenhouses and conservatories.

The significant thing is that mould growths need food in order to prosper, and they find it in organic matter. They feed on the oils and other organic substances in decorative materials, such as in paints, wallcoverings, paste and size; it is true that many modern materials have a much lower proportion of organic content than traditional materials like glue size and flour paste, but they still contain some substances on which mould can develop, such as for instance on the plasticizer in emulsion paint. Many decorators are under the mistaken impression that emulsion paint is immune; emulsion paint is not a fungicide and cannot kill mould growth. It follows that under suitable conditions almost any kind of decorative product may become infected, and the problem is aggravated in places where condensation is heavy. Infection is especially likely to occur in such places as bakeries, breweries, dairies, etc. The spores may be carried by wind or air currents and may travel a considerable distance, infecting plaster and woodwork far from the original seat of the trouble.

People tend to think that mould growths occur only occasionally in isolated buildings, but periodically there are outbreaks that cover immense areas and even occur on a countrywide scale. There was a sharp rise in the incidence of mould growth as a serious problem affecting decoration in the late 1940s when premises which had been blitzed in the war lay derelict for a long time; fungoid growth developed unchecked, and the spores were carried by the winds to spread the infection on a very wide scale. Thirty years later in the 1970s there was the start of a new outbreak arising from a totally different set of circumstances, and this has developed in the 1980s into a considerable nuisance. It was largely the result of a successful advertising campaign. The Government encouraged people by advertising and by cash inducements to seal up their premises and retain as much heat as possible in the interests of fuel economy; advice was given about methods of preventing heat losses, and grants were available for loft insulation. Many commercial firms took advantage of this wave of publicity, particularly in the promotion of double glazing, and here again the selling point was the saving in fuel costs. Whether the saving in fuel is as great as the government or the double glazing firms predicted is open to question; what is beyond question is that throughout the country we now have damp conditions due to the condensation of moisture in domestic premises on a scale previously unheard of, and the widespread development of mould growth has become a very serious problem.

When mould is encountered the first essential is to discover the cause of any damp which is present and to take adequate steps to prevent its recurrence; where condensation is the cause, some means of ventilating the premises must be found. The treatment is then to remove all infected matter by means of scraping, burning off or stripping, avoiding any undue disturbance which would cause the spores to be blown about and distributed over a wider area; the debris is then destroyed by burning. After this the infected area is washed down with a suitable fungicide, several types of which are on the market, and is then kept under observation for at least a week; should the growth show any sign of recurring the surface should be washed for a second time with the fungicide. Two applications are usually sufficient to check the growth except in persistent cases. The surface may then be decorated; a fungus- or mould-resistant paint may be used, or alternatively the priming coat may be thinned with naphtha which has good fungicidal properties. If the plastered surfaces are to be papered it is essential to use a paste which incorporates a fungicide, and to avoid the use of glue size.

Mould stains The disfigurements caused by mould or fungoid growth.

Mouldings Ornamental and continuous lines of projections or grooving used to embellish the face of a structure and showing, in profile, a complex series of curves; they may for instance, form part of a cornice, may surround the panels in a piece of woodwork, may surround a door or may be part of a capital or arch, etc. Any individual part of a moulding is called a member, and any member which is ornamentally carved is said to be enriched.

Mucilage A viscous substance found in various kinds of plants. When a vegetable drying oil, such as linseed oil, is being prepared for use as a constituent of paint, the oil extracted from the seed pods is filtered and then stored in tanks until the mucilage settles to the bottom and the oil becomes clean and fit for use. Oil intended for making varnish is heated, and this makes the mucilage coagulate and settle out.

Muffle A pad of cloth tied and secured round the top of the stile of a ladder in order to prevent its damaging or marking the surface upon which it rests.

Mullions Vertical posts or uprights dividing a window into two or more lights.

Multi-colour paint (also known as multi-fleck paint, flecked paint, etc.) A type of material which enables several colour combinations to be applied simultaneously in one single application. Such paints are widely used, especially in the decoration of public buildings, schools, hospitals, office blocks, municipal buildings, and the like, and are now being increasingly used in hotels, theatres, etc., and domestic buildings.

The type most frequently used consists of colour particles or globules which remain separate in the dried film, being insulated from each other by an aqueous colloidal solution which prevents them from merging. The finished effect resembles that of spatter (q.v.) in appearance, although the spots of colour do not stand out in high relief as in spatter. They are applied by spray; normal spray equipment can be used, provided the air pressure is kept low, but the best results are achieved by using a spray head of the internal mix type. Airless spray tends to disturb the particle shapes because of the high pressure involved. The paint can be applied direct on most types of surface but it is not suitable for use on expanded polystyrene. On new surfaces the use of a primer coat is recommended; previously painted surfaces may require the application of a sealer coat. In this country the material is restricted to internal surfaces, but in countries with a dry climate it can be used outdoors; even on inside work it should not be applied when humid conditions prevail as excess moisture interferes with the film-forming properties. The coating builds up to three or four times the thickness of a conventional paint film, so the coverage is low, averaging about three square metres per litre. The shelf life when the material is stored in 5-litre containers is about four to six months, but deterioration is more rapid when large containers are stored. Intermixing two different colours of the same brand is not impossible but is difficult because vigorous stirring affects the particle size.

Multi-colour paints for brush application have been developed, notably in Denmark, and are available here. They consist of a coarse emulsion of white spirit-soluble paint in an acrylic resin emulsion paint.

A more recent development is an interior wall finish with a wide range of multi-colour effects produced either with varying degrees of metallic glitter or devoid of glitter. The painting system consists of the application of a base coat of specially formulated emulsion, designed to give the maximum amount of film "build" and with the drying retarded so as to make it receptive to an application of dry flakes. This application is the second part of the process, and consists of spraying dry PVA flakes on to the tacky base coat, and dry metallic flakes are incorporated to produce the glitter effect. The final stage is the application of a tough, chemically resistant lacquer coat. This type of material offers the considerable advantage that no masking up is required because the sprayed coating takes the form of dry flakes which do not adhere to a dry surface, and this represents a great saving of time and money compared with the normal multi-colour painting process. The type with the highest degree of glitter produces a very striking and attractive effect which is much appreciated in the decoration of discotheques, theatres, hotels, in fact in any place of entertainment.

There are many reasons why multi-colour paints are such a popular choice for the treatment of public buildings. It is said that the surface does not develop a charge of static electricity and for this reason it does not attract dust or dirt and remains cleaner than a conventional paint film. It is also resistant to grease and oil stains. It dries to a hard film with a fairly high resistance to abrasion, and it can be washed with soap and water or with solvent cleaners. These factors mean that to some extent graffiti can be removed with a fair amount of success, although of course there is no means of countering the mindless vandals who arm themselves with sharp steel instruments to score deeply into any clean paint surface they find.

It is claimed that if the paint surface is damaged, small local repairs can be carried out with the spray gun and that such repairs are hard to detect, but this would depend upon the length of time that had elapsed since the initial coating had been applied. It is sometimes said that the very thick paint coating helps to mask surface irregularities, but this is debatable; there is no reason why a single coating of multi-colour paint should be more effective in this respect than the equivalent thickness of paint applied in three or more separate coatings; in any case the paint, however thick, is bound to follow the contours of the surface.

The main objection to multi-colour paints is on aesthetic grounds. The colour flecks can look attractive when seen as a small colour sample, but the results can be disappointing when the paint is used on a large area; obviously there are limits to the size of the colour particles, and the flecks are too small to be effective when used on a large expanse of wall, being out of scale. Similarly, some of the colour combinations are pleasing when seen in isolation on a shade-card sample but can be disagreeable when used on a large area. It must be said, however, that in recent years some manufacturers have gone to considerable trouble to overcome these difficulties, and multi-colour finishes are now available in a very attractive range of colourings, so much so that interior decorators are much more ready to specify these paints on high-quality work than they were a few years ago.

Multi-stipple effects Broken colour effects produced by a technique in which three or four colours are stippled on to a ground of wet matt oil paint;

one painter lays in the ground with a generous coating and a second painter follows up immediately with the stippling colours, which are stippled into the ground colour with a fair degree of force. The stipple colours blend with each other and into the ground, producing a soft, mottled effect.

Multi-stippler A type of hair stippler once devised and marketed by the Leyland Paint and Varnish Co., but now no longer obtainable, although many people still possess them. It has the same surface area as an ordinary hair stippler, but the working face is divided up into four sections, each section consisting of a miniature stippler, with a gap between them. A special dipper can was supplied with the stippler, and this had four compartments into which the miniature stippler heads fitted with room to spare all around. A separate colour is placed in each compartment, and the stippler and dipper can are used together to produce multi-stipple effects.

Multiple jet cap An air cap, or that part of a spray gun which directs the air into the stream of fluid in order to atomize it, comprising 5, 7, 9 or more orifices as opposed to the conventional type of cap with only 3 orifices. The advantages provided by a multiple jet cap include better atomization of viscous materials such as synthetics and greater uniformity of spray pattern.

Multiple plate stencils Stencilled patterns produced by means of the design being cut from two or more plates accurately registered one to another. Various features can be obtained in this way which would not be possible with single plate stencils—for example, a pattern may be produced in which no ties are obvious and blank spaces are filled, or in which outline treatments are achieved.

Munsell colour system A system of colour definition based on hue, value and chroma, hue distinguishing red from blue, green from yellow, etc., value being related to the lightness or darkness of the colour, and chroma being the strength of the colour.

The system was devised by Albert H. Munsell, an American artist, with the object of replacing vague and confusing colour terms with a clear and specific method of notation. He set himself to describe colour psychologically, i.e. in terms of visual sensation, without concerning himself with the physical variables involved; his method was to establish a series of coloured shapes varying equally in all directions, in the domain of colour, in terms of visual appearance.

It is obvious that terms such as "light blue", "dark green", "shell pink", etc., are much too vague and imprecise to give any real indication of what is intended; the reason the terms are vague is that they do not supply sufficient data to describe the colours adequately. Munsell's system provides all the information required, because it describes colour by a three-dimensional notation. The clarity of this system can be illustrated by a simple analogy; if we were to attempt to describe a wooden box it would not be sufficient merely to say that the box was 900 mm long; it would still not be sufficient if we added a second dimension and said it was 900 mm by 600 mm wide. By adding a third dimension, however, and saying that the box measured 900 mm by 600 mm by 300 mm deep, we provide a complete description.

Munsell defined the three dimensions or "variables" of colour as being *hue* (that which distinguishes red from yellow, green from blue, etc.), *value* (the lightness or darkness of a colour as related to black and white) and *chroma* (the strength or purity of the colour). These he constructed into a three-dimensional colour solid, often termed the "Munsell Colour Tree", which has a vertical axis passing from black to white through a graduated scale of greys. Radiating from the axis there are horizontal branches graded from neutral grey to full colour or hue. There are ten basic hues, consisting of five principal hues (namely, red, yellow, green, blue and purple) and five intermediate hues (namely, yellow-red, green-yellow, blue-green, purple-blue and red-purple). Each of the ten basic hues is divided into ten parts, to make a circular scale of a hundred finely graded hues.

The Munsell system enables any colour to be described precisely, which is far more satisfactory than the use of vague terms such as dove-grey, willow green, etc. What is more, it is flexible enough to permit of further expansion. A complete Munsell reference for a colour defines the hue, the value and the chroma in that order; for example, a colour corresponding to what is sometimes known vaguely as Georgian green has the Munsell reference of 7.5 GY 7/4; 7.5 GY refers to the basic hue of green-yellow, 7 to the value on a scale of ten ranging from black (0) to white (10), and 4 refers to the chroma on a scale ranging from neutral grey to full strength at any given value level. Neutral greys, having no hue or chroma, are specified by the value figure prefixed by "N", e.g. N6.

Muntins The vertical parts of a framed or panelled joinery construction which lie between the panels and span the distance between the various horizontal rails.

Mural decoration From the Latin *murus*, a wall; the adornment of walls by means of surface decoration in oil colour, water colour or fresco, by mosaics or by carvings in wood, stone, terra-cotta, marble, etc. The term is also understood to include the decoration in similar manner of vaults and ceilings. To the painter and decorator, mural painting implies a composition carried out in some material such as oil paint or emulsion paint, applied either directly to the wall or to a fabric such as canvas which is then affixed to the wall; it consists of a complete composition, design or picture which may occupy a large area of wall space, a whole wall or a series of walls extending around a room, and as such it is an integral part of the background decoration of the room as opposed to an easel picture or other movable object. Present-day mural treatments include the hanging of photographic reproductions of scenery and aerial views which are prepared in the form of large sheets, and decorators' merchants stock a range of coloured scenic reproductions printed for hanging as mural decorations.

N

Nail heads The nails used to fix building boards in position may rust if a water-thinned material such as emulsion paint is applied directly upon them; rusting may also occur if they are sunk below the surface and the cavity filled with a water filler. If the boards are primed with oil paint after fixing, this difficulty does not arise, but if they have been primed before fixing the nail heads should be touched in with primer before any waterbased material is applied.

Nail holes The cavities in woodwork, etc., where nails have been punched down should be filled with a hard stopping after priming and before any subsequent coats are applied.

Nail stock brush A brush with a binding of leather or strip metal which is secured by nails to a wooden handle. (**NLC**)

Naphtha A volatile and highly flammable solvent, water-white in colour and with a disagreeable odour, which is used in the preparation of various kinds of paint products and which is obtained by the distillation of coal-tar, petroleum or shale oil. It is sometimes used in priming paints and stains for woodwork because of its penetrative powers and its fungicidal properties, being especially useful for timber with a high resinous content and for primers to be applied to areas which have been infected with mould and fungoid growths. As a primer, however, its use should be restricted to bare unpainted surfaces, as it exerts a powerful solvent action which dissolves normal paint films and might therefore dissolve any previous coatings. Naphtha is widely used by paint manufacturers and incorporated into anti-fouling paints, certain quick-drying synthetic media and various kinds of bituminous materials.

Naphthalene An aromatic hydrocarbon obtained by the distillation of coal-tar. It is used as a starting material in the production of phthalic anhydride and in the preparation of dyestuff intermediates.

Naphthenate driers Drying agents, widely used in modern paint manufacture, obtained by fusing metallic salts with naphthenic acid.

Naples yellow A pigment composed of lead and antimony; originally it was found occurring naturally on the slopes of Vesuvius. It is now obsolete; present-day "Naples yellow" is an imitation prepared by tinting zinc oxide with cadmium and ochre. (**NLC**)

Natural order (of colour) The order in which colours of maximum purity will occur if arranged in a circle so as to progress from the lightest tone to the darkest, e.g., yellow, orange, red, purple, violet, blue, blue-green, green and back to yellow, yellow being the lightest colour (nearest to white) and violet to the darkest (nearest to black). If black is added to the light colours and white to the dark colours so that yellow becomes the darkest colour and violet the lightest, the natural order is reversed and a circle of discords is produced in which each hue is discordant with its neighbouring hue.

Natural oxides Oxides of iron occurring naturally in many parts of the world and prepared for use as pigments by a simple process of grinding and levigation.

Natural resins Substances of vegetable origin derived from the exudations of various types of trees, as opposed to synthetic resins produced artificially, which are used in the production of varnishes and paints.

Neat Unadulterated

Needle oak A name sometimes given to the method of imitating oak grain by means of cutting or incising the paint film or the underlying wood with patent tools.

Negative stencil A stencil pattern designed so that the background is cut out and the ornament forms the ties.

Neoprene A form of synthetic rubber produced from butyl chloride which may be vulcanized with zinc oxide.

Neoprene glue An adhesive, made from neoprene, used for hanging certain kinds of wallcoverings, and especially heavy-duty contract wallhangings.

Neoprene paint A paint usually supplied as a two-pack material based on the synthetic rubber substance known as neoprene (q.v.) and used in situations where a high resistance to weather and chemicals is required. Although generally applied as a multi-coat system, it can be used as a single coating where there is no splash or spillage, provided care is taken to avoid misses. It forms a tough rubbery coating, but is generally available only in black or grey.

Nets See *Safety nets.*

Neutral The state of having no definite or determinate character—hence, for example, "neutral plaster", a gypsum plaster which because it is free from lime and is therefore non-alkaline has no harmful chemical effects upon a superimposed paint; "neutral colour", a colour in which no single hue quality predominates, etc.

Neutralize To render inoperative or ineffective, to counteract. For example, when a surface has been stripped with a caustic paint stripper the residue of alkaline material which remains may be neutralized by washing the surface with a weak acid solution such as vinegar; the difficulty, of course, lies in determining at what point true neutrality is attained and when the substance present in the surface shows a reaction of neither acidic nor alkaline character, and for this reason the painter's attempts to neutralize a surface are usually of a loose and non-scientific character.

Newel An upright post, at the top or bottom of a staircase, supporting the handrail; also applied to the central shaft from which the steps of a winding stair radiate.

Nibs Small particles of foreign matter such as pieces of paint skin or coagulated medium, grit, etc., embedded in a paint film and projecting above the surface so that they feel rough to the touch and mar the appearance of the surface. The term can also be applied to minute specks of roughness present on a surface which is about to be decorated, e.g., small specks of grit or mortar, etc., on a plastered wall.

Niche A recess in a wall hollowed like a shell to hold a statue or ornament.

Nigrosine A blue-black dyestuff, obtained from aniline hydrochlorates, used in spirit stains to produce black.

Nitro-cellulose materials Lacquers, enamels, etc., produced from nitro-cotton, which is prepared by treating cellulose in the form of cotton fibre with nitric and sulphuric acids. The other ingredients are the solvents and diluents used to dissolve the nitro-cotton and maintain it in solution, the plasticizers added to give flexibility, and various resins which impart gloss and adhesive properties. See *Cellulose*.

Nitro-cotton See above.

No-fines concrete A mixture of concrete consisting of coarse aggregate and cement without the admixture of sand.

Nominated sub-contractor A firm of contractors specified, generally by an architect, to supply and fix certain materials or to carry out certain specialist work under a prime cost sum on a bill of quantities contract. Sometimes the nominated sub-contractor is an individual person rather than a firm, e.g. a mural painter, heraldic artist, gilder, or grainer.

Nominated supplier A person or firm nominated, generally by an architect, to supply certain materials under a prime cost sum on a bill of quantities contract, the materials to be fixed or applied by the main contractor.

Non-bleeder gun A spray gun fitted with an air valve which shuts off air when the trigger is released, the trigger controlling both air and fluid. This type of gun is used with compressor units having a pressure-controlling device.

Non-convertible coatings Coatings which dry by the evaporation of the solvent, no "cure" or chemical reaction taking place in the film. They include chlorinated rubber, cyclized rubber, vinyl resins, cellulose finishes, knotting, etc.

Non-ferrous A term used to define substances which do not contain iron, e.g. aluminium, a non-ferrous metal.

Non-polar solvents Paint solvents which are not electrically conductive. In electrostatic spraying, should it be found that the conductivity of the paint is too high, it is sometimes possible to correct it by adding a non-polar solvent instead of using a polar solvent; this may effectively reduce its conductivity. Examples of non-polar solvents are amyl acetate, mineral spirits, toluol, and xylol among many others.

Non-reversible material A material which when dry is not softened up by the application of further coatings.

Non-yellowing paints Paints formulated with pigments and media of a type that will provide a finish capable of maintaining its whiteness longer than conventional alkyd resin paints.

Novamura The brand name of a unique and very beautiful kind of wallcovering developed and produced by ICI at their works at Hyde in Cheshire. It consists of foamed polyethylene without any paper backing, and it feels delightfully soft and warm to the touch. With this product it is the wall that is pasted, not the wallhanging; a special adhesive is supplied for the purpose and the dry wallhanging is hung straight from the roll and pressed into contact with the wall. It is very light in weight and is thus easily applied to ceilings, but in fact ease of application is one of the distinctive features of the product wherever it is used; there is no difficulty in fixing the material behind pipework and around fitted units. Novamura is fully washable and is resistant to steam and water vapour. It is dry-peelable and can therefore be removed very easily when the time comes for redecoration.

Nozzle The opening through which the paint emerges from a spray gun and through which the abrasive is ejected in blast-cleaning equipment.

In the case of airless spraying the nozzle tip is made of tungsten carbide to resist the abrasive action of the paint. The tip eventually becomes worn and needs replacing; the actual life of the tip depends on several factors but is chiefly dependent on the type of material that is being sprayed, silicates being particularly erosive, although even the titanium oxide used in decorative paints has a marked abrasive effect. The orifice through which the paint is ejected is usually elliptical, and there is an angled slot or deflector groove immediately beyond the orifice to force the atomized paint into a predetermined fan pattern.

In the case of air-propelled spraying a large nozzle size is used when spraying heavy, coarse or fibrous materials so as to prevent clogging; viscous materials require small nozzle sizes to facilitate thorough atomization. The nozzle size also varies according to the type of feed which is being used, whether suction feed or pressure feed. The size is identified by a letter stamped on the collar of the needle and on the outer edge of the fluid tip.

In the case of blast-cleaning equipment the design of the nozzle has an important effect on the efficiency of the process; the type with a venturi tube or narrowed throating inside the cylinder increases the velocity of the abrasive, and produces a more regular cleaning pattern than a straight cylindrical nozzle. The inner casing of the nozzle is lined with tungsten carbide or a special alloy to resist the harshness of the abrasive action.

Numerals The symbols employed to express a number. The numerals in normal usage in this country are incorrectly described as Arabic numerals but are actually of comparatively recent origin.

Nut oil Walnut oil

Nylon A general term for a wide range of recently developed materials which while having no exact counterparts among natural products are similar in chemical composition to proteins. Nylon can be produced in many forms such as powders, sheets, solutions and yarns, the latter being at present of most interest to the painter and decorator. Nylon can be produced in several ways; a common method is to react adipic acid and hexamethylene together under heat to form a polymer which is then extruded to form a continuous filament, the filament then being drawn out or stretched to give the material the properties of a textile fibre. The outstanding properties of the fibre are its very high tensile strength, lightness in weight, elasticity, resilience, resistance to abrasion, low moisture absorption, resistance to alkalis and oils, and immunity to mould or fungoid growth and insect attack.

Nylon brushes Brushes with a filling composed of nylon filament. Because of the scarcity and price of hog hair the use of man-made fibres as an alternative is of great importance.

Nylon brushes offer several definite and distinct advantages over other types of filler. In the first place, they are remarkably hard-wearing and resilient; comparative tests have proved that when bristle brushes and nylon brushes are subjected to a similar degree of hard usage for an equal length of time, the length of the nylon has been found to have decreased only minimally when the bristle has been completely worn down. In the second place, nylon is far cheaper than bristle and the gap in price is constantly widening. In the third place, nylon is not adversely affected by paint solvents nor by alkaline materials. It should be noted, however, that nylon brushes are not suitable for the application of creosote or any material of an acidic nature.

On the other hand, nylon brushes have certain disadvantages compared with hog hair. When dipped into the paint kettle the brush does not become charged with paint as effectively as a bristle brush, and when charged it does not spread the paint so efficiently; this means that it does not produce quite such a level or even coating, and in addition the rate of application is slowed down. Nor can the paint be laid off as satisfactorily, and this can often result in a coarse and ropey finish. The manufacturers do what they can to improve the spreading qualities of the filament by grinding it down so as to make it taper towards the tip, and they also treat it so as to produce an artificial flag at the tip of each length of filament; naturally, though, when the flag is worn away it cannot be replaced, whereas the flag of a hog hair bristle is constantly renewed as the brush wears down throughout the life of the bristle. A further drawback is the springiness of nylon filament which leads to the paint being splashed around far more than when a bristle brush is in use.

Nylon ropes Strong alkali-resistant ropes; their higher degree of stretch makes them capable of absorbing shock loads, but is not a desirable feature in ropes intended for use in suspended scaffolds. See *Synthetic ropes*.

O

Oak A hardwood of the greatest interest and importance to the painter and decorator. The oak is a tree of the genus Quercus, which is widely distributed throughout the world; there are some 250 different species, of which the best known and most important commercially are the European oaks (which include English oak and Austrian oak), American oak and Japanese oak. "Australian oak", however, is quite unrelated.

At one time the oak covered large areas of Great Britain, and was an important factor in its economy. Quite apart from its vital role in the development of the nation's sea power, it was the material that the Anglo-Saxon people turned to for domestic building, it was the timber used in the fine roofs, the benches and the stall work that were such important features of medieval churches, it was widely used in Tudor domestic building not only in the main structures but also for panelling, and at least from Norman times up to the Restoration in the 17th century it was the principal wood used for furniture. Although the last period in which extensive planting took place was the Napoleonic wars, it would appear that the long tradition of the use of oak coupled with the beauty and the distinctive grain of its timber have made an indelible impression on the tastes of the British people so that to this day there is a constant demand for oak effects in decorative work, a steady market for wallpapers, relief goods and veneers for the simulation of oak panelling, and a call for the painted and grained imitation of oak which exceeds that of any other type of wood imitation.

The colour of natural oak varies from a rich honey colour to a yellowish brown. The heartwood grain markings, although similar to ash, are far more rugged and varied in shape and a peculiar feature is that the outer edges of the elliptical curves are sharply spiked and tend to open out into spoon-like shapes at the extremities. Due to the breadth of the medullary rays, oak wood presents a most beautiful silver-grain or flash when cut on the quarter. The wood takes stain well but shows to better advantage if left unstained so that its unrivalled natural colour and grain are not obscured.

Oak graining is generally carried out in oil graining colour, which should afterwards be overgrained in Vandyke to develop the subtle variations of highlight. Much of the commercial graining that is seen is hopelessly crude in colour, due to the fact that the ground colour is too muddy and the stain made too warm in an effort to redeem it. For natural oak a ground colour of white and raw umber alone may be used, for medium oak and pollard oak the white may be tinted with raw umber and golden ochre, for dark oak burnt umber and golden ochre stainers are used and for antique oak the pigments are burnt umber, ochre and black. The stainers used to make the graining colour for each of these types are respectively raw umber, raw umber and raw sienna, burnt umber and raw sienna, and burnt umber and black. The grain markings may be produced by the wipe-out process or by pencilling in with a one-stroke writer. The characteristic pore markings are sometimes added by means of a check roller. An excellent imitation of oak can be produced with patent graining wheels of various kinds which are used to cut or incise the grain markings and pores into the ground colour or into the wood itself prior to staining.

Oak timber is used for various constructional purposes, including door frames, window frames, sills, staircase treads and risers. The painting of these and similar oak surfaces is complicated by three factors: (i) the wood contains a high proportion of tannin which may retard the drying of the primer coat, (ii) the close grain prevents penetration of the primer, thus affecting adhesion, unless the primer is thinned down with 10 percent of white spirit to assist penetration, (iii) the pronounced and open pores cannot be bridged satisfactorily with undercoatings or finishes, the paint tending to recede from the edges of the gaps; this necessitates filling the pores after priming, and a good proprietary brand of exterior grade paste filler is recommended. Gypsum filler does not accommodate itself sufficiently to the movement of the timber.

When oak is used for exterior doors and gates, especially on church work, historic buildings, and substantial domestic properties, the wood is sometimes given a preservative treatment of boiled oil so as not to obscure the natural beauty of the grain, the oil being applied copiously and the surplus wiped off after a lapse of some two hours, the work being then rubbed briskly with a soft cloth to produce a slight sheen. It is important that the wood should be thoroughly clean before the treatment is undertaken, and that the finish should be maintained in good condition by periodic re-oiling. The drawback of this traditional treatment is that dirt tends to cling to the surface, and for this reason it is no longer used to the same extent that it was a few years ago. The problem is to find a suitable treatment which will give the required protection without spoiling the appearance of the wood; clear varnish for instance is unsuitable because a gloss finish of any kind detracts from the appearance of oak. Today a range of transparent wood finishes is available and the various manufacturers should be consulted as to the choice of a product best suited for the particular location and exposure conditions in question. One of the leading firms specializing in wood finishes produces an excellent material consisting of a combination of high-grade alkyd resins and non-wax polymers which, in a three-coat system, gives an attractive transparent finish which yields very satisfactory results. For interior work the choice is much wider, and includes a variety of wood preservatives and catalyst wood finishes. It should be noted that whenever iron, in the form of wedges or nails, is in contact with newly cut oak a blue-black stain of the same composition as writing ink rapidly forms, due to the action of the wood's natural tannin upon the metal.

Oak combing roller Alternative term for check roller.

Oak grain finisher A small brass roller with fluted lines running along the drum, mounted on a wooden handle. It is used for finishing the lines made by a check roller by carrying them right into the angle at the edge of a panel.

Oak varnish An old-fashioned term given to ordinary grades of short-oil varnish for interior work, made from less expensive resins than church oak varnish. (**NLC**)

Obeche A tree found in tropical West Africa producing a soft, light timber which is known as Nigerian whitewood or West African satinwood and which is used in coach-building and shop-fitting.

Oblique projection A projection is a method of linking together the plan and elevations of a room or building so as to present a three-dimensional picture. An oblique projection is the simplest form of this, and is produced by drawing an elevation of one wall with lines drawn at 45° from each corner to correspond with the length of the side walls, to the same scale as the elevation, and with lines drawn from these points to complete the view. The three-dimensional appearance of the room is immediately apparent, but of course it seems to be distorted compared with a perspective drawing; for this reason its use by decorators is confined as a rule to working drawings from which measurements can be read off.

Obliterating power Opacity.

Obliteration Obscuring or effacing any previous markings, pattern or colour on a surface.

Ochre A yellow earth pigment derived from sands and clays found in many parts of the world including Britain, France, Italy, India and America, and consisting of a mixture of silica, alumina and hydrated oxide of iron. Like all earth colours, ochre is a variable pigment, subject to considerable differences in colour, texture, opacity and staining strength from one sample to another. It is one of the oldest pigments known, having been used from the very earliest times. It is prepared by grinding and levigation and produces a rather dull brownish yellow which is stable, permanent and fast to light but which is rather a poor drier.

Offset match Another term for a drop pattern wallpaper. See *Drop pattern*.

Off-white A term applied to a material which is obviously not a pure white but which is so close to white that it cannot be called by any definite colour name.

Oil A viscid liquid, greasy or soapy to the touch, which is lighter than water, insoluble in water, soluble in ether and usually soluble in alcohol. The term covers three classes of substance, as follows:

(i) Fatty or fixed oils, of vegetable or animal origin. These can be subdivided into three groups, namely;

(a) drying oils, such as linseed oil, tung oil, poppy seed oil, etc., which when exposed to the air absorb oxygen and undergo a chemical change whereby they become tough leathery solids;

(b) non-drying oils, such as castor oil, olive oil, palm oil, tallow, etc., which ferment on exposure; and

(c) semi-drying oils such as croton oil, grape seed oil, etc., which are intermediate between the other two.

(ii) Mineral oils, distilled from peat, shale, etc., which are used as illuminants.

(iii) Essential or volatile oils which are chiefly of vegetable origin and are used in medicine and perfumery.

The oils used as binding agents in the manufacture of paint and varnish, which are clearly of most interest to the painter and decorator, belong to the first class, i.e., the fatty oils, and in particular to the group known as the drying oils, although certain non-drying oils (e.g., castor oil) can be processed in such a way as to develop a structure similar to that of tung oil whereby they can be usefully incorporated into paint media.

Oil absorption The quantity of oil required to convert a specific quantity of dry pigment to a stiff paste. This factor is of fundamental importance in paints and enamels as it affects such properties as the consistency, opacity, gloss, etc.

Oil-based paste filler A ready-made filler for levelling surface cracks and indentations in woodwork, which is suitable for both outdoor and indoor use. It is supplied in tins, ready for immediate use. It dries rather slowly, and has the advantage of having very little absorbency, which means that the paint applied upon it does not sink to any appreciable extent. The woodwork must be primed before the filler is applied. After application it is rubbed down with waterproof sandpaper.

Oil-bound water paint A decorative coating consisting of a good-quality pigment such as lithopone or titanium oxide, which has as its binding agent an emulsion of oil in water or, in some cases, an emulsified oil varnish. It is supplied in paste form to be beaten up just before use, and is thinned with water and applied with a broad distemper brush. It has a pleasing matt finish, is tolerant of damp, and is resistant to alkaline action. For a considerable part of the first half of the 20th century it was the principal material used for the decoration of ceilings and was also widely used as a coating for walls in good-class decorative work. It has now been completely superseded by emulsion paint in Britain although it is still used to a limited extent in some parts of Europe. (**NLC**)

Oil filler See *Japan filler*, for which this is an alternative term.

Oil gloss A straight linseed oil paint composed of a base pigment tinted as required and thinned to a working consistency with linseed oil and turpentine. (**NLC**)

Oil gold size Oil gold size is a mordant for gilding consisting of a thickened or partially oxidized oil. Formerly it was prepared by exposing linseed oil to the air for long periods in shallow vessels until it became fatty; at this stage it was pigmented with ochre, driers were added and it was then thinned down with boiled oil or varnish. Modern ready-made oil gold size is prepared from stand oil and is supplied pigmented ready for use. It is available in varying drying speeds; as a general rule the slower its speed of drying, the more lustrous the finished gold will appear. It is used in the gilding of carved or modelled work, for gilding large wooden or metal letters and for large areas where a solid gold background is required for lettering or decoration. It must be applied over a surface which has been adequately sealed to render it non-absorbent and must be well brushed out because of its tendency to creep and develop ridges and fat edges. After application it must be protected from any possible settling of dust until such time as it is tacky enough to gild. It is not suitable for sign work or decorative work where sharply defined shapes are to be produced, nor for areas where it would be exposed during the drying period to the effects of the weather. It possesses the great advantage of holding its tack for a considerable period, thereby making it easy to apply the gold evenly. It should not be used as the mordant for metals other than gold leaf or for bronze powders because of the discolouration which takes place due to the oxidation of the oil.

Oil length Originally a term used to describe the ratio of oil to resin in a varnish medium, but now applied to paint to denote the proportion of drying oil in a medium or binder. Thus, the term "long-oil" defines a medium in which the proportion of drying oil is 70 percent or more, "medium-oil" where the proportion is between 50 and 70 percent, and "short-oil" where the proportion is lower than 50 percent, generally in the order of 45 to 50 percent. As a general rule all paints intended for outdoor use are in the long-oil range.

Oil paint A paint in which the binder consists of a drying oil or an oil varnish and which dries by the oxidation or polymerization of the binder.

Oil varnish A varnish composed of drying oil and resin, together with driers and thinners (as opposed to a spirit varnish or a water varnish).

Oiling in A process carried out after a surface has been filled and levelled; the substance used is actually a half-and-half mixture of varnish and turps, not oil. When the filling has been completed satisfactorily, thoroughly rubbed down and is quite dry, a thin coat of varnish and turps is applied and allowed to dry. The object is to seal the porosity of the filler. Failure to oil in results in ropey brushwork due to the uneven absorption of the subsequent coats of paint, thereby destroying the whole object of the filling process. It is not generally realized that work which has been properly filled and oiled in requires no further rubbing down, thus ensuring a saving of time.

Oiling of woodwork A treatment whereby hardwoods such as oak, teak, etc., are coated with oil as a preservative. The wood should be dry and should be well cleaned down before treatment. Boiled linseed oil is applied copiously and after two hours the surplus oil is wiped off. A further oiling is carried out after 48 hours, and thereafter at weekly intervals for five or six weeks. The final application should be followed by a brisk rub down with a soft cloth in order to produce a sheen. Periodically the work should be cleaned down and re-oiled to maintain it in good condition. The first coating of oil should be thinned with some 15 percent of white spirit or turpentine or some 10 percent of naphtha in order to ensure its penetrating the wood. The subsequent coats should be of neat oil.

Oily woods Certain woods such as cedar and teak have an oily nature which has an adverse effect upon any paint or varnish coatings applied to them, by slowing down the drying of the coating and by preventing it from adhering properly. If this fact is not taken into account before the wood is primed there is a strong possibility that the coating will subsequently peel and flake off. To cope with this problem it is sometimes recommended that the wood should be washed down with acetone, which is scrubbed into the surface with a stiff brush, but care must be taken to allow the acetone to evaporate completely before any form of surface coating is applied. Generally, however, a thorough wash with white spirit is quite strong enough for the purpose. It is most important that the first coating or primer should be of an adhesive nature. When a clear wood finish is specified, the first coat should be thinned with the solvent recommended by the manufacturer. When a paint treatment is required, an aluminium primer is generally the most satisfactory, but some paint manufacturers produce a primer specially formulated for such woods.

Oiticica oil An oil obtained from the nuts of a tree found in Northern Brazil, which approximates very closely to tung oil in its properties.

Old oil gold size The same material as oil gold size; the terms are interchangeable.

Oleo-resin Some confusion exists about this term, which is not always used with a clear understanding as to its meaning, and which is interpreted in two different ways.

(i) Strictly speaking, an oleo-resin is a natural mixture of a volatile essential oil and a resin; it is derived from a substance exuded from various types of trees in semi-fluid form which solidifies on exposure to air but remains soft and plastic. In some cases oleo-resins are used as plasticizers to prevent materials such as spirit varnishes from becoming too brittle.

(ii) The term is far more frequently used today to define a binder, medium or varnish composed of a fusion of vegetable drying oils with either natural or synthetic resins.

Ombré effects Blended colour effects produced by the use of tinted glaze medium.

One-coat paints A type of finish offered by various paint manufacturers to appeal to the customer who is anxious to eliminate labour costs and obtain as economical a job as possible. Such paints are formulated with high-opacity pigments, and in some cases are thixotropic. Their success depends largely upon the condition of the existing finish; clearly they are most likely to be satisfactory where the existing surface is free from defects. Under these circumstances many established finishes would be equally successful in obliterating in one coat although possibly their use would demand a higher level of application skill than the one-coat finish. Where the existing finish is damaged or in poor condition, some form of pre-treatment is required and the one-coat finish offers no particular advantage. On new surfaces a primer is required, together with a sufficient degree of undercoating to provide enough "build" for the finish. Even where conditions are suitable for the material it must be realized that because a single coat is thinner than a full paint system it provides less protection.

One stroke (also called one-stroke brush or one-stroke writer)
A sable hair brush set in a metal ferrule; the "length out" of the hair is shorter than that of the normal signwriting brush, and the width is usually greater; the ferrule is splayed out and flattened so that the brush itself is flat in shape and is chisel edged. One-strokes are available in several widths and are designed to produce work with short rapid strokes; they are extremely useful for ticket writing and poster work.

Onyx A variety of quartz with variously coloured layers, formerly a very popular subject for marbling.

Opacity The obliterating power or "hiding power" of a paint, i.e. its ability to obscure the colour of the underlying surface. The opacity of a paint depends upon the nature of the pigment (for example, titanium has much greater opacity than any other commercial white pigment) and upon the amount of pigment used in relation to the medium. Scientifically the opacity depends on the amount of light reflected by the particles of pigment, which in turn depends on the difference between the refractive index of the pigment and that of the medium. The paint technologist measures the opacity of a pigment by the Contrast Ratio method. (See *Contrast ratio*.)

Opaque The opposite of transparent; impenetrable to the sight.

Optical mixture To the painter and decorator dealing with pigmentary colours, this term describes the effect produced when small intermingled though separate specks of colour are viewed from a distance. Thus, if a surface were painted yellow and then spattered with blue, at a certain distance the separate primary colours would no longer be distinguishable and the effect would be that of a vibrant bright green. Optical colour mixtures are usually more brilliant than the plain allover coatings produced by a mechanical mixture of the same colours.

Optical tape measure A device which enables the person using it to measure objects at any distance between two and thirty metres without moving from the spot. It is of immense value to estimators, especially those whose work involves the measurement of large industrial sites and premises. It is particularly useful, for example, in situations where an expanse of structural steelwork needs to be measured in areas where the presence of dangerous chemical fumes, moving machinery and other hazards make ordinary access impossible. The measure consists of an instrument with a focusing dial which is adjusted until the images in the view-finder merge together into one, when the distance is read off from the scale. This instrument is remarkably cheap in price. Larger models are available which allow distances of up to a thousand metres to be measured, but since they are very expensive and because such long distances are not met with even on big industrial painting projects there is no point in considering them.

O

Or The heraldic term for gold.

Orange chrome An orange pigment made by treating normal lead chromate with caustic soda or quicklime.

Orange lead Also known as orange mineral. A pigment similar to red lead but paler in colour. It is manufactured by oxidizing white lead, whereas red lead is made by oxidizing a material called massicot, which is the yellow monoxide of lead.

Orange peeling A fault in a spray-applied paint film, taking the form of an uneven surface which resembles the outside of the skin of an orange. There are several possible causes of the fault and they are all generally bound up with incorrect methods of application. Incorrect thinning of the paint, or using paint in so viscous a condition that when it strikes the surface it will coalesce but cannot flow out, will lead to orange peeling; so also will using too low an air pressure so that the paint is not properly atomized and cannot flow out after application. Holding the gun too far from the work and using too high an air pressure, especially when spraying lacquer, is another cause, due to the solvent evaporating before the material has had time to flow out; if, on the other hand, the gun is held too close to the work, the solvent is dried out too rapidly because of the action of the compressed air striking the surface. Careless working resulting in overspray or in overloading a surface which is setting up is a further cause of orange peeling.

Orange shellac The best quality of shellac.

Orbital sander A sanding machine for the rubbing down of flat surfaces; the rubbing face consists of a felt covered platform measuring about 175 mm by 75 mm, to which a waterproof abrasive paper is clipped; when in action, the platform moves with a circular motion similar to the movement of the hand in manual rubbing down.

Oregon fir See *Columbian pine*.

Organic A term used in technical literature, relating to paints and decorative products derived from substances and compounds obtained from living growths containing carbon. Organic chemistry is the study of the compounds of carbon, although a few simple compounds such as carbon dioxide are usually included in inorganic chemistry.

Organic colours Pigments consisting essentially of carbon compounds; they are produced by precipitating organic dyestuffs or by coupling organic intermediates.

Oriental lacquer A thick milky emulsion obtained from the sap of the tree *Rhus vernicifera*, native to China. The emulsion is heated to purify it and forms a natural lacquer which will dry readily in darkness provided the atmosphere is cool and damp, but which remains tacky indefinitely if exposed to light and warmth. See *Lacquer*.

Ormolu See *Water gilding.*

Ostwald theory The theory of colour and light as related to the craft of a painter, explained in a book entitled "Letters to a Young Painter on the Theory and Practice of Painting" by a German scientist, Wilhelm Ostwald, who lived from 1853 to 1932. An English translation of the book appeared in 1907. Ostwald attempted to establish absolute values for artists' pigments. The Ostwald colour circle is based upon eight basic hues, namely yellow, orange, red, purple, blue, turquoise, sea green and leaf green.

Outrigger The horizontal or almost horizontal tubes projecting outwards from the face of a building, to which are attached the pulley blocks from which a cradle is suspended.

Oval brush See *Varnish brush.*

Overgrainer A brush used in graining for the purpose of producing a series of parallel lines, in thin glaze colour, either in oil or water media. It is a thin long-haired brush with a filling of hog hair set in a metal ferrule; very often the ferrule is packed with wood or with cork composition. The width may vary; the usual widths are 38 mm and 63 mm. The overgrainer is charged with colour and is then passed through an ordinary hair comb in order to break it up into separate strands. In addition to the normal type of overgrainer there are variations known as pencil overgrainers and fantail overgrainers which are especially useful for certain types of wood grain.

Overgraining A process carried out with thin glaze over the top of figure graining in order to simulate the subtle light and shade effects seen in natural wood. It is usually carried out in a water medium such as Vandyke brown but oil medium may also be employed. Though often omitted on the grounds of economy, it is very necessary if an accurate representation of true wood grain is desired, for it is impossible to convey a really natural effect in one single figuring operation.

Overhead expenses A term meaning the costs incurred in operating a business which are not directly chargeable to any particular job or contract. They are generally known today as "establishment charges" and the two terms have the same meaning. For a fuller definition, see *Establishment charges.*

Overlap and repair adhesive An adhesive material usually supplied in small tubes, for the purpose of allowing overlapping seams to be fastened down when vinyl wallcoverings are being hung. The adhesive can also be used for making small repairs where wallpaper already attached to a wall surface has been damaged.

Overspray A term used in spray painting to mean paint which travels beyond the confines of the area which is to be painted. Excessive overspray leads to uneconomical working through loss of paint, and overspray falling on a previously painted surface is a frequent cause of orange peeling.

O

Ox hair Hair obtained from the ears of oxen, used as the filler for various kinds of artists' brushes and fine brushes used for lettering, lacquering, etc.

Ox hair blender A flat chisel-ended brush set in a metal ferrule at the end of a very long slender handle. The hair is only short and the brush itself quite a small one. It is used for blending light and dark colours in the production of shaded effects in lettering.

Oxalic acid A sour, highly poisonous acid derived from vegetable matter which sometimes is used for bleaching out natural woods such as oak, although it is not as useful or effective as the proprietary bleaches which are available.

Oxford ochre A soft transparent ochre with a peculiar brownish-yellow tone found in pockets in the ironstone deposits which occur over a large part of Oxfordshire. The supply is now practically exhausted. (**NLC**)

Oxidation A chemical process whereby substances take up or combine with oxygen. Of importance to the painter in connection with the oxidation of metals, etc., when exposed to the air, the oxidation of vegetable drying oils, and so on.

Oxides Compounds formed by the union of chemical elements with oxygen.

Oxy-acetylene equipment Equipment involving the use of a mixture of oxygen and acetylene to produce an intensely hot flame, such as, for example, flame-cleaning equipment.

Ozone A condensed form of oxygen containing 3 atoms to the molecule, whereas the oxygen molecule only contains 2 atoms. It is present in very small quantities in the lower atmosphere, its occurrence being probably due to electrical action and particularly to the electrolysis of water; its presence is supposed to explain the bracing effect of sea air. Ozone is a powerful oxidizer attacking and destroying organic matter, bleaching vegetable colouring-matter and attacking most metals. It has a pronounced effect upon paints applied in coastal districts or exposed to marine atmospheres, causing the initial drying to take place at a rapid rate but also accelerating the whole process of oxidation and thereby hastening the ultimate breakdown of the film through chalking and perishing.

P

Paint A substance consisting of finely powdered insoluble materials, chiefly pigments, suspended in a liquid binding medium, which is applied in liquid form and which when exposed to air or under the influence of heat has the power of changing to a dry adherent film.

Paint agitator A device fitted to a pressure feed tank in a spray painting outfit as a means of stirring up the paint in the tank. The agitator may be connected to a manually operated handle which the operator turns when stirring is required, or it may be mechanically operated.

Paint bucket See *Paint scuttle.*

Paint can or paint kettle The container in which paint is placed ready for brush application. A wide range of sizes and shapes is available. Some paint cans are straight sided; others are tapered, which makes for easy stacking and storage. The smaller types of can are to be preferred for good-quality decorative finishes such as gloss paint; the larger types are more favoured by the industrial painting contractor. The desirable features of a paint can are that it should be treated to prevent rusting, that it should have a fairly sharp lip to facilitate the removal of surplus paint from the brush, that it should be robust enough to withstand repeated burning out and cleaning and that it should have a lip shaped to prevent paint running down the outside face.

Some paint kettles are now made of a strong plastic material.

Paint colours for building purposes There is a British Standard of this name, BS 4800. When introduced in 1972 it comprised 88 colours, but it was revised in 1981 and now includes 100 colours (including black and white). Each colour is identified by a code consisting of three parts. The first part denotes the hue, and consists of an even number with two numerals (e.g. 04 for red, 20 for yellow, and so on); the second part denotes greyness and consists of a single letter (e.g. B, D, E, etc.); the third part denotes weight and consists of odd numbers with two numerals ranging from 01 to 55. Thus, colours with the same first part are of similar hue (e.g., 04 E 53 is a bright scarlet red, 04 D 45 is a maroon colour, etc.); colours with the same letter are in the same greyness grouping (e.g., 06 E 56 which is an orange colour has the same greyness grouping as 04 E 53 which is bright red); colours with the same final part are of similar weight (e.g., 24 C 33, a pale lilac colour, is of similar weight to 04 C 33 which is a blend of pink and cream—and incidentally these two colours have the same greyness grouping too).

The object of introducing BS 4800 was to satisfy the needs of the construction industry and its associated industries for a standardized range of colours, providing a reasonable amount of choice within the limits of economical production, and catering for all types of materials including paints and other building materials. At that time, in 1972, the intention was stated of introducing a basic range for the co-ordination of colours for all building purposes, and this occurred in 1976 when a further British Standard, BS 5252, was issued. As a development of this, several other British Standards have appeared providing colour ranges for specific branches of the construction industry and for use in particular aspects of building work. It is therefore important that BS 4800 should not be considered in isolation, but should be linked in conjunction with BS 5252 and its various offshoots. It is also very important indeed that the painter and decorator should be aware of how the system has evolved and thoroughly conversant with the way it operates.

BS 5252: 1976 is entitled "Framework for Colour Co-ordination for Building Purposes" and provides 237 systematically related colours from which specific ranges may be selected. It is co-ordinated in terms of the three visual attributes on which BS 4800 is based, namely hue, greyness, and weight. BS 5252 has 12 hues. The greyness scale shows any of those hues graduated from "clear" and thence through shades containing increasing amounts of grey, and there are 5 groups of greyness. The weight distinguishes the apparent lightness of any hue or greyness, and there is a range of 8 "weights" applicable to each greyness group. In BS 5252 the colours are arranged to show these relationships clearly, and the key numbers to be used by the manufacturers of paints and other building products in addition to their own brand names for the colours are stated. The Standard is called a framework because it provides the basis for further colour selections to be made. A supplement to the Standard has now been issued under the title of BS 5252 F—"Framework for Colour Co-ordination for Building Purposes; Colour Matching Fan." It contains patches measuring 64 mm square of all the colours, and is used to facilitate the matching of colours.

Other British Standards have now been issued which, together with BS 4800, are part of the co-ordinated framework envisaged in BS 5252, one of which is of particular interest to painters and decorators. They are as follows:
BS 4900: 1976, "Vitreous Enamel Colours for Building Purposes", in respect of colours applied to metals for use as interior or exterior claddings.
BS 4901: 1976, "Plastic Colours for Building Purposes", in respect of colours covering opaque plastics products such as laminates and moulded or extruded components.
BS 4902: 1976, "Sheet and Tile Flooring Colours for Building Purposes".
BS 4903: 1979, "External Colours for Farm Buildings". This of course concerns the many people engaged in painting and decorating in rural areas. It specifies 40 preferred colours for external use on farm buildings. The interesting and significant thing about this is that it clearly shows how the principles of co-ordinating colour planning are being systematically extended to cover every aspect of commercial enterprise. This Standard is based on the conclusions set out in a lengthy document on a seemingly unrelated topic, namely BS 5502, "The Code of Practice for the Design of Buildings and Structures for Agriculture".
BS 4904: 1978 (1985), "External Cladding Colours for Building Purposes" which specifies 38 preferred colours for external cladding in aluminium, asbestos-cement, opaque glass, opaque plastics, and steel.

There are also Standards relating to safety signs; these are dealt with under the heading *Safety signs—British Standards*.

Paint conductivity meter A device which measures, and thereby helps the painter to adjust, the electrical conductivity of the paint when using an electrostatic handgun.

Paint harling A process used for the protection of the exterior steelwork of steel-clad houses, which has been employed more extensively in Scotland than elsewhere. The process is carried out in four stages, as follows:

(i) The surface is carefully prepared and cleaned, and all loose bolts, rivets, etc., made good.

(ii) A rust-inhibitive priming coat is applied and allowed to dry hard. A thick coat of viscous paint (which until recently was composed of paste white lead, stand oil and gold size), pigmented to the desired colour, is applied and allowed to become tacky.

(iii) Paint-coated granite chips are thrown on to the tacky surface by hand, and the whole surface then allowed to dry hard. The granite chips are coated with paint in a concrete mixer some eight hours before they are to be used.

Paint harling produces an extremely durable finish even when used in very exposed conditions. For the best results the work should be carried out by men trained in this operation and the process should be carefully organized and supervised. When the surface becomes dingy due to accumulated soot and grime, it can be washed down to remove the dirt and a coat of paint applied by spray. If the harling itself is damaged the affected area is cleaned down to the bare steel and a further application of primer, thick paint and granite chips applied to match up to the surrounding area.

Paint pad A device for applying paint, introduced for the benefit of the amateur painter and not worth the consideration of the professional decorator. It consists of a flat rectangular plastic holder attached to a handle; a detachable mohair or foam-rubber head is fastened to the holder, and it is this which spreads the paint. The pads are made in assorted sizes, the smallest being intended for cutting in windows, the dimensions of the largest being 150 mm × 100 mm. Some makes have wheels at the side of the plastic holder to assist in cutting in.

Paint pump (1) The essential part of the airless-spray system, by which the paint is pressurized. Three types of pump are available, the pneumatic pump driven by compressed air, the hydraulic pump driven by petrol engine or electric motor, and the diaphragm pump also driven by petrol or electricity.

(ii) A fluid pump driven by compressed air and used to convey paint to a spray gun directly from the large drums in which paint is delivered to a site; it is a useful time-saving device on large-scale painting contracts.

Paint remover A liquid which is applied to a painted surface in order to soften the old paint and bring it to such a condition that it can be stripped off. It may take the form of a caustic paint remover, which is an alkaline material acting by saponifying the binder medium in the old paint film, or a spirit paint remover, which consists of a solvent material powerful enough to dissolve the old coating. Spirit paint remover is the more expensive of the two but in nearly every case it is a far more satisfactory stripper to use. Paint remover is employed where burning off would be an unsuitable method of stripping, such as on surfaces like plaster or metal which are good conductors of heat, or on delicately carved or moulded work, on narrow glazing bars in close proximity to glass, on woodwork which is to be restored to its natural condition and where scorch marks would be disastrous, and in localities where flammable materials are stored. See also *Hot-air paint stripping*; *Peel-away paint stripper*; *Spirit paint remover*.

Paint roller See *Roller*.

Paint scuttle Also known as a paint bucket or paint tank. A big container for holding paint, designed for the application of paint by rollers on large areas. Various sizes are available, the largest having a capacity of 10 litres. A mesh or ridged insert is provided to ensure that the roller is evenly charged with paint. The container is fitted with strong supporting hooks so that it can be attached to ladders or steps.

Paint shaking machine or paint rejuvenator A machine into which tins of ready mixed paint which have been kept in stock for a considerable time may be clamped and subjected to a vigorous agitation, thus restoring the contents to their original condition without a lengthy period of manual stirring.

Paint stripper A term sometimes used for paint remover.

Paint tank See *Paint scuttle*.

Paint testing All paint materials are subjected to rigorous testing by the manufacturers to ensure the maintenance of the quality of existing lines and to develop new products with improved properties. Tests are carried out under actual normal working conditions approximating as closely as possible to the conditions which pertain on the site; in addition, a number of techniques have been evolved for testing some specific aspect of a paint's performance and for providing a reasonably reliable assessment of its properties without a great deal of delay. The following are some of the tests in common use.

Durability. The durability of a paint is tested on small panels placed on exposure racks in various parts of the country and subjected to the effects of the sun, rain, frost, etc. Because of the length of time required to gain information by this method, use is also made of accelerated weathering tests in which the panels are placed in a rotating drum and exposed to a constant succession of ultra-violet irradiation from a carbon arc and saturation with a water spray in order to simulate rapidly the conditions leading to breakdown.

Viscosity. This is tested by means of the flow cup in which the rate of flow through a standard sized hole is measured, or by a torsion viscometer or paddle viscometer in which a cylinder on a spindle or a paddle is immersed in the material, rotated, released and the amount of overswing measured, or by a falling ball viscometer in which the passage of a metal ball through the material is timed.

Opacity. The hiding power of a paint is tested on cards or boards divided into chequered or striped patterns in black and white, or by the use of opacity meters or by means of a device whereby a tapering space between two glass plates is filled with paint and the point at which the material ceases to be transparent is noted.

Colour. Comparisons of colour are made with the human eye, which is more sensitive than instruments, although for some purposes use is also made of colorimeters or spectrophotometers.

Drying time. This is tested by sprinkling a painted surface with sand and noting at what point the sand can be dusted off without injury to the surface. Another test involves the use of what was formerly called the "mechanical thumb" but is now known as a plunger, which simulates the twisting action of the human thumb when pressed down on a painted surface. The plunger is tipped with a commercial quality of natural rubber, and this rubber tip is covered with a piece of clean cloth with no folds or creases in it; the plunger is rotated by an electric motor. The drying time can also be ascertained by a form of scratch test in which a pointed needle is drawn through a paint film alongside a graduated scale and the spot at which the film ceases to flow together is noted and recorded.

Hardness. This is tested by a form of scratch test in which weights of increasing value are placed on a needle travelling across the paint film until scoring takes place; another instrument for the purpose is a hardness rocker, which consists of two hoops, a pendulum and a calibrated scale, the number of pendulum swings being governed by the tackiness or otherwise of the surface; the mechanical thumb is also used.

Adhesion and elasticity. These are measured by means of the bend test in which a strip of painted metal is bent around a hinge, or by a drop test in which weights are dropped on to a painted panel. A simple test is to score the surface with a knife or coin.

A highly sophisticated test recently developed is the "pull-off test" for measuring the adhesion of paints and varnishes. It is identical with the test prepared by the International Organization for Standardization, and makes use of a tensile tester and test cylinder. A sample of the paint or varnish is applied to a suitable substrate; the faces of the test cylinder are coated with an adhesive such as cyanoacrylate, a two-component solventless epoxide, or peroxide-catalysed polyester, and the test sample brought into contact with them. When the adhesive has fully cured, the test assembly is placed in the tensile tester and force is applied uniformly across the test area; the tensile strength needed to break the assembly is recorded.

Water resistance. Tests are used to note how much water is absorbed by a paint film and also to what extent the paint allows the passage of moisture.

Further tests are listed in BS 3900.

Wet-edge time. This is tested on a prepared panel measuring 610 mm × 305 mm. One half of the panel is painted with the material under test, applied with a 25 mm brush and laid off, care being taken to avoid producing an abnormally thick or thin edge. Approximately two minutes before the specified wet-edge time of the material has elapsed, the operative begins to apply paint to the second half of the panel, arranging it so that the two edges can be worked together at the specifed wet-edge time, and the paint is then crossed and laid off. The panel when dry is examined for any imperfections such as lack of continuity in the film, absence of levelling, and variations in colour.

Brush and flow properties. A large-scale test is used to assess the brush and flow characteristics of primers, undercoats, finishing coats and water-borne paints. Two test panels are prepared, one to be coated with the material under test and the other with a comparable material of an agreed standard. Both materials are applied and laid off, and differences in their application properties are carefully observed and recorded. When the test panels are furnished with suitably designed mouldings, the same test can be used to observe other properties, such as the tendency of the material to retract from sharp edges and protuberances. The same testing procedure can be used to assess the comparative performances of complete paint systems.

A great many other tests are listed in BS 3900—see below.

Paint testing—British Standards, BS 3900 At one time, separately numbered standards were issued to define individual tests for specific paint properties, but in 1965 the British Standards Institution introduced a different system under which all forms of paint testing would be correlated under one numerical heading. This was envisaged as a continuing process whereby every aspect of paint testing would be tabulated, with new pamphlets being constantly prepared and added, so that eventually there would be a complete dossier on the subject, to be kept continually up to date. This has now become a very extensive series of documents, produced and presented in such a form that they can be filed together to make a comprehensive volume covering every aspect of paint testing. It is issued as BS 3900, with the title "British Standard Methods of Test for Paints", and is still being regularly reviewed and with new additions being made. The more recent documents in this series correspond with the standards produced by the Technical Committee of the International Organization for Standardization, of which the United Kingdom is a constituent member.

All the items in BS 3900 are classified in clearly defined groups which identify the particular area of testing to which they belong.

It is useful to understand the system, as this helps a person with an inquiry to locate the information required without wasting time in unnecessary searching. For example, in the title "BS 3900: Part F 11: 1985", the first part, BS 3900, shows that it is one of the British Standard methods of test for paints; the second phrase, Part F 11, shows that it is the eleventh paper to have been published in Group F, which is the group dealing with Durability tests on paint films; the final number, 1985, is the date of publication. The subject-matter of this document has the full title of "The determination of resistance to cathodic disbonding of coatings for use on land-based buried structures" and is one of the more recent sections to be published.

The subject areas of the various groups are as follows:

Group A—Tests on liquid paints (excluding chemical tests). This is one of the groups which concerns the working decorator most closely, because the tests are closely allied to practical application methods; it includes guidance on the sampling of paints, varnishes, etc., the examination and preparation of samples for testing, the preparation of panels prior to painting, paint application, and so on. The large-scale brushing test referred to in a previous entry is in this group.

Group B—Tests involving chemical examination of liquid paints and dried paint films. This is obviously of greater relevance to the paint technologist than to the decorator.

Group C—Tests associated with paint film formation. This group contains items such as the test for wet-edge time, surface drying time, freedom from residual tack, etc., and is therefore of great interest to the decorator.

Group D—Optical tests on paint films. Although these tests are for laboratory use, the notes concerning their use contain certain guidelines that the decorator should be aware of; for example, in the tests for the visual comparison of colours, which is a matter of practical importance to the decorator, the standard (after warning the observer to avoid eye-fatigue) goes on to give a specific warning not to view pastel colours immediately after comparing strong colours.

Group E—Mechanical tests on paint films. This again is directed to laboratory staff members, but the nature of the tests is of considerable interest to the decorator. Many of the tests referred to in the section about adhesion and elasticity in the previous entry on Paint Testing (including the pull-off test for adhesion) are to be found in this group.

Group F—Durability tests on paint films. This again is a group with a mainly scientific content, but it contains many items which the decorator would do well to study, such as for example the test for resistance to humidity in the form of continuous condensation, as well as the tests for resistance to humid atmospheres containing sulphur dioxide and resistance to hot fats, etc. The test concerning land-based buried structures referred to in a previous paragraph comes within this section.

Group G—Environmental tests on paint films (including tests for resistance to corrosion and chemicals). This group is probably of more concern to people employed in a supervisory capacity or involved in drawing up specifications than to working decorators.

Group H—Rating schemes. This is a recent addition to the series, and one that is of great importance to the painter and decorator. The story of how it was introduced is very interesting. In the late 1970s the British Standards Institution realized the need for a new section to deal with the evaluation of certain painting defects, and work was put in hand. In 1980, BS 3900: Part H 1: 1980 was published, presenting a system of evaluation and rating schemes for the degrees of blistering in paintwork and of rusting on painted metal. This, however, had to be revised only two years later to conform with a parallel document issued by the International Organization for Standardization. Our European confederates have a tendency to prefer a rigmarole of jargon to a simple statement of fact, and their standard bears the resounding title of "ISO 4628/1—1982; Paints and Varnishes—evaluation of degradation of paint coatings—destruction of intensity, quantity and size of common types of paint".

The first paper under the new scheme was H1, describing the system of evaluation and the method of rating. This was followed in 1983 by the publication of four new standards.

BS 3900: Part H 2: 1983 is called the "Designation of Degree of Blistering" and is a most useful document. It is illustrated by a series of photographs showing blisters of various size, graded from 1 to 5, and another series of photographs showing varying densities of blister concentrations in paintwork, again ranging from 1 to 5. It is a very simple matter for any person conducting an inquiry into the incidence of blistering on a site to compare the photographs with the defective paintwork, and in the negotiations that take place the size-rating of the largest blisters and the greatest degree of density are quoted.

BS 3900: Part H 3: 1983 is the designation of the degree of rusting. This too is illustrated with photographs of rust nodules graded from 1 to 5 and photographs showing the density of the rusting from 1 to 5.

BS 3900: Part H 4: 1983 is the designation of the degree of cracking. This is illustrated by line drawings in black ink. There are five drawings of varying degrees of cracking *without* any differential direction, that is to say, cracking in random shapes; and there are also five drawings of cracking *with* differential direction, that is, striated lines of cracking running in a roughly parallel direction.

BS 3900: Part H 5: 1983 is the designation of the degree of flaking. This too is illustrated by drawings, but in this case the shape and form of the flakes is depicted in solid black, that is to say, the flakes are shown not in outline but in the mass. Here again there are two sets of drawings graded from 1 to 5, one set showing random distribution of flakes and the other showing flakes with differential direction.

Paint tray A shallow container for paint, designed for the application of paint by roller. It is used in a horizontal position. The inside of the tray is deep at one end and inclined upwards to a shallow end; the sloping part is pressed into a pattern of grooved ridges, so that as the roller is withdrawn from the deep end surplus paint is squeezed out, thus ensuring an even distribution of paint on the ceiling or wall surface. Various sizes of tray are available to accommodate varying widths of roller.

Painter's colic A disease contracted by the absorption of lead into the system over a long period. See *Lead poisoning*.

Painting conditions The outside factors prevailing at the time that paint is applied and which might be expected to have a bearing on the life of the paint film, e.g., the atmospheric conditions such as rain, frost, or dew on exterior work, or the condensation of moisture or the presence of large quantities of dust in the atmosphere on indoor work.

Painting mittens These have been developed to facilitate the painting of metal railings, pipes, etc. They consist of lambswool mittens with a polythene lining, which the operative wears like a glove; by rubbing his mittened hand backwards and forwards over the surface the operative is able to spread the paint. While this is probably the most primitive form of paint application ever invented, it must be admitted that painting railings by brush application is not a pleasant occupation and leads to the clothing and skin being spattered with paint splashes; the use of mittens results in less splashing.

Pale Weak in colour.

Palette (i) A flat board, generally with a thumb piece, used by artists as a tablet on which to mix colours.

(ii) The range of pigments used to carry out a piece of decorative work; for example, we say; "In painting this mural the decorator restricted himself to a palette of lemon chrome, ultramarine blue and Indian red" or "To imitate this marble we use a palette of raw sienna, burnt sienna and indigo blue", etc.

Palette board A plain piece of board used by the decorator as a substitute for an artist's palette on which to place small quantities of colour and to carry out colour mixing.

Palette knife A knife with a very flexible blade, used for mixing or matching small quantities of colour. Many sizes are available. The decorator usually employs a palette knife with a blade of between 100 mm and 300 mm in length, with its two edges parallel, and terminating in a semicircular end. The artist generally employs a shorter and smaller type of palette knife with the edges tapering and terminating in a sharply rounded end.

Palimpsest A manuscript on a previously used parchment or other material from which the original writing was erased to make room for the new script. The term is also now applied to illuminated manuscripts and monumental brasses which are turned over and used on the reverse side. In recent years the term has been used even more loosely to describe any example of a surface or ground which has been re-used, and in this sense it can be applied to a decorative painting carried out on the reverse side of a canvas or painted panel.

Panel A distinct compartment raised above or sunk below the level of a wall, ceiling or door surface. The term is also loosely applied to an isolated piece of ornament or an isolated and free-standing piece of rigid material such as hardboard or wood upon which a sample of some decorative effect can be executed for demonstration purposes.

Panelling effects The treatment of flat surfaces such as walls or ceilings in order to give the impression of panelling. The term includes: the hanging of relief materials to imitate the appearance of actual wood panelling; the hanging of wallpaper in such a way as to form compartments of one pattern surrounded by a stiling of a different pattern; the application of plastic paint so that compartments of one type of texture are surrounded by a stiling of a different texture; the division of a wall into panels of texture or pattern separated from one another by real or imitation wooden stiles and rails, etc.

Pantograph A device used for making exact copies of a drawing on a larger or smaller scale.

Paper A thin flexible substance made up of the interlaced fibres of rags, straw, wood, etc.

Paperhanger's roller See *Felt-covered roller*.

Paperhanging The technique of applying wallpapers to areas such as walls, ceilings, etc.; the term also includes the hanging of relief materials, real and imitation wood veneers, fabrics such as silk, tapestry, canvases, grasscloths, etc., and coated fabrics such as, for example, PVC fabrics.

Paperhanging brush Also termed "papering brush", "putting on brush", "sweep", "laying on brush", "smoothing brush", and "paperhanger". A brush used in the application of wallpaper for the purpose of laying on and smoothing the paper down into its correct position. It is usually, although not always, a wire drawn brush; that is to say, the separate tufts of bristles are set into individual holes in the wooden handle and secured on the reverse side of the base piece with wire binding. The handle is shaped to fit the hand comfortably and snugly and is usually about 250 mm in length and 63 mm in depth. The "length out" of the bristles is normally between 63 mm and 75 mm.

The bristles are set in rows and the brush graded accordingly; a one-row or two-row brush is usually suitable for light and delicate papers, a three-row or four-row brush suitable for papers of average weight and consistency, while brushes with more than four rows of bristles are generally suitable for very heavy papers and relief materials. This, however, is not an invariable rule. Very fine brushes intended for delicate papers are sometimes made with three, four or five rows of bristle, but the tufts are very small and are so closely packed that there are as many as thirty-five in a row; on the other hand, a single-row brush made with very big strong tufts and only about eight tufts to the row is sometimes sold for heavy papers.

A conscientious paperhanger intent upon the quality of his work would never restrict himself to using only one papering brush, but would wish to carry two or three of different types, selecting them carefully so as to equip himself to deal with any kind of paper from the most delicate to the heaviest and coarsest.

Paraffin A colourless, tasteless, odourless, solid fatty substance produced from the dry distillation of coal, shale, lignite, peat, etc. In Great Britain the word is applied quite inaccurately to a substance properly called kerosene, which is an oil distilled from petroleum, coal or bituminous shale.

Paraffin blowlamp A blowlamp constructed for use with kerosene. The fuel is drawn up a brass tube from inside the body of the lamp, the tube being curved round in a U-shape around the nozzle. Kerosene does not vaporize as readily as petrol; an essential feature of a paraffin lamp is therefore a pump which is used to build up the pressure when lighting and maintain pressure during operation. The running costs of a paraffin lamp are very low, being about half those of a petrol lamp, and the lamp is more satisfactory than a petrol lamp in windy weather. On the other hand, the nipple tends to clog up very easily with a carbon deposit, and a paraffin lamp needs more time spending on its maintenance than a petrol lamp, which helps to outweigh the difference in cost between the two fuels. Nevertheless, it must be said that when properly maintained a paraffin lamp gives an excellent flame. A poorly maintained lamp does not burn the fuel completely and tends to deposit a light smearing of greasy matter on the surface which is being stripped; it is therefore essential that the surface should be thoroughly rubbed down before priming, preferably by a wet process.

Paraffin blowlamps are not used to any great extent in present-day practice.

Paraffin wax A white translucent material obtained by the fractional distillation of petroleum; it is crystalline in structure, resistant to both acids and alkalis, is soluble in mineral oils and is slightly soluble in turpentine, crystallizing out on standing. It is used in the manufacture of certain kinds of flat varnish and also as a stiffener in spirit paint removers.

Parapet A low or breast-high wall or fence provided as a protection on balconies, bridges, terraces and flat roofs. A parapet is an essential feature in the erection of outriggers for the suspension of a cradle from a flat roof; if no parapet exists, a dummy parapet must be provided in order to cant the outriggers.

Parchment The skin of calves, sheep, goats, etc., prepared for painting and manuscript writing.

Parchment size A clear weak size made by boiling scraps of parchment and straining the resultant liquid. It is sometimes used by the decorator to even up the lustre of a gilded surface and protect the surface from the accumulation of dirt. The size is applied with a soft squirrel hair mop. When it becomes soiled it can be washed off, taking the deposit of dirt with it, and a fresh coating of size laid on.

Pargetting The covering of the exterior of a building (including the timbers) with a tough lime plaster mixed with ox-hair; sometimes it is decorated in moulded or combed patterns. Such a finish is often coated with an exterior quality of emulsion paint.

Parian cement A hard burnt plaster of the anhydrous (Class D) group, similar to Keene's cement and subject to the same painting procedures.

Paris white The finest grade of ordinary whiting, used as an extender in some cheap kinds of oil paint. (**NLC**)

Parti-coloured Partly of one colour, partly of another; variegated.

Paste A term loosely used to describe any soft plastic mixture, but in every European language it refers in its literal sense to flour; it is derived from the word *pasta* which occurs in Latin, Greek, Old French and Italian and is the word from which our English word paste arose. Flour paste is of course the traditional adhesive used for paperhanging.

Today there is a very wide range of pastes and adhesives available to the decorator. Until recently flour paste was the only paperhanging adhesive, for although pure starch paste was used for expensive and delicately coloured papers, starch itself is a constituent of flour. When paste powders were first introduced they too were made from flour, and some of these paste powders still have a limited sale. The advent of wallcoverings with an impervious face coating meant that the paste trapped behind them tended to remain moist for a long time, and it became desirable to find an adhesive that would not putrefy under these conditions; cellulose pastes were introduced for this purpose, and these pastes are still in common use to a very considerable extent.

The present trend is towards the production of a range of adhesives each ideally suited to one specific type of wallcovering. This is an exciting development because it means that good-quality modern wallhangings can be applied with the certainty of giving complete satisfaction to the customer, without the risk of unexpected failures and disappointments. There are adhesives based on acrylic, PVA and other synthetic resins, synthetic rubber, etc., some of which are air-drying and others which set on contact. The range now includes

(a) Ready-to-use pastes for lightweight cloth-backed and paper-backed vinyls which allow the paperhanger plenty of time to manoeuvre the paper into the correct position and which dry to a strongly adherent transparent film;

(b) Thixotropic pastes based on synthetic resins for the hanging of heavy-duty paper-backed and cloth-backed hangings including textiles and vinyls, which have a strong initial tack capable of gripping these heavy materials;

(c) Pastes containing acrylic co-polymers which dry to a transparent film, for hanging foam-backed vinyls and other wallhangings where resistance to the migration of plasticizers is required;

(d) Thixotropic pastes based on synthetic resins for the hanging of lightweight textiles, fibreglass, treated fabrics, paper-backed vinyls, etc., which have the distinctive property of reducing to a minimum the wetting of the wallhanging so as to prevent shrinkage, and

(e) Thixotropic water-resistant pastes for hanging materials such as foam-backed vinyls and heavy cloth-backed vinyls under "wet-room" conditions.

All these pastes can be applied by brush, roller or spatula, and are usually (though not necessarily) applied to the wall rather than to the wallhanging. The manufacturers of these pastes supply explicit instructions and recommendations which help the decorator to select the adhesive which is precisely correct for any type of material and any particular site conditions.

Paste board A hinged and folding board, usually supported on a trestle, employed by the paperhanger as a surface upon which to lay wallpaper during the operations of shading, cutting up, pasting and folding. The standard length of a paste board is 1.83 metres. There is no standard width. Most pasteboards are far too narrow to permit clean and careful working. For best results a paste board when opened should give a width of at least 610 mm but quite a number of patterns are on sale which fall to as low as 530 mm wide.

Paste colours The name given to the range of the commoner pigments such as ochre, Venetian red, burnt umber, etc., when ground in oil and supplied in the form of a stiff paste for use in hand mixed paints. (**NLC**)

Paste driers or patent driers Drying agents mixed with extenders such as barytes, etc., and ground to a stiff paste with linseed oil for use in hand-mixed paints. (**NLC**)

Paste filler A filling composition mixed thickly enough to be applied by knife.

Paste powders Proprietary materials consisting of flour paste prepared as a powder which is chemically neutral and which will keep indefinitely. Hot-water paste powders are brought into use by mixing them to a batter with lukewarm water and then adding boiling water to scald the mixture, which must be allowed to cool before use. Cold-water paste powders are in ready-made form and simply need to be reconstituted by the addition of water.

Pastel colours Colours in which the purity is reduced by the addition of grey.

Pasting machine A device whereby wallpaper can be pasted evenly, smoothly and quickly without the use of a paste brush. Various kinds have appeared on the market. Basically they all consist of a paste container, a pasting roller, and two pressure rollers secured by a tension bar to hold the paper in contact with the pasting roller. In some cases the paste container is placed on the floor close to the skirting board and a full roll of paper is inserted in the machine; the paper is pulled through the rollers in an upward direction, ready to be hung on the wall; the lower end of the paper is cut off and the machine moved along ready for the next piece to be hung. In other types the machine is secured to the paste board and the paper pulled out along the board ready to be folded and cut, which is a quicker and less cumbersome method.

Pasting machines have been available to the trade since the 1950s but they have never been a success commercially, most decorators having tended to ignore their existence completely. Of course, a few paperhangers are more venturesome and are prepared to give them a trial; some of the people who use them have found the machines to be very satisfactory both as regards cleanliness of working and speed of operation, and claim that they produce significant savings in labour costs without any loss of quality.

Patch painting or patch priming The touching in or priming of localized areas in order to bring them forward to a state corresponding more closely to the surrounding areas. It may happen, for example, that in preparing a piece of woodwork such as a window frame it may be necessary to burn off the sill while the remainder of the work only requires rubbing down; in this case the sill will be patch primed to compensate for the loss of film thickness compared with the adjacent work. Similarly, if painted plaster work is being prepared for repainting and any patches are laid bare, or if a local area has been made good or replastered such as, for example, round a newly fitted fireplace, the rubbing down is completed and the work allowed to dry out, after which the bare patch is primed to stop porosity before any coating is applied to the whole wall.

Patching up Making good defects in a structure such as holes in plaster work, etc., or repairing a damaged area of decorative work in such a way as to make it correspond with the surrounding areas.

Patent driers See *Paste driers*. (**NLC**)

Patent knotting A solution of shellac in methylated spirit used to seal the resinous content of knots. (See *Knotting*.)

Patina The gloss produced by age or by continuous hand polishing on woodwork.

Pattern combing The manipulation of wet tinted glaze with steel graining combs in order to produce a free-hand pattern by exposing the ground colour.

Pattern roller A fairly wide roller the drum of which consists of a cylinder of rubber, cork or wood which is cut away in parts so as to form a pattern raised above the surrounding areas. The roller is charged with colour from a shallow tray, the surplus paint removed, and the roller then passed in a vertical or horizontal line across a previously painted surface. Some care is needed to produce an even and regular application of paint, but provided the choice of colours is suitable a pleasing result can be obtained, the main objection being the repetitive effect of numerous lines of pattern.

Pattern staining A disfigurement which occurs principally on ceilings and which takes the form of some localized areas becoming much darker than the remainder of the surface. It is commonly seen on plaster ceilings where the shape and pattern of the underlying joists and lathing is clearly revealed; it is also seen on ceilings constructed with building boards even when the surface has been skimmed with plaster, the position of the nails used in fixing the boards being indicated by local darkening.

Pattern staining is due to the deposit of smoke and dust particles on the surface and this is caused by the difference in thermal conductivity between the plaster or building board and the wood or metal of which the joists, laths or nails are composed. The trouble usually occurs on ceilings above which there is another room which is normally at a lower temperature or above which there is a roof loft or open space. It is commonly supposed that the disfigurement is caused by the passage of air through the plaster, but this is not so; the actual cause is that the air on the upper side of the ceiling seeks to become equal in temperature to the air in the room below, and, when the warm air of the room strikes the ceiling, heat is transferred from one side to the other. But plaster is a better conductor of heat than wood; where wooden laths and joists exist, therefore, the passage of the heat is obstructed, but in the spaces between the laths the passage is clear. More heat can therefore pass through the spaces and consequently more dirt is attracted to these parts. In cases where the underlying structure is of metal, however, or where expanded metal lathing has been used, it is the areas backed by the metal that are the better conductors of heat, and it is to these areas that most of the dirt will be attracted. In the same way, the metal nails securing building boards are apparent because they provide an easier path for the passage of heat than do the surrounding areas.

The only real cure for the trouble would be to equalize the temperature on both sides of the ceiling, which is usually impracticable. To some extent the trouble can be alleviated by insulating the spaces between the joists above the ceiling with some material such as slag wool or vermiculite, or by lining the face of the ceiling with a building board of low thermal conductivity. Surface treatments such as could be applied by the decorator do not provide a thick enough coating to be effective; to a very limited extent, however, a textured surface, such as a coating of plastic paint or a heavy relief paper, will break up the surface sufficiently to make the regularity of the pattern staining less obvious.

Pattress A colloquial term for the wooden base of a gas or electric light fitting or an electric light switch.

Pebbling A word sometimes used instead of "orange-peeling".

Peelable wallcoverings Wallpapers which are easily stripped when redecoration is required; the top surface peels away, leaving the paper backing intact.

Peel-away paint stripper A proprietary material for removing old paint and varnish films, even those of quite considerable thickness, in one clean and fairly quick operation. It consists of a powder which is mixed with water and applied to the painted surface; after application a re-usable fibre cloth (supplied with the product) is pressed into contact with the material, which is then allowed to dry. When it is dry the cloth is peeled away, bringing with it the entire paint film and leaving the surface clean and dry. The surface is then washed down and is ready to be redecorated.

This material offers several advantages compared with other methods of paint stripping. There are no unpleasant or toxic fumes, and of course there is none of the risk of charred woodwork which is always a possibility when blowtorches or blowlamps are used. Paint and varnish films can be removed from woodwork, plaster, metal or any other type of surface, and because the material conforms to the contours of the surface it removes paint just as effectively from mouldings, window bars or textured areas as it does from plain level surfaces. It will penetrate as many as fifteen or more coatings, and because it reduces the coatings to the form of a paper-like sheeting there is none of the sticky mess associated with conventional liquid paint removers. It is especially useful in restoration work, and has been used for this purpose at some of the nationally famous institutions.

One of the drawbacks, apart from the expense of the material, is that it will not remove cellulose products and is not always effective in removing paint from wooden surfaces where a water-thinned acrylic primer has been used.

Peeling A fault which is similar in all respects to flaking and is caused by the same factors, namely inadequate preparation or the use of unsuitable material. (See *Flaking*.)

Peeling of wallpaper, in the sense that the edges of the paper become loose and begin to curl away from the underlying surface, may be due to careless pasting, as a result of which the edges are starved of paste, or may be caused by inadequate preparation whereby the surface to which the paper is applied bears a deposit of loose dry powdery material; or in the case of vinyl wallpaper it may be due to the edges having been overlapped.

Pencil A term which is often used rather loosely; decorators very often apply the term to any kind of signwriting brush, and some people go so far as to describe any small form of artists' brush as a pencil. It is more accurate to reserve the term "pencil" for a signwriting brush of the long-haired variety terminating in a point, as opposed to a "writer", which is chisel edged. The best type of pencil is made from red sable, although ox hair pencils are made for use on rough surfaces. The sable may be set in quill or in a metal ferrule.

To avoid any possible confusion between the signwriting brush and the familiar instrument used for drawing, a good habit to cultivate is that of always referring to a black lead pencil by its full name.

Pencil overgrainer An overgrainer consisting of a series of small pointed brushes similar to writing pencils set in a row along a metal-bound wooden stock. Several sizes are available in varying widths. The best kind has pencils of sable hair, but this makes an expensive brush. The pencils should be spaced irregularly so as to give variation of width between the lines. Pencil overgrainers are excellent for the imitation of many woods, being particularly useful for American walnut. In the USA a pencil overgrainer is called a "pipe brush".

Pentaerythritol A form of alcohol used in the paint industry; it is used to neutralize rosin when making ester gums, and to react with acids such as phthalic anhydride in the making of alkyd resins.

Pentimento A term for what occurs when coatings of oil paint become more translucent with the passage of time due to a change in the refractive index of the medium. The process is a very gradual one.

Perilla oil A drying oil obtained from Manchuria and the East Indies; it is superior to linseed oil both in drying rate and polymerization rate.

Perishing The breakdown of a paint film through age, resulting in loss of flexibility, adhesion and cohesion and revealed by the development of such conditions as chalking, cracking, flaking, etc.

Permanent Fadeless, fast to light; a term used in describing pigments.

Permanent green A mixture of viridian, which is a hydrated oxide of chromium, with cadmium yellow or zinc chrome.

Permanent orange An orange pigment of the azo class, which is fast to light and has good tinting strength but rather poor opacity.

Permanganate of potash Used by the French polisher to make a water stain for wood; a very weak solution is used to give oak colour and a slighter stronger solution mixed with a little ammonia to give walnut. (**NLC**)

Permeable Penetrable; allowing the passage of fluids; for example, water-thinned materials such as emulsion paint possess a certain degree of tolerance for damp because if used on a plaster surface which is not completely dry the moisture can pass through the film and escape without forcing the film away from the surface, a property which is due to the permeability of the film.

Perspective drawing The representation of solid objects as the eye actually sees them, i.e., with receding parallel lines converging to a point on the horizon or eye level, so that distant objects appear smaller than objects of the same size closer to the viewer. Perspective drawings are widely used by interior designers and decorators in order to convey to a prospective client an impression of the actual appearance of a finished scheme.

Perspex paint for ships' hulls A type of paint which forms a layer of perspex similar to the perspex sheeting used for aircraft windows and cockpit canopies. It was introduced in 1983 and has led to such phenomenal savings in cost as to result in the closing down of the naval dockyards at Chatham and Gibraltar and to a considerable curtailment at Portsmouth. These savings occur because the dry-docking of warships for the purpose of painting the hulls, which formerly took place every 18 months, is now only needed at intervals of 3 years because of the use of this paint. The paint itself is remarkably cheap in price. One of its outstanding features is that as the ship moves through the water the paint is polished by the friction, while a toxic chemical incorporated in the paint prevents the growth of weeds and barnacles.

Petrifying liquid A thin emulsion sometimes used for thinning down an oil-bound water paint. Completely obsolete in Britain. (**NLC**)

Petrol A fuel obtained by refining natural petroleum and used for internal combustion engines and as a heating fuel. Its chief use to the painter, as distinct from its everyday use in motor vehicles, is as a fuel for blowlamps and for the compressors which operate spray plant, power tools, etc.

Petrol blowlamp A lamp designed to use petrol as its fuel; a cotton wick inside the lamp draws the petrol up a brass tube to the nozzle which, being hot, causes the fuel to vaporize. When the lamp is warm, pressure is maintained automatically, and there is therefore no necessity for a pump; some patterns of petrol lamp are, however, fitted with a pump, which is used to increase the pressure when the lamp is first being lighted.

Although petrol is more expensive than kerosene, and the running costs of a petrol lamp therefore higher, a petrol lamp is cleaner in operation and requires less time to be spent in stripping it down and cleaning for maintenance purposes. It tends to lose its pressure in windy weather; this can be prevented to some extent by the use of an asbestos-lined metal wind-shield which, however, adds to the weight of the lamp.

Petrol engines Petrol-driven compressors have a great advantage in that they can be used on any site irrespective of whether electrical power is available or not; their disadvantages are that they are noisy, they produce poisonous exhaust fumes, and they constitute a fire risk, and for these reasons there may be objections raised to using them in public buildings.

Petroleum A natural oil composed of hydrocarbons occurring at many places in the earth's crust, and from which are derived lubricants, fuels for heating, lighting and power, and a wide range of chemical products such as solvents, plastics, synthetic rubber, synthetic fibres, dyestuffs and pigments.

Petroleum Regulations Act, 1936 and 1973 Under the terms of the Act, "petroleum" includes petrol products and oil made from coal, shale, peat and other bituminous substances. "Petroleum spirit" is petroleum which has a flashpoint of below 73°F (22.8°C) when tested in the manner described in the Act. This means that many of the solvents used in paint may be affected by the Act. The provisions laid down include the following:

(i) A licence must be obtained if more than 3 gallons (13.638 litres) of petroleum spirit are to be kept in storage.

(ii) Petroleum spirit must be stored in glass or metal containers, but plastic containers may also be used, provided that the plastic conforms to the specification included in the Act.

(iii) The containers and the store where they are kept must be clearly marked with the words "Petroleum spirit" and "Highly flammable".

Phenol Carbolic acid.

Phenol formaldehyde resins Also called phenol resins and PF resins. These materials, produced by the interaction of phenol and formaldehyde under a variety of conditions, were the first synthetic resins to be made on a large scale. The earliest phenol resins were thermosetting, suitable for moulding but insoluble in oil. The next stage was to cook the resins with rosin at a fairly high temperature, the acidity of the rosin being neutralized by the introduction of glycerine, which produced "reduced" or "modified" PF resins which have a tendency to yellowing but which are used in undercoatings and gold sizes. From these were developed a class of rosin-free resins, known as "100 percent" or "pure" phenolic resins, which are highly water-resistant and durable and which if cooked with tung oil possess very good resistance to alkalis and to the destructive effects of industrial and marine atmospheres.

Phosphating The name given to various processes which have been developed to increase the corrosion resistance of bright sheet steel and light-gauge sections and to limit the spread of rust from damaged areas and edges; these processes are widely used in the automobile and similar industries and are adapted to the large-scale production of sheet metal articles to prevent rust creep from damaged parts. The metal is degreased and freed from rust and is then treated, either by dipping or spraying, with a solution of metal phosphates and phosphoric acid. In the "thin coating" or "accelerated" process the metal is immersed for five minutes at 75° to 85°C (167° to 185°F), or subjected to power spraying for one minute; in the "thick coating" process used for nuts, bolts and castings the metal is immersed for an interval of 15 to 60 minutes at boiling point. The thicker coating which is produced is unsuitable for articles to be finished in high gloss paint as it causes an appreciable loss of gloss.

The application of phosphating to structural steelwork has been limited by the difficulties of handling heavy plates and sections, but plant is now in operation in which heavy steel components of up to 10 metres in length can be phosphated.

Phosphorescent pigments Specially prepared sulphides of certain metals such as zinc and cadmium. Paints containing these pigments continue to glow for a time when the source of light is removed. These paints contain only a small proportion of binder, and are not very durable. See also *Luminous paints.*

Phosphoric acid washes Surface washes for the preparation of structural steelwork and domestic fittings prior to painting; various proprietary brands are available. They are usually in concentrated form and require diluting with three parts of water before use. They are used cold and are applied either by brush or spray; after application they are allowed to remain on the surface long enough to react with any light rust which is present, and the residue is then removed with hot water washing. In their present stage of development their usefulness on structural steelwork is very limited, although their performance is improved if the surface is first freed of heavy rust and scale by mechanical cleaning.

Photomurals Large-scale photographic prints used as mural decoration, either applied directly to the wall surfaces or mounted on suitable backing boards and then framed. For a long time they have been used chiefly because of their low cost as compared with a painted mural, and the subject-matter has been confined to outdoor scenes of landscapes or buildings—very often rather crude and offensive in colour—and to aerial photographs in monochrome or colour. Today there is a much more imaginative approach, and interior designers are producing very skilful and decorative images which are an art form in their own right. Photomurals in black and white, single colour or any combination of colours are produced to meet the exact requirements of a client, and they are being widely used, especially in public buildings such as hotels and restaurants, offices and boardrooms, high-class stores, banks, etc.; there are, for instance, some excellent examples in the Concorde lounge and in many of the major airports. Photomurals are particularly useful in difficult areas such as long corridors, for which purpose large-scale photographs several metres long are produced, or in rooms with subdued lighting where photographic prints can be trans-illuminated to make an effective colour treatment without detracting from the intimate atmosphere of the area. The drawback of colour photography used to be its tendency to fade, but the prints can now be treated so as to become as long-lasting as the surface to which they are applied. Some interior decorators are now heavily engaged in firing photographs into glass and ceramic ware, or etching them by laser into stone and wood.

Phthalic anhydride A substance which when combined with glycerine forms the basis of alkyd resins.

Phthalocyanine pigments Organic pigments with a very complex structure, with outstanding properties of chemical and physical resistance, capable of withstanding temperatures of up to 200°C (392°F) and with a very high tinting strength. They are fast to light even when reduced, and they are insoluble in all paint media. The basic pigment is phthalocyanine blue, which is so important in present-day paint manufacture that it has virtually superseded Prussian blue. It is available both in a green-shade and a red-shade form. When the green-shade form is mixed with organic arylamide yellow it produces a range of lightfast greens which have none of the defects associated with chrome greens, and the red-shade form is used to produce violet pigments.

Physical change A change which takes place whereby a substance undergoes an alteration in form and sometimes in volume but no alteration of weight or chemical composition occurs, as opposed to a chemical change in which a new substance is formed. For example, water which is in liquid form can undergo a physical change and become a solid substance, ice, under the effect of cold, and can become a gas, steam, under the effect of heat. In neither case is the change permanent and when the temperature rises above the freezing point or drops below the boiling point of water the substance reverts to its liquid state.

As an illustration of the difference between physical change and chemical change, if a piece of iron is melted, made to expand or contract, or magnetized, it undergoes a physical change. If it is made to rust, i.e., to oxidize, a chemical change occurs.

Picking out (or picking in) Treating a small localized area in some special way that distinguishes it from the surrounding areas: e.g., treating one individual member of a moulding or cornice with a different colour from the remainder, treating some individual piece of ornament in order to emphasize it by comparison with the surrounding surfaces, etc.

Picking up An indefinite term which is used in two very different ways. (i) In one sense it is used as being synonymous with "lifting", and means disturbing or softening a previous coating when applying a subsequent coat. (ii) In another sense it refers to keeping a wet edge in paintwork alive by joining it up with a new area and blending the two together so that no lap is visible.

Pickle A solution of caustic soda used to strip paint or polish from a surface or to clean painters' tools and utensils. See *Caustic paint remover* and *Caustic pickle*.

Pickled pine Common pinewood from which paint has been stripped. From the 18th century onwards pinewood has been used for panelling; its introduction for the purpose may have been due to its cheapness compared with oak or to the fact that the available oak was required for shipbuilding. Rooms panelled in pine were generally painted and it is only comparatively recently that the grain of pinewood itself has been appreciated; nowadays, however, the effect of pine from which paintwork has been stripped is esteemed by many people as providing a quiet background which shows off furnishing fabrics to advantage. There is also some call for the painted imitation of pickled pine; when this is required an off-white ground is used and the graining colour may be made up from raw and burnt umber and ultramarine.

Pickling (i) The traditional meaning of this term is the removal of paint, varnish or polish by means of an alkaline paint remover. (ii) In modern trade parlance, pickling refers to the process of removing rust and mill scale from structural steel before erection by means of immersing it in a bath containing both an acid solution and an inhibitor to prevent the metal from being unduly attacked by the acid. Pickling may be carried out with a cold solution of hydrochloric acid or a hot solution of sulphuric acid, followed in either case by a thorough rinsing with warm water. Until fairly recently a final rinse with a solution of slaked lime was given, but this practice has been discontinued. The usual practice is for the pickled steel to be primed while still warm after rinsing. A further method which is very much favoured by many authorities is one in which the metal is immersed in a solution of sulphuric acid, then washed with warm water and finally immersed in dilute phosphoric acid, no subsequent washing being required; this method leaves a slightly protective phosphate film on the steel.

Picture rail A length of horizontal moulding separating the frieze from the wall filling, and from which pictures may be suspended.

Picture varnish A protective coating composed of a spirit-soluble resin dissolved in a volatile solvent which lends itself to easy removal and restoration.

Pier A mass of masonry, as distinct from a column, supporting the arch or superstructure of a bridge. The term is also sometimes used rather loosely to mean a stone or metal pillar.

Pigments Insoluble substances in finely divided form which impart colour and opacity to a paint; they may also possess some other property, such as the power to inhibit rusting, resistance to some specific form of chemical attack, resistance to heat, etc., which enhances their value for some particular purpose.

Pilaster A rectangular feature in the shape of a pillar, but projecting only about one sixth of its breadth from a wall.

Piling A defect which occurs when a quick-drying paint is applied by brush and begins to set up during application, resulting in a thick uneven film.

Pine The name given to a large and important group of coniferous trees providing softwoods for building and constructional purposes. It covers such woods as Scots pine (a tree native to Britain), Cembran pine, Columbian pine, Weymouth pine (white or yellow pine), pitch pine (a very resinous tree and consequently providing a very durable wood), Corsican pine, etc.

Pinholing A defect in a painted or varnished surface in which the film is marred by the occurrence of minute craters which are slightly rough to the touch and which allow the passage of moisture. There are several possible causes. A frequent cause of pinholing in varnish is faulty application technique. If varnish is shaken up or poured carelessly it becomes frothy, the froth consisting largely of tiny air bubbles; similarly, the common practice of working a brush into a canful of varnish and wiping the brush on the lip of the can causes an accumulation of froth to form. If varnish is applied in this condition some of the air bubbles are conveyed to the work and tend to burst as the varnish is setting. The utmost care should be exercised to prevent the formation of air bubbles when dealing with varnish. Pinholing may also be due to the presence of grease on the surface, and frequently follows when cissing has occurred. It may also be due to the use of a cheap, poorly blended varnish.

Pinholing is often seen in spray applied paint coatings and may often be traced to the presence of small quantities of grease or moisture in the air line. It may also occur in a paint coating when a quick-drying material is applied over a very porous surface.

Pink primer The traditional primer for wood, which was composed of a mixture of white lead and red lead, possessing the easy-brushing qualities of the white lead plus the ability to set firmly (even when locked within the pores of the timber and thus shut off from the air) conferred by the red lead. Present-day pink primers are generally made with leadless pigments.

Pipe identification colours See *Colour coding*.

Pitch The most widely used type of pitch is the black residue left over from the distillation of coal-tar, but the term also covers a great variety of dark brown or black resinous substances obtained from petroleum, pinewood, and oils and fats of various kinds.

Pitch paper A type of paper used in the treatment of damp walls, especially before the hanging of wallpaper. It consists of a stout brown lining paper coated on one side with pitch, and is supplied in rolls of the same size as normal wallpaper. It is hung with ordinary paperhanger's paste, preferably used fairly round, and it is the pitch coated side which is pasted and placed in contract with the wall.

Pitch pine A wood with bright colour and bold contrasting grain. It is usually grained in oil colour working with raw sienna, burnt sienna and burnt umber graining colour over a warm cream ground; the figuring may very well be put in with a one-stroke writer.

Pitting The formation of holes, pits and craters in a metal surface due to corrosion or due, sometimes, to the injudicious use of pneumatic chisels and hammers for descaling.

Plan A drawing of the various parts of any floor or storey of a building, projected upon a horizontal plane.

Plank The usual term for what is more correctly known as a scaffold board. Planks can be made from many kinds of timber, both softwood and hardwood, such as Canadian spruce, European spruce, Douglas fir, Western hemlock, East African camphor wood, etc., and should be free from defects such as spiral grain, splitting, shakes or decay. The slope of the grain should not exceed one in twenty on the edge or one in twelve on the face. The timber should as far as possible be free from knots.

The thickness of a plank is related to its length. A plank 38 mm (1½ in.) thick should not exceed 2.75 m (9 ft), a 50 mm (2 in.) plank should not exceed 3.35 m (11 ft), and a 75 mm (3 in.) plank should not exceed 3.96 m (13 ft). According to the Construction Regulations the width of a plank should not be less than 200 mm (8 in.) or, in the case of boards or planks not exceeding 50 mm (2 in.) in thickness, not less than 150 mm (6 in.). In ordinary working practice, however, a width of between 230 mm (9 in.) and 280 mm (11 in.) is more usual and more comfortable to work on.

The ends of a plank may be treated to help prevent splitting; they may be rounded or cut off at an angle of 45°, and in addition they may be bound with galvanized hoop iron or be finished off with strips of hardwood, the latter being less likely to cause injury to the hands or damage to polished floors. Planks should be tested at regular invervals.

Plant A rather vague term meaning the tools, machinery and apparatus used by an industrial concern; in the case of the painter and decorator the term would be held to include spray equipment, compressors, steam strippers, scaffolding, etc.

Plaster A material applied in plastic state to provide a uniform finish to ceilings and walls; external plaster finishes are usually termed "renderings". For fuller details of the various types see *Gypsum plasters* and *Lime plaster*.

Plaster-based filler A filler supplied by various manufacturers in packets in dry form, to be mixed with water immediately before use; it is intended for filling shallow holes and cracks in plaster and for filling the grain in woodwork. It is quick-setting and very absorbent when dry.

Plaster/cellulose-based filler A filler supplied by various manufacturers in packets in dry form, to be mixed with water immediately before use. It is intended for filling shallow holes and cracks in plaster and for filling the grain in woodwork. It sets more slowly than a straight plaster-based filler, and is absorbent when dry.

Plaster of Paris Hemihydrate gypsum plaster, Class A. Neat plaster of Paris is used for making good cracks and holes in plaster work; it is eminently suitable for the purpose because it hydrates and sets up very rapidly, because it expands slightly as it sets and therefore grips the existing plaster work very strongly, and because it is chemically inert and does not therefore exert any adverse effect upon superimposed paint etc.

Plaster stopper Plaster of Paris mixed with water immediately before use, for making good deep cracks and holes in plaster (see *Plaster of Paris* above). Today a proprietary brand supplied in packet form is generally used. The holes should be thoroughly wetted first, otherwise the moisture in the stopper will be absorbed by the surrounding plaster before the stopper has had time to set; when this happens the stopper will be powdery and loose when it dries and will tend to fall out.

Plasterboard A type of building board composed of a layer of gypsum on either side of which is a layer of very stout paper or fibre; the paper is tightly adhering because the gypsum contains a small quantity of glue. Plasterboard is quite inert and is perfectly safe to paint; the side which it is intended shall be exposed when the board is fixed in position is generally finished in ivory colour, and the surface is ready for immediate decoration. See also *Gypsum plasterboard*.

Plastic paint A decorative material which is applied to interior wall and ceiling areas and which while still wet can be manipulated in many ways to produce an extremely wide variety of textures; it can also be modelled to produce decorative motifs, can be applied through stencil plates to form decorative borders and can, when dry, be carved to produce sculptured effects. When dry it can be painted and glazed and wiped to produce an enormous range of broken colour effects. It is probably due to the very wide range of possibilities that it presents, and the fact that many decorators have used it with considerably more ingenuity than discretion, that it has become rather unpopular in recent years; when carefully applied to produce an evenly distributed and subdued texture, and coloured and finished with reasonable restraint, it is a useful decorative medium, especially for the decoration of public buildings. It is essential that the surface to which it is applied should be adequately sealed so as to be non-absorbent. Contrary to common belief, it is not effective in masking open joints in unplastered brickwork or cavities in plaster work; if an even texture is to be produced the surface must be reasonably smooth.

Plastic paper A wallpaper embossed and coloured in such a way that when it is hung it gives the appearance of a wall surface treated with plastic paint. The better qualities of plastic paper are of the duplex variety.

Plastic prints Wallpapers upon which a pattern has been printed with a friable relief material similar to plastic paint. The back of the paper is usually smooth. Plastic prints need careful handling when they are being hung; any undue creasing or sharp bending will lead to the plastic material becoming dislodged, excessive soaking will lead to the softening and crumbling of the plastic matter, and careless use of the papering brush will damage the pattern. These papers have been superseded by more modern techniques of wallpaper manufacture. (**NLC**)

Plastic wood A ready-made cellulose-based stopper usually supplied in tubes but also occasionally in tins, which is used for filling holes and cracks in woodwork when a clear wood finish is required. Plastic wood sets very quickly and can be sandpapered to give a smooth surface. It is usually tinted to match the colour of the wood.

Plasticizer A non-volatile substance which is incorporated into a paint, lacquer or varnish during manufacture in order to increase the flexibility of the dried film.

Plinth The projecting moulded or stepped base of a building; also applied to the lowest square member of the base of a column.

Plumb bob or plumb line A weight suspended on a length of string, used to ensure accuracy in the setting out of any vertical work and to make sure that wallpapers and borders are truly vertical instead of being tilted at an angle when hung.

Plywood Thin layers of wood, with the grain running in different directions, glued together under pressure. The introduction of synthetic resin-bonded plywoods that do not soften under damp conditions has led to the increased use of plywood in situations where solid wood was formerly used.

Pneumatic A term used to describe anything which acts by means of air, as for example, "pneumatic tyre"—a tyre containing air, "pneumatic motor"—a motor driven by air, etc.

Pneumatic piston pump A type of pump in an airless spraying unit, deriving its power from compressed air supplied by an air compressor. The pump multiplies the input pressure very considerably, the pressure ratio ranging between 23:1 and 66:1.

Pneumatic tools Tools and appliances operated by compressed air, e.g., pneumatic chisels and hammers for the descaling of steelwork, etc.

Pock marking A term used in many parts of the country to denote orange peeling, and sometimes used to refer to the pits and depressions which occur when a partially dry paint film is exposed to a shower of rain.

Podger A tool used in the erection of tubular scaffolding for tightening up the couplers.

Poise The standard unit of viscosity used in paint technology to define the consistency of a paint or medium as measured by a viscometer. Whenever the poise is quoted the temperature is also recorded; this is most important because the viscosity of a paint varies considerably according to fluctuations in the temperature, decreasing as the temperature rises and increasing as it drops.

Polar solvents Paint solvents which are electrically conductive. They are used in electrostatic spraying to adjust the conductivity of the paint itself. The De Vilbiss Co. Ltd lists eleven solvents as being polar; of these, methanol is the one with the greatest degree of conductivity, and methyl isobutyl ketone the one with the least conductivity.

Pole gun A gun with an extension measuring 1300 mm (52 in.) or 2000 mm (80 in.) used in airless spraying to increase the area of work that can be sprayed without the use of a scaffold, or to reach awkward spots without erecting additional scaffold.

Pole ladder Otherwise known as a builder's ladder. Pole ladders are those with half-round sides or stiles of softwood which are made from straight poles selected for their freedom from defects; the poles are sawn into halves down the centre and the two stiles of a single ladder consist either of the two halves of one pole or two sections from separate poles suitably matched. They are used for general building work and wherever a single ladder of considerable length is required. They usually range in length from 3 metres to about 20 metres, although longer ones are sometimes used.

Polish See *French polish*.

Polishing varnish A quick-drying hard short-oil varnish made for use on furniture and other woodwork as an alternative to French polish; the resin used is hard enough to withstand polishing. It has the advantage of being more resistant to the effects of hot water, alcohol, etc., than French polish.

Pollard oak Wood displaying a large number of small knots and an irregular curly figure, due to the pollarding of the tree, i.e., the lopping off of the top part of the tree or of the main branches in order to encourage it to form a large number of side shoots. Willows and poplars are normally the only types of tree to be pollarded nowadays, but there is a constant demand for an imitation of pollard oak effects in graining; the effect is generally reserved for the panels of doors, etc., so as to contrast with the plainer rails and stiles; it is carried out in oil medium on a light buff ground, the graining colour being made up from burnt umber, raw sienna and burnt sienna, and should always be overgrained.

Pollution Pollution of the atmosphere with smoke, soot, sulphur fumes, etc., is an important factor in the premature breakdown of paint films in industrial areas. In certain factory premises the concentration of chemical gases in the atmosphere is considerably higher than the normal industrial pollution and the life of the paint film may be very severely reduced in consequence. The corrosion of steelwork is greatly accelerated by chemically polluted atmospheric conditions.

Poly- "Poly" when used as the prefix to a word means "many"; thus, for example, painting in polychrome means using several colours, a polygon is a figure with many angles or sides, etc.

Polychromatic finishes Translucent shot-silk effects produced in cellulose and synthetic finishes and very popular in the fields of industrial finishing and motor car work. They are obtained by the suspension of small polished particles of beaten flakes of aluminium, bronze, copper or brass in the medium. They present a most attractive appearance when newly done, but they oxidize very rapidly and change tone; this makes it very difficult to touch up or refinish any local areas because of the impossibility of matching the paint exactly. Normally, when subjected to outdoor exposure polychromatic finishes need the application of a protective lacquer.

Polychromatic painting Painting in several colours, as opposed to monochrome painting.

Polychromes Wallpapers which are lightly embossed with an all-over miniature pebble-dash effect and which are printed in several colours, the colours being distributed in irregularly shaped patches and not forming any definite pattern.

Polyester finishes These are polyester lacquers consisting of polyester resin normally dissolved in styrene, and are widely used for wood finishes, especially in industrial finishing.

Polyester resin fillers Unsaturated polyester resins are used in the production of solvent-free fillers which are completely stable in that they are virtually free from shrinkage. They are used mainly in vehicle-body repair work on metal and fibreglass surfaces. They have a very short pot life.

Polymer A name given to a synthetic resin in which large molecules are formed by the chemical process of polymerization. See the next entry on polymerization.

Polymerization A term relating to the formulation of plastics; its particular relevance to the painter and decorator is its use in connection with the drying and setting of various substances employed in the formulation of surface coatings. The term, together with its associated terms such as "polymer", "co-polymer", etc., although perfectly clear to paint technologists, cause some difficulty to practical decorators, who wish that the composition of paint products could be explained in a simpler way. It is, however, impossible to understand the principles involved in the behaviour of modern materials without some preliminary knowledge of chemistry, and any attempt to simplify such terms as "polymerization" to the point where they are perfectly clear to the layman, as attempted in the following paragraphs, must inevitably lead to some dilution of what is, in fact, a very complex subject.

Polymerization may be described as a phenomenon in which a large number of similar molecules combine together to form a single multiple molecule, the compound thus formed being termed a "polymer" or "polymeride". In this connection a molecule can be defined as the smallest particle of a substance that is capable of independent existence while still retaining its characteristic chemical properties, a definition which would hold good except in the case of crystalline salts.

There are certain naturally occurring substances such as cellulose, starch, etc., which consist of relatively simple units repeated many times over in their structure, which are known as polymers. Chemists have, however, discovered methods of linking together the molecules of various other substances to form synthetic polymers. These may be classified under two main headings.

Addition polymers are formed by linking together the molecules of a substance end-to-end so as to form a long chain, many hundreds or even thousands of units in length. There is no change of substance involved, the resulting "long chain molecules" being composed of the same basic units as the initial compound. They are nearly always "thermoplastic", i.e., they can be repeatedly softened and resoftened by applying the appropriate heat and pressure treatment, provided they are not decomposed or degraded. The properties of any given addition polymer can be altered or modified by increasing or decreasing the length of the polymeric chain, the chain length being controlled by varying such conditions as the temperature and pressure under which the polymerization takes place. Examples of addition polymers which are of interest to the painter and decorator are certain of the vinyl resins which at ordinary temperatures are hard plastics but which can be modified by the addition of plasticizers to form rubber-like materials for many purposes, e.g., polyvinyl acetate, which is the resin most frequently employed in the U.K. in the formulation of emulsion paints, and polyvinyl chloride, which when dissolved in solvents and laid on a backing of cloth fabric gives a wide range of coated-textile wallcoverings and materials such as leathercloth which are used both as wallhangings and as upholstery materials.

Condensation polymers are formed by linking together a large number of basic units by means of a reaction between two different molecules during which water or some other simple compound is eliminated. It is important that a catalyst or accelerator should be present in the polymer-producing reaction; otherwise polymerization would not take place at all or would proceed so slowly as to be uneconomical. These polymers are "thermosetting", i.e., they become permanently rigid under the action of heat. This is because the molecules instead of being linked in simple chains are converted into a mass of molecules cross linked in three dimensions. This process is not capable of repetition, a thermosetting polymer being destroyed by further heating. Examples of condensation polymers relevant to the painting and decorating trade are phenol-formaldehyde resins, urea-formaldehyde resins and alkyd resins.

Co-polymerization is a term used for a process of addition polymerization in which two or more distinct species of molecules are involved, each one of which species is capable of polymerizing by itself. The product is known as a "co-polymer".

All the explanation given above relates to the present developments in the field of synthetic resins, but the principles of polymerization also apply to several of the older painting materials. For example, the "stand oil" used to produce old-oil gold size, and which in former days was used in the manufacture of Dutch enamels, is obtained by the polymerization of linseed oil by heating it to a temperature of 300°C (572°F) with all air excluded; up to 250°C (428°F) no change in structure takes place, but above this figure polymerization occurs and the oil increases in viscosity and density. In the same way when certain oils such as tung oil, safflower oil, etc., are so treated they are converted into a gelatinous material. An interesting example of a natural thermoplastic polymer in everyday use is shellac, a compound which under certain conditions shows marked qualities of elasticity. Polymerization also plays some part in the process by which a traditional oil paint (composed of drying oil, pigment, drier and thinner) sets and hardens. At one time it was stated dogmatically that such a paint dried entirely by the oxidation of the oil content after the thinner had evaporated, but it is now believed that the oxidation of the oil is a phase followed by a gradual process of polymerization.

Polypropylene ropes Strong low-stretch ropes which are acid- and alkali-resistant and are very suitable for use in scaffolding, particularly in situations exposed to destructive industrial conditions. See *Synthetic ropes*.

Polystyrene Polystyrene resins are derived from the monomer styrene, which is a liquid product of the petroleum industry. On its own this forms a resin by polymerization which, although it has important properties of resistance to light, heat and chemicals, is only used to a limited extent in the paint industry, mainly in metallic paints and fluorescent paints. It can, however, be foamed to produce expanded polystyrene which has very low thermal conductivity and good sound-insulating properties, and this is pressed into sheets for use on ceilings and walls in areas liable to condensation. When the monomer styrene is co-polymerized with butadiene or acrylic esters it produces resins with a high level of water-resistance and durability, and these are used as binders in paints for exterior masonry.

Polythene A proprietary term for what is more strictly known as "polyethylene". A type of synthetic rubber produced by the polymerization of ethylene, which is tough, light and flexible and possesses high resistance to water and chemicals. It is not widely used as a surface coating material, but is of interest to the painter in a different connection. Dust sheets made from polythene are now being extensively employed, the special advantage that they offer being the fact that they are impermeable to moisture. This is obviously a great advantage when any operation involving the use of large quantities of water is being carried out; when washing down is in progress or when wallpaper is being stripped, polythene sheets afford greater protection to floors and furniture than conventional fabric sheets. On occasions when it is impracticable to remove the carpets during redecoration, or when theatres or cinemas are being decorated, the use of waterproof dust sheets is clearly a great benefit, and should some mishap occur whereby a paint can is overturned the risk of severe damage is considerably lessened. Heavy grades of polythene are available for use as substitutes for tarpaulins and as temporary glazing on building sites, and have actually been used as an all-over protection for the side of a building enabling exterior painting to be carried out in wet weather.

Polyurethane foam This is used as a backing material for certain kinds of modern textile wallcoverings. A most interesting development is a polypropylene wallcovering on a backing of polyurethane foam which has many distinctive features. It is applied by a special technique of stretching, and the adhesive is only used around the perimeter of each wall. The wall surface needs no preparation except at the edges round the perimeter of each wall where the adhesive is applied. The wallcovering is applied horizontally and continuously off the roll, so there are no joints at all, just a complete unbroken covering of the material. The material itself is very thick and has a soft spongy texture; it has excellent sound-deadening and heat-insulating properties, and is produced in very attractive designs.

Polyurethane foam fillers These are proprietary products sold in a cartridge complete with a cleanser. They consist of polyurethane foam, and are intended chiefly for filling cracks and holes in plasterwork, but can also be used for woodwork, metalwork and fibreglass surfaces. They can be used to fill quite large cavities, because the filler itself expands to twice its original volume after about one hour. After application, when it is set, the filler can be sanded down and is ready for painting or any other decorative treatment. Protective gloves should be worn when using these products.

Polyurethane lacquers These lacquers are of considerable interest and importance both in industrial finishing and in painting and decorating, and many formulations are in use to provide for a wide variety of purposes. They are available both as clear transparent lacquers and as pigmented coatings. Clear lacquers are available for wood finishing, panelling and timber cladding, boat finishing, etc., and pigmented types are obtainable to give a range of household paints of exceptional hardness, and materials for ship painting, etc.

The name polyurethane covers a variety of materials based on similar types of resin but modified in various ways to meet some particular need or develop some special characteristic. In general, the properties for which polyurethane coatings are notable are film hardness, toughness and flexibility, extreme resistance to abrasion, water resistance, and durability under conditions of both indoor and outdoor exposure. As a rule their adhesion is excellent, but if they are applied on top of conventional paint coatings they tend to act as paint strippers due to the strength of the solvents employed in their formulation. After curing they develop high resistance to chemicals and solvents, and very little progressive change takes place in the coatings, as compared with conventional paint systems.

There are three main types in use. One type is a two-pack system consisting of a polyester or polyether resin blended with a polyisocyanate resin curing agent immediately before use. The two materials must be kept separate until required and it is important that the curing agent should be kept in a completely moisture-proof container. The two packs must be mixed together in the precise proportions recommended by the manufacturer. The pot life varies from two to 24 hours according to the purpose for which the coating is made, the pot life depending on such factors as the type of resin employed, the temperature at the time of application, etc. These coatings can be applied by brush or spray, and on mass production work a catalyst spraying system may be employed. They are air drying and are hard dry in four to six hours; full curing is complete after two or three days, after which time the coating will be impervious to the solvents from subsequent coats; it is therefore essential that when two or more coats are required they should be applied without undue delay, otherwise adhesion may suffer.

The second type is a one-pack system intended for stoving, and contains blocked adducts; these are resins in which the isocyanate groups are blocked by reaction with phenols or alcohols. When heated the phenols or alcohols split off allowing the isocyanates to react with the polyester. Their properties resemble those of the first type.

The third type is a one-pack system which is cured by moisture, the moisture from the atmosphere causing polymerization. They become touch dry in one to two hours and can be recoated after four or five hours. They can be applied by brush or spray. This type includes a range of pigmented coatings suitable for normal household painting, available in both eggshell and gloss finish; these paints possess exceptional properties of hardness and resistance to scratching and abrasion, and under certain circumstances can be applied over existing coatings of conventional paint, provided, of course, that these are hard and in sound condition.

Polyurethane is also blended with silicone and incorporated into certain high-class alkyd gloss paints (one-pack) for ordinary painting and decorating purposes.

It should be noted that the Timber Research and Development Association does not recommend the use of polyurethane lacquers on exterior timbering. The association states that although they possess good durability there are also drawbacks to their use, the most serious of which is the virtual impossibility of satisfactorily maintaining a weathered coating because of the poor adhesion of subsequent coatings.

Polyurethane paint A two-pack material composed of urethane resins mixed with a catalyst just before use, and used in situations demanding resistance to chemical attack. It is considered to be rather more weather resistant than the epoxy paints. Polyurethane-pigmented floor paints, which are also two-pack materials, have a high degree of resistance to wear as well as resistance to acids, alkalis and detergents.

Polyvinyl acetate Popularly known as PVA. A series of colourless resins obtained by the polymerization of vinyl acetate. They form the basis of the bulk of the emulsion paints produced in the U.K. at present. They give a film with a good performance and require very little plasticization, but they tend to stimulate corrosion if used on steel. An important feature is their permeability to water vapour, which allows them to be used on damp porous surfaces.

Polyvinyl chloride Popularly known as PVC. A synthetic resin produced by the polymerization of vinyl chloride under heat and pressure, which resembles rubber in its properties, is resistant to many chemicals, is non-flammable and is a good electrical insulator. It is used more in the plastics industry than in paint, its application to the painter and decorator's work being in the field of coated fabrics. See also *Leathercloth* and *PVC coated fabrics*.

Popping An alternative term for the defect in plastering known as blowing. See *Blowing*.

Poppy oil or poppy seed oil A drying oil obtained from the seeds of the opium poppy, produced mostly in India and the Levant. It is a very pale oil with a slow drying rate and, owing to its scarcity, it is too expensive to be used in ordinary commercial practice. It is, however, employed in artists' colours, its paleness and slow drying being an asset to the artist and mural painter. Fine tube colours are sometimes ground in it.

Poron The brand name for a type of foamed polystyrene used in sheets on ceilings and walls to minimize condensation, and also supplied in the form of acoustic tiles.

Porosity A term which is very often used loosely as an alternative to absorbency. To be precise, however, the porosity of a building material such as brick, stone, plaster, etc., is the ratio of pore space to the total volume of the material, and the pores do not usually absorb water to their full extent, their absorbency being governed by the capillary attraction they are able to exert.

Porous The condition of having pores or passages along which fluids may travel.

Portable compressor A piece of spray equipment in which the complete outfit is mounted on a wheeled chassis and equipped with handles. The portable compressor is the only type suitable for normal painting and decorating work, since the work of a stationary compressor is obviously limited to factory or workshop production methods.

Porter A type of marble, also known as "Black and Gold", which is found in the Apennines. It has a black background clouded with grey, and is strongly veined with chain-like formations in yellow.

Portico A porch or vestibule with columns.

Portland cement The essential constituent in concrete, cement rendering and asbestos-cement sheeting, and also used in the backing material for gypsum plasters, Keene's cement and exterior renderings such as stucco. It is produced by burning limestone with clay or shale at a high temperature until it forms a clinkered mass, which is then cooled and ground to a fine powder. When the plasterer mixes Portland cement with water, part of the water combines chemically with the cement, causing it to set hard.

Portland cement is highly alkaline, and until it has completely dried out it will rapidly attack and destroy any oil paint applied to the surface. Since the surface may remain active for a very considerable period it should always be tested with litmus before painting is undertaken. In the past a great deal of faith was placed in washing the surface of Portland cement with a zinc sulphate solution to "neutralize" the alkali; this practice is most undesirable not only because it is ineffective as a neutralizing agent but also because it defeats its own object by rewetting the cement and because it may lead to trouble due to the zinc sulphate crystallizing beneath the paint.

Positive stencil A stencil plate in which the ornament itself is cut out.

Pot life A term chiefly used in connection with two-pack materials to denote the length of time that they will remain in usable condition. Two-pack materials consist of two components, namely a base and an activator or catalyst, the two components being mixed immediately prior to application. Once the components are mixed, gelation may take place very rapidly, and the length of time which elapses before gelling occurs is termed the pot life. The pot life is dependent upon such factors as the type of material, the type of solvent, the solids content and the temperature at the time of mixing.

Pounce A device for transferring the outline of a design on to a wall surface quickly and without causing damage to the surface. The design is drawn out on cartridge paper or detail paper, and holes are then pricked into the paper at close intervals along the outline. The paper is then held in contact with the wall while a "pounce bag" containing dry powder colour is lightly beaten against the lines; the dry colour passing through the pricked holes on to the wall leaves a mark sufficiently clear for the decorator to work to.

Pounce bag A small home-made bag generally consisting merely of a piece of cloth secured at the neck with an elastic band, in which dry powdered pigment is placed for the purpose of pouncing a design.

Pouncing Applying a drawing by pounce.

Pound brush Also called a "ground brush". It was the old-fashioned round brush made of hog hair bristle of up to 150 mm in length, which had to be bridled before use and needed a very careful "breaking-in" period. It has now been completely superseded by the 75 mm-wide flat brush. (**NLC**)

Powdered pumice An abrasive consisting of finely pulverized pumice stone which is used, with water as the lubricant, for felting down varnished or gloss-painted surfaces or for rubbing down paintwork between coats. It is an excellent material for the purpose, but has the disadvantage that any particles left behind after its use lead to very obvious bittiness occurring in the succeeding coats; it is particularly difficult to remove all traces of the powder from the quirks of mouldings.

It is rarely used now except for preparing exhibition panels and display work; even on the highest class of domestic decoration it has been mostly superseded by waterproof abrasive papers. (**NLC**)

Powered access equipment Hydraulic or electrically-operated equipment designed for use where a comparatively small area of work is difficult to reach, and when the cost of erecting scaffold would be much too high in proportion to the labour cost of the actual paint application. Various types of this equipment are available, each adapted for particular kinds of work.

One type consists of a platform on the end of a crane-like boom which can be raised to a vertical height of 30 metres (about 100 ft) and can swing around to any point within a 30-metre diameter; the boom is mounted on a vehicle turntable which can be placed in any desired position and which is controlled either from the turntable or from the platform itself. The platform is surrounded by a sturdy guard-rail for the safety of the operatives. This equipment is very useful for overhead work on busy thoroughfares or on awkward gable walls or tall masts, etc., and provides an excellent means of painting bridges both underneath the span and on the vertical faces. It is also ideal for signwriting work in busy localities and for fixing prefabricated sign-work in difficult areas.

Smaller versions are available with either a one-man or two-man platform, and these are very useful for lofty repetition work of short duration, such as the painting of lamp standards along stretches of road.

Another type of equipment is a tower which consists of a platform mounted on a sturdy pillar, the pillar rising vertically from a wheeled base member with struts that can be extended from each corner to give stability. Various sizes are available, some reaching a height of 23 metres (about 75 ft) when free-standing or 60 metres (about 200 ft) when fitted with wall ties. The equipment can be towed by ordinary commercial vehicles and is quickly assembled on the site. Movement is controlled from the working platform. This type is very useful on big-scale repetition work, such as for example the painting of window frames on tall large factory buildings, office blocks, hospitals, etc., and for painting a large number of isolated units spread out over a considerable distance.

A third type consists of a large working platform mounted on a mobile chassis, the platform being raised or lowered by an expanding metal frame extending and contracting on the concertina principle. The whole of the movement is controlled from the platform with a lever which operates the ascent and descent, forward and backward motion, steering and locking. Because of the size and capacity of the working platform this type of equipment is very useful in industrial painting operations.

Power-operated platforms See above.

Power sources for compressors, etc. See *Compressors—source of supply*.

Po-yok oil A drying oil from West Africa, with characteristics midway between those of linseed oil and tung oil.

Pozzolana See under *Fly ash*.

Precipitation Also called "colour striking". A method of preparing pigments by mixing together two soluble salts so that they react with one another to form one or more insoluble compounds; the pigments prepared in this manner include titanium white, Prussian blue, lithopone, lead chromates, etc.

Prefabricated A word used to describe such things as the component parts of a building, manufactured prior to their being delivered and assembled on a site.

Prefabricated sheets A term covering the various types of wallboards and sheetings used for the dry-lining of structures.

Premature A word used to describe something that occurs too early, before its proper time, as for example when we speak of "the premature breakdown of a paint film", "the premature setting of an adhesive", "the premature drying-out of plaster", etc.

Preparation The treatment given to a surface prior to the application of any paint or decorative material. It is a well-known fact that correct and thorough preparation is absolutely essential if the best results are to be obtained with any painting or decorating material; it is also well known that preparation is very often carried out badly and inadequately and is sometimes ignored altogether.

Pre-pasted papers Otherwise known as "ready-pasted papers". These are wallpapers which are supplied with the back surface already coated with an adhesive substance, the adhesive being activated by contact with water.

The usual method of hanging pre-pasted paper is as follows. After the paper has been cut up to the required lengths, a cut length is loosely rolled up with the pattern inwards; it is immersed in a trough of cold water for one or two minutes (as recommended on the manufacturer's instructions relating to that particular paper) and then withdrawn vertically and applied to the wall. The pattern is matched and the paper smoothed down with a sponge or damp cloth to exclude bubbles and wrinkles, and the waste is then trimmed off at the top and the base. The procedure for hanging long lengths, such as on staircase walls, is slightly different. The roll is completely immersed and then back-rolled in the water, then withdrawn from the water and allowed to drain before hanging; the roll is held in one hand and a short length is applied to the wall and smoothed into position with the other hand, progressing downwards as the roll comes down the wall. This same procedure can be used when hanging the paper on ceilings.

Pre-pasted papers which had already been widely used in the USA were introduced into the U K in 1961 but made practically no impact on the purchasing public. They were reintroduced in 1971 with greater success, and now account for the major part of wallpaper production.

Preservative A substance which has the power of giving protection against injury or decay. In the broadest sense all paints and decorative materials act as preservatives to the surface on which they are applied. In the narrower sense the term is usually reserved for fluids such as creosote and more especially the fine modern range of wood preservatives, preservative woodstains, etc., which are used to protect woodwork in situations where a paint treatment would not be appropriate. It can also refer to substances which are added to various decorative materials to prevent them from putrefying, e.g., the inhibitors added to certain kinds of wallpaper pastes to prevent decomposition.

Pressure drop A term used in air-propelled spray painting to signify the lowering of air pressure between the source of air and the spray gun itself. Pressure drop is usually caused by friction between the flowing air and the walls of the hose through which it passes.

Pressure feed brush A paint brush, the hand-piece of which is connected by means of a flexible hose to a pressure feed paint container; when a button on the hand-piece of the brush is pressed the bristles are automatically charged with paint. The brush is used in exactly the same way as a normal paint brush, and paint only flows when the button is pressed. The fact that constant dipping into a paint can is eliminated leads to a saving of time in application, and it is also claimed that there is less splashing than with an ordinary brush and less waste of paint.

The pressure feed brush was designed primarily for the industrial contractor engaged in heavy structural work and employing unskilled or semi-skilled labour. Its use is largely confined to industrial work, decorators having tended to adopt a conservative attitude towards it.

Pressure feed cup A type of fluid container attached directly to an air-propelled spray gun, and designed for use with enamels, plastics and other materials too heavy for suction feed and in situations where only a comparatively small quantity of material is to be sprayed. There are two types of pressure feed cup; the regulator type is equipped with an air regulator which allows the pressure on the fluid to be varied, whereas in the non-regulator type the pressure on the fluid is the same as the atomizing air pressure.

Pressure feed tank A type of paint container used in air-propelled spray painting. It consists of a robust steel cylindrical tank, heavily galvanized on both inside and outside, fitted with a clamp-on lid, inlet and outlet taps and valves, and a safety valve. The pattern commonly used by the decorator is also equipped with a pressure gauge or gauges, and is generally fitted with an agitator which may be either manually or mechanically operated. The capacity of the tank may vary between 4.5 and 270 litres (1 to 60 gallons), and obviously the higher the capacity the longer it will be possible to operate without interruption; in the type of work carried out by painting contractors the limiting factor is the size and weight of tank that can be conveniently handled, moved around the site, and hoisted when necessary on to a scaffold.

The pressure feed tank provides a constant flow of large quantities of paint at an accurately controlled pressure to the spray gun, and is an essential part of the outfit for all normal sized operations. It would be impracticable to engage in any spray work on a commercial scale without it, if only because of the frequent interruptions required for replenishing the supply of paint. In most cases the use of a double regulator type is an advantage as it permits fluid and atomizing pressures to be varied according to local operating conditions, e.g., for allowing adjustments to be made when the gun is operated at a considerably higher level than the tank, etc.

Pressure-reducing valve See *Air transformer*.

Pressure switch A device included in a spray outfit to break the circuit when maximum pressure is reached in the air receiver, the circuit closing again when the pressure drops to the minimum setting.

Pretreatment A term covering such things as solvent wiping, grease removal, abrasive treatments, rust removal by various processes, and pickling processes, applied to metal surfaces prior to painting in order to improve the durability of the paint system by ensuring better adhesion, restricting corrosion, etc.

Pretreatment primers Also termed "wash primers", "wash coats" and "etch primers". Solutions used as a chemical pretreatment for metals. Their value as a treatment for non-ferrous metals such as zinc and aluminium, in order to improve the adhesion of paint, is well established and they are now being increasingly used in the surface preparation of steel. They normally consist of an etching agent such as phosphoric acid to which is added a film-forming synthetic resin called polyvinyl butyral, and a substantial proportion of chromate pigment. They are usually supplied in two parts to be mixed immediately before application in accordance with the manufacturer's instructions, the mixture remaining workable for about eight hours, but there are also some one-part primers available. Application is by brush or spray.

There is a widespread belief that the use of a pretreatment primer is a substitute for a normal coat of paint, but in fact the film which is formed is very much thinner than a conventional paint film and it is therefore important that a normal priming coat should be applied without delay and should be followed by a full paint system. It is also important to note that thorough cleaning of the surface is essential before the pretreatment primer is applied.

A type of pretreatment primer has been developed which is based on the anti-corrosive properties of tannin, and is recommended by some authorities for use on steel. It is claimed that the film which it forms will last much longer than that of the normal etching primer, and that its use is therefore preferable in situations where an immediate follow up with priming paint is impracticable. Further advantages claimed are that it is not dangerous to the skin, that it gives off no fumes, and that it has a blackening effect upon the metal which clearly shows up any areas that have been missed. On the other hand, the tannin will not form a film on a greasy surface or on a surface that has been chemically cleaned.

Whatever type of pretreatment primer is used on steel it is necessary, if good results are to be obtained, that mill scale and heavy rust should be removed prior to application.

Pricing Preparing an estimate; assessing the layout and dimensions of a structure in order to discover the price that needs to be charged for decorating it according to the customer's requirements.

Pricking wheel A device which facilitates the making of a pounce; it consists of a wheel of small diameter, from the outer edge of which a number of points protrude, mounted on a wooden handle in such a way that it can rotate easily.

Primary colours The fundamental basic hues which cannot themselves be formed by a mixture or combination of any other hues, and from mixtures and combinations of which all other colours can in theory be formed. The primary colours in pigments are red, yellow and blue; the primary colours of light are red, green and blue.

Prime cost sum A sum of money provided in a bill of quantities for work that is to be carried out by a nominated sub-contractor, or for materials or goods to be obtained from a nominated supplier; the contractor is entitled to a reasonable profit on such an item, and a percentage is added to the prime cost sum for this purpose.

Primer The first coat of paint to be applied to any surface; the basis or foundation of the entire paint system, upon the stability of which the success of the whole system depends, and therefore a factor of the utmost importance in any paint system.

The functions of a primer may be listed as follows:

(i) To provide a durable and protective coating which acts as a bridge between the underlying surface and the remainder of the paint system, enabling subsequent coats to fulfil their proper purpose.

(ii) To satisfy the absorption of porous materials such as timber, plaster, etc., while still leaving sufficient binding medium at the surface to bind the pigment adequately and hold up the subsequent coats.

(iii) To provide adhesion on non-porous materials such as zinc, aluminium or glass.

(iv) To form a barrier over chemically active materials such as new lime plaster, asbestos-cement sheeting, concrete, etc., which will prevent the alkaline content of these materials from attacking and destroying the paint film.

(v) To inhibit the corrosion of ferrous metal surfaces.

(vi) To form a coating upon radiators, heating pipes, etc., which will withstand the effects of heat and prevent it from softening, cracking or discolouring subsequent coats.

As a general rule it is most desirable that a primer should be applied by brush even if subsequent coats are to be applied by roller or spray.

Priming (a) The application of a primer, usually regarded as a task requiring little skill but actually an important one and essentially one calling for patience and care.

(b) The word "priming" is often used as a synonym for "primer".

Priming coat First coat; primer.

Process white An opaque, water-mixed white prepared from blanc fixe, used by interior decorators in making working drawings and decorative schemes, especially when executing black-and-white drawings for reproduction by printing.

Profile In its true sense this is a drawing of the side view of an object, and more especially a drawing of the human face, but today the meaning has broadened to include an outline drawing of the vertical section of a building or of the contours of any projecting architectural members such as mouldings. The word is actually derived from a Latin word meaning to draw in outline.

Profile is also a technical term with two meanings related to painting and decorating:

(i) The first meaning goes one stage further than the definition given in the paragraph above. It refers to anything which projects outwards from the face of a building's surface, such as a moulding, and it is also applied to any object which projects outwards and presents a sharp edge such as, for instance, a section of angle iron. The importance to the painter is that paint coatings have a marked tendency to recede or draw away from any sharp edges at the time of application, and this means that on the edges of doors, mouldings, etc., the dried paint film is much thinner than on the rest of the surface, so much so that the edges look quite bare and the underlying wood grins through. In the case of the industrial painter this is of even greater concern because the arrises and sharp edges of angle iron and structural steel members are places where the paint film is not thick enough to protect the metal properly and the paint soon breaks down, allowing rusting to begin and to spread rapidly.

The difficulty could be overcome if arrises and sharp edges were slightly rounded before any question of painting arose. At one time competent carpenters and jointers took a pride in rounding off the edges of woodwork with a plane or a spokeshave before handing the work over to be painted, but in present-day conditions these extra little matters of care and attention are usually forgotten. As always, it is the decorator who is held responsible for any defects that are apparent, and to the layman it appears obvious that any weakness in the paint coating must be the fault of the painter. The edges of angle iron are not generally very sharp because of the difficulty this would cause in handling the metal, but it is still very sound practice to use micaceous iron oxide paints for undercoating ferrous metals as these paints have the remarkable property of lying along the edges without any tendency to recede as other paints do.

(ii) The second meaning of the term "profile" refers to the blast-cleaning of metal when the abrasives etch the surface of the metal and roughen it. This roughness is of great value in promoting the adhesion of paint to the cleaned metal. The pattern produced by the abrasives is called the profile, and this varies according to the type of abrasive used; small round abrasive particles called "shot" produce a rounded profile, while the small angular particles known as "grit" produce an angular profile.

Profit margin The percentage added by the contractor to an estimate to yield a reasonable cash return over and above all the costs incurred. In preparing an estimate of painting work, the probable cost of labour is assessed, the cost of materials and the price of hiring plant and equipment are added, and the establishment charges proportional to the outlay are then included. Up to this point only the actual cost of producing the work has been reckoned. The profit margin is the contractor's remuneration, allowing for replacing old stock and extending the firm's trading position by expansion and growth.

Progress report A report prepared by a supervisor showing the progress of work on a particular site and making any special observations on matters relating to the rate of progress. The purpose of the report is to make sure that progress is proceeding at the proper rate in keeping with the target figure, and if the progress rate is lagging behind schedule, to analyse the cause and suggest means of improving it. For this purpose a regular progress report is essential on every contract, and especially in the case of a large operation.

On small-scale domestic work progress is usually checked visually by a daily visit of the employer or manager, but on a contract of any significant size a weekly progress report is the general rule. For it to be effective the supervisor must have on hand a copy of the dimensions and labour cost figures on which the estimate was based, and all work that has been done since the previous visit is measured and checked against these figures, the extent of the work completed being compared with the amount of money so far spent in the form of wages. Any divergence calls for immediate investigation, otherwise the contract may continue to fall behind schedule to the point where it is no longer possible to retrieve the situation, so that the contract is certain to make a loss.

Propane A flammable gas sometimes used as the fuel to operate a blowtorch or other piece of equipment. See *LPG containers*.

Protection The protection of a surface from decay or corrosion is one of the principal reasons for the application of paint.

Protection of Eyes Regulations Statutory Instrument 1974, No. 1681: 1974, the Protection of Eyes Regulations, gives definitions of various kinds of "eye-protectors" including goggles, visors, spectacles and face screens and also of free-standing fixed screens attached to a building or structure. It makes the important point that whatever type of protection is provided must be suitable for the person to whom it is supplied, and also that it must conform with an approved specification and must be marked to indicate the purpose for which it was designed.

The processes for which eye-protectors are required by statute are listed, and they include the blasting of concrete by compressed air, the cleaning of buildings by shot or other abrasives, cleaning by high-pressure water jets, chipping of metal, chipping or "scurfing" of paint, slag, rust or other corrosion from the surface of metals by hand tools or portable power-driven tools, and the maintenance of any plant which contains or has contained acids, alkalis, dangerous corrosive substances, or any substances injurious to the eyes.

Protective clothing, equipment, gear, etc. For many of the operations and with many of the materials used in both domestic and industrial painting it is most important that the operatives should be supplied with protective gear, and equally important that the gear provided should actually be worn by the operatives. Decorators engaged mainly on domestic work tend to think that these matters don't concern them and that protective measures are only needed on industrial work, but this is not the case; certain kinds of lacquers, for instance, give off vapours of such a toxic nature that not only is a respirator necessary but it must be the particular kind of respirator which provides an independent air supply, and there are many operations where it would be foolish not to use some form of protection for the hands.

For protective equipment to be of any use there are certain cardinal rules to observe:

(a) The gear must be the correct type for the particular work in hand.
(b) The operatives must have been trained in the correct way of using the gear, and it is the individual operative's duty in law to understand and employ the correct method.
(c) The gear must be the right size and a proper fit for the individual operative to whom it is supplied, and items such as safety helmets and respirators should be the personal property of the individual to whom they were issued and should not be regarded as interchangeable between one person and another.
(d) The gear must be in good condition when supplied and must always be maintained in good condition.
(e) It is the individual's responsibility to see that any particular clothing, equipment or gear provided is actually used and worn at all the appropriate times. A safety helmet or respirator is not providing any protection if it is hanging on a peg in a rest room on another part of the site. Quite apart from the folly of taking unnecessary risks whilst at work, it must be stressed that in the event of an operative sustaining an injury the operative's claim for

damages would not be upheld in a court of law if it was proved that protective gear had been supplied but was not being worn at the relevant time.

Information about specific items of protective equipment are given under the following headings: *Aprons, Barrier creams, Ear plugs, Eye protection, Gauntlets, Respirators, Safety belts, Safety footwear, Safety helmets, Safety nets*, and *Visors*.

Protractor An instrument taking the form of a graduated semicircle used to set out and measure angles.

Proud Projecting above the level of the surrounding surface; on a higher plane. Thus we may speak of a nail which has not been properly driven home as "standing proud" of a surface, or of applying a filling composition in such a way that it "stands proud" of the surrounding area so that it can be rubbed down when dry to become level with the rest of the surface.

Provisional sum A sum of money provided in a bill of quantities for work or costs that cannot be foreseen, or which cannot be correctly estimated until work is in progress; e.g. a considerable quantity of "making good", the necessity for which is not disclosed until some existing material is removed from a surface, or extra coatings needed to deal with an unstable coating not revealed until stripping is taking place.

Prussian blue A blue pigment prepared by precipitating a ferric salt such as ferrous sulphate with a solution of potassium ferrocyanide. It varies in colour from a slightly greenish blue to a blue tinged with violet, and it has a characteristic bronze lustre, although non-bronzing blues are made for certain special purposes. The colour of Prussian blue is intense and it has very great staining strength, yet in spite of its strength it is notable for its great transparency. It is resistant to acid but is readily attacked by alkali and will discolour rapidly if used on new plaster, cement, concrete, etc., unless the surface has been adequately sealed with an alkali-resisting primer. Prussian blue has now been largely superseded by phthalocyanine blues.

Pugging A term used to describe the mixing of a pigment with medium in such a way that the pigment becomes "wetted" and forms a thick paste. The process is carried out, in the course of paint manufacture, in a pug mill.

Pulley A grooved wheel over which a rope is passed, used in lifting operations of various kinds, e.g., in the rigging of gin wheels, cradles, bosun's chairs, etc.

Pulley block or sheave block A wooden block or a metal frame in which pulley wheels are mounted and which is usually furnished with a long swan-necked hook. A single pulley block contains one wheel only, a double pulley block contains two wheels, and so on.

Pulley systems Pulleys are used in many ways and provide what is known as a "mechanical advantage", which is a means of easing the physical labour involved in raising heavy loads by reducing the amount of manual effort required. A specific pulley system is selected to give the most efficient method for the particular job in hand.

The mechanical advantage to be gained by each system can be worked out quite easily. The mechanical advantage is found by dividing the weight of the load by the force needed to lift it; for example, if by the use of pulleys a load of 300 lb can be lifted with a force of 30 lb the mechanical advantage would be $300 \div 30 = 10$.

The simplest pulley system consists of a single pulley block mounted on a scaffold or high up on a building as a gin wheel for the purpose of hoisting materials and equipment. This gives no mechanical advantage at all; in fact, the force required to raise the load is slightly higher then would be needed to pick up the load from the ground by hand, because the frictional drag of the rope passing over the wheel has to be overcome as well. The rope hanging over the wheel touches the ground at both sides when the wheel is not in use, so its length is double the distance from the ground to the pulley block. This system would be of no use in rigging a cradle as the effort required by the operatives to raise themselves, the cradle and their equipment, would be too exhausting and would be quite impracticable.

The next system is one that can be used for cradles but still makes quite a heavy demand upon the operatives. It consists of two single pulley blocks at the top of the building and two single pulley blocks mounted on the cradle, one at each end, and on each side of the cradle the length of rope is now three times the height of the building. The force needed to lift the weight of the cradle plus the operatives, as divided between the pulleys, is now half the total weight, so the mechanical advantage is 2, not allowing for frictional losses, and the length of the ropes is three times the height of the building. A system with two double pulley-blocks at the top and two single pulley blocks on the cradle gives a mechanical advantage of 3, and the length of the ropes is four times the height of the building. The use of double pulley blocks both at the top of the building and on the cradle gives a mechanical advantage of 4, and the rope is five times the height. Treble pulley blocks at the top and double pulley blocks at the cradle give a mechanical advantage of 5, and the rope is six times the height. Treble pulley blocks both at the top and on the cradle give a mechanical advantage of 6 and the rope is seven times the height.

Clearly the greater the number of pulley wheels, the greater is the mechanical advantage. For instance, if a cradle were to be occupied by two operatives with a combined weight of 320 lb and the cradle itself with its associated equipment weighed 100 lb, totalling 420 lb, the use of the system with treble pulley blocks at both the top and on the cradle would mean that the force needed to raise it would be $420 \div 6 = 70$ lb, 35 lb for each operative, and this would make for very easy working. But there are other factors to take into account. Because the rope extends for a distance of 7 times the height of the building the operatives would have to pull each rope a distance of 7 metres in order to raise the cradle 1 metre. But an even greater disadvantage would be the length of rope required. If the building were 20 metres high each rope would be 140 metres long, and it would be extremely difficult to keep it neatly coiled and to avoid getting it tangled.

The choice of a pulley system for any particular job resolves itself into making the physical demands on the operatives tolerable without using an unwieldy length of rope. The second of the systems just described, that of using a single pulley block top and bottom, is in fact the method which is practically always used by one of the large scaffolding firms specializing in supplying cradles for hire. Many contractors prefer the third or the fourth system, and one of the biggest firms in the North of England uses the fifth system practically all the time.

Further information about the use of pulleys is provided, complete with illustrations, in *Painting and Decorating* by Hurst and Goodier (Charles Griffin & Co. Ltd).

Pulling The term used to describe the drag or pull on the wrist which is felt when viscous materials such as varnishes or enamels are being applied by brush. It is due to the resistance to the free movement of the brush set up by the viscosity of the material.

Pulling over The process of levelling a nitro-cellulose lacquer film, particularly on wood, by applying a pullover solution with a pad.

Pulling up The softening of a previously applied coat of paint when a further coat of paint or varnish is being applied. See *Lifting*.

Pullover solution A levelling solution used to bring nitro-cellulose lacquers to a perfectly smooth finish resembling French polish; it is applied by means of a pad and smooths out irregularities by pulling the cellulose coating from one spot to another to produce a level film. The solution is composed of organic solvents which only partially dissolve the lacquer film.

Pulps These are the cheapest variety of patterned wallpapers, in which the natural colour of the paper itself forms part of the finished surface. Pulps are usually thin papers. They must not be oversoaked, otherwise the colour printed on them tends to loosen; they should be hung immediately after pasting. Largely superseded by modern methods of wallpaper production.

Pulverized fuel ash See *Fly ash*.

Pumice blocks Regular rectangular shaped abrasive blocks made up from powdered pumice and very often containing a mild detergent for attacking the grease on a painted surface. They are useful for broad work but are inclined to be cumbersome on panelled surfaces. It is most important that when pumice blocks are being used the surface should be thoroughly rinsed off with clean water immediately after rubbing, in order to remove all traces of detergent from the surface before any paint is applied.

Pumice stone A substance of volcanic origin; a light form of acid or silica-rich lava which became spongy and porous due to the escape of steam or gas while the lava was cooling. Pumice stone is used as an abrasive, with water as the lubricant, and is especially useful for the initial cleaning down and preparation of previously painted and enamelled surfaces prior to redecoration. Pumice stone is supplied in lumps of varying size and is prepared for use by cutting a lump across with an old hacksaw blade so as to provide two pieces each presenting a flat face; the faces are then rubbed on a wet stone to make them smooth. The operative then takes a piece in each hand; after wetting the painted surface he uses one piece to rub the surface with a circular motion. The stone soon becomes clogged up; to prevent this, and to maintain the stone in useful condition, the two pieces are periodically rubbed together.

A good quality of pumice stone will float in water. A poor quality sinks, which indicates that it is not porous enough to abrade a painted surface properly.

Pump filter A cylindrical wire-gauze filter fitted in a casing on the filter manifold at the pump outlet in an airless spraying unit.

Puncheon Any vertical tube, used in the erection of tubular scaffolding, which is not supported upon the ground or upon a base plate.

Pure stainers Pigments supplied in concentrated form, not reduced nor mixed with extenders.

Purity The strength or intensity of a colour, denoted in the Munsell system by the word "chroma" and also sometimes referred to as "saturation".

Purlin A horizontal beam or member in a roof construction, resting upon the principal rafters and supporting the common rafters and the roof covering.

Purple of Cassius A purple dye, used in glass manufacture for the production of ruby glass, made by precipitating a solution of tin chloride with a solution of gold chloride; the precipitate forms a powder which contains colloidal gold and tin hydroxide. Gold was already familiar as a glass pigment in the early 16th century, but this particular material was developed by Andreas Cassius in Hamburg in the mid-17th century and was rapidly accepted throughout the glassworks of Bohemia.

Its interest to painters and decorators lies in the fact that a fault has occasionally been known to occur on gilded work, especially in coastal districts, and when gold leaf has been applied to painted surfaces on yachts and boats; the defect takes the form of a purple stain which spreads into the surrounding paintwork. This fault has been attributed to a complex reaction between the gold, the paint pigments and media and salt spray which produces a compound similar to purple of Cassius.

Purpure The heraldic term for the purple tincture.

Putlog A horizontal tube or other member in a tubular or pole scaffold, spanning from a ledger to the wall of the building. The putlog may be a tube specially made for the purpose with one end flattened to form a tongue about 75 mm in length, or it may be an ordinary tube to which a detachable end-piece called a putlog end is added. In either case the whole of the flattened end should be bedded in the brickwork or stonework of the building.

Putlog coupler A non-load-bearing coupler used in the erection of tubular scaffold for the purpose of fastening a transom or putlog to a ledger.

It is perfectly adequate for this purpose but should never be used for coupling standards to ledgers where a full load-bearing coupler is necessary.

Putlog end or putlog head A flattened blade or tongue with a fitting which enables it to be attached to a normal plain-ended tube in order to convert the plain tube into a putlog.

Putlog scaffold A scaffold consisting of a single row of standards set some 1.3 metres from the wall and joined by ledgers. The putlogs are supported at one end by the ledgers and at the other end they are inserted in joints in the brickwork or stonework. Putlog scaffolds are used mainly in the erection of new buildings, and are therefore of less interest to the painter and decorator than independent scaffolds, but they cannot be completely overlooked because of the occasions when a painter engaged on a new building uses a builder's scaffold which is already in position.

Putrefaction The decomposition and decay of animal and vegetable matter due to a chemical change brought about by bacteria; it is generally accompanied by an unpleasant odour. Such materials as glue size are liable to putrefy fairly quickly. Exposure to persistently damp conditions can lead to the putrefaction of various decorative materials and may give rise to the occurrence of mould and fungoid growths.

Putty A stiff dough-like composition used for stopping holes and cracks in woodwork prior to painting and also for bedding the glass in window frames. A good quality putty is made from whiting ground in raw linseed oil. Cheap grades of putty are very often made with non-drying mineral oils and are unsatisfactory in every respect.

Ordinary linseed oil putty is not suitable for bedding glass in metal window frames, as it takes too long to harden; furthermore, if the window is exposed to the sun the frame becomes hot which causes the putty to sag and even, in extreme cases, to run, and this tendency to sag may continue for a very long time. Various proprietary putties are available for use on metal windows; if ordinary putty is used it should be stiffened by the addition of a hardening agent such as red lead or gold size.

Putty knife A knife used for stopping holes and cracks with putty or hard stopping, and for bedding glass into window frames. Two patterns are available, one of which terminates in a pointed end, the other resembling a chisel knife except that its end is slanted; the choice is entirely one of individual preference. The blade of a well-made putty knife should be continued right through to form an integral part of the handle; the blade should be fairly stiff in order to press the putty well home.

Puttying up The process of stopping holes and cracks with putty. It is important this should be carried out *after* priming. If putty is applied to bare wood, or if the holes and cracks have not been satisfactorily sealed with paint, the bare wood absorbs the oil from the putty and leaves the putty in a powdery and crumbling condition.

PVA Polyvinyl acetate.

PVC Polyvinyl chloride.

PVC-coated fabrics Wallcoverings which consist of woven cotton, finely woven linen, or non-woven fabrics, coated on the face with polyvinyl chloride, and supplied in a very wide range of attractively coloured patterns. They have many outstanding features, notably the fact that they are extremely durable and very highly resistant to abrasion, being far more durable and resilient than any painted surface. They are strongly resistant to chemicals such as detergents, which makes them ideally suitable for use in situations subjected to rough usage. They are washable, impervious to moisture, and fast to light; grease, alcohol and other stains can easily be removed from them.

When PVC-coated fabrics were first introduced they were often presented in the form of leathercloths both as wallcoverings and upholstery fabrics, and there was a tendency to think of them in terms of restaurant and ship decoration where their hard-wearing qualities were more important than matters of appearance. This has changed and they are now used much more widely, being available in patterns and colourings suitable for any kind of decorative scheme and for the most fashionable establishments. Of course, their resistance to hard wear is still their strongest asset, and they are an obvious choice for the decoration of public buildings such as hospitals, schools and hotels, especially in corridors and other high-traffic areas. But they are by no means restricted to these places alone, and they form a large section of the range of contract wallcoverings for use in business houses, offices and boardrooms, banks, luxury hotels and high-class stores, and they are also widely used in domestic decoration.

PVC-coated fabrics are supplied in a variety of lengths and widths. For domestic work many people prefer rolls of similar dimensions to ordinary wallpaper, to be hung with the edges butted in the usual way, but there are extra-wide rolls of various dimensions for large contract areas where the object is to eliminate joints as far as possible. For this purpose each wall area is measured up accurately and the material ordered accordingly, the fabric being sold in cut-lengths by the metre.

Most of the fabrics are supplied ready-trimmed, but for those which do need trimming the technique is to hang one length, hang the next length to overlap it by about 50 mm, cut through the two lapped edges and then remove the two 25 mm selvedges to form a perfect butt joint.

Some of the fabrics can be hung with ordinary paperhanger's paste, usually a cellulose paste, but because the material is impermeable to moisture it is essential that the paste should contain a fungicide. Generally, however, one of the adhesives of the types specially prepared for these fabrics is used. In all cases the manufacturer's recommendations about adhesives and instructions about hanging techniques should be carefully followed.

PVC-coated papers These consist of a tough PVC coating on a paper backing, and while they are obviously not as robust as PVC-coated fabrics they do possess to a great extent the same features of washability and resistance to abrasion, chemical attack and the action of detergents, and they are of course less expensive and are very easily hung. They are less easily soiled than ordinary wallpapers and are resistant to oils, fat and grease.

In their early days they were regarded as an offshoot of leathercloth manufacture but are now recognized as a normal part of the wallpaper industry and available in as wide a range of patterns and colourings as other papers. As well as being supplied in the standard wallpaper dimensions, there are extra-width papers available for wall-partitioning and for large contract surfaces in hotels, offices, schools, hospitals and other public buildings. One type produced in Holland has a very strong paper backing and is patterned with a coating that simulates the appearance of leather, and this material, as well as being a wallhanging, is also suitable for counters and bar fronts, doors, panels and display units.

Various adhesives are on sale which have been specially formulated for PVC-coated papers. Ordinary paste may also be used for some of them, but it is important that it should contain a fungicidal agent, because the coated paper is completely impervious to moisture and the paste therefore tends to remain moist for a long time, especially on a non-absorbent surface. After hanging, the edges of the paper should be wiped over with a moistened cloth to remove any paste which may have strayed on to the front surface. The edges must be accurately butted; PVC-coated paper will not stick to itself, so overlapping joints will not stick down.

Pyroxylin An alternative term for nitro-cellulose, generally referring to the more soluble types.

Q

Quartering Cutting a log of wood lengthwise along its radius, thus exposing the ray figure caused by the pith rays and showing the highly decorative "edge" grain or "silver" grain; hence "quartered oak", etc.

Also a term used in heraldry to denote the sub-division of a shield into equal quarters in which are placed the various coats of arms its owner has inherited.

Quercitron The North American black or dyer's oak, from the bark of which a yellow dye is prepared. (**NLC**)

Quicklime Calcium oxide; lime produced by heating limestone or chalk to drive off carbonic acid gas, and not yet slaked. See *Lime*.

Quicksilver See *Mercury*.

Quiet colour Receding colours such as greys, greens and blues are sometimes referred to as "quiet" colours, as opposed to reds and yellows which are inclined to be strident and assertive.

Quill The hollow stem or barrel of a bird's feather. Signwriters' brushes are sometimes set in quills, which are fitted on to wooden handles by the purchaser. Many signwriters prefer this pattern of brush to the type which is set in a metal ferrule, maintaining that the quill, being flexible, has less tendency to cut the delicate sable hair when the brush is in use.

Whereas writers in metal ferrules are graded numerically for size, those set in quill are classified according to the bird from which the quill was obtained. They range in order of size from the lark, which is the smallest, to the swan, which is the largest, the full range being as follows: lark, crow, duck, extra duck, small goose, goose, extra goose, small swan, swan, large swan.

The fitting of a handle to a new quill brush is an operation requiring some care; otherwise, the quill will be split and the brush ruined. The handle should be very carefully shaped and pared to the size of the quill, being finally smoothed down with sandpaper until it is an exact fit. The quill should then be dipped in hot water for a few minutes, taking care that the sable hair does not become wet. When the quill has become flexible the handle is gently inserted; after a few minutes it will be found that the quill has hardened and has taken a firm grip on the handle.

Coachpainters' riggers and liners are often set in quill, but it is not usual to fit a handle to these brushes.

Quirk Strictly speaking the sharp V-shaped recess in a moulding, between the moulding proper and the fillet or soffit; very often the word is loosely used to describe any deep cavity or incision.

R

Racking rope The rope that secures a cradle or bosun's chair to the downhaul, i.e. that part of the fall by which vertical movement is controlled.

Radial stippler A device used in the production of broken colour effects in glaze and paint, and also for texturing plastic paint. It consists of a circular aluminium plate to which rounded strips of rubber are attached, the strips radiating from the centre. The aluminium base is fitted with a wooden bridge handle. The stippler is used with a swirling motion. Radial stipplers have not been on sale for many years, but some decorators still possess them and they are occasionally used.

Radiation The emission of rays of light or heat; the transfer of heat or light from one body to another without raising the temperature of the intervening medium. This is the principle of heat transfer upon which infra-red drying is based.

Radiator brush Sometimes called a "flag". A small flat paint brush mounted on the end of a long strong wire handle, and designed for conveying paint to the less accessible parts of a heating radiator.

Rag rolling A method of producing a broken colour effect in tinted glaze medium. The general method adopted is to lay in a previously painted ground with glaze medium following up with the hair stippler; then, while the glaze medium is still wet, a chamois leather dipped in white spirit and well wrung out is tightly twisted up, taken between the fingers and thumb of both hands, and passed over the glaze with a rolling action from top to bottom. This has the effect of removing patches of glaze and revealing the ground colour. The leather should be rolled with an irregular twisting motion; if rolled in straight lines a somewhat mechanical effect is produced. Although the term specifically speaks of "rag" rolling, rag is not usually employed because of the lint which such material deposits on the surface. Provided the ground colour and glaze colour are well chosen, rag rolling can produce very charming effects.

Rails The horizontal members of a framed or panelled joinery construction.

Raker A term used in connection with tubular scaffolding to signify an inclined tube having a bearing upon the ground or on an adjacent structure.

Raking out A term used in reference to making good defective plaster work; the clearing of all loose and unsound material from a crack, usually with a knife or shavehook, before new stopping is inserted.

Random match Also called "Free match". A term applied to a wallpaper with a random pattern and no specific matching points.

Raw linseed oil The oil obtained by crushing the seeds of the flax plant, filtered and refined in order to clarify it ready for use.

Raw sienna A yellow-brown earth colour consisting chiefly of iron oxide and containing smaller amounts of silica, alumina, oxide of manganese and calcium carbonate, found principally in Sicily and Italy and taking its name from the Italian town of Siena. It is a somewhat transparent pigment, and for this reason is very useful in the tinting of glazes, when it makes a rich golden colour, and in the mixing of graining colour. Due to its manganese content it is a better drier than ochre although otherwise similar in composition.

Raw umber An earth pigment similar in composition to ochre and sienna but containing a higher proportion of oxide of manganese and consequently a good drier. It is a good stainer and, like all the earth pigments, is fast to light, durable and inexpensive to produce.

Reaction The chemical action of one substance on another.

Ready bound A term used about spirit colours such as drop black, etc., to signify that they have been ground with a small quantity of varnish medium and merely need thinning with white spirit to make them ready for use. The term distinguishes them from colours ground in turps which need the addition of varnish medium before they are used.

Realwood A very thin veneer of actual wood, fastened to a backing of thin flexible card, which is supplied in large sheets. It is used in conjunction with stiles and rails to form panelling effects with panels of any desired dimensions; after hanging it is stained to the required colour and varnished, when it is practically indistinguishable from genuine wood panelling.

Receding colours Colours which have the effect of making the surfaces to which they are applied appear more distant than they actually are. It is generally stated that blues, greens and greys fall into this category. It should be noted, however, that this statement is only true if it is qualified and that blue, for example, may actually be an *advancing* colour in relation to its adjacent colours or surroundings. Decorators should beware of the increasing tendency to accept glib definitions and sweeping dogmatic statements about colour as being necessarily true under all circumstances.

Red One of the primary colours, both of light and of pigment. Used in colour coding to signify danger and to call attention to the presence of fire appliances.

Red cedar A timber which is widely used for exterior claddings in modern construction. It is said to be the only exterior softwood cladding which needs no protective treatment, which accounts for its popularity, but in practice some form of treatment is usually specified to improve its appearance by taking away its rawness, and this sometimes causes difficulty. A varnish treatment is not satisfactory because red cedar contains an oil which interferes with the drying of the varnish. A treatment with a Madison sealer or with one of the modern preservative woodstain systems is preferable.

Red lead A bright orange-red pigment prepared by oxidizing molten lead until a yellow crust called massicot is formed; the massicot is ground, washed and levigated, and then roasted again to cause further oxidation until the desired colour is obtained.

Red lead is an oxide of lead which contains some free or uncombined monoxide of lead; when the pigment is mixed with an oil or varnish medium the free monoxide combines readily with the medium and causes it to oxidize. For this reason red lead possesses the property of drying and hardening even when it is not exposed to the air, and therefore when it is drawn into the pores of an absorbent surface such as wood or plaster it is able to set hard. The film which it provides is very tough and highly protective, due to the lead soap which forms from the interaction of the pigment and the medium. There are certain difficulties about using straight red lead as a primer for woodwork, quite apart from its toxic properties; the feeding of the pigment with the medium and its marked tendency to settle have the unavoidable result of causing ropey brushwork which shows through the subsequent coatings and mars the appearance of the finished paintwork. For this reason it was the usual custom to use a pink primer for woodwork, consisting of a mixture of red and white lead which combined the advantages of both pigments without their drawbacks. Under today's stringent lead paint regulations it is now rarely used.

The chief value of red lead, however, is in the field of anti-corrosive painting; it is a rust inhibitive pigment which actively discourages the formation of rust by electrolytic and chemical action. In spite of the considerable volume of research which has taken place into the problems of corrosion and the various treatments that have been evolved, no other pigment has yet been found as a fully effective substitute for use on normal structural steelwork. It is particularly useful for steelwork which is to be left exposed for a long period during and after erection without any further paint treatment, especially if a straight red lead/linseed oil mixture is employed to give the requisite film thickness. In locations exposed to a heavy concentration of chlorine or sulphur, however, red lead may be an unsuitable primer.

Red lead is not used in finishing coats because, like all lead pigments, it is affected by sulphur contamination in the atmosphere. Red lead paints can be applied by brush or roller, but spray application is not advisable and when used is subject to stringent precautions. It is advisable to wear PVC gloves or gauntlets when applying red lead paints by any method.

It should be noted that the use of red lead paint in any form is now subject to the Control of Lead at Work Regulations, 1980, and the Approved Code of Practice deriving from these regulations. Section 4 of the Code deals with the assessment of work which exposes persons to lead, and indicates the types of work likely to lead to a significant level of exposure; these include the spraying of lead paints other than those conforming to BS 4310: 1968 or low solubility lead compounds. Section 6 of the Code lays down an absolute requirement that any rubbing down or scraping of lead paint must be done by wet methods. Section 7 of the Code requires that any person exposed to airborne lead must be furnished with and must wear suitable respiratory equipment, and this applies to the spraying of lead paints generally, including red lead paints.

Red lead/graphite primer A primer in which up to 20 percent of the total weight is composed of graphite and the remainder of red lead. This produces a paint which works and spreads much more easily than straight red lead and does not settle to the same extent. It produces a thinner film, which some authorities think is less suitable than a straight red lead/oil paint for steelwork to be left exposed for long periods.

Red lithopone A pigment composed of a mixture of cadmium sulphoselenide co-precipitated with barium sulphate.

Red oxide An iron oxide pigment prepared by calcining a yellow oxide of iron such as ochre at a high temperature. For a long while it was popularly regarded as an ideal pigment for the priming of iron and steel; it is now generally realized that red oxide has no rust inhibitive properties and that in fact the cheaper grades actually stimulate corrosion.

Reducer An American term for a paint thinner.

Reducing power The strength of a white pigment; the extent to which a white pigment when mixed with a definite proportion of coloured pigment is able to produce a pale tint, the strongest white pigments producing the palest tints.

Redwood This coniferous tree, native to the USA, is the largest and tallest in the world and reaches an immense age. The timber is used for constructional purposes. After the first seasoning the wood tends to assume a violet tint, a discolouration which stains or bleeds into any superimposed paint. The wood should be primed with aluminium primer to prevent this, and in some cases it is necessary to apply a sealer coat of thin shellac.

Reflected colour Colour which is reflected from one brightly coloured surface upon another.

Reflex gun A type of gun, used in airless spraying, which incorporates an air valve. The air, which is controlled by a separate button, can be used to remove loose dust from a surface before paint is sprayed. This type of gun can only be used with a pneumatic pump, and an air line from the pump to the gun is needed.

Relief A moulded, carved or stamped design which stands out above a plane or curved surface, the extent to which it projects being more or less in proportion to the object depicted in the design.

Relief effects Several methods can be employed by decorators to impart some degree of relief to a flat and level surface. One obvious method is to apply a coating of plastic paint, which can then be manipulated by means of combing or stippling to produce a pattern; a variant of this is to use sprayed plastic to produce spatter effects. An interesting extension of these is the production of imitation stonework, the wall being marked out in an ashlar pattern resembling the joints in stonework with the narrowest type of masking tape; plastic paint is applied and stippled, and as it is setting the masking tape is carefully peeled off; when the plastic paint is dry it is painted in an appropriate colour and the joint lines picked out in a lighter colour resembling a grouting of cement. Another variation is to use a stencilling technique with plastic paint to give a more formal and distinct textured appearance of relief.

Relief effects can also be obtained without actually texturing the wall surface at all, by using the technique of painting in monochrome to produce the appearance of sculptured stonework, modelled plasterwork, or carved woodwork motifs. This technique was widely used in the past and can be seen in many of the historic buildings in the care of English Heritage or the National Trust. A very fine example of an extremely large scheme carried out in this way is the Painted Hall of the Royal Naval College at Greenwich, painted by Sir John Thornhill in 1700 in Sir Christopher Wren's famous building. In the present-day decoration of theatres, churches, hotels, etc., this technique is being used with great success.

Relief goods Decorative materials consisting of pre-formed relief designs, either hollow backed or solid backed, to be applied by the painter and decorator. See the entries under the headings of *Anaglypta*, *Supaglypta*, *Lincrusta* and *Metallized panels*.

Remote cup outfit A piece of air-propelled spray equipment designed to combine the advantages of a full-scale pressure feed set-up with the portability of a suction or gravity cup attached directly to the gun. It consists of a pressure feed cup of 2.2 litre capacity fitted with controls to balance the flow of air and fluid, and is connected to the gun by short lengths of air and fluid hose (usually about 1200 mm (4 ft) long).

Removable sprayhead An air-propelled spray gun assembly consisting of an air cap, fluid needle and sprayhead body, designed as a complete unit which may be detached from the main body of the gun in one section. Its use offers several advantages, such as making possible quick changes from one material to another and facilitating cleaning. In case of damage to the front portion of a gun, the sprayhead may be replaced without the expense of obtaining a complete new gun.

Rendering (a) In constructional work this means a coating of cement, mortar, stucco or other material applied to an external wall to produce a smooth surface and prevent the penetration of damp.

(b) In architectural draughtsmanship the term means the accurate projection of shadows on an elevational drawing.

(c) In interior decoration a designer or decorator often speaks of a drawing produced for a client as being "a water-colour rendering" or "a rendering in gouache", etc.

Repetitive pattern A pattern or design which can be repeated or reproduced several times over by a process such as stencilling, silk screening, etc.

Residual current contact breaker A safety device for use with electrical equipment which detects even the smallest amount of electricity flowing to earth and cuts off the current instantaneously. See *Electrical equipment—safety precautions*.

Resin (natural) A natural resin is an adhesive flammable substance formed by secretion in trees and plants, exuding naturally from many of them, in particular from trees such as fir or pine, and which hardens on exposure to air.
Recent or *virgin* resin is obtained from living trees, generally as a result of a deliberate incision being made in the trunk; the resin exudes in the form of globules or tears, which solidify when exposed to the atmosphere.
Fossil resin is obtained from trees which lived many centuries ago; it is dug up from the ground in locations where it has rested since the trees in which it was formed decayed in past ages; it occurs at depths varying from about 1 metre to 14 metres. It is very much harder than recent resin.

Resin generally has a glassy appearance and a slightly yellow-brownish colour. It is soluble in oil when heated, and in certain solvents, but is insoluble in water. It is amorphous, i.e. it has no tendency to crystallize, and has no definite melting-point. Its importance to the decorator lies in its use as a constituent of varnish. Fossil resin is used in the manufacture of decorators' varnishes. Recent resins, which are softer, are used in making picture varnish, map varnish, etc. For a very long time varnishes made from natural resins were of the utmost importance to the painter and decorator, but they have now been very largely superseded by synthetic resins.

Shellac, which is a constituent of knotting, is a form of resin which does not exude from a tree but occurs as a result of insect parasites collecting in swarms and feeding on the sap of a tree; the twigs eventually become embedded in the mass of sticky substance they produce.

Resin (synthetic) Originally the term was meant to apply to a chemically produced substance which resembled a natural resin in appearance and properties, but it now has a much broader application and is used to describe materials which bear little or no resemblance to natural resins, which offer qualities that are not to be found in any natural product, and which are made under perfectly controlled conditions so that they are uniform and consistent in character. Synthetic resins include polymerized condensates, in which two substances are heated together in the presence of a catalyst and the product subsequently polymerized (e.g., phenolic resins, alkyd resins, etc.) and direct polymerization products in which a substance is polymerized in the presence of a catalyst (e.g. vinyl resins, coumarone resins, etc.) each having their own special properties; the formulation can be controlled to produce a material suited to meet a particular set of conditions such as a peculiarly corrosive environment or a distinctive type of atmospheric pollution. In general it may be said that synthetic resins impart to a paint film a greater measure of flexibility, a higher degree of chemical resistance, better flow and more rapid setting than is obtained with natural products.

Resinous timbers Certain woods such as Columbian pine, pitch pine, etc., are extremely resinous, so much so that when they are used in construction the resin has a strong tendency to exude not only from the knots but all over the surface of the wood. This has the effect of forcing off any paint which is applied to the surface, causing it to develop a large crop of blisters. For these timbers an aluminium primer is better than an ordinary wood primer; it is non-penetrative, and clings to the surface by means of the adhesiveness of the medium, the leafing effect of the aluminium flakes forming a metallic barrier of sufficient mechanical strength to hold back the resin.

Respirator A piece of apparatus worn over the mouth and nose to filter inhaled air or to prevent the inhalation of toxic gases.

There are many operations in painting and decorating for which the wearing of a respirator is essential, such as the spraying of paint—especially lead-based paint—working in confined spaces or in situations where there are fumes and dust, and operations which involve the use of substances which if inhaled are dangerous to health.

Several types of respirator are available including the mouthpiece and noseclip type, the half-mask covering nose and mouth, and the full facepiece covering eyes, nose and mouth, and they are classified as either the cartridge type or the canister type according to the method by which the air is filtered. The cartridge type consists of either a full facepiece or a half-mask holding a replaceable cartridge which contains some absorbent or adsorbent material. The canister type is a full facepiece with absorbent or adsorbent material in a replaceable canister.

Respirators for protection against dust include the general purpose type most commonly used by painters and decorators; for trades and occupations subjected to a much heavier concentration of dust there are positive-pressure powered respirators set in a hood which covers the head down to the shoulders, or a blouse covering head and shoulders down to the waist and wrists, and high-efficiency respirators. Respirators giving protection against gases include canister types and cartridge types. Respirators giving protection against both gases and dust include canister types and cartridge types with a particular filter suitable for various specific types of gas.

For most painting and decorating operations a multi-purpose respirator of the half-mask or full facepiece type with a cartridge filter is the best choice, because the appropriate cartridge filter can be selected in conjunction with the type of facepiece most suitable for the conditions under which the work is to be performed. In some cases, however, a respirator with a separate air supply (more properly described as "breathing apparatus") is required; for example, if certain polyurethane paints are being sprayed, because of the highly toxic nature of the free isocyanates released. The same precautions are necessary when certain materials which are not in themselves toxic but which produce giddiness or extreme nausea are being sprayed, and in any situation where work is taking place in an atmosphere deficient in oxygen.

It is most important that respirators should be properly fitted to the person to whom they are supplied. All respirators have certain limitations. When air is drawn through the filter the lungs may produce a negative pressure in the facepiece, causing unfiltered air to enter between the facepiece and the face. If the person using the respirator wears spectacles, or if the needs of the particular job require the wearing of eye-protectors, the facepiece may be prevented from fitting properly. Canisters or cartridges giving protection against certain specific gases may not be effective against other kinds of contaminant, and for this reason the type of material which the respirator is expected to exclude should be checked against the types of contaminant specified on the container. Perhaps what is most often overlooked is that canisters and cartridges have only a limited life and need to be replaced at frequent intervals. It is most important that respirators should be comfortable for the wearer and should fit closely without chafing, and that they should be the personal property of the person to whom they are issued. On no account should they be jumbled up at the end of a day's working so as to be handed out the next day indiscriminately and used on a communal basis.

The legal requirements concerning the use of respirators are covered by the Construction (Health, Safety and Welfare) Regulations and the Control of Lead at Work Regulations.

Respiratory protective equipment A term given to any kind of device which protects its wearer from the harmful effects of a contaminated atmosphere. There are many ways in which the atmosphere may become contaminated, especially in locations where industrial operations are taking place. Some industrial processes produce fumes and dust. Other processes involve the use of toxic substances which give off dangerous gases. In some processes chemical substances are used which combine with oxygen in the air, leaving the atmosphere deficient in oxygen, particularly if the operation is taking place in a small enclosed and unventilated space. Even without the presence of harmful chemicals, the operatives who are working in a confined space may soon exhaust the supply of oxygen just by the act of breathing, taking in oxygen every time they inhale and giving out carbon dioxide when they exhale.

The position is complicated by the fact that the atmospheric contamination may arise from more than one source; it is possible for both dust and toxic gases to be produced at the same time and in one operation, and if the process is taking place in a confined space there may be oxygen deficiency as well. And there is an added complication in that each of the contaminating elements may have harmful effects on other parts of the body as well as on the lungs, so that as well as needing respiratory protective equipment the operatives may also require special clothing to protect them against corrosive substances, radioactivity and other dangers.

There are two forms of respiratory protective equipment. The first is a device that filters the atmosphere to prevent the passage of contaminating substances, so that the operative is breathing clean air. This is the respirator in one of its many forms, discussed in some detail in the preceding entry. The second is a device which receives a supply of clean air from an outside source, so that the operative is not dependent on the atmosphere in the immediate vicinity of the workplace. This is known as "breathing apparatus". It is used in situations where a filter would not be able to remove harmful substances from the atmosphere, such as where the atmosphere has been polluted with highly toxic matter or where the atmosphere is deficient in oxygen, i.e. where there is not sufficient oxygen to support life.

There are two main types of breathing apparatus, the air-line type and the self-contained type.

The air-line type can be fed either by a fresh-air line or by a compressed-air line. In the fresh-air-hose apparatus the air is drawn from a clean source along a hose with a large diameter by the breathing action of the wearer, which may be assisted by manually-operated or motor-operated bellows. Compressed-air-line apparatus is again divided into two types; one of these has a "demand valve" in the system which enables the wearer to receive air as and when it is needed, while the other type maintains a constant flow of clean air. In self-contained breathing apparatus, air or oxygen is supplied to the wearer from a cylinder or other form of container which is an integral part of the apparatus.

Where the painter and decorator needs breathing apparatus, either when using materials which give off toxic gases or when working in confined spaces, it is the self-contained type which is usually employed, the other types being mainly (though not invariably) intended for the more heavy industries. One drawback of self-contained breathing apparatus is that it restricts the wearer's movements; the apparatus is bulky and cumbersome, and this causes difficulty when the operative has to negotiate a very small opening to enter the working area or where the working space itself is limited. The wearer of the apparatus needs to be in good physical condition.

There is a British Standard, BS 4275: 1974, entitled "The Selection, Maintenance and Use of Respiratory Protective Equipment".

Retardant or retarder An ingredient added to a substance or mixture with the object of delaying or slowing down a certain occurrence; for example, megilp added to graining colour to delay the setting, the agglutinant added to a hemihydrate gypsum plaster to slow down the set, the materials added to cellulose lacquers to retard the evaporation rate, etc.

Retiring colours Synonymous with "receding colours".

Reveal The surface at right angles to the face of a wall, at the side of an aperture, doorway or window.

Reveal pin A device embodying a screw-jack, used in erecting tubular scaffolding in order to secure a puncheon into a window opening for the purpose of tying-in the scaffold to the building.

Reversible In painting and decorating this term is applied to any paint or surface coating which softens up under the action of a solvent, e.g. cellulose lacquer.

Reversing alternate lengths A method employed in the hanging of plain, semi-plain and mottled wallpapers in which no definite pattern is apparent, in order to avoid any shading effect being noticeable. Such papers are sometimes slightly darker on one side than the other; if hung in a straightforward manner this slight difference of colour or tone is seen along each edge. The reversing of the alternate lengths is carried out during the cutting up of the paper, so that when it is hung each dark edge is alongside another dark edge and each light edge alongside another light edge.

Several of the modern textile wallcoverings are hung with the alternate lengths reversed.

Ribbon gold Transfer gold leaf made up in the form of rolls, to be applied by means of a gilding wheel. The rolls vary in width from 9.5 mm to 76 mm and are usually 20 metres long.

Ridgely A household name in the painting trade; the trade name for a wide variety of tools and other items of decorators' equipment such as paste tables, trimmers, graining tools, etc.

Rigger A colloquial term for a coachpainter's liner, set in quill.

Right-angled coupler Also known as a hinged coupler or a double coupler. The load-bearing coupler used in tubular scaffolding to connect standards and ledgers at the principal node points.

Rinsing Washing or cleaning a surface by means of the application of liberal quantities of clean water.

Rise and fall clauses Clauses included in contract documents to protect the contractor against fluctuations in the cost of materials, wage rates, lodging and travelling allowances, and other contingencies arising after the signing of a contract and before the completion date. The adjustments are net, and do not provide any increase in the profit margin.

Riser The vertical front of a step in a staircase.

Rivelling Also called "shrivelling" and "wrinkling". A defect in a gloss film taking the form of wrinkles which appear during the drying period, usually caused by an unduly heavy or liberal application of varnish or gloss paint whereby the surface skins over, while the material underneath is still soft.

Road paint or road line paint A quick drying and bitumen-resistant material composed of Manila resin dissolved in industrial spirit with the addition of a plasticizer and a suitable pigment, used for painting lines and traffic indications upon road surfaces.

Robots Many of the operations in large-scale industrial production, including paint spraying, which at one time were done by hand are now performed by robots. The first move in this direction was the process of automatic spraying, described under that heading. The next stage was the introduction of robots in the early 1970s. A survey carried out in Germany in 1983 by the Kommerzbank revealed that in the ten years up to 1982 nearly 7000 German workers had lost their original jobs as a result. The first robots were clumsy devices, heavy, immobile, and restricted to performing one single task, but they had to a great extent taken over many operations such as spot-welding and paint spraying. But the design of robots has improved out of all recognition, and now there is a second generation of "intelligent robots" equipped with sight and a delicate sense of touch, and these are able to perform a variety of multiple tasks in a wide range of industries.

Similar developments are taking place in other countries. Not only does the Volkswagen company estimate that second-generation robots do practically 50 percent of all work in the car industry, but it is also reckoned that already 15 percent of all assembly work in American industry as a whole is performed by robots.

Rogue peaks A term used in connection with blast-cleaning to describe odd peaks of metal that are left projecting above the general level of the surface after the cleaning is completed. The rogue peaks need to be removed with a nylon scourer or scraper before any paint is applied.

Roller (1) A revolving drum mounted on a handle and covered with some fabric or other kind of material which will pick up paint from a suitably shaped container and will transfer the paint to a wall or ceiling surface to produce an even coating. If used under favourable conditions of work suited to the technique, the roller gives good results and makes a significant saving in labour costs. Over a given area, roller application is more then twice as quick as brush application; even allowing for cutting in and for the cleaning of the roller after use it is still between 40 percent and 50 percent quicker on suitable work. Generally speaking, a suitable site for roller application would be one with large plain areas and relatively few window or door openings or features involving cutting in. The advantage in speed of application is increased on rough surfaces such as fair-faced brickwork, roughcast, etc., or on lightly textured surfaces such as a relief wallcoverings, plastic paint, etc. A further advantage is that the roller often gives better covering than the brush.

Considerable improvements have been made in the design of rollers. The earliest type had a sleeve consisting of polyurethane foam or some similar material, which absorbed a great deal of paint and was therefore extremely wasteful and difficult to clean. When spirally-wound mohair rollers were introduced they were much better, and those with short pile were the first kind of rollers that would apply gloss paint satisfactorily. The cost of mohair, however, is very high, and for this reason natural lambswool was often used as a substitute; unfortunately wool has the drawback of absorbing the thinner from the paint, especially in the case of water-thinned materials such as emulsion paint, and this causes matting of the fibres. But the principle of the spirally-wound mohair roller is still used in an adapted form for the application of gloss paints. The chief material now used for roller sleeves is a synthetic fibre, the quality and length of which can be accurately controlled, and which discharges the paint very effectively. The design of rollers themselves has also been modified, and apart from heavy-duty rollers the spindle assembly is no longer used. In present-day rollers a sleeve without a core is fitted on to a spring cage frame which rotates on a spindle.

Rollers are generally either 304 mm, 229 mm, 178 mm, or 51 mm wide, with a diameter of either 38 mm or 44 mm. The 229 mm and 178 mm sleeves are supported on a single-arm cage frame; the 304 mm sleeves are either fitted to a double-arm spigoted frame or supplied with a double-arm roller with two

152 mm cage frames. There are also extra wide rollers for industrial painting purposes, curved rollers or flexible rollers for painting pipework and corrugated sheeting, and long-handled crevice rollers for painting the backs of radiators. Extension poles can be fitted to rollers to extend the distance that can be painted from one spot.

Paint rollers can also be used in conjunction with airless spray equipment, two kinds of roller being available for the purpose. One kind consists of an extension arm which is fitted to the front of the airless gun, the roller being mounted at the other end; the paint flow is controlled by pressure on the gun trigger. The other kind consists of an extension arm which is attached to the paint hose with a fitting similar to that used for coupling spray guns; in this case the paint flow is controlled by a trigger fitted on the extension.

(2) A tool used by paperhangers. It may take the form of an angle roller or a seam roller for pressing down and helping to minimize the joints in wallpaper, or it may be a felt-covered or rubber-covered broad roller to be used instead of a paperhanging brush for smoothing down delicate wallpapers such as satins or flocks.

(3) A tool intended to transfer a repeating pattern in paint on to a wall surface. See *Pattern roller*.

Roller coating A term used to describe an industrial finishing process whereby paint is applied by rollers to flat metal articles; the process is extensively employed in the production of food containers and in the manufacture of metal signs.

Roman alphabet The symbols devised by the Romans to represent the various sounds made by the human voice in speech. They were probably derived from the Etruscan alphabet, which in turn had been derived from the earlier Greek. Records written in the Roman alphabet have been found dating as far back as the seventh century B.C., but it was not until the first century B.C. that examples became common; in this century, however, they became so frequent as to be innumerable. By this time the Etruscan characters had been adapted and various additions from the Greek alphabet incorporated to form the classic Roman alphabet of twenty-three characters which is the basis of the characters now in use in the Western world.

To the painter and decorator the term "Roman alphabet" is generally taken to mean the series of symbols found in the monumental Roman inscriptions, the forms of which were directly evolved from the use of the chisel, and which reached their fullest stage of development towards the close of the first century B.C. The supreme example is generally held to be the inscription on the base of the Trajan column at Rome dating from A.D. 114. It is considered that lettering of this period reached a peak which for legibility and beauty has never been surpassed.

The characters or symbols in the Roman alphabet each have their own particular basic shape, varying in width from the O and the Q which are as broad as they are high, through the slightly narrower letters C, G and D to the narrowest letters of all, which are the E, F and L (except, of course, for the I). As a general rule, the vertical strokes of the characters are the "thick" strokes, their width being about one-eleventh of the height, and the horizontal strokes are the "thin" strokes and are about two-thirds as wide as the thick strokes; the exception to this rule is the N, in which the oblique stroke is thick and vertical strokes thinner. The strokes are terminated at top and bottom with serifs which develop naturally from the shaping of the stroke. The distinctive quality of Roman lettering is the subtlety of its formation, the strokes being shaped or curved gradually out to the serif, the curved forms of such letters as the R and the B being modified so as to form a strong angle with the adjacent forms, and so on. This subtlety is completely lost if any attempt is made to reduce it to mechanical forms. Mechanical methods of production, whereby the proportions of the letters are based upon a system of numbers and the strokes of the letters are formed with instruments such as rulers and compasses, should never be applied to Roman lettering.

Roof ladder A properly constructed roof ladder consists of a long wooden frame which is laid upon the sloping surface of the roof from the edge to the apex. Projecting battens are secured across the framework at regular intervals to provide footholds; a hook made of metal tubing, shaped so as to pass over the ridge and grip the other side of the roof, is bolted on the end of the framework, and small wheels are mounted on the upper part of the ridge hook to facilitate pushing the ladder up the roof.

Root of oak The wood obtained by cutting across the base of the tree where the growth of the root system is developed; the grain is very much twisted and curled and the wood is dark in tone. The graining is undertaken in much the same way as pollard oak.

Ropes In order to comply with the Construction Regulations, ropes used for scaffolding should be of good construction, sound material, adequate strength, suitable quality, and free from patent defects; if they are defective through contact with acid or other corrosive substance they are to be discarded. They should be inspected for possible damage at least every six months, and in fact it is good policy to inspect them after each occasion of use, and to facilitate this they should be marked (e.g., with a copper sleeve on which an identifying figure is stamped) and a record kept of the inspections.

Manila or sisal ropes treated with a water repellent are generally used for scaffold work, but synthetic fibre ropes offer considerable advantages over these, especially in situations where they are exposed to the risk of damage by corrosive liquids such as cleaning compounds which might affect their strength. See *Synthetic ropes*.

Ropey See *Ropiness*.

Ropiness Also known as "ribbiness" or "tram lines". A defect in paintwork, whereby the brushmarks fail to flow out and are extremely conspicuous. It is generally due to faulty workmanship; the following are some of the possible factors leading to its occurrence:

(i) Uneven or careless application of the paint.
(ii) Piling too much paint upon the surface.
(iii) Overbrushing the paint until it has begun to set.
(iv) Using paint of too round or thick a consistency.

(v) Failing to keep the edges of paintwork alive, so that newly applied paint disturbs that which is already setting.
(vi) The use of dirty or clogged up brushes.
(vii) Insufficient sealing of the porosity of preceding coats, leading to the too rapid absorption of the medium of the newly applied paint.

Rosewood A type of tree found in Brazil, Argentina, the West and East Indies and India. The wood, which is brown, red-brown or a dark brown which is almost black, has a striped grain suggestive of marble markings, and is used for veneering, furniture and cabinet making and shop-fitting. The grained imitation of rosewood may be carried out in oil or water colour with a graining colour of Vandyke brown, mahogany lake and black on a ground of bright terra-cotta. Overgraining is carried out with mahogany lake and black.

Rosin See *Colophony*, which is another term for rosin.

Rotary disc sander A sanding machine consisting of a flexible rubber or composition disc attached to a drill chuck; a disc of abrasive paper of the appropriate grade is fastened to the disc pad by a central screw or by means of an adhesive. It is used for preparing new woodwork or previously painted surfaces, or for the removal of rust from steelwork or for re-surfacing floors. It can also be used for polishing, if fitted with a lambswool mop, or for removing rough surfaces from welds if fitted with a carborundum grinding wheel.

It is very rapid in action and can be used on curved surfaces, but it is a difficult tool to control, and can easily damage the surface unless handled carefully.

Rotary screen printing A highly sophisticated modern system used to print a very wide range of wallpapers. Basically it consists of a screen which is a seamless nickel cylinder, with perforations of varying sizes, and a stainless steel squeegee blade adjusted to regulate the printing pastes that are passed through the screen. The design is engraved by coating the screen with a thin, light-sensitive lacquer, wrapping it with a film containing the design, and exposing it to light, so that the perforations shut off from the light-source are fully opened, and these form the design. The system is suitable for the application of several different kinds of pastes, inks and dispersions, both in the form of coatings and of printed designs. Among them are compact and foamable PVC plastisols, transparent PVC, printing inks, lacquer coatings, aqueous dispersions both for coating and printing papers and for washable top-coats, foamable acrylate dispersions, and adhesives both for laminating top textile and paper and for applying flock materials, as well as for making pre-pasted papers.

The range of wallcoverings produced by rotary screen printing is thus very extensive. It includes conventional wallpapers coated and subsequently printed with aqueous dispersions, washables, compact vinyl wallpapers subsequently embossed, and three-dimensional vinyl papers; the latter are produced in many forms such as textured, highly foamed products with a white overprint, imitations of fabrics, yarn laminates and ceramic tiles, and papers with small relief patterns.

Rotation dip or roto-dip A method of paint application which is a development or extension of normal paint dipping and which is employed in many branches of mass production industrial surface coating, especially in the motor car industry, where the process is used for the phosphating and priming of car bodies. The object to be treated is secured to a horizontal spit and is passed along a conveyor line to be rotated through tanks which contain the requisite fluids and paint.

Rotogravure Formerly called "Rotary photogravure". A process used in wallpaper production. A photo-engraving process is employed to etch the design into the surface of chrome-plated copper-faced cylinders. Ink is applied to the roller, any excess being removed with a steel "doctor blade", and the ink left in the etched design is transferred to the smoothly calendered paper which has previously been grounded with colour. As many as six colours can be printed in one pass, producing very subtle tonal and additive colour effects.

Rottenstone A mild abrasive taking the form of a very finely powdered soft yellowstone which was used in the hand polishing of varnished work, linseed oil being used as the lubricant. Now completely obsolete. (**NLC**)

Rouge roi A highly decorative fossiliferous marble quarried extensively in Belgium; its colour varies from deep fawn to rich red-brown, the surface being broken with irregular patches of grey and soft white interspersed with strong veins of opaque white. It is generally imitated on a ground of light grey or white.

Roughcast Sometimes called pebble-dash or harling. A form of external plastering, normally consisting of two coats of mixed cement and sand, in which a coating of pebbles or gravel is thrown on to the second coat before it is set.

Roughing in A term used in the making good of defective plaster work to apply to the backing or rendering coat which is used when extensive repairs are necessary. It generally consists of one part of a retarded hemihydrate plaster gauged with three parts of clean sand.

Round A term used by the painter to describe a paint or similar material of stiff consistency which, when applied, produces a fairly thick film giving a high degree of "build". A paint is said to be too round when it is too stiff to allow of easy brushing and requires thinning before it can be properly applied.

Round brush An alternative name for a pound brush. (**NLC**)

Round coat A full coat of heavy bodied paint.

Rubber (i) A material produced by the coagulation and drying of the latex which is contained in numerous species of trees, shrubs and plants; the chief source of natural rubber is the tree *Hevea brasiliensis* grown in Malaya,

Ceylon and Indonesia. Natural rubber, although tough and elastic at normal temperatures, becomes hard in winter and soft and sticky at summer temperatures; this thermal instability is overcome by a process of vulcanization whereby the rubber is mixed with sulphur and subjected to heat treatment.

(ii) The tool used in the application of French polish. It consists of a pad of cotton wool which is saturated with polish; the pad is covered with a piece of lintless cotton or linen cloth which has previously been well washed to remove all traces of dressing or lime.

Rubber combs Tools made of rubber, used in graining for the purpose of imitating the straight grain of wood. They lift the graining colour from the ground more cleanly than steel combs. Rubber combs with teeth of varying widths can be purchased, a familiar pattern being the triangular shaped combs which present three separate sides each with a different tooth arrangement. Many grainers, however, prefer to make up their own combs by cutting notches in the edge of a piece of rubber flooring; with the home made article it is possible to devise teeth of varying widths and of a size and pattern suited to the individual piece of work in hand.

Rubberized fabric A material sometimes used on damp surfaces prior to hanging wallpaper. It is elastic enough to conform to surface irregularities, and can be carried over shallow mouldings and cornices if necessary. It is important that the adhesive recommended by the manufacturers of the product should be used.

Rubber-set brushes Brushes in which the bristles or hairs are locked into place in a cement made of vulcanized rubber.

Rubber stippler A tool used in producing broken colour effects and also very useful for texturing plastic paint. It consists of a flat wooden base upon which are set a number of thin flat pieces of rubber arranged in a variety of ways. The broken colour effect is obtained by squeezing the face of the stippler upon a surface laid in with wet tinted glaze; the rubber strips remove the glaze and expose the ground colour. It will generally be found that the glaze, instead of being removed cleanly, tends to form into thick ridges which stand proud of the surface and remain fairly soft for a long while; a further criticism is that rubber stippling often produces an unpleasant mechanical effect. Unless it is very carefully carried out and the colours chosen with great discretion, rubber stippling is notable for the ugliness of the effect it produces.

Rubberseed oil An oil sometimes used in paint manufacture, derived from the seeds of the tree *Hevea brasiliensis*.

Rubbing block A flat piece of wood or a pad of cork, felt or rubber of a size which can conveniently be held in the hand, and over the face of which a piece of sandpaper is stretched; the object of the rubbing block is to ensure that the pressure of the hand is distributed evenly over the whole face of the sandpaper during the process of rubbing down.

Rubbing compound A mildly abrasive paste used for burnishing nitrocellulose finishes, either by manual or mechanical methods, in order to produce a high degree of gloss.

Rubbing down A term covering all the various processes of preparation in which an abrasive substance is passed over a surface prior to painting.

Rubbing in The application of a thin film of graining colour on to a painted ground prior to executing a piece of figure graining. The term probably derives from the fact that the graining colour has to be applied very sparingly and brushed very vigorously with a rubbing motion in order to spread it out evenly enough and thinly enough for the purpose.

Rubbing-in brush A short well-worn brush, usually not exceeding 50 mm in width, which is reserved for rubbing in graining colour and is kept perfectly clean for the purpose, being never dipped into an opaque paint.

Rubbing varnish A hard short-oil varnish not intended as a finishing varnish but as a material which will withstand rubbing down with abrasives such as powdered pumice or waterproof sandpaper prior to the application of further varnish coatings. Now obsolete.

Rumbling See *Tumbling*.

Run lines Straight painted lines, produced by means of a lining fitch and straightedge, so called because if the lining fitch is used correctly the lines are produced by long rapid strokes.

Runs Runs are defects in a painted surface, occurring most commonly in gloss films but by no means restricted to these, which take the form of localized swellings where an excess of paint has flowed downwards and stands proud of the remainder of the surface. Runs are generally due to the material being unevenly distributed. They may also be caused by the accumulation of excess quantities of paint in various kinds of surface irregularities such as holes or cracks or in mouldings, the excess paint continuing to flow when the surrounding paint has set.

Rust The product of the corrosion of iron or steel, due largely to electrolytic action. It consists mainly of hydrated ferric oxide with some basic ferrous or ferric carbonates also present. See further under *Corrosion*.

Rust creep A term used to describe the action which takes place when the paintwork protecting an area of iron or steel is broken or damaged, and the rust which forms on the exposed metal is not limited to the area of damage but tends to spread outwards beneath the surrounding paintwork, leading eventually to the paint being pushed off and to widespread corrosion taking place. Rust creep is accelerated by the presence of salt due to electrolytic action (see the paragraph on *Salt* for further details). The presence of a phosphate coating under the paint stifles the electrolytic action and restricts the spread of rust.

Rust-inhibitive pigments Pigments which check the tendency of iron and steel to corrode, by precipitating a thin protective film on the surface of the metal. They are said to render the metal "passive". Pigments known to possess rust-inhibitive qualities include red lead, zinc chromate, zinc dust, zinc phosphate and calcium plumbate.

Rust-stimulative pigments Pigments such as graphite, Prussian blue, Venetian red, and certain red oxides which, if used so that they are in direct contact with iron or steel, will actually promote the formation of rust. They are, of course, perfectly safe to use in undercoats or finishing coats, provided the metal has first been primed with an inhibitive pigment. In some cases they possess qualities which make them desirable as ingredients in a primer. Graphite, for instance, is rust-stimulative but it has considerable water-excluding properties which make it valuable, so it is often mixed with an inhibitive pigment as a component in primers for iron or steel; provided the proportion of the inhibitive pigment is high enough to counteract the stimulative action of the graphite, it gives excellent results. Another example is red oxide, which though rust-stimulative in itself is a useful ingredient in a metal primer if mixed in the right proportions with zinc chromate or red lead.

Rutile A mineral and commercial form of titanium dioxide with a characteristic crystalline structure.

S

Sable (i) A type of animal hair obtained from a creature of the polecat family called the kolinski. It is a very slender and fine hair, yet is also very strong and resilient; for this reason it is an ideal material for signwriters' brushes, fine artists' brushes and water-colour brushes. The best quality is known as red sable.

(ii) The heraldic term for black.

Sable liner A sable brush set in quill, similar to a sable writer or pencil but with longer hair. It is used for running fine lines on woodwork. In church decoration, for example, the horizontal runs of intricate carving on an oak rood screen are separated by mouldings extending along the whole length of the screen, and the operation of picking out and gilding the individual members of the mouldings calls for a lot of dexterity to produce a line of consistently even width; for such a purpose no other tool is as effective as a sable liner. In high-class domestic work and period decoration the sable liner is used for painting lines around door panels, etc. The technique is to hold the liner by the quill with the thumb and forefinger, guiding it by running the middle finger along a moulding or beading. On plain woodwork with no mouldings, a straightedge can be used as a guide for the finger. Sable liners are graded in size according to the kind of bird's quill used as the ferrule. The largest is the goose, and the smallest is the lark. With the lark size it is possible to produce painted lines as fine as pen-and-ink lines ruled on paper.

Sable writers and pencils The correct term for signwriters' brushes made of sable. Sable writers and pencils have much longer hair than artists' brushes or water-colour brushes; this is necessary so that the brush can hold a sufficient quantity of paint to produce a stroke of reasonable length before needing to be recharged. Sable is the only hair which when long enough for this purpose still retains its shape and remains springy and flexible. The writer is a brush with a chisel edge, while the pencil is pointed; for most purposes the writer gives greater scope. Writers and pencils can both be obtained set either in a metal ferrule or in a quill, but most signwriters today prefer the metal ferrule type.

Sable writers and pencils are expensive, and they are delicate tools that are easily damaged. They should be used with care to avoid causing them damage, and when not in use they should be kept in a suitable brush-case, secured in such a way that the hair is fully protected. After use all traces of paint must be removed, otherwise the hair will become stiff and rigid, but the cleaning needs to be done very carefully to prevent any injury to the hair.

Sables The colloquial term used by signwriters to denote signwriting brushes made from sable hair.

Sacrificial coatings A term used for coatings which offer cathodic protection to iron and steel to prevent corrosion.

Corrosion is a natural process in which a metal returns to the state of the ore from which it was extracted; in the case of a steel structure, corrosion causes a progressive and destructive weakness in the structure. There are two ways of protecting the metal from corrosion. One method is to seal it with a very strong impervious layer so that its surface cannot be reached by a gas or a liquid, but this is not practicable for structural steelwork. A protective coating obtained for instance by the vitreous enamelling process where a covering of glass is produced, or by a process in which the metal is totally encased in plastic, would be physically impossible, quite apart from the immense cost involved. The second method is to provide cathodic protection by means of a sacrificial coating.

Sacrificial coatings act on the same principle as an electric cell. If a plate of zinc is immersed in a vessel containing a corrosive fluid such as sea-water it will be attacked in some degree, and if in another similar vessel a plate of steel is immersed in the fluid it will become rusty. But if the two plates are put together in one container in such a way that they are touching each other or are connected to each other by an electrical conductor, it will be found that the zinc is being attacked at a more rapid rate but that the steel plate will not corrode. What is occurring is that a primitive form of electric cell has been made in which the zinc is acting as the anode and is sacrificing itself in order to protect the steel which is the cathode. If a piece of steel is in contact with a piece of zinc of the same dimensions the zinc will dissolve away and the steel will not be attacked until the zinc has disappeared. Zinc is not the only metal to behave in this way; aluminium is another example of a metal that is anodic when in contact with steel.

Sacrificial coatings for structural steelwork may consist of a layer of metal applied by hot-spraying by specialist contractors, or paint coatings such as the zinc-rich primers, etc., used in industrial painting. These paints consist of a high concentration of metallic zinc powder in non-saponifiable media such as chlorinated rubber or epoxy resins. See also *Cathodic protection*.

Safety belt A device intended to prevent an operative from falling when working in a precarious situation where the provision of a safe working platform or other effective form of scaffold is not possible, and where a safety net which would prevent a fall cannot be used. It consists of a belt made of webbing, leather, nylon or terylene, with or without a harness, and a length of rope or wire rope, with a double-lock snap hook at the end attached to a safe anchorage point. It is desirable that the belt should also be attached to an inertia reel device similar to a car seat belt; the reel itself is attached to a firm anchorage point and allows freedom of movement, but in the event of a fall or indeed of any sudden jerk the reel clamps tight and checks the fall.

There is a British Standard, BS 1397: 1979, entitled "Specification for Industrial Safety Belts, Harness and Safety Lanyards". It stipulates that a safety belt should be capable of adjustment to fit the wearer round the waist, the adjustors to be provided with devices that self-lock securely on the belt.

Safety chair A development from the normal type of bosun's chair, intended to give a greater measure of security to the occupant. Several patterns are available; the essential features of all of them are that the framework is of metal, that a back rest is provided, that the operative is compelled to sit with his legs astride the suspension unit or a portion of the metal framework, and that either a safety chain is provided or else the framework itself ensures that the operative is completely enclosed at waist level; the object of these features is to make it impossible for the operative to slip out of the chair even if for any reason he should become unconscious. No part of the chair must be liable to become accidentally detached.

There is a British Standard, BS 2830: 1973, entitled "Suspended Safety Chairs and Cradles for use in the Construction Industry".

Safety feet Devices consisting either of rubber suction pads or of adjustable metal units which are attached to the stiles at the base of a ladder to prevent it from slipping when in use on smooth floors. While ladders fitted with these devices are useful for factory work, the general experience seems to be that operatives tend to place too much reliance upon them and to pull out the foot of the ladder much too far for safety, defeating the purpose of the device.

Safety footwear Boots or shoes fitted with internal steel toe-caps, to give protection against falling objects and to prevent injury caused by striking the toes against hard objects. Modern safety footwear is available in a wide range of styles and sizes and is indistinguishable from normal footwear. It is not much used in the painting and decorating trade, but is a wise safety precaution for those engaged in factory work or work on building sites. A particular hazard on building sites is the litter of odd pieces of wood lying on the ground with nails projecting upwards; this is a very frequent source of serious and painful accidents.

Safety harness A device used in conjunction with a safety lanyard attached to an anchorage point; a chest harness incorporates a chest belt with shoulder straps linked by strong fabric either at the front or the rear, capable of supporting the torso. Many safety officers today are of the opinion that a full safety harness is preferable to a safety belt in all situations where this type of equipment is needed. A general-purpose safety harness is available which incorporates thigh straps and shoulder straps.

Safety helmet A piece of safety equipment rarely used in normal domestic decorating but which is a necessity where work is in progress on a building site—in fact no reputable building firm would allow anybody access to a site unless wearing one. A great many serious accidents are caused by falling objects, and it should be remembered that the rate of acceleration of any falling object is 32 feet per second per second (i.e. it falls 32 feet in the first second, 64 feet in the next, 96 feet in the next, and so on) which means that even a very small object such as, say, a nut or a bolt, can strike anybody who happens to be in its path with the impact of a rifle bullet. The value of a safety helmet is demonstrated by the number of building operatives who have been struck by potentially lethal objects such as long pointed steel rods, etc., and yet have survived without injury because their heads were properly protected. Any form of work that exposes a person to the risk of falling objects demands the use of a safety helmet; it would be foolish to think of working on a block of flats, for instance, where toys and other objects may inadvertently be dropped from a balcony or window, and helmets should always be worn by anyone using cradle equipment.

Modern safety helmets are generally made of resin-bonded fibreglass with a head harness of polythene. It is most important that the helmet should be adjusted to fit properly; if it grips too tightly it is uncomfortable and likely to give the wearer a severe headache, while if it is loose it does not afford any real protection and may in fact drop off.

Safety lanyard The line connecting a safety belt or safety harness to an anchorage point.

Safety sheets, safety nets These are very often the only safeguard for operatives engaged in roof work, the painting of bridges, etc.

(i) Safety sheets. Also called "protection sheets" or "man-catching protection sheets". They consist of canvas sheets strong enough to support the weight of a person falling into them. They are available in various sizes, the usual ones being 6 m × 4.5 m, 6 m square, and 9 m × 4.5 m. The canvas should be reinforced with diagonal webbing and should be rot-proofed.

Safety sheets, however, have several drawbacks and may in some cases actually create dangers, and may certainly give operatives an entirely false sense of security. The problem is that however well they are secured the tension in them is uneven so that some parts are taut while other parts are slack. The tendency if someone falls on a part that is tightly stretched is for the sheet to rip and burst apart, allowing the unfortunate person to dive straight through with no means of arresting the fall. On the other hand anyone falling on a slack area may find that the sheet behaves like a trampoline, and many cases have occurred of operatives bouncing up off the sheet into the air and falling down again outside the perimeter of the sheet. Another difficulty is that all sorts of things may also fall into the sheet and present unexpected hazards. Cases have been recorded where a discarded cigarette end has fallen into a sheet which has already collected a fair amount of spilled paint and solvent splashes, setting the sheet on fire, and the operatives working above the sheet have been badly burned and in some instances fatally burned before they could escape. For this reason safety nets give a much greater measure of protection than sheets.

(ii) *Safety nets.* These consist of a mesh of man-made fibre ropes which are much lighter in weight and more manageable than sheets, and which are not affected either by chemical pollution or exposure to weather conditions. In present-day safety nets the difficulty of unequal tension has been overcome. The best form of net is the type in which the ropes, instead of being knotted and tied at the joints, pass at each point of intersection between a strong plastic disc with four holes in it, the holes being large enough to allow the ropes to slide freely; because of this the whole net automatically adjusts itself and presents a uniform level of tension over its entire area, capable of absorbing the force of any weight that falls into it.

Safety signs—British Standards Safety signs are dealt with in BS 5378, "Safety Signs and Colours", published in various parts. BS 5378: Part 1, 1980 is entitled "Specification for Colour and Design". It describes a system of safety colours and signs giving information for use in the prevention of accidents, and for warning of health hazards and certain kinds of emergency. BS 5378: Part 2, 1980, is entitled "Specification for Colorimetric and Photometric Properties of Materials". It identifies the above properties of materials used for safety signs as specified in Part 1. BS 5378: Part 3, 1982 is a specification for signs additional to those given in BS 5378 Part 1. It gives further examples of safety signs following the principles laid down in Part 1, and also gives advice on the selection and use of safety signs.

It should be noted that from January 1986 it became compulsory by law for all safety signs to comply with BS 5378.

Safflower seed oil A drying or semi-drying oil derived from the seeds of a plant grown in India, Egypt, Asia Minor, the USA, and Australia. It oxidizes at a slower rate than linseed oil, and is used in the manufacture of non-yellowing alkyd resins. It is also used in artists' colours, and a yellow dye is obtained from the flower of the plant.

Saffron A water stain derived from a bulbous plant of the crocus family, and used in making wood stains.

Sagging Another term for curtaining. See *Curtains* and *Curtaining*.

Sags A defect in spray painting caused by using too high an air pressure, especially during the application of a gloss paint. The surface of the paint is disturbed by the force of the air travelling over it, causing the paint to sag.

Salt The name given to a class of compounds which can be regarded as acids the hydrogen of which is wholly or partially replaced by a metal. A typical example is sodium chloride, otherwise known as common salt, which is a compound of the metal sodium with the gas chlorine and which is found in large deposits in many parts of the world and is present in dissolved condition in sea water.

Common salt sets up a strong corrosive action upon iron and steel, a factor which is of great importance when considering the protective treatment of these metals where they are to be exposed to marine atmospheres, and which also affects the treatment of motor car bodies because of the practice in large towns and cities of distributing salt on the roads to clear ice and snow in the winter. Should the paint film protecting the metal be broken or scratched, the exposed metal begins to corrode and rust is formed. The salt which is present acts as an electrolyte; the rust assumes anodic polarity and is surrounded by a cathodic area where caustic soda is formed. The caustic soda, being alkaline, saponifies the priming paint and loosens the whole paint system on either side of the damaged part. When the loosened paint peels off, the newly exposed metal rapidly corrodes and the electrolytic action proceeds at an accelerated rate.

Common salt is a hygroscopic material, i.e., it readily imbibes moisture from the atmosphere. This is a factor which sometimes assumes great importance to the painter and decorator. If sea sand has for any reason been incorporated into building materials there is a strong tendency for the affected areas either to remain permanently damp or persistently to become damp in periods of humid weather; in the same way, property which is subjected to damage by flooding from sea water is likely to be badly affected by persistent damp. See *Deliquescent salts.*

Salt spray test A test applied by paint manufacturers to metal finishes in order to assess their anti-corrosive properties. It involves spraying a painted panel with salt solution at frequent intervals.

Salubra The proprietary name given to a range of imported wallpapers with a washable smooth surface.

Sampling procedures It sometimes happens that painters working on a contract site are required to provide samples of the materials they are using to the authority for whom the contract is being carried out. This may be just a routine formality to ensure that the materials conform to the specification, in which case the whole procedure is perfectly amicable, but it may be because the authority suspects rightly or wrongly that the contracting firm is using sub-standard materials or that the contractor's employees are tampering with the materials, perhaps by over-thinning or mixing them with some other substance, in which case there could be some ill-feeling. Where there is any possibility of a dispute between the authority and the contractor it is important that the painters concerned in the matter should be aware of the correct procedure.

The request is usually made by some official directly or indirectly employed by the authority. It could be the clerk of works or a person nominated by the architect, or in the case of a public authority an official appointed by the corporation. On a contract for an industrial firm it would usually be the works engineer. Normally, any of these people would know how to conduct the matter. In some cases, however, such as on a large building site, it might be an over-zealous general foreman, in which case it is important for their own protection that the painters should see that the proper procedure is observed.

Very often in the case of a routine check the sample is taken from an unopened container chosen at random from those stored on the site. On the other hand, the request might be for a sample of the material actually being used at a given time by an individual painter, taken from the painter's can. In such a case it is as well if taking the sample is deferred until the foreman painter is present, and if there is any suspicion that the material has been tampered with it would be wise for the painters to insist that an independent witness is present, preferably a person of some standing and authority.

The essential thing is that *two* samples should be taken. Two perfectly clean containers are required which can be fastened and sealed, preferably with screw-top lids. When the sample is taken from an unopened tin, the lid of the tin is removed, the material stirred very thoroughly with a clean stir-stick or spatula, and a sample poured into each of the containers. When the sample is taken from a paint can the material should likewise be stirred with a clean stick and poured into both containers. If possible the containers should be filled to about 95 percent of their capacity. The lid of each container is screwed on and is immediately secured with adhesive tape; it is advisable for one of the parties present, or for two people representing both the authority and the contractor, to sign each of the tapes and add the date; sometimes the authority may insist that the tapes are further secured with sealing wax to ensure that they will not be tampered with in any way. Next, two good-sized labels are prepared; on each label is clearly written a precise description of the material in the containers, the name of the contractor, the address of the site and the location on the site where the material is being applied, the date, and any other relevant information; one label should then be placed on the *body* of each container, *not* on the lid. The authority's representative takes possession of one container and the other is retained by the contractor's representative who should make sure that it is delivered as soon as possible to the contractor's offices. When a dispute is possible the contractors will probably hand it to their legal advisers for safe keeping.

All this is very important because the authority will arrange for their sample to be analysed, and should they be dissatisfied with the result the contractor's sample can be analysed by an independent paint chemist. It has been known for an authority to insist on having three samples taken, one for their own use, one for the architect's retention, and one for the contractor.

There is a British Standard relating to sampling (BS 3900: Part 1: 1965) but this is concerned mainly with samples taken from bulk consignments and tested in a paint manufacturer's laboratory.

Sand blasting A method of removing rust and scale from steelwork prior to painting, leaving a roughened surface to which paint adheres readily. The method is particularly useful in the preparation of cast iron where the use of wet treatments based on acids or alkalis might lead to chemicals being trapped in the porous casting, giving rise to blistering in the paint film. At one time it was quite widely used in naval dockyards for exterior ship painting, but it is no longer employed on site work, and in factory processes its use is strictly controlled because of the health hazards involved.

Sand dry The point at which a paint film is dry enough for dry silver sand sprinkled on the surface to be removed by means of a soft hair brush without suffering damage.

Sander or sanding machine A machine used for the process of sanding. Many brands of sander are now on the market, and in the modern machines the pads to which the abrasive paper is attached may consist of felt, cellular rubber or sponge rubber, and tubular rubber which is specially suitable for use on curved surfaces. See also the entries under the headings of *Belt sander*, *Orbital sander* and *Rotary disc sander*.

Sanding An abrasive process used to level a surface before the application of a decorative or protective coating; sanding may be applied to a variety of surfaces but the term is chiefly used in connection with the preparation of wood. In woodworking factories and in workshops devoted to the manufacture of furniture, large power feed drum sanders and belt sanders are employed; to the painter and decorator, the sanding machines in most common use are portable tools, which may be powered either by electricity or compressed air and which may take the form of belt sanders, rotary discs, or orbital sanders. For most types of work orbital sanders are the most suitable but for wood which is to be stained or clear finished the final sanding should be carried out with the belt sander; otherwise, scratches across the grain will mar the appearance of the work.

The most usual abrasive is a garnet paper, but for the harder types of wood an aluminium oxide paper is more suitable, being tougher. In the interests of economy on labour costs it is best to use the coarsest grade of grit that will produce a sufficiently smooth finish.

Sanding sealer A hard sealer coat applied to wood, in order to fill the grain without obscuring it, prior to sanding.

Sandpaper The most commonly used of all the abrasive materials; it consists of stout cartridge paper coated with glue and strewn with powdered glass, sand or flint. It should be stored in a dry place; otherwise, the glue becomes soft and the grit is loosened.

Sanitary wallpaper A type of wallpaper which is now completely obsolete, having been replaced by the modern washables. It was printed in oil colour and was generally varnished after application, being intended for use in steamy atmospheres. (**NLC**)

Sans serif Literally, "without serif". A type of plain block alphabet devoid of serifs. See *Gill Sans*; *Univers*.

Sapele A West African light-coloured mahogany with grain markings of a rather stripy appearance, widely used in construction work.

Saponification The process by which an oil or fat is decomposed by reaction with an alkali and converted into a soap. It affects the work of the painter and decorator when oil paint is to be applied to an alkaline surface in the presence of moisture, the free alkali attacking the oil and decomposing it, causing free glycerine to be released. This results in the paintwork blistering, discolouring, losing its gloss and becoming soft and sticky. The affected areas often develop drops or runs of a sticky brown liquid; in really severe cases the whole of the paintwork becomes sticky and liquefied. Surfaces which affect paint in this manner include new plaster, concrete, cement, asbestos-cement sheeting, etc. Portland cement products are very highly alkaline. Pure lime plaster alone is not particularly destructive to oil paints but if contaminated by soluble alkali from the backing material it becomes highly destructive; gypsum plasters are not in themselves harmful to oil paint but lime is sometimes added to them by the plasterer in order to make them work more easily, and they may be contaminated by alkaline material brought forward from the backing. When an oil paint system is to be applied to such surfaces they should be given ample time to dry out, and should then be sealed with alkali-resisting primer.

Saponification can also be produced by failure to remove the detergents used in preparing a surface for repainting, or when paint has been removed from a porous surface by means of a caustic paint stripper if sufficient care is not taken to neutralize or remove all trace of the stripper. Emulsion paints are not affected in this way as they contain no oil, but alkaline matter in the presence of moisture may cause emulsion paint to discolour or may affect the film in other ways.

It should be noted that although alkaline attack only takes place when moisture is present, so that if the surface is completely dry it should in theory be safe to apply oil paint directly upon it, any penetration of water into the surface at a subsequent date may re-activate the alkali and cause saponification.

It has been indicated that saponification is generally due to the alkaline nature of the surface to which the paint is applied. It is also possible, however, for paint applied to a completely inert surface such as wood or metal to be saponified by external attack, if alkaline materials or solutions are allowed to splash it or encroach upon it.

Sapwood The younger, outer zone of wood in a tree trunk, lying nearest to the bark, generally softer and often paler than the remainder of the timber. The word is very often used wrongly by the painter and decorator, who confuses sapwood with heartwood, and speaks of a piece of heartwood graining as "a sap".

Sash tool A round brush, bound either with string or metal, of a size suitable for cutting in window putties. Now superseded by the 25 mm paint brush. (**NLC**)

Sash window A window formed with sashes, i.e. with sliding, glazed frames running in vertical grooves.

Satin finishes A name often applied to wall paints which dry with an eggshell sheen.

Satin paper Wallpaper grounded with distemper which is then polished and glazed to produce a satin-like sheen before printing, the drawback being that the glazed surface cracks easily during application. Superseded by modern methods of wallpaper production. (**NLC**)

Satinwood A very light-coloured wood used in furniture and cabinet making; a somewhat darker wood also known as satinwood is used for constructional purposes. The light wood can be imitated by a similar process to that used in mahogany graining; the graining colour is made up from raw sienna, burnt sienna and raw umber, on a ground of yellowish white, and the work is overgrained with a very thin glaze of blue-black or ivory-black.

Scaffold board The correct term for what is more commonly known as a plank. See *Plank*.

Scaffold board clip A device for anchoring scaffold boards to tubular scaffold either in a vertical position (for toe-boards) or in a horizontal position.

Scaffolding A temporary framework consisting of poles or metal tubes and planks, etc., on or from which work may be performed during constructional or maintenance operations on a building, or by means of which access may be obtained to the working area.

Scagliola An imitation stonework effect. Scagliola itself is generally confined to indoor work and consists of fine plaster of Paris mixed with glue, which is polished after application, and into which pieces of gypsum and marble may be embedded. This term is sometimes used to refer to paint treatments giving similar effects.

Scalding An operation carried out in the process of glass gilding, in which very hot water (*not* boiling, because of the danger of cracking the glass) is lightly swabbed across the face of the gold leaf with a squirrel hair mop in order to improve the lustre; it has the effect of dissolving and clearing any traces of gelatine that remain between the gold and the glass to mar the appearance of the gold. The operation needs to be carried out extremely carefully, especially in frosty weather.

Scaling Another term for flaking.

Scarlet A bright red colour tending towards orange.

Scarlet chrome A lead chromate pigment obtained by replacing part of the chromium radical with molybdenum.

Schedule A schedule is a document which supplies information about certain design features in a single building or in a group of buildings such as a housing estate, hospital complex, etc. It enables the operatives working on the site to identify what treatment is required at every location on the site.

In relation to painting and decorating, a schedule gives a complete, concise and accurate guide to the type of finish (e.g. emulsion paint, gloss paint, etc.) and the colour to be used on every item in every location on the site.

Schedules are only used where the rooms are so numerous and repetitive as to become confusing. On normal domestic decorating work a schedule is never used; it would be quite unnecessary. Even on larger contract work, schedules are rarely required; in a structure where the types of finish are fairly uniform and only a limited range of colours is specified, the information needed to identify the individual parts is usually incorporated in the specification.

The situation is very different on a very large contract such as for a school or hospital for example, where there is a complex system of rooms, each with its own type of wall surface, its own layout of cupboards and similar built-in furniture, its own individual colour scheme, etc. In such a case a schedule will almost certainly be provided to itemize all the information the painter needs about each separate location, and very often drawings will also be supplied by the architect so that each specific area mentioned in the schedule can be located.

A typical "finishing and colour schedule" for the painting of a hospital could consist of several pages, each ruled off with vertical lines at varying distances, and with the wording arranged to read horizontally. The first column (a narrow one) would give the room numbers as shown on the drawing. The second column would identify the rooms by name, e.g. women's surgical ward, side ward, sister's office, doctor's interviewing room, ward kitchen, sluice, bathroom and so on. The next column might be headed "ceiling", and beside each room would be inserted a code letter indicating the type of finish and a code number indicating the colour. Further columns would be headed "walls", "cupboards", "built-in furniture", "fittings", "skirting board", "floor", etc., and in each case the type of finish and the colour would be indicated and probably the type of substrate would also be named.

The contractor usually receives several copies of the schedule. The foreman in charge of work on the site obviously needs one (probably more than one, as they tend to become dog-eared and obscured by paint splashes) and the charge hands responsible for various areas each need one; the contractor's supervisory staff each need a copy so that they can check on whether or not the work is being done correctly; other copies will be retained in the contractor's office for consultation purposes and to enable supplies of the right materials and colours to be ordered.

Schedule contract A type of contract sometimes used for work done under the auspices of a Government department or public authority. A document is prepared by quantity surveyors in which the work is itemized. It differs from a bill of quantities in that each item is priced at rates stipulated by the quantity surveyors themselves in what is called a "schedule of prices", instead of being priced by the contractor. The schedule of prices may have been specially drawn up for the particular contract in hand, or it may be a printed schedule applicable to several contracts and published by the department or authority concerned. When the work is completed, the contractor is paid a sum of money calculated by applying the prices in the schedule to the actual quantity of work performed. This type of contract is chiefly used for emergency measures where it is necessary for the work to be put in hand immediately before the full implications are known and before a bill of quantities could be drawn up.

Scorching Scorching is liable to occur when a surface is being burned off if the lamp or torch flame is allowed to linger in one spot. It is permissible and indeed desirable to scorch any large knots in order to extract as much of the resin as possible, but scorching of any other part of the wood is to be avoided as it destroys the cellular properties of the timber and has an adverse effect upon the adhesion of the paint.

Scotch glue The best quality cake glue.

Scots pine A general purpose softwood, the one most widely used in the building trade for constructional purposes, formerly known as fir but now almost universally called Scots pine.

Scraper A tool with a thin steel blade, used for such purposes as the stripping of paint, stripping wallpaper, and removing loose or scaly matter from a flat surface.

Scrim A thin strong type of muslin, sold in long rolls of varying widths, and used by the decorator for the preparation of bad surfaces prior to paperhanging. It is particularly useful when papers or fabrics have to be hung on woodwork; unless scrim is hung first the movement of the wood soon causes the paper to split.

There are two methods of applying scrim; one method is to paste the surface of the wood, hang the scrim dry, and then apply paste all over the face of the scrim; the other method is to dip the scrim in paste, wring it out, apply it to the wood and secure it with tacks, the tacks being removed when the work is dry. As the scrim dries out it shrinks and the wrinkles disappear.

Narrow rolls of scrim are available for covering the joints in building boards.

Scrubbable wallpapers A clumsy term used by retailers to describe wallpapers that can be washed with a soft brush and a mild detergent.

Sculptured wallpapers Textured, highly foamed vinyl wallpapers giving the effect of carved stonework, modelled plasterwork, etc., usually with a white overprint as a protective finish.

Scumble A semi-transparent stain or glaze which is applied over a hard dry ground of a different colour; while the scumble is wet it is manipulated in such a way as to expose portions of the ground colour. It differs from a glaze in that it is used to produce a broken colour effect by means of a sharp distinction between the scumble colour and the ground colour, whereas a glaze is used solely to modify the ground colour and is similar in colour to the ground.

The essential features of a scumble are that it should remain open long enough to be manipulated but should retain the markings made in it without flowing out. A scumble may be made of oil colour or water colour; oil scumbles today are chiefly the proprietary brands of scumble stain, but it is sometimes desirable to make up a mixture of transparent glaze medium and various stainers to suit a particular job; water scumbles are hardly ever used now but can be made up with powdered pigments bound with fuller's earth with the addition of a little glycerine to retard the drying.

Scumble stain A semi-transparent oil stain, often of a rather pronounced colour, used for graining (especially brush graining) and other broken colour effects. Some excellent proprietary brands of scumble stains are available which work far more smoothly than home mixed varieties and which have the capacity to remain open longer for manipulation without the drawback of flowing out and losing their clarity; proprietary scumbles are usually ready for immediate use, merely requiring thinning with white spirit and sometimes easing out with oil. Scumble stain may also be used as a stain applied directly to bare wood.

Scumbling The production of broken colour effects by means of scumbles applied over appropriately tinted grounds, and suitably manipulated. The methods by which the effects are achieved include graining, brush graining, combing with steel or rubber combs, rag rolling, rubber stippling, rolling with crinkled paper, and, in the case of plastic painted or other textured surfaces, wiping with soft cloth to reveal the highlights.

Dark brown scumbles are often applied over metallic paints and then wiped to produce antique leather or oxidized effects. When water scumble is used for this purpose it may be applied directly on to the metallic paint, but if oil scumble is being used the metallic paint should be given a buffer coat of clear lacquer before scumbling is commenced.

Scurf Any scaly matter on a surface.

Scurfing The act of chipping, scraping or otherwise removing scaly matter from a surface, especially a metal surface. The term is used in official literature; for example, in Statutory Instrument No. 1681: 1974, The Protection of Eyes Regulations, the listed processes for which eye-protection must be provided and used includes "the scurfing of paint, slag, rust or other corrosion from the surface of metals by hand tools or portable power-driven tools".

Sealers Liquids, which may be either clear or pigmented, and which are used to reduce the suction of absorbent surfaces, to bind down previous coatings or loose material, or to prevent any soluble matter on or in the surface from damaging the new paint system. The term includes such materials as quick-drying varnishes for checking porosity, stabilizing fluids for binding down loose matter, shellac solutions for treating the knots in timber or for preventing bleeding in its various forms, and aluminium powder, which may be used in conjunction with other sealer materials such as shellac and which is also used for preventing bleeding.

Some sealers also act as primers, and are often sold as "Primer-Sealers".

Sealing coat Sealer.

Seam roller A narrow roller used by paperhangers in order to press down the joints in paper and render them less conspicuous. It should not be used on an embossed wallpaper.

Seasoned timber Wood which has been treated in such a way as to reduce drastically its moisture content in order that it may become stable and may be used without serious risk of distortion. Timber which is freshly felled very often has a moisture content of 100 percent of its oven-dry weight, i.e., its moisture content accounts for half the total weight of the log. Wood which has been seasoned naturally in the open air has a moisture content of about 15 percent of the oven-dry weight. Natural seasoning is a lengthy process, and for this reason much timber nowadays is artificially seasoned or "kiln dried"; the moisture content of artificially seasoned wood is often as low as 10 percent of the oven-dry weight. From the painter's point of view, the low moisture content of kiln-dried timber presents certain disadvantages, as it means that the wood tends to take up moisture from outside sources, and considerable fluctuation may take place.

Second coating Applying the second coat of paint on top of a previous coat.

Secondary colours Colours produced by the combination of two primary colours, e.g., orange composed of red and yellow, green composed of blue and yellow, and purple composed of red and blue.

Seediness Also called "pepperiness". A defect in a gloss paint film, taking the form of evenly distributed minute specks. It is generally due to the use of a coarse or insufficiently ground pigment but it may also develop in a paint which has been stored for a long period.

Selective treatment The treatment of one or more walls in a room, or of some particular feature of the interior or exterior of a building, in such a way as to make it markedly different from the remaining areas, e.g., the painting of one wall in a different colour from the remainder, or the use of some special pattern or texture on one particular wall or feature. Selective treatments are justified when there is some legitimate reason for emphasizing a feature, when used to add interest to what would otherwise be a dull and pedestrian scheme, or when used to compensate for the difference between a heavily shaded wall and a wall receiving strong sunlight. When used just for the sake of producing novel effects they tend to become irritating.

Selenium red Cadmium red.

Self-adhesive Capable of being attached to a surface without the application of some additional adhesive, e.g., self-adhesive masking tape, which is supplied ready for use and which sticks to a surface on contact, pre-pasted wallpapers, etc.

Self-adhesive backing Certain decorative products, the facing of which would not withstand the amount of handling involved when an adhesive is spread over the back by brush or spatula (e.g. metallic vinyl display sheeting, etc.) are supplied with a self-adhesive backing covered with a protective film. The material is cut exactly to size, and after the protective film is peeled off is carefully placed in position, the contact adhesive thus exposed making an immediate bond with the surface requiring decoration.

Self-chalking line A snap line which, when withdrawn from its container, is automatically charged with chalk or powdered colour.

Self-etching primers Primers which when sprayed or brushed on aluminium-coated or zinc-coated surfaces, chemically etch the surface to leave a firmly adhering "wash" coating of zinc chromate that makes a firm foundation for subsequent paint coatings. It is essential that the metal-coated surface be degreased before the etching primer is applied.

Self-lubricating abrasives See *Abrasive papers*.

Selvedge Strictly speaking, a narrow strip of different material woven along the edge of cloth, to be removed or hidden when the cloth is seamed, but in relation to painting and decorating the term refers to the strip running along each side of a roll of wallpaper and which is trimmed off before the paper is hung. The purpose of the selvedge is to protect the edges of the paper from damage while it is in storage or when it is being transported from one place to another. Practically all wallpapers today are supplied ready-trimmed, with each roll individually wrapped in a tightly bound film of polythene, but certain hand-made wallcoverings are still supplied with a selvedge.

Semi-drying oils Oils which dry more slowly than linseed oil but have less tendency to yellowing on exposure. They are used in the manufacture of non-yellowing alkyd resins. They include dehydrated castor oil, safflower seed oil, sunflower seed oil, soya bean oil and tall oil.

Semi-gloss The term applied to a material which is designed to present a higher degree of gloss than a flat or eggshell sheen product but which has not the mirror-like appearance of a full gloss paint.

Separation See *Floating*.

Sequence of coats The principle underlying the formation of a sound paint system, whereby each separate coat is mixed in such a way that it contributes some definite characteristic to the system as a whole. Opinion has always been sharply divided as to the most satisfactory sequence of coats, some authorities maintaining that flat coats and oily coats should alternate throughout the system while others contend that each coat should be made progressively more oily and elastic than the previous one. The matter is no longer of importance; the drying mechanism of modern finishes is not subject to the limitations of old-time products, and the undercoatings supplied by the manufacturers are formulated to build up a carefully balanced system.

Set pattern Sometimes called a "straight match". The term refers to a wallpaper in which the pattern repeats horizontally, i.e., the matching points on both the left- and right-hand sides of the paper are at the same level. When the paper is cut into lengths, each length will comprise the same number of repeats and will be cut top and bottom at the same point in the pattern.

Setting out The preliminary marking out of a piece of work as a guide to the actual execution.

Settling Separation of a pigment from the medium whereby it no longer remains in suspension but sinks to the bottom of the container where it forms a hard solid cake. Certain heavily pigmented materials tend to settle if kept in storage for long periods; this tendency can be checked to some extent by inverting the tins on the shelves at regular intervals or by using a paint-shaking machine.

Sgraffito or graffito A method of producing an ornamental device by scratching through a layer of plaster to reveal a differently coloured ground. The technique is a very old one, and examples are to be seen in the ancient town of Pompeii. The process has been adapted in many ways for painted decoration; sgraffito effects are sometimes used in plastic paint, for example. It is occasionally employed as a purely painted treatment; on a dry and hard painted ground a flat paint (usually with glaze medium added to retard the set) is laid in, and the ornament is then boldly drawn in the wet paint. Very often an indiarubber is used to remove the paint cleanly. Sgraffito is essentially a freehand technique and needs to be carried out confidently without any niggling.

Shade Strictly speaking, a colour darkened by the addition of black. The word is very often used loosely and incorrectly; people frequently speak of a shade when they mean a colour, or speak of a "pale shade" when they mean a tint.

Shade card A card upon which several small samples of colours are mounted in order to exhibit the colour range of a manufacturer's product or to describe or correlate certain groupings of colours.

Shading (i) The process of comparing several rolls of wallpaper with one another to ascertain that the colour in each case is exactly the same. In spite of the great care that is taken at the wallpaper mills it occasionally happens that slight variations of colour occur between one batch and another, and it is important that the paperhanger should "shade" the papers in good light before trimming them or cutting them up.

(ii) A term used in signwriting to denote painting an inscription in such a way as to make it appear that each individual letter is a solid three-dimensional object projecting outwards from the surface. It is carried out by painting what purports to be a shadow to each letter, in the position where a shadow would be cast upon the background surface if the letters were solid and a bright light were coming from one single point. Sometimes the shading is in black, but very often all attempt at realism is discarded and shading becomes a means of providing a pleasing multicolour effect. The purist despises shading, and indeed shading would be out of place on work demanding a dignified piece of lettering; nevertheless, there are occasions when shading is a legitimate method of enriching a signboard.

For shading to be successful, certain points should be observed:

(a) The shading colour should be markedly deeper in tone than the colour of the letters; otherwise, the shape of the letters becomes confused.

(b) A narrow gap should be left between the edge of the letters and the edge of the "shadow".

(c) The perspective of the shadows should be exaggerated.

It is generally considered that shading to the right of the letters gives a more effective appearance than shading to the left, but that shading to the right takes longer to execute.

Sharp coat A thin coating of paint which has been well thinned down with white spirit and which contains a minimum of oil, e.g., the type of paint mixture used in "following the trowel".

Sharp colour or sharp paint A colloquial term for any rapid drying paint yielding a flat film.

Shavehook A tool used in burning off, especially designed for removing paint from mouldings. It is used with a pulling motion and is therefore less liable than a knife to cause damage to the contours of the moulding. Three patterns are available, namely those with triangular heads, those with pear-shaped heads and those with combination heads offering a variety of different shapes suitable for various contours.

Sheariness A defect in a paint film similar to flashing. The term can be applied to any film which exhibits an uneven degree of gloss, but is chiefly used to refer to eggshell or semi-gloss films in which localized glossy streaks are seen or in which small areas are pulled up. It may be due to overbrushing, or to failure to keep the edges alive so that a partially set area of paint is disturbed. It may also be due to applying the material on an excessively porous surface or a surface which has been inadequately sealed and undercoated.

Sheave block See *Pulley block.*

Sheen The slight degree of gloss or lustre seen on an eggshell finish or semi-gloss finish.

Shelf life The length of time that a paint or other decorative material will remain in usable condition when placed in storage.

Shellac A spirit soluble resin formed from the secretion of insect parasites which attach themselves to the branches of trees, the twigs eventually becoming encrusted with the substance. The chief source of supply is India. The best quality is known as orange shellac, cheaper grades being called button shellac or garnet shellac. White shellac is made by bleaching the resin with alkali.

Shellac forms the basis of French polish and of many kinds of spirit varnish. When dissolved in methylated spirits it is used by the painter as knotting, to prevent the resin from the knots in timber from bleeding into a paint film; it is also used as a sealer to prevent various other substances from bleeding.

Shelling Another term for flaking.

Sherardizing A method of treating iron and steel in order to obtain a rust-proof surface; it consists of heating the iron or steel in the presence of zinc dust in such a way that an amalgamation of the two metals takes place, an iron-zinc alloy being formed. Provided the bare metal is thoroughly prepared and cleaned, a high degree of protection is afforded. Since sherardizing is a heat treatment carried out in enclosed containers of limited size, there are certain obvious limitations to its use. It is, however, employed in the manufacture of steel window frames, iron railings, gates and door furniture of various kinds as well as in many other fields which are not of direct concern to the painter. It is also used for the treatment of steel scaffold couplers and of the metal fittings on other types of scaffolding equipment such as steps, etc.

When sherardized surfaces are to be painted it is generally found that they are roughened enough to give good paint adhesion and no further pre-treatment is necessary.

Ship's bottom paint Anti-fouling paint containing poisonous ingredients to deter the formation of marine growths.

Shop priming Priming paint applied to wooden or metal articles while they are still in the workshop prior to delivery on the building site. In theory this is the ideal treatment, since the articles are given a good measure of protection under ideal conditions before they are subjected to outdoor exposure; in practice the quality of the priming paint very often leaves much to be desired, and the shop priming proves a most unsatisfactory foundation for a painting system.

It should be remembered that even when the shop priming is of excellent quality there is always the possibility of the film being damaged in course of transit to the site, and that the primed articles should be inspected and any damage rectified immediately they arrive on the site.

Short oil A term applied to a paint medium which contains a low proportion of drying oil in relation to its resin content. It is usually understood to mean that the proportion of drying oil is between 45 and 50 per cent. Generally speaking a short-oil paint is more lustrous but less elastic than a long-oil product and is liable to craze or perish if subjected to outdoor exposure; its use is therefore restricted to interior work.

Shot blasting A process of cleaning steelwork by directing metallic shot toward the surface at high velocity by means of compressed air. The term is often used indiscriminately to refer to both shot and grit blasting and this may cause confusion, especially as there are several different kinds of shot. It is advisable to be more precise and to use the more correct term "blast-cleaning" which covers the whole range of operations whereby steelwork is cleaned by directing abrasive particles at the surface. See the entries *Abrasive* and *Blast-cleaning*.

Shot silk effects Effects whereby a painted object appears to change its colour according to the position of the viewer. Such effects may be achieved on a textured surface, such as a wall textured in plastic paint, by careful manipulation of a spray gun. A typical method is as follows:

The whole surface is coated with aluminium or bronze and allowed to dry; the surface is next sprayed lightly with one colour with the spray gun held at an angle to the work so that only one side of the depressions and cavities in the surface is struck; the surface is then sprayed again with a different colour with the gun held at a different angle, and so on. By this means three or four colours may be superimposed on the metallic ground.

For industrial finishing, a polychromatic metallic cellulose is produced which, with a special technique of spray gun application, gives a two-tone translucent shot silk effect.

Shrivelling See *Rivelling*.

SI units In the modern world-wide developments of science and industry there are obvious disadvantages in using two separate and dissimilar systems of measurement, the Imperial system and the metric system. In the early

1960s, therefore, it was agreed internationally to adopt in every country a simplified and rationalized version of the metric system, known as the Système International, shortened to SI.

From the painter and decorator's point of view the effect is that:
Length is measured in millimetres (mm), metres (m), kilometres (km)
Weight is measured in grams (g), kilograms (kg)
Volume is measured in millilitres (ml), litres (l)
Force is measured in newtons (N)
Pressure is measured in bars (b)*
Energy is measured in joules (J)
Horsepower is measured in kilowatts (kW)

Siccative An alternative term for *driers*. (**NLC**)

Sienna A type of marble distinguished by its warmth and richness of colour, with groups of stone-like shapes of various sizes linked by fine veining. It is imitated on a white ground with a palette of raw sienna, burnt sienna, chrome yellow, Indian red, ultramarine blue and white; the effect should be of soft masses of pale cream, rosy red, grey and deep yellow, with veins of purple, reddish grey and brown.

Sign kit A small toolbox containing tubes of fine colours, tins of gold size of various drying times, a screw-top jar for turps, a number of dippers, a chalk line and folding rule, an expanding mahlstick and, of course, a set of signwriting brushes.

Silica The oxide of the metal silicon obtained from quartz, flint and similar materials. It is used in the manufacture of Japan fillers, and also as an extender and suspending agent in certain types of paint.

Silicate water paints Water paints based on sodium silicate or potassium silicate. Their main feature is their non-flammability, which places them in group 1 of the available fire-retarding paints, but they are not greatly used by the painter and decorator because of their alkaline nature which restricts the number of pigments that can be used with them and because they cannot be followed up with normal oil paints unless sealed with alkali-resisting primer. They tend to cause efflorescence to develop if they are used on plaster, concrete or brickwork.

Silicon The non-metallic element best known in the form of silica.

Silicone resins A group of resins containing a substantial proportion of silicone, which is a plastic-like substance built up from rings or chains of silicon and oxygen atoms. Paints based on silicone resins have outstanding properties of heat resistance and are largely unaffected by acids, alkalis, salt solutions or oils. In the production of such paints the silicone resin may be combined with an organic resin such as; say, a phenolic, epoxy or an alkyd

---

*1 bar = 10^5 N/m^2 = 10^5 pascals = 1.02 kg/cm^2 = $14\frac{1}{2}$ lb/in^2

resin, producing a range of heat-resisting paints for industrial finishing and also air-drying paints with very useful properties.

A paint which is pigmented with aluminium powder and with silicone resin as the sole medium is used in industrial painting. It is capable of withstanding temperatures in excess of 540°C (1000°F) and is used for the surface coating of steel smoke-stacks and factory chimneys, boilers, heaters, mufflers, etc. Its adhesion to steel surfaces is not so positive as that of conventional coatings; it is therefore essential that the surface should be thoroughly cleaned and all organic paints, scale and rust removed. The full heat and corrosion resistance of the paint is not developed until it has been stoved at a temperature of between 200° and 250°C (392° and 482°F) in order to polymerize the resin; this presents no obstacle, however, as although it would clearly be impossible to apply normal stoving techniques to such huge articles as boilers and smoke-stacks, these temperatures are reached when the articles are put into use. The resistance of silicone resin paints to organic solvents is poor until the paint has been cured.

Silicone resins are also used in waterproofing or water-repellent fluids on building surfaces such as brickwork, stonework, reconstituted stone, cement, concrete, cinder block, stucco, etc., for which purpose they are very effective. The fluid is applied by brush or spray, preferably during a good spell of fine weather. It operates not by filling the surface pores but by lining them with a water-repellent film which inhibits capillary absorption, with the result that water falling on the treated surface does not form a continuous film but remains in the form of droplets which run off.

Water-repellent fluids based on waxes, oils, fats or metallic soaps cause a noticeable alteration in the tone and texture of the surface to which they are applied; fluids based on silicone resins are completely colourless, and a fugitive dye is incorporated so that they can be used without the possibility of any parts being missed, the dye disappearing after a few days. Another point is that products containing wax or fat encourage dirt retention which eventually darkens the surface, but silicone-based products have no such effect. The fluid penetrates to a distance of between 1.5 and 6 mm according to the porosity of the surface. It should be noted that while the use of the fluid allows masonry to breathe and does not therefore hinder the drying-out of the structure, the presence of soluble salts in the structure may give rise to trouble; the salts are prevented from rising to the surface in solution, and may therefore be deposited within the pores at the depth to which the repellent fluid has penetrated, causing the treated surface to spall. Water-repellent fluids, therefore, should not be used until efflorescence has ceased to form.

Silicone resins are also used in the manufacture of furniture polishes and car polishes. It is very important that any surface known to have been maintained with periodic applications of furniture polish should be most carefully cleaned down before paint is applied to it. This remark applies with even greater force when any motor vehicle is being repainted or resprayed; it should be assumed that silicone polishes have at some time been applied, and great care taken to remove all traces of polish during the preparation.

Silk The fabric made from the fine soft glossy fibre spun by the larvae of certain moths, especially the silkworm. Silk in various forms is sometimes used as a wall fabric or wallcovering.

Silk screening A method of reproducing an unlimited number of repeats of a motif or pattern, used a great deal by commercial artists and very useful to the decorator as a technique with possibilities beyond those of conventional stencilling. Silk screening has many advantages. It produces a design in solid colour, unlike a stencil which is often weak and patchy, and it is excellent for reproducing intricate patterns involving a lot of detail. But the greatest advantage is that there are no ties to break the continuity of the design. With an ordinary stencil, ties are essential to hold the stencil plate together; in cutting a stencil of a simple letter "O" for example, at least two ties are necessary, otherwise the central part of the letter would simply fall out, but in silk screening the central part is supported by the fabric, so there are no breaks in the letter shape.

Certain manufacturers produce ready made silk-screen designs, but some decorators prefer to design and cut their own. The technique briefly consists of using a wooden frame with a silk screen stretched across it; the design is cut into a masking material, very often a shellac coated paper, which is then pressed into contact with the silk so that the mesh is blanked off except where the design occurs. Printing is carried out by placing the frame in the required position and drawing colour across the screen with a rubber squeegee, the colour passing through those parts where the mesh is exposed.

Silk wallcoverings These are available in many different forms.

Fabrics are the oldest form of wallhanging, in use long before paper was known, and from the earliest days silk was prized as the finest and richest of all the fabrics. Silk wallcoverings were first used in China where the weaving of silk originated, but it took a very long time for information about the material to spread to the Western world, and although a small amount of silk was used in the Roman empire for items of clothing, no silk looms were set up in Europe until the 12th century A.D. Yet by the end of the 13th century when splendid tapestries and brocades were being used on a lavish scale in the manorial halls and domestic areas of castles, silk hangings had already become an established feature in the trappings surrounding people of wealth and distinction.

Some of the firms producing silk fabrics for present-day interior decoration concentrate on the traditional patterns; a notable example is the long-established Gainsborough Silk Weaving Co. Ltd.of Sudbury, Suffolk. There are other firms such as Ian and Marcel who specialize in hand-painted silks of great subtlety and charm, using aniline dyes in combination with a rubber solution resist, which have the advantage that colours can be blended into one another and that there is no limit to the number of colours and shades used in any one design. Naturally these are expensive products for clients who are prepared to pay a high price to have a completely individual decorative scheme, unique to them alone. Helen Sheane Wallcoverings Ltd of Banbury, Oxfordshire, produce a very wide range of lovely silk wallcoverings of a plainer kind which exploit the weave of the material in many fascinating ways to give delightful sparkling effects and subtle light-and-shade gradations; their products are available across an extremely wide price range, bringing the pleasure of distinctive silk wallhangings within reasonable reach, and catering for the sort of customer whose work is carried out by a good painting and decorating firm. In the field of contract wallcoverings the firm of Ernest

Turner (Northdown House) Ltd offers an extensive range of textile hangings in which silk is combined with various other fabrics such as wool, jute, cotton, linen, viscose and polyester.

Silking A defect in a varnish or gloss film taking the form of very fine wrinkled lines which give the film a silky sheen. The wrinkles usually follow the lines made by the brush; on dipped or flow-coated articles they appear in the direction of the flow. The defect is usually due to a fault in the medium.

Silks The name given to emulsion paints that have a greater degree of sheen than the matt finish type and will withstand more cleaning. (**NLC**)

Silver grain The grain markings exposed when a log is cut quarterwise.

Silver leaf The metal silver prepared in the form of thin leaves for use in a similar manner to gold leaf. It is supplied in books of 50 leaves, each leaf measuring 115 mm by 115 mm. Silver leaf tarnishes very rapidly when exposed to the air, and in fact the edges of each leaf tend to tarnish while it is still in the book; the leaf needs a protective coating of clear lacquer immediately after application.

Silvering The silvering of glass to make mirrors is carried out with an ammoniacal silver solution mixed either with Rochelle salt (sodium potassium tartrate) or with a nitric acid–cane sugar–alcohol mixture; the solution is poured on to chemically clean glass where it deposits a film of silver. This is washed clean, given a protective coating of varnish, and then coated with a protective film of paint.

Simplex paper An inexpensive embossed wallpaper, consisting of a single layer of paper which passes through inked steel rollers with the pattern in relief, so that both printing and embossing take place in one operation. The embossing is less pronounced than that of a duplex paper in which the patterned paper is laminated on to a backing paper, and it is further reduced by the fact that some of the relief flattens out as the paper is being pasted and hung.

Single section ladders Ladders which are constructed as a single unit, as opposed to extension ladders in two or three units.

Sinking Any local loss of gloss or sheen in a paint film, due to absorption of the medium by the undercoats or to the porosity of the surface to which the paint is applied.

Size See *Glue size*.

Size bound distemper A composition of common whiting and glue size. See *Distemper*. (**NLC**)

Size brush The name loosely given to the flat squirrel-hair brush used for applying the isinglass in glass gilding.

Skewings The unavoidable waste entailed by gilding operations. In loose leaf gilding some surplus is bound to occur through overlapping of edges, etc., just as in any glass sign work it is impossible to work precisely to the shapes of the letters; in transfer gold operation it is impossible to clear all the leaves completely, especially if very small lettering is being gilded; any waste of this kind, known as the "skewings", is carefully collected and retained until there is a sufficient quantity to be returned to the gold beaters, who will make a cash allowance for it.

Skimming The thin top film of a plastered ceiling or wall surface.

Skin glue size The finest quality of glue size, practically colourless.

Skin protection When matters of health and welfare are being considered, the care of the skin is often overlooked. Many of the materials used in the painting trade contain harmful chemicals and irritants, the effects of which are aggravated by some of the techniques employed, yet the general attitude is one of total apathy, or worse. Even today it is common to see workers scrubbing their hands and arms and even their faces with solvents to remove paint splashes, robbing their skin of the natural oils that are essential to it. Yet protecting the skin is so easy.

Obviously any operation involving the use of caustic substances or acids calls for the wearing of heavy-duty PVC gloves or gauntlets; when dry materials are being used, light cotton gloves give enough protection as a rule. But for normal painting work, gloves of any kind would be a needless restriction; they prevent the free use of the fingers and interfere with the sense of touch.

For most work the best form of protection is a barrier cream, properly applied and rubbed well into the cuticles and the webs of the fingers before work commences, and the use of a suitable cleansing cream after the work is finished. Barrier creams have been very much improved in recent years, with a range of special types available each giving protection against some particular form of contaminant; the drawback of these is that the operatives may not notice that the type they are using is completely ineffective against the substances they are actually encountering on that particular site. Another point is that other parts of the body as well as the hands may be exposed to the harmful substances, the arms for example, and especially the face. Century Oils Ltd., of Stoke-on-Trent, produce a universal barrier cream which gives protection against all forms of both wet and dry contaminants, eliminating the risk of using the wrong type of barrier. It is an excellent product which contains a high proportion of film-forming waxes to protect the wearer against the effects of abrasion, and in spite of being non-greasy to the touch it contains glycerine and natural fats which nourish the skin. This firm has gained a great reputation over many years for its protective products. It also produces excellent cleanser creams for use at the end of the working day. One which is of special interest to painters and decorators is a liquid skin cleanser which removes paint splashes, ingrained dirt and grease from the skin and can be used without water and afterwards wiped off with a towel or tissue; ideal for sites where washing facilities are inadequate or non-existent.

It seems certain that there will soon be a big increase in the extent to which barrier creams and cleanser creams are used in industry generally and in painting and decorating in particular. Under the terms of the Packaging and Labelling of Dangerous Substances Regulations which came into force on 1st January 1986, it became compulsory for warning notices and labels to be prominently displayed on a wide range of products which hitherto had been supplied in plain containers. The warning labels carry details of (a) the designation of the substances, in most cases the chemical name, (b) the classification (e.g. "harmful") and the corresponding hazard label, (c) the risk phrases (e.g. "may cause fire"), (d) the safety phrases (e.g. "keep container dry"), and (e) the name and address of the manufacturer and supplier. Certain materials used in painting and decorating are specifically mentioned in the Regulations; they include paints and varnishes containing more than 0.5 percent lead, cyanoacrylate adhesives, certain preparations containing isocyanates, certain preparations containing sensitizers, and certain preparations intended to be sprayed. It is clear that as painters and other operatives see these warning notices and are made aware of the possible hazards, they will increasingly demand that proper protective materials are supplied to them; in particular, barrier creams, etc.

Skinning The formation of a surface skin on a film of paint or on a quantity of paint in a container, due to contact with the air.

Skip A rather primitive form of suspended scaffold which used to be extremely popular and is still used to some extent in the woollen and cotton towns of the North. It consists of a wicker basket fitted with wheels which enable it to run down a wall surface. It is suspended by block, pulley and rope, and accommodates one man who is able to lower himself as desired. In the Construction Regulations a skip comes under the same provisions as a bosun's chair, and is only to be used in situations where a more elaborate scaffold or a full cradle is impracticable or unreasonable. It must be at least 762 mm deep and must be carried by two strong bands of metal.

Skirting board The board running round the base of the wall of a room.

Slaked lime Calcium hydroxide, or quicklime which has been slaked by the addition of water.

Slate filler A Japan filler composition made up of slate powder and Japan gold size; it is an extremely good and strong filler, but needs to be rubbed down smooth within a reasonable length of time after application, otherwise it sets extremely hard and difficulty is experienced in getting it really smooth.

Slate powder A very finely ground powder consisting of aluminium silicate, obtained from slate, which is used to make up slate filler.

Sleepiness or sleepy gloss The condition of a gloss film in which the natural glossiness is reduced as the material dries, but not by any process allied to blooming. It may be due to the application of the gloss over an unsuitable undercoat, an undercoat which is unduly absorbent, or an undercoat which is not completely hard and within which some solvent is trapped which subsequently escapes through the gloss. It may also be due to some defect in the formulation of the gloss material itself.

Sleeve The fabric or natural skin covering around the rotating head of a paint roller, which picks up the paint from the bucket or tray and distributes it over the wall or ceiling surface.

Sleeve coupler A coupler used in tubular scaffolding to join two tubes end to end; the term refers specifically to the type of coupler which grips the outside face of the tubes, as opposed to a joint pin which grips the internal surfaces.

Slip or slide (i) The condition of a surface whereby a material applied to it can be moved around with some freedom. Slip is an important characteristic in a surface upon which wallpaper is being hung. One of the objects of applying glue size to a surface is to impart some measure of slip, so that the paper can be moved around until it is in the correct position rather than that it should stick immediately upon contact.

(ii) The term is sometimes used to describe a paint with low surface tackiness, such as graphite paint, etc., which can be brushed out very thinly.

Slung scaffold A scaffold suspended from wire bonds from the underside of the roof or ceiling of a building where a scaffold built from the ground would be impracticable, e.g., in a theatre or cinema where normal performances are not to be interrupted, in railway stations, etc. The ledgers are usually about 3 metres apart and the transoms about 1.2 metres apart. The scaffold is close boarded to provide a broad working platform.

Slushing A term used to describe a method of applying paint to inaccessible surfaces, by which paint is flooded on freely and the surplus allowed to drain off.

Smoke stains A frequent source of trouble on plaster work in the vicinity of chimney breasts due to smoke continually eddying around the surface or seeping through to the surface from the chimney by means of hair cracks. Such stains, unless cleaned off and sealed, will bleed into new paintwork.

Smudge A paint mixture made up with the residue of paint left over in tins or returned from jobs; traditionally, the material used for painting the inside of gutterings, etc. (**NLC**)

Snap line A length of string or twine which is rubbed with a piece of chalk, held firmly at each end, and plucked in the centre to give a clean straight line when setting out a piece of decorative work.

Soaking Causing a material to absorb as much moisture as possible, e.g., repeatedly wetting wallpaper in order to soften it prior to stripping. Sometimes the term is used to indicate that some measure of control is exercised in the application of moisture such as, for example, when speaking of a wallpaper being allowed to soak for, say, ten minutes, meaning that when it is pasted and folded it should be laid aside for a period of ten minutes before it is hung; in the same way one can speak of "oversoaking" a wallpaper, i.e., allowing it to remain pasted and folded for too long a time before hanging it, which leads to excessive stretching.

Soap A substance composed of the salt of an alkali and fatty acid, which possesses detergent and cleansing properties.

Soft distemper Another term for size distemper. See *Distemper*. (**NLC**)

Soft soap A blend of vegetable and animal oils saponified with caustic alkali used by the painter in washing down prior to decoration.

Softener A brush used in graining for the purpose of softening the markings, for relieving any harshness or crudity from the work, and for blending. Hog hair softeners are used for oil colour; badger softeners are reserved for water colour.

Softwood Coniferous timbers such as fir, spruce, pine, etc., used for constructional purposes. Although the wood is sometimes quite hard, they are all known by the general term of softwood.

Soirette papers Self-coloured satinette wallpapers with a low-relief pattern.

Sole plate A strong plank of wood to which the base plates are screwed or spiked when a tubular scaffold is being erected on soft or uneven surfaces; it forms the basis of the scaffold and distributes the weight evenly over a wide area. Sole plates should also be used with an internal scaffold in situations where it is necessary to protect the floor from damage, such as, for example, when erecting a scaffold on a wood block floor.

Solid emulsion paint Emulsion paint intended for roller application, and supplied in the form of a solid jelly. The jelly liquefies as soon as the roller is brought into contact with it, and it then spreads easily over the surface to which it is applied, though remaining drip-free. It is useful in various situations, such as when a ceiling needs to be re-coated but the existing wallpaper must not be disturbed and must be kept free from splashes.

Soluble Capable of being dissolved—hence "water soluble" is a term applied to a substance which will dissolve in water, "spirit soluble" to a substance which will dissolve in alcohol, etc.

Solution A liquid with some substance or substances dissolved in it.

Solvent A liquid used in the manufacture of a paint or decorative coating in order to dissolve or disperse the film-forming constituents with the object of making the mixture thin enough and fluid enough for easy application; the solvent evaporates from the film after application and therefore does not become part of the dried film. The solvent is also referred to as the "thinner".

Soya bean oil A semi-drying oil extracted from the ground beans of the soya plant, and used in the manufacture of non-yellowing alkyd resin paints.

Spacing The arrangement of individual letters in a word or an inscription, and of the separate words in an inscription, in such a way as to produce an even and regular effect which makes for good legibility. The object is to make the area of the space between each of the letters appear to be the same, allowing for the differences in contour and shape of each individual letter. Good spacing is one of the most important aspects of lettering and demands a keen eye and a sense of proportion which can only be cultivated with conscious effort and constant practice; there is no means of employing mechanical aids.

Spanish red oxide A brightly coloured oxide of iron pigment with good staining properties, found in Spain.

Spanish white Another term for Paris white.

Spar varnish A boat varnish formulated in such away as to give exceptional water resistance.

Spatchel filler An oil-based filling composition developed in the early 1970's in Germany and used very widely on the Continent, but not introduced into the U.K. until much later. It is an excellent material for filling all kinds of surface indentations, but is particularly suitable for use on broad areas and for filling and surfacing wood grain, especially regular grooved grain markings. It is supplied in ready-mixed form as a smooth paste, and is applied with a small flexible plastic spatula; it is extremely smooth in composition and spreads very easily—it literally spreads like soft butter and is sometimes called "butter filler". The technique is to apply it very generously and spread it rapidly in one operation, when it dries to a beautifully smooth surface which usually does not need to be rubbed down when dry, being ready for immediate painting; there is no necessity for "oiling-in" before painting. It does not shrink after application, and therefore there is no need to apply a film which lies "proud" of the surface; where, however, it *does* stand proud of the surface it rubs down very easily. The manufacturers claim that it can safely be applied to bare wood because it acts as its own primer, but this is not a thing to be recommended.

Spatter or splatter A spraying technique whereby paint is ejected from the spray gun in such a manner as to fall on the surface in thick blobs which remain separated and which do not flow together to form a continuous film. This is achieved by using an air pressure too low to atomize the paint and sufficient merely to eject it. Spatter is carried out with a plastic paint composition or with unthinned emulsion paint to produce a low-relief treatment known as spray plastic; the surface is coated up by spray or brush with emulsion paint to produce a solid coating, and when this is dry it is followed up by spattering in one, two, three or more colours differing from the ground, the darkest colour being spattered first and the lightest colour last; the spray gun is used with a circular motion with the trigger continuously pressed.

Spatula A tool with a broad flexible blade, originally used for spreading plaster and for mixing pigments, but now used for a variety of operations which involve spreading some soft paste-like composition. A special kind of spatula is recommended for the application of many of the adhesives made to be used with present-day wallcoverings; this is the V-notched spatula, which has notches 1.5 mm deep and 1.75 mm wide in the blade, the notches being 1.75 mm apart; the adhesive is usually spread on the wall surface rather than on the wallcovering.

Specific gravity The ratio of the weight of a given volume of a substance to the weight of the same volume of water at a temperature of 4°C.

Specification A detailed statement giving precise particulars of the preparatory work to be done, the materials to be used and the extent of the work to be undertaken on a particular site by a painting contractor.

Spigot An alternative term for a joint pin used in tubular scaffolding.

Spirit colour A very thin fluid consisting of a coloured pigment alone with no white added, the fluid being well thinned down with white spirit and containing just enough varnish medium to bind the particles together. It is purely and simply a decorative coating with no protective properties at all; it is applied over a suitably prepared, painted and undercoated surface. After application, when dry, it is varnished.

Spirit paint remover A paint remover consisting of a powerful solvent with the addition of a thickening agent to enable it to cling to the surface to be stripped and also to retard evaporation of the solvent. It is used in circumstances where burning off would be unsuitable (see *Paint remover*) and operates by dissolving the old film.

Correctly used, a spirit paint remover is extremely effective; cases have been recorded of paint films composed of as many as eighty separate coatings being stripped by one application. A great many people regard it as ineffective, due to the fact that its correct use is rarely understood. A very common fault, due to impatience, is to apply the paint remover and then begin to scrape the surface after an interval of only a few minutes; this is quite useless as well as being very wasteful of material. The proper technique is to apply the paint remover and allow it to stand for some twenty minutes until it begins to etch the surface of the old paint film. At this point a second application is given, and for this purpose the remover is piled on very liberally. No attempt is made to use a scraper until the entire film is softened, a process that may take several hours, but when this stage is reached stripping is thorough, clean and simple.

Spirit paint remover is more expensive than caustic paint stripper but is much more effective and leaves no harmful residue to damage the new paint system. If any residue at all remains it consists of the wax that is sometimes used as the stiffening agent, and this may retard the drying of the new paint coating; after stripping, therefore, the surface should be cleaned down with white spirit to remove any residual wax.

Some paint removers are flammable and should not be used in situations where the vapour given off from them can come into contact with a naked flame. Whatever type of spirit paint remover is in use, the room should be well ventilated; otherwise, the vapour given off may give rise to unpleasant symptoms of nausea.

Spirit stain A solution of spirit-soluble dye such as nigrosine, turmeric, gamboge, etc., in industrial alcohol, very often with the addition of a resin such as shellac as binder. It is a very penetrative stain and evaporates rapidly, for which reason it is a difficult material to apply evenly. (**NLC**)

Spirit varnishes Varnishes made by dissolving resins in industrial spirit, sometimes with the addition of a plasticizer of either castor oil or balsam. Shellac is the principal resin used, but manila, mastic, damar and sandarac are sometimes employed. (**NLC**)

Spiriting off or spiriting out The last stage in French polishing, in which the last traces of oil are removed from the work and a brilliant finish produced by burnishing the surface. It is performed by drawing a rubber moistened with methylated spirit repeatedly across the surface, or by applying a dilute acid solution with the palm of the hand over the work (which also has the effect of hardening the film of shellac) or by the use of grinding rubbers.

Splicing of ladders Increasing the effective height of a ladder by lashing another ladder securely to its face by means of ropes passed round the rungs and stiles. It is generally carried out with the ladders standing upright.

Splicing ropes Ropes used for lashing ladders together. They should be at least 6 metres in length in order to give the requisite number of turns round rungs and stiles.

Split complementary A variation or extension of the method of using two contrasting colours to form a complementary colour scheme, made by taking one hue and contrasting it with the hues immediately to the right and left of the hue directly opposite to it on the colour circle. For example, on the Munsell system the complementary colour to red is blue-green; a split complementary based on red as the main hue would have blue and green as the other two hues, since blue and green lie on either side of blue-green on the circle.

A split complementary combination gives three hues to work with instead of only two as in a complementary pair; this gives more hue variety, when building up a scheme, without the risk of discord which would result from picking three hues at random.

Split spray A defective spray pattern resulting in bands of paint of uneven thickness being applied, due to the atomizing pressure, fluid pressure and spray width being wrongly adjusted.

Splitheads Also known as "splits" and "bandstands". Adjustable supports with which a working platform can be quickly and safely erected. They consist of a tripod base, which nowadays is generally made to fold up for ease of transport, and a centre prop surmounted by a swivelling fork head into which one or two planks can be fitted on edge, the planks acting as ledgers to support the platform. They generally extend to a maximum height of almost 3 metres.

Sponge An essential part of a painter's kit. Natural sponges are a primitive form of animal life, those sold commercially being found in the Eastern Mediterranean. Synthetic sponges are now generally used both for domestic decoration and for industrial work; these hold a greater quantity of water and their flat face covers a bigger area at one sweep.

Sponge stippling A decorative effect readily produced in emulsion paint or occasionally in matt or eggshell paint finish. The technique consists of painting the wall surface with a suitable colour in the normal manner and allowing it to dry; the colours to be stippled on are then mixed and a little of the darkest of these colours is placed on a flat palette board. A dry natural sponge, cut across the centre to present a flat face, is used to pick up the colour from the board and transfer it to the wall; the stippling is carried out with a light dabbing motion, the wrist being continually turned to and fro so as to avoid any regularity in the pattern. This is followed by stippling in each of the other colours in turn, the lightest colour being applied last of all.

Spontaneous combustion Ignition of a substance without the direct application of a flame, which is particularly liable to occur with substances susceptible to oxidation. Rags and cloths which have been used for graining, for wiping out scumble, and for glazing effects should never be left crumpled up at the close of a day's work but should be opened up and spread out to dry, preferably in the open air, because of the danger of spontaneous combustion.

Spot price An estimate of price arrived at purely by a visual examination of the work, without the aid of any measurements, and based upon the estimator's fund of experience which enables him to compare the extent of the work mentally with previous jobs he has handled.

The trained estimator uses spot pricing as a check on the accuracy of his work. He compares his spot price with the price he arrives at by carefully working out all his figures and measurements; should there be any startling discrepancy between the two it may very well indicate that some significant figure has been omitted from or multiplied wrongly in his calculations, and he is warned of the advisability of rechecking his figures.

Spot priming A term used, especially in the painting of structural steelwork, to mean stripping off the paint from small local areas and touching in these areas with priming paint prior to applying a coat of paint over the entire surface. It is generally carried out when the condition of the surface does not demand complete paint removal but when small local patches have been subjected to abrasion or damage.

Spout brush or striker A long-handled brush used for bridge work, for roof work, for painting the mouths of spoutings, etc. The brush head is set at an angle to the handle.

Spray booth A compartment or enclosure used in premises devoted to industrial finishing or motor vehicle work, designed to confine spray painting operations and to extract the fumes and overspray resulting from these operations.

Spray gun The essential part in every spray set-up, being the tool that directs the atomized paint to the surface which is being painted.

Spray gun extension A rigid extension, 1200 mm in length, which is fitted to the air and fluid inlets of a spray gun and which includes a device enabling the trigger of the gun to be operated from the other end of the extension. Its purpose is to enable the operative to spray high walls, ceilings and other features which are out of reach without the use of scaffolding.

Spray gun tips The changeable parts of an airless spray gun which control the width of the spray pattern and also control the fluid flow.

Spray painting A method of paint application whereby a controlled stream of paint is broken up or atomized and directed on to a surface in the form of a fine mist, the chief advantage of the method being speed of application and the ease by which a relatively smooth film can be produced.

Spray pattern The pattern produced by the paint which is ejected from a spray gun and directed to a surface when the trigger is pressed once and then released while the gun is kept stationary. The pattern can be adjusted to suit the particular job in hand. The pattern may be distorted if the settings or pressures are wrongly adjusted, if the gun is clogged with dirt or dried paint, or if the gun has been damaged by careless handling or cleaning.

Spray plastic See *Spatter*.

Spray silvering The application of silvering to glass by means of spray equipment. For this purpose on mass production work a twin-headed spray gun is used.

Sprayhead Part of an air-propelled spray gun; an assembly consisting of air cap, fluid tip and fluid needle.

Spreading capacity or spreading power The area covered by a given quantity of paint, varnish or other decorative fluid when applied in a normal manner over a suitable surface. It is generally expressed in terms of square metres per litre (or per 5 litres) of material, although paste materials are reckoned in square metres per kilogram. It is influenced by many factors, such as the porosity, and texture of the surface, the method of application and the skill of the operative. It should be remembered that the figures quoted by manufacturers for their products are often based upon application under ideal conditions, such as on a non-porous surface at a carefully controlled temperature, with no waste involved.

Springwood That part of the annual ring of a tree's growth which forms in the spring, which is relatively soft and spongy compared with the denser summerwood, and which therefore tends to absorb stain and paint more freely.

Stabilizing fluid A viscous fluid used to reduce the suction of an absorbent surface and to bind down previous coatings or loose material prior to painting.

Stable Unchanging: a product is said to be stable if under normal conditions of use it retains its characteristics.

Staggered joints A term used in tubular scaffolding, to refer to the practice of arranging that the end-to-end joints in standards should be at varying heights and that the joints in ledgers should be at varying lengths along the scaffold, a practice which is very necessary to prevent the occurrence of lines of weakness along which the scaffold might break apart.

Staging A working platform of any kind. See also *Lightweight staging*.

Stain (i) A discolouration or blemish.

(ii) A fluid used to colour a surface by penetrating it without obscuring it. Woods of good quality may be stained to enhance the appearance of the grain markings or to make them harmonize with other woodwork in a decorative scheme; inferior woods may be stained to hide defects or for reasons of economy by providing a very cheap method of colouring the wood.

The term "stain" includes several different types of material:

WATER STAIN consists of vegetable dyes such as logwood, saffron, etc., in solution; it tends to emphasize the grain markings, especially in the case of a softwood, because it penetrates freely into the springwood but is rejected by the hard resinous summerwood. It has the drawback of raising the grain of the wood.

SPIRIT STAIN consists of spirit-soluble dyes such as nigrosine, turmeric, etc., in solution with shellac. It evaporates quickly and for this reason is difficult to apply evenly; it tends to subdue the grain markings, and if used too strongly it gives a "bronze" semi-opaque effect.

OIL STAIN consists of semi-transparent pigments such as sienna, crimson lake, etc., ground in a drying oil and thinned with white spirit; it is less penetrative than water stain or spirit stain and can therefore be applied more evenly, especially on softwood. Because the colouring-matter is pigmentary it tends to subdue the grain markings.

VARNISH STAIN is a pigmented hard varnish which lies as a top coating on the wood rather than penetrating it.

CHEMICAL STAIN is used by the French polisher; it consists either of an aqueous solution applied directly to the wood, or of a material such as ammonia that fumes the wood.

Present-day wood-stains as produced by the leading paint manufacturers are not included in any of these categories, as they are formulated to present other features of a moisture-repellent or protective nature to the timber or to provide a more sophisticated type of finish. By definition they are not true stains; a true stain is a solution containing a soluble dye, and pigmentary materials do not give the same measure of purity and transparency.

Stainers Coloured pigments ground in a paint medium, which can be added to a paint in order to change or modify its colour.

Staining strength or staining power The degree to which a coloured pigment imparts colour to a white pigment, assessed by grinding a definite weight of coloured pigment with a specified weight of opaque white pigment and comparing it with the tint produced with a known standard.

Stand oil A drying oil, generally best quality linseed oil, which has been polymerized by heat treatment without the addition of driers. It is very pale in colour, and has outstanding qualities of flow.

Standard A term used in pole or tubular scaffolding to mean a vertical tube, column or support which transmits the load to the ground or to a base plate.

Standard method of measurement A document issued jointly by the Royal Institute of Chartered Surveyors and the National Federation of Building Trades Employers to provide a uniform basis for measuring building work generally, including painting and decorating.

Standing ladder A ladder with rectangular sides or stiles. This type of ladder is neither so heavy nor so robust as a pole ladder, and is used where lightness is required. Standing ladders are not usually made more than 8 metres in length.

Standing part That portion of the suspension rope on a cradle or bosun's chair which stands between the top pulley block and the point of suspension.

Starch A carbohydrate which is found in rice and all kinds of grain.

Starch paste A fixative made by beating up starch with a little cold water to form a creamy batter which is then scalded with boiling water until it thickens. It forms a fine colourless paste which is excellent for hanging delicate papers, but has now been superseded in everyday practice by the modern range of adhesives. (**NLC**)

Starved A term applied to a surface the porosity of which has not been satisfied by the coats of paint applied to it, resulting in a patchy film.

Steam cleaning A method sometimes used for cleaning the stone fabric of a building; provided steam alone is used the fabric suffers no ill effects. The work is usually carried out by specialists in this field.

Steam jenny A piece of heavy-duty equipment used by some transport undertakings for degreasing and stripping the paint of vehicle bodies prior to painting.

Steam stripper A piece of equipment which strips wallpaper and other forms of wallhanging very quickly and efficiently, leaving the plastered surface clean and sterile. It is especially useful for stripping materials which do not yield readily to applications of water or similar methods, such as wallcoverings made with an impervious substance on the face, papers that have been coated with emulsion paint, relief materials coated with paints of various kinds, and even such impenetrable materials as Lincrusta. There is a container in which water is heated, the steam which is generated being conveyed through a flexible hose to the "concentrator", a rectangular plate the inner face of which is punctured by rows of perforations and on the outer part of which a handle is mounted. The concentrator is held for a short time in contact with the wall or ceiling area so that the steam penetrates and softens the wallcovering, which is then removed with a scraper. Without a steam stripper the removal of the wallcovering would be a laborious process of jabbing at the material with a knife, which would inevitably cause damage to the plaster; the use of the steam stripper eliminates this, which not only results in a great saving of time and effort but also means that less time needs to be spent on making good the damaged wall surface. It should be noted, however, that if the concentrator is held too long in one position the steam may penetrate the skimming of the plaster which may as a result be buckled and lifted.

Many steam strippers operate from an LPG cylinder, but today electrically powered steam strippers are being increasingly used in preference to these, because they are less cumbersome and can so much more easily be lifted from place to place as the work proceeds. It is very important that whatever type of steam stripping equipment is in use, the working area must be well ventilated.

Stearic acid A hard wax-like saturated fatty acid derived from animal and vegetable fats and oils. It is the basis of metallic stearates used as flatting and gelling agents, and some of its esters are used as plasticizers.

Steel Steel, which is made by a variety of processes, consists of iron combined with carbon in various proportions. When assembled for the load-bearing framework of buildings and other engineering structures it is known as structural steelwork. It corrodes rapidly in the presence of air and moisture, and corrosion is accelerated by a smoke or chemically polluted atmosphere, by sea air and so on. The arrest of corrosion and the protective treatment of steel are among the most important aspects of the painter's work.

Steel combs Tools used in graining for the portrayal of coarse grain. They are rectangular in shape, one edge being divided to form a number of narrowly separated teeth. A wide choice is available, the combs themselves ranging from narrow to broad, and the teeth also ranging from fine to coarse. When combs are purchased the teeth are set at regular intervals, but the grainer very often breaks out several teeth in order to form an irregular pattern. Useful effects are gained by using broad combs wrapped round with cloth followed by fine combs taken across at a slight angle. Combs should be wiped clean after every stroke.

Steel straightedges These are available in several lengths, and are used for various purposes such as, for example, in conjunction with a sharp knife or Stanley knife for trimming certain kinds of wallcoverings by means of cutting through the vertical overlaps to produce a perfect butt joint.

Steel wool An abrasive material which is available in several grades varying from very fine wool to coarse steel shavings; it has several applications to painting and decorating. The finest grades may be used for rubbing down both old and new paintwork; the medium grades provide an excellent material for stripping paint and polish from intricately carved or modelled work when used in conjunction with paint remover, and are also useful for the preparation of non-ferrous metals, in order to roughen their surface and provide a key for paint; the coarse grades are used for rough scouring. According to the needs of the particular surface, steel wool may either be used dry or lubricated with water; when used for removing rust from steel, it is lubricated with paraffin or white spirit. It is important that all traces of the steel wool are removed before paint is applied; there is a tendency for fine specks of the metal to be left embedded in the surface or to become bound to the surface by the paint coating, and these can cause trouble through subsequently rusting and staining the paint film. Gloves should be worn to protect the hands while steel wool is being used.

Stencil A thin plate from which a pattern or design is cut out; the plate is laid upon the surface which is to be decorated, and colour is applied through the voids or cut out portions so as to reproduce the design on the surface and, of course, by moving the position of the stencil plate the design can be reproduced many times over. The stencil plates used by the decorator generally consist of paper, but for certain purposes they may also be made from thin cardboard, sheet zinc or lead foil. It is essential that the stencil plate should be strong and robust enough to hold together as a complete unit, and for this reason the pierced sections of the plate are held together with "ties"; the art of designing a stencil is to arrange that the ties form an integral part of the pattern.

Stencil brush A round brush with the bristles set in a metal ferrule, mounted on a short stubby handle; the brush is so shaped as to present a circular flat working face. The method of using a stencil brush is to pour a little colour on to a flat palette board, moisten the tips of the brush with the colour and then stipple the colour gently and sparingly with a backwards and forwards dabbing motion on to the surface which is to be decorated; under no circumstances should the brush be dipped into a can of paint, otherwise it will pick up far too much colour and produce a smudgy, untidy piece of work with paint straying under the plate beyond the bounds of the design.

Stencil brushes are made in several sizes. After use the tips should be moistened in solvent and the brush then washed out with soap and water; after the brush has been washed and rinsed it should be wrapped around with a piece of stout paper, secured with an elastic band to bring it back tightly into shape and to prevent the tendency for it to splay outwards. When a stencil brush is being purchased it is important to see that the handle fits the hand comfortably; otherwise, prolonged use will lead to chafing and blistering of the skin.

Stencil cutting The process of preparing a stencil plate. One of the most effective methods for practical purposes is as follows:

(a) The design is drawn out accurately on a sheet of stout cartridge paper. Accurate setting out is essential, especially with a multi-plate, all-over pattern, in which any error, however slight, is magnified by each repetition.

(b) The portions to be cut out are painted in with strong poster colour, and the paper then pinned up and examined from a distance. This enables the decorator to judge the probable effect of the completed work and to decide whether the pattern is well balanced; the effect cannot be properly judged when only a pencil outline has been drawn in.

(c) The paper is oiled with a cloth soaked in raw linseed oil; this makes the paper easier to cut.

(d) The paper is placed on a piece of heavy plate glass, and the pattern cut out with a suitable knife which is kept well sharpened.

(e) The completed plate is coated on both sides with shellac knotting to stiffen it up, and to make it possible to clean the plate by wiping paint off.

Stencil knife A short knife with a wooden handle, made especially for stencil cutting and supplied by a decorators' merchant. The knife should be sharpened periodically while in use; otherwise, it will tend to produce ragged edges.

Stencil paper A dark brown oiled paper sold specially for stencil cutting. Many decorators, however, prefer to work on white cartridge paper, as described under the heading *Stencil cutting*.

Stencil pin A stout pin set in a fairly large plastic or composition head, which is used for pinning a stencil plate into position.

Stencilling Producing a decoration with stencil plates; the paint may be applied in many ways, such as by stencil brush, spray or sponge stipple. The work must be carried out carefully to avoid any paint creeping under the plate and blurring the work.

Stepladder A single-section ladder, with rectangular stiles, and with rectangular treads which should, as far as possible, be horizontal while the ladder is in use.

Steps Stepladders with a hinged frame which swings back to make them self-supporting. They are made of softwood and need to be of sturdy construction, since they are constantly subjected to hard use. Steps should be fully extended while in use; otherwise they are liable to kick. If used on uneven ground the feet should be packed so as to stand firmly and solidly. The ropes should be long enough to prevent any possibility of the steps closing while in use. Bricks should not be placed on the treads in order to raise a plank to extra height. The practice of standing on the lower rails at the back of the steps is a dangerous one. Care should be taken to maintain steps in good condition; they should not be painted because of obsuring defects and adding to the weight, and the ropes should be inspected periodically and checked for fraying and the hinges checked for corrosion.

Stibnite The ore from which the pigment antimony is obtained.

Stickiness Stickiness which persists in a paint film, which has been applied long enough to have become hard and dry under normal conditions, may be due to inadequate preparation and the presence of grease; stickiness which occurs in a film which has previously dried is generally due to saponification.

Stipple A term with several meanings. As a general rule, to stipple a surface means to strike a wet newly-painted surface repeatedly and systematically with a brush specially designed for the purpose with the object of levelling out the coat of paint and eliminating brushmarks. It can also mean the use of a fitch, stencil brush or sash tool to add a little paint of a different colour to a previously painted surface, or the production of a broken colour effect or a textured finish by partially lifting the wet paint or wet glaze with a rubber stippler. When paint is applied to a sheet of glass or a glass sign in order to obscure it, the coating may be levelled out more satisfactorily by stippling with a soft cloth than by using a stippling brush.

Stippler A type of brush specially designed for some form of stippling. Unless it is qualified by some distinctive description, the word is usually understood to refer to a hair stippler, which consists of a large number of wire-drawn tufts of soft hog-hair arranged on a flat base plate, and made so as to present a flat rectangle of hair; this type of stippler is used for levelling out a coat of paint and eliminating the brushmarks, or for blending colours in order to produce a gradation of colour on a large area, or for levelling up an area of tinted glaze prior to rag rolling, rubber stippling, scumbling or other broken colour effects. See also *Hair stippler*. A modification of the hair stippler is the "two-row stippler" (q.v.) which is used to perform similar operations in a confined space.

Special kinds of stipplers are available for specific purposes. Rubber stipplers of various patterns and shapes are made for the production of broken colour effects and textured plastic paint effects. A radial stippler may also be used for broken colour work and plastic paint effects. A type of stippler was produced at one time by a well-known firm of paint manufacturers and was made on the same principle as a hair stippler except that the face was divided into four separate rectangular areas; this tool was used in conjunction with a metal tray also divided into four sections, a different colour of paint being placed in each section, and was designed to produce a broken colour effect by adding the four different colours simultaneously to a previously painted ground.

Stippling The process of striking a painted surface with a stippler or similar tool for any of the purposes described in the previous paragraphs.

Stockholm tar The material from which crude tar is obtained.

Stop To stop a surface is to fill up the holes and cracks in it with a suitable stopping. It should not be confused with the application of filler; stopping is applied to a definite hole or cavity, whereas filling is used for the treatment of shallow indentations in the surface.

Stop tar knotting A material usually consisting of a compound of shellac and manila in industrial spirit, with the addition of a plasticizer to render it more elastic. It is used to prevent such materials as tar, creosote, bituminous paint, bronze paint or oil soluble dyes from bleeding into a superimposed paint film.

Stopping A stiff paste used to fill up holes, cracks and similar defects in a surface; in the case of woodwork it may consist of putty, or better still of a hard stopping, applied after the priming coat is dry, while in the case of plastered surfaces it may consist of plaster of Paris, Keene's cement or a proprietary brand of filler.

Stoving Used in industrial finishing. The process of drying and hardening a paint coating by means of the application of heat, either by convection in a stoving oven, or by radiation in which infra-red equipment is used. The term is taken to mean drying at a temperature of above 65°C (150°F), as opposed to forced drying in which only moderate temperatures are employed.

Stoving materials Used in industrial finishing. Known variously as stoving enamels, stoving finishes, stoving paints, etc., these are materials which are dried by heating, irrespective of the type or source of heat applied, as opposed to air-drying materials

Stoving oven Used in industrial finishing. A thermostatically controlled oven into which a painted article is placed and in which heat is transferred to the article by convection in order to dry the paint.

Straight match See *Set pattern*.

Straightedge The type of straightedge used by the decorator is generally a length of bevelled wood, and is employed in conjunction with a lining fitch for the production of straight painted lines. For some purposes, however, such as in mitring Lincrusta strapping or the knife trimming of certain kinds of wallcoverings, a steel straightedge is used.

Strainer A sieve which allows fluid to pass through but which prevents the passage of lumpy matter, skins or other foreign bodies. Normally it consists of a truncated cone of light sheet-metal, sometimes called a gravity strainer, in the base of which a circular rimmed piece of gauze is fitted; the gauze, popularly known as the "strainer bottom", is replaced when worn or clogged up. The strainer is placed on top of a paint can and the fluid strained through, its passage being often assisted by strokes of a fitch or 25 mm tool. The usual size of strainer is some 200 or 225 mm at the top and 88 to 112 mm at the base, with gauzes to fit; the gauze is available in varying degrees of mesh. Until recently, miniature strainers could be purchased and these were very useful for dealing with small quantities of enamel, etc., for high class work; unfortunately, these seem to be no longer obtainable. On the other hand, it is now possible to buy disposable strainers which are cheap enough to be discarded immediately after use and which, because no cleaning out is necessary, represent a saving in labour that more than compensates for their purchase price.

Straining The sieving of paint in order to trap out skins and foreign bodies; most essential if paintwork is to be free from nibs and especially necessary when paint is to be applied by spray if gun blockages are to be avoided.

Straining cloth Fine-mesh lintless cloth, which is secured to the top of a paint can by means of an elastic band and through which varnish or enamel is allowed to strain by gravity.

Striker Alternative term for a spout brush.

Striking (i) To the painter this term means the harmful penetration of a material by some liquid substance. For instance, on rushed work a painter might decide to save time by adopting the dubious practice of hanging the wallpaper first and then applying gloss paint to the woodwork immediately after, thus doing the two operations in one day; but unless the paint is very carefully cut in so as to leave a slight gap, the medium from the paint will almost certainly "strike into the paper" causing unsightly stains where it has penetrated along the edges.

(ii) To the paint manufacturer, striking means the same as precipitation.

Stripe painting Applying additional coats of paint, usually primer, along the angles of structural steel to give them extra protection.

Strippable papers See *Dry-strippable papers*.

Stripper A word sometimes used loosely to refer to a paint remover.

Stripping The removal of some previous coating from a surface, e.g., the removal of old wallpaper or old paint.

Stripping knife A broad knife used for paint or wallpaper removal.

Stucco Also known as "Roman cement". A hydraulic cement obtained by burning a naturally occurring cement rock consisting of clay and limestone; the material was widely used in the 18th and 19th centuries as an external rendering for buildings. The word is an Italian one which has passed into the common speech of several languages and is often used rather loosely to describe any type of plaster rendering.

Styptic knotting Styptic is a general term covering certain medical preparations which arrest bleeding; the term "styptic knotting" is derived from this and means a white or colourless knotting used instead of the normal orange shellac knotting to arrest the bleeding of knots in woodwork which is to be finished in white or light-coloured enamel. This was necessary in the days when enamels had very little opacity and knots coated with dark knotting were plainly visible through the finish. Present-day gloss paints with high opacity have made styptic knotting totally obsolete. (**NLC**)

Styrene Also called "vinyl benzene"; a liquid produced from benzene and ethylene (i.e., from coal and petroleum) which polymerizes on heating to form a solid resinous substance. This can be reacted with the oil component of an alkyd resin to produce a wide range of air-drying paints and stoving finishes.

Sublimation The process of converting a solid substance, first to a vapour by heating and then back again to a solid by cooling.

Sublimed blue lead A grey pigment consisting of basic lead sulphate; it is a rust-inhibitive pigment and is used under strict control as a primer for iron and steel, especially in locations exposed to a polluted atmosphere, e.g., on gas-producing plant, etc.

Sublimed white lead A basic sulphate of lead produced by the sublimation of lead sulphide. (**NLC**)

Substrate A jargon word which is now very widely used in the technical literature relating to the painting trade. It is a rather misleading term. To be precise, in scientific terms a substrate is among other things a substance on which bacteria, fungi, etc., are grown. It would be better if we were to use the word "stratum" which means a layer or a set of successive layers of any deposited substance, and from which is derived the word "substratum" meaning a sunken layer or substance lying underneath. And that is really what is meant by the word "substrate" when it is used in our technical literature; it means whatever is lying underneath. But the confusion comes from the fact that the word is used very loosely. It can refer to the substance or the surface on which a decorative material is applied, such as the wood, plaster, etc., to which paint, wallpaper etc., is applied, but it is also sometimes used to refer to the existing coatings of paint present on a surface to which a new paint system is applied.

Suction Strictly speaking, the act or process of sucking, i.e., the production of a vacuum in a confined space causing a fluid to enter under atmospheric pressure. In the painting trade the term is used rather loosely as an alternative term for absorbency.

Suction cup A small paint container used in air-propelled spraying which is attached to the under part of a spray gun and which allows the atmospheric pressure to enter and force the paint up to the fluid tip when a current of air is flowing and creating a vacuum at the orifice of the gun.

Suction feed gun A spray gun, used in conjunction with a suction cup, in which a stream of compressed air creates a vacuum which causes the atmospheric pressure to force paint up from the cup. It is used in spraying small quantities of thin material such as cellulose, synthetic enamel, bronze, etc., and where frequent changes of colour are involved.

Suede A soft pliable form of leather, smooth and velvety to the touch, derived from the skin of a kid, and not given any sort of treatment or dressing to harden or polish the face.

Suede finishes Industrial finishes owing their effect to the presence of fine wrinkles, produced by inducing the paint film to skin over under controlled conditions. These materials may be air drying but as a general rule they are made as stoving finishes.

Suede floor paint A non-slip floor paint with considerable resistance to the weather and used for the decks and walkways of ocean-going vessels; one brand is produced by ICI under the name of Suede Deck and Floor Paint.

Suede substitutes Various materials are produced to simulate the effect of suede in wallhangings. Probably the most luxurious of these is the suede effect made of viscose rayon flock on a paper backing, a most attractive material, soft and warm to the touch and with the added advantage of being supplied in flame-proofed form.

Suede wallcoverings These delightful wallcoverings are soft and warm to the touch and have a pleasantly mottled matt finish. Helen Sheane Wallcoverings Ltd., of Banbury produce these in various attractive colourings ranging from a light fawn to "slate" which is a deep soft grey.

Sugar soap A soluble alkaline soap preparation used by the painter and decorator for washing down paintwork, for preparing old paintwork for repainting or for stripping old paintwork, the sugar soap being added to water in varying quantities to produce a solution of the strength suitable for the particular purpose required. Its chief constituent is washing soda, which is mixed with yellow bar soap and to which is added a small quantity of crude palm oil and a small amount of Russian or Swedish turpentine.

When sugar soap is used for washing down, work should commence at the lowest parts of the walls or woodwork and should proceed upwards; this is to prevent any soap solution from running down a dry surface and causing streaks to appear. The soap solution must not be allowed to dry on the surface, nor must it be allowed to remain on the surface long enough to soften the paintwork; as soon as possible the whole of the area that has been wetted and washed should be swilled off with clean water, rinsed well with several changes of clean water and then sponged and leathered off. If any of the soap is left behind it is liable to attack the new paint film and lead to local saponification.

Sulphurized oil See *Vulcanized oil.*

Summerwood The harder, denser portions of the annual rings of a tree's growth, less absorbent to stain and paint than the spongier springwood.

Sunflower seed oil A drying oil used in the manufacture of non-yellowing alkyd resins.

Supaglypta A hollow-backed high relief material with a greater depth of pattern than Anaglypta and which retains its emboss extremely well.

Surface cleanliness A matter of great importance in relation to the blast-cleaning of steelwork. The success of the operation depends to a very great extent on the degree of cleanliness achieved. While there is no exact method of measuring the cleanliness, it can be defined and controlled. BS 4232: 1967, "Surface Finish of Blast-Cleaned Steel for Painting" specifies three degrees of surface cleanliness and the type of paint surface for which they are appropriate.

The 1st Quality is when the whole surface of the steel shows blast-cleaning pattern and the bare steel is entirely free from contamination and discolouration; this is the quality required for the reception of chemically resistant paints which are to be subjected to the most demanding conditions of exposure.

The 2nd Quality is when the whole surface shows blast-cleaning pattern and at least 95 percent of the surface is completely clean; tightly bonded millscale is permissible on up to 5 percent of the whole surface and up to 10 percent on any single square of 25 mm sides. This is the quality required for chemically resistant paint systems such as epoxide and vinyl resin paints, and is also the standard desirable where the best results are required for conventional paints exposed to fairly corrosive conditions.

The 3rd Quality is when the whole surface shows blast-cleaning pattern and at least 80 percent of the surface is clean bare steel; tightly bonded millscale is permissible on up to 20 percent of the surface with not more than 40 percent on any single square of 25 mm sides. This is the minimum requirement for steelwork to be painted with conventional paint systems exposed to mildly corrosive conditions.

To assist in the recognition of these qualities there is a photographic scale illustrating and defining the various stages of rusting and treatment. This is the European scale of degree of rusting for anti-corrosive paints, and is available from the Paintmakers' Association of Great Britain. It comes under its French title, "Échelle Européenne de Degrés d'Enrouillement pour Peintures Antirouille".

Similar standards for the surface cleanliness of steelwork are specified by the Swedish Standards Organization and the Steel Structures Painting Council, USA. The Swedish standards are defined by means of a set of professionally produced photographs; the American standards simply employ a verbal definition.

Surface dry The term used to describe a paint film which is dry on the surface but still soft and tacky underneath.

Surface tension The force which acts at the surface of a liquid, tending to make it behave as though it were enclosed in an elastic membrane. Surface tension has an important bearing upon the capillarity of liquids.

Surfacer A pigmented filler composition applied to a slightly uneven surface and which, when sanded down, presents a smooth level surface upon which the paint system is applied.

Suspended scaffold A suspended scaffold is defined in the Construction (Safety, Health and Welfare) Regulations as being a scaffold suspended by means of ropes or chains and capable of being lowered or raised by such means.

Suspending agent A substance incorporated in a paint formulation in order to keep the pigments in suspension and prevent or delay settlement, e.g. asbestine, mica, silica, etc.

Suspension A liquid in which particles of solid matter are held up or suspended, either because the particles are very small or because the liquid is highly viscous.

Suspension point The point of connection between a bosun's chair or one side of a cradle and the suspension rope or bottom pulley block used for suspension.

Suspension rope The rope passing through the pulley block or blocks for suspending a cradle or bosun's chair, commonly referred to as the "fall".

Sweat out A defect in plaster work whereby the plaster fails to achieve its proper strength and hardness due to the fact that the surface was sealed too early, and while still containing moisture, by an impervious paint system.

Sweating A defect in a paint or varnish film whereby oily matter from the undercoats exudes through the surface causing it to become permanently tacky; the defect is often due to the application of a quick-drying coating over an insufficiently hard undercoat. The term is also very often loosely and incorrectly used in the trade to refer to the condensation of moisture upon structural surfaces.

Sweating back A defect in which a dry paint or varnish film develops tackiness when ageing, due to the hydrolysis of the glycerides present.

Swedish scale The Swedish standards for the recognition and definition of the degrees of surface cleanliness of blast-cleaned steelwork; they are illustrated by coloured photographs which are used alongside the actual cleaned steel for purposes of comparison. As in the British system, three degrees of cleanliness are defined. On the Swedish scale SA3 corresponds with our 1st Quality, SA 2.5 with our 2nd Quality, and SA2 with our 3rd Quality.

Sweet chestnut A wood which is very similar in appearance and properties to oak, but with very narrow pith rays as a result of which it lacks ray figuring.

Swivel coupler A coupler used in tubular scaffolding for joining tubes at any angle other than a right angle, and intended for use in forming diagonal bracings.

Sword liner A brush set in a quill, used by coach painters for the freehand production of painted lines, and so called because the shape of the working surface resembles the shape of a scimitar.

Sycamore A highly decorative whitish or honey coloured wood with most pleasing and subtle mottled markings, although when exposed to light and air it tends to develop a somewhat unpleasant yellowish colour. The imitation of sycamore is sometimes called for in modern decorative schemes and may be carried out with a graining colour of raw sienna, Vandyke brown and ultramarine blue on a white or cream ground; for the best results watercolour graining should be used.

Symbols used in labelling paint tins See *Classification, Packaging and Labelling of Dangerous Substances.*

Synthetic paint A term used very loosely in the trade to describe any type of paint containing some proportion of synthetic resin medium. The term is derived from the word "synthesis" which means the composition or building up of a complex whole by the union of two or more substances; many painters are under the mistaken impression that the word means that a synthetic material is an inferior substitute.

Synthetic resins These are produced from non-resinous forms of materials by chemical reaction processes. They include urea-formaldehyde, maleics, phenolics, alkyds, acrylics, melamines, epoxies, vinyls, silicones, etc., from which film-forming media of varying oil-lengths are obtained for use in decorative and industrial paints. See *Resin (synthetic).*

Synthetic ropes Ropes produced from man-made fibres, which offer distinct advantages over those produced from natural fibres because of their greater strength, low moisture absorption, and resistance to alkalis, soap solutions, oils and petroleum. They are especially useful for scaffolding purposes and for the suspension of cradles in situations where a high concentration of chemical substances is encountered or where the ropes are liable to be fouled by alkaline solutions in the course of operations involving the cleaning of buildings. Many forms of synthetic rope are available, including *Nylon* which is a strong alkali-resistant rope with a high degree of stretch which enables it to absorb shock loads but which makes it unsuitable for some purposes, *Terylene* which is a very strong and flexible acid-resistant rope and which, because of its low even stretch, is preferable to nylon for suspended scaffolds, *Polypropylene* which is a low-stretch rope highly resistant to acid and alkali and therefore suitable for destructive industrial conditions, and which is available in a variety of textures, and *Polythene* which is a fairly stiff rope resistant to acid and alkali. The manufacturers of synthetic ropes should be consulted for advice and information about the most appropriate type of rope for any specific purpose.

T

Tack rag A device for removing dust and grit from a surface prior to painting. It consists of a length of cotton fabric impregnated with a non-drying tacky or adhesive substance and folded so as to form a pad of convenient size for handling. When passed across a piece of work it picks up any dust which is present, the dust clinging to the pad, in contast to a duster brush, which flicks the dust away but sends it swirling into the surrounding air from whence it gradually settles back again on to the work. A tack rag is designed in such a way that when one face has become clogged up and too dirty for further use it can be folded over to present a fresh clean face, a process which can be repeated several times over so that one pad provides thirty-two clean faces.

Tack rags are widely used in industrial and coach painting, but are not yet used to a great extent in painting and decorating and certainly not used as much as they should be. In the initial stages of a job, at the burning off, rubbing down and priming stages, it is probable that the conventional duster brush is more effective than a tack rag in clearing away the debris, but in the later stages of the work when undercoats are being applied, and particularly in the finishing stages when gloss materials are being used, the tack rag is undoubtedly the most efficient form of dust removal and ensures a much cleaner piece of work than can be achieved with a duster.

Tackiness Stickiness; a paint or varnish which has begun to set, has lost its initial wetness and fluidity and has become sticky is said to be tacky. An essential feature of gilding with oil gold size or Japan gold size is that the gold size must have reached the right degree of tack before the gold leaf is applied.

Talc A magnesium silicate used as an extender in paints; French chalk is a well-known variety of talc.

Tall oil Obtained as a by-product when wood pulp is being prepared for paper manufacture; when purified it is used as an ingredient in non-yellowing alkyd resins.

Tallow A substance composed of the harder and less fusible fats of animals, especially beef or mutton fat, which is sometimes incorporated into limewash (see *Limewash*) and is also used in glass embossing for the purpose of building up a wall round a piece of glass to form a reservoir which will hold the acid while the etching is in progress.

Tannin An astringent substance found in various types of wood, notably in oak (see under *Pretreatment primers* for its use as an anti-corrosive for steel). Whenever iron wedges or nails are in contact with newly cut oak a blue-black stain similar in composition to writing ink is formed, due to the action of the tannin in the wood upon the metal.

Tar black A cheap coal-tar product used for such purposes as treating wooden posts which are to be contact with the soil, etc. (**NLC**)

Tarnishing The formation of a film of discolouration on the exposed face of a metal, destroying the lustre. Some metals are very susceptible to tarnishing, silver being notorious in this respect. See *Silver leaf*.

TBT—tributyl tin A toxic compound used in certain kinds of anti-fouling paints for ships' hulls. The resin base of such paints, especially in its co-polymer form, dissolves slowly and releases its toxic agent at a controlled rate. The paint has a longer effective life than other types of anti-fouling paint, which is in itself an economy and has the extra advantage that the ships coated with it require repainting at less frequent intervals and therefore spend less time out of commission.

Paints based on TBT are very popular with yachtsmen but decidedly unpopular with conservationists, who claim that the toxic exudation is responsible for the decline in the number of oysters around the coasts of Britain. The French have banned these paints altogether; in the U.K. the Department of the Environment banned the use of paints containing more than 7.5 percent of TBT as from January 1986, but most of the paint which is sold contains less than this and therefore does not come under the ban.

Teak An Asiatic tree the wood of which is used for various constructional purposes, such as dock and waterside work, woodwork for the chemical industry, coach and wagon construction and for doors, windows and gates, and also for furniture and cabinet work, especially for such items as laboratory benches, etc.; it is, of course, widely used in the shipbuilding industry. Its colour ranges from deep yellow to dark brown and indeed almost to black. Its value is enhanced by the fact that it exists in abundant quantities, and it is superior to all other woods in its freedom from movement. It contains a natural oil and feels oily to the touch; the natural secretions of some woods have a corrosive effect upon any metal which is in contact with them, but the oil contained in teak actually has a preservative effect upon metal fittings, bolts, etc., which are adjacent to it. When teak is to be painted the oil content presents a difficulty by preventing the paint from drying; it is necessary to wash the work down either with acetone or white spirit, and some firms supply a special teak sealer which acts as a primer and is followed by normal undercoats.

Tekko The name given to a range of metallic silk-faced wallpapers with the appearance of damask. It is important that the wall surfaces to which they are applied should be perfectly smooth and completely free from nibs, as the metallic sheen of the paper shows up every defect in the surface.

Telescopic scaffold Scaffolding equipment which is designed to be adjustable in length or height, e.g., telescopic scaffold boards used by house decorators, telescopic mobile towers used by highways departments for the maintenance and painting of lamp standards, etc.

Tempera One of the earliest painting techniques ever practised, and still occasionally used for decorative or mural work. The pigments are ground in water and bound with egg yolk, mixed white and yolk of egg, milk, or glue.

Template A pattern or mould, usually made of thin card, thin wood or metal, used as a guide in the shaping or setting out of a piece of decoration.

Terebene A solvent obtained by treating turpentine with sulphuric acid, the product being steam distilled. The material is seldom seen nowadays. (**NLC**)

Terebine A very strong liquid drier which is rather dark in colour and produces a somewhat brittle film. Its only use today is as a drier in graining colour, but when used for this purpose it needs to be added very sparingly, otherwise it will cause the dried film to crack. (**NLC**)

Terra alba Alternative term for gypsum or calcium sulphate.

Terre verte See *Green earth.*

Tertiary colour A colour produced by mixing two secondary colours, e.g., olive green produced by mixing purple and green.

Terylene ropes Very supple, strong and hard-wearing acid-resistant ropes, with a low and even degree of stretch, eminently suitable for use with suspended cradles. See *Synthetic ropes.*

Texture Originally applied to the distinctive feel and appearance of a woven fabric, imparted by the arrangement of its threads; and more generally applied to the sensation produced by any material which by the disposition of its structure or components offers a distinctive tactile and/or visual experience.

Texture paints Paints deliberately made to produce a rough finish; for example, plastic paints, made to remain pliable long enough to be manipulated to a low relief pattern, or paints to which sand, powdered pumice or similar materials are added for various purposes.

Textured wallcoverings A general term covering any kind of material which is hung on to a smooth wall surface to provide some measure of relief. It includes wallpapers with varying degrees of emboss such as simplex, duplex, etc., ingrain or woodchip papers, high-relief goods such as Anaglypta, Supaglypta, etc., vinyl textured wallcoverings, and the very wide range of textile wallcoverings which include hessian, canvas, wool, jute, vinyls of many kinds, etc., and the foam-backed textile hangings such as Lesura.

Thermal wallcoverings Various kinds of wallcoverings are available which provide thermal insulation and reduce heat losses in the rooms where they are applied, and usually they also have very good sound-insulating properties. Some consist of woven glass-fibre textiles of quite considerable thickness, others are made of a mixture of natural and man-made fibre textiles on a substantial backing of polyurethane foam, and some incorporate a layer of aluminium to reflect some of the heat that would otherwise be transmitted through the wall.

Thick edges See *Fat edges.*

Thickening A decrease in the fluidity of a paint material, due generally to the loss of some of the solvents by evaporation, but also sometimes allied to "fattening".

Thinners Volatile liquids added to paints in order to make them more fluid and bring them to a workable consistency. The essential features of a thinner are that it should be colourless so as not to affect the colour of the paint to which it is added, that it should be completely miscible with the paint at a normal working temperature, that it should completely evaporate and form no part of the dried paint film but should not evaporate so quickly as to make application difficult, and that it should act only upon the medium and not react with the pigment to cause precipitation. In the case of house painters' materials it is also necessary that the thinners should not be powerful enough to disturb or soften up the previous coatings. The thinner most widely used by the painter and decorator is white spirit; emulsion paints are, of course, thinned with water. The thinner for cellulose is generally a material which does not dissolve the nitro-cellulose but merely dilutes the solvent; petroleum and coal-tar distillates are used for the purpose, and it is important that the selected thinner should evaporate at the same rate as the solvent. For this reason it is essential that the correct thinner specified by the paint manufacturer for use with any particular cellulose product should always be used.

Thinning Adding a thinner to a paint or allied substance in order to render it more fluid and bring it to a suitable consistency for the intended method of application, whether it be spray, brush, etc. The thinning of paint for this purpose is perfectly legitimate, and in fact if the paint were applied in too ropey a condition several serious defects might develop in the film; nevertheless, in some quarters the idea is prevalent that thinning is a form of adulteration which should not be allowed to occur, and in some cases the paint manufacturers foster this idea by offering to "guarantee" their products provided they are used exactly as supplied. It should be noted that a reasonable degree of thinning improves the adhesion of the paint to certain types of surfaces by helping it to penetrate; on hardwoods, for example, the addition of a greater quantity of thinners than usual is to be recommended in order to secure this penetration. On the other hand, of course, over-thinning should most certainly be avoided; the effect of adding too much thinner is that a given quantity of the medium is forced to cover too great an area and the proper cohesion of the pigment particles is affected. This may result in the material lying on the surface in an underbound or powdery condition.

Thinning ratio The proportion of thinners to paint recommended by the manufacturers of a product in order to give the most satisfactory results.

Thixotropic paints Paints which have a jelly-like structure which is broken down when the paint is stirred, shaken or heated or when it is subjected to the shearing action of a brush or a roller, and which return to their jelly-like state a short time after the shearing action ceases. The advantages are that they do not require stirring before use, that no settlement takes place while the material is in storage, that they are easy to apply, that they can be used with large brushes without any dripping or splashing (thus leading to economy in time and material) and that runs and sags are not likely to occur because the material reverts to its high viscosity before such defects can form. Thixotropic paints should not be confused with materials possessing false body; glaze medium, for instance, possesses high viscosity which breaks down under the shearing action of a brush, but its viscosity is resumed immediately the brushing ceases and before the brushmarks have time to flow out; with thixotropic paints, however, an interval occurs between shearing and the resumption of high viscosity during which the brushmarks do flow out.

Thixotropy can be imparted to certain normal paint formulations by means of modifications and additions made during manufacture; for instance, a thixotropic alkyd can be made by adding a polyamide resin into the alkyd resin cook, yielding a paint with all the normal properties of an alkyd resin as well as thixotropic qualities.

Two drawbacks are met with in thixotropic paints. One is that such paints do not possess the property of filling any surface depressions or indentations in the way that a conventional paint does; instead of this the thixotropic materials closely follow the contours of any defects in the surface. The other drawback is that they tend to sweat when stored and this tendency is increased with any rise in temperature such as that, for instance, caused by exposure to sunlight; the defect may often be overcome by shaking or stirring the paint vigorously and then allowing it to resume its high viscosity.

Thixotropic red lead primer A primer for iron and steel similar to conventional red lead but with a slight modification to produce a jelly structure. Its advantages over the traditional material are that it does not settle in the can and that it flows out to a film reasonably free from brushmarks. When used on clean steel its performance does not seem to be inferior to that of the conventional red lead primer.

Thixotropy From a Greek work meaning "changing by touch", the condition whereby a material possesses a high viscosity while allowed to rest undisturbed, undergoes a reduction in viscosity when shaken or stirred, and resumes its high viscosity when the disturbance ceases.

Tie-in or tying-in A necessary measure in order to give a tubular scaffold stability. An independent scaffold needs to be tied-in to the building, throughout its length. The best method is to extend certain of the transoms to pass through window openings and to couple them to tubes placed inside the building and wedged against the inner wall. Where this is not feasible, some of the transoms are coupled to puncheons wedged into the window openings and tightened by means of reveal pins; when this method is employed a greater number of ties should be provided to compensate for the lesser strength of each individual tie. Ties normally should be provided at the level of the second vertical lift from the ground, and thereafter at every second lift.

Ties (i) Those parts of a stencil pattern which are included in order to hold the plate together and impart strength to it.

(ii) Tubes used to couple a scaffold to some rigid construction in order to form a tie-in to the building.

Tint That which is produced when a colour is lightened or reduced by the addition of white.

Tinters Alternative term for stainers.

Tinting Adjusting the colour of a paint to the precise colour that is required, by means of adding small quantities of stainers.

Tinting strength The staining power of a coloured pigment.

Tip cleaner A device fitted to an airless spray gun which allows a blocked tip to be reversed so that the blockage can be ejected, after which the tip is brought back to its original position.

Tips See *Spray gun tips.*

Titanium dioxide Also known as titanium white. It is a white pigment with remarkable properties. It has far greater opacity and tint resistance than any other white pigment, it is non-toxic, it does not react adversely with paint media and therefore there is no danger of "livering" occurring in any paint pigmented with it, and it is resistant to chemical concentrations in the atmosphere and is therefore not affected by sulphur fumes. It is expensive, but because of its great opacity a high degree of pigmentation is not needed to produce a paint of good hiding power, and it can also be added to paints formulated with other pigments so as to improve their opacity. Titanium dioxide is obtained from the mineral ores ilmenite and rutile, and according to the method of manufacture it can be produced in two forms; these are known as the anatase and the rutile grades. The anatase grade is a cold bluish-white, and if used in exterior finishing paints it causes them to chalk rapidly on exposure. The rutile grade is a slightly creamy white but gives finishes which are resistant to exterior exposure. It is the rutile grade which is of main interest to the painter and decorator; this is the grade that is used in decorative gloss paints, undercoats and emulsion paints, and also in marine paints and in many materials formulated for industrial painting. The anatase grade is used in industrial finishing in the production of household equipment, etc., and for interior work in hospitals and similar places where a brilliant white appearance is required.

Titanium nickel yellow A pigment obtained by the addition of salts of nickel and antimony to titanium hydroxide before calcination. It is a dull yellow in colour but produces clean bright tints when reduced with white. It has excellent heat-resisting properties and is used in the manufacture of heat-resisting paints.

Toe boards Scaffold boards or lengths of wood turned on edge, and running along the boundary of a working platform; together with the guard rails they form a protection to prevent the fall of persons, materials or tools from the platform. Under the Construction Regulations it is required that boards or some other suitable form of barrier be provided on any platform from which it might be possible to fall a distance exceeding two metres (6 ft 6 in.). The height of the toe board or barrier is to be at least 150 mm (6 in.) and the distance between the toe board and guard rail must not exceed 765 mm (30 in.). These measurements were amended under the terms of the Construction (Metrication) Regulations which came into force on 9th November 1984.

Toluol A colourless solvent obtained from coal-tar; because of its low-boiling and fast-evaporating properties it is used as a solvent for hot-sprayed coatings.

Tone A word which is frequently misused. It refers to the amount of light reflected from the surface of a colour irrespective of all other characteristics. From this it will be seen that in a colour circle the colour of lightest tone is yellow and that of deepest tone is violet; when white is added to a colour a lighter tone is produced while the addition of black deepens the tone; the tone is also modified by the amount of light falling upon it and hence the amount of light that can be reflected.

Tooth A characteristic of a dried paint film into which has been mixed a quantity of coarse or abrasive pigment. Tooth improves the rubbing properties and the adhesion of a paint; paints which are to be applied to a smooth non-absorbent surface may have tooth imparted to them by the addition of a crystalline pigment such as silica. Pigments such as graphite are liable to scale due to their greasy nature; this tendency can be checked by adding silica to them to give tooth.

Tosher A slang term used to describe an operative, generally an unskilled workman, employed on rough industrial painting work.

Touching in Applying colour to a very small area.

Transfers Designs for decorative devices, trade marks, etc., which are prepared and printed on thin backing sheets in such a form that they can be affixed to a suitable surface and the backing sheet peeled off; they are available as individual items or in strips or sheets that can be cut into separate items or torn off along perforated lines. There are various types of transfers sold, including the water type in which water-soluble adhesive is the fixative, the spirit type in which a spirit-soluble gum is used, and the heat fixing type in which a thermoplastic resin or gum coating is used with the application of heat; in all these types the adhesive is present on the backing sheet as a thin coat applied after the device has been printed. In addition there is a varnish type, which does not carry an adhesive but to which a varnish coating is applied by the painter, and also a slip-off type which is an extension of the water type. The actual process of application varies according to the particular type of transfer which is being used, but provided the manufacturers' instructions are followed the operation presents no difficulty; the main considerations are to see that the surface to which the transfer is to be applied is perfectly clean, to ensure that no air bubbles are formed and to see that the backing is peeled off without pulling up any part of the transfer design with it.

Translucent A term applied to a substance or material which although not transparent allows light to pass through it.

Transom A term used in scaffolding to denote a short tube spanning between two ledgers and at right angles to them; transoms are spaced at suitable intervals in order to support scaffold boards or a working platform. In an independent scaffold the transom performs the same function as a putlog in a putlog scaffold. Also (in building) a horizontal bar across a window.

Travelling cradle A type of scaffold in which a steel or aluminium alloy track slung from outriggers carries the jockeys from which the cradle is suspended; this permits the cradle to be moved not only up and down but also from side to side in either direction as required.

Tread The horizontal upper part of a step on a staircase, between the vertical risers.

Trestle A trestle consists of two frames or sections hinged together in such a way that when they are closed they lie flat and when open they form a firm support, resting on four feet, for one end of a working platform. The frames consist of rectangular softwood stiles into which cross-bars or bearers, also rectangular and capable of supporting the working platform, are morticed and tenoned. Trestles are generally available in lengths varying between 2 and 4.5 metres when closed. A single trestle is generally referred to in the trade as a pair of trestles.

Trestle scaffold A scaffold in which two or more pairs of trestles are used to provide the supports for a working platform. The Construction Regulations have widened the term to include any scaffold in which the supports for the platform are splitheads, folding stepladders, tripods or similar movable contrivances. The Regulations further lay down that trestle scaffolds (a) shall not be so situated that a person working on the platform might fall a distance of more than 4.5 metres (15 ft); (b) shall not consist of more than one tier if folding supports are used, and (c) shall not be erected on a scaffold platform unless the trestles or supports are firmly attached to the platform and are adequately braced and unless sufficient space is left for the transit of materials along the platform. These requirements are in addition to the usual provisions that the trestle, etc., shall be of sound material, adequate strength and properly maintained.

Trichlorethylene A powerful chlorinated solvent, used as a degreasing agent for metal prior to painting.

Tricresyl phosphate A plasticizer added to cellulose to make it more flexible.

Trimmer A device for removing the selvedge from a roll of wallpaper. In fact practically all wallpapers are now produced in ready-trimmed form, so trimmers are very rarely used. (**NLC**)

Trimming The process of removing the selvedge from wallpapers and other wallcoverings before hanging. On the rare occasions when a wallpaper is supplied with a selvedge, a wheel trimmer and straightedge is usually the most effective method of removing it cleanly. Certain fabric wallcoverings require trimming, but this is usually done by hanging the material in such a way as to overlap the previous length by about 50 mm and then cutting through the overlap on both lengths with a sharp knife or Stanley tool, thus forming a perfect butt joint.

Trowel A tool used by the painter primarily for making good defective plaster work prior to decoration. Plastic paint is sometimes applied with a floating trowel when heavy relief effects are required.

True contrast The contrast obtained by placing side by side two colours which are exactly complementary; in light, by any pair of colours which when added together will produce white light (e.g., yellow and blue, red and blue-green, purple and green); in pigmentary colours, by any pair of colours which when mixed together will produce neutral grey.

Tubular scaffold A form of scaffolding composed of a series of hollow metal tubes, suitably coupled. The tubes may consist of either steel or aluminium alloy; steel tubes may be welded, seamless or close jointed and should be galvanized to make them resistant to corrosion or should be painted or varnished throughout their length; aluminium tubes are seamless and are not usually given any form of surface treatment to protect them from atmospheric attack. Aluminium is, however, softened by alkaline materials and therefore if the scaffold is to be in contact with wet cement, concrete, etc., for any length of time the tubes should be painted. Aluminium alloy tubes are sometimes preferred to steel because of their lightness, but they are not as strong as steel and therefore the deflection of alloy tubes used as horizontal beams is higher than that of steel tubes subjected to the same load; for this reason the standards need to be set more closely together to reduce the deflection of the ledgers.

The selection of tubes and couplers and the whole process of the erection, maintenance and dismantling of tubular scaffold is covered by numerous provisions of the Construction (Safety, Health and Welfare) Regulations, which should be carefully studied by anyone concerned with the use of such scaffolds.

Tumbling or rumbling A method of paint application used in industrial finishing for the treatment of small articles which cannot be satisfactorily coated by other methods. It consists of placing the articles in a drum together with a small quantity of paint, the drum being rotated until the surface of the articles is completely covered. The articles are then placed on a wire mesh to be dried, usually by stoving.

Tung oil See *China wood oil.*

Turkey red An artificial red oxide with high opacity, produced by calcining yellow iron oxide at a relatively low temperature.

Turkey umber A type of umber obtained from Cyprus, and owing its name to the fact that it was originally exported through Turkey. (**NLC**)

Turk's head A large coarse-haired round brush with the hairs set in pitch, mounted on a wooden stock which is attached to a long wooden handle; it is used for limewashing and for rough work generally. (**NLC**)

Turmeric A plant with long leaves and cream flowers, grown in Ceylon, from the rhizomes of which a fine yellow dye is produced that is used in spirit stains. (**NLC**)

Turpentine A solvent obtained by distillation from the oleo-resin of the pine tree. When the trees are eventually felled, having reached the point where they fail to yield any further, a stronger solvent with a pungent smell is obtained by steam distillation from the pinewood stumps and this is known as wood turpentine.

Turpentine is practically the ideal paint solvent. It is clear, limpid and colourless, it evaporates almost completely, leaving no visible residue when exposed in a thin film, and while it readily dissolves all vegetable and mineral oils it does not dissolve the linoxyn formed by the drying of a paint film, for which reason it does not disturb previously applied coatings. In trade practice today, however, it has been completely superseded by white spirit which is considerably cheaper. (**NLC**)

Turpentine substitute White spirit. Also termed turps substitute and known colloquially as sub-turps.

Twin-headed spray gun A type of spray gun designed to spray a protective coating and a catalyst simultaneously so that the two materials mix in the spray pattern after they have left the gun and before they reach the surface. The instantaneous mixing in atomized form eliminates the problem of spraying formulations which have too short a pot life to be mixed before use. The gun is used for spraying various types of two-pack material, including polyurethane lacquers, and can also be used for spray silvering.

Two-knot distemper brush See *Distemper brush.* (**NLC**)

Two-pack materials A term used to describe certain modern materials, such as, for example, the amine-cured epoxy resin coatings, which are supplied in two packs one of which consists of an activator or catalyst which is to be added to the paint immediately before use. When the two materials have been mixed together the pot-life of the product is short, gelation taking place within a few hours.

Two-pack stopper A stopper based on polyester, for use on woodwork and metalwork. The activator is added to the base immediately before use. It sets quickly to a very hard finish.

Two-row stippler A very narrow hair stippler consisting, as the name implies, of only two rows of tufts of hair instead of the usual 175 mm by 125 mm or 150 mm by 100 mm flat surface of the full-sized stippler. It is intended for use in locations too narrow to be reached by a normal stippler, and to enable stippling to be carried right into the angles of sharp corners or into the corners of panels and mouldings.

U

Ullage The air-space above the contents of a closed container. The commonest example relating to painting and decorating is the air-space left above the level of the paint, i.e., between the paint and the lid, in the container in which the paint is supplied. The ullage is necessary to allow for any expansion of the contents that might take place due to temperature changes, etc.

Ulstron ropes Multi-filament polypropylene ropes of soft texture. See *Synthetic ropes*.

Ultramarine blue A fine rich blue pigment with a reddish cast, a colour which is not easily matched with other pigments. It has been used since ancient times, and for many centuries it was a natural product prepared from a semi-precious mineral called lapis lazuli, but this is now only used as an artists' colour. Present-day ultramarine is produced artificially from a mixture of silica, china clay, sulphur and soda ash, subjected to prolonged calcination.

Ultramarine is resistant to alkalis but is very sensitive to acids. When ground in an oil medium it has a strong tendency to settle and cake in the container, the colour of the paint becoming progressively lighter as the work proceeds, and particles of the separated pigment tend to work up under the brush and produce an unfortunate streakiness. Because of these drawbacks its use in oil media is largely restricted to mural and decorative work, but it is an excellent pigment for use in water-thinned paints. Low-grade ultramarine reduced with terra alba is sold as "lime blue" for correcting the colour of limewash.

Ultramarine green A pigment produced in the process of making ultramarine blue; it is reduced and sold as "lime green".

Ultramarine violet Similar in properties to ultramarine blue, but with slight differences of composition and processing.

Ultra-violet rays Non-visible light rays of short wavelength, occurring just beyond the violet end of the spectrum, which are very destructive to paint and varnish films. Known also as actinic rays.

Umber A natural brown earth pigment derived from coloured clays composed of hydrated silicate, the colouring being due to the presence of iron oxides and a high proportion of manganese oxide. The best quality comes from Cyprus and is known as Turkey umber, but umber is also found in Italy, France, the USA and Great Britain. Like all the earth pigments it is permanent, stable and cheap to produce; it is a much better drier than ochre or sienna because of its manganese content, manganese being a powerful drying agent. It possesses good staining strength; the natural product, raw umber, has a peculiar greenish cast and when mixed with white it produces a fine range of cool subtle colours. Raw umber can be calcined to produce burnt umber, which is a rich dark brown colour and when mixed with white gives a much warmer range of colours. Burnt umber has only moderate staining strength, but is very useful in the production of stains and graining colour because of its partial transparency.

Undercoats The coatings applied to a surface after priming and filling or, in the case of previously painted work, after the preparation. The main functions of undercoats are to provide "build" or film thickness, opacity, and the most suitable ground for the reception of the finishing coat, while filling small local depressions in the surface.

Univers A form of sans serif alphabet now widely used. Designed by Adrian Frutiger in the 1950's, it is very similar in appearance to Gill Sans except that none of the capital letters is pointed.

Universal primer A priming material consisting of a drying oil/resin type of medium tinted with white or light-coloured pigments, useful on small-scale maintenance work for the patch-priming of various types of surface such as wood, metal or plaster.

Unseasoned timber Timber which still contains an excessive quantity of moisture; when a tree is freshly felled its moisture content is equal to a hundred percent of the net weight of the timber, and thorough seasoning is required to allow the bulk of this moisture to dry out before the wood is fit for use in joinery. The painting of unseasoned wood is always most unsatisfactory. The contraction of the wood as further drying out takes place loosens the adhesion of the paint film and forces it off, and the pressure of the contained moisture seeking to escape causes blistering, peeling and flaking to occur. If the wood is painted on both sides to that the moisture is completely trapped inside, the wood itself may become rotten.

UPVC Unplasticized polyvinyl chloride. A thermoplastic material used in the production of several items employed in modern building work, such as in various kinds of wall claddings, rainwater goods, window frames, etc. It does not require any protective painting.

UPVC, painting of The impact resistance of new UPVC products may be impaired if normal types of paint are applied on them, although after an interval of from 7 to 10 years the risk becomes negligible. But in fact the decorator is often required to paint them so that they will conform to the colour scheme of the remainder of the structure. When this is the case the method of preparation is exactly the same both for new goods and for components that have undergone a considerable period of weathering. The procedure is to wash them well with a warm detergent solution, followed by rinsing them off thoroughly with plentiful quantities of clean water, afterwards allowing them to dry. They should not be rubbed down with abrasives as this also has the effect of reducing their impact resistance. If impact resistance is not a matter of major importance, ordinary alkyd resin paints can be used; a gloss coating can be applied directly to the surface, but it is better to use an undercoat followed by gloss. It should be remembered, however, that continual painting defeats the purpose of using these components, so it is better to use long-life coatings at less frequent intervals. Another point to remember is that UPVC is thermoplastic, so that if the components are exposed to direct sunlight it would be most unwise to paint them a markedly darker colour than the original colour of the plastic, because the use of dark colours increases the heat absorption of the paint and the underlying surface, and this would adversely affect the plastic.

Urea resins These are practically colourless resins made by combining urea, which is a white crystalline solid, with formaldehyde; they are thermosetting resins and are used in the manufacture of stoving enamels.

Urethane paint A one-pack material composed of urethane-modified oils or alkyds, producing a chemically resistant high gloss paint which is easier to use than chlorinated rubber or epoxy-ester paint.

Urethane/pitch A chemically resistant paint composed of urethane resins combined with coal tar pitch, with properties similar to coal tar/epoxy paints. It has the capacity to cure even at low temperatures and in areas of high humidity. It is usually spray-applied.

V

Vacuum straining A very quick and efficient method of straining paint. It is particularly used on large-scale industrial painting operations, especially those on which airless spray equipment is in use, where a considerable quantity of paint needs to be strained. The basis of the system is that the strainer is connected to the air line, the air valve being turned on when paint is poured into the strainer; this forms a vacuum which draws the paint rapidly through the gauze mesh.

Value The word is used in the Munsell colour system to denote the tone value, i.e., the lightness or darkness, of a colour.

Value cost contract A type of contract on which the sum of money paid to the contractor is calculated as a percentage of a carefully worked out valuation of the work actually completed, based on an agreed schedule of prices. It provides the contractor with a strong incentive to see that the work is carried out economically and efficiently, because if the final cost is below the valuation the contractor's remuneration is increased.

Vandyke brown A deep brown, richer in colour than burnt umber, which used to be derived from a natural peaty earth found in Germany but is now prepared by the partial decomposition of beechwood bark or cork. It is a semi-transparent pigment and besides being sold as an artists' colour it is used by the decorator in making up graining colour and glazes for graining. Although it has a most attractive rich colour it is a very unsatisfactory material to use. It is a very poor drier and has a retarding effect upon oil, and it is very prone to fading; it is used chiefly in water medium, but even in this form it has a bad effect upon the drying of a superimposed varnish film. It is also strongly inclined to cracking.

The material which is sold to the decorator nowadays is not usually true Vandyke brown but an imitation made up from ochre, oxide of iron and lampblack; this is a more durable material but lacks the richness of colour of genuine Vandyke.

Varnish A transparent coating based upon drying oils and natural or synthetic resins. Usually it is designed to present a lustrous protective finish, but it is sometimes formulated to provide a matt finish of a less protective nature.

The traditional form of varnish was known as "oil varnish" and was composed of a hard fossil resin combined with a drying oil, with the addition of a drying agent and a volatile solvent; the two main classifications were long-oil varnishes, intended for outdoor exposure, and short-oil varnishes for indoor work; and within these classifications there were numerous varieties of varnish each formulated for some specific type of work.

Today practically all varnishes are based on synthetic resins such as alkyds, epoxies and polyurethanes; for situations subjected to very severe outdoor weathering conditions a long-life varnish composed of phenolic resin and china-wood oil medium is often used. These are all one-pack materials. Two-pack epoxy and polyurethane varnishes are oil-free.

Varnish brush An oval brush with a filling of fine pure bristle in a stout metal ferrule. An oval brush is the best type for the application of varnish because its shape lends itself to the production of a good, evenly spread film. In fact it is also an ideal brush for applying gloss paint.

Varnishing The application of varnish, the main object of the operation being to produce an even level film free from runs, sags and pinholing and not marred by dust or bittiness. It is essential that varnish should be applied firmly and confidently; if the coating is rubbed out too bare it is practically impossible to obtain an evenly distributed film and the usual result is the formation of runs and the production of a finish with a starved appearance.

Vegetable fibre Coarse material used as the filling for cheap brushes for the application of alkaline materials and for washing down. See *Fibre brushes.*

Vehicle The liquid components of a paint, consisting of the binding medium and the thinner; so called because it "carries" the pigment, or holds it in suspension. See *Medium.*

Veiling The formation of a cobweb pattern during spraying.

Veining horn Another term for graining horn.

Venetian red Originally a natural red iron oxide pigment found in Italy, now generally produced by calcining yellow oxide of iron at a high temperature. It has a strong yellowish or brick red colour and has good staining strength.

Venice turpentine The oleo-resin of the Tyrolean larch. (**NLC**)

Ventilation The provision of a means whereby air can circulate freely in an enclosed area, or by which the air in such an area can be purified.

It is obviously most important that there should be adequate ventilation in any working area where materials producing toxic fumes are in use, or where the operations present the risk of explosion or fire hazards, in addition of course to any safety precautions relating to the particular process. What is less obvious but equally important is that in confined spaces the oxygen in the air is quickly exhausted unless proper measures are taken to provide ventilation; also that in ordinary working areas where materials which in themselves are not toxic are in use (e.g., normal paints, adhesives, etc.) members of the workforce may be affected by symptoms of nausea, sickness or dizziness if the room is not properly ventilated. Similarly when equipment such as steam strippers are in use and the atmosphere becomes excessively humid, the working area should be well ventilated to protect the health of the employees.

On a long-term basis, lack of ventilation causes many problems of another kind, and these are becoming increasingly prevalent. During the 1970's there were several vigorous campaigns sponsored by the Government aimed at conserving fuel and energy, and government subsidies were made available to property owners and tenants to encourage them to instal roof-loft insulation, the double glazing of windows, and the filling of cavity walls with foamed insulating materials. The saving of fuel costs, very often highly exaggerated and based on dubious figures, has become a positive mania exploited by the manufacturers of numerous products, and householders resort to applying thermal insulating materials to walls and ceilings and even to putting draught-proofing strips around the doors. The cumulative effect of these measures is the total elimination of ventilation, especially in properties where the chimney openings have been sealed because of the Clean Air Act. The result has been an enormous increase in the incidence of mould growths encouraged by the condensation of moisture, and this has now reached epidemic proportions. The cost to the country in terms of ill-health among the public and of the deterioration of property is impossible to estimate.

Verd antique Also called Verde Antico or Vert Antique. A beautiful serpentine marble showing irregularly shaped and variable sized patches of white, dark green and black interspersed with a fine network of streaks in various tints and shades of green. There are various methods of imitating the marble, and it may be worked on a ground of white, black or grey.

Verdigris A green crystalline substance, copper acetate, which forms on the surface of copper which is exposed to the atmosphere. Metallic paints based on copper bronze, if not protected by lacquer, are liable to discolour due to the formation of verdigris.

Vermiculite A flaky porous mineral substance which is extremely light in weight and which readily absorbs and retains air and moisture. It is used in the building industry to produce materials for thermal insulation. Vermiculite plasters have excellent acoustic properties, together with anti-condensation and heat-insulating qualities. Vermiculite is also used to a limited extent in finely ground form as a paint filler.

Vermilion A very expensive red pigment consisting of sulphide of mercury which has been used from ancient times; originally it was obtained from a mineral called cinnabar, but it is now produced artificially. It is a fine bright red colour with good opacity, but because of its cost is rarely used except as an artists' colour and for high-class decorative work.

Vert The heraldic term for green.

Vert de mer A marble with a greenish black ground with pronounced veining in white and varying tints and shades of green.

Vinegar A weak solution of acetic acid obtained from various dilute alcoholic fluids; it is used by the painter for neutralizing the effects of caustic paint removers.

Vinyl-based filler A composition supplied as a smooth paste in ready-mixed form, which is used for filling cracks and shallow holes in plaster. It has good adhesion and when dry it presents a somewhat absorbent surface.

Vinyl distempers and vinyl water paints Names that are sometimes given to certain brands of emulsion paint intended solely for interior use and for situations where they are not exposed to severe conditions of wear; they are therefore cheaper than normal emulsion paints.

Vinyl grain filler A quick-setting composition supplied as a smooth paste in ready-mixed form for filling indentations and surface cracks in woodwork. It is absorbent when dry.

Vinyl resins A large group of resins derived from polymerized vinyl acetate or vinyl chloride or a combination of the acetate and chloride polymerized together. As well as being used in the plastics industry they are of great importance in paint manufacture, forming the basis of most of the emulsion paints produced today and being used for other products such as etch primers, protective coatings resistant to splashing or fumes from water solutions of acids, alkalis and salts, etc. In industrial finishing they are used in lacquers for roller coatings. They are also used very widely in the production of vinyl wallpapers and other wallhangings.

Vinyl wallcoverings See *PVC-coated fabrics* and *PVC-coated papers*.

Vinyl wallpapers These were introduced shortly after the development of PVC-coated fabrics and are now the most important single group of papers in present-day production. They are composed of paper which is coated or laminated with PVC and are printed in special inks and dyes which are fused into the surface. They are resistant to chemical attack and withstand washing and mild scrubbing with detergents, and have a reasonable degree of resistance to abrasion or mechanical damage; they are therefore suitable for use in situations where they are subjected to fairly severe treatment. When redecoration is needed, the PVC facing can be peeled away dry from the paper backing. Vinyl is also applied to many wallhangings which have a delicate appearance but are actually quite strong, a notable example being the range of vinyl flocks.

Violet pigment See *Carbazole violet*.

Viridian See *Guignet's green*.

Viscometer An instrument for measuring the viscosity of a paint. Torsion or paddle viscometers and falling-ball viscometers are described under the heading of *Paint testing* but these of course are laboratory instruments for paint technologists. The form of viscometer used by the operative painter as a means of maintaining the quality of a finish from one batch of paint to another is the flow cup, the most popular type of which is the Ford cup. This is of greater importance in industrial painting and vehicle painting than in normal painting and decorating work.

V

Viscose A chemical form of cellulose from which one kind of artificial silk is made. As such it is the constituent of many forms of wallhanging both for domestic work and for contract wallcoverings.

Viscosity The internal resistance to motion or flow possessed by a liquid, which is measured in terms of the force required to overcome it. For practical purposes it can be understood as the "stickiness" of a fluid.

The more viscous a liquid is the more slowly it flows. The viscosity of a paint medium is therefore clearly of the utmost importance, having a direct bearing upon the ease or lack of ease of its application, and its suitability for application by various methods such as by brushing, spraying, dipping, etc.

For certain industrial painting operations the viscosity of the material is a critical factor in the success or otherwise of the painting system, and for this reason it is important that it should be accurately assessed. Details of a method of determining the viscosity are given in BS 3900: Part A6. It should be noted, however, that this method cannot be applied to thixotropic paints, the apparent viscosity of which is not an indication of their true viscosity.

Visor A form of eye-screen, hinged to become the movable part of a helmet and which also gives some measure of protection to the face; it is used in situations where the eyes are at risk, either through the splashing of caustic substances or the impact of hard particles of material in the course of such operations as chipping, scraping, or wire-brushing. Advice should be sought from a reputable manufacturer of safety equipment as to the best type for any particular purpose.

Volatile A word meaning "readily evaporating", derived from the Latin *volare*, to fly. Hence we speak of a "volatile solvent", meaning a paint solvent which evaporates freely when exposed to the air, leaving no part behind in the dried paint film.

Volatilization A process used in the preparation of certain pigments including antimony white, carbon black, zinc oxide and basic lead sulphate, in which the raw materials are heated and converted to gases from which the pigment is deposited on cooling. Pigments produced by this process are characterized by their fineness and smoothness of working.

Vulcanized oil Also called sulphurized oil. A vegetable drying oil, e.g. linseed oil, perilla oil, etc., which has been reacted with sulphur or sulphur chloride. Such an oil possesses a higher degree of chemical resistance than the untreated oil, but the outstanding feature of a vulcanized oil is its ability to set very rapidly even while the paint film of which it is a part is still quite wet; because of this property it is possible to include it in a paint formulation which permits a second coat to be applied before the first coat is dry, without picking up, such formulations being the basis of the wet-on-wet process.

Vulcanized rubber An insoluble cement made of a compound of rubber and sulphur subjected to heat treatment, which is used to lock the bristles of a brush firmly into place.

Vynaglypta A solid-backed low-relief material, similar in appearance to Lincrusta, and produced by embossing a thick vinyl coating on a pulp paper backing. It is supplied in a white washable finish, but can be coated to any desired colour with emulsion paint, etc., after hanging.

W

Wainscot oak Another term for quartered oak.

Wallboards Building boards and sheetings used to form a rigid lining construction for walls and ceilings; the term includes hardboards, plasterboards, fibre boards, insulating boards, etc., details of which are given under the appropriate headings.

Wall brush or flat wall brush A rather vague term which refers to a flat paint brush of a sufficiently large size to be used to apply flat and semi-gloss oil paint economically to broad surfaces. In various parts of the country it is known by colloquial terms such as wallboard, wallband, weatherband, etc. The term "wall brush" can be used to refer to brushes of various widths such as 75 mm, 100 mm, 125 mm, 150 mm and 175 mm.

Wall claddings Non-structural (i.e. non-load-bearing) coverings to interior or exterior walls.

Wallpaper Wood-pulp paper upon which colour is applied either in the form of a regularly repeated pattern of specific size or as a random effect devoid of any regularly repeated feature; the design may be enhanced by embossing or some other form of relief. It is supplied in rolls that can be cut to any required length by the paperhanger, and the width is such that the cut lengths can conveniently be handled by the paperhanger working singly, and pressed into contact with a ceiling or wall surface by means of a suitable adhesive.

Wallpaper can be classified either as machine printed or hand printed. Machine printing is a mass-produced process taking advantage of all the latest technological developments, whereas hand-printed papers are printed usually from silk screens but occasionally from blocks, each colour being printed separately and each roll of paper being treated individually. Obviously hand printing is very slow compared with a mechanical process, and it would be quite impossible to satisfy even a fraction of the demand for wallpaper by this means. In fact, of course, the overwhelming majority of papers are machine printed, and hand printing accounts for only a tiny proportion of wallpaper production. But although machine printing is very rapid, the initial cost of bringing a pattern right through from the design stage into production is very high, and the paper can be sold cheaply only if its sales are on a big enough scale to be economically viable. Hand-printed papers appeal to customers who want to have something of an individual nature rather than buy a pattern which is widely available on the mass market, or who wish to have a pattern printed to a particular colour scheme. One great advantage is that hand printing can be used to produce patterns with an unusually large repeat; the dimensions of the rollers used in machine printing set a definite limit on the length of the repeat.

In recent years the methods of wallpaper production have altered considerably. At one time the majority of papers were printed in distemper colours, with a very small proportion printed in oil colours and subsequently varnished for use in steamy atmospheres. Today, vinyls account for the greater part of wallpaper production and the old sanitary papers and varnished papers have been rendered obsolete. Similarly, a high proportion of present-day papers are pre-pasted, and practically all are supplied in ready-trimmed form. Many papers are now produced with a view to making their removal easier when the time comes for redecoration.

Wallpaper, history of The definitive work giving an accurate description of the development of wallpaper production from its earliest days to the first part of the 20th century was published in 1926. It is called *A History of English Wallpaper, 1509–1914* by A. V. Sugden and J. L. Edmondson, and was published by the great firm of Batsford. It is a truly magnificent book, and it would be quite impossible for anyone now or in the future to produce a comparable book because so much of the source material has vanished for ever. The sheer physical size of the book is amazing—it measures 336 mm × 267 mm × 51 mm thick—but what is far more to the point is the superb quality. It must be one of the most handsome volumes ever printed. There are 70 wonderful colour plates and 190 half-tone illustrations. The cost of producing the blocks was borne by the old Wallpaper Manufacturers Ltd., and accounted for more than would ever be raised by the sale of the book. The history is traced from the tapestries and painted cloths of the 15th and 16th centuries and the oldest surviving patterned paper, a pomegranate design measuring 406 mm × 280 mm made in 1509, through the 18th-century developments, the famous pioneer designs, the Chinese papers and their English imitations, and the late Georgian period; then on to the introduction of machinery, the work of William Morris, Owen Jones and Walter Crane, and the evolution of techniques in washable, embossed and flock papers and the raised materials for relief decorations. Then follows a fascinating account of all the wallpaper mills, based on the mill records. This book is unique; nothing of the kind had ever been attempted before, and now many of the historic wallpapers have perished and disintegrated, the mill records have been dispersed or destroyed, and most of the firms no longer exist.

Wallpaper pasting machine See *Pasting machine*.

Wallpaper, standard dimensions From 1963 onwards the size of a roll of machine-printed wallpaper of British manufacture has been standardized at 10.05 metres long (11 yards) by 533 mm wide when trimmed. Prior to this the length was 11½ yards. The reduction was made so that British paper would conform to the dimensions used by Continental manufacturers. The British Standard Specification was amended accordingly in August 1963.

The strange thing is that some Continental wallpapers on sale in Great Britain are not made to these dimensions, and in some cases there is a considerable variation. American manufacturers use a different standard; their wallpapers are supplied in rolls of 6.4 metres (7 yards) or in double rolls of 12.8 metres (14 yards), the width being 533 mm.

Walnut A highly decorative wood obtained from a tree of the Juglandaceae family which is native to Asia Minor but which is now widely distributed in many parts of the world. It is used to a considerable extent in furniture manufacture and cabinet making, being a wood that works easily and takes a good polish. The grain is rather obscure, but the colouring gives a strong impression of grain markings. Walnut shows very great variations of colour ranging through grey-brown, grey-green, greyish yellow and grey-red, the curly bands of the contrasting tones flowing over the surface regardless of the boundaries of the annual rings. Burred wood, obtained from the Mediterranean countries, is in very great demand by cabinet makers. Walnut is a favourite wood with grainers and the methods of imitating the wood are legion. It may be grained in either oil or water medium.

Warp laminates or warps Also known in America as "Warp laid yarns". These have been fairly recently introduced into the range of textile wallcoverings. They take their name from the process of weaving, in which the warp consists of parallel threads through which the weft is passed at right angles to form the woven fabric. In warp laminates, however, the weft is dispensed with and only the warp is used; this is carefully laid on to a paper base coated with adhesives, the threads running in parallel lines. One of the benefits is that the material is hung like wallpaper, lengths being placed side by side, but no joints are visible as they are concealed by the strands of fabric.

Various kinds of fabric are used in manufacturing the laminate. It has been found that linen, wool and natural silk are the most satisfactory as they do not readily attract smoke and dust. Cotton does not attract them either, but unfortunately when it does become soiled it is difficult to clean. Man-made fibres are not a success, as they have a strong tendency to attract dirt and are not easily cleaned when part of a wall fabric. Jute has been tried but has the disadvantage of fading very rapidly.

Wash coat See *Pre-treatment primers*.

Wash-down brush A coarse fibre brush which can be used for washing down with alkaline detergents without sustaining damage.

Wash primer See *Pre-treatment primers*.

Washability The extent to which dirt can be removed from a decorated surface without damaging the face of the decoration.

Washable distemper A mixture of whiting, borax and lime, bound with casein, which when hard can to some extent be sponged down. Now completely obsolete in Great Britain. (**NLC**)

Washables The name used by wallpaper manufacturers and retailers for papers with a coating that gives them a washable surface.

Washing down Removing grime from a painted surface, or washing a painted surface preparatory to repainting, often with the aid of sugar soap. See *Sugar soap* for further details.

Water colours Artists' colours made by grinding suitable pigments into aqueous gums or shellac solutions.

Water gilding This is a gilding process used on very high-class work, that produces either the very highest degree of shine or lustre or else the most exquisite matt finish. It is an extension of the tip-and-cushion method of gilding, and it is a very highly skilled specialist operation.

A special kind of water size is used. "Burnish size" produces the high-lustre gilding; it consists of parchment or gelatine size with the addition of pipeclay and blacklead in its composition. "Matt size" produces the matt finish, and this contains pipeclay, Armenian bole and other ingredients. Both burnish size and matt size are supplied in ready-prepared form by the gold-beating firms from whom gold leaf is obtained.

In both burnish and matt gilding the initial stages of the water-gilding process are exactly the same. First the surface to be gilded is bodied up with several coats of gelatine size and whiting. This is followed by five or six coats of either burnish size or matt size applied with a camel-hair brush; each coat is allowed to dry hard and is then rubbed down with a very fine grade of sandpaper. When the work is fully bodied up, the surface is gilded with water alone; this is done by wetting the size freely with a camel-hair brush fully charged with water, and the loose-leaf gold is applied immediately by the tip-and-cushion method. This requires great speed and dexterity, because the water is very quickly absorbed into the size; the gilder usually holds both the camel-hair brush and the tip in the same hand, and lays the gold leaf as soon as the water is passed over the surface.

When the gilding is dry, the next stage depends on whether a brilliant lustrous or a matt finish is required. For the lustrous finish, the gold is polished by rubbing it lightly and carefully with an agate burnisher, and this produces a mirror-like finish that looks exactly like solid gold. For the matt finish the dry gold is coated with clear parchment size which is sometimes coloured with a few drops of ormolu. Ormolu is prepared from white shellac dissolved in spirits of wine and tinted with "dragon's blood". Sometimes a piece of ornamental work is carried out partly in matt gold and partly in burnished gold to provide a contrast.

Water gilding is used where the very finest quality of gilded work is required, and it demands the highest level of craftsmanship on the part of the gilder. Examples are to be seen in various well-known buildings. In one of the brochures produced by Campbell Smith & Co. Ltd., the famous firm of decorators, showing examples of their work, there is an illustration of the stone reredos in the chapel of Eton College where water gilding finished with the agate burnisher was used with superb results.

Water paint The term is not used indiscriminately for any water-thinned material but is applied specifically to an oil-bound water paint. This material has now been completely superseded by emulsion paints.

Waterproof sandpaper An abrasive made for the wet rubbing down of paintwork, which is cleaner and more effective than dry rubbing down. Wet rubbing down is compulsory by law for any painted surface containing lead. See *Abrasive papers*.

Water-repellent fluids Colourless, or relatively colourless, liquids intended to increase the resistance to rain penetration of porous and absorbent walls that are substantially free from cracks. They may consist of solutions or emulsions of water-repellent substances such as waxes, oils, resins or fats, or of metallic soaps such as aluminium stearate, but those in general use today are based upon silicone resins. The liquids are applied by brush or spray, preferably during a spell of dry weather. Before they are applied the surface should be carefully examined and all defects made good. For further details, see under *Silicone resins*.

Water resistance The ability of a surface coating to resist the passage of water in liquid form.

Water size See *Water gilding*.

Water stain A stain consisting either of vegetable dyes in solution or of semi-transparent pigments bound with gum arabic. See *Stain*.

Water-thinned paints This term can be very misleading; it appears to be self-explanatory, and it would be logical to use it in reference to any sort of coating that is thinned with water, but in fact there are many water-thinned materials which are not usually referred to in this way. For instance, emulsion paint is very rarely described as "water-thinned paint"; the specific term "emulsion paint" is nearly always used for the sake of clarity.

Generally speaking, the term is used to define products developed by paint technologists as alternatives to traditional coatings. In industrial finishing processes the advantages of water-thinned paints are (a) reduced fire hazards, and (b) the elimination of the heavy wastage caused by the evaporation of highly volatile solvents. An obvious example relates to the use of cellulose products, where a significant proportion of the cost goes to pay for a large quantity of expensive solvents which evaporate rapidly, presenting the risk of fire and explosion, and which form no part of the finished coating. In the car industry today considerable use is made of water-thinned primers, primer-surfacers, and other coatings.

In the case of painting and decorating, the value of water-thinned paints lies chiefly in the saving of time which results from being able to apply primer, undercoats and finishing material in quick succession, in the speed at which the paints can be applied and in the absence of residual paint odour. A typical example is the use of acrylic paints in present-day decoration.

Wax The name given to various animal, vegetable or mineral substances which possess a certain lustre and resemble fats in that they are lighter than water and melt upon heating. Beeswax, which is secreted by bees and is obtained by heating the honeycombs in water, is used in the preparation of wax polishes and wax stains. Paraffin wax, the most important of the mineral waxes, is used in the manufacture of certain kinds of flat varnish and also as a stiffening agent in spirit paint removers.

Wax stains Preparations composed of semi-transparent pigments mixed with beeswax and thinned with turpentine, used for the treatment of hardwoods. They are brushed on and allowed to dry, and then polished with a short soft-haired polishing brush or a piece of coarse fabric.

Weather-boarding See *Clapboard*.

Weathering Undergoing the effects of exposure to the atmosphere, e.g., the weathering of a paint film when subjected to outdoor exposure, the weathering of new steelwork in order to loosen the mill scale, etc.

Webbing A fault which occasionally develops in a paint film during drying, and which takes the form of a fine network of wrinkles extending over the surface. It is similar to frosting and is generally caused by the swelling of the partially dried surface skin.

Welding primer A material formulated to allow welding without the joint being weakened and without the production of toxic fumes. It is less protective than any of the inhibitive primers, and for this reason the welded area should be re-primed as soon as possible.

Wet edge Also termed the "live edge"—see the section under this heading.

Whenever a large surface area is being painted, the customary procedure is to paint and lay off the work in sections, blending each section into the previous one while the paint is still fluid enough for this to happen without any laps becoming apparent. For example, if a flush door is being coated with gloss paint the upper part of the door is laid in and the paint levelled by means of crossing it and laying it off; the lower part is then painted, joining it into the edge of the upper portion. If a large wall is being painted it is often necessary for two or more painters to work together as a team. The first painter lays in an approximately square section and levels it off, and then begins to lay in another section which joins the first section along its vertical edge; meanwhile the second painter begins to lay in a section below the first one, joining the two sections together along their horizontal edge. According to the size of the wall there may be a third painter following the second, a fourth following the third, and so on, although normally a wall of such dimensions would call for spray application. In each case the wet edge is where one section joins the previous one. In each and every case and whatever the method of application the important thing is that the edges must be joined up while the paint is still "open" and the edges "live"—in other words, while it is still sufficiently fluid to blend without showing any joints or laps.

Wet-edge time The length of time that a film of a given brand of paint remains sufficiently fluid for the edges to be joined up without laps becoming apparent. The wet-edge time depends chiefly on the formulation of the paint, but it can be affected by atmospheric conditions, fluctuations of temperature and the absorbency of the surface. See also the sections relating to wet-edge time under the headings of *Paint testing* and *Paint testing—British Standards*.

Wet-on-wet A system of paint application used in industrial finishing whereby several coats are applied by spray at short intervals, each coat being applied while the previous coat is still wet. This is made possible by the use of vulcanized oil which possesses the property of setting rapidly while the paint of which it is a constituent is still wet.

Wet-or-dry sandpaper See *Abrasive papers*.

Wet rubbing down Any system of rubbing down paintwork that involves the use of a liquid lubricant; it is generally understood as referring to the use of a waterproof abrasive paper in conjunction with water, although occasionally other substances such as pumice stone may still be used with water, and when steel wool is being used to remove rust from iron or steel the lubricant is white spirit. Under the terms of the Approved Code of Practice for the Control of Lead at Work Regulations, there is in section 6 an absolute requirement that wet rubbing down must be used on lead-painted surfaces.

Wetting The ability of a paint medium to spread uniformly and rapidly over the surface of the pigment particles. This is a matter of great importance in paint formulation; if the pigment is merely dispersed in the medium and not thoroughly wetted, the particles tend to fall through the medium and settle in a hard cake at the bottom of the container. Surrounding the pigment particles, and very often firmly attached to them, is a layer of moist air and sometimes a layer of gas, and it is necessary that the medium should be able to expel these substances and take the place that they ocupied; the wetting power of the medium is the extent of its ability to do this.

Whirling In industrial finishing, a method of speeding up the drying of small painted articles by means of centrifugal action.

White Japan A very loose and inaccurate term sometimes used by painters to mean an ordinary white gloss paint. (**NLC**)

White lac Shellac which has been bleached with alkali.

White lead A basic carbonate of lead which for untold years has been the most important material for the protective painting of property in Britain. In this respect it has many outstanding and unique characteristics—its ability to combine with drying oils and thus produce a lead soap to form a tough, leathery, elastic film of very great durability; its opacity; its smooth brushing properties making for easy application; and the fact that it breaks down by a gentle chalking action rather than by cracking, thus being more easily and cheaply prepared for repainting than other types of paint. Its greatest drawback is its toxic content, which has led to its virtual withdrawal from the market in conformity with EEC requirements. (**NLC**)

White plastic wallpaper An embossed paper with a white vinyl overprint.

White shellac A material used in the preparation of ormolu. See *Water gilding*.

White spirit A solvent produced by the distillation of crude petroleum which has now almost completely replaced turpentine as the paint solvent in normal use in the trade, being considerably cheaper and for all practical purposes just as effective. It is sometimes known as turps substitute and in some quarters the term is still used disparagingly, but a good quality of white spirit is colourless and evaporates without leaving any residue.

Cheap grades of white spirit should be avoided, as any residue which fails to evaporate does not oxidize and take its place as part of the film as residual turpentine does, but remains greasy and may retard the hardening of the paint film.

White textured paper An embossed paper similar to Anaglypta.

Whitewash Any cheap form of distemper based on whiting loosely bound with glue, glue size, casein or similar binder. (**NLC**)

Whiting A material prepared by grinding and pulverizing natural chalk. It is one of the two constituents of putty, the other being linseed oil. At one time it was very widely used in decorating, being the sole constituent of distemper apart from a very small quantity of glue size added as the binder; in this connection it has the strange property of losing its opacity when mixed with water and regaining it as the water evaporates. Distemper is now completely obsolete except for scenic painting, where its great luminosity and its total absence of sheen make it unrivalled for use under the powerful stage lighting.

Wiped glaze effects Broken colour effects that are sometimes used on plastic paint. The textured plastic paint, when dry, is coated with paint to reduce its porosity and brought to an eggshell finish. When this is dry a lightly tinted scumble glaze is applied over the whole surface and hair-stippled to distribute the colour evenly; a soft rag is then drawn over the surface so that the glaze is removed from the relief portions but is retained in the hollows, which enhances the appearance of the texture.

Wiping out The production of decorative effects by means of lifting part of a coating while it is still wet in order to reveal the ground, e.g., in glazed and scumbled effects, in figure graining, etc.

Wire brush An abrasive tool with a rubbing surface formed with clumps or tufts of stiff steel wire, used for the removal of rust and mill scale from iron and steel surfaces, and for general harsh scouring purposes.

Wire-drawn brush A brush in which the bristle is drawn through holes in the base of the brush in separate tufts and secured on the reverse side by wire. Brushes set in this way are usually those which are to be used dry, such as dusters, paperhangers' brushes, etc.

Wood alcohol A crude alcohol known also as wood naphtha or wood spirit, which has good solvent properties but is not generally used because of its toxic qualities; it is sometimes used in paint removers.

Wood chip boards Also known as "Particle boards".

Building boards consisting of chips or particles of wood and a resinous binder, compressed to form a thick high-density board. Various grades of surface finish are available, some being smooth and ready for immediate painting, and others being rather coarse and needing to be filled before painting.

Wood chip papers Another name for "Ingrain papers". Wallpapers consisting of stout substantial pulps into which wood chips and various kinds of fibrous material are introduced during manufacture so as to produce a texture. They are very popular, as when used on uneven or cracked plasterwork they tend to conceal the defects in the surface. Some are supplied in attractive colourings that are complete in themselves and need no further treatment, but many of them are supplied in a form which is intended to be coated with emulsion paint after application.

Wood oil See *China wood oil.*

Wood preservatives Fluids made for the protection of timber in situations where a paint treatment would be impracticable. They generally consist of either coal-tar derivatives, creosote, spirit-soluble metallic compounds such as copper or zinc naphthenates, or water-soluble metallic salts such as zinc chloride, mercuric chloride, copper sulphate, etc.

Wood stains A general term covering a very wide range of materials used to protect and to enhance the appearance of both exterior and interior woodwork. All the major manufacturers offer a complete range of such materials. They are available for both hardwoods and softwoods, with exterior qualities suitable for such diverse surfaces as smoothly finished doors and window frames, for the variable finishes of fascias and claddings, garden sheds and garden furniture, benches, etc., and for the rougher woodwork of fencing, trelliswork and gates, as well as interior qualities for doors, panelling, boarded ceilings, cabinets, shelving, and both structural and decorative woodwork of all kinds.

A great deal of care and research has been given to the formulation of these materials, and the types of system recommended and the ingredients used vary considerably from one manufacturer to another. It is advisable to obtain information from several makers in order to compare them and make a selection best suited to the particular piece of work in hand.

Wood turpentine See *Turpentine.*

Wood wool slabs These are a form of building board composed of long wood fibres loosely bound up with Portland cement, and having a very open surface. Generally they are rendered or plastered after fixing. If, however, a paint or emulsion paint coating is to be applied directly on the bare slabs, spray application is advisable, but if an oil paint is being used an alkali-resisting primer is needed because of the highly alkaline nature of the cement.

Wool Wool must be the oldest textile known to the human race, and used for clothing ever since sheep and goats were first reared by men. Most people only think of wool in terms of clothing and carpets, but it was used for making rich tapestries and other wallhangings from early days. Today it is available to the decorator in many forms. Laminated woollen wallcoverings are of particular interest both for their subtle colourings and because they present an all-over texture with no joints visible. Those sold for domestic decoration are very little thicker than ordinary wallpapers, and provide a material of great distinction and charm at reasonable cost. The contract wallcoverings are considerably more substantial, and provide a most luxurious texture with great varieties of rich colour within each single pattern. The firm of Ernest Turner Ltd markets a fine range of what are called Barra wallcoverings which are produced entirely in the UK; they consist of 100 percent new wool yarn laminated to a tough paper backing, which gives a strong resilient material of great stability, ideal for hotels, restaurants, offices and public buildings of all kinds. The finish is soft, warm and pleasant to the touch, and the irregularly spaced bands of colour ranging from pale creams to deep warm browns give a gorgeous rich appearance.

Working rules These form an agreement drawn up jointly by the employers' and operatives' associations to define the conditions of employment in all branches of the construction industry, e.g., wage rates, allowances for night work, overtime, travelling time, holiday pay, safety procedures, employment of young persons, the procedures for dealing with disputes, termination of employment, etc. In addition to the national working rules there are regional working rule agreements relating to the variations in certain localized areas. Revisions and amendments are published in printed form from time to time.

Wrap-back A defect in electrostatic spraying whereby paint is deposited on the gun handle and on the operator, caused by holding the gun too far away from the object which is being sprayed.

Wrap-round effect A term used to describe a particular feature which occurs in electrostatic spraying, in which the paint not only coats the near-side of the article facing the spray but also travels round to the far side, with the result that an even coating of paint is applied all round the object. This is due to the fact that the atomized particles of paint are electrically charged and the object to be sprayed is earthed; the paint is electrically attracted to the earthed object.

Wren Sir Christopher Wren who lived from 1632 to 1723 was an architectural genius without parallel, and yet by training he was a scientist and his first building was not erected until 1662 when he was 30 years old. At that time he was the Savilian Professor of Astronomy at Oxford. He came into prominence as an architect as a result of the Great Fire of London in 1666, after which his whole life was devoted to construction. Most people think of him solely in terms of St. Paul's Cathedral which is indeed a great work, the building of which extended over a period of 35 years, but it was only one of a vast number of works he carried out. Probably his most outstanding feat was immediately after the Great Fire; in the disaster 443 acres were gutted and 13700 houses destroyed, yet Wren's drive and ability were such that he rebuilt the area and rehoused the homeless people in just under 3 years. This was without the benefit of motor transport, electrical gear, or computers.

Wren's other building work included several Royal palaces including Hampton Court and a huge new palace at Winchester, numerous college buildings at Oxford and Cambridge, the Observatory and the Royal Naval College at Greenwich, the Guildhall, the Royal Exchange, the Royal Hospital at Chelsea, many city livery halls, several fine houses, and 51 churches in the City of London alone. Each of his 51 churches was an architectural masterpiece, each was unique, totally different from one another, and each one filled with superb craftsmanship of all kinds—stone masonry and sculpture, carved woodwork, wrought ironwork, modelled plasterwork, painting and gilding. In everything he did he surrounded himself with wonderful craftsmen, choosing them with the greatest care and from then onwards treating them as equals. And when towards the end of his days inferior men made his life a misery with their jealousies and intrigues, he treated them with quiet courtesy and dignity.

Wren is included in this dictionary because he, probably more than any other architect of any period, appreciated the value of craftsmanship and was aware that the success of any project depends upon the existence of a proper understanding between architect and craftsmen. He realized that however brilliant the architect may be as a creative designer, the finished building will be unsatisfactory unless the craftsmen are able to interpret the design with imagination, insight and skill. Once he knew that a member of his team was reliable he had the confidence to let that person execute the work to the best of his ability and bring his own distinctive skills to bear upon it. For this reason his relationship with his craftsmen brought out the very best in them. He recognized their skill and practical knowledge without which his designs could not be translated into fact, and they for their part recognized his genius—a perfect combination. The records show that he loved to meet them socially on equal terms, dining with them at the end of the day, and that they regarded it as the greatest honour and privilege to be members of his team.

Unfortunately subsequent developments in the organization of building work have led increasingly to the depression of the crafts into a totally subservient role, widening the gap between the designer and the practical craftsman till there is no longer any point of contact between them, and reducing the status of the crafts to the level of semi-skilled or unskilled labour with no responsibility for the outcome of a project. This is not good for the image of the industry, not good either for the professional people or the craftsmen, and not good for the consumer, the general public.

Wrinkling See *Rivelling*.

Writer A sable signwriting brush terminating in a chisel edge, as opposed to a "pencil", which is pointed.

Writer's gold size See *Japan gold size*.

Wrought iron Very pure iron mixed with a little slag in the form of iron oxide or silicate, which is rolled and hammered after it leaves the furnace. The slag forms fibres in the iron which make it different from cast iron which is crystallized metal. Wrought iron resists rusting; it is very tough but can be hammered into shape. When new it is generally covered with a thin layer of millscale.

Xylol A solvent obtained by the distillation of coal tar. It is highly flammable, although in comparison with toluol it is less flammable and evaporates more slowly, but it evaporates far more quickly than white spirit. Because of its evaporation rate it is not greatly used in paints intended for brush application, but some of the non-convertible paints such as chlorinated rubber contain a high proportion of xylol in their thinner. Xylol is also widely used in spray-applied industrial finishing products, both stoving and air-drying.

Yellow One of the primary colours. Yellow pigments include yellow ochre, yellow oxide of iron, zinc chrome, certain cadmium pigments, and titanium nickel yellow which is used in heat-resisting paints.

Yellowing The discolouration of a paint on ageing whereby it develops a progressively deepening yellowish tinge. This is most noticeable in white and light grey paints and in clear varnish finishes.

Yorkshire pattern distemper brush See *Distemper brush.*

Z

Zinc A bluish-white metal element found in many parts of the world. It is permanent in dry conditions but is liable to corrode in both alkaline and acidic conditions. A number of alloys are formed by combining zinc with other metals. Probably the most significant use of zinc in building is as a protective coating for steel; for this purpose it is applied by various methods such as hot dipping, hot spraying, electro-galvanizing, etc.

Zinc surfaces, whether in the form of sheet zinc or galvanized iron, present certain difficulties in respect of paint coatings. When normal paints are applied to new zinc or zinc-coated surfaces they tend very quickly to develop extensive flaking and peeling, especially when exposed to the weather. This is partly due to the smooth greasy nature of the metal which offers little adhesion to paint, and partly to the fact that a chemical reaction takes place between the metal and the paint medium which causes loosely adhering zinc soaps to form at the surface. If, however, the metal is allowed to weather for a period of about six months the surface becomes inactive and paint will adhere fairly well. In this case a first coat of either calcium plumbate primer or zinc chromate primer should be used.

When an immediate paint treatment is required, some form of chemical pre-treatment is necessary. The most satisfactory of these, after any rust that is present has been removed, is a two-pack etching primer. This should be followed by a coat of calcium plumbate primer, or if the use of lead is prohibited a coat of zinc chromate primer. In the case of previously painted galvanized iron, rust should be removed by wire-brushing and then the same priming procedure followed.

Structural steelwork when exposed to severe corrosive conditions is often given a hot-sprayed metal coating of zinc. When this is done, and it is intended that it should be reinforced with a painting system on top, an etching primer should be applied as a sealer to the zinc coating within 48 hours, otherwise corrosive products may develop which would affect the adhesion of the paint.

Apart from considerations of the painting of zinc-coated surfaces, the main interest of zinc to the painter is its use as a constituent of paint. Zinc pigments offer a number of attractive qualities, including fineness of particle size, good colour retention, and strong anti-corrosive properties.

Zinc chloride A white deliquescent substance made by dissolving zinc in hydrochloric acid, which is used in certain kinds of wood preservative fluid to discourage fungoid growths.

Zinc chromate primer A priming paint with very useful rust-inhibitive properties. It is not affected by exposure to sulphuretted hydrogen, and is particularly useful for the shop priming of steel because it can be safely left for several months before the succeeding coats are applied. It is also useful where obliteration with a minimum number of coats is required and where a red lead primer would be too strong in colour to be covered easily. Zinc chromate can be incorporated in several different types of medium and can therefore be adapted to brushing, spraying or dipped application and to either air-drying or stoving paints. As it is non-poisonous there is no restriction upon spraying it. Zinc chromate primer is generally considered to be the most suitable primer for use on the metal aluminium.

Zinc chrome A pale lemon pigment with very poor opacity; it is mixed with Guignet's green and certain blue pigments to produce a range of greens.

Zinc dust A material of pronounced rust-inhibitive properties made by the vaporization of metallic zinc. Its main use is in primers for the protection of steelwork. See *Zinc-rich primers*.

Zinc naphthenate A compound which is soluble in white spirit and in naphtha and which gives rot-proofing solutions with toxic properties that are effective against woodworm and other wood pests.

Zinc oxide A permanent white pigment produced by the volatilization of metallic zinc which, because of its fine texture, was widely used in enamels and gloss paints made with oil or varnish media. Since the introduction of titanium oxide and of alkyd and other synthetic resins, its use for these purposes has declined and very little is now used. An extremely fine colloidal type of zinc oxide is used, however, in combination with other pigments in order to give increased gloss retention in certain kinds of gloss paint today. It is also used in cellulose nitrate lacquers for industrial finishing, and it is used as an artists' colour under the name of Chinese white.

Zinc phosphate primer A recently developed primer with very strong anti-corrosive properties. It is non-toxic and is compatible with a wide range of media. Its qualities are such that it is replacing red lead as a primer for steelwork and many authorities consider it to be better than zinc chromate for priming steel.

Zinc-rich paints or zinc-rich primers Paints made entirely with zinc dust and medium. In most cases the zinc dust content is between 92 and 95 percent of the dried film, but there is one type in which the proportion of zinc dust in the dried film is only 80 percent. The small amount of medium is generally of the non-oxidizing type; polystyrene, epoxies, acrylics, vinyls, and chlorinated or isomerized rubber are used. Zinc dust is also used in an inorganic zinc silicate primer in which the medium is a silicon ester.

Zinc-rich primers have very powerful rust-inhibitive properties, and are of great value in the priming of steel, which they protect by means of an electrochemical action due to the fact that the metal particles are in contact with each other and with the steel; the paint film behaves in the same way as a film of metallic zinc in the presence of an electrolyte. It is claimed that the rust-inhibitive action of zinc-rich paints is so strong that they will protect steelwork from further corrosion even if it is rusty when they are applied, but obviously the cleaner the metal surface at the time of application the more effective they will be; in fact, for all practical purposes the rule is that blast-cleaning is essential where zinc-rich primers are to be used.

Some difficulty may be experienced in choosing a suitable undercoating and finishing system to apply on top of a zinc-rich primer, due to the reaction between the metallic zinc and the medium in the superimposed paint whereby the medium is embrittled and the top coats flake.

Zinc silicate primer See *Zinc-rich paints* above.

Zinc spraying The coating of iron and steelwork with metallic zinc. See *Metal spraying*.

Zinc stearate Used as the lubricant in self-lubricating abrasive papers. See *Abrasive papers*.

Zinc tetroxychromate A greenish-yellow pigment with poor opacity; it is used in metal primers of various kinds, but its chief use is in etch primers.